The Proceedings of the Seventeenth West Coast Conference on Formal Linguistics

The Proceedings of the Seventeenth West Coast Conference on Formal Linguistics

edited by
Kimary Shahin, Susan Blake
& Eun-Sook Kim

Conference held at the
University of British Columbia
1998

Published for the
Stanford Linguistics Association
by the
Center for the Study of Language and Information

Contents

Specificational Pseudoclefts as Lists

ARTEMIS ALEXIADOU & ANASTASIA GIANNAKIDOU[+]
ZAS-Berlin & ILLC-University of Amsterdam

1. Introduction

In the recent literature, it has been argued that Greek lacks specificational pseudoclefts (SPPs). The goal of this paper is to show that this is not true. We will present evidence suggesting that Greek *has* not one but two types of SPPs, and we will show that these two types instantiate a distinction between equation and specification as a distinction between object-identity and set-theoretic identity.

The term "pseudocleft" refers to copular constructions where one of the phrases surrounding *be* is a wh-element (usually a free relative), cf. (1):

(1)   What John is is silly.

Following Merchant (1998), we will refer to the non-wh-part as the *pivot* of the pseudocleft, and to the wh-part as the *nonpivot*. We will see later on that

[+] We thank the audience of WCCFL XVII for their feedback, Hamida Demirdache, Javier Gutiérrez-Rexach, Orin Percus, and especially Chris Kennedy for his very helpful comments. Many thanks also to numerous native speakers of Greek for judgements, to Josep Quer for helping us understand the Spanish and Catalan data, and finally to Jason Merchant for discussion and detailed comments on an earlier draft.

1

nonpivots do not always contain a wh-phrase. Higgins (1979), following Akmajian (1970), argues that pseudoclefts may be *predicational*, or *specificational*. The two readings for sentence (1) are illustrated in (2a) and (2b), respectively:

(2)   a.   John is P. Being P is silly. or, P-hood is silly (predicational)
        b.   John is the following: silly.   (specificational)

Under the predicational reading, (1) has a subject-predicate structure, but under the specificational reading, it does not. Rather, "the pseudocleft functions as a list, in which the subject is the heading and the predicate complement is an item on the list" (Higgins 1979:5). Higgins envisioned lists are (possibly open) sets of individuals or properties, so (2a) expresses something like $\{P|$ P is a property that John has$\}$ = $\{$silly,...$\}$.

Because the semantic structure of a SPP is superficially comparable to that of an equative identity statement like *The Morning Star is the Evening Star* (extensively discussed in the philosophical literature), many authors analyzed SPPs as equative sentences on a par with identity statements (cf. Rapoport (1987), Heycock & Kroch (H&K) (1996)). Higgins (1979), however, insisted on keeping the two apart. For Higgins, identity statemens equate two objects, but SPPs do something different: they express a relation between the heading of a list and its contents. In this paper we adduce evidence supporting Higgins's position, and we spell out a formal analysis of specification as set theoretic equation.

The paper is organized as follows. In section 2, we discuss Greek SPPs, taking Iatridou & Varlokosta's (I&V 1998) claim that there aren't any as the point of departure. We point out the problems encountered with this claim, and present some novel data which seriously question the empirical scope of it. Data from Spanish and Catalan will also be discussed in this connection. Then, building on Higgins, we propose a formal distinction between equation and specification in section 3, and in section 4 we show that this distinction can handle successfully the relevant facts.

2. Is it True that Greek Lacks Specificational Pseudoclefts?

Pseudoclefts in Greek are discussed in Veloudis (1979) and more recently in I&V (1998). Because each analysis discusses different sets of data, Veloudis and I&V reach strikingly different conclusions: Veloudis (1979) presents data supporting the existence of Greek SPPs, but I&V conjecture that Greek lacks SPPs. The facts to be presented in this section will support the conclusion reached by Veloudis.

2.1 Iatridou and Varlokosta 1998
Unlike English, Greek exhibits two types of pseudoclefts, one involving a wh-free relative (FR), and one not. The nonpivot of the familiar English-

type is introduced by the FR pronoun *oti* 'what(ever)', and will be referred to as *free relative pseudocleft* (FRP). Alternatively, the nonpivot may be introduced by the demonstrative *afto* 'this.neut.sing' followed by *pu* 'that'. Masculine, feminine, and plural forms may also be used. We will refer to this type as a *demonstrative pseudocleft* (DemP). I&V argue that the specificational reading is unavailable in either case, illustrating with examples with plain copular nonpivots like (3):

(3)   a.   *Afto pu ine o Pavlos ine vlakas.
            this that is the Paul is stupid
            'What Paul is is stupid.'
    b.   * Oti ine o Pavlos ine vlakas.
            what(ever) is the Paul is stupid
            '*Whatever Paul is is stupid.'

Note that specificational readings in such cases are unavailable with *ever*-FRs in English, as evidenced by the ungrammaticality of the English translation in (3b) (an issue to which we return in section 4).[1]

    I&V rule out sentences like (3) using three assumptions. First, they assume that *oti* and *ever*-FRs denote universal quantifiers. Second, they follow Williams (1983) (see also Heggie (1988), Moro (1992)) in assuming that SPPs contain inverse predication, where the nonpivot is the predicate, and the pivot is the subject. Third, it is assumed that demonstratives can never be used predicatively. In these terms, FRPs are ruled out because they are universal quantifiers, and thus cannot type-shift to a predicative interpretation as is required by inverse predication. DemPs are ruled out because it is claimed that demonstratives can never be used predicatively (a claim empirically unjustified, as we see below).

    Under I&V's account, languages that resemble Greek in employing demonstrative-like elements in pseudoclefts are expected to give rise to the same kind of ungrammaticality, since the demonstrative-like element will not be able to contribute a predicate. Although I&V do not provide the relevant data, this prediction appears, at first glance, to be borne out in Spanish and Catalan (data from Josep Quer (p.c)):

(4)   ??El que és en Joan és idiota.   Catalan
            the that is the John is stupid

---

[1] In support of their argument, I&V note the absence of connectivity effects in Greek pseudoclefts. Though space prevents us from going into this issue, we should emphasize that connectivity effects are not entirely absent. Veloudis (1979a) presents grmmatical data involving anaphors and in Alexiadou & Giannakidou (1998) we showed that principle C effects and case connectivity are also visible. NPI-licensing is still bad, but note that data from NPI-licensing in pseudoclefts are quite marginal in English too:
(i)   ?What John forgot to buy was any books, versus
(ii)   * What John forgot to buy was anything.

(5)   ??Lo que es Juan es idiota.   Spanish
             the that is John is idiot
             'What John is is an idiot.'

Although the ungrammaticality in these languages is not as sharp as it is in Greek (?? versus *, probably because a demonstrative is used in Greek but a definite in Spanish/Catalan), it is present.[2]

Though this type of data can be accounted for by I&V, moving to a larger set of data makes it impossible to maintain their hypothesis.

2.2   Problems with Iatridou & Varlokosta 1998

We summarize below the main problems we see with I&V's account:

(a) SPPs are available in Greek (see also fn2 for Spanish/Catalan).

(b) The ungrammatical SPPs with copular nonpivots become grammatical if material is added to the nonpivot. The effect is very robust and is observed in Spanish and Catalan too.

(c) That FRs are universals is quite controversial. In fact, Alexiadou & Giannakidou (1998) present arguments as to why Greek FRs are not universals, and apply tests which suggest that Greek FRs pattern with plural definites rather than with universals (see also Giannakidou (1997a)). As we did in those studies, we will adopt here an analysis of FRs as plural definites, in the spirit of Jacobson (1995), and more recently Dayal (1997) (but see Wiltschko (1998) for an analysis of FRs as indefinites).

(d) Invoking inverse predication for specificational sentences is empirically and conceptually unjustified (cf. Rapoport (1987), H&K (1996)).

(e) There are significant differences between DemPs and FRPs which are largely ignored in I&V, but which will be shown to have important consequences as to how the SPP domain is partitioned.

Points (c) and (d) have been thoroughly discussed in the literature, so we will not elaborate here. Because the rest concerns the specifics of I&V's analysis of Greek SPPs, it will be helpful to go into the details.

2.2.1 Greek Specificational Sentences are Available

Greek exhibits SPPs with both DemPs and FRPs. This is illustrated in great detail in Veloudis (1979a,b). The majority of his examples involve agreeing

---

[2] Note, however, that the Catalan and Spanish sentences improve considerably in the S(ubject)-V(erb) order. Compare (4) and (5) to (i) and (ii), respectively:

(i)   ?El que en Joan és és idiota.
(ii)   ?Lo que Juan es es idiota.

The improvement, not observed in Greek, casts doubt on the crosslinguistic validity of I&V's claim. Moreover, (4) and (5) become impeccable if modified, for instance by adding an adverbial in the (non)pivot (J. Gutiérrez Rexach, p.c.). This connects to the improvement mechanism which we dub "addition effect" and we discuss in the next subsection.

demonstratives (cf. (6)), but pseudoclefts with neuter demonstratives and FRs are generally fine too:

(6) Aftos pu filise ti jineka su itan o Petros.
    this.masc that kissed the wife yours was the Peter
    'The one who kissed your wife is Peter.'
(7) Afto pu agorase o Petros itan afto to palio leksiko.
    this that bought the Peter was this the old dictionary
    'What Peter bought was this old dictionary.'
(8) Oti efaje o Petros oli mera itane patates.
    what(ever) ate.3sg the Peter was potatoes
    'What Peter ate all day was potatoes.'

Crucially, FRPs are more restricted than DemPs: pivots of FRPs are more selective than those of DemPs, which may contain various types of NPs. Singular count nouns, for instance, are fine in DemPs (cf. (7)), but are excluded from FRPs, as we see in (9):

(9) *Oti   agorase o Janis itan afto to palio leksiko.
    what(ever) bought John was this the old dictionary
    '*Whatever John bought was this the old dictionary.'

We come back to this contrast in section 4. For now, let it just be noted that the grammatical sentences presented here are quite unexpected for I&V.

2.2.2. The 'Addition Effect'
Although the SPPs with plain copular nonpivots in (3) are ungrammatical, the SPPs below are fine:

(10) Afto pu dhen ine o Janis ine vlakas.
     this that not is the John is stupid
     'What John isn't is stupid.'
(11) Afto pu episis ine o Janis ine tsigounis.
     this that also is the John is miser
     'The other thing John is is a miser.'
(12) Afto pu prepi na ine o Janis (ja na pari ti doulia) ine dinamikos.
     this that must subj. is the John (so subj. take the job) is dynamic
     'What John must be (in order to get the job) is dynamic.'

These sentences contrast with (3) in one important way: material has been added to the copular nonpivot; negation *dhen* 'not' in (10), *episis* 'also' in (11), and the modal *prepi* "must" in (12).[3] 'Addition' improves only DemPs.

---

[3] I&V very briefly discuss a similar example (1997: fn. 30):
(i)   Afto pu dhen m'aresi ston Kosta ine to chiumor tu.

As we see below, FRPs in Greek as well as *ever*-FRs in English remain ungrammatical:

(13) *Oti   dhen ine o Janis ine vlakas.
       what(ever) not is the John is stupid
       '*Whatever John isn't is stupid.'
(14) *Oti episis ine o Janis ine tsigounis.
       what(ever) also is the John is miser
       '*Whatever else John is is a miser.'
(15) *Oti   prepi na ine o Janis ine dinamikos.
       what(ever) must subjunctive is the John is dynamic
       '*Whatever John must be is dynamic.'

An explanation of this contrast is offered in section 4. 'Addition' improves copular DemPs also in Spanish and Catalan (data from Josep Quer).

(16) a.   El que en Joan no és és idiota.   Catalan
            the that the John not is is stupid
      b.   Lo que Juan no es es idiota.   Spanish
            the that not is the John is stupid
            'What John isn't is stupid.'
(17) a.   El que també és en Joan és garrepa.   Catalan
            the that also is the John is miser
      b.   Lo que también es Juan es agarrado.   Spanish
            the that also is the John is miser
            'The other thing John is is a miser.'
(18) a.   El que en Joan ha de ser és decidit.   Catalan
            the that the John must subj. is is decisive
      b.   Lo que Juan tiene que ser es decidido.   Spanish
            the that must subj is the John is decisive
            'What John must be is decisive.'

These facts are extremely problematic under I&V's analysis, unless one of their crucial assumptions is abandoned: that demonstratives (and, by extension, definites) do not receive predicative interpretations. But if this is given up, I&V's explanation for plain copular nonpivots doesn't go through anymore: if demonstratives admit predicative uses, it is no longer obvious what rules out plain copular nonpivots in the first place.

In fact, contrary to I&V's (1997: 15, fn. 21) claim, it can be shown that demonstratives can indeed be used as predicates (the same can be shown for definites, but space prevents us from elaborating):

What I don't like about Kostas is his humor.
Note, however, that sentences like (i) are fine even without negation. I&V admit that here we are dealing with a "superscriptional" (=heading of the list in Higgins's terminology) use of the nonpivot, but they do not explore the consequences of this position.

(19) A: John is very hard-working.
      B: Ne, afto (akrivos) ine (ke olo ti doulia skeftete).
          yes this (exactly) is   and all the job thinks
          'Yes, that he is (and he is always thinking of work).'

Such uses of demonstratives abound. We take it that the predicative interpretation of a demonstrative becomes possible by a type-shifting operation like Partee's IDENT, which is the inverse of IOTA: it takes an *e*-type expression as its input and yields <*e,t*> as its output.

Thus far, we have reached two conclusions. First, Greek *has* SPPs. Second, FRPs and DemPs are semantically different. A successful analysis of SPPs should be able to account for this difference in a simple way.

3. Equation versus Specification

We propose that SPPs come in two varieties: either as equative, or as truly specificational. As we see in (20), equation and specification both involve some instance of identity. In equation, we have identity between *objects* (which must be of the same type, equation is thus subject to matching constraints, see also H&K (1996)). Specification, on the other hand, involves set-theoretic identity: α and β are coextensive sets.

(20) a   *Equation*
           α = β, where α and β range over elements of the same type.
           Possible types are: e, <e, t>, and functional types.
      b   *Specification*
           α = β, where α and β are coextensive sets, α specified by
           predicate notation {x| P(x)}, and β by list notation {a,b,c}.

Formalizing specification as in (20b) is consistent with Higgins's view of SPPs expressing identification between the heading of a list and its contents. Specified sets may consist of individuals, or properties.

The distinction between equation and specification we propose here should not be translated into an ambiguity of the copula *be*. Following Williams (1983) and Partee (1985), we assume that there is one unambiguous *be*, we believe, however, that equation and specification involve more structure than predication. One possible way to represent this is by postulating equative and specificational small clauses under *be*, extending the proposals in Heggie (1988), Carnie (1995) and H&K (1996). In order to compositionally derive the desired readings, we would then have to say that the heads of these small clauses belong to different types, since they combine with arguments of different types (an individual in equation, but a set in specification). Space prevents us from going into the details here.

In this context, and given the empirical distinction between DemPs and FRPs, two hypotheses are plausible. We may want to argue that equation and specification map onto FRPs and DemPs respectively. Alternatively, we may allow DemPs to be ocassionally equative. We will see below that only this weaker hypothesis can be faithfull to the facts.

4. An Analysis of Specificational Pseudoclefts in Greek

The proposed distinction between equation and specification must account for the following issues. (i) The difference between FRPs and DemPs. (ii) The exclusion of plain copular nonpivots. (iii) The 'addition' effect. (iv) The difference between English and Greek with respect to copular nonpivots. First, we deal with (i) and then we address the issues (ii)-(iv).

4.1. Two Types of Specificational Pseudoclefts
(a) *Demonstrative pseudoclefts as specificational sentences*
Consider first the straightforward cases: DemPs with pivots containing count or mass nouns. The demonstrative nonpivot receives its regular interpretation: a singular referring term as (23):

(21) Afto pu efaje o Petros itane patates.
      this that ate the Peter was potatoes
      'What Peter ate was potatoes.'
(22) Afto pu agorase o Petros itan afto to palio leksiko.
      this that bought the Peter was this the old dictionary
      'What Peter bought was this old dictionary.'
(23) $[\![$ afto pu efage o Petros $]\!] \Rightarrow \imath x$ [ate (P,x) $\wedge \neg \exists x'$[ate (P, x') $\wedge$ x'< x]]

The question is how the pivot is interpreted. The examples in (24)-(26) help us answer this question.

(24) Afto pu efaje o Petros itane patates, pagota, fistikia ke proino.
      this that ate the Peter was potatoes ice creams, nuts and breakfast
      'What Peter ate was potatoes, ice creams, nuts and breakfast.'
(25) Afto pu efaje o Petros itane, metaksi alon, pagoto.
      this that ate the Peter was among others the ice-cream
      'What Peter ate was, among other things, ice-cream.'
(26) Afto pu efaje o Petros itane, ja paradigma, pagoto.
      his that ate the Peter was   for example ice-cream
      '?What Peter ate was, for example, ice-cream.'

The pivot in (24) contains more than one item, indicating that there were more than one thing that Peter ate. Yet this does tell us that the nonpivot is interpreted as a set. One could argue that a collective interpretation of the objects (which would license the 'part of' relation and thus the plural interpretation of the demonstative clause) is possible. The felicity of *among other things* and *for example* in (24) and (26) is, in this respect, decisive. *Among other things* and *for example* have been used as diagnostics for nonexhaustive, *mention-some* readings (cf. Groenendijk & Stokhof (1984), Merchant (1998)). The appropriateness of nonexhaustive modification indicates that in these cases the nonpivot is interpreted as an open set, rather than as an (atomic or plural) individual. Note that nonexhaustive set modification is fine in the English *what* sentences too. We conclude that the pivots in (21) and (24)-(26) are intepreted as sets specifying what Peter ate; (25), (26) have the same representation (25'):

(21') $[\![(21)]\!]$= > {x|Peter ate x} = {potatoes}
(24') $[\![(24)]\!]$= > {x| Peter ate x} = {potatoes, nuts, ice-cream, breakfast}
(25') $[\![(25)]\!]$ = > {x| Peter ate x} = {ice-cream,...}

Likewise, (22) has the logical form in (27). Modification by *among others,* and *for example* is possible, as we see in (28):

(27) $[\![(22)]\!]$= > {x| Peter bought x}= {this old dictionary}
(28)   Afto pu agorase o Petros itan, ja paradigma/metaksi alon, afto to
        this that bought the Peter was, for example/among other, this the
        palio leksiko.
        old dictionary
        'What Peter bought was, for example, this old dictionary.'
        'What Peter bought was, among other things, this old dictionary.'

Nonneuter DemPs, like (29) cannot be analyzed as specificational. Note that the pivot may not contain more than one item, and modification by *among others,* and *for example* is not tolerated, as is shown (30) and (31). If we want to talk about more than one individual, the plural form *afti* "ones.masc.pl" must be used instead (in Greek as well as in English):

(29)   Aftos pu filise ti jineka su itan o Petros. (Veloudis (1979a:13))
        this.masc.sg that kissed the wife yours was the Peter
        'The one who kissed your wife was Peter.'
(30)   * Aftos pu filise ti jineka su itan o Petros ke o Pavlos.
        '*The one who kissed your wife was Peter and Paul.'
(31)   *Aftos pu filise ti jineka su itan metaksi alon/ja paradigma o Petros
        '*The one who kissed your wife was, among others/for example, P.'
(32)   Afti pu filisan ti jineka su itan o Petros ke o Pavlos.
        'The ones who kissed your wife is Peter and Paul.'

Agreement, present in nonneuter DemPs but absent in neuters, has thus an intepretative effect: it licenses equative readings in DemPs. Cases like (30) and (31) are type mismatches (recall that equated objects must of the same type). If this is correct, then we have to assume that agreement information is relevant at the level at which pseudoclefts are interpreted.

(b) Free relative pseudoclefts as equations
The simlest case here is provided by FRPs with two FRs, like (33). Since we take it that *oti*-FRs denote plural individuals, the FRPs at hand express an equation between two plural individuals as in (36):

(33)   Oti aresi stin Elena ine oti sixenete o Petros.
        what(ever) likes in-the Elena is oti detests the Pete
        'What Elena likes is what Peter hates.'
(34) $[\![$ oti aresi stin Elena $]\!]$ => ιx [like (E,x)$\wedge\forall$x' [like (E, x')$\rightarrow$ x' < x]]
(35) $[\![$ oti sihenete o Petros $]\!]$ => ιx [hate (P,x) $\wedge\forall$x' [hate (P,x')$\rightarrow$ x'< x]]
(36) ιx [like (Elena, x) $\wedge$ $\forall$x' [like (Elena, x')$\rightarrow$ x' < x]] =
        ιx [hate (Peter, x) $\wedge\forall$x' [hate (Peter, x')$\rightarrow$ x' < x]]

It is also conceivable to treat the (33) as involving properties rather than individuals, in which case the ι would range over objects of type <e, t>. Pseudoclefts with *afto pu* in both positions express the same equation, this time between unique atomic individuals, as illustrated below:

(37)   Afto pu aresi stin Elena ine afto pu sixenete o Petros.
        'What Elena likes is what Peter hates (namely cooking).'
(38) $[\![$ afto pu aresi stin E. $]\!]$ => ιx [like (E, x)$\wedge\neg\exists$x'[like (E,x') $\wedge$ x' < x]]
(39) $[\![$ afto pu sihenete o P. $]\!]$ = > ιx[hate (P,x) $\wedge\neg\exists$x'[hate (P,x') $\wedge$ x' < x]]
(40) ιx [like (Elena, x) $\wedge \neg$ $\exists$x'[like (Elena,x') $\wedge$ x' < x]] =
        ιx[hate (Peter, x) $\wedge\neg$ $\exists$x'[hate (Peter, x') $\wedge$ x' $\leq$ x]]

Appending something like *metaksi alon to majirema* "among other things cooking", which we use as diagnostics for specificational readings, would yield ungrammaticality here. Equations of functional types (cf. Groenendijk & Stokhof (1984), Engdahl (1986), Chierchia (1993), Sharvit (1997)) are also available, but we omit consideration for space reasons.

    Consider, finally, the ungrammatical (9), repeated here as (41):

(41)   *Oti   agorase o Janis itan afto to palio leksiko.
        what(ever) bought John was this the old dictionary
        '*Whatever John bought was this old dictionary.'

(41) is bad because its pivot is defined on atoms and not on plural individuals as is required for the purposes of equation. (41) will therefore be ruled out as a type mismatch, as shown (44):

(42) $[\![$ oti agorase o P. $]\!]$ => ιx[bought (P,x) $\wedge\forall$x'[bought (P,x')$\rightarrow$ x' < x]]

(43)   ⟦ afto to palio leksiko ⟧= >ιx [x∈ ⟦old dictionary⟧∧ ¬∃x'[x'∈ ⟦old
        dictionary⟧ ∧ x' < x]]
(44)   ιx[bought (Peter, x) ∧∀x'[bought (Peter, x') → x' < x]] ≠
        ιx [x∈ ⟦old dictionary⟧∧ ¬∃x'[x'∈ ⟦old dictionary⟧∧ x' < x]]

Such mismaches do not arise with specification, so the DemP counterpart of
(41), (22), is fine. We predict here that if we insert a plural individual in the
pivot, (41) will improve. This prediction is borne out, as illustrated in (45)
with a mass noun (a plural definite would give a samilar result):

(45)   Oti efaje o Petros oli mera itane patates.
            what(ever) that ate the Peter was potatoes
            'What Peter ate all day was potatoes.'

We conclude that the empirical contrast between FRPs and DemPs can be
successfully captured by the distinction between equation vs. specification
we defined in (20).

4.2. Copular Nonpivots in Greek and English
Recall the ungrammatical examples repeated here as (46):

(46)   *Afto pu /oti ine o Pavlos ine vlakas.
        'What Paul is is stupid.'
        '*Whatever Paul is is stupid.'

Consider now what the demonstrative version of this example would mean.
Because we have a demonstrative, the nonpivot would probably be
something like (47a), namely the unique property that John has (implicity
assumming that *afto* is crosscategorial). The pivot identifies that unique
property with the property of being stupid, as in (47b):

(47)   a.   ⟦ afto pu ine o Janis ⟧ = ιP [John is P]
        b.   ιP [John is P] = {stupid}

However, what we see in (47b) is not a wellformed list. Rather, it yields an
equation between a unique property and a singleton set containing that
property, which in turn is not a wellformed equation: it violates the
matching requirement because α and β are not of the same semantic type.
Cases like (47a) are thus excluded because, on the one hand, they are not
wellformed lists, and on the other, they cannot yield wellformed equations.
        Addition of material in the nonpivot suspends uniqueness and
renders a set interpretation possible. To see this, consider the case of
negation in (48) and the possible translations of the nonpivot in (49a,b):

(48)   Afto pu dhen ine o Janis ine vlakas.
            this that not is the John is stupid
            'What John isn't is stupid.'
(49)   a.   ⟦ afto pu dhen ine o Janis ⟧ = ιP [John is ¬ P]
       b.   ⟦ afto pu dhen ine o Janis ⟧ = λP [John is ¬ P]

According to (49a) the nonpivot denotes the unique property that John does not have. But this is not the right interpretation for the nonpivot, as shown by the fact that possible continuations like the ones in (50), which void uniqueness and indicate a set interpretation, are legitimate:

(50)   a.   Afto pu dhen ine o Janis ine vlakas, kutos ki akindhinos.
            this that not is the John is stupid silly and harmless
            'What John isn't is stupid, silly and harmless.'
       b.   Afto pu dhen ine o Janis ine, metaksi alon, akindhinos.
            'What John isn't is, among other things, harmless.'

Hence, the *afto pu* nonpivot is not equivalent to the unique property that John does not have. Rather, negation opens up the domain and it enables the creation of a set which will specify properties that John does not have. The nonpivot will enumerate these properties. The right interpretations for (48) and (50a,b) are then (51a,b,c), respectively:

(51)   a.   {P| John is not P} = {stupid}
       b.   {P| John is not P} = {stupid, silly, harmless}
       c   {P| John is not P} = {stupid,...}

In other words, the set containing the property of being stupid is included in the set containing the properties that John does not have, and the set {stupid, silly, harmless} is a subset of the same set in (51b).

     Likewise, *episis* 'also' in (52) opens up the domain and enables the creation of a set which will include additional properties of John, as in (53). The property of being a miser would be included in that set:

(52)   Afto pu episis ine o Janis ine tsigounis.
       'The other thing John is is a miser.'
(53)   {P|John is also P} = {miser}, or {miser} ⊆ {P|John is also P}

The modal in (54) has exactly the same effect, but this time we have a set of possible properties of John's:

(54)   Afto pu prepi na ine o Janis ine dinamikos.
       this that must subjunctive is the John is dynamic
       What John must be is dynamic.
(55)   {P| J. is possibly P}= {dynamic}, or {dynamic}⊆{P|J. is possibly P}

The Catalan and Spanish facts presented in 2.2.2 are amenable to exactly the same analysis, but space prevents us from probing into the details. The 'addition' effect is thus accounted for under the assumption that DemPs are specificational in the sense of list identifying. In our analysis, it is also predicted that addition will have no effect in FRPs, since these are equational, and equations of the form in (47b) are illformed. The ungrammatical examples in (13)-(15) show this prediction to be fully borne out.

As we see in the the translation of (46), plain copular *what* nonpivots are grammatical. Does this follow from our system? The answer is positive. Assuming, following Partee (1985), and Jacobson (1995) that *what* is crosscategorial, reference to properties, as is required for the interpretation of this sentence, is licit. Because *what,* unlike the demonstrative *afto,* is not by default associated with (unique) reference, it may denote a set, in this case a singleton:

(56) $\{P|\ \text{John is P}\} = \{\text{stupid}\}$

Note that this is consistent with Jacobson's view that *what*-FRs start out as sets and then they type-shift to individuals. As our English informants tell us, it is possible to manipulate the context in such a way so that *among other things,* and *for example* modification on *what*-SPPs would be possible, as expected, since we are dealing with specifications.

Finally, why are -*ever* FRPs excluded? (We refer now to the * translation of (46)). The answer is straightforward. *Whatever* is excluded for the same reason Greek FRPs are excluded: -*ever* FRs would always contribute individuals and would thus give rise to illformed equations. An additional constraint here would be imposed by the nature of free choice quantification (see Dayal (1997), Giannakidou (1997b)).

We showed how our analysis handles the relevant Greek facts, and we presented a couple of tests diagnozing set intepretations in specificational pivots. Our analysis extends directly to Spanish and Catalan. Izvorski (1997) presents some discussion of Bulgarian demonstrative SPPs, supporting the distinction between equation and specification made here and the ensuing predictions, as regards the availability of set intepretation in DemPs and the 'addition effect'. It would be interesting to see whether our account can predict the behavior of SPPs in more languages, but this unfortunately will have to be left for future research. Another important task is to identify precisely what types of expressions can induce the 'addition effect'. We have discussed here negation, 'also', and deontic modals (epistemic modals have the same effect) as cases in point for Greek, note, however, that in Spanish and Catalan various kinds of modification in the nonpivot are able to bring about the set intepretation, even word order (cf. fn.2). For a more refined understanding of the 'addition effect', more research towards identifying and restricting the set of possible inducers is required.

5. Conclusion

Two conclusions should be drawn from this paper. First, Greek *has* specificational pseudoclefts. Spanish/Catalan were shown to be similar in this respect. Second, there is considerable empirical support for a distinction between equation and specification, connecting to Higgins's original view of the heterogeneity of the non-predicational domain. Iatridou &Varlokosta's (1998) account cannot be maintained in the light of these conclusions. Greek, Spanish, and Catalan do form a natural class in terms of excluding plain copular nonpivots, but this was shown to follow not from the analysis proposed in Iatridou & Varlokosta, but from the inability of plain copular nonpivots to be intepretated as predicates *by default*.

References

Akmajian, A. 1970. On Deriving Cleft Sentences from Pseudocleft Sentences. *Linguistic Inquiry* 1:140-168.

Alexiadou, Artemis & Anastasia Giannakidou. 1998. Equation and Specification in the Semantics of Pseudoclefts. *ZAS Working Papers in Linguistics*, ZAS Berlin.

Chierchia, Gennaro. 1993. Questions with Quantifiers. *Natural Language Semantics* 1: 181-234.

Dayal, Veneeta. 1996. Quantification in Correlatives. In E. Bach et al. eds., *Quantification in Natural Language*. Dordrecht: Kluwer.

Dayal, Veneeta. 1997. Free relatives and *ever:* identity and free choice readings. To appear in SALT VII.

Engdahl, Elisabet. 1986. *Constituent Questions.* Dordrecht: Kluwer.

Giannakidou, Anastasia. 1997a. *The Landscape of Polarity Items.* Doctoral dissertation, University. of Groningen.

Giannakidou, Anastasia. 1997b. *Linking sensitivity to limited distribution: the case of free choice. Proceedings of the 11th Amsterdam Colloquium,* ILLC, University of Amsterdam. 139-144.

Groenendijk, J. & M. Stokhof. 1984. *Studies on the Semantics of Questions and the Pragmatics of Answers.* Doctoral dissertation. University of Amsterdam.

Heycock, Caroline. and Antony Kroch. 1996. Pseudocleft connectivity: Implications for the LF interface. Unpublished manuscript, University of Edinburgh and University of Philadelphia.

Higgins, Roger. 1979. *The Pseudocleft Construction in English.* Garland.

Jacobson, P. 1995. On the quantificational force of English free relatives in E. Bach et al. eds., *Quantification in Natural Language*. Dordrecht: Kluwer.

Iatridou, Sabine and Spyridoula Varlokosta. 1998. Pseudoclefts Crosslinguistically. *Natural Language Semantics* 6: 1-26.

Izvorski, Roumyana. 1997. On the type of 'be' and on the nature of the wh-clause in Specificational Pseudoclefts. Paper presented at the Workshop on the Syntax and Semantics of (Pseudo-)clefts, ZAS Berlin, December 1997.

Merchant, Jason. 1998. Pseudosluicing: elliptical clefts in Japanese and English. Ms. *ZAS Working Papers in Linguistics*, ZAS Berlin.

Moro, Andrea. 1992. *The Raising of Predicates*. Doctoral dissertation. University of Venice.

Partee, Barbara. 1985. Ambiguous Pseudoclefts with Unambiguous Be. Proceedings of NELS 16:354-366.

Partee, Barbara. 1987. Noun Phrase Interpretation and type-shifting Principles. In J. Groenendijk et al., eds., *Studies in Discourse Representation Theory and the Theory of Generalized Quantifiers*. Dordrecht: Foris.

Rapoport, Tova. 1987. *Copular, Nominal and Small Clauses: a Study of Israeli Hebrew*. Doctoral Dissertation, MIT.

Sharvit, Yael. 1997. *The Syntax and Semantics of Functional Relative Clauses*. Doctoral Dissertation. Rutgers University.

Veloudis, Jannis. 1979a. *Pseudo-cleft and cleft sentences: some evidence from Modern Greek*. MA Thesis, University of Reading.

Veloudis, Jannis. 1979b. Observations on the general Characteristics of clefts and pseudo clefts [in Greek]. Scientific Bulletin of the School of Philology of the University of Thessaloniki, volume IH 41-56.

Williams, Edwin. 1983. Semantic vs. Syntactic Categories. *Linguistics & Philosophy* 6:423-446.

Wiltschko, M. 1998. The Syntax and Semantics of Free Relatives. This volume.

Wherefore Lost English Verb Movement[*]

MARK D. ARNOLD

University of Maryland

1. Introduction

The narrow scope of this paper is a presentation of new evidence concerning the loss of V-to-I raising in English; on a broader level, the new evidence provides insights concerning the Language Acquisition Device — namely that the acquisition of syntactic mechanisms is driven by syntactic triggers.

Though such a claim seems to be a tautology, it nonetheless requires empirical motivation. Roberts (1993) and Rohrbacher (1994), though differing in the details, adopt the basic assumption that the acquisition of V-to-I raising is driven by the acquisition of the morphological paradigm for verbal inflection: given a sufficiently rich paradigm for verbal inflection, verb movement is acquired; the disappearance of a sufficiently rich morphological paradigm entails that verb movement is no longer acquired. The evidence presented here illustrates: 1) the descriptive and explanatory inadequacy of the morphology-based explanations, and 2) the accuracy of the predictions made by assuming that

---

[*] I wish to gratefully acknowledge the generosity of Anthony Kroch and Ann Taylor for making the Penn-Helsinki Parsed Corpus of Middle English freely available for research via anonymous ftp. I am also indebted to Doug Jones for showing me how to write an executable file.

verb movement was no longer acquired as a consequence of the loss of the syntactic trigger for verb movement.

Given the view that syntactic triggers drive the acquisition of syntactic mechanisms, the problem is to provide an explanation for the loss of the syntactic trigger for verb movement. The most obvious candidate in that regard is the spread of periphrastic *do*: as *do* spread through the language, examples of verb movement disappeared from the primary linguistic data. However, shifting the focus to *do* simply restates the problem: why did periphrastic *do* spread through the language?

In Arnold (1996, 1997), I show that 1) *do* spread for grammatical rather than sociolinguistic reasons, and 2) numerous diachronic details — including the spread of *do* — can be best explained by adopting a unified analysis of P-stranding, ECM, and *that*-deletion. In brief, the analysis is that P-stranding, ECM, and *that*-deletion are all instances of a novel LF incorporation mechanism in which a functional head incorporates into the verb which governs it.[1] Given the novel incorporation mechanism underlying P-stranding, ECM, and *that*-deletion, *do* spread through the language because use of *do* allowed the verb to remain in VP, thus providing a derivation with shorter movement for the LF incorporation of the relevant functional head(s).[2] In other words, the proposal is that the spread of *do* occurred as the result of the spread of P-stranding, ECM and *that*-deletion.

As intuitively unfathomable as such a proposal might seem at first glance, this paper presents new evidence from the Penn-Helsinki Parsed Corpus of Middle English which provides very strong support for the analysis. In fact, the diachronic details presented here are of the sort which would have probably remained unnoticed had there not been a proposal which predicted a correlation between verb movement and the relevant constructions.

In order to clarify the connection between the proposal for the spread of *do* and the particular predictions which were tested in the Corpus, I present first an overview of the work which led to the research reported on here. Given that introduction, I turn to the details of the findings in the Corpus.

---

[1] In fact, all three constructions had restricted forms in Old English (OE); the analysis provides an account for why all three constructions became generalized during Middle English, as well as providing an account for such subtle diachronic details as e.g. the chronological similarity between the loss of verb raising and the obligatory deletion of *that* in so-called *that*-trace contexts. See Arnold (1995a, 1996, 1997) for complete discussion of the full range of diachronic facts.

[2] Of course, given Chomsky's (1995) numeration, derivations with 'do' are not comparable to derivations with verb movement; see Arnold (1995a,b) for discussion of the implications of this proposal for Minimalism.

2. The Proposal

As a matter of illustrating the empirical breadth of the proposal, the following list presents the chronological details addressed in earlier work:

(1) transitive verbs which had selected Dative complements in Old English (e.g. *help*) start showing novel passive forms (e.g. *The men were helped*) in the 13th century; however, indirect objects (also marked Dative in Old English) did not appear as the subject of passive for 100-150 years after the appearance of the novel direct object passives (see Denison (1993));

(2) the eventual innovation of indirect object passives (IOPs) ((1) above) aligned with the statistically significant use of periphrastic *do* : both first appeared with clear regularity at the end of the 14th century, and both remained relatively rare until the end of the 15th century (see Ellegard (1953) on *do*, and Denison (1993) on IOPs);

(3) the disappearance of quasi-double object constructions (e.g. *Mary gave to John a book*) occurred in the same century in which verb movement had clearly given way to the widespread use of *do*, namely the latter half of the 16th century (see Visser (1963-1973) on double object constructions and Ellegard (1953) on *do*);

(4) the innovation of complex prepositional passives (e.g. *John was taken advantage of*) paralleled the delayed innovation of IOPs (see Denison (1993));

(5) deletion of *that* in *that*-trace contexts hit 100% in the 16th century (see Bergh and Seppanen (1992));

(6) deletion of *that* in ECM and control structures (e.g. *Mary convinced him that to go*, *Mary expected that him to go*) approached the modern standard in the 16th century (see Visser (1963-1973));

(7) from 1400-1700, the relative frequency of periphrastic *do* was higher with transitive verbs than with intransitives; with respect to different sentence types, the relative frequency of *do* was highest with negative questions, then affirmative questions, then negative declaratives and was lowest in affirmative declaratives (see Ellegard (1953)).

By adopting an incorporation analysis of P-stranding, ECM, and *that*-deletion, the various diachronic developments outlined in (1) - (7) can be seen to be the various consequences of a single underlying development rather than accidental similarities. And crucially, the morphology-based approaches to the loss of verb movement are at a loss to provide any insight about the chronological similarities outlined in (1) - (7).

As noted above, the proposal is that the consequence of the novel incorporation constructions was an increase in the use of *do*: *do* allowed the V head to remain in VP, thus allowing for a shorter movement when incorporating the relevant head into the verb.

(8) a. <u>P-stranding</u>   b. <u>ECM</u>   c. <u>ø-Complementizer</u>

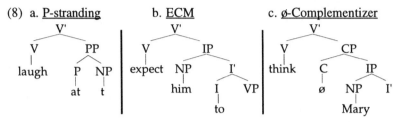

For the various constructions in (8), movement of the verb out of VP would require LF incorporation of either P, infinitival-*to*, or the null complementizer to cross the VP projection. However, as illustrated in (9) using a hypothetical P-stranding structure, use of *do* in (9b) allows incorporation to occur within the VP:

(9)   a. <u>neg. Q with V-to-I-to-C</u>:
      -P must cross three X^{max} for incorporation into V
      $[_{CP} [V_i+I]_j [_{IP} t_j [_{NegP} [_{VP} t_i [_{PP} P [_{NP} (e)]]]]]]$
      b. <u>neg. Q with *do*</u>:
      -P crosses no X^{max} for incorporation into V
      $[_{CP} do_j [_{IP} t_j [_{NegP} [_{VP} V [_{PP} P [_{NP} (e)]]]]]]$

Given that the derivation with *do* requires shorter movement in order to converge, it blocks the derivation with verb movement. Under this analysis, we can understand why *do* spread through the language, and we have an explanation for the patterns found by Ellegard. First, since a transitive verb is more likely than an intransitive to have a complement containing an element which will incorporate into it, *do* was used more frequently with transitives than with intransitives; second, the distinctions in the relative frequency of *do* in different sentence types follow from the overall degree of complexity in the different structures; (10a-d) represent structures with overt verb movement and a stranded P which must incorporate into the raised V head:

(10)   a. <u>Neg. Q</u>:
       -two instances of form chain, incorporation crosses three X^{max}
       $[_{CP} [V_i+I]_j [_{IP} t_j [_{NegP} [_{VP} t_i [_{PP} P [_{NP}]]]]]]$

   b. <u>Aff. Q</u>:
   -two instances of form chain, incorporation crosses two X^{max}
   $[_{CP} [V_i+I]_j [_{IP} \quad t_j [_{VP} \quad t_i [_{PP} P [_{NP}]]]]]$
   c. <u>Neg. Decl.</u>:
   -one instance of form chain, incorporation crosses two X^{max}
   $[_{IP} \qquad V_i [_{NegP} [_{VP} \quad t_i [_{PP} P [_{NP}]]]]]$
   d. <u>Aff. Decl.</u>:
   -one instance of form chain, incorporation crosses three X^{max}
   $[_{IP} \qquad V_i [_{VP} \quad t_i [_{PP} P [_{NP}]]]]$

It is worth noting that the relative frequency of *do* in affirmative declaratives barely climbed above 10% even during the period when use of *do* in affirmative declaratives was not yet restricted to emphatic contexts as it is now. This fact is important when considering the analysis of *do* offered by Watanabe (1993).

Watanabe adopts a Minimalist view of *do*, but he places the discussion in the context of how Procrastinate influences the acquisition device: given that *do* allows verb movement to Procrastinate, the acquisition device ultimately adopts *do* rather than verb movement. However, Watanabe's analysis encounters two empirical problems, one specific to the acquisition of verb movement, and one more generally related to cross-linguistic interrelations between synthesis and periphrasis.

With respect to the acquisition of verb movement, van Kampen (1997) reports that children learning Dutch initially overgeneralize their use of *doen* but then fairly quickly abandon the overuse and adopt the adult V-raising grammar. The initial overgeneralization by Dutch children is (at least superficially) explained by Watanabe's analysis: children overuse *doen* due to a bias in the acquisition device which favors the periphrastic form. However, the fact that Dutch children override the bias in the acquisition device and converge on grammars with verb movement poses the following question for Watanabe's analysis of *do*: why didn't children acquiring early Modern English abandon their biased use of *do* and hypothesize verb raising grammars just as Dutch children do?

Furthermore, in addition to the specific empirical problem posed by children learning Dutch, Watanabe's analysis faces a broader problem, namely the cross-linguistic tendency for the availability of a synthetic form to block the use of a periphrastic form (see Poser (1992)). For example, the availability of *faster* in English blocks the use of *more fast*:

(11)   a. Mary is faster than Bill.
        b. *Mary is more fast than Bill.

On the standard assumption that synthetic forms indicate instances of head movement, Watanabe's analysis predicts that periphrastic forms would generally block synthetic forms, contrary to observation. In other words, if the spread of periphrastic *do* was the consequence of a bias in the acquisition device which favors periphrasis over synthesis, then we would expect periphrasis to be the more generally adopted strategy; however, given that synthesis is the more generally adopted strategy, Watanabe's analysis provides no explanation for the spread of *do*.

Thus, given the cross-linguistic observation *vis a vis* synthesis and periphrasis, as well as van Kampen's observation concerning the acquisition of Dutch, Watanabe's explanation for the spread of *do* is empirically inadequate. Moreover, just as with the morphology-based accounts of the loss of verb movement, Watanabe's analysis offers no explanation for the range of diachronic parallels outlined in (1) - (7).

3. Extending the Analysis and Searching the Corpus

The proposal outlined above was originally developed to address the spread of *do*; however, as the majority of the texts in the Penn-Helsinki Corpus predates the widespread use of *do*, the specific details of the proposal must be slightly modified in order to test the theory.

To that end, recall that the operative force in the analysis is the economy provided by *do* in constructions with P-stranding, ECM, or *that*-deletion: *do* allowed the verb to remain in VP and thus allowed for shorter LF incorporation of the relevant functional head. If the proposal is right, we expect the following situation to emerge: in those cases where a writer could select between two grammatical forms, e.g. P-stranding versus pied-piping, the presence of a V head in VP would have increased the likelihood of the use of P-stranding; likewise, in clauses with clear evidence that the verb had raised out of VP, P-stranding would have been disfavored.

Of course, the problem is that in many clauses with a simple tensed verb, there is no definitive way to establish whether the particular sentence corresponded to an instance of V-raising or affix-hopping. In other words, *Mary likes John* could correspond to either its Middle English form, as in (12a), or its modern form, as in (12b):

(12)　　a.　[Mary [likes$_i$　[　t$_i$　　[John]]]]
　　　　　b.　[Mary [(pres) [likes [John]]]]

The necessary approach, therefore, is to focus the research on clauses which provide clear evidence of the location of the V head. For the purposes of automatic searches in the corpus, there are two syntactic details which I take to provide clear evidence of either V-raising or V *in situ*: 1.) following Pollock (1989), the location of the Neg head relative to a finite V, or 2.) the presence of a non-finite V. (The second possibility, i.e. non-finite V, occurs when either tense is carried on a modal/auxiliary or the clause is infinitival.)

3.1 Some Details about the Corpus

The Penn-Helsinki Parsed Corpus of Middle English is a collection of ASCII files which contain annotated sentences from a variety of Middle English texts. Each sentence from a given manuscript constitutes a separate token, and the annotation scheme provides low-level syntactic parsing as well as part of speech tags and locations of traces/elisions, e.g. s = subject, vt = tensed verb, a = auxiliary, p = preposition, %- = trace/empty. A sample token is given in (13).

(13)   ([f Al men 1[L [c-1 +tat] %s-1 r % [at wyll] [v her] [p of +te sege of Jerusalem], L]1] [l her] %[s +ge]% [at may] [v her] [p of gret meraculs 2[L [c-2 +tat] %d-2 r % [s almytty God] [vt wro+gt] 2.1[UP [a to] [v schow] [d his goodnys UP]2.1 L]2 and of gret vengans 3[L [c-3 +tat] %d-3 r % [s he] [vt toke] [p for syn] . L]3])(SIEGE,70.1)

Moreover, Kroch and Taylor (1995) provide a program which divides all of the sentences in a file into all of the separate clauses which make up the sentences. The result of applying this program to the token in (13) produces the tokens in (14). The research reported here was conducted on files in which each clause is a separate token, as in (14).

(14)   ([f Al men %L%] [l her] %[s +ge]% [at may] [v her] [p of gret meraculs %L% and of gret vengans %L%])(SIEGE,70.1)

(1[L [c-1 +tat] %s-1 r % [at wyll] [v her] [p of +te sege of Jerusalem] , L]1)(SIEGE,70.1)

(2[L [c-2 +tat] %d-2 r % [s almytty God] [vt wro+gt] %UP% L]2)(SIEGE,70.1)

(3[L [c-3 +tat] %d-3 r % [s he] [vt toke] [p for syn] . L]3)(SIEGE,70.1)

(2.1[UP [a to] [v schow] [d his goodnys] UP]2.1)(SIEGE,70.1)

Additionally, the files in the corpus are divided chronologically into four periods: M1, 1150-1250; M2, 1250-1350; M3, 1350-1420; M4, 1420-1500. This distinction is particularly helpful for testing the predictions of the incorporation analysis for the following reason. Given the proposal that the novel incorporation constructions (P-stranding, ECM, and *that*-deletion) spread during Middle English, it is insightful to compare the patterns found in the earliest texts to those in the latest. Throughout the discussion, I will make clear which subsets of files were searched for given patterns.

A final note concerns the particular searches which were conducted. First, in order to research the correlation of *that*-deletion with verb movement, the most certain diagnostic was the position of the tensed verb relative to Neg; as noted above, when the tensed verb precedes Neg, I assume that the sentence exhibits V-raising. Second, for P-stranding, the diagnostic used was the presence of a non-finite V; I assume that a non-finite V occurs in the VP and therefore provides a very local incorporation site for the stranded P. Finally, due to the coding conventions in the corpus, there is no automatic way to distinguish ECM from control structures; thus, testing the predictions *vis a vis* ECM is left for future work.

3.2 *That*-deletion

Before turning to the specific correlation between *that*-deletion and verb movement (as indicated by Neg), it is worth considering the basic pattern of *that*-deletion in the earliest texts compared to the latest. Of the eleven files in the earliest period, only six have an example of deleted *that*, and the overall relative frequency of *that*-deletion is 12% (17/138). By contrast, all 14 files with M4 designation contain at least one example of deleted *that*, and the overall frequency is 39% (247/641). These general numbers provide clear evidence that the option of deleting the sentential complementizer *that* spread during Middle English.

Turning now to the more specific prediction, the search required "rebuilding" of clauses such that the status of the complementizer (overt versus null) could be correlated with the position of the governing verb. In other words, given that the relevant detail for *that*-deletion is the position of the verb which governs the complementizer, and given that the sentences in each file had been divided into separate clauses, it was necessary to reconcatenate a *that*-clause with the clause it was originally embedded in. Once the clauses were appropriately rebuilt, the search could then determine the correlation between certain verb movement — as indicated by a tensed verb preceding Neg — and deleted *that*.

The findings are quite striking: of the 27 tokens in which Neg intervenes between the tensed verb and the complementizer position, there are only three cases of *that*-deletion — and all three are examples of the same construction:

(15)   a.   cmaelr4.m4
            (1.1[H [w-1 the whiche] [s thou] [vt woldist] [- not]
            %T% H]1.1) (1.1.1[T %s-1 r % [vt were] [m doon] [p
            to the] . T]1.1.1)(AELR4,16.68)
            . . . which you would not want done to you.
        b.   cmdocu3.m3
            (2[L [c-1 that] %s-1 r % [vt wolde] [- nought] %T%
            L]2) (2.1[T [s her falsnesse] [at had] [v be] [m knowen
            ]   :   [p   to   owre   lige   lorde   ]   .   T]2.1   )
            (DOCU3,PET,196.114)
            . . . that it would not be the case that her falseness
            become known to our lord.
        c.   cmpriv.m4.m4
            ([s I] [vt wolde] [- nott] %T% %L%) (1[T [s that
            letter] [vt were] [m seyn] [p wyth som folkys] , T]1)
            (CMPRIV,JPASTON,449.579)
            I would not want that letter to be seen by certain people.

Even if we make nothing of the fact that all three tokens are examples of the same construction, the rate of *that*-deletion when Neg intervenes between the verb and the complementizer is only 10% (3/27), well below the average of 30% (366/1228) for the periods (M3 and M4) in which the tokens are found.

However, further investigation of the construction in (15) suggests that such examples of *that*-deletion are themselves special cases requiring further study. Searching for all examples like those in (15) reveals that *that*-deletion in such *wold(e)* constructions is 58% (18/31), far above the 30% average for the M3 and M4 periods. Based on the higher than average rate of *that*-deletion in *wold(e)* constructions, I set them aside for further study. Given the evidence to set aside the three tokens in (15), the final result offers strong support for the theory being tested: there are no instances of *that*-deletion when Neg intervenes between the governing verb and the complementizer position. This fact follows directly from an analysis in which the possibility of deleting *that* is restricted whenever the verb has raised out of VP.

3.3 P-stranding
For P-stranding, the automatic searches become a bit more complex for two related reasons. First, P-stranding was quite productive in relative clauses in Old English; thus the early texts — when searched without regard to clause type — actually have a higher rate of P-stranding than of pied-piping, contrary to what we might expect given the standard view that the productivity of P-stranding was a Middle English innovation. Second, given the high rate of P-stranding in the earliest texts, a superficial glance at the corpus suggests that P-stranding was actually disappearing during Middle English, contrary to the standard view.

Table 1 shows that P-stranding was more common than pied-piping in six of the eight files from the M1 period, while Table 2 shows that pied-piping was more common during in 13 of 15 files in the M4 period.

Table 1: Stranded-P versus Pied-P in M1 texts

FILE	TOTAL	STRDP	% STR	PIEDP	% PP
cmancriw.m1	31	19	61.29	12	38.71
cmhali.m1	29	13	44.83	16	55.17
cmjulia.m1	23	20	86.96	3	13.04
cmkathe.m1	24	16	66.67	8	33.33
cmmarga.m1	31	21	67.74	10	32.26
cmpeterb.m1	2	2	100.00	0	0.00
cmsawles.m1	9	6	66.67	3	33.33
cmvices1.m1	23	11	47.83	12	52.17

overall frequency stranded-P in M1:   62.79
overall frequency pied-P in M1:   37.21

Table 2: Stranded-P versus Pied-P in M4 texts

FILE	TOTAL	STRDP	% STR	PIEDP	% PP
cmaelr4.m4	3	2	66.67	1	33.33
cmcapchr.m4	17	1	5.88	16	94.12
cmcapser.m4	4	1	25.00	3	75.00
cmcaxpro.m4	37	0	0.00	37	100.00
cmedmund.m4	5	2	40.00	3	60.00
cmfitzja.m4	23	2	8.70	21	91.30
cmgregor.m4	6	1	16.67	5	83.33
cminnoce.m4	25	3	12.00	22	88.00
cmkempe.m4	25	12	48.00	13	52.00
cmmalory.m4	18	4	22.22	14	77.78
cmoffic4.m4	8	1	12.50	7	87.50
cmpriv.m4	65	23	35.38	42	64.62
cmreynar.m4	16	5	31.25	11	68.75
cmreynes.m4	28	7	25.00	21	75.00
cmsiege.m4	4	3	75.00	1	25.00

overall frequency stranded-P in M4:   23.59
overall frequency pied-P in M4:   76.41

Given the numbers in Tables 1 and 2, it appears that P-stranding was disappearing during Middle English: the rate for P-stranding drops from 62.79% to 23.59%.

However, when relative clauses are considered separately, a different pattern emerges. Table 3 shows that the apparent disappearance of P-stranding is actually due to a significant shift from P-stranding to pied-piping in relative clauses:

Table 3: Stranded-P versus Pied-P in Relative Clauses versus Non-relatives

	Relative Clauses		Non-relatives	
	% stranded-P	% pied-P	% stranded-P	% pied-P
M1	69.84	30.16	43.48	56.52
M4	18.14	81.86	51.06	48.94

Notice that P-stranding in relative clauses drops from 69.84% in M1 to only 18.14% in M4; this dramatic shift, quite possibly due to influence from Norman French and/or Latin, accounts for the apparent obsolescence of P-stranding represented in Tables 1 and 2.

Furthermore, of particular significance is the fact that P-stranding in non-relative clauses increases during the same period, i.e. even though pied-piping very nearly becomes the rule in relative clauses, the fact that P-stranding increases in non-relative clauses provides evidence to support the standard view that the productivity of P-stranding was a Middle English innovation. Moreover, the patterns in Table 3 illustrate that the relevant constructions to search in the context of this paper are those cases in which P-stranding occurs in non-relative clauses.[3]

Recall that the prediction is that the presence of a V head in VP will increase the likelihood that P-stranding will occur. In other words, if the proposal for the incorporation analysis of P-stranding is right, there should be a higher than average rate of non-finite verbs in those clauses which contain stranded-Ps. As Table 4 shows, the prediction obtains: the frequency of non-finite verbs is nearly three times higher than normal when the clause also contains a stranded-P.

Table 4: Rates of non-finite V in:
-all non-relative clauses vs. non-relative clauses with stranded-P
-comparing M1 texts to M4 texts

	% non-finite V	
	all clauses	clauses with stranded-P
M1	24.59	65.00
M4	29.44	83.33

This pattern also obtains when the entire corpus is searched:

---

[3] I leave for future work a completely unified analysis of the progress of P-stranding during Middle English.

Table 5: Rates of non-finite V in:
      -all non-relative clauses versus non-relatives with stranded-P
      -all texts in the corpus

% non-finite V	
all clauses	clauses with stranded-P
27.56	71.01

Tables 4 and 5 illustrate the accuracy of the prediction when clause type is controlled for, i.e. setting aside relative clauses allows the pattern to stand out. Another similar research control arises if we consider that P-stranding due to A-movement was not at all possible in Old English, and thus another way to test the incorporation analysis would be to target so-called pseudo-passives, i.e. passive constructions in which A-movement creates a stranded-P.

Again, we expect that clauses with pseudo-passives should have a higher than normal rate of non-finite verbs. As before, the results are very compelling: the relevant verb is non-finite in all 35 tokens in which an overt subject is co-indexed with the trace of a stranded-P. Additionally, when the search is broadened to allow for empty subjects, i.e. A'-movement of the subject of a passive, only three of the additional nine tokens contain finite verbs. Thus, even without attempting to explain away the apparent counter-examples, the frequency of non-finites in pseudo-passives is 93%, well above the normal frequency for non-finites of 27.56%.

4. Implications of the New Evidence

To close, there are two issues which are important to keep in mind. First, the findings are very robust: with respect to *that*-deletion, recall that there were no instances of deleted *that* when Neg intervened between the verb and the complementizer position; with respect to P-stranding, the frequency of non-finite verbs was three times the normal rate when the clause contained a stranded-P, and for the most clear-cut examples of pseudo-passive, every example of P-stranding co-occurred with a non-finite verb. The robustness of the findings argues strongly in favor of the incorporation analysis.

Second, these robust findings were found precisely because the incorporation analysis predicts a correlation between these novel Middle English constructions and the potential for verb movement. By contrast, in addition to the fact that the morphology-based accounts of the loss of verb movement are unable to address the original diachronic details outlined in (1) - (7) above, these new findings concerning the correlation of verb movement with other constructions are completely mysterious under the morphological analyses. Likewise, building an economy bias into the acquisition device in order to explain the spread of *do* allows for no explanation of the patterns presented here.

The broad implication is that the loss of verb movement in English was a matter of the loss of the syntactic trigger for verb movement, i.e. the spread of periphrastic *do* meant the disappearance of the syntactic trigger for verb movement. The findings reported here provide strong support for the proposal that the spread of *do* was tied to the spread of P-stranding, ECM, and *that*-deletion. While it is entirely likely that the morphological paradigm of verbal inflection had to collapse before verb movement could be lost, the *coup de grace* came from the spread of periphrastic *do*.

References

Arnold, Mark D. 1997. "Double Object Constructions and Indirect Object Passives: Problems Posed by History", in the Proceedings of the 15th Annual Meeting of the West Coast Conference on Formal Linguistics, 1-15. CLSI: Stanford.

Arnold, Mark D. 1996. "A Unified Analysis of Preposition Stranding, ECM, and *that*-deletion", in the Proceedings of the 26th Annual Meeting of the North East Linguistic Society, 1-15 GLSA, University of Massachusetts: Amherst.

Arnold, Mark D. 1995a. Case, Periphrastic *do*, and the Loss of Verb Movement in English. PhD dissertation, University of Maryland.

Arnold, Mark D. 1995b. "The History of Periphrastic *do*: An Argument for Lexical Insertion at Spell-Out", in the Proceedings of the 25th Annual Meeting of the North East Linguistic Society, 121-134. GLSA, University of Massachusetts: Amherst.

Bergh, Gunnar B. and Aimo S. Seppanen. 1992. 'Subject Extraction in English: The Use of the *That*-Complementizer', in Fernandez, Fuster, and Calvo, (eds.), *English Historical Linguistics 1992*, 131-144. Philadelphia: Benjamins.

Chomsky, Noam. 1995. Minimalist Program. Cambridge: MIT Press.

Dension, David. 1993. *English Historical Syntax: Verbal Constructions*. New York: Longman.

Ellegard, Alvar. 1953. *The Auxiliary* do: *The Establishment and Regulation of its Use in English*, Behre, F. (ed.), Gothenburg Studies in English. Stockholm: Almqvist and Wiksell.

Kampen, Jacqueline van. 1997. First Steps in Wh-movement. Wageningen: Ponsen and Looijen.

Kemenade, Ans van. 1987. *Syntactic Case and Morphological Case in the History of English*. Dordrecht: Foris.

Kroch, Anthony and Ann Taylor. 1995. Penn-Helsinki Parsed Corpus of Middle English Texts. Anonymous ftp: babel.ling.upenn.edu/ facpapers/tony_kroch/mideng-corpus.

Pollock, Jean-Yves. 1989. "Verb Movement, UG, and the Structure of IP", *Linguistic Inquiry*, 20: 365-424.

Poser, William. 1992. "Extending Morphological Blocking into Syntax" in Sag, I. and A. Szabolcsi (eds.) *Lexical Matters*, 111-130. Stanford: CLSI 24.

Roberts, Ian. 1993. *Verbs and Diachronic Syntax: A Comparative History of English and French*. Boston: Kluwer.

Rohrbacher, Bernard (1994). *The Germanic VO Languages and the Full Paradigm: A Theory of V-to-I Raising*. PhD dissertation, University of Massachusetts, Amherst.

Visser, Fredericus Theodorus. 1963-1973. *An Historical Syntax of the English Language*. Leiden: E.J. Brill.

Watanabe, Akira. 1993. *Agr-Based Case Theory and Its Interaction with the A-Bar System*. PhD dissertation, MIT.

Chinese-Type Questions in English*

ADOLFO AUSÍN

University of Connecticut

1. Introduction

In this paper I will discuss questions like the one that appears in (1a). The sentence in (1a) has the form of a yes/no question. As such it can be answered as in (1b). However there is at least another possible way of answering (1a): the answer in (1c) seems to be quite reasonable for a question like (1a). So, it seems that the yes/no question in (1a) can be answered as the Wh-question in (2).

(1)   a.   Do you want something?
        b.   Yes, I do.
        c.   A beer.
(2)   What do you want?

Assuming that the type of answers that a question can have is an indication of the structure that the question has, I will propose that the question in (1a) can have a structure quite similar to the one of the sentence in (2). The structure that they share, when (1a) is answered with (1c), is the one that appears in (3):

(3)   C [you want [wh+something]]

---

* I am thankful to the members of the Linguistic Department at the University of Connecticut, the audience of WCCFL XVII, Esther Torrego, Ignacio Bosque and Juan Uriagereka, for questions, suggestions and support of different kind. I am also indebted to Enrique López, Norberto Moreno, Pilar Pérez, Natalia Sánchez and Jose Luis Sancho for grammaticality judgements.

Taking advantage of the feature movement hypothesis defended in Chomsky (1995), I will propose that in (3) there are two options: either the whole *[wh+something]* moves to C, and then we would get (2); or only the wh- part of it moves, and then we would get (1a).[1]

The evidence that I will use to support my proposal is that the relation between the indefinite pronoun and the matrix Comp is subject to locality constraints. In other words, I will use the same argument that Huang used to justify the existence of LF wh-movement in Chinese. However, the final result will be somewhat similar to Watanabe's (1992) proposal on operator movement in Japanese.

2. Some antecedents

The idea that wh-words are complex units and that syntactic operations play a role in their making is quite old within the generative grammar. In fact, it is as old as the generative grammar, since that idea can be traced back to *LSLT* and *Syntactic Structures.* The proposal in those works appears exemplified and simplified in (4). A definite pronoun is generated in-situ. This pronoun can be optionally moved to a sentence initial position. Later a wh- morpheme will be attached to it. In the morphophonemics, *wh+it* will be turned into *what.*

(4)   a.   John ate it   Chomsky (1955:436-7, 1957:69 fn.2)
           b.   it John ate
           c.   wh-it John ate
           d.   What did John eat

Soon after this some other variants of the same idea were pursued. The main two characteristics of these new approaches to question formation were: first, that the pronoun that is associated with the interrogative (and relative) pronoun is the indefinite; and second, that the wh- morpheme is associated with the pronoun before the pronoun moves to the sentence initial position. In (5), Chomsky's (1964) proposal is exemplified. *Wh+something* is inserted in the complement position of *admire,* and then moved to the sentence initial position. See also Klima (1964:252-3), Katz and Postal (1964:79ff).

(5)   a.   John admire wh-someone   Chomsky (1964:38)
           b.   wh-someone John admires
           c.   who does John admire

---

[1] This will not be the only explanation that I will consider for the facts in (1). Two more explanations will be considered in addition to the one that has been mentioned: one based on quantifier raising and the other based on unselective binding.

Relating interrogatives with indefinites explains some facts regarding the similar distribution of these two elements. The contrast in the sentences in (6) is explained if one assumes that interrogatives and indefinites share some properties. The examples in (6) show that *else* can go with indefinite and interrogative pronouns, but not with definite expressions.[2]

(6)   a.   Who else was at the party?   Bach (1971:157)
        b.   Someone else was at the party.
        c.   *The man else was at the party.

Ross (1969) took advantage of the relation between interrogative and indefinite pronouns in his analysis of what he called "sluicing", illustrated in (7):

(7)   Somebody just left – guess who.   Ross (1969:ex. 2a)

Placing the wh- morpheme in the wh-word instead of in the beginning of the sentence was crucial to explain the possibility of having multiple questions, as Katz and Postal (1964) explicitly argue. If the wh- morpheme were attached to some element already placed at the beginning of the sentence then we would not have an explanation for the possibility of having multiple wh-questions as in (8).

(8)   When did John see whom?   Katz and Postal (1964:106)

3. Some considerations from Chinese

The Chinese influence in this proposal is twofold. On one side the sentences that I am dealing with contain indefinite pronouns interpreted as interrogative pronouns. Interestingly enough, in Chinese the lexical item that is used as a wh-word in wh-questions is the same as the one used as an indefinite pronoun in some contexts, as can be seen in the examples in (9), taken from Li (1992):

(9)   a.   Ta yiwei wo xihuan <u>shenme</u>?   Li (1992: ex. 1a,b)
            he think I   like   what
            '<u>What</u> does he think I like?'

---

[2] As pointed out by Howard Lasnik (p.c.), the observation does not seem to be completely accurate since *else* does not seem to pick out indefinites, but some type of quantifier expressions as shown by the sentences in (i) and (ii):
(i)   Everybody else went to the party.
(ii)   Nobody else liked the talk.

b. Ta yiwei wo xihuan <u>shenme</u>.
    he think I   like   what
    'He thinks that I like <u>something</u>.'

In (9a) *shenme* is used as "what" according to Li's translation. In (9b), the same word, *shenme* is interpreted as an indefinite. Li's translation of (9a) is "What does he think I like?" However, since in (9b) *shenme* is translated as *something*, there is an alternative translation of (9a) identical to Li's. The only difference is that instead of using *what*, *something* is used, as shown in (10):

(10) Does he think that I like something?

Note that (10) is a good translation of (9a) only if (10) is interpreted as a wh-question, and not as a yes/no question. Since (10) is the most literal translation of the Chinese (9a), I will call that type of sentences, Chinese-type questions. Specifically, with this name I want to refer to yes/no questions that have an indefinite pronoun and to the fact that this indefinite pronoun can be interpreted as an interrogative pronoun.

Sentences like the ones in (1a) and (10) share another important characteristic with the Chinese counterparts. Huang (1982) showed that, although Chinese does not have overt wh-movement, the distribution of the wh-words is subject to locality constraints similar to the ones that rule wh-movement in languages with overt wh-movement. Huang's proposal was that there is wh-movement in languages that do not display it overtly. Again, interestingly enough, the distribution of indefinite pronouns interpreted as interrogative pronouns seems to be subject to some locality constraints. This is the second reason why I am calling the sentences in (1a) and (10) Chinese-type questions. In section 5 we will see some of these locality constraints.

4. Are we dealing with a pragmatic phenomenon?

When I have talked to some people about what I am calling Chinese-type sentences, a typical reaction has been to attribute the wh-question interpretation of these yes/no questions to some kind of discourse rule that requires answers to be as informative as possible. Consider again the sentence in (1), repeated here:

(1) a. Do you want something?
     b. Yes, I do.
     c. A beer.

It's quite probable that an answer like (1b) is not going to satisfy the information needs of the person who asked (1a). Under this view, (1c) would be a "better behaved" answer in terms of conversational cooperativeness, maybe along the lines of Grice's maxim of quantity:

(11)   Make your contribution as informative as it is required (for the current purposes of communication) (Grice (1975)).

If this were the whole story, it would not be interesting from a syntactic (or semantic) point of view. But also, it would be somewhat unexpected that we find that the distribution of these pronouns is subject to locality constraints similar to the ones that we found in other parts of the grammar and in other languages.

We can check the accuracy of the pragmatic account by forcing the yes/no interpretation of a yes/no question. We can do that by adding *or not*. The pragmatic account would expect that this addition would cause no change. However, the account that I will propose expects that the interpretation of the indefinite pronoun as an interrogative pronoun should not be possible since I will claim that in these cases we are not dealing with real yes/no questions. Let's consider the following sentences. From here on, I will always provide the question with an answer. The grammatical judgement will be about the appropriateness of the question/answer pair.

(12)   Did you say that somebody called? Mary.
(13)   a.   *Did you say that somebody called or not? Mary.
        b.   *Did you or did you not say that somebody called? Mary.

The contrast between (12) and (13) tells us that the pragmatic account does not seem to be on the right track. If the possibility of having *Mary* as an answer to the question in (12) is due to some additional specification of an implicit affirmative answer, then there is no reason why we cannot have the same answer in the sentences in (13).[3]

---

[3] Note that although I am defending that in the sentences that I am worried about (for instance, (1a) and (10)) pragmatics does not have much to say, I am not claiming that pragmatics should not explain the adequacy of other types of question/answer pairs. For instance, that (ib) is a good answer to (ia) is probably just a pragmatic phenomenon. Interestingly, this type of combinations seems to be quite different from the one we have seen in the text, since it does not accept "long distance" questions, as shown by the oddity of the dialogue in (ii) if the answer is intended to refer to the moment in which John left:

(i)   a.   Did John leave?
        b.   Ten minutes ago.
(ii)   a.   Did you say that John leave?
        b.   #Ten minutes ago.

5. The facts

5.1. English

Let's take a look at more English examples. The judgements are contrastive rather than categorical. The fact that the judgements are about question-answer pairs makes the task of judging these sentences especially difficult. I have abstracted away from variation and tried to focus on contrasts.[4]

The sentences in (14) show that the indefinite interpreted as an interrogative pronoun can appear in any argument position: subject in (14a), object in (14b) and prepositional object in (14c).

(14) a. Did somebody call? Your mother.
      b. Do you want something? A beer.
      c. Did you speak with someone? With Mary.

The sentences in (15) show that the indefinite pronoun can be an adjunct: temporal in (15a) and locative in (15b).

(15) a. Did you see Mary sometime last week? On Monday.
      b. Did you see Mary someplace? In the market.

The sentences in (16) show that neither *somehow* nor *someway* likes to have an interrogative interpretation, a fact to which we will come back in section 6.

(16) a. *Did he fix your car somehow? With a screwdriver.
      b. *Do you want your burger someway? Burnt.

The sentences in (17) show that the indefinite pronoun with an interrogative interpretation can appear in embedded sentences. That is, the indefinite does not need to appear in the matrix sentence in order for it to be interpreted as an interrogative in the matrix clause.

(17) a. Did you say that someone talked to John? Peter.
      b. Did you say that Mary saw someone? John.
      c. Did you say that Mary saw you somewhere? In the market.

---

[4] The status of some of these examples, both in English and Spanish, sometimes changes for some speakers if the answer is preceded by *Yes*. Even more, in some languages, some sort of affirmative answer is required. This could be relevant and interesting to look at. However, since there are clear contrasts without the use of that affirmative answer, I will focus on these contrasts. The same can be said about the use of *anything* or *anyone* instead of *something* or *someone*.

In the sentences in (18) we can see that the distribution of *somebody* with an interrogative interpretation is not sensitive to the subject constraint when the indefinite appears within an NP. There is no difference between subject position, as in (18a,c) and object position, as in (18b,d). In this respect, the indefinite pronoun with an interrogative interpretation contrasts with the typical instances of wh-movement. In (18a,c) the interrogative interpretation of the indefinite pronoun is fine even though the indefinite appears within the subject of the clause. However, the subject constraint does show up when the indefinite pronoun is additionally embedded within a sentence as in (18e).

(18) a. Did somebody's father come to the meeting? John's.
 b. Did Mary hit somebody's father? John's.
 c. Were jokes about somebody told at the meeting? About John.
 d. Did they tell jokes about somebody at the meeting? About John.
 e. *Did the fact that Mary hit someone surprise you? John.

The sentence in (19) is an example of the adjunct condition. In this case everybody has a clear judgment that the sentence is ungrammatical.

(19) *Did John leave after someone came in? Peter.

In (20) we have some crucial sentences involving wh-island violations. Unfortunately the judgements are not very clear. Some speakers like them all (with the exception of the one with *somehow* in (20e), which is irrelevant since the sentences in (16) were already ungrammatical). For some other speakers there seems to be a difference based on the argument-adjunct asymmetry. For those speakers, there is a clear contrast between (20a&c) and (20b&d).

(20) a. Are you wondering whether to fix something tonight? The computer.
 b. (*)Are you wondering whether to see *Casablanca* sometime next week? On Monday.
 c. Are you wondering where to put something? The computer.
 d. (*)Are you wondering what to put somewhere? On the table.
 e. **Are you wondering whether to fix your car somehow? With a screwdriver.

5.2. Spanish

Although all the examples until now are from English, the phenomenon is found in other languages as well. For instance, in Spanish we find a similar phenomenon. Below are some examples that illustrate this. Note, however, that in the general discussion of the problem (in section 6) I will focus on English.

(21)   a.   Dijo Juan que se iba   a quedar con alguien? Con María.
                  said Juan that SE going to meet with someone? With María
                  'Did Juan say that he was going to meet with someone? With María.'
        b.   *Dijo Juan que se iba a quedar con alguien o no?
                  said Juan that cl going to meet with someone or not?
                  Con María.
                  With María
                  'Did Juan say that he was going to meet with someone or not? With María.'

(22)   Ha llamado alguien? María.
        has called someone? María
        'Has someone called? María.'

(23)   Viste a María algún día? El lunes.
        Saw to María some day? The Monday.
        'Did you see María someday? On Monday.'

(24)   *Lo hiciste de alguna manera? Rápidamente.
        Cl did   of some way   quickly
        'Did you do it somehow? Quickly.'

(25)   Dijiste que alguien vino a verte?   María.
        said   that someone came to see-you? María
        'Did you say that someone came to see you? María.'

(26)   Les   pediste que te   esperaran en algún sitio?
        to-them asked   that for-you waited   in some place?
        En el metro.
        In the subway
        'Did you ask them to wait for you someplace? In the subway.'

(27)   Vino el padre de alguien a la fiesta? El de Juan.
        came the father of someone to the party? The of Juan
        'Did the father of somebody come to the party? Of Juan.'

(28)   Pegó María al   padre de alguien? Al   de Juan.
        hit   María to-the father of someone? To-the of Juan
        'Did María hit the father of someone? Of Juan.'

(29)   *Te enfadaste cuando vino alguien?   Juan.
        you-got upset when came somebody? Juan
        'Did you get upset when someone came in? Juan.'

(30)   *Te   enseñó Juan qué   libro poner en algún sitio?
        to-you showed Juan what book put   in some place
        En la   estantería.
        On the shelf
        'Did Juan show you what book to put somewhere? On the shelf.'
(31)   *Te   enseñó Juan dónde colocar algo?   El ordenador.
        to-you showed Juan where to put something? The computer.
        'Did Juan show you where to put something? The computer.'
(32)   *Te preguntó Juan dónde viste a alguien? A María.
        to-you asked Juan where saw to someone to María
        'Did Juan ask you where you saw someone? Mary.'
(33)   Te enseñó Juan cómo arreglar algo?   El   ordenador
        cl taught Juan how fix   something The computer
        'Did Juan teach you how to fix something? The computer.'

Without going into details, the pattern that arises from these facts is that
wh-violations seem to be worse than in English. The only wh-violation that
seems to be accepted is the one with *how* in the embedded clause, as in (33).
It does not seem to be a random fact since in English, even those who
would not accept any wh-violations would like the English version of (33).
Chomsky (1973:244-5) has already noted this quite liberal behavior of
embedded interrogatives headed by *how* in the case of wh-movement, as
shown in (34). Chomsky (1973:245, fn26) suggested that expressions like
know-how could be lexicalized.

(34)   What crime does the FBI know how to solve? (Chomsky's (1973)
        ex. (59))

Again, the fact that the distribution of interrogative *something* patterns in
such a similar way as wh-movement seems to be quite meaningful.

6. The explanation(s)

The explanation that I think is the right one is based in terms of feature
movement. However, other explanations are conceivable. Before I give
more details about my proposal, let's consider two alternatives. One based
on Quantifier Raising (QR) and Absorption and the other based on
unselective binding.

6.1. QR and Absorption
One could think that the appropriate way of characterizing these facts is in
terms of QR and absorption. Let's assume the following:

(35) a. Yes/no questions have a yes/no operator.
  b. Indefinites undergo QR to a position close enough to the yes/no operator.
  c. Indefinites and the yes/no operator can undergo absorption and the result of this absorption is an interrogative pronoun.

Under these hypotheses, the interpretation of a sentence like (36) would be as illustrated in (37). In (37a) the structure after QR is shown. An informal representation of the interpretation of (37a) appears in (37b). And (37c) is the result that we would obtain after the yes/no operator and the existential quantifier undergo absorption. The representation in (37c) is quite compatible with a wh-question-type answer. The interpretation in (37c) is probably the same one that is assigned to (38).

(36) Did somebody call?
(37) a. Wh [somebody [t called]]
  b. ?Yes/No [∃x [x called]]
  c. ?x [x called]
(38) Who called?

The problems with this approach are the ones that appear in (39):

(39) Problems:
  a. It relies on QR, which does not seem to have a clear status in the current framework.
  b. QR is sometimes considered clause bound and we have seen that indefinite pronouns with interrogative interpretations can appear in embedded sentences.
  c. Yes/no operators cannot undergo absorption (cf. *I wonder whether Peter bought what).

6.2. Unselective binding
There is an increasing literature in which the interpretation of wh-in-situ is done by unselective binding as initially proposed in Pesetsky (1987): Reinhart (1995), Tsai (1994) and some others.

One could argue that the same mechanism that is used to unselectively bind wh-in-situ can be used to interpret indefinite pronouns as an interrogative. This approach is quite appealing and can explain some interesting correlations. For instance, this approach could very nicely explain why neither (40) nor (41) is possible:

(40) *Do you want your burger somehow? Burnt.
(41) *Who left how?

It seems reasonable to attribute the ungrammaticality of these two sentences to the fact that neither *how* nor *somehow* have an open position that can be unselectively bound by a wh- operator in C.

However, this approach does not seem to be able to explain the locality constraints that determine the distribution of the indefinites with interrogative interpretation.

Reinhart (1995) claims that one of the advantages of the unselective binding approach to wh-in-situ is that it can explain why wh-in-situ does not seem to be subject to any locality constraints on its distribution, provided that it can be unselectively bound. This is what explains the grammaticality of (42).

(42)   Who fainted when you attacked whom?   (Reinhart's (1995) ex. (27a))

However, we have seen that interrogative indefinite pronouns are subject to some locality constraints. Thus, (22) repeated here is ungrammatical. This casts doubts on the unselective binding approach. If *whom* can be unselectively bound in (42), there is no reason why *someone* should not be unselectively bound in (22).

(22)   *Did John leave after someone came in? Peter.

The same conclusion can be drawn from the analysis of sluicing that Chung, Ladusaw and McCloskey (1994) propose. According to these authors, the best way to characterize sluicing is through what they called IP recycling: the IP is copied into the sluiced part. The relation between the wh-word and the indefinite pronoun is done through binding. The advantage of this treatment is that there is no movement, and therefore, they can explain why Subjacency and the ECP do not seem to play any role in some cases of sluicing. This is exemplified in (43). After IP recycling we get (44).

(43)   ?Irv and someone were dancing together, but I do not know who. (example from Ross (1969), Chung, Ladusaw and McCloskey (1994) ex. (88a))

(44)   Irv and someone were dancing together, but I do not know who [Irv and someone were dancing together].

However, the distribution of indefinite pronouns with interrogative interpretation is subject to some locality constraints, as we have seen in several examples. Most of these examples are fine in the sluiced version, as shown in (45), the sluiced version of (22).

(45)   John left after someone came in but I cannot remember who.

6.3. Feature movement

The proposal that I think is more accurate in dealing with the facts is based on feature movement. Under this proposal (46) underlies both (47) and (48), if (48) is answered as indicated.

(46)   C [you want [wh+something]]
(47)   What do you want?
(48)   Do you want something? A beer.

In order for the proposal to work I need to assume that in English (and Spanish) wh-words can be optionally decomposed by syntactic operations. If the whole lexical item moves, we get (47). If only the wh-feature moves, we get (48).[5,6]

This approach can arguably explain the locality constraints which rule the distribution of interrogative indefinite pronouns since some type of movement is involved in these sentences. The precise way in which this can be done is not still clear to me, partly because the facts are not crystal clear.

Note that the explanation that the unselective binding approach had for the ungrammaticality of (40) and (41), repeated here, can still be kept under the feature movement approach, since the feature movement approach is not incompatible with unselective binding.

(40)   *Do you want your burger somehow? Burnt.
(41)   *Who left how?

However, the feature movement approach has a big problem I still do not have a solution for. Imagine that we start with the structure in (49), and we decide to move the wh-feature of the subject. Then we should get (50), which is ungrammatical.

(49)   C [[wh+someone] want [wh+something]]
(50)   *Does somebody want what?

One possible way of explaining the ungrammaticality of (50) is to relate it with the impossibility of having a pair-list interpretation in (51):

---

[5] This is quite reminiscent of the operator movement proposal made in Watanabe (1992) for Japanese.

[6] Under this approach, a problem that remains to be solved is the different presuppositions that (47) and (48) convey. The question in (47) presupposes that the addressee wants something, whereas (48) has no such presupposition.

(51)   What does somebody want?

If the impossibility of the pair-list interpretation in (51) is attributed to the impossibility of *somebody* and *what* undergoing absorption, then we would have an explanation for the ungrammaticality of (50). One could argue that (50) is ruled out by the impossibility of *what* being associated with the matrix C, which is already "linked" to *somebody*. In other words, both the ungrammaticality of (50) and the lack of a pair-list interpretation in (51) would be explained if we assume that "real" wh-words cannot undergo absorption with interrogative indefinite pronouns. If so, the ungrammaticality of (50) would not be a problem for the feature movement approach to the interrogative interpretation of indefinite pronouns.

7. Conclusion

To conclude, in this paper I have presented new data and proposed three analyses. Future research should improve some of these proposals or maybe develop a new one that can shed additional light on these facts. Although the specific details are not crystal clear yet, it seems that we have new evidence for the old idea that indefinites and interrogatives are closely related. As Howard Lasnik likes to say, "sometimes old ideas are not merely interesting, they can be even right."

8. References

Bach, Emmon. 1971. Questions. *Linguistic Inquiry* 2:2.153-166.

Chomsky, Noam. 1955. *The Logical Structure of Linguistic Theory*. New York: Plenum Press. 1975.

Chomsky, Noam. 1957. *Syntactic Structures*. The Hague: Mouton.

Chomsky, Noam. 1964. *Current Issues in Linguistic Theory*. The Hague: Mouton.

Chomsky, Noam. 1973. Conditions on Transformations, in S. Anderson and P. Kiparsky, eds., *A Festschrift for Morris Halle*. New York: Holt, Rinehart and Winston.

Chomsky, Noam. 1995. *The Minimalist Program*. Cambridge, Mass.: MIT Press.

Chung, Sandra, William Ladusaw and James McCloskey. 1994. *Sluicing and Logical Form*. UC Santa Cruz.

Grice, H.-Paul. 1975. Logic and Conversation, in P. Cole and J. Morgan, eds., *Syntax and Semantics* 3.41-58. New York: Academic Press.

Huang, C.-T. James. 1982. *Logical Relations in Chinese and the Theory of Grammar*. Doctoral dissertation, MIT.

Katz, Jerrold J. and Paul M. Postal. 1964. *An Integrated Theory of Linguistic Descriptions*. Cambridge, Mass.: MIT Press.

Klima, Edward S. 1964. Negation in English, in J. A. Fodor and J. J. Katz, eds., *The Structure of Language. Readings in the Philosophy of Language.* Englewood Cliffs, NJ: Prentice-Hall.

Li, Y.-H. Audrey. 1992. Indefinite Wh in Mandarin Chinese. *Journal of East Asian Linguistics* 1.125-155.

Pesetsky, David. 1987. Wh-in-situ: Movement and unselective binding, in E. J. Reuland and A.G.B. ter Meulen, eds., *The Representation of indefiniteness*. Cambridge, Mass.: MIT Press.

Reinhart, Tanya. 1995. *Interface Strategies.* OTS Working Papers. Utrecht.

Ross, John R. 1969. Guess who? in R. Binnick et al., eds. *Papers from the Fifth Regional Meeting of the Chicago Linguistic Society.* 252-286. Department of Linguistics, University of Chicago, Chicago, Ill.

Tsai, W.-T. Dylan. 1994. *On Economizing the Theory of A-bar Dependencies.* Doctoral dissertation, MIT.

Watanabe, Akira. 1992. *Wh- in situ, Subjacency, and Chain Formation.* MIT Occasional Working Papers in Linguistics, 2. MITWPL.

Resultatives and Zero Morphology

OLGA BABKO-MALAYA

Rutgers University

1. Introduction[*]

This paper proposes that resultative constructions are formed by affixation of a zero perfectivising verbal prefix. This hypothesis, as shown in the paper, explains the behavior of two types of resultatives in English: transitive and intransitive resultatives discussed in Carrier and Randall 1992.

Examples of transitive and intransitive resultatives are given in (1)-(2):

(1) Transitive resultatives
   a. John watered the tulips flat
   b. The grocer ground the coffee beans into a fine powder
   c. They painted their house a hideous shade of green

(2) Intransitive resultatives
   a. The joggers ran their Nikes threadbare
   b. The kids laughed themselves into a frenzy
   c. He sneezed his handkerchief completely soggy.
                              /Carrier and Randall 1992, p.173/

As the data in (1)-(2) illustrate, transitive resultatives are derived from transitive verbs, whereas intransitive resultatives are based on intransitive unergative verbs.

---

[*] I am indebted to Maria Bittner, Jane Grimshaw and Roger Schwarzschild for discussions and valuable comments.

As discussed in Carrier and Randall 1992, the two types of resultatives differ with respect to nominalization, selectional restrictions and other phenomena which suggest that the postverbal NP in transitive resultatives is the argument of the verb, but the postverbal NP in intransitive resultatives is not. The differences between the two types of resultatives are shown in the paper to follow from the hypothesis that formation of resultatives involves affixation of a zero perfectivising prefix.

The paper proceeds as follows. Section 2 presents the first argument in favor of the presence of a zero prefix in resultative constructions, which is based on Myer's generalization, discussed in Pesetsky 1995. The syntactic analysis of the two types of resultatives and its consequences with respect to nominalization and long-distance extraction of resultative phrases are discussed in section 3. Section 4 proposes a semantic analysis of the transitive and intransitive resultatives, and shows how this analysis explains the 'direct object restriction' (Simpson 1983, Levin and Rappaport 1995) on the resultative phrases, as well as their selectional properties. Finally, section 5 provides cross-linguistic evidence for this analysis, based on parallel behavior of overt perfectivising prefixes in Russian.

2. Myer's Generalization (Pesetsky 1995)

The first piece of evidence for the presence of a zero prefix in resultatives comes from what Pesetsky 1995 calls "Myer's generalization": "Zero derived words do not permit the affixation of further derivational morphemes" (Myers 1984). This generalization is used in his work as a test for zero morphology. For example, an explanation of the ungrammaticality of the following nominals is given under the assumption that the nominalizing suffixes are attached to zero derived verbs, and therefore, are ruled out by Myer's generalization.

(3) a. *Bill's growth of tomatoes /Chomsky 1972/
b. * their gift of Bill books
c. * the book's annoyance of Bill
/Pesetsky 1995/

The assumption that formation of resultative construction involves affixation of a zero morpheme, therefore, leads us to expect that a similar pattern can be observed with resultative constructions. This prediction, as the data in (4)-(6) show, is borne out:

(4) a. Bill grew the tomatoes big
   b. the growth of tomatoes
   c. *the growth of tomatoes big

(5) a. He destroyed the town to rubble
   b. the destruction of the town
   c. *the destruction of the town to rubble

(6) a. He removed the dishes away
   b. the removal of the dishes
   c. *the removal of the dishes away

3. Syntactic Structures

The assumption that resultative constructions are derived by affixation of a zero prefix, as is shown in this section, predicts that there are two possible syntactic representations of the resultative construction. These structures are argued for to correspond to the transitive and intransitive resultatives, illustrated in (1) and (2). The proposed analysis is further shown to explain the fact that in both structures the resultative phrase behaves like an argument of the verb (Simpson 1983, Rothstein 1983, Carrier and Randall 1992 among others), whereas the behavior of the postverbal NP is different in the two constructions.

3.1. A Proposal

Let us adopt the view on the morphological component, advocated in Baker 1988, Borer 1991, Kratzer 1994 among others, according to which morphology determines well-formedness of combination of morphemes regardless of whether the morphemes are combined together prior to the syntax, or as the result of incorporation. According to this proposal affixes can either be base-generated as sisters of V, or they can be the heads of separate projections, and adjoin to verbs as the result of head movement.

Following the proposal in Kratzer 1994, let us further assume that affixes head a separate projection if and only if they have an argument to realize. In the case of transitive resultatives, the postverbal NP is selected by the verb, and therefore is generated in the Spec of VP position. The resultative prefix is base-generated as a sister of V, as the structure in (7a) shows. In the case of intransitive resultatives, on the other hand, the postverbal NP is not an argument of the verb, but rather is introduced by the prefix. The resultative prefix, therefore, heads a separate projection, and adjoins to the verb as the result of incorporation.

(7) (a)Transitive Resultative   *(b) Intransitive Resultative*

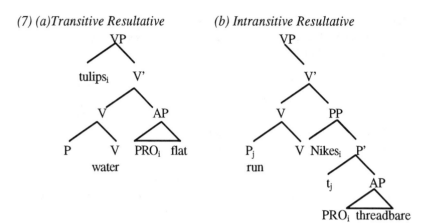

The structures in (7) are based on the assumption that external arguments are introduced outside of VP projection. Specifically, as is discussed in more detail below, the present analysis follows the proposal in Kratzer 1994 that external arguments are not the arguments of the verbs, but rather are introduced syntactically by independent functional heads.

3.2. Resultative phrases are lexically governed by the verb

First, the analysis given above predicts that in both structures the resultative AP is lexically governed by the verb. In the case of transitive resultative, the resultative phrase is the complement of the verb, whereas in the case of intransitive resultatives, the domain of government is extended as the result of incorporation of the prefix (Baker 1988).

This prediction accounts for the observation in Rothstein 1983, Levin and Rappaport 1995, among others, that in languages like Icelandic result denoting adjectives can incorporate left to the verb[1]:

(8) a. þeir máluðu húsið hvítt
     they painted house the white

---

[1] The Icelandic examples cited in the literature are based on transitive resultatives. This phenomenon, however, is a general property of resultative constructions in Icelandic, independent on whether the resultative is transitive or not.

b. þeir hvítmáluðu húsið
they whitepainted house the
/Levin and Rappaport 1995/

Another consequence of this analysis is based on long-distance extraction
of resultative phrases out of wh-islands, discussed in McNulty 1988,
Carrier and Randall 1992:

(9) Extraction of resultative phrases out of transitive resultatives
a. ?How flat do you wonder whether they hammered the metal?
/McNulty 1988/
b. ? How shiny do you wonder which gems to polish?
c. ? Which colors do you wonder which shirts to dye?

(10) Extraction of resultative phrases out of transitive resultatives
a. ?How threadbare do you wonder whether they should run their sneakers?
b. ?How hoarse do you wonder whether they sang themselves?
c. ?How dry do you wonder whether the sun baked the field?
/Carrier and Randall 1992/

As the data in (9)-(10) show, extraction out of wh-islands for both
transitive and intransitive resultatives results in a Subjacency violation,
rather than ECP violation, as in the case of extraction of adjuncts, subjects
or depictives:

(11) Long-distance extraction our of adjuncts, subjects and depictives:
a. * How$_i$ do you wonder whether to punish these boys t$_i$?
b. * Who$_i$ do you wonder [which boys]$_j$ t$_i$ should punish t$_j$?
c. * [How angry]$_i$ does Mary wonder whether John left t$_i$?
/Carrier and Randall 1992/

The contrast between (9)-(10) and (11), therefore, is predicted, given that
resultative APs in (7) are lexically governed by the verb.

3.3. Resultative Nominalization

The data discussed in this section illustrates the first difference between the
two types of resultatives. As discussed in Carrier and Randall 1992,
transitive and intransitive resultatives show different behavior with respect
to *ing$_{of}$* nominalization, i.e. nominals derived by *-ing* suffix that take *of-*
NPs:

(12) *Transitive resultative nominals*
a. The watering of tulips flat is a criminal offense in Holland
b. The slicing of cheese into thin wedges is the current rage
c. The Surgeon General warns against the cooking of food black

(13) *Intransitive resultative nominals*
a. *the drinking of oneself sick is commonplace in one's freshman year
b. *the talking of your confidant silly is a bad idea
c. *What Christmas shopping means to me is the walking of my feet to
pieces   /Carrier and Randall 1992, p. 201/

Let us adopt a proposal in Abney 1987, that this type of nominals is derived by affixation of a nominalizing suffix *-ing* to a verb presyntactically. In this respect *ing*$_{of}$ nominals are different from the other types of *-ing* nominals, which are derived by nominalizing maximal projections: VP or IP.

Given this analysis, we can show that the contrast in (12)-(13) follows from the structures proposed above and two independently motivated assumptions (i) morphological subcategorization of a resultative prefix does not allow it to be adjoined to nouns[2], and (ii) presyntactic derivation precedes syntactic incorporation.

In the case of transitive resultative nominals, the nominalising suffix *-ing* attaches to a prefix-verb combination, as (14) shows[3]:

(14)

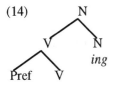

---

[2] This restriction seems to be a general property of all perfectivising operators, such as particles in English, and overt perfectivising prefixes in Slavic languages, which cannot be adjoined to nouns.

[3] The suffix *-ing* in this case is attached to a zero derived verb. Under the approaches which assume that this affix is derivational, this structure violates Myer's generalisation However, as discussed in Pesetsky 1995, Myer's generalisation applies only to a certain type of suffixes, specifically those which cannot in general be adjoined to already suffixed verbs (cf.Fabb 1988), independent on whether they were derived by overt or zero affixes. The suffix *-ing* , therefore, patterns with other suffixes which can be adjoined to already suffixed verbs. Examples of such suffixes are *-er* and *-able*, which, as discussed in Pesetsky 1995, violate Myer's generalisation.

This structure cannot be derived for intransitive resultative nominals, where the prefix is adjoined to a verb in the syntax, as the result of head movement. Nominalization, on the other hand, is done presyntactically, and therefore precedes the syntactic incorporation of the resultative prefix.

Another possible structure is given in (15). In this structure the verb nominalizes in the lexicon, and then the prefix is adjoined to it as the result of head movement. This structure, however, is ruled out by the morphological subcategorization of the prefix, since it is adjoined to a noun, and not a verb.

(15)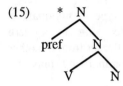

4. Semantic Interpretation

This section shows that given the syntactic structures discussed above, and the rules of compositional semantics in Bittner 1994, 1998, the two types of resultatives have different logical translations. The proposed semantic analysis is shown to account for the aspectual properties of the resultative construction (Dowty 1979, Hoekstra 1988, Van Valin 1990, Pustejovsky 1991 and others), as well as the fact that resultative phrases cannot be predicated of the subjects and indirect objects (Simpson 1983, Levin and Rappaport 1995). Finally, the section discusses different behavior of the two types of resultatives with respect to their selectional properties (Carrier and Randall 1992).

4.1. The semantics of the resultative prefix

The analysis given below relies on Dowty 1979 decomposition approach, according to which semantic representation of sentences is derived by means of aspectual operators DO, CAUSE and BECOME. In Dowty 1979 these operators are part of the lexical representation of a verb. The present analysis, however, assumes in the spirit of Generative Semantics (e.g. McCawley 1968) that decomposition can be done in the syntax. More specifically, I assume that aspectual operators are affixes, which, as has been discussed above, can adjoin to the verb either presyntactically, or as the result of incorporation. The predicate DO, for example, under this analysis is a zero affix which projects a separate constituent that introduces an agent.

The resultative prefix is composed from the operators CAUSE and BECOME, and is defined as a 3-place relation between the denotations of a verb, a noun phrase, and a resultative phrase:

(16) $\lambda P \lambda q \lambda y$ CAUSE (P(y), BECOME(q))[4]

For example, the logical translation of the sentence in (17) is given in (18):

(17) John wiped the table clean
(18) DO(j, CAUSE(wipe$_{<e,t>}$(the-table), BECOME(clean(the-table))))

Transitive verbs like 'wipe' in this analysis, following Kratzer 1994, are analyzed as properties, predicated of the internal argument. The external argument, on the other hand, is introduced by the aspectual operator DO[5], which denotes a relation between a proposition and an agent (Dowty 1979). The sentence in (17) is predicted to be true, therefore, in case John is an agent of the proposition which says that wiping of the table causes the table to become clean.

One of the consequences of this analysis concerns aspectual interpretation of resultative constructions, which denote Vendler/Dowty accomplishments, independent on lexical aspectual properties of the verb. For example, although the verb in (19) is an activity, the resultative construction derived from this verb is an accomplishment, as the durational phrases illustrate:

(19) John ran (for an hour/*in an hour)
(20) John ran the pavement thin (*for an hour/in an hour)

If a causative reading associated with a resultative construction comes from the semantics of the resultative prefix, then this aspectual shift is explained.

---

[4] All logical expressions below are intensions (cf.Church 1940). The variables P, Q in the expressions below are of the type <e,t>; variables p, q are of the type t, and x, y are individual variables.
[5] In this respect the present analysis differs from Kratzer 1994, where external arguments are introduced by thematic operators.

4.2. Compositional derivation

The example in (21) below illustrates compositional derivation of the transitive resultative given in (17). The structure in (21) adopts the proposal in Kratzer 1994, that external arguments are not the true arguments of the verb, but rather are introduced syntactically, by the heads of a VoiceP projection.

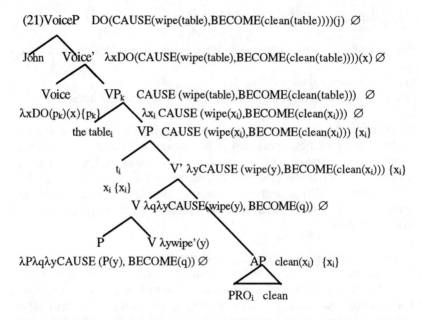

(21) VoiceP   DO(CAUSE(wipe(table),BECOME(clean(table)))))(j) $\varnothing$

John   Voice' $\lambda x DO(CAUSE(wipe(table),BECOME(clean(table)))))(x)$ $\varnothing$

Voice VP_k CAUSE (wipe(table),BECOME(clean(table))) $\varnothing$
$\lambda x DO(p_k)(x)\{p_k\}$ λx_i CAUSE (wipe(x_i),BECOME(clean(x_i))) $\varnothing$
the table$_i$ VP   CAUSE (wipe(x_i),BECOME(clean(x_i))) $\{x_i\}$

t_i V' λyCAUSE (wipe(y),BECOME(clean(x_i))) $\{x_i\}$
$x_i \{x_i\}$
V $\lambda q\lambda y$CAUSE(wipe(y), BECOME(q)) $\varnothing$

P   V λywipe'(y)
$\lambda P\lambda q\lambda y$CAUSE (P(y), BECOME(q)) $\varnothing$ AP   clean(x_i) $\{x_i\}$

PRO$_i$ clean

The translation rules and the semantics of empty categories and traces are adopted from Bittner 1994, 1998. Each translation has two coordinates: an expression and a store. The store is a set of variables (as in Rooth and Partee 1982). The filtering component requires that the store in the final translation must be empty. PRO and traces in this analysis are translated as indexed variables, which are kept in store. Variables from the store can be bound in case the index of the variable coincides with the index of one of the sister constituents. For example, given that the index of x_i coincides with the index of the NP 'the table$_i$' adjoined to VP in (21), the translation of the lowest VP can undergo the binding rule, so that the resulting translation can be combined with the NP by function application[6].

---

[6] Definite noun phrases are assumed in the derivations to be of the type e. This assumption is made to simplify the structures, and nothing crucial for the purposes of this paper hinges upon it.

The derivation of the intransitive resultative is based on one additional operation which is called substitution binding in Bittner 1998. In this operation every occurrence of a stored variable is substituted by a functional complex, such as P(x) for p. This operation applies to the translation of the predicate DO in the derivation of intransitive resultatives in (23), given that the translation of the VP in this case is a property, and the predicate DO requires a proposition as its argument. Application of this operation, motivated by independent phenomena in Bittner 1998, allows us to preserve a uniform translation for the predicate DO. Given these assumptions, the translation of the sentence in (22) is as in (23):

(22) John run the pavement thin

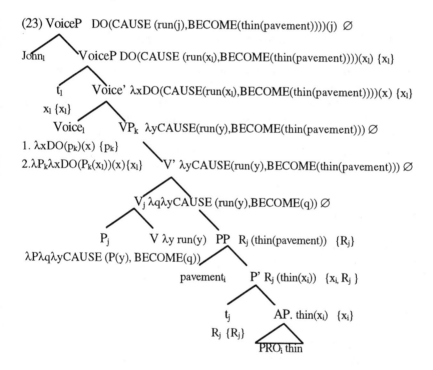

(23) VoiceP DO(CAUSE (run(j),BECOME(thin(pavement))))(j) $\emptyset$

John$_l$ VoiceP DO(CAUSE (run(x$_l$),BECOME(thin(pavement))))(x$_l$) {x$_l$}

t$_l$ Voice' λxDO(CAUSE(run(x$_l$),BECOME(thin(pavement))))(x) {x$_l$}

x$_l$ {x$_l$}

Voice$_l$ VP$_k$ λyCAUSE(run(y),BECOME(thin(pavement))) $\emptyset$

1. λxDO(p$_k$)(x) {p$_k$}

2.λP$_k$$\lambda$xDO(P$_k$(x$_l$))(x){x$_l$}   V' λyCAUSE(run(y),BECOME(thin(pavement))) $\emptyset$

V$_j$ λqλyCAUSE (run(y),BECOME(q)) $\emptyset$

P$_j$ V λy run(y)   PP R$_j$ (thin(pavement)) {R$_j$}

λPλqλyCAUSE (P(y), BECOME(q))

pavement$_i$ P' R$_j$ (thin(x$_i$)) {x$_i$, R$_j$ }

t$_j$ AP. thin(x$_i$) {x$_i$}

R$_j$ {R$_j$}

PRO$_i$ thin

Let us note that under this analysis the external argument of the verb *run* is semantically analyzed as the argument of both the verb and the predicate DO. This assumption departs from Kratzer 1994, who follows Marantz 1984 in the assumption that all external arguments are not the true arguments of the verb. Under the present analysis transitive verbs are properties, predicated of internal arguments, whereas intransitive verbs are properties predicated of external arguments. Syntactically, however, as in Kratzer 1994, all external arguments are introduced by functional heads.

4.3. Direct Object Restriction

One of the consequences of these derivations is a restriction on possible interpretations of resultatives, discussed in Simpson 1983, Levin and Rappaport 1995 among others, according to which resultative phrases can only be predicated of the postverbal NP, but not of the subject, or of an oblique complement. The sentence in (24a) from Levin and Rappaport 1995, for example, cannot be interpreted as in (24b):

(24) a. Terry wiped the table clean
    b. #Terry became clean as the result of wiping the table

This fact follows from the compositional derivation of the resultative constructions. Given that the prefix adjoins to the verb (either presyntactically or as the result of incorporation), the only noun phrase which can fill the argument position in the translation of the prefix is the NP which is generated in the Spec of VP position. If this position is associated with the direct object position, as Kratzer's analysis suggests (cf. also Larson 1988, Hale and Keyser 1993 among others), then the Direct Object Restriction is explained.

4.4. Selectional properties

Now let us turn to the consequences of the derivations given above with respect to the differences between transitive and intransitive resultatives. These differences are shown to follow from the final translations of the two types of resultatives given in (21) and (23) and repeated here in (25b) and (26b):

(25) a. John wiped the table clean
    b. DO(CAUSE(wipe(table), BECOME(clean(table)))(j)

(26) a. John run the pavement thin
    b. DO(CAUSE(run(John), BECOME(thin(pavement)))(j)

The translations in (25b) and (26b) differ in the following respect. In the case of transitive resultatives the postverbal NP fills the argument position of both the verb and the resultative predicate. In the case of intransitive resultatives, on the other hand, the argument of the verb is an external argument, whereas the postverbal NP fills only the argument position of the resultative phrase.

This assumption predicts the difference in the selectional restrictions between the two types of resultatives, discussed in Carrier and Randall 1992, which are illustrated in (27)-(29) below:

(27) a. The bears frightened the hikers
      b. The bears frightened the hikers speechless.
      c. *The bears frightened the campground.
      d. *The bears frightened the campground empty

(28) a. The baby shattered the porringer
      b. The baby shattered the porringer into pieces
      c. *The baby shattered the oatmeal
      d. *The baby shattered the oatmeal into portions

(29) a. *The joggers ran their Nikes
      b. *The kids laughed themselves
      c. *He sneezed his handkerchief
                    /Carrier and Randall 1992/

The data in (27)-(28) illustrate that selectional properties of the verbs are preserved in the case of transitive resultatives. Selectional properties of the verbs are usually attributed to theta-role assignment under sisterhood (Chomsky 1981). Under this approach, the fact that transitive resultatives select for the postverbal NPs, as well as resultative phrases (see data in (8)-(10)), is used as evidence for the ternary branching of the resultative constructions (Rothstein 1983, Simpson 1983, Carrier and Randall 1992, among others).

As discussed in Bittner (to appear), we can maintain binary branching in the syntax if we shift the semantic selection from the syntax into semantics. The fact that postverbal NPs in the case of transitive resultatives must satisfy selectional restrictions of the verb follows under this approach from the logical representation, given that they serve as semantic arguments of the verb. If verbs are partial functions, defined on certain classes of arguments compatible with their meaning, then selectional properties of

the verbs follow from the tools of the compositional semantics (cf. also
Bittner (to appear)).

5. Parallel Behavior of Overt Perfectivising Prefixes in Russian

The hypothesis that resultative constructions are derived by affixation of a
zero perfectivising prefix is further supported by parallel behavior of overt
perfectivising prefixes in languages like Russian. As the following
sentences illustrate, the perfectivising prefix 'pere' in (30a) preserves the
adicity of a verb, i.e. the number of its arguments, whereas in (30b) it
changes an intransitive verb into a transitive one.

(30) a. Ivan **pere**pisal   pis'mo
         Ivan pere-write letter-ACC
         Ivan rewrote the letter

     b. Ivan **pere**krichal otca
         Ivan pere-shout father
         Ivan outshouted the father

(31) a. Ivan pisal   pis'mo
         Ivan wrote-IMP letter-ACC
         Ivan was writing a letter

     b. *Ivan krichal otca
         Ivan shouted father

Given syntactic assumptions discussed above, we can suggest that in (30a)
this prefix is base-generated as the sister of the verb, whereas in (30b) it
projects a prepositional phrase, and adjoins to the verb as the result of
incorporation. This analysis predicts that perfective verbs in the examples
in (30) are similar to transitive and intransitive resultatives in all respects
except for Myer's generalization.

Consider for example the data in (32). As in the case of resultative
constructions in English, Russian perfective verbs can undergo ing_{of}
nominalization only if the prefix is base-generated as the sister of the verb:

(32) a. **pere**pisyvanije pis'ma
        the rewriting of the letter

b. *perekrichanije otca
the outshouting of the father

A similar pattern can be observed with respect to adjectival passive formation:

(33) *Adjectival passives from transitive resultatives*
a. the stomped-flat grapes
b. the spun-dry sheets

(34) *Adjectival passives from intransitive resultatives*
a. *the danced-thin soles
b. *the run-threadbare Nikes
/Carrier and Randall 1992, p.195/

(35) **perepisannoje pis'mo**
rewritten letter

(36) *perekrichannyi otec
outshouted father

An analysis of adjectival passive is beyond the scope of this paper. However, the data above supports the hypothesis that resultatives are derived by affixation of a zero perfectivising prefix, given that parallel behavior of the two types of resultatives and perfective verbs in Russian under this analysis is not unexpected.

References

Abney, S..P. 1987. *The English Noun Phrase in its Sentential Aspects* Ph.D. Dissertation, MIT

Baker, M. 1988. *Incorporation. A Theory of Grammatical Function Changing.* Univ. of Chicago Press, Chicago

Bittner, M. 1994. "Cross-Linguistic Semantics", *Linguistics and Philosophy 17:* 5, 57-108

Bittner, M. 1998. "Cross-Linguistic Semantics for Questions", *Linguistics and Philosophy 21:* 1-82.

Bittner, M. (to appear) "Concealed Causatives", to appear in *Natural Language Semantics*

Borer, H. 1991. "The Causative-Inchoative Alternation: A Case Study in Parallel Morphology". *The Linguistic Review 8:* 119-158.

Carrier, J. and J. Randall. 1992. "The Argument Structure and Syntactic Structure of Resultatives", *Linguistic Inquiry 23:* 173-234.

Chomsky, N. 1972. *Studies on Sematics in Generative Grammar,* The Hague: Mouton

Chomsky, N. 1981. *Lectures on Government and Binding.* Dordrecht: Foris

Church, A. 1940. "A Formulation of the Simple Theory of Types", *The Journal of Symbolic Logic 5,* 56-68.

Dowty, D. 1979. *Word Meaning and Montaque Grammar,* Dordrecht:Reidel

Fabb, N. 1988. "English Affixation is Constrained only by Selectional Restrictions", *Natural Language and Linguistic Theory 6,* 527-540.

Hale, K. and S.J.Keyser 1993. "On Argument Structure and the Lexical Expression of Syntactic Relations" in K. Hale and S.J. Keyser (eds.) *The View From Building 20: Essays in Linguistics in Honor of Sylvan Bromberger,* The MIT Press, Cambridge/Mass.

Hoekstra, T. 1988. "Small Clause Results", *Lingua* 74: 101-139

Kratzer, A. 1994. "The Event Argument and the Semantics of Voice". Univ. of Massachusetts ms.

Larson, R. 1988 "On the Double Object Construction", *Linguistic Inquiry 19:* 335-394

Levin, B. and M.Rappaport Hovav. 1995. *Unaccusativity.* The MIT Press, Cambridge/Mass.

Marantz, A. 1984 *On the Nature of Grammatical Relations.* The MIT Press, Cambridge/Mass.

McCawley, J.D. 1968 "The Role of Sematics in a Grammar" in E.Bach and R.Harms (eds.) *Universals in Linguistic Theory* Holt, Rinehart, and Winston, New York, 124-169.

McNulty, E. 1988. *The Syntax of Adjunct Predicates.* Ph.D. Dissertation, Connecticut, Storrs.

Myers, S. 1984 "Zero-derivation and Inflection", *MIT WPL 7,* Dept. of Linguistics and Philosophy, MIT, Cambridge/Mass.

Pesetsky, D. 1995 *Zero Syntax: Experiencers and Cascades* The MIT Press, Cambridge/Mass.

Pustejovsky, J. 1991. "The Syntax of Event Structure". *Cognition 41:* 47-81

Rooth, M. and B. Partee 1982. "Conjunction, TYpe Ambiguity and Wide Scope 'Or'", *Proceedings of WCCFL 1,* Stanford Univ. California, 353-362.

Rothstein, S. 1983 *The Syntactic Forms of Predication,* Ph.D Dissertation, MIT, Cambridge [Published in 1985 by Indiana University Linguistics Club,Bloomington]

Simpson, J. 1983. "Resultatives" in L.Levin, M.Rappaport, and A.Zaenen, eds. *Papers in Lexical-Functional Grammar,* Bloomington: Indiana University Linguistics Club: 143-157.

Van Valin, R.D. "Semantic Parameters of Split Intransitivity", *Language 66,* 221-260.

obabko@rci.rutgers.edu

On the Interpretation of *there* in Extentials

SJEF BARBIERS & JOHAN ROORYCK

HIL/ Leiden University

1. Introduction[*]

In this paper, we would like to show that a large number of properties of existential sentences which have been noted in the pragmatic literature (Ward and Birner (1995) and references cited therein), can be derived from the syntactic configuration generated by the presence of *there*. We claim that existential *there* makes three syntactic and semantic contributions to a sentence, as listed in (1):

(1)   I.   *There* is a topic, base-generated in spec,TopP;

       II.   *There* denotes a relation between a hearer-<u>new</u> part and a hearer-<u>old</u> whole.

       III.   *There* is a proform of the complement of Top, i.e. FocP. It forces FocP to be interpreted as a relation between a hearer-new part and a hearer-old whole. Put differently, FocP is an instantiation of the relation denoted by *there*.

---

[*]   We would like to thank the *WCCFL XVII* audience for questions and comments. Thanks also go to Ana Arregui, Marcel den Dikken, Jenny Doetjes, Arantzatzu Elordieta, Helen de Hoop, Aniko Liptak, Olaf Koeneman, Michael Rochemont, Guido Vanden Wyngaerd, and Chris Wilder for suggestions and discussion. The usual disclaimers apply.

The structure of the paper is as follows. We will first go into some background assumptions with respect to the syntactic configuration and principles involved in *there* sentences (section 2), before evaluating the empirical consequences of this proposal in section 3. In this section, the so-called 'definiteness restriction' on the subject in *there* sentences will be shown to follow from properties of FocP. Various well known restrictions on the predicate in *there* sentences will be related to the part-whole relation forced by *there*. Finally, we present some curious new data involving restrictions on extraction from *there*-sentences, which will be elegantly derived from Chomsky's (1995) Minimal Link Condition. In section 4, we investigate further consequences of our analysis for the distribution of *there*, and for the impossibility of topical object preposing in Dutch.

2. Assumptions

Following Rizzi (1995), we assume a layered structure for the left edge of CP as in (2). The reader is referred to Rizzi (1995) for motivation of the relative order of ForceP, TopP and FocP. We assume that a constituent in specTopP is interpreted as hearer-old information. *There* is base-generated in SpecTopP. It involves old information, as is also evidenced by the fact that it is phonologically destressed. *There* is coindexed with the complement of Top: FocP. FocP should thus be viewed as the associate of *there*. The (indefinite) subject of *there*-sentences receives case in SpecIP position (see also Lasnik 1995). We assume that a constituent in SpecFocP is interpreted as hearer-new information. The subject moves from SpecIP to SpecFocP position, and is interpreted as hearer-new information. This configuration requires that the verb move up to Top position in *there* sentences.

(2)

ForceP
- spec
- ForceP
  - Force
  - TopP
    - *there* j (= topic)
    - TopP
      - Top
      - FocP j (= comment)
        - *subject* i (= hearer-new)
        - FocP
          - Foc
          - IP (= presupposition)
            - t i
            - IP
              - I
              - (AgrOP)
                - (object)
                - (AgrOP)

In addition to the assumptions spelled out in (2), we assume (an informal version of) Chomsky's (1995) Minimal Link Condition, stating that no more than one spec-position can be skipped. The idea that SpecFocP is associated with hearer-new information and SpecTopP with hearer-old information has a corollary: the opposite information values of SpecTopP and SpecFocP entail that a constituent cannot move from SpecFocP to SpecTopP, since this would provide such a constituent with a contradictory information status.

3. Consequences

3.1 Conditions on the subject

Let us first evaluate the consequences of the representation in (2) with respect to the properties of the subject. Since Milsark (1974), it is well known that the subject in *there* sentences displays a so-called Definiteness effect. This term is however quite misleading, since at least some definites can actually occur as the subject of *there* sentences, as shown in (3) (Milsark (1974), Rando and Napoli (1978), Reed (1982), Ward and Birner (1995)). The contrast in (3c-d) shows that definite DPs which can only be interpreted as 'hearer-old' topics such as the pronouns *het* and *it*, cannot appear as subjects in *there*-sentences.

(3)   a.   Er is ook nog JAN
        b.   There's also John
        c.   Er is ook nog DIT/*het
        d.   There is also THIS/*it
        e.   Er staan de mooiste bloemen in de tuin
            I. 'There are very nice flowers in the garden'
            II. # 'The most beautiful (of a given set of) flowers are
            in the garden'
        f.   Er staan veel bloemen in de tuin
            I. 'There are many flowers in the garden'
            II. # 'Many of the flowers are in the garden'

We would like to explore the idea that the so-called Definiteness effect is not a consequence of partitive case-assignment (Belletti (1988)), but of the configurationally determined 'hearer-new' information status of the subject in *there* sentences. The idea that the subject in SpecFocP must be interpreted as hearer-new can explain both the preference for indefinite subjects and the conditions determining the appearance of definite subjects in *there*-sentences.

Putting information-status aside, the difference between definite and indefinite DPs is that definite DPs are identifiable, while indefinite DPs are not: i.e. the identity of indefinite DPs cannot be ascertained (Ward and Birner (1995)). Placing a definite DP in SpecFocP, where it configurationally receives 'hearer-new' information status, gives rise to a potential conflict, since identifiable DPs are 'hearer-old' in the unmarked case. For definite DPs to appear in SpecFocP, this potential conflict must be solved by the context. One way to solve this conflict involves an interpretation by which definite, i.e. identifiable DPs, are nevertheless presented as new. This is the case in the 'forget' context which licenses the definite subject in (2a-c): the subject, though identifiable by virtue of its definiteness, is nevertheless interpretable as new information via the 'forget' context. As Ward and Birner (1995) note, the 'forget' context is just one of several possibilities for solving this conflict.

The interpretation of the superlative subject in (3e) can be explained in a similar way. The subject in (3e) only has an absolute superlative interpretation, and not the expected relative superlative interpretation. In our view, this can be explained as follows. The relative superlative interpretation is partitive and requires a given, i.e. identifiable set of flowers. The presence of the subject in the configurationally 'hearer-new' SpecFocP precludes an interpretation of the DP as identifiable. As a result, the only remaining interpretation for the DP in (3e) is the absolute superlative interpretation which does not require reference to an identifiable set. A similar analysis holds for the absolute and relative interpretation of *veel* 'many' in (3f).

This analysis has a number of consequences for the position of the subject in sentences without *there*. We argue that subjects in such sentences usually occupy the position that *there* occupies in (2). The contrast between *there-* and *there*-less sentences can be represented as follows:

(4)   a. $[_{TopP}$ there are $[_{FocP}$ [these people]$_i$ $[_{IP}$ t$_i$ in the garden]]]
      b. $[_{TopP}$ [these people]$_i$ are $[_{FocP}$ ___ $[_{IP}$ t$_i$ in the garden]]]

In other words, subjects move from SpecIP to SpecTopP, skipping SpecFocP in accordance with the Minimal Link Condition. As a result, subjects acquire hearer-old status and avoid the hearer-new status associated with SpecFocP. With respect to (5a-b), the effects of (3) can now be observed in reverse: the relative superlative interpretation is required, because the DP in SpecTopP must be interpreted as hearer-old information. The same partitive interpretation applies to (5b).[1]

---

[1]   As Helen de Hoop (p.c.) correctly observes, the absolute interpretation of the superlative in (5a) and the absolute interpretation of *veel* 'many' in (5b) are available, provided that the superlative and *veel* 'many' are stressed. We take this marked intonation pattern to indicate that the subject is interpreted in a position lower than its surface position (cf. similar effects in *ALL people didn't call*, where *all* takes narrow scope with respect to negation). More specifically, we take the subject to be interpreted in SpecFocP in these cases. Alternatively, we could assume that there is no TopP in such cases.

(5) a. De mooiste bloemen staan in de tuin
         the nicest flowers are in the garden
         I. #'There are very nice flowers in the garden
         II. 'The most beautiful (of a given set of) flowers are
         in the garden
     b. Veel bloemen staan in de tuin
         I. # 'There are many flowers in the garden'
         II. 'Many of the flowers are in the garden'
     c. Een plant staat *(doorgaans) in de tuin
         a plant is usually in the garden

The sentence (5c) represents an interesting case. An indefinite DP subject in SpecTopP gives rise to a potential conflict: indefiniteness usually corresponds to unidentifiability, whereas SpecTopP configurationally endows a constituent with 'hearer-old' information status. The properties of unidentifiability and 'hearer-old' information status are difficult to reconcile, and create a potential interpretive conflict. This conflict can however be solved through a generic interpretation for the sentence, which is one way of allowing unidentifiable indefinites to be interpreted as 'hearer-old'. In terms of configurational information requirements, the case in (5c) can be considered the mirror image of the definiteness constraint in (3).

The analysis presented here relies heavily on the idea that constituents acquire part of their interpretation by movement, in this case, their information status. This is not an uncommon view. It can be found in Diesing's (1992) work on the interpretation of indefinites, and in Bennis' (1995), Postma's (1995) work on the Dutch *Wh-* word *wat* 'what', whose interpretation as an indefinite or as a *Wh-* NP varies with its configurational position, as illustrated in (6-7).

(6)   Jan at wat   (7)   Wat at Jan
         John ate what   what ate John
         I. 'John ate something'   I. # 'John ate something'
         II. #'What did John eat' II. 'What did John eat'

With respect to alternative analyses of *there* sentences, it is important to point out that our analysis both precludes an approach in terms of covert subject raising and an analysis in terms of feature raising (Chomsky (1995)). Adapting the analysis developed here in terms of a feature-based framework for movement, raising of a 'hearer-old' feature to *there* would erroneously predict that subjects could be 'hearer-old' when in a position lower than SpecTopP. By contrast, in our analysis, subjects can only acquire a 'hearer-old' or 'hearer-new' interpretation through overt movement to the position where this interpretation is assigned.

3.2 Conditions on the predicate

In addition to the restrictions on the subject, *there*-sentences also involve restrictions on the predicate. We have assumed that *there* is a proform of FocP, and that it denotes a relation between a hearer-new part and a hearer-old whole (cf. 1.II). It follows that FocP must denote a relation between a hearer-new part and a hearer-old whole (cf. 1.III).

Before developing the consequences of this view, we would like to present some initial evidence that a part-whole interpretation of *there* is necessary. The new-part-of-old-whole analysis makes it possible to present a unified analysis of Dutch 'expletive' *er* 'there' and quantitative *er* 'of-it'. In (8), quantitative *er* can be taken to represent a relation between 'hearer-old' sharks and the 'hearer-new' ones seen by me.

(8)   Over haaien gesproken, ik heb er (twee) gezien
        talking about sharks, I have there two seen

Since quantitative *er* requires a part-whole analysis, the null hypothesis is that existential *er* 'there' also has such an interpretation.

We then have to investigate how this part-whole relation of *er,* and, by extension, *there,* would surface in the context of existentials where *er* is coindexed with a FocP as in (2), rather than with an NP as in (8). It is our contention that the part-whole relation of *there* in existentials is realized on the FocP it is coindexed with, and more in particular on the predicate contained in this FocP.

The effects of this relation can be observed in the well-known restriction of the predicates in *there*-sentences to stage-level and nonstative predicates, as illustrated in (9) and (10) (Milsark (1974)):

(9)   a.   Er is een student beschikbaar/*intelligent
        b.   There is a student available/*intelligent
(10)   a.   Er viel een boek op de grond
               there fell a book on the ground
        b.   *Er kost een boek een gulden
               there costs a book a guilder

These data can be accounted for as follows in terms of the part-whole relation imposed by *there.* Stage-level predicates and nonstative predicates can be viewed as part-whole relations inherently, in the sense that they are true for only part of the temporal axis associated with the subject. By contrast, individual-level predicates and stative predicates are generally true for the entire temporal axis associated with the subject, and as a result they are inherently not part-whole. The 'stage-level/ nonstative' restriction on the predicate in *there* sentences can thus be reduced to the requirement that the predicate be interpretable as part-whole.

There are some additional indications that this account of the restriction in terms of 'part-whole' relations is on the right track. Sentences with individual and stative predicates are greatly improved if the subject contains a Focused indefinite quantifier. This is illustrated by (11):

(11)   a.   Er zijn maar TWEE studenten intelligent
        b.   There are only TWO students intelligent
        c.   Er kost maar EEN boek een gulden
            there costs only one book a guilder

By focusing the indefinite quantifier in the subject, a partitioning is imposed on the numerical axis associated with the subject: the predicate is true for part of this numerical axis, and false for the rest of the axis (Barbiers (1995)). This partitioning fulfills the part-whole requirement. Since IP can be identified with AgrSP/TP, and since AgrS has the index (i.e. the features) of the subject, a part-whole relation defined on the subject is a part-whole relation defined on IP, and, by extension, on FocP.[2]

    An important consequence of this analysis is that it falsifies Milsark's (1977) classical account of the unavailability of individual level predicates in *there*-sentences. Milsark (1977) relates the ungrammaticality of individual level predicates in *there* sentences to the fact that these same predicates are also ungrammatical with an indefinite subject in the canonical subject position. In other words, (12a) is ungrammatical because (12b) is.

(12)   a.   *There was a basketball player tall
        b.   *A basketball player was tall

However, the contrast in (13) shows that this cannot be quite true: while (13a) can be improved by a generic interpretation (cf. supra), (13b) cannot.

(13)   a.   A basketball player *(usually) was tall in those days
        b.   *There was (usually) a basketball player tall in those days

The analysis advocated here provides two distinct explanations for the sentences in (13a-b). The sentence (13a) is ungrammatical without a generic interpretation because an unidentifiable indefinite DP is in the 'hearer-old' SpecTopP. The sentence (13b), by contrast, is ruled out because *tall* is an individual level-predicate, precluding a part-whole relation.

---

[2]   Olaf Koeneman (p.c.) points out that the part-whole relation we posit on FocP is difficult to trace in impersonal and objectless passives such as (i):

i.   Er werd gedanst   ii.   Er werd naar huis geschreven
    There was danced   There was to home written

We assume an analysis for the intransitives in (i) parallel to that of the transitives with an empty object in (ii). The intransitive in (i) can be taken to involve an indefinite empty (cognate) object. This implicit object is the subject of the *there* impersonal passive. Being indefinite and in SpecFocP, the empty object denotes unidentifiable 'hearer-new' information.

3.3 Conditions on extraction from *there*-sentences

In this section, we turn to the predictions of the structure in (2) with respect to extraction from *there*-sentences. A crucial property of this structure is that it involves three subsequent filled Specifier positions: *there* in SpecTopP, the subject in SpecFocP, and the trace of the subject in SpecIP. Let us now suppose, following Rizzi (1995), that movement proceeds via Specifier positions only, and assume Chomsky's (1995) Minimal Link Condition. Under these conditions, the predictions made by the structure in (2) are as follows.[3]

First of all, everything dominated by IP is trapped, and cannot be extracted. SC-predicates, low adverbials such as manner adverbs, and objects in transitive expletive constructions (TECs) cannot be preposed, regardless of their information status. This is so because in the structure for *there*-sentences in (2), preposing would involve movement of a constituent to SpecForceP, skipping three filled Specifier positions and thus violating the Minimal Link Condition. The correctness of this prediction can be evaluated in (14) through (16):

(14)   **Small clause predicates**
  a.   *[$_{PP}$ In de sloot/*slechts in EEN sloot]$_i$ is er iemand t_i
         gesprongen
         in the ditch/only in one ditch is there someone jumped
  b.   *[$_{PP}$ Op de tafel/*slechts op EEN tafel]$_i$ heeft er iemand
         'n kop t_i gezet
         on the table/only on one table has there someone a cup put
  c.   [$_{PP}$ Op de tafel]$_i$ heeft Jan een kopje t_i gezet

(15)   **Low adverbials**
  a.   *PERFECT$_i$ heeft er iemand dat probleem t_i opgelost
         perfectly has there someone that problem solved
  b.   PERFECT$_i$ heeft Jan dat probleem t_i opgelost
         perfectly has John that problem solved

---

[3] As the reader will notice below, we take SpecForceP to be the only landing site for *Wh*-elements and a possible landing site for Focused constituents. Here our assumptions diverge from Rizzi's (1995). The reason is that languages such as Dutch show ordering restrictions in the extended CP domain that differ from those in Italian, but that are nevertheless compatible with the ordering of functional projections proposed by Rizzi (1995). A second difference between Rizzi's proposal and ours is that Rizzi (1995) allows for recursion of TopP below FocP. This low TopP does not seem to be available in Dutch, and can be shown to be immaterial for the argument in the main text.

(16)   **Objects in TECs**[4]

    a.   *[$_{DP}$ Hoeveel boeken/wat/dat boek]$_i$ heeft er iemand t_i
            meegenomen?
            how many books/what/this book has there someone taken

    b.   Er heeft iemand drie boeken/dat boek meegenomen
            there has someone three books/that book taken

    c.   Drie boeken/dat/dit boek/*het heeft Piet meegenomen
            three books/that/this book/*it has Pete taken

The sentences (14c), (15b) and (16c) show that *there*-less sentences do not exhibit these restrictions on preposing. Movement to SpecForceP in these cases complies with the Minimal Link Condition, since no more than one Specifier, that involving the subject, needs to be skipped.

A second prediction of our assumptions is that the subject, and high adverbials that can be base-generated as adjuncts to FocP, can prepose by moving to SpecForceP. This is so because they only have to skip SpecTopP, in compliance with the Minimal Link Condition. This can be verified in (17a-b), (17d) and (18a-d):

(17)   **Subjects**

    a.   [$_{ForceP}$ [Hoeveel mensen]$_i$ vroegen [$_{TopP}$ er t_i om geld?]]

    b.   [$_{ForceP}$ [Maar TWEE mensen]$_i$ hebben [$_{TopP}$ er t_i om geld
            gevraagd]]
            only two people have there for money asked

    c.   *[$_{ForceP}$ Zij hebben [$_{TopP}$ er om geld gevraagd]]
            they have there for money asked

    d.   [$_{ForceP}$ [How many people] were [$_{TopP}$ there asking you for
            money today]]

    e.   *[$_{ForceP}$ [Who] is [$_{TopP}$ there asking you for money]]

(18)   **High adjuncts**

    a.   [$_{FceP}$ [$_{PP}$ Slechts in één kamer] heeft [$_{TopP}$ er iemand gebeld]]
            only in one room has there someone called

---

[4]   Olaf Koeneman (p.c.) mentions the following potential counterexample to our generalization that objects in TECs cannot be preposed:

i.   Welk boek heeft er nou NIEMAND gelezen?
    'which book has there now nobody read'

Koeneman (p.c) also points out that this construction involves additional restrictions which are not a general property of TECs. First of all, sentences such as (i) require the presence of modal-like elements such as the particle *nou* or the (affirmative) adverbial *altijd wel*. Secondly, the subject must be negative and focused, as shown in (ii):

ii.   *Welk boek heeft er nou IEMAND/ een jongen gelezen?
    'which book has there now nobody/ a boy read'

The complex interaction of conditions licensing sentences such as (i) makes it unclear whether the sentence in (i) falsifies our generalization. We will leave this problem for further research.

b.   *[$_{ForceP}$ [$_{PP}$ In de kamer] heeft [$_{TopP}$ er iemand gebeld]]
      In the room has there someone called

c.   *[$_{ForceP}$ [$_{PP}$ Daar] heeft [$_{TopP}$ er iemand gebeld]]
      there has there someone called

d.   [$_{PP}$ In de kamer/daar] heeft Piet gebeld
      in the room/there has Pete called

However, movement of subjects and high adverbials is subject to a condition involving their information status. Only 'hearer-new' (non D-linked) subjects and adjuncts can prepose, because they proceed via or originate in FocP and must skip SpecTopP, the position where a constituent is identified as 'hearer-old' information. The contrast between the successfully preposed 'hearer new' subjects in (17a-b) and the unfelicitously preposed 'hearer old' subject in (17c), as well as the difference between the felicitous 'hearer new' preposed PP in (18a) and the unfelicitous 'hearer old' preposed PPs in (18b-c), show that this prediction is correct.

It is important to point out that the analysis outlined here makes more accurate predictions with respect to extraction out of *there-* sentences than that presented in Belvin and den Dikken (1997). Belvin and den Dikken (1997) propose an analysis of *there*-sentences in which the entire sentence is generated in the specifier of a projection containing *there*. They then proceed to derive the restrictions on extraction from *there*-sentences from the general ban on extraction from left branches. This predicts however that no extraction at all should be possible out of *there*-sentences, contrary to fact.

By contrast, the analysis outlined here makes a fine-grained distinction between extractions that are excluded by a strong structural condition such as the Minimal Link Condition (SC-predicates, manner adverbials, TEC objects); and extractions that are allowed by the Minimal Link Condition, but constrained by the properties of the positions available for movement *in casu* the ('hearer-new') information-status associated with SpecFocP (subjects, high adjuncts).

4. Further consequences

In this section, we would like to explore some further consequences of the analysis outlined above. These include preposing of objects in transitive clauses, the relation between *there* and its associate FocP, and the relation between *there* and IP with respect to Case, agreement, and stylistic inversion.

4.1 Why objects cannot be real topics

Travis (1984) and Zwart (1993) observe that the object of a transitive clause cannot be preposed as a topic. The focalized object *jou* 'you' in (19a) contrasts with the necessarily topical *je* 'you' in (19b). Such a restriction does not apply to subjects, as (19c) shows.

(19) a.   Jou hebben we gezien   c.   Je/Jij hebt ons gezien
           you have we seen   you have seen us
      b.   *Je hebben we gezien
           you have we seen   (cf. Travis (1984), Zwart (1993))

The sentence structure we have assumed in (2) affords an explanation for this observation. The structure of a transitive clause without *there* is as in the bracketed structure in (20).

(20)   [$_{ForceP}$ _ Force [$_{TopP}$ _ Top [$_{FocP}$ _ Foc [$_{IP}$ **subject** I
        [$_{AgrOP}$ **object** AgrO]]]]]

Preposing the object necessarily involves movement to SpecFocP: the object can only skip one Specifier at a time, in this case SpecIP, but not SpecFocP. In SpecFocP, the object is identified as hearer-new information. Therefore, it cannot subsequently move to SpecTopP, where it would be marked as hearer-old information, since this would provide the object with contradictory information status. This explains the contrast between (19a) and (19b): the pronoun *je* inherently is an 'hearer-old' topic, and therefore must move to SpecTopP. Since it can only do so by moving through SpecFocP, it receives a contradictory interpretation and the sentence is ruled out. The focalizable *jou* does not encounter this problem. The subject *je* in (19c), however, can reach SpecTopP, skipping only SpecFocP.

 For the same reason, IP-adjoined temporal and locative adjuncts can reach SpecTopP, as in (21a).

(21) a.   [$_{TopP}$ [$_{PP}$ Tijdens de vakantie] [Top zou [$_{FocP}$ ZO'N boek
           [$_{IP}$ t$_{PP}$ [$_{IP}$ zelfs Jan niet lezen]]]]] (observation Neeleman 1994)
           during the vacation would such a book even John not read
      b.   *Tijdens de vakantie zou ZO'N boek je niet lezen
           During the vacation would such a book you not read
      c.   *Tijdens de vakantie zou 't zelfs Jan niet lezen
           During the vacation would it even John not read

The data in (21b-c) support the labeling and bracketing in (21a). As we have shown, reduced subject and object pronouns must license their interpretation by overt movement to SpecTopP. The presence of the adjunct in SpecTopP blocks movement to SpecTopP, hence these reduced pronouns cannot be licensed.[5]

---

[5]   Sentences containing both a reduced subject and a reduced object pronoun at first sight would require two SpecTopPs to be licensed, contrary to our assumptions here. However, we propose that such sentences must be analysed as involving cliticization of the object pronoun to the verb before movement of this cluster to Top.

4.2 *There* and the associate status of FocP

We have taken the position that *there* in existential constructions is not an expletive, but makes the semantic contributions outlined in (1). Moreover, *there* is coindexed with the complement of Top, FocP. In this way, existential *there* strongly resembles expletive *it* in (22) for which Moro (1991) and Rooryck (1997) have also proposed a nonexpletive analysis.

(22) a. It seems that John will come
     b. The situation at hand (= it) resembles a typical situation
         in which John will come.

For Moro (1991) and Rooryck (1997), *it* in (22b) is a pro-CP coindexed with the CP complement of *seem*. Rooryck (1997) makes this relation more explicit by providing a semantic rationale for the relation between pro-CP *it* and the CP complement of *seem* along the lines of (22b): *seem* in (22a) expresses a relation of resemblance between a token situation expressed by *it* and a type-interpreted CP.

The question now arises as to the difference between *there* and *it*. The sentences in (23-24) show that *there* and *it* are in complementary distribution.

(23) a. Het/*er schijnt [$_{CP}$ dat Jan zal komen]
     b. It/*there seems [$_{CP}$ that John will come]
(24) a. Er/*het schijnt [$_{FocP}$ iemand te komen]
     b. There/*it seems [$_{FocP}$ to come someone]

In our view, this is because *there* and *it* make different syntactic and semantic contributions to the sentence. Pro-CP *it* and CP denote situations, while *there* is a proform for FocP and denotes a part-whole relation.

Comparing pro-CP *it* and pro-FocP *there* also raises another question. The traditional expletive analysis for (22) raises the problem of why the CP cannot move into the position of the expletive, yielding sentences such as (24b).

(25) a. It seems [$_{CP}$ that John came]
     b. *[$_{CP}$ That John came] seems t$_{CP}$

Rooryck (1997) solves this problem by assuming that *it* is a token of the situation-type denoted by CP, and that both *it* and CP are necessary because *seem* establishes a resemblance relation between token and type.

The question now likewise arises why FocP cannot move into the position of *there*, SpecTopP. In other words, why is *there* necessary?

(26) a. There came a man into my room
     b. *[$_{TopP}$ [$_{FocP}$ a man t$_i$ into my room]$_j$ [$_{Top}$ came$_i$ t$_j$]]

Within the analysis developed here, the answer to this question is straightforward. FocP denotes 'hearer-new' information. As such, it cannot be moved into a 'hearer-old' SpecTopP, since that would provide FocP with contradictory information status.

4.3 *There* and IP: Case, agreement, stylistic inversion

One of the advantages of the analysis presented here is that it requires no special mechanism for (partitive) case assignment to the subject in English and Dutch. Nominative Case and subject agreement are licensed in SpecIP. The configuration in (2) also accounts for the fact that V in Top has scope over subject in SpecIP, and that the subject cannot bind into a PP lower than *there*, but higher than the subject at surface structure as in **There seem to each other$_i$ to be some of the applicants$_i$ eligible for the job* (Lasnik (1992), attributed to L. Davis; den Dikken (1995)).

The analysis is however left with a problem with respect to agreement and Case in raising contexts. As can be observed in (27), agreement in raising structures is with the subject in the embedded clause:

(27) $[_{TopP}$ There $[_{IP1}$ seem $[_{IP2}$ to be students in the garden]]

In the analysis presented here, this is quite unexpected, since the subject *students* remains in the embedded clause, agreeing with the local I, and not with the matrix I. As a result, our analysis would predict that there is no way to ensure plural agreement on the matrix verb *seem*, since the subject does not raise to the extended projection of the matrix *seem* at any point in the derivation. Correspondingly, the embedded infinitival I does not assign Case to the subject, and the configuration does not allow Case to be assigned by *seem*. Under a feature-movement analysis, agreement with and case-assignment by *seem* are straightforward.

The solution we propose for this problem is as follows. First of all, we take sentences with raising verbs followed by an infinitival complement to involve a monoclausal structure, in line with ideas proposed by Cinque (1997). Secondly, we follow Barbiers (1998) in assuming that English and Dutch are underlyingly SOV, and that the different surface positions of the verbs in these languages are the result of a difference in spell-out, as indicated in (28).

(28)   a.   That $[_{TopP}$ there [seem to be] $[_{FocP}$ students
              $[_{IP}$ students [seem to be] $[_{VP}$ in the garden [seem to be]]]]]
        b.   Dat $[_{TopP}$ er [lijken te zijn] $[_{FocP}$ studenten
              $[_{IP}$ studenten [lijken te zijn] $[_{VP}$ in de tuin [lijken te zijn]]]]]

The agreement and Case properties in raising structures now follow in the same way as for the cases discussed above: case on the subject and agreement on the verb are licensed in IP.

A final issue brought up by our analysis concerns the configurational status of IP as the presuppositional complement of Foc in (2). This implies that IP can move to SpecTopP. There seems to be evidence that this is indeed the case. Stylistic Inversion is analyzed by Rochemont and Culicover (1990) as preposing of a remnant VP. In our analysis, this proposal can be advantageously reformulated as involving movement to SpecTopP of a remnant IP as in (29).

(29)   [$_{TopP}$ [$_{IP}$ Into the room nude] j [Top walked$_i$ [$_{FocP}$ a man
         no one knew [Foc t$_i$ t$_j$]]]]]

The advantage of our analysis is that it explicitly captures the information status of the different constituents. The IP acquires 'hearer-old' status, while the subject represents the only new information in (29).

Given that Case of the subject is licensed in SpecIP in *there*-sentences, SpecFocP should in principle be available for constituents other than the subject. The presentational *there* construction seems to be a case in point (Rochemont and Culicover (1990: 29(52a-b)))

(30)   a.   [$_{TopP}$ There walked [$_{FocP}$ [$_{IP}$ into the room] [$_{IP}$ the one man
                she had no desire to see t$_{IP}$]]]
         b.   * There was the one man she had no desire to see in the room.

In (30a), a segment of IP moves into SpecFocP, stranding the subject in SpecIP. We have already assumed (cf supra) that IP can be identified with the subject, since IP equals AGR$_S$P/ TP, and AGR$_S$P has the phi-features of the subject. As a result, movement of the segment of IP is formally equivalent to movement of the subject, but yields slightly different information status results. More specifically, this correctly predicts that the definiteness restriction on the subject is relaxed when the segment of IP moves to SpecFocP. Recall that we derive the definiteness restriction from our assumption that the subject acquires 'hearer-new' status in SpecFocP. Since the subject remains in SpecIP in (30), it does not receive the 'hearer-new' information status hence need not be indefinite. As (30b) shows this prediction is correct.

5.   Conclusion

The results of our analysis can be summed up as follows:
1.   The so-called definiteness restriction on the subject in *there*-sentences, and apparent exceptions to this restriction follow from our assumption that

the subject always moves to SpecFocP where it is identified as 'hearer-new' information.

2. The 'individual-level/ stative' restriction on the predicate in *there*-sentences can be derived from the part-whole relation imposed by *there*. Apparent exceptions involving Focus on an indefinite quantifier within the subject corroborate this idea.

3. The analysis makes a fine-grained distinction between extractions from *there*-sentences that are excluded by the Minimal Link Condition (SC-predicates, manner adverbials, TEC objects), and extractions allowed by the Minimal Link Condition that are only possible for constituents with a 'hearer-new' information status.

4. *There* is not an expletive, but a pro-form of FocP, and thus similar to the CP pro-form *it* in *seem* contexts.

References

Barbiers, Sjef. 1995. The syntax of interpretation. Diss. HIL/ Leiden University.
Barbiers, Sjef. 1998. English and Dutch as SOV languages and the distribution of CP complements. to appear in: R. Kager et al. eds. *Linguistics in the Netherlands 1998.*
Bennis, Hans. 1995. The meaning of structure: The *wat voor* construction revisited, in M. den Dikken and K. Hengeveld eds. *Linguistics in the Netherlands 1995,* 25-36
Belletti, Adriana. 1988. The case of unaccusatives. *Linguistic Inquiry* 19.1-94.
Belvin, Robert and Marcel Den Dikken. 1997. *There* happens *to, be, have. Lingua* 101.151-183.
Cinque, Guglielmo. 1997. Adverbs and functional heads. A cross-linguistic perspective. to appear, Oxford University Press.
Chomsky, Noam. 1995 *The Minimalist Program.* MIT Press, Cambridge (Mass.)
den Dikken, Marcel. 1995. Binding, expletives and levels. *Linguistic Inquiry* 26.347-354.
Diesing, Molly. 1992. Indefinites. Cambridge: The MIT Press
Lasnik, Howard. 1992 Case and Expletives: Notes toward a Parametric Account. *Linguistic Inquiry* 23:3.381-405.
Lasnik, Howard. 1995. Case and expletives revisited: On greed and other human failures. *Linguistic Inquiry* 26:4.615-634.
Milsark, Gary. 1974. Existential sentences in English. Doctoral dissertation, Cambridge: MIT.
Milsark, Gary. 1977. Towards an explanation of certain peculiarities of the existential construction in English. *Linguistic Analysis* 3:1.1-29.
Moro, Andrea. 1991. The raising of predicates: Copula, expletives and existence. *MIT Working Papers in Linguistics* 15.119-181.
Neeleman, Ad. 1994 *Complex Predicates.* Diss. Utrecht University.
Postma, Gertjan. 1995 *Zero Semantics.* Diss. Leiden University.
Rando, E.mily and Donna Jo Napoli. 1978. Definites in *there* sentences. *Language* 54.300-313.
Reed, Ann. 1982. *Contextual reference.* Bloomington: Indiana University Linguistics Club.
Rizzi, Luigi. 1995 The fine structure of the left-periphery. Course material for GISL 1996.
Rochemont, Michael and Peter Culicover. 1990. English focus contructions and the theory of grammar. Cambridge: Cambridge University Press.
Rooryck, Johan. 1997. On the interaction between Raising and Focus in sentential complementation. *Studia Linguistica* 50.1-49.
Travis, Lisa. 1984. *Parameters and effects of word order variation.* Ph.D diss. MIT.
Ward Gregory and Betty Birner. 1995. Definiteness and the English existential. *Language* 71.722-742.
Zwart, Jan-Wouter. 1993. *Dutch Syntax: A Minimalist Approach.* Diss. University of Groningen

Ability Modals and their Actuality Entailments*

RAJESH BHATT

University of Pennslyvania/Massachusetts Institute of Technology

1. Proposal

I show that the English ability modal *was able to* is ambiguous between two readings which can be paraphrased as 'managed to' and 'had the ability to'. In languages where the presence of genericity is marked morphologically, these two readings are expressed by distinct forms. I provide an analysis that derives these two readings from an underlying predicate *ABLE*. It is proposed that *ABLE* has the semantics of an implicative verb like 'manage to'. The 'had the ability to' reading is derived by combining *be able to* with a *Gen* operator.

2. The Ambiguity of *was able to*

(1) can be embedded in two quite different kinds of contexts as indicated in (2a, b).

(1)   John was able to eat five apples in an hour.

(2)   a. Yesterday, John was able to eat five apples in an hour. (past episodic)

      b. In those days, John was able to eat five apples in an hour. (past generic)

*I am much indebted for very helpful discussion to Martin Hackl, Irene Heim, Sabine Iatridou and Roumyana Izvorski. I have also benefitted from comments by Probal Dasgupta, Dave Embick, Kai von Fintel, Lisa Matthewson, David Pesetsky, Kalyanamalini Sahoo, members of the LF-reading group at MIT, and audiences at the WCCFL at UBC, the ConSOLE in Lisbon, and the GLOW in Hyderabad. Thanks are also due to Patrick Hawley for directing me to some of the philosophical literature on this topic.

(2a) implicates that John actually ate five apples in an hour. I will refer to this implication as the **actuality implication** (leaving open, at this point, the question of whether it is an implicature or an entailment) of (2a). If an ability attribution attributes an ability P to an individual x, the actuality implication corresponding to this ability attribution states that the ability is realized by x. This is shown in (3).

(3)   a.   Ability Attribution: $ABILITY \ (P)(x)$

   b.   Actuality Implication: $P(x)$

(3) abstracts away from issues of tense and temporal modifiers. I assume that any temporal modifiers that modify the ability attribution in (3a) will be inherited by the actuality implication in (3b).

Cancellation of the actuality implication leads to a certain oddness.

(4)   Last night, a masked assailant attacked me on my way home. I was able to wrestle him to the ground. #But I didn't do anything since I am a pacifist.

The two readings associated with *be able to* allow different interpretive possibilities for indefinite/bare plural subjects.

(5)   A fireman was/Firemen were able to eat five apples.

   a.   Yesterday at the apple eating contest, a fireman was/firemen were able to eat five apples. (Past episodic, actuality implication, existentially interpreted subject)

   b.   In those days, a fireman were/firemen were able to eat five apples in an hour (Generic, no actuality implication, generically interpreted subject)

In its most natural interpretation, (5a) has a 'managed to' reading i.e. there is an actuality implication. The indefinite subject *a fireman* (or the bare plural subject *firemen*) receives an existential interpretation. On the other hand, (5b) has a 'had the ability to' reading. There is no actuality implication and the indefinite subject *a fireman* (or the bare plural subject *firemen*) can only be interpreted generically.

There seems to be a link between the availability of a non-generic reading and the presence of an actuality implication. The 'managed to' reading (the actuality implication reading) of *be able to* is available in the simple past tense, but not in the simple present. In English, non-states in the simple past tense are ambiguous between a past generic and a past episodic reading, while non-states in the simple present tense only have a present generic reading. To investigate this link further, I will now consider languages where generic readings are marked by aspectual morphology, typically imperfective aspect.

3. Crosslinguistic Evidence

In languages where imperfective aspect appears on generic sentences (sentences in the perfective aspect lack generic readings), we find that when the ability modal occurs with imperfective aspect, there is no actuality implication. However, when the ability modal occurs in the past perfective, there is an actuality implication. Further, in these languages, the actuality implication seems to be uncancelable so I will be referring to it as the actuality entailment.

3.1 Greek
When the ability modal is in the imperfective, the assertion of the ability can be followed by a clause asserting that the ability was not actualized (cf. 6a). However, when the ability modal is in the past perfective, the modal assertion cannot be followed felicitously by a clause asserting that the ability was not actualized [1] (cf. 6b).

(6) a. Borusa   na sikoso   afto to trapezi ala δen
        CAN.impfv.1s NA lift.non-pst-pfv.1s this the table   but NEG
        to sikosa
        it lift.impfv

        '(In those days), I could lift this table but I didn't lift it.'

    b. Boresa   na tu miliso   (# ala δen tu
        CAN.pst-pfv.1s NA him talk.non-pst-pfv.1s   but NEG him
        milisa)
        talk.pst-pfv

        'I was able to talk to John (but I did not talk to him).'

The presence of the actuality entailment when the ability modal is in the past perfective can also be seen by the contradictoriness of the examples in (7).[2]

(7) a. # O Yanis borese   na skotosi   ton Petro 3 fores
        the John CAN.pst-pfv NA kill.non-pst-pfv the Peter 3 times

        'John managed to kill Peter three times.'

    b. # Boresa   na aftoktoniso
        CAN.pst-pfv NA kill-self

        'I managed to kill myself.'

---

[1] Judgements by Sabine Iatridou

[2] The corresponding examples in the imperfective are not contradictory. (7a) with the ability modal in the imperfective means something like 'On three occasions, John could have killed Peter'. Similarly, (7b) means something like 'I could have killed myself'. Sentences similar to (7) will also be discussed in the context of Hindi. There too the contradictoriness vanishes if the ability modal is put in the imperfective. Similar facts obtain in Bulgarian and Catalan.

3.2 Hindi

Like the Greek ability modal in the imperfective aspect, the Hindi ability modal *sak* in the imperfective[3] lacks an actuality entailment. This can be seen by the fact that they can be followed by a clause asserting the non-actualization of the ability (cf. 8a).

There is an actuality entailment when the ability modal is in the past-perfective. The assertion cannot be followed by a clause asserting the non-actualization of the ability (cf. 8b).

(8) a. Yusuf havaii-jahaaz uṛaa sak-taa   hai/thaa   (lekin vo
         Yusuf air-ship   fly   CAN-impfv be.Prs/be.Pst but   he
         havaii-jahaaz nahĩĩ uṛaa-taa   hai/thaa
         air-ship   Neg fly-impfv be.Prs/Be.Pst

         'Yusuf is/was able to fly airplanes but he doesn't/didn't fly airplanes.'

     b. Yusuf havaii-jahaaz uṛaa sak-aa   (# lekin us-ne havaii-jahaaz
         Yusuf air-ship   fly   CAN-Pfv   but   he-erg air-ship
         nahĩĩ uṛaa-yaa)
         Neg fly-Pfv

         'Yusuf could fly the airplane, but he didn't fly the airplane.'

The presence of an actuality entailment when the ability modal is in the past perfective is also demonstrated by the contradictoriness of (9a, and b).

(9) a. # Yunus Yakub-kaa tiin baar khoon kar sak-aa
         Yunus Yakub-Gen 3   times murder do CAN-Pfv

         'Yunus could murder Yakub three times/on three occasions.'

     b. # mE apne-aap-ko maar sak-aa
         I   self-Acc   kill can-Pfv

         'I could kill myself.'

3.3 General pattern

The pattern that emerges across the languages [4] where the perfective/ imperfective distinctions is marked on ability modals is shown in (10).

---

[3] In addition to genericity, the Greek imperfective has an additional 'event-in-progress' reading. The Hindi imperfective lacks this reading, which is realized by a separate progressive marker. Because of the absence of the 'event-in-progress' reading, *-taa*, the marker of imperfective aspect, is sometimes glossed as 'Hab(itual)'.

[4] The same facts obtain in Bulgarian (Roumyana Izvorski p.c.), Catalan (Sergi Casals, Miguel-Angel Hernando-Cupido, Luis Lopez, Josep Quer, and Maria Isabel Oltra-Massuet p.c.) and French (Philippe Schlenker p.c.). The facts in Albanian (Dalina Kallulli p.c.), Basque (Karlos Arregui-Urbina p.c.), Galician (Carmen Rio-Rey p.c.), Brazilian Portuguese (Luciana Storto p.c.), and Spanish (Olga Fernandez p.c.) are substantially similar though not identical to Bulgarian, Catalan, French, Greek, and Hindi.

(10) a. Past (Pfv(**CAN**) [VP]) = *managed-to*

　　　b. Past (Impfv(**CAN**) [VP]) = *had-ability-to*

The two readings associated with *be able to* (in the past) are realized in these languages by distinct forms. Across languages, imperfective aspect primarily makes two distinct semantic contributions - the semantics of an event in progress and the semantics of genericity. The semantic contribution relevant here is the semantics of genericity. This can be seen by the fact that the Hindi imperfective marker -*taa* only contributes the semantics of genericity, the 'event-in-progress' reading being marked by a specialized progressive marker.

4. The Actuality Implication and its relationship with Ability

Does an ability modal with an actuality implication still have an ability component to its meaning? At first it seems that it does. However, looking at a wider array of facts suggests that an ability modal with an actuality implication does not have an ability component to its meaning.

Ability modal sentences with an actuality implication do not just mean that an event related to the embedded predicate took place. If they did, then the sentences in (11) would have been fine on the readings indicated in parentheses.

(11) a. *Yesterday, it was able to rain here. (Yesterday, it rained here)

　　　b. # The mailman was able to be bitten by a dog yesterday. (The mailman was bitten by a dog yesterday)

Also, if all that was asserted was that an event related to the embedded predicate was actualized, the oddness of (12) would be puzzling.

(12) # A woman in Watertown was able to win 3 million dollars in the lottery yesterday.

A plausible explanation for the oddness of (11a, b) and (12) is that they do not constitute good ability attributions. This explanation presupposes that ability modal sentences with an actuality implication involve an ability attribution. However, the oddness of (12) vanishes if the context makes it clear that winning the lottery involves some kind of sustained (non-minimal) effort.

(13) After buying lottery tickets regularly for several years, a woman in Watertown was finally able to win 3 million dollars in the lottery yesterday.

The manner in which the oddness of (12) is alleviated in (13) suggests that ability modals with an actuality implication do not necessarily involve an ability attribution and that what was wrong with (12) was not that no ability was involved but that the context did not indicate that some effort went into the action. Once that was fixed, (12) (cf. 13) improved considerably (also see §4.2).

4.1 Relationship with Implicative Verbs

The oddness of (12) and the manner in which this oddness is ameliorated are similar to the oddness of (14) involving the implicative verb *manage* and the manner of the amelioration of this oddness.

(14) a. # A woman in Watertown managed to win 3 million dollars in the lottery yesterday.

  b. After buying lottery tickets compulsively for several years, a woman in Watertown finally managed to win 3 million dollars in the lottery yesterday.

We saw that the odd (12) and (14a) became acceptable, if the context indicates that some effort went into the action. How is this component of the meaning of *be able to* and *manage to* represented? I will argue that this component of their meaning is represented as a conventional implicature. To this end, I will introduce some tests developed by Karttunen & Peters (1979) for identifying conventional implicatures.

Karttunen & Peters (1979) argue that the meaning of an implicative verb like *manage* is best represented in terms of its assertion and its conventional implicature as in (15).

(15) John managed to sit through the Chinese opera.

  a. Assertion: John sat through the Chinese opera.

  b. Conventional Implicature: Sitting through a Chinese opera requires some effort for John.

They base this distinction upon the fact that the parts of the meaning of (15) indicated in (15a) and (15b) behave differently with respect to entailment patterns and presupposition projection. For example, (16a) entails (16b) but not (16c).

(16) a. I just discovered that John managed to sit through the Chinese opera.

  b. I just discovered that John sat through the Chinese opera.

  c. I just discovered that sitting through a Chinese opera required some effort for John.

The facts with *was able to* with an actuality implication seem similar.

(17) a. I just discovered that John was able to sit through the Chinese opera.

  b. I just discovered that John sat through the Chinese opera.

  c. I just discovered that sitting through a Chinese opera required some effort for John.

The pattern in (17) suggests that the part of the meaning of *was able to* that makes cases like (11a, b) and (12) odd is part of the conventional implicature of *was able to* and not part of its assertion.

4.2 More *was able to* without ability

(18b) is another case where we seem to have just an actuality entailment without an accompanying ability attribution.

(18) (from Thalberg 1969)

    a. Yesterday, Brown hit three bulls-eyes in a row. Before he hit three bulls-eyes, he fired 600 rounds, without coming close to the bulls-eye; and his subsequent tries were equally wild.

    b. Brown was able to hit three bulls-eyes in a row.

    c. Brown had the ability to hit three bulls-eyes in a row.

From (18a), we can conclude (18b) but not (18c). Brown could have hit the target three times in a row by pure chance and he does not need to have had any ability for (18b) to be true.

If we accept that *was able to* can be used in the absence of any actual ability attribution, we have an argument that shows that treating actuality implications as implications of an associated ability attribution cannot be correct. As (13) and (18b) show, actuality implications are present even in the absence of an ability attribution to entail them. So the actuality implication cannot be the implication of an associated ability attribution. The actuality implication (and its associated conventional implicature) is all there is.

We can still ask the question of whether the actuality implication is cancelable or not and on the basis of (13) and (18b), we can say that it is not cancelable. Therefore, it is either part of the assertion (or entailed by the assertion) or part of the conventional implicature. The entailment pattern in (17) suggests that what we are calling the actuality implication constitutes the assertion of (17a). I will, however, continue to refer informally to the 'managed to' reading of *be able to* as the actuality entailment of the ability modal.

4.3 Conclusions from Section 4

When an ability modal has an actuality entailment, there is no ability attribution. In fact the term 'actuality entailment' as defined in (3) is misleading because it suggests that there is an ability attribution that entails the actuality entailment. The actuality entailment is all there is. The actuality entailment has as part of its meaning that the relevant event involved some effort on the part of the subject. This part of the meaning is part of the *conventional implicature* of the ability modal. (11a) is bad because no effort is involved and hence the conventional implicature of the ability modal is not satisfied, and not because of a pragmatically odd ability attribution.

5. Compositional Derivation

5.1 Existential Readings with *be able to*

We have seen in (5) that bare plural/indefinite subjects of *was able to* can receive both a generic and an existential interpretation. The existential interpretation of a bare plural/indefinite subject of *was able to* was accompanied by an actuality entailment (cf. 5a). But is it, in general, necessary for an ability modal to have an actuality entailment, in order for its indefinite subject to be interpreted existentially? The following examples seem to be cases where there is no actuality entailment and yet the indefinite subject receives an existential interpretation.[5]

(19)   a.   Yesterday, at the apple eating contest, a fireman was able to eat fifty apples in an hour. I know because I had seen him drink an illegal performance enhancing potion. However, he never ate any apples at the contest because the judges caught him and barred him from the contest.

       b.   Last Tuesday, in Schenectady, a five year old girl was able to lift 500 kilograms. The scientists were able to detect her ability by measuring her muscle stress. She never actually lifted anything because she was straightjacketed throughout Tuesday to prevent her hurting herself. It is speculated that she had temporary acquired superhuman strength due to demonic possession.

However, if we look at bare plurals the facts go in the other direction. Consider (19a, b) with the indefinite subjects replaced by the corresponding bare plural subjects. Then, it does not seem possible to interpret the bare plural subjects existentially.

Diesing (1992) and Kratzer (1995) show that existential readings for indefinite subjects are available only when existential readings for bare plural subjects are also available. The seemingly existential readings in the absence of an actuality entailment in (19) are not true existential readings but are instead instances of specific indefinite readings, which are always available. [6] Therefore, from the absence of existential readings with bare plural subjects in the absence of an actuality entailment, I conclude that existential readings are only available when there is an actuality entailment.

---

[5]For a few speakers, (19a, b) are quite odd. For most other speakers, the temporary ability without any accompanying actualization reading is available. I am unable to explain this variation in judgements currently.

[6]It is instructive to look at the case of ability modals in the present tense. There is no actuality entailment and existential readings for indefinite and bare plural subjects are not available (cf. i).

i   a.   A fireman is able to do fifty pushups in a minute.

    b.   Firemen are able to do fifty pushups in a minute.

However, even here, in (ia), the indefinite can be interpreted specifically as in 'a fireman, namely Michael'.

It follows from the above conclusion that instances of momentary/ short-lived ability (cf. 19) and instances of more long term abilities are not truly distinct with respect to genericity/ILP-hood. This is a welcome result since in the languages which mark the perfective/imperfective distinction on ability modals, long term abilities and momentary abilities are both realized by the same form: an ability modal in the imperfective.

5.2 Back to Compositional Derivation

The goal is to try and connect the two readings of *be able to*: *managed to* and *had the ability to*. I assume that underlying the two readings of *be able to* is one predicate which combines with different operators to yield the two readings. I will call this predicate *ABLE*.

What kind of predicate is *ABLE*? It could be a stative stage level predicate, a stative individual level predicate, or a non-stative. On the basis of the absence of existential readings in the English simple present, it could be argued that *ABLE* is not a stage level predicate. However, as has been discussed by Fernald (1994) and Glasbey (1997), the absence of existential readings for bare plural subjects is not the most reliable test for stage-levelhood. Glasbey (1997) notes it is difficult to get an existential reading for *plates* in (20a), while an existential reading is obtained without difficulty in (20b).

(20)   a. Plates were dirty.

       b. The hotel inspector filed a bad report on Fawlty Towers. The standard of service was, he said, disgraceful. Plates were dirty, cutlery was bent and the floors were thick with grease.

The exact explanation of these facts is beyond the purview of this paper. What is relevant is that there are many adjectival stage-level predicates that do not allow existential readings for their bare plural subjects. So the absence of existential readings does not prove that *ABLE* is not a stage-level predicate.

This leaves us with the following options: either *ABLE* is a stative (ILP or SLP) or it is a non-stative. Both these options will be explored in the two following sections.

5.2.1 *ABLE* is a stative

I will make the following set of assumptions about the interaction of tense and aspect, and the English tense-aspect system in particular: the feature $+/-$bounded, which is introduced by the aspectual morphology, is available to the semantic computation. In the present tense, the +bounded feature is not available.[7] Languages vary in how they realize the feature $+/-$bounded. Languages like Greek, Hindi, Spanish etc. realize the +bounded feature as perfective aspect and the [−bounded] feature as imperfective aspect. How these features are realized in English is shown in (21) taken from Anagnostopoulou, Iatridou & Izvorski (1997).

---

[7]This $+/-$bounded feature should not be confused with telicity. See fn. 2 of Anagnostopoulou, Iatridou & Izvorski 1997 for a definition.

(21) a. non-stative, [unbounded]-> Progressive
      b. non-stative, [bounded] |
      c. stative, [unbounded] |-> non-Progressive
      d. stative, [bounded] |

To derive the actuality entailment, we need to basically stipulate it.

(22) $ABLE_{stative}(\mathcal{P})(x) + [+\text{bounded}] \leftrightarrow \mathcal{P}(x)$ (Actuality Entailment)

When there is no [+bounded] feature around, we just get the normal ability attribution. Consequently, in languages which realize the [+bounded] feature by perfective aspect, ability modals in the perfective have an actuality entailment. Since there is no [+bounded] feature in the imperfective, ability modals in the imperfective lack an actuality entailment.

In English, states in the past tense can have either the [+bounded] feature or the [−bounded] feature. Consequently, an ability modal in the past tense may or may not have an actuality entailment.

However, treating *ABLE* as a stative is problematic. Firstly, the actuality entailment has to be stipulated. Further this stipulation is quite unexpected given the general pattern of how stative predicates combine with perfective aspect in Greek (also in Bulgarian and Hindi): when [+bounded] combines with a state (i.e. when a state appears in the Perfective), it yields an inchoative interpretation cf. (23).

(23) (from Anagnostopoulou, Iatridou & Izvorski 1998)

      O Jannis agapise   tin Maria to 1981
      the Jannis love-pst-perf-3sg the Mary in 1981

      'John started loving/fell in love with Mary in 1981.'

Hence, our actuality entailment stipulation is rather shaky on consistency grounds too.

Finally, the conventional implicature that appears with the actuality entailment (see §4.1) also has to be stipulated. In comparison, the other approach, which treats *ABLE* as a non-stative implicative verb, seems more promising and it is to that that we turn next.

5.2.2 *ABLE* is a non-stative implicative verb
We assume that *ABLE* is a non-stative implicative verb with a conventional implicature somewhat similar to *manage to*.

The fact that in the episodic past in English, and past perfective in Bulgarian, Catalan, Greek, Hindi etc., there is an actuality entailment does not come as a surprise, but instead follows from our assumption that *ABLE* is an implicative verb.

(24) John managed to eat the pizza → John ate the pizza.

The predicate embedded under the implicative verb is evaluated with the matrix tense specification.

The interpretive possibilities available to bare plural/indefinite subjects of *be able to* follow from our analysis of *be able to* as a non-stative predicate. The English past tense allows for both episodic and generic readings of non states but the English present only allows for generic readings (cf. 25a, d). These are exactly the possibilities found with *be able to* (cf. 25b, e) (and also with *managed to* cf. 25c, f).

(25) a. Firemen lift heavy cinder blocks. (only gen.)

b. Firemen are able to lift heavy cinder blocks. (only gen.)

c. Firemen manage to lift heavy cinder blocks. (only gen.)

d. Firemen lifted heavy cinder blocks. (gen./∃)

e. Firemen were able to lift heavy cinder blocks. (gen./∃)

f. Firemen managed to lift heavy cinder blocks. (gen./∃)

The conventional implicature discussed in §4.1 survives to the actual ability attribution. It is somewhat odd to attribute trivial abilities such as the ability to lift one's finger. However, such ability attributions become perfect if the context makes it clear that they are not trivial for the person to whom the ability is being attributed.

(26) a. # Timmy is able to breathe.

b. Timmy had a terrible car accident as a result of which he lost control over most of his muscles. Thankfully, he is able to breathe.

So (26a) is odd because its conventional implicature is not satisfied. Once the conventional implicature is satisfied, as in (26b), the oddness vanishes.

The LFs in (27) show how the ability attribution reading ('had the ability to') of *be able to* is derived. In Bulgarian, Catalan, Greek, Hindi etc. the *Gen* operator is contributed by the semantics of imperfective aspect.

(27) a. (In those days,) A fireman was able to eat five apples.
          LF: Past (*Gen* (*ABLE* (eat-5-apples)) (**fireman**))

b. A fireman is able to eat five apples.
          LF:*Gen* (*ABLE* (eat-5-apples)) (**fireman**)

The absence of actuality entailments is not surprising since the LFs in (27a, b) do not entail the corresponding generic sentences. Also consider the fact that (28a) does not entail (28b).

(28) a. John manages to sit through a Chinese opera.

b. John sits through a Chinese opera.

It may be argued that the analysis offered here suffers from the problem of too strong truth conditions. Even in the generic, implicative verbs need some verifying instances. Consider (28), which can presumably not be said unless John has on some occasions sat through a Chinese opera. Such a need for verifying instances seems absent with *be able to*. However, this problem only arises if we identify the semantics of *be able to* with the semantics of *manage to*. Not all generic sentences require verifying instances. Consider the following examples of generic sentences from Carlson (1995).

(29)   a.   This machine crushes up oranges and removes the seeds.

      b.   The Speaker of the House succeeds the vice president.

      c.   Sally handles the mail from Antarctica.

Carlson (1995) notes that (29a-c) seem quite possibly to be true even under circumstances where the corresponding episodes do not ever take place. So it is not the case that all generic sentences require verifying instances. Lawler (1973) and Dahl (1975) have noted that generic sentences can have two quite different readings as can be seen in (30).

(30)   John drinks beer.

(30) has a 'universal'/ habitual reading under which John habitually drinks beer (all the time or on the relevant drinking occasions) and an 'existential'/ dispositional reading that says that John does not object to drinking beer. It seems the dispositional reading does not require verifying instances while the habitual reading does. Why it is the case that (27a, b) only involve the dispositional flavor of genericity, however, still remains to be explained.

    Another potential problem is Hackl (1998)'s analysis of ability *can/is able to* as an individual level predicate. Hackl argues that with respect to compatibility with locative modifiers and quantificational adverbs, *can/is able to* pattern with individual level predicates like *be intelligent* and not derived generics like *eat pizza*. The point he makes about *can/is able to* can be extended to non actuality entailment *was able to* also. Are his analysis and the current treatment of the *had the ability to* ability attribution as a derived generic compatible? I think yes, if we use a recent analysis of individual level predicates developed by Chierchia (1995). Chierchia's analysis treats individual level predicates as *derived* inherent generics. He derives the differences that exist between individual level predicates and transparently derived generics from lexical properties of individual level predicates and not from an appeal to the underived status of individual level predicates. The relevant features of his account can be adopted by us to give the derived generics in (27) individual level properties. So there is no contradiction between assuming individual level properties for the 'had-the-ability-to' ability attribution and treating it as a derived generic.

    A problem that I do not have much to say about at this point is the incompatibility of *be able to* with the progressive. If *be able to* is a non-stative predicate, we expect it to be compatible with the progressive. This expectation is not met.

(31)   * John was being able to eat the pizza.

While I do not have an explanation, I would like to note that other implicative verbs are not perfect in the progressive either.

(32) ? John was managing to eat the pizza.

Further, the ill-formedness of (31) may very well have something to do with the fact that adjectives in English do not generally occur in the progressive.

6. Conclusions

To conclude: I propose that sentences like 'John was able to lift the truck' are ambiguous between a 'managed to' implicative verb-like reading which asserts that John actually lifted the truck and says nothing about John's abilities and a 'had the ability to' reading which asserts that John has the ability to lift the truck. Furthermore, the implicative verb reading is only available in non-generic (perfective) environments, while the 'had the ability to' reading is only available in generic (imperfective) environments. In his 1971 paper on implicative verbs, Karttunen writes:

> If the quarterback in 46a (= 'In the last game, the quarterback was able to complete only two passes') did not in fact complete two passes, it is very improbable that anybody would regard 46a as true. (pg. 355)
>
> What remains to be explained , however, is why *be able* and other similar verbs in contexts like 46a, *which I am unable to describe in any general way*, must be interpreted as giving not only a necessary but a sufficient condition for the truth of the embedded sentence. (pg. 356) (emphasis mine: RB)

The paper gives a general characterization of the environments where *be able to* behaves like an implicative verb and makes a proposal as to why *be able to* behaves the way it does.

  I will end this paper with a related puzzle. *be able to* is not peculiar in its interaction with aspect. There seems to be a class of verbs which behave like implicative verbs in the perfective and attribute ability in the presence of genericity. Consider the pattern with the Greek verb *epitrepo* 'permit'.

(33) a. i   karta mu epetrepse   na xrisimopiiso tin vivliothiki
           this card me allow.pst.pfv   use   the library

           'This card permitted me to use the library.' (I used the library)

      b. i   karta mu epetrepe   na xrisimopiiso tin vivliothiki
           this card me allow.impfv   use   the library

           'This card permitted me to use the library.' (I don't have to have used the library)

An understanding of the interaction of *be able to* with aspectual morphology will help us to understand the closely related behavior of verbs like the Greek *epitrepo* 'permit'.

References

Anagnostopoulou, E., S. Iatridou, and R. Izvorski (1998) "On the morpho-syntax of the Perfect and how it relates to its meaning," in P. N. Tamanji and K. Kusumoto, eds., *Proceedings of NELS 28*, Amherst, Massachusetts, GLSA, 1–17.

Carlson, G. N. (1995) "Truth Conditions of Generic Sentences: Two Contrasting Views," in G. N. Carlson and F. J. Pelletier, eds., *The Generic Book*, University of Chicago Press, Chicago, 176–223.

Chierchia, G. (1995) "Individual-level Predicates as Inherent Generics," in G. N. Carlson and F. J. Pelletier, eds., *The Generic Book*, University of Chicago Press, Chicago, 176–223.

Dahl, Ö. (1975) "On Generics," in E. L. Keenan, ed., *Formal Semantics of Natural Language: Papers from a Colloquium Sponsored by the King's College Research Centre*, Cambridge University Press, Cambridge, England, 99–111.

Diesing, M. (1982) *Indefinites*, Linguistic Inquiry Monographs 20, MIT Press, Cambridge, Massachusetts.

Fernald, T. B. (1994) *On the Nonuniformity of the Individual- and Stage-level effects*, Doctoral dissertation, University of California, Santa Cruz, Santa Cruz, California.

Glasbey, S. (1997) "I-level predicates that allow existential readings for bare plurals," in A. Lawson, ed., *Proceedings of SALT VII*, Cornell University, Ithaca, NY, Cornell Linguistics Club, 169–179.

Hackl, M. (1998) "On the semantics of ability attributions," unpublished manuscript, Massachusetts Institute of Technology.

Karttunen, L. (1971) "Implicative Verbs," *Language* 47:2, 340–358.

Karttunen, L., and S. Peters (1979) "Conventional Implicature," in C.-K. Oh and D. A. Dinneen, eds., *Presupposition*, Syntax and Semantics 11, Academic Press, Inc. Harcourt Brace Jovanovich, New York, 1–55.

Kratzer, A. (1995) "Stage-level and Individual-level Predicates," in G. N. Carlson and F. J. Pelletier, eds., *The Generic Book*, University of Chicago Press, Chicago, 125–175.

Lawler, J. (1973) *Studies in English generics*, University of Michigan Papers in Linguistics 1, University of Michigan Press, Ann Arbor, Michigan.

Thalberg, I. (1969) "Austin on Abilities," in K. T. Fann, ed., *Symposium on J. L. Austin*, Humanities Press Inc., New York, 182–205.

A Restrictive/Non-Restrictive Distinction in Possessive Nominals

JOSÉ BONNEAU, PIERRE PICA & TAKASHI NAKAJIMA
McGill University, CNRS-Paris, & Toyama University

1.   Introduction

Kayne, (1994) provides an analysis that unifies the properties of relative clauses with those of Nominal Possessives, and Adjectival constructions, in that all these construction involve a D° and a CP. There is however no systematic proposal as to how his structural account could capture the various relationships expressed in possessive nominals. We propose rephrasing Kayne's hypothesis in the light of the leading ideas of Kayne (1998), that the Restrictive/Non-Restrictive distinction found in Relative Clauses corresponds to the Inalienable versus Alienable distinction of the Nominal Possessive constructions in French, hereby giving new evidence for the hypothesis according to which the two constructions are configurationally related. We propose to extend this distinction to adjectives, hereby giving new evidence in favor of Kayne's analysis. This enables us to account for several previously unaccounted or even unnoticed facts. Our hypothesis suggests that the very same phenomena are at stake in various domains of the grammar which involves distinct Grammatical Categories. We discuss in the conclusion some consequences potentially relevant for the general architecture of the grammar, in the light of the minimalist program sketched in Chomsky (1995), and many subsequent works.

2.   On the Restrictive vs Non-Restrictive Distinction

2.1. Restrictive vs Non- Restrictive Relative Clauses
It is generally assumed that both Restrictive Relative Clauses (RRC) and Non-Restrictive Clauses (NRRC) have the same structure at spell-out.

Kayne (1994) attempts to capture the fact that NRRC are not in the scope of the article at the level of semantic interpretation by assuming covert movement of the IP to Spec DP at this abstract level as in (2):

(1) [$_{DP}$ l'[$_{CP}$ [$_{NP}$ homme$_i$] que [$_{IP}$ [$_{VP}$ je vois e$_i$]]]]]
([$_{DP}$ the [$_{CP}$ [$_{NP}$ man$_i$] that [$_{IP}$ I see e$_i$]]]])

(2) [$_{DP}$ [$_{IP}$ je vois e$_i$]$_j$ l' [$_{CP}$[$_{NP}$ homme$_i$] que [$_{IP}$ e$_i$] $_j$]]]] (NRRC only)

This amounts to saying that while (1) represents both RRC and NRRC at PF, the difference between (1) vs (2) represents the difference between RRC and NRRC at LF. This analysis is problematic in the light of Kayne (1998), according to which covert movement is not part of UG, the most important cases of covert movement being restated in terms of overt syntactic operations.

Assuming that (1) is a common structure for both RRC and NRRC, we are led to suggest, much in the spirit of Kayne (1998), that, while (1) is the full fledged structure of RRC at PF; it is not the full fledged structure of NRRC at this level.

In the case of NRCC, we assume that overt movement of the remnant VP outside DP, followed by further movement of the whole DP, as illustrated in (3a) and (3b) respectively:[1]

(3) a. [$_{VP}$ je vois e$_i$]$_j$ [$_{DP}$ l' [$_{CP}$ [$_{NP}$ homme$_i$] que [$_{IP}$ [$_{VP}$ e$_i$]]$_j$]] $\Rightarrow$
     b. [$_{DP}$ l' [$_{CP}$ [$_{NP}$ homme$_i$] [que [$_{IP}$ [$_{VP}$ e$_i$]] $_j$]]$_k$ [$_{VP}$ je vois e$_i$]$_j$ [$_{DP}$k]

According to this analysis, RCC, and NRRC have a very different structure at Spell Out, at least in languages where NRRCs are signaled by an intonation break (see Safir (1986), among many others). While the fact that raising of the 'Predicative Noun' into the Spec of Comp in both NRRC and RRC (cf. Vergnaud, (1974)) might explain some similarities between the two constructions, we take the contrast between (1) on the one hand and (3.a) and (3.b) on the other hand, to be responsible for a series of contrasts between NRRC and RRC. (3.a) in particular expresses the fact that the relative clause acts 'as if' it is not in the scope of the Determiner. We take the difference between (1) and (3.b) to be responsible for various contrasts in the literature. [2]As Kayne notes following Emonds, (1979), stacked relatives are only possible if all are RRC, or if all are restricted but the last:

(4) a . Le livre qui est sur la table, que j'ai lu hier
         (the book that is on the table, that I read yesterday)

---

[1] See Kayne (1998) for a general hypothesis concerning the functional categories that could trigger these movements, which we adopt from Kayne.

[2] See also section 32 below, where it is suggested that the movement illustrated in (3.b) might be triggered by PF features not accessible to semantic interpretation.

b. *Le livre, qui est sur la table que j'ai lu hier
(the book, that is on the table which I saw yesterday)

We would like to relate the ungrammaticality of (4.b) to the fact that NRCC can modify a relational noun such as 'soeur', as opposed to RRC (see section 3.1 and footnote (2)):

(5) a. Sa soeur, que Jean admire, est toujours présente
(his mother, that Jean admires, is always present)
b. *Sa soeur que Jean admire, est souvent présente
(his mother that Jean admires, is always present)

Note finally that a NRRC cannot be used to modify a quantified antecedent such as 'tout le monde' (everyone), as illustrated in (6):

(6) *Jean a parlé à tout le monde, qu'il connaissait
(Jean spoke to everyone, that he knew)

2.2 Restrictive vs Non-Restrictive Possessive Constructions

Our analysis in terms of overt movement of the distinction between NRRC and RRC suggests that there is much more structure above DP than what is usually assumed in the literature. This point was already suggested by the properties of Possessive Nominals (see in particular Kayne (1993), (1994). Extending Szabolcsi's (1981), (1994)'s analysis of Hungarian Noun phrases, Kayne (1994) proposes that the structure of a Possessive Nominal like (7) is close to that illustrated in (8):

(7) la table/mère de Jean
(lit. 'the table/mother of Jean')
(Jean's table/mother)

(8) [DP la [CP [NP table/mère$_i$] de [IP Jean e$_i$]]]]

This amounts to saying that Possessive Nominals with 'de' have a structure akin to that of RRC, and that the possessed noun has moved into the Spec of 'de', now interpreted as a nominal complementizer. Kayne's analysis of possessive constructions raises the question of whether Possessive Nominals, akin to NRRCs exist. We would like to claim that they do, and that they correspond to Possessive Nominal's constructions involving the element 'à', illustrated by (9):

(9) la table à Jean
(lit. 'the table to Jean')
(Jean's table)

Let us suggest, extending our analysis of NRRC to NRR Possessive Constructions (NRRPC), that the structure corresponding to (9) involves an overt movement of the N to Spec CP as in (10):

(10) [$_{DP}$ la [$_{CP}$[$_{NP}$ table$_i$] à [$_{IP}$ [$_{NP}$ Jean e$_i$]]]]]

This operation, which amounts an extension of Vergnaud's raising analysis of RC to nominal constructions is, in our terms subject to further overt movement of the remnant NP [Jean e$_i$] outside DP, as illustrated in (11.a), followed by further movement of whole DP, as illustrated in (11.b):

(11) a. [$_{NP}$Jean e$_i$] $_j$ [$_{DP}$ la [$_{CP}$[$_{NP}$ table$_i$] à [$_{IP}$ [$_{NP}$ e $_i$] $_j$]]
     b. [$_{DP}$ la [$_{CP}$[$_{NP}$ table$_i$] à [$_{IP}$ [$_{NP}$ e i] $_j$]]]] $_k$ [$_{NP}$Jean e$_i$] $_j$ [$_{DP}$]$_k$

In (11.a) the NP following the complementizer like element 'à' is not in the scope of the article, much as the VP is not in the scope of the article in the NRRC in (3.a). Note that, as expected under the present analysis, 'à' is clearly intotanionally set off in (12.a), where 'voisin de table' is not inalienably possessed by 'Jean' while this is not the case with 'de' in (12.b):

(12) a. le voisin de table à Jean
         (lit. 'the neighbor at the table to Jean')
     b. le voisin de table de Jean
         (lit. 'the neighbor at the table of Jean')

That is, while NRRPC pattern with NRRC, Restrictive Relative Possessive Nominals (RRPN) pattern with RRC.

3. On the Restrictive vs Non-Restrictive Distinction

3.1 On Restrictive vs Non Restrictive Possessive Nominals
Our general hypothesis captures in structural terms the traditional intuition according to which Possessive Nominals are related to Relative Clauses (cf. Benveniste (1960a), among others). We would like to draw a parallelism between the restrictive vs. non restrictive interpretation of relative clauses, and the inalienable and alienable interpretations of Possessive Nominals : While in RCC the head of the relative forms a complex predicate bound by D° (a relation which can be mediated by a 'that' complementizer in English), while in NRRC the D° bounds the Noun alone and the NRRC is predicated and the whole relative clause is predicated of the whole DP. (cf. McCawley (1981); Stowell (1981); and Larson & Segal (1995), for a brief survey of what is at stake

We would like to suggest NRRCs, just like NRRPCs, express a permanent (inalienable) relation between two entities. This is not the case of

RRCs and RRPNs which express a non-permanent (alienable) relation. Note moreover that the observation that NRRC does not allow indefinite in Possessive Nominals, as illustrated in (13):[3]

(13) a. *un livre à un enfant
          ('a book to a child')
      b. ? un livre à l'enfant
          ('a book to the child')
      c. *le livre à un enfant
          (the book to a child)
      d. le livre à l'enfant
          ('the book to the child')

That our general analysis is on the right track is supported by the fact that NRRPC favors strongly inalienable possession, as illustrated by (14), inspired from Kayne (1994):

(14) a. *la conférence à hier
          (the conference to yesterday)
      b. la conférence d'hier
          (the conférence of yesterday)

Note that one can hardly speak of 'possession' in (14.b) where the relation between 'conférence' and 'hier' seems reducible to predication, as already expressed by Benveniste's concept of 'appertainance'.[4] It is conceivable,

---

[3] Example (13) is reminiscent of (i) bellow :

(i)   un mur, qui est rouge, s'est écroulé
     (a wall which is red, felt apart)

where 'un' needs to be interpreted as a partitive. Note that the hypothesis according to which NRRC expresses a permanent (inalienable) property is supported by (ii) bellow:

(ii)   ?* le mur, qui est en face de moi à ce moment-ci, est rouge
      (the wall ,which is in front of me à ce moment précis, is red)

If one assumes that DP raising expresses the fact that NRRCs do not form a new NP, that is, are not part of the Noun Phrase, then the constraint on stacking follows. See for a configurational approach, Kayne (1994)'s Chapter 3 according to which stacking of NRRC is blocked by illicit movement of a predicate out of a left branch (in the terms of the present analysis, by illicit movement of something (the NRC) contained in a Specifier).

[4] See Benveniste (1962), who uses examples like 'la couleur de la forêt' (the color of the forest). Of interest here is the concept of 'non-possessable Noun', clearly related to natural elements in some Amerindian languages (see Crowley (1996) and Richards (1973), among many others. See also Bonneau & Pica (1996)). Kayne develops an analysis according to which what Benveniste calls 'appartainance' constructions have to be analyzed in terms of relative clauses. From this point of view the fact that we do not find structures like (i) might be reducible to stacking constraints on NRRCs:

(i)   *l'imbécile de Jean de Paul
     (lit. 'the imbecile of Jean of Paul')

from the point of view developed in the text, that 'à' in NRRPC is associated with an empty element. This element moves to some higher position in a structure like (11.a), perhaps to allow long distance movement of 'Jean' in Spec CP, and further movement of the whole DP further up, much in the spirit of Kayne 1993's analysis of auxiliary selection.[5] If it is right that 'avoir' is the spell-out of 'être+a' as his analysis suggests, implementing the intuition of Benveniste (1960a), then it is not inconceivable that 'à' is the spell-out of 'de+à'. This might in turn explain why 'à' is, in Possessive Nominals, restricted to human possessor (Kayne (1975), Milner (1978), Tremblay (1989), Bonneau & Pica (1996), among others), while no such a restriction seems to be observed with NRRC. This is illustrated in (15) which shows that the DP following 'à' cannot be an inanimate:

(15) * le pied à la table
      ('the foot of the table)

The ungrammaticality of (15) strongly suggests that inalienable possession is associated with the concept of a permanent and active process, as strongly argued for in Bonneau & Pica (1996). The analogy we draw between RC and Possessive nominals allows us furthermore to account for the following contrast reminiscent of (4) of section 1, above:

(16) a.   la voiture de Pierre de Jean
           ('the car of Pierre of Jean')
           ('the car of Pierre's that John has')
     b.   * la voiture à Pierre de Jean
           ('the car to Pierre of Jean')

Example (16) shows that the stacking properties observed with RRC versus NRRC (see Emonds (1979)) can be reproduced within Nominal Possessive Constructions: While RRPC, that is constructions with 'de', do stack, constructions with NRRPC do not. More precisely NRRPC stacking is subject to the very same conditions that usual RRCs, as illustrated by (17), which should be compared with (4) above:

(17) a.   * la voiture à Pierre à Jean
           ('the car to Pierre to Jean)

On the other hand it is conceivable that the ungrammaticality of such structures derives from some interpretative principles. We leave this topic aside, for further research.

[5] On the fact that 'à' might not be in the same position as 'de', see Kayne (1998: 160, note 43), and Kayne (1975). A parallelism between 'de' and 'à' and 'avoir' and 'être' is already suggested in Milner, (1982).

b.   ? la voiture de Pierre à Jean
      ('the car of Pierre to Jean')
      (the car of Pierre's that Jean has)

Example (17.a) which involves stacking of two NRRPC is out as expected, while (17.b) which involves a RRPC followed by a NRRPC is marginal at best, as expected in the present framework. That is (17.b) is akin to (18) where a Non-Restrictive Relative Clause follows a Restrictive Relative Clause :

(18) Je viens de lire le livre qui parle de nos ancêtres, que Paul m'a donné
      (I just read the book which speak about our ancestors, that Paul gave me)

3.2 On Restrictive vs Non Restrictive Possessives in French
The analysis of stacking we have proposed above seems compatible with the following paradigm :

(19) a. son livre à Jean
          ('his book to Jean')
          (the book that he has, that belongs to Jean)
      b. son livre de Jean
          ('his book of Jean')
          (the book that he has, that is Jean's)

Let's assume that the structure of a possessive element like 'son' in (19.b) is akin to that of a Non-Restrictive Adjectival Relative Clause, as illustrated in (20):

(20) $[_{DP} D° [CP son_i [de [livre e_i]]]]$

The element 'son' can raises further to D° in (20) where it acquires the φ-features of D°, and can be interpreted as a pronominal like element. While the stacking properties follows, that is, (19.b) is an example of stacking of two restrictive relative clauses and (19.a) an example of a RRCPC followed by a NRRPC, the judgments depend on the lexical item associated with the possessive. Hence, observe the following paradigm :

(21) a. sa soeur à Jean
          (his sister to Jean)
      b. *sa soeur de Jean
          (his sister of Jean)

One natural question that arises at this point is whether a 'son' corresponding to a Non-Restrictive Adjectival Relative Clause do exists. We believe that it does - and corresponds to a structure like (22.b) & (22.c), which illustrates the fact that 'son' is not in the Scope of D°:

(22) a. [$_{DP}$ D° [CP son$_i$ [à [IP [$_{NP}$livre e$_i$]]]]]
(Raising of 'son' in Spec CP) =>
b. [livre e$_i$] $_j$[$_{DP}$ D° [CP son$_i$ [IP à [[e] $_j$ e$_i$]]]]
(Raising of the remnant DP outside Spec DP) =>
c. [DP D°][CP son$_i$ [IP à [[e] $_j$ e$_i$][livre e$_i$] $_j$[]]
(Raising of the whole DP)

We believe that this derivation where 'à' incorporates into 'son' corresponds to a meaning of a Non Restrictive Adjectival relative Clause within which 'sa' expresses inalienable possession.

Our analysis, which amounts to saying that there are two possessive adjectives 'sa' in French, corresponding respectively to a (restrictive) 'pronominal possessive' 'sa' and to a restricted 'reflexive (adjectival) possessive', is supported by the fact that long distance possessives akin the Scandinavian 'sin' can be detected in French, as first observed in Bonneau & Pica (1996):

(23) a. L'on$_i$ souhaite toujours que l'on dise du bien de sa$_i$ femme
(One always wishes that one praise (SUBJ) his (own) wife)
b. *L'on$_i$ souhaite toujours que Paul dise du bien de sa$_i$ femme
(One always wishes that Paul praise (SUBJ) his (own) wife)

The contrast illustrated in (23) is, in our terms, blocked by a specific element 'Paul' in (b) reminiscent of similar contrasts with long distance 'soi', which can only be detected with bare quantifier antecedents in French (see Pica (1982), (1984)).[6]

If the analysis of so called 'adjectival possessives' is on the right track, one could say that 'sa' is a Non-Restrictive Possessives when it is associated with a relational Noun (such as body parts, kinship terms) or a Noun expressing social activities. [7] This might explain the status of (24b), where the NRRC precedes the RRC. This hypothesis also explains the status of (24.a). The possessive associated with the kinship term 'soeur' is interpreted as a NRRC, as is 'sa soeur à Jean', but NRRC do not stack.[8, 9]

---

[6] See also Pica (1998). The analysis developed in the text suggests that there is a parallelism between Possession and Reflexivization, as suggested in Pica (1992).
[7] See the notion of 'Personal Sphere' in Bally (1926).
[8] Example (24.a) is nevertheless grammatical in some dialects of French - where 'à' is not intonationally set off. We interpret this fact as indicating that for some speakers the 'à + N' phrase is interpreted as a kind of doubling of the clitic-like element 'sa'.
The analysis of (20.a) in the text might be extended to (i), which is ungrammatical for most speakers.

(i)   *Je connais la soeur qui est belle à Jean

(24) a. ? sa soeur à Jean
        (his sister to John)
     b. *sa soeur de Jean
        (his sister of Jean)

Before turning to other types of adjectival RCs, let us examine the ungrammaticality of (6) above, restated here as (25) :

(25) *Jean a parlé à tout le monde, qu'il connaissait
     (Jean spoke to everyone, that he knew)

The generalization seems to be that a NRCC cannot have a quantifier within its scope. This would follow if the quantifier is stuck inside the relative clause itself. That this might be on the right track is indicated by the following contrast, inspired from Kayne (1975):

(26) a. le voisin de table à chacun/tous   (group reading only)
        ('the neighbor at table to each/all')
        (everyone's neighbor at the table)
     b. le voisin de table de chacun/tous (group or quantificational reading)
        (lit. the neighbor at table to each/all)
        (everyone's neighbor at the table)

(27) a. la mère à chacun/tous   (group reading only)
        (lit. the mother to each/all)
        (everyone's mother)
     b. la mère de chacun/tous   (group or quantificational reading)
        (lit. the mother of each/all)
        (everyone's mother)

The group reading corresponds to a non quantificational interpretation according to which for all x there is only one person (next to him), or one

---

(lit.'I Know the sister who is beautiful to Jean')
(I know John's sister who is beautiful)

Compare with (ii), whose properties seem to pattern like other cases of stacking :

(ii)   la soeur de Jean qui est belle   (RRC + RRC)
      (the sister of Jean who is beautiful)

The marginal character of (iii) might be related to the ungrammaticality of (5.b), in the text.

(iii) ??   la soeur qui est belle de Jean   (RRC +RRC)
      (the sister which is beautiful of Jean)

[9] The fact that the possessive adjective corresponds to two elements is also supported by the aspectual constraints studied by Godard (1986,), as reinterpreted in Bonneau & Pica (1996).

mother. Put in syntactic terms, the quantifier is interpreted within the scope of the determiner associated with the 'head' of the relative clause. The quantificational reading on the other hand corresponds to an interpretation where the quantificational element can take scope over the $D°$, perhaps by overt movement to the Specifier of a Distributive Phrase as in Kayne (1998). These contrast pattern together with the contrast between (25) and (28):

(28) Jean a parlé avec tout le monde qu'il connaissait
     (Jean has spoken with everybody he knew)

This is reminiscent of our observation that in (3.a) the relative clause acts 'as if' it is not in the scope of the Determiner. Let us assume that the last movement (3.a) is triggered by PF features (related to word order). If this kind of feature is not accessible to semantic interpretation, we can derive the facts alluded to above in a straightforward fashion. In a more general way the parallelism between Relative Clauses and Possessive Nominals supports our claim that both constructions involve the same general mechanisms made available by UG.

4. On Restrictive vs Non Restrictive Adjectives in French

If we assume as in Kayne (1994) (see also Smith (1964)) that adjectives involve RC constructions, we expect to find a restrictive vs. non-restrictive distinction in this syntactic area too. That is, we expect all adjectives to enter in a common structure, as illustrated in (29):

(29) $[_{DP} D° [_{CP} [_{AP} grand_i] [_{IP} [_{NP} pays] e_i]]]$ (RC + NRRC)
        $[_{DP} D° [_{CP} [_{AP} big]_i [_{IP} country e_i]]]$

One further expects that overt movement of the remnant NP outside DP, followed by movement of the whole DP, as illustrated in (30a) and (30b) respectively:

(30) a. $[_{NP} pays e_i]_j [_{DP} le [_{CP} [_{AP} grand_i] [_{IP} [_{NP} e_i]]_j]]] =>$
     b. $[_{DP} le [_{CP} [_{AP} grand_i] [[_{IP} [_{NP} e_i]] _j]]_k [_{NP} pays e_i]_j [_{DP}]_k]]$

That this might indeed be the case is suggested by the following examples where 'grand' must be interpreted as 'great' in (31.b), hereby expressing an inalienable (non restrictive) property of 'Paul', while it is most naturally interpreted as 'big' in (31.a), where it expresses an alienable property: [10] [11]

---

[10] See Bonneau & Pica (1996) for a larger class of examples.
[11] We would like to suggest that while (31.a) in the text illustrates stacking, (31.b) does not, as the ungrammaticality of (i) suggests.

(31) a.   le grand pays de Paul
        (the big country of Paul)
   b.   le grand pays à Paul
        (lit. the great country to Paul)
        (Paul's great country)

That is, we would like to suggest that a certain class of adjectives expresses inalienable properties when they are employed with social noun or kinship terms such as 'pays' 'mère' etc. , which are inherently non-restrictive (see Benveniste (1960b)). Interestingly this non-restrictive adjective seems to express permanent (non-specific) properties and are compatible with long distance reflexivization as illustrated by (32) where 'grand' must be interpreted as 'big' (non restrictive) in (32.b), not as 'great' (restrictive) in (32.a):[12]

(32) a.   On$_i$ souhaite toujours que les gens disent du bien de son$_i$ grand pays
        (One always wihses that people praise (SUBJ) his great country)
   b.   *On$_i$ souhaite toujours que Paul dise du bien de son$_i$ grand pays
        (One always wihses that people say praise (SUBJ) his big country)

5. Conclusion

While the analysis developed in the text leaves many areas unexplored, it suggests clearly that the very same mechanisms are playing a role in what used to be considered distinct constructions of the Grammar. If the analysis developed in the text is on the right track, the very same Restrictive/Alienable versus Non-Restrictive/Inalienable distinction seems to play a role in various types of Relative Clauses, Possessive Nominals and Adjectival Constructions, as well as in the process of Reflexivization.

(i)   * le grand pays à l'homme que je connais
       (The great country to the man that I know)

That is, as suggested in note (6) above 'à+N' seems, in some constructions, to play a mere role of identificaton of the relative clause Possessor, as in clitic doubling construction. Perhaps related is 'mon ami à moi' ('my friend to me'). This suggests that the absence of stacking with NRC might be due to an interpretative according to which NRC establish an unique relation between two objects x and y and that inalienable relationship holdS of two objects only (as opposed to part-whole relationship). We hope to be able come back to this topic in the next future.
[12] See on that matter which suggests some relationship between Possession and Reflexivization (as suggested in note 6), Pica (1982), Pica (1985) and Pica & Tancredi, (1988).

We hope that our analysis, which puts to fore a number of hitherto unobserved empirical phenomena will shed some new light on the notion of alienability (and its alleged relationship with aspect), while making possible a better understanding of languages where the usual categorial distinctions of Indo-European languages seems masked (see among many others, Rodrigues (1996)).

While the nature of the syntactic movement involved needs to be investigated in more detail (but see Kayne (1998)), the analysis developed in the text, according to which all interfaces interact with the very same syntactic level accounts in a straightforward way for interaction of phonological factors, such as intonation breaks and semantic interpretation.[13] As pointed out in the text, it remains to be determined which elements are visible for each interface (the Conceptual/Intentional and the Articulatory/Perceptual interfaces) and how sound and meaning are paired together. Precise answers to these questions are of crucial interest for a minimalist approach to language and its interaction with other faculties, whose exact nature still needs to be determined.

---

[13] See for a discussion, Higginbotham (1995,) among others.

7. References

Bally, Charles. 1926. L'expression des idées de sphère personnelle et de solidarité dans les langues indo-européennes, In Fankhauser, F & J. Jakob eds., *Festschrift Louis Gauchat*. Aarau: H. R. Sauerlander. 68-78.

Benveniste, Emile. 1960a. 'être' et 'avoir' dans leurs fonctions linguistiques. *Bulletin de la Société linguistique de Paris*. 54. fasc 1. Paris. 52-62.

Benveniste, Emile. 1960b. *Le vocabulaire des institutions européennes*. Minuit: Paris.

Benveniste, Emile. 1962. Pour l'analyse des formes casuelles : Le génitif latin. *Lingua* XI. 10-18.

Bonneau, José and Pierre Pica. 1996. From 'Appartainence' to Possession : Predicative and Relative Constructions in French Nominals. Ms, McGill University & CNRS.

Chomsky, Noam. 1995. *The minimalist Program*. Cambridge Mass: MIT Press.

Crowley, Tim. 1996. Body parts and Part-whole Constructions in Paamese Grammar. in Chappell, Hilary, & William McGregor eds. *A Typological Perspective on Body Part Terms and Part-Whole Relation*. Mouton: Berlin. 383-432.

Emonds, Joseph. 1979. Appositives Relatives have no Properties. *Linguistic Inquiry* 10. 211-243.

Godard, Danièle. 1986. Les déterminants possessifs et les compléments de nom. *Langue Française* 72. Larousse: Paris. 102-122.

Higginbotham, James. 1995. Semantic Computation, Ms. Sommerville College.

Kayne, Richard. 1975. French Syntax: The Transformational Cycle. MIT Press: Cambridge Mass.

Kayne, Richard. 1993. Towards a Modular Theory of Auxiliary Selection. *Studia Linguistica* 47. 3-31.

Kayne, Richard. 1994. *The Antisymmetry of Syntax*. MIT Press: Cambridge Mass.

Kayne, Richard. 1998. Overt vs Covert Movement. Ms, New York University.

Larson, Richard & Gabriel Segal. 1995. *Knowledge of meaning. An introduction to Semantics Theory*, MIT Press: Cambridge Mass.

McCawley, James. 1981. The Syntax and Semantics of Relative Clauses. *Lingua* 53. 99-149.

Milner, Jean-Claude. 1978. *De la syntaxe à l'interprétation*. Paris: Le Seuil.

Milner, Jean-Claude. 1982. Les génitifs adnominaux en français, in *Ordres et raisons de langue*. Paris: Le seuil. 69-94.

Pica. Pierre. 1982. Liage et contiguïté, in J. C. Milner (Ed.), *Recherches sur l'Anaphore*. Cahier de l'URA 642. Paris. 119-164.

Pica, Pierre. 1985. Subject, Tense and Truth : Towards a Modular Approach to Binding,in Jacqueline Guéron, Hans Obenauer, & Jean-Yves Pollock .eds, in*Grammatical Representation*, Dordrecht: Foris. 258-291.

Pica, Pierre. 1992. The Case for Reflexives or Reflexives for Case. *Papers from the 26th Regional Meeting of the Chicago Linguistic Society*, Volume 1, Chicago. 363-378.

Pica, Pierre. 1998. On the Theoretical Implications of the Properties of 'se' and 'soi' in French. Ms. CNRS.

Pica, Pierre and Chris Tancredi. 1998. Anaphoric Thoughts and Self Identification. Ms. CNRS & Yokohama National University.

Richards, John. 1973. *Dificuldades na Analise da Posessao Nominal na Lingua Waura.* Seria linguistica 1, 1. Summer Institute of Linguistics: Brasilia. 11-28

Rodrigues, Aryon. 1996. Argumento e Predicado em Tupinambe. Ms. National University of Brasilia.

Safir, Ken. 1986. Relative Clauses in a Theory of Binding and Levels. *Linguistic Inquiry* 17. 663- 689.

Smith, Carlota. 1964. Determiners and Relative Clauses in a Generative Grammar of English. *Language* 40. 37-52.

Stowell, Tim. 1981. *Origins of Phrase Structure.* Doctoral Dissertation, Massachusetts Institute of Technology: Cambridge Mass.

Szabolcsi, Anna. 1981. The Possessive Construction in Hungarian: A Configurational Category in a Non-configurational Language. *Acta Linguistica Academiae Scientiarum Hungaricae* 31. 261-289.

Szabolcsi, Anna. 1994. The Noun Phrase, in Ferenc Kiefer & Katalina Kiss eds. *The Syntactic Structure of Hunagrian,* Syntax and Semantics 27. Academic Press : San diego. 179-265.

Tremblay, Mireille. 1989. French Possessive Adjectives as Dative Clitics, in John Fee eds. *Proceedings of the 8th West Coast Conference on Formal Linguistics.* CSLI. Stanford (distributed by Cambridge University Press). 399-413.

Vergnaud, Jean-Roger. 1974. *French Relative Clauses.* Doctoral Dissertation, Massachusetts Institute of Technology. Cambridge Mass.

Predicable Participles*

CLAUDIA BORGONOVO & SARAH CUMMINS

Université Laval

1. Introduction

This paper examines -*en* participles ("past" participles) in English, French, and Spanish, and the conditions that enable them to appear within a DP — what makes them predicable. We propose that DP-internal predication by participles is accomplished via BE, which licenses three interpretations of the participle. This proposal offers an explanation for cross-linguistic variation in grammaticality and insights into the aspectual readings available to DP-internal participles.

Across languages, participles of transitive verbs are generally able to predicate within DP, and their aspectual class does not influence their acceptability. (1a) shows participles of stative verbs, (1b) participles of processes, both punctual and durative, and (1c) participles of Transitions, Pustejovsky's (1995) term covering both accomplishments and achievements — that is, complex events made up of a process that culminates in the attainment of a state.

---

*We would like to thank Peter Ackema, Päivi Koskinen, and Sara T. Rosen for valuable discussion and comments, and our Laval colleagues Silvia Faitelson-Weiser, Darlene LaCharité, Alan Manning, and Philippe Prévost for comments on an earlier version of this work.

(1) a. <u>States</u>
    a respected scholar, a well-loved tale, a collection admired for
        centuries
    un savant respecté, un conte bien-aimé, une collection admirée
        depuis des siècles
    un sabio respetado, un recuerdo querido, una colección admirada
        desde hace siglos

   b. <u>Processes</u>
    scribbled notes, a rented room, balls kicked towards the goal
    des notes gribouillées, une chambre louée, des balles envoyées vers
        le but
    notas garabateadas, una pieza alquilada, las pelotas pateadas al arco

   c. <u>Transitions</u>
    a broken window, a well-sharpened knife, furniture painted since
        the fall
    une fenêtre cassée, un couteau bien aiguisé, des meubles peints
        depuis l'automne
    una ventana rota, un cuchillo muy afilado, los muebles pintados
        desde el otoño

Participles of intransitive verbs do not appear so freely within DP, and the correct generalization on this use is not clear-cut. A widely-accepted view (e.g. Hoekstra (1984, 1986); Ackema (1995)) relates to argument structure or mapping patterns: unaccusative, but not unergative, participles have a DP-internal use, as illustrated in (2).

(2) *a fallen leaf/ *the worked man*
    une feuille tombée/*l'homme travaillé
    una hoja caída/*el hombre trabajado

But not all unaccusatives participles can appear within a DP. Zaenen (1993) and Levin and Rappaport Hovav (Levin and Rappaport (1986, 1989), Levin and Rappaport Hovav (1995)) have proposed that telicity is an additional requirement. This explains the unacceptability of (3): *live*, like its counterparts *vivre* and *vivir*, although classified as unaccusative, does not form a predicable participle because it is not telic.

(3) **the man lived in Paris/*l'homme vécu à Paris/*el hombre vivido en*
    París

A first question, then, is why aspectual class is irrelevant for transitive verbs but a determining factor for intransitives. A second problem becomes apparent when this requirement is examined from a cross-linguistic perpsective. With the reasonable assumption that, across languages, verbs display broad consistency in syntactic and aspectual classes, it is surprising to note variation in the ability of intransitive participles to appear within DP, as illustrated in (4). In each case, French has a predicable participle of a telic unaccusative, while English and Spanish do not.

(4) a.   *les participants partis après 4 heures / *los participantes partidos después de las 4 / *the participants left after 4*

    b.   *les invités arrivés après moi / *los invitados llegados después de mí/ *the guests arrived after me*

    c.   *les élèves montés au deuxième étage / *los alumnos subidos al segundo piso / *students gone up to the second floor*

    d.   *les spectateurs entrés après le lever du rideau/ *los espectadores entrados después de levantado el telón/ *the spectators entered after the curtain*

If argument structure and aspectual class are sufficient to characterize predicable participles, this variation is unexpected and unexplained. We propose instead an account of all DP-internal predication by *-en* participles that explains this cross-linguistic variation and correctly predicts behaviour in other languages. Our account, by appealing to a universal syntactic condition and a finer-grained semantic feature than aspectual class, teases apart subtle interpretational differences available both cross-linguistically and within a single language, while unifying certain facets of sentential and DP-internal participial predication.

2. Predication via BE

Considering all DP-internal uses of participles together, we formulate a condition on the licensing of participles, which extends to restrictive modification in general. We propose that DP-internal participles are licensed via BE. This general condition accounts not only for typical, widespread patterns but also for the cross-linguistic variation we have noted. Our hypothesis also predicts systematic patterns in the interpretation of predicable participles, including certain ambiguities that have been largely unnoticed.

    A few preliminary assumptions should be stated. As is clear from the examples above, we are not establishing an *a priori* distinction between "adjectival" and "verbal" participles or between prenominal and postnominal uses in English. We ignore the issue of obligatory adjuncts with participles (cf. Grimshaw and Vikner (1990)). In short, we are considering all participles that appear within DP, whether before or after the noun, whether alone or with an adjunct, as instances of the predicative use of the participle, the point of interest to us at this stage.

    We follow current research in assuming that all *-en* participles, whether in a verbal passive, a perfective, or a DP, largely share the same characteristics (cf. Ackema (1995); Cowper (1989, 1995)). The main assumption is that the participial morpheme -*en* is assigned the external theta-role of the verb it attaches to. This explains why participles of transitive and unergative verbs do not predicate of the external argument of the base verb, since the relevant theta-role is no longer available to be assigned under predication.

We take predication to be the expression of a semantic relationship, the assignment by a predicate of its external theta-role to an argument. We follow Higginbotham (1995) and others in considering that modification (the relationship that exists within a DP between the head noun and most adjectives, some prepositional phrases, and all -*en* participles) involves the same semantic relationship as other forms of predication. (cf. Williams (1994); Crisma (1996:69): "...the relation of attributive modification...[is] after all a special case of predication".) We propose that predication is accomplished within DP via BE, in the same way that the predication of properties is accomplished at the sentential level. Here we are merely making explicit what semanticists have assumed: a red ball is a ball that is red, and "a batted ball is a ball that has been batted" (Higginbotham (1985:566)).

The structure we propose to make DP-internal predication via BE syntactically explicit is given in (5).

(5) <u>Predication via BE within DP</u>

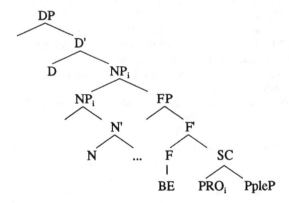

This structure contains an unnamed functional projection FP, headed by BE, a functional head without semantic content (following Ritter and Rosen's (1997) proposal for sentential BE; cf. Kayne (1993, 1994)). In French, English, and Spanish, BE is phonetically realized only when dominated by Tense. BE takes a Small Clause complement whose predicate constituent, in the case of interest here, is the participial phrase. The subject of the Small Clause is PRO, controlled by the head NP.

This simplified tree omits any functional projections between DP and NP, such as AgrP, NumberPhrase, DefinitenessPhrase, since they are not relevant here. Agreement between participle and head could be achieved by an

AgrP projection, if that is how one chooses to handle agreement facts. This structure is compatible with two views of how surface order between the noun and participle (or other restrictive modifier) is achieved, both involving adjunction of the participle to NP, as in Valois (1996), Siloni (1995), and others. Adjunction could be to the right in Romance and to the left in English, with heavy participle movement to the right. Or a universal structure could be devised, with the participle adjoined to the left, and an AgrP projection to which the N moves overtly in Romance and covertly in English. Nothing in the rest of this paper hinges on the choice between these two possibilities.

The essential claim that the tree in (5) makes, in a maximally simple form, is that a DP-internal participle is structurally associated with a head NP via BE and it is interpreted via BE. Thus interpretation of the predication within a DP is handled in the same way sentential interpretation via BE is. Association of a participle with BE licenses three interpretations:

(6) Interpretations of a participle via BE
 • passive, available to transitive verbs
 • perfective, subject to parametric variation
 • stative, available to verbs that depict a state

The passive interpretation is the typical result of the association of the participle with BE: a batted ball is a ball that has been batted; a respected scholar is a scholar who is respected. The -en morpheme's semantic feature of [past] in combination with an eventive verb gives a perfective aspectual reading (that is, the batting event is over); with a stative verb, the past feature gives the reading that the state existed previously (a respected scholar is one who is already respected).[1]

The perfective interpretation is available to the participles of verbs that select BE as the perfective auxiliary.

A stative interpretation is available to the participles of verbs that denote the right kind of semantic entity in the participial form. To determine what this right kind of semantic entity is, it is necessary to look more closely at DP-internal predication by the participles of intransitive verbs. As we saw above, it has been claimed that their ability to predicate depends on their aspectual class; it turns out, in fact, that a factor other than telicity is crucial.

Levin and Rappaport Hovav (Levin and Rappapport (1986), Levin and Rappaport Hovav (1995)) cite data such as *a recently appeared book, a newly emerged scandal* as evidence that telic unaccusatives in English form perfective adjectival participles. But in fact such participles appear very reluctantly as DP-internal modifiers (cf. Pesetsky (1995)). Levin (1993) and

---

[1] Note that this same distinction holds in sentential uses of the participle: with *She has batted since the third inning,* the batting event is over; with *I have respected her since 1990,* the state of respecting is not over, but existed previously.

Levin and Rappaport Hovav (1995) list about 80 verbs that could be considered telic unaccusatives in English; these are classified as verbs of inherently directed motion, appearance, occurrence, disappearance, and internally caused change of state. Participles of this last class do predicate freely within DP of any semantically compatible argument, as shown in (7a). The few change-of-state participles that do not display this ability are exemplified in (7b).

(7) a. *rusted pipes, tarnished dreams, wine fermented in casks, decayed vegetation, metal corroded by exposure to the elements, leaves wilted and withered, swollen fingers, blistered palms, the molted skin of a serpent*

b. **bloomed/*blossomed/*flowered honeysuckle vines, *stagnated bayous, *mouldered muffins*

But the situation is reversed for the sixty or so verbs in the other semantic classes: only a few are as productive as the change-of-state verbs:

(8) *fallen trees, escaped convicts, lapsed coverage, expired leases, vanished treasure*

The particples of the remaining telic unaccusatives are either utterly unable to predicate within DP, as in (9a); or else they are extremely restricted — either because they can appear only prenominally (9b) or only postnominally (9c), or because their arguments and modifiers are much more restricted in a DP-internal use than in tensed propositions (9d-f).

(9) a. **receded tides, *fled civilians, *mountain-climbers plunged to their deaths, *an accident occurred in the night, *a madman burst into the room, *subsequently ensued events*

b. *departed guests/*guests departed in a huff*

c. *a repairman come to check the pipes/*a recently come repairman*

d. *descended testicles/*descended hikers, *descended miners, *descended weather balloons*

e. *a recently appeared book/*a recently appeared explorer, *a recently appeared planet*

f. *recently arrived guests/*tardily arrived guests, *early arrived guests, *already arrived guests, *hurriedly arrived guests, *subsequently arrived guests*

The same pattern is repeated in Spanish: the telic unaccusatives that appear freely as DP-internal participles are those that depict a change of state; a few other telic unaccusatives crop up, but they are exceptional.

(10) a.   *las mareas retiradas, *los civiles huidos, *los alpinistas
          precipitados a su muerte
          'receded tides, fled civilians, mountain-climbers plunged to their
          death'
     b.   un libro recientemente aparecido/*un explorador recientemente
          aparecido, *un planeta recientemente aparecido
          'a recently appeared book, a recently appeared explorer, a recently
          appeared planet'
     c.   testículos descendidos/*caminantes descendidos, *mineros
          descendidos, *globos meteorológicos descendidos
          'descended testicles, descended hikers, descended miners, descended
          weather balloons'

These examples show that predicability is dependent on much more than telicity. "Telic unaccusative" does not adequately characterize the class of participles of intransitive verbs in Spanish and English that are able to predicate within a DP. The data instead suggest a condition for a stative interpretation via BE.

(11) Stative interpretation via BE
      DP-internal predication is available to participles of intransitive verbs
      that are Transitions culminating in a fully-specified state.

This refinement distinguishes between two types of telic unaccusatives: those that depict a change of state, such as rot, and those that depict a change of location, such as arrive. Both verbs are Transitions, composed of an activity or process that culminates in a state, but they differ in the nature of this final state. That of rot is a lexically-specified property; the lexical representation of the verb specifies that the argument acquires the property, an accidental quality resulting from the process or activity that precedes it. This is what we mean by "a fully-specified state". In the case of arrive, the final state is not a quality but a location; the argument cannot be said to have acquired a quality.

Other linguists have made this distinction in decompositional semantic representations. For example, Pustejovsky (1995) explicitly introduces at, a kind of semantic primitive, in the lexical representation for arrive in (12a); this element is absent from the representation of change-of-state verbs. Jackendoff (1990) distinguishes states that refer to a "property" from those that refer to a "place". Thus, this semantic difference has been noted, but not exploited to account for the different syntactic behaviour of verbs of the two types.

(12) a.　　　　*arrive*　　　　b.　　　　*rot*

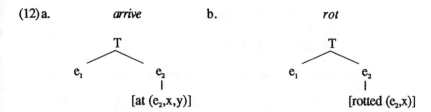

[at (e₂,x,y)]　　　　　　　　　　[rotted (e₂,x)]

The verbs whose participles appear freely within DP in English and Spanish are those that depict a quality the argument acquires by virtue of a Transition; those that depict a Transition to a location are less felicitous. But certain verbs are able to express both. Some verbs of disappearance or inherently-directed motion also imply the acquisition of a quality; these are more acceptable than those that express a simple change of location (cf. examples (9d-f) and (10b) and (c) above). The verb *fall* in English (*caer* in Spanish) is particularly illustrative of this distinction: it resists a DP-internal use when it refers only to downward movement to a location; predication works best when the verb expresses acquisition of a quality — that is, a transition to a fully-specified state.

(13) a.　*ángeles caídos, fallen angels* (= corrupted)
　　　　un guerrero caído, a fallen warrior (= dead, killed),
　　　　hojas caídas, fallen leaves (= dead)
　　b.　*??un chico caído, ?a fallen child* (= on the ground)
　　　　??libros caídos, ?fallen books (= to the floor)

In (13a), the participles are interpreted as expressing the acquisition of a quality—corrupted or dead. The (b) examples are difficult because no interpretation is readily available: the passive interpretation fails, because *fall* and *caer* are not transitive verbs; the stative interpretation fails, because no specified state is referred to; and the perfective interpretation fails because active perfectives are not associated with BE in English and Spanish.

French patterns differently. In French, there is general consistency in the ability of telic unaccusatives to appear as DP-internal participles, whether or not they culminate in a fully-specified state.

(14) a.　*une lettre parvenue à destination*
　　　　'a letter reached its destination'
　　b.　*un accident survenu sur l'autoroute*
　　　　'an accident occurred on the highway'
　　c.　*les secouristes venus trop tard pour sauver les passagers*
　　　　'rescuers come too late to save the passengers'

d. *des alpinistes descendus au refuge*
'mountain-climbers descended to the hut'

e. *des arbustes fleuris, des bananes pourries, une bombe explosée, du lait aigri*
'flowered shrubs, rotted bananas, an exploded bomb, soured milk'

Like their counterparts in Spanish and English, French participles of change-of-state unaccusatives, as in (14e), predicate freely within DP. The cases where French contrasts with Spanish and English comprise verbs of directed motion and appearance, disappearance, and occurrence. These are typically Transitions culminating not in a fully-specified state, but a location.

Therefore, these participles are not interpreted as specified states: they denote the wrong kind of semantic entity. Nor can they be interpreted as passives, since they are intransitive. But, unlike their counterparts in English and Spanish, these participles are associated lexically with the auxiliary BE in a fashion parallel to passive participles' association with BE: these verbs select *être* to form the periphrastic perfect tense in French.

(15) a. *La lettre est parvenue à destination.*
'The letter reached its destination.'

b. *L'accident est survenu sur l'autoroute.*
'The accident occurred on the highway.'

c. *Les secouristes sont venus trop tard pour sauver les passagers.*
'The rescuers come too late to save the passengers.'

d. *Les alpinistes sont descendus au refuge.*
'The mountain-climbers descended to the hut.'

The third interpretation is therefore available in French. BE licenses a perfective interpretation, because BE is a perfective auxiliary in French.

3. Predictions

3.1 Cross-linguistic predictions

Our analysis predicts that constructions similar to the French examples in (4) and (14) should be grammatical for other languages which associate these verbs with BE in perfective tenses; the prediction is confirmed by Italian and Dutch counterparts of such constructions, given in (16) and (17), respectively. The underlined participles are forms of verbs that select the BE auxiliary (*zijn* in Dutch and *essere* in Italian) to form periphrastic perfect tenses.

(16) a. *I bambini arrivati dopo le 5 devono attendere fuori.*
'The children arrived after 5 must wait outside.'

b. *Gli studenti partiti alle 5 devono tornare alle 6.*
'The students left at 5 must return at 6.'

(17) a. *De vroeg binnengekomen kinderen zullen ook weer vroeg moeten vertrekken.*
'The children entered early entered must also leave early.'
b. *De na vijven gearriveerde gasten zullen niet worden toegelaten.*
'The guests arrived at 5 will not be admitted.'

3.2 Aspectual readings

Predication via BE can give rise, then, to three interpretations of the participle: passive, specified state, and perfective. As noted, passive participles are generally allowed, whether they are derived from aspectually simplex stative verbs, as in (18); from aspectually simplex eventive verbs that do not necessarily entail a change of state in their objects (19); or from aspectually complex transitions that do entail such a change-of-state (20).

(18) a. *a respected scholar, a cherished keepsake, a well-loved story*
b. *un savant respecté, un souvenir chéri, un conte bien-aimé*
c. *un sabio respetado, un recuerdo querido, un cuento muy amado*

(19) a. *the batted ball, the bottle shaken well, a missed opportunity*
b. *la balle frappée, le biberon bien agité, une occasion ratée*
c. *la pelota bateada, el biberón bien sacudido, una ocasión desaprovechada*

(20) a. *the murdered prince, the finished picture, the watered rows*
b. *le prince assassiné, le tableau terminé, les rangées arrosées*
c. *el príncipe asesinado, el cuadro terminado, los canteros regados*

With aspectually simplex passive participles, the aspectual reading available depends on the aspectual type of the verb. States give rise only to a stative reading, as in (21); here the adverbials headed by *for, pendant,* or *durante* are compatible only with statives, while *in an instant, en un instant,* and *en un instante* are compatible only with eventives.

(21) a. *a scholar respected for decades/un savant respecté pendant des décennies/un sabio respetado durante décadas*
b. **a scholar respected in an instant/*un savant respecté en un instant/*un sabio respetado en un instante*

Aspectually simplex processes give rise only to the eventive reading :

(22) *the balls batted since three o'clock/les balles frappées depuis 3 h/ las pelotas bateados desde las 3*
= balls that someone has batted since three o'clock
≠ balls that have been batted (in a batted state) since three o'clock

However, our analysis predicts that passive participles of verbs that depict a Transition culminating in a specified state will be ambiguous between a stative and an eventive reading. Predication by such participles can be licensed in two ways. Each gives rise to a different aspectual reading. Licensing as a passive results in an eventive reading; licensing as a fully-specified state results in a stative reading. The prediction that both readings are available for participles of this class is borne out in all three languages, as shown in (23). (23a), for example, can have either an eventive reading — there was a painting event since Tuesday — or a stative reading — a painted state has existed since Tuesday.

(23) a.   *les meubles peints depuis mardi/the furniture painted since Tuesday/los muebles pintados desde el martes*
         = someone painted the furniture since Tuesday (eventive)
         = the furniture has been in a painted state since Tuesday (stative)
     b.   *protesters imprisoned since noon/des manifestants emprisonnés depuis midi/los manifestantes encarcelados desde las 12*
         = the imprisonment(s) took place after noon (eventive)
         = the protesters have been languishing in prison since noon (stative)

Turning to intransitive verbs, in English and Spanish these are licensed only by the specified-state condition, and they have only a stative reading:

(24) a.   *blistered feet, corroded pipes, fermented cider, tarnished dreams*
     b.   *pies ampollados, caños corroídos, sidra fermentada, sueños arruinados*
         = feet that are in a blistered state, etc.
         ≠ feet that something has blistered, etc.

It is worth noting that in English many change-of-state intransitives have a transitive causative variant, and attempts to force an eventive reading on participles of such verbs often result in a passive interpretation, as shown in (25). Our account predicts this as well: licensing as a specified state gives rise to only the stative reading; the eventive reading would have to come from licensing as a passive.

(25) a.   *seeds germinated in April*
         = someone germinated the seeds in April
         ≠ the seeds germinated in April
     b.   *cliffs eroded in the winter*
         = something eroded the cliffs in the winter
         ≠ the cliffs eroded in the winter
     c.   *cider fermented in 1993*
         = someone fermented the cider in 1993
         ≠ the cider fermented in 1993

Intransitive participles licensed as perfectives in French by virtue of their association with BE are predicted to have only an eventive reading, not a stative one. This prediction is borne out, by and large. A stative reading is not available to the participles in (26).

(26) a. *un accident survenu en un instant/*pendant un long moment*
'an accident (that) occurred in an instant/for a long while

   b. *les lettres parvenues au ministère depuis la grève*
= 'letters that have reached the ministry since the strike'
≠ 'letters that have been at the ministry since the strike'

   c. *les enfants accourus en un clin d'oeil/*pendant vingt minutes*
'the children (who had) rushed up in a trice/for twenty minutes'

However, there are a few such verbs that give rise to both a stative and an eventive reading, such as those in (27):

(27)   *les spectateurs arrivés/partis/disparus depuis une heure*
'the spectators (who) arrived/left/disappeared in the last hour'
'the spectators (who have been) here/gone/missing for an hour'

We have no clear explanation at this point for the availability of a stative reading. Bouchard (1995: 236-243) attributes the availability of both the eventive (or "active") reading and the stative reading of such participles in tensed clauses to the fact that verbs like *arriver* and *partir* depict an instantaneous transition, with no internal development. However, Bouchard was comparing such verbs to only two other similar verbs (*aller* 'go' and *venir* 'come') that do not allow the stative interpretation. It is not clear how *survenir* 'happen suddenly', for example, which allows only the eventive reading, necessarily expresses more internal development than *arriver* and *partir*.

DP-internal predication by an -*en* participle requires some aspectual complexity in the verb. Transitive verbs possess this complexity, regardless of event type, by virtue of their two arguments, one of which is associated with the source, originator, initiator of a situation, and the other with the target, goal, delimiter, undergoer. Single-argument verbs possess aspectual complexity only when they express a change of state or a change of location. All -*en* participles refer to the end of an eventuality (with "end" not necessarily being taken in a temporal sense): this end is associated with the object of a transitive verb or the culminating state of a verb that depicts a Transition (or with both). We can hypothesize that, in the case of telic unaccusatives — those intransitive verbs that have the aspectual complexity for participial predication — the fact that both fully-specified states and locations are licensed in French by association with BE results in a merger of the two kinds of culmination, making both a stative and an eventive reading more widely available, where semantically feasible. This idea also suggests an explanation for why certain intransitives culminating in a location rather than a fully-specified state are licensed as DP-internal participles, even though they select the perfective auxiliary *avoir* rather than *être*. Such verbs are semantically similar to verbs that select *être*, but in the vagaries of the French auxiliary-selection system, they wind up with *avoir* rather than *être*. Some examples are given in (28).

(28) a. *un homme surgi de l'ombre*
     ' a man loomed up out of the mist'
  b. *des Haïtiens immigrés au Canada depuis 1990*
     'Haitians immigrated to Canada since 1990'
  c. *la boue jaillie*
     'the spurted mud'

Our account makes a final prediction: intransitive verbs culminating in a specified state that are associated with perfective BE will have an eventive reading not available to those that have no such association. The stative reading is available by virtue of the semantics of the verb, and the eventive reading is available by virtue of licensing as a perfective via BE.

This is the case with French *mourir* 'die', which selects the auxiliary *être*. In (29), the participle *mort* may be assigned either a stative reading or an eventive reading.

(29) a. *l'homme mort depuis midi*
     'the man (who has been) dead since noon'
  b. *l'homme mort il y a une heure*
     'the man (who) died an hour ago'

In the Spanish example of (30), only the stative reading is available to *muerto*. Licensing as a specified state is the only licensing available, since Spanish does not use BE as a perfective auxiliary.

(30) a. *el hombre muerto desde hace 3 días*
     'the man (who has been) dead for three days'
  b. *?el hombre muerto a las 3*
     'the man (who) died at three o'clock'

The same situation arises with certain pronominal verbs. All pronominal verbs in French select *être* as the perfective auxiliary, while their counterparts in Spanish uniformly select *haber*. Our account predicts that the participles of pronominal verbs expressing culmination to a specified state will be licensed as statives in both French and Spanish, as in (31).

(31) a. *la fille évanouie depuis midi*
     'the girl (who has been) in a faint since noon'
  b. *la niña desmayada desde el martes*
     'the girl (who has been) in a faint since Tuesday'

Further, we predict that an eventive interpretation will be available to such participles in French, by virtue of association with perfective BE, but not in Spanish. The prediction is once again confirmed.

(32) a. *la fille évanouie il y a 10 minutes*
        'the girl (who) fainted 10 minutes ago'
     b. *?* la niña desmayada a las 3*
        'the girl (who) fainted at 3 o'clock'

4. Conclusion

We have proposed that all DP-internal uses of *-en* participles are instances of predication, and that predication by participles within DP is accomplished in the same way that their sentential predication is: by a structural association with BE. Interpretation is also accomplished via BE, which licenses a passive, a stative, and a perfective interpretation. The passive interpretation is available to all transitive verbs. The stative interpretation requires a particular semantic entity: a specified state resulting from a transition. The perfective interpretation via BE requires that the verb in question select BE as a perfective auxiliary. The availability of a DP-internal use for the participles of intransitive verbs and the aspectual readings available to all types of participles are predicted from this account of the licensing of participial predication.

References

Ackema, Peter. 1995. *Syntax Below Zero*. Utrecht: Onderzoeksinstituut voor Taal en Spraak.
Bouchard, Denis. 1995. *The Semantics of Syntax*. Chicago: University of Chicago Press.
Cowper, Elizabeth A. 1989. Perfective [-en] *is* Passive [-en]. Proceedings of the Eighth West Coast Conference on Formal Linguistics, 85-93.
— 1995. English Participle Constructions. *Canadian Journal of Linguistics* 40(1): 1-38.
Crisma, Paola. 1996. On the Configurational Nature of Adjectival Modification, in K. Zagona, ed., *Grammatical Theory and Romance Languages*. Amsterdam: John Benjamins Publishing Company, 59-71.
Grimshaw, Jane and Sten Vikner. 1990. Obligatory Adjuncts and the Structure of Events, ms. Brandeis University and University of Geneva.
Higginbotham, James. 1985. On Semantics. *Linguistic Inquiry* 16: 547-593.
Hoekstra, Teun .1984. *Transitivity: Grammatical Relations in Government-Binding Theory*. Dordrecht: Foris.
— 1986. Passives and Participles, in F. Beukema and A. Hulk, eds., *Linguistics in the Netherlands*. Dordrecht: Foris, 95-104.
Jackendoff, Ray. 1990. *Semantic Structures*. Cambridge: MIT Press.
Kayne, R.S. 1993. Toward a Modular Theory of Auxiliary Selection. *Studia Linguistica* 47: 3-31.
—1994. *The Antisymmetry of Syntax*. Cambridge: MIT Press.
Levin, Beth. 1993. *English Verb Classes and Alternations*. Chicago: University of Chicago Press.
Levin, Beth and Malka Rappaport. 1989. An Approach to Unaccusative Mismatches. Proceedings of NELS 19, GLSA, University of Massachusetts, Amherst, 314-328.
— 1986. The Formation of Adjectival Passives. *Linguistic Inquiry* 17(4): 623-661.
Levin, Beth and Malka Rappaport Hovav. 1995. *Unaccusativity: At the Syntax-Lexical Semantics Interface*. Cambridge: MIT Press.

Pesetsky, David. 1995. *Zero Syntax*. Cambridge: MIT Press.
Pustejovsky, James. 1995. *The Generative Lexicon*. Cambridge: MIT Press.
Ritter, Elizabeth and Sara T. Rosen (1997). The function of *have*. *Lingua* 101:3/4.295-321.
Siloni, Tal. 1995. On Participial Relativizers and Complementizer D^0: A Case Study in Hebrew and French. *Natural Language and Linguistic Theory* 13:3. 445-487.
Valois, Daniel. 1996. On the structure of the French DP. *Canadian Journal of Linguistics* 41:4. 334-376.
Williams, Edwin (1994). *Thematic Structure in Syntax*. Cambridge: MIT Press.
Zaenen, Annie. 1993. Unaccusativity in Dutch: integrating syntax and lexical semantics, in J. Pustejovsky ,ed., *Semantics and the Lexicon*. Dordrecht: Kluwer, 129-161.

Faithfulness and Contrast: The Problem of Coalescence

TRISHA CAUSLEY
University of Toronto

1. Introduction[*]

This paper explores the role of input representations and contrast in Optimality Theory. I argue that current views of the role of input representations (e.g. Prince and Smolensky (1993), Itô, Mester, and Padgett (1995), Smolensky (1996)) are inadequate in accounting for vowel coalescence and deletion patterns that are associated with particular inventory types. Attempts to explain the patterns with Faithfulness constraints alone end up missing important inventory-based generalizations, or are simply unsuccessful.

In answer to this problem, I propose an account of vowel deletion/coalescence phenomena which relies crucially on the representation of segments in the input. Input representations are related to the place markedness of a segment type which is in turn linked to the presence or absence of place contrasts in an inventory (Steriade (1987), Avery & Rice (1989), Rice & Avery (1993), Goad (1993), Dyck (1995)).

In this paper, I start by outlining briefly the role that markedness plays in place assimilation patterns and describe one way of accounting for these patterns in Optimality Theory (§2). Place assimilation generalizations are relevant to the discussion of vowel coalescence phenomena in that they share many similarities, and parallel Optimality Theoretic accounts are available for both. Next, I describe the types of coalescence phenomena that

---

[*] Thanks to the members of the phonology project in the Department of Linguistics at the University of Toronto for their helpful comments. This research was funded in part by a SSHRCC grant (410-96-0842) to E. Dresher and K. Rice, and a SSHRCC doctoral fellowship (752-96-1729).

I am considering, asserting that certain vowel assimilation, coalescence, and elision phenomena are a unified set of processes, motivated by the same set of constraints (§3). In the next section I look at different vowel coalescence/ elision patterns which are associated with particular vowel inventories (§4). I contrast two different ways of accounting for the phenomena: one relying crucially on contrast-driven input representations, and one relying on feature-specific Faithfulness constraints. I argue that only the first analysis allows us to capture the relationship between inventory shape and the behaviour of particular segments in coalescence. Finally, I present patterns found in languages with asymmetrical inventories and demonstrate the problems these type of systems pose for a feature-specific Faithfulness account of coalescence (§5).

2. Place markedness and assimilation asymmetries

Asymmetries in cross-linguistic place assimilation patterns are linked to markedness relations between segments: unmarked elements tend to be targets and not triggers while marked elements tend to be triggers and not targets (Kiparsky (1985)). Thus, in place assimilation patterns, we often see a [coronal] + [labial] sequence becoming [labial][labial] while a [labial]+[coronal] sequence remains [labial][coronal].

This raises the question of why unmarked elements are susceptible to assimilation while marked elements resist. Given the markedness constraint hierarchy *dors, *lab >> *cor (Prince & Smolensky (1993)), these patterns are completely unexpected: assimilation seems to preserve a more marked feature at the cost of losing a less marked feature, creating less harmonic forms.

Feature-specific Faithfulness constraints may appear to be a direction to follow in search of a solution. The Max-Feature set of constraints requires the preservation of input features. They are relativized to particular features and may be ranked freely with respect to one another. The constraints governing [labial] and [coronal] features are given in (1).

(1) Feature-Specific Faithfulness constraints:
      a.   MAX-LAB
              Every [labial] specification in the input has a
              correspondent in the output.
      b.   MAX-COR
              Every [coronal] specification in the input has a
              correspondent in the output.

The ranking MAX-LAB>>MAX-COR means that, in a [coronal]+[labial] input sequence which undergoes assimilation, the [labial] specification will be maintained at the expense of the [coronal] specification. However, such a solution requires a "reverse hierarchy" where Faithfulness is more sensitive to marked elements (i.e. Faith$_{marked}$ >>Faith$_{unmarked}$). If this pattern is a universal one, this ranking, which is inexplicably the mirror image of the markedness hierarchy, is a fixed one. As we will see in the next section, a similar asymmetry is often found in vowel hiatus resolution patterns, and a similar problematic feature-specific Faithfulness account is available.

3. Coalescence, Elision, and Assimilation: A unified approach

Vocalic hiatus resolution gives rise to several different processes. The relevant processes here are vowel coalescence, assimilation, and elision. As Casali (1996), (1997) points out, in most languages, the outcome of vocalic hiatus resolution is determined by position (e.g, preserve V_1 over V_2, or assimilate an affix vowel to a stem vowel.) However, where positional factors are not at issue, the patterns depend on the nature of the segments involved. That is, when the coalescence of two particular vowels produces the same output regardless of their input order, the output must be determined on the basis of the vowels themselves. When two vowels X and Y come together in any order and Y is always deleted, it must be something about the nature of X that keeps it from being deleted and something about the nature of Y that prevents it from surfacing at the expense of X. It is these types of cases that are treated here. I summarize the relevant patterns schematically in (2).

(2)

Deletion/Elision	X + Y, Y + X -> X
Assimilation	X + Y, Y + X -> XX
Coalescence	X + Y, Y + X -> Z
	l l l l l
	x y y x x

The differences between these processes are a result of additional considerations irrelevant to the present discussion.[1] Importantly, they share a basic similarity which is that the outcome of these processes is determined by the features of the input segments. Thus they are treated together here as one process that works to preserve certain features at the expense of others.

What is interesting about the processes in (2) is that, parallel to the assimilation asymmetries discussed above, X is the more marked segment type of the pair. As in assimilation, in the output of a [coronal]+[labial] vowel sequence, it is the coronal feature or vowel that is lost and the [labial] that is preserved. How do we account for this asymmetry? I will contrast two alternatives. One alternative relies on feature-specific Faithfulness constraints. The relative ranking of these constraints drives the maintenance of certain features (and thus certain vowels) over others. The other alternative relies on the representations of input segments: it is the structure of the segments involved which determines the output. I will show that only the second alternative allows us to capture the apparent relationship

---

[1] For a detailed analysis of these processes and their similarities, see Causley (in preparation).

between the outcome of hiatus resolution and the number of contrasts in an inventory.

4. Hiatus resolution and Inventory shape

4.1 Assimilation/Coalescence/Elision in four and five-vowel inventories

Dogrib, a Northern Athapaskan language, displays a pattern of coalescence commonly found in languages with four and five vowel inventories.

(5)   Dogrib Vowel inventory[2] (Causley (1995a))

ı			į
e	o	ę	ǫ
	a		ą

In Dogrib, a vowel-vowel sequence arising from affixation often undergoes coalescence. Both the front vowels /i/ and /e/ will coalesce with the back vowel /o/ for an output back vowel, regardless of the relative order of the underlying vowels as in (4). Since positional factors are not determining the quality of the output vowel, it must be either the segmental content of the input segments or the ranking of feature-specific Faithfulness constraints which determines the output.

(4)   a.   go+įdì   k'ała gǫǫdì   'you're (sg) still alive'
        b.   go+èkw'ǫ̀   goòkw'ǫ̀   'our jaw'
        c.   ye+odzı   yoodzı   'corner'
        d.   ʔɑr+ı   ʔɔɔ   'spruce bough'

Similar coalescence patterns are found in a language with a five-vowel inventory such as Afar. Like Dogrib, in Afar coalescence front vowels assimilate to non-front vowels. Rose (1993) gives the following vowel inventory and coalescence data for Afar:

(5)   Afar Vowel inventory

i	u	i:	u:
e	o	e:	o:
	a		a:

The data in (6) demonstrate that /e/ assimilates to /o/ regardless of their relative ordering.

(6)   a.   da'ro e'xe   da'rooxe   'I gave grain'
        b.   diidaa'le oob'be   diidaa'loob'be   'I heard a bee'

---

[2]Orthographic note: the diacritic in ı, ę, ǫ, ą indicates nasality.

Since the vowel-vowel sequences do not surface in these languages, we can assume that a constraint such as NoHiatus (given in (7)) or another constraint prohibiting two adjacent non-identical vowels[3] is ranked above any constraints prohibiting coalescence (such as UNIFORMITY (McCarthy & Prince (1995)), *MULTIPLE CORRESPONDENCE (Lamontagne and Rice (1995))).

(7)   NoHiatus: *VV
       No vowel-vowel sequences.

The question to be addressed now is: how do we determine the quality of the output vowel? In particular, how do we ensure that the output of a front vowel-back vowel coalescence is always back regardless of the ordering of the input vowels?

       One alternative is to call upon the feature-specific Faithfulness constraints from (3) to decide between keeping the features of the front vowel or the back vowel. This analysis is shown in the tableau in (8).

(8)   Input $/V_1 + V_2/$ [i + u]
                   | |
               [cor]$_1$ [labial]$_2$

Candidates	Max$_{lab}$	*VV	Max$_{cor}$
☞ 1. V_1 V_2 [u] \ / [lab]$_2$			*[cor]$_1$
2. V_1 V_2 [i] \ / [cor]$_1$	* ! ([lab]$_{2)}$		
3. V_1 V_2 [i + u] | | [cor] [lab]$_2$		*!	

Since it is always the [coronal] specification that is lost, Max$_{cor}$ is ranked below Max$_{lab}$ and *VV. This means that a coronal vowel will assimilate (or delete, if input morae are not to be preserved) as in candidate 1 in (8), instead of losing a [labial] specification as in the second candidate, or failing to resolve the hiatus as in the third candidate. The ranking between Max$_{lab}$ and *VV cannot be determined from this data, since both are satisfied in the output forms. Not included in this tableau are constraints which rule out alternative hiatus resolution strategies such as glide insertion or formation of a complex segment (e.g. /ü/). Note that such constraints must be ranked above the Max$_{cor}$ constraint in order to compel its violation. We will return to this issue in the next section.

---

[3]Note that long vowels, or vowels with linked features, are excluded.

Thus, the ranking of Max$_{lab}$ over Max$_{cor}$ gets the desired result: the output vowel will always carry the [labial] specification over the [coronal] one. While this account works, it faces the same criticism as the parallel account for the place assimilation facts described in §2: Faithfulness is inexplicably partial to marked elements and a reverse markedness hierarchy obtains in the Max$_{feature}$ constraint set.

4.2 Coalescence in an inventory with front-central contrast

When we examine hiatus resolution in languages which have a three-way place contrast in their inventory, a different pattern emerges. In these types of inventories, the place features of a front vowel are not lost in the interest of preserving the features of a back vowel. Instead both front vowel and back vowel place features are maintained in the output.

The Korean vowel inventory has central vowels at the high and mid heights. The inventory is given in (9).

(9)   Korean vowel inventory (Sohn (1987))

<table>
<tr><td>i</td><td>ɨ</td><td>u</td></tr>
<tr><td>e</td><td>ə</td><td>o</td></tr>
<tr><td>æ</td><td>a</td><td></td></tr>
</table>

When vocalic hiatus is resolved, the central vowels /ə/ and /ɨ/ assimilate to other vowels as demonstrated in (10). A sequence of front and back vowels is resolved through coalescence giving a front rounded vowel as in the examples in (11).

(10)	a.	is-ɨmyən	iimyən	'to connect'
	b.	p'yam	p'æm	'cheek'
	c.	pe-ə	pee	'to cut'
	d.	kæ-ə	kææ	'to fold'
	e.	cu-ə	coo	'to give'
(11)	a.	kwemul	kömul	'monster'
	b.	wisəŋ	üsəŋ	'hypocrisy'
	c.	p'yocok	p'öcok	'sharp'

The Chaha vowel inventory also includes central vowels (12). As in Korean, the central vowels are subject to assimilation in hiatus contexts, while glide insertion breaks up a front-back and back-front vowel sequences.

(12) Chaha (Semitic) vowel inventory (Rose (1993))

<table>
<tr><td>i</td><td>ɨ</td><td>u</td></tr>
<tr><td>e</td><td>ə</td><td>o</td></tr>
<tr><td></td><td>a</td><td></td></tr>
</table>

As demonstrated in (13) /ə/ assimilates to preceding or following vowel.[4] In (14), front-back and back-front sequences are resolved through glide insertion.

(13)	a.	yə-ef	yef	'let him cover with a lid'
	b.	yə-od	yod	'let him tell'
(14)	a.	Turi-u	?Turiwu/Turiyu	'he is an expert'
	b.	gəβəre-ugə	βərewu/?gəβəreyu	'he is a farmer'

In these types of pattern, neither [cor] nor [lab] is lost. Only central vowels assimilate. These patterns may be accounted for using the same constraints as in the tableau in (8), except the constraint Max$_{cor}$ needs to be re-ranked in these languages so that it is satisfied at the expense of constraints against glide formation and formation of the complex segment /ü/.

(15)   Input /V₁ + V₂/   [u + i]

        | |

        [lab]₁ [cor]₂

Candidates	Max$_{lab}$	Max$_{cor}$	*VV	
1. V₁ V₂ [u] \ / [lab]₁		*!		
2. V₁ V₂ [i] \ / [cor]₂	*!			
3. V₁ V₂ [i u] [lab]₁ [cor]₂			*!	
☞ 4. V₁,₂ [ü] / \ [cor]₁ [lab]₂				*Korean: coalesce to give front-rounded vowel*
☞ 4. V₁ C V₂ [iyu] [cor]₁ [lab]₂				*Chaha: insert epenthetic glide*

As with the patterns discussed in §4.1, the [labial] feature cannot be lost as in the second candidate in (15), and the hiatus cannot be left unresolved as in the third candidate. However, because Max$_{cor}$ rules out a candidate lacking the [coronal] specification (candidate 1), the vowels either coalesce to give a front rounded vowel (Korean) or glide insertion breaks up the cluster

---

[4]The central vowel /ɨ/ only appears in epenthetic contexts so it does not occur in situations where hiatus could potentially arise.

(Chaha). In both cases, both [coronal] and [labial] are maintained. Of course, other constraints are violated by these optimal outputs, but what is important is that the Max_{cor} constraint out-ranks such constraints and is able to rule out the assimilation or deletion of a [coronal].

The problem with such an account is that, although these patterns correlate with the shape of the inventory (i.e. the presence vs. absence of the central vowel), the ranking of Max_{cor} is unrelated to inventory shape, we should not expect to find any relationship between the number of contrasts in a inventory and the patterning of segments in coalescence or assimilation.

4.3 Summary

To summarize briefly at this point, we have seen that the pattern of coalescence demonstrated in a language is related to the place contrasts in the vowel inventories. In languages with a simple front-back contrast in the inventory, a front + back vowel sequence resulted in a back vowel in the output. In languages with a front-central-back contrast, central vowels delete or assimilate when adjacent to a front or back vowel. A front + back vowel sequence results in an output with both front and back place features. Thus, there is a link between the patterning of front vowels and the shape of the inventory.

Interestingly, a similar relationship is found between the number of height contrasts in an inventory and the height coalescence patterns demonstrated by a particular language (Goad (1993), Casali (1996)). Again, a feature-specific Faithfulness account like the one discussed above is unable capture this type of relationship. The next section proposes an alternative account of these facts, making direct reference to the contrasts in a system.

5. The Importance of Input

5.1 Contrast and segment structure

In §4, we saw that the presence vs. absence of contrasts in an inventory affected the patterning of segments (specifically, front vowels) in coalescence patterns. In this section, I propose an account of these deletion/coalescence phenomena which relies crucially on the representations of segments in the input. This represents a departure from the position taken in most current OT literature that the role of input representations is minimal, and that segmental patterning can be determined on the basis of output constraints alone (cf., e.g., Itô, Mester, and Padgett (1995), Smolensky (1993)).

Following on recent work on segment structure (Avery and Rice (1989), Rice and Avery (1993), Dyck (1995)) the representations I propose directly encode segmental markedness in the structural complexity of the representation. The complexity of the representations is related to the presence or absence of contrasts in an inventory: since pairs of contrasting places of articulation are distinguished by the presence of a feature on one of the pair, additional contrasts imply additional complexity in the representations. Thus in systems with only a front-back contrast, back vowels are marked with a place feature and front vowels do not need to be marked with place to distinguish them in the inventory. In systems with a front-central-back contrast, both the front and back vowels are marked for place to contrast them with the central vowel. Therefore we expect segments to behave differently (particularly in terms of phonological activity-shown as perseverence under deletion, assimilation or coalescence) depending on what they contrast with.

5.2 Four and five vowel systems (Dogrib and Afar)

To minimally contrast front vowels from back vowels in systems with only a front-back contrast, the back vowels receive a [labial] specification; front vowels are placeless. Thus the representations in this type of system are as in (16).

(16)   i   u   e   o
        | |
     [labial]   [labial]

The Faithfulness constraint that is required under this account is a general featural Faithfulness constraint Max-F that preserves input features by requiring that they have an output correspondent. A tableau is given in (18) demonstrating the combined effects of the input representations in (16) and Max-F.

(17) Max-F: Every feature in the input has a correspondent in the output.

(18)   Input /V_1 + V_2/   [i + u]
                    |
              [labial]$_2$

	Candidates	Max-F	*VV
☞	1. V_1 V_2 [u] \ / [lab]$_2$		
	2. V_1 V_2 [i] \ / [cor]	*! <[lab]$_2$>	
	3. V_1 V_2 [i u] | | [lab]$_2$		*!

A front vowel-back vowel sequence in these four and five vowel systems has only a single [labial] feature in the input, therefore the constraint Max-F will rule out a candidate such as the second one which lacks a [labial] specification. The third candidate fails to resolve the hiatus, so the first is optimal.

5.3 Inventories with central vowels (Korean, Chaha)

Recall that the pattern in this type of system is one where central vowels combine with front and back vowels to give front and back vowels respectively. On the other hand, front + back vowel sequences are resolved through the insertion of an epenthetic glide (Chaha), or coalescence to give front rounded vowel (Korean).

In a view where input representations are contrast-driven, the presence of central vowel forces [coronal] on front vowels (Rice and Avery (1993)) as in the representations in (19):

(19)
```
     i  e          ɨ  ə          u  o
     Pl            Pl            Pl
     |                           |
     cor                         lab
```

In a central vowel-front vowel sequence, the front vowel is marked with [coronal] and the central vowel is placeless, therefore the best candidate for the tableau in (20) is the first one in which the central vowel assimilates to the front vowel and the [coronal] specification is maintained.

(20)   Input /V₁ + V₂/ [ɨ + i}
```
              |
           [cor]₂
```

Candidates	Max-F	*VV

☞ 1. V₁ V₂ [i]
   \ /
  [cor]₂		

2. V₁ V₂ [ɨ]
   \ /
   ?
	*! <[cor]₂>	

In a front-back or back-front sequence, the input will involve both a [labial] and a [coronal] specification. This means that Max-F will rule out any candidate that lacks an output correspondent for these features. Therefore the optimal candidate(s) will have both of these features intact as in the fourth and fifth candidates in (21).

(21)   Input /V_1 + V_2/ **[i + u]**
            | |
         [cor]$_1$ [lab]$_2$

Candidates	Max-F	*VV

1. V_1 V_2 **[u]**
    \ /
    [lab]$_2$
	*!
	 <[cor]$_1$>	

2. V_1 V_2 [i]
    \ /
    [cor]$_2$
	*!
	 <[lab]$_1$>	

3. V_1 V_2 [u i] 		 [cor]$_1$ [lab]$_2$		*!

☞   4. $V_{1,2}$ [ü]
     / \
  [lab]$_1$ [cor]$_2$		

☞ 5. V_1 C V_2 **[uwi]** 		 [cor]$_1$ [lab]$_2$		

Korean: coalesce to give front-rounded vowel

Chaha: insert epenthetic glide

5.4 Summary

As we have seen, the phonological activity (shown as perseverance under deletion, assimilation, or coalescence) is linked both to segmental markedness and to the presence of contrasts in an inventory.

An account of these patterns relying on contrast-driven input representations makes explicit the link between phonological activity, markedness, and contrast. Contrasts determine the representations; the complexity of the representation determines the relative markedness of a segment. Phonological activity is an artifact of the presence vs. absence of structure on a segment: if a feature is present in the input, it is preserved because it is under the purview of Faithfulness.

Under a feature-specific Faithfulness account, this same relationship is not captured. Instead, marked features are singled out by Faithfulness. Unmarked features may or may not be preserved under Faithfulness, but there is *no expected link* between inventory and activity of a particular feature.

6. Asymmetrical Inventories: one central vowel

A final interesting inventory type is one with a front-central-back contrast at one height, and a front-back contrast at another. Wahgi, a language of the East New Guinea Highlands, has a high central vowel but no mid central vowel (22).

(22)   Wahgi Vowel Inventory (Philips (1976))

i   ɨ   u

e   o

a

A vowel deletion process in the language deletes[5] the high central /ɨ/ and the mid front /e/ when adjacent to a stressed vowel.

(23)   a.   /endɨ eti'/ →   [endɨ ři]   'one only'
        b.   /pe'ne áŋ/ →   [pén áŋ]   'at the garden'
        c.   /nɨ-ipɨm/ →   [nipɨm]   'he spoke'
        d.   /pɨ-ipɨm/ →   [pipɨm]   'he knew'

In the next two sections I contrast two ways of accounting for these facts. As will be shown, this type of pattern is not easily explained in a feature-specific Faithfulness account, yet falls out naturally from an account making reference to contrast-driven input representations.

6.1 Feature-specific Faithfulness

Under feature-specific Faithfulness, the behaviour of different segments is explained through the ranking of output constraints alone; there are no constraints on the input representations. This means that both front vowels in this type of inventory should be similarly specified for place. Thus, in the tableaux in (24) and (25), the front vowels in the input are specified as [coronal].

(24)   Input /e_1 + o_2/

         | |

         $[cor]_1$ $[labial]_2$

Candidates	Max$_{lab}$	*VV	Max$_{cor}$

☞ 1.   o
  |
  $[lab]_2$
			*$[cor]_1$

2.   e
  |
  $[cor]_1$
	*! $[lab]_2$		

Since the input front vowel /e/ is lost in favour of a back vowel, we know that Max$_{lab}$ must be ranked above Max$_{cor}$. Also, since hiatus is resolved at the expense of violating Max$_{cor}$, we know that *VV is ranked above

---

[5]There are other processes described by Philips (1976) which assimilate or delete the vowel /ɨ/ before or after another vowel, but it is difficult to ascertain what exactly is happening since there are few examples. There are also some rule of vowel harmony and suffix allomorphy which appear to be interacting in the data.

Max_{cor}. The ranking *VV, $Parse_{lab}$ >> $Parse_{cor}$ compels the deletion of /e/ in the interest of saving /o/. However, the problem with this approach is that the same ranking will not give the non-deleting output in the case of i + u.

(25)   Input $/i_1 + u_2/$

        | |

    $[cor]_1$ $[labial]_2$

Candidates	Max_{lab}	*VV	Max_{cor}
☞ 1. u 	 $[lab]_2$			*<$[cor]_1$>
2. i 	 $[cor]_1$	*! <$[lab]_2$>		
3. i u 		 $[cor]$ $[lab]$		*!	

6.2 Constrast-driven Input Representation

The proposal argued for here is that input representations have a great deal to do with the way segments pattern in the output. Input representations are contrast-driven, therefore the representations for the vowels in the Wahgi inventory are as in (26). Contrastively specified for place, only one front vowel (at the same height as the central vowel) is marked for front. The mid vowel does not contrast with a central vowel at the same height, therefore it does not bear a coronal specification. Therefore, we expect both the central and the non-contrastively front vowel to pattern as a natural class of unmarked segments.

(26)   i   e, ɨ   u o

       Pl   Pl   Pl

       | |

     cor   lab

In the input, a high front vowel has a [coronal] specification , as in (28), while the mid vowel does not, as in (27). This means that the mid vowel will be subject to assimilation/deletion and the high vowel will not.

(27)   Input /e + o/
            | |
               $[lab]_2$

Candidates	MaxF	*VV
1. e	*! $<[lab]_2>$	

☞ 2. o
    |
   $[lab]_2$		

(28)   Input /i + u/
           | |
         $[cor]_1$ $[lab]_2$

Candidates	MaxF	*VV

1. i
   |
  $[cor]_1$
	*! $<[lab]_2>$	

2. u
   |
  $[lab]_2$
	*! $<[cor]_1>$	

☞ 3. i   u
   | |
  $[cor]_1$ $[lab]_2$
		*

7. Conclusion

A representational account of markedness based on contrast ties together the relationship between the number and type of phonemic distinctions in a language and the phonological activity of feature specifications. This paper has demonstrated the advantages of such an approach in accounting for the vowel coalescence, assimilation, and deletion patterns associated with different vowel inventories. In this account, a general notion of Faithfulness is maintained, and specific features need not be referred to. Instead, Faithfulness requires only that all input elements have correspondents in the output.

On the other hand, a feature-specific Faithfulness account misses the relationship between the contrasts present in an inventory and the behaviour of a particular segment. The different patterns may receive satisfactory accounts on a language-by-language basis through the ranking of different Faithfulness constraints. However, the different rankings required for different patterns share an unexpected connection to the inventory of the language. Why should a particular ranking be associated with a particular inventory type, when inventory type is determined by a separate set of contraint rankings? Further, in the case of asymmetrical inventories, a feature-specific Faithfulness account expects to have similar patterns of coalescence obtain at all heights, regardless of the contrasts present.

References

Avery, Peter and Keren Rice. 1989. Segment Structure and Coronal Underspecification. *Phonology* 6.2: 179-200.

Casali, R. 1996. Resolving Hiatus. Doctoral Dissertation, UCLA.

Casali, R. 1997. Vowel Elision in Hiatus Contexts: Which Vowel goes? *Language* 73.3: 493-533.

Causley, Trisha. 1995a. Vowel assimilation in Dogrib. ms., University of Toronto.

Causley, Trisha. 1995a. Markedness and Underspecification in Optimality Theory. In P. Koskinen and C.Smallwood (eds.)*TWPL* 15.2.

Causley, Trisha. In preparation. Complexity and Markedness in Optimality Theory. Doctoral Dissertation, University of Toronto.

Dyck, Carrie. 1995. Constraining the Phonetics-Phonology Interface. Doctoral Dissertation, University of Toronto.

Goad, Heather. 1993. On the Configuration of Height Features. Doctoral Dissertation, University of Southern California.

Itô, J., A. Mester, and J. Padgett. 1995. Licensing and Underspecification in Optimality Theory. *Linguistic Inquiry* 26.4: 571-613.

Kiparsky, Paul. (1985) Some consequences of Lexical Phonology. *Phonology Yearbook* 2: 85-138.

Lamontagne, Greg, and Keren Rice. 1995. A Correspondence account of coalescence. *UMOP* 18: 249-384.

Lombardi, Linda. 1995. Why Place and Voice are Different: Constraint Interactions and Feature Faithfulness in Optimality Theory. ms., University Maryland, College Park. ROA-105.

McCarthy, John J. and Alan Prince. 1995. Faithfulness and Reduplicative Identity. *UMOP* 18: 249-384.

Phillips, D.J. 1976. *Wahgi Phonology and Morphology*. Pacific Linguistics Monograph Series 36. Linguistic Circle of Canberra, Canberra.

Prince, Alan and Paul Smolensky. 1993. *Optimality Theory: Constraint Interaction in Generative Grammar*. To appear, MIT Press. TR-2, Rutgers University Cognitive Science Center.

Rice, K. D. and Peter Avery. 1993. Segmental Complexity and the Structure of Inventories. *TWPL* 12.2: 131-153.

Rose, Sharon. 1993. Coronality and Vocalic Underspecification. *TWPL* 12.2: 155-176.

Smolensky, Paul. 1993. Harmony, Markedness, and Phonological Activity. Talk given at ROW I. UMass: Amherst.

Smolensky, Paul. 1996. The Initial State and Richness of the Base. ms., The Johns Hopkins University.

Sohn, H.-S. 1987. On the representation of vowels and diphthongs and their merger in Korean. *Chicago Linguistic Society* 23: 307-323.

Steriade, Donca. 1987. Redundant Values. *Proceedings of CLS* 23: 339-362.

Reconstruction in Dislocation Constructions and the Syntax/Semantics Interface

CARLO CECCHETTO & GENNARO CHIERCHIA

Kanda University, COE (Tokyo) & Università degli Studi di Milano

1. Introduction

According to a simplified view of the syntax/semantics interface, the interpretative properties of a moved constituent having to do with predicate arguments relations (i.e. theta assignment) are determined at the base position, while other interpretative properties, typically those having to do with the Binding Theory (BT), scope and variable binding, are determined by the position a constituent occupies after its movement. However, it has been known for a long time that this simplified picture is not really adequate. There are cases in which the semantic effects of movement are undone. These are generally referred to as "reconstruction effects". With the minimalistic turn, the hypothesis that scope and binding are interface phenomena has lead Chomsky (1995) to revive the idea that movement is, in fact, copying and traces are full blown, phonologically silent replicas of the displaced constituent. This has important consequences for reconstruction effects. It is no longer necessary to "put back" what had been moved, for its copy already is where we need it (see Chomsky (1995), Heycock (1995), Fox (forthcoming), among many others, for discussion). While this line of inquiry is promising, the issue remains of dependencies that do not appear to involve movement and yet display an analogue of reconstruction effects ("connectivity"). A famous case in point is that of pseudoclefts (Higgins (1973) is the classical reference). In the face of these phenomena, several different approaches can be pursued. As we see it, they can be classified in three main groups. The first is to pose what tantamounts to a rule of reconstruction (by analogy with, say, the rule of quantifier lowering). An approach along these lines has the advantage that, suitably liberalizing LF copying/movement, it can hardly fail to be descriptively adequate. The disadvantage is that it does not seem to shed much insight on why reconstruction/connectivity effects show up where they do. The second line is to take a closer look at the constructions that appear not to involve movement and hope that, in fact, they do, albeit in less familiar ways (Heycock and Kroch's (1996) approach to pseudoclefts, as well as Boskovic's (1997), can be seen as interesting attempts in this direction). The third approach crucially calls into play interpretative mechanisms. On this view, it is the way chains and other relations at a distance are interpreted that induces reconstruction/connectivity, possibly in interaction with syntactic devices (Jacobson (1994), Chierchia (1995) and Sharvit (1997) are explicit recent tries that exemplify this trend). In this paper we provide what we take to be new evidence in favor in the third family of approaches. We discuss Clitic Left Dislocation (CLLD) in Italian and, building on Cecchetto (forthcoming), show that it falls into two separate patterns. The first (involving DPs) is optimally analyzable in terms of movement (pace Cinque (1990)). The second, however, (involving PPs) cannot be so analyzed and must instead be viewed as a case of base generated topic. Yet, in spite of this, it displays connectivity effects. What is interesting about this situation is that the differences between the two kinds of CLLD are quite localized. This actualizes, for once, the often invoked "everything else being equal" condition, thus making the choice of movement vs. not movement hard to miss. Whether our proposal is right or not, we do seem to have a novel type of connectivity phenomena, particularly recalcitrant to a purely syntactic treatment.

Our paper is organized as follows: we present in section 2 the relevant properties of CLLD. In section 3 we introduce our analysis of this construction and in section 4 we show how it derives its properties in a principled way. Section 5 is devoted to the consequences of our approach. Among other things, we argue that the dislocation of dative PPs is a most clear example of an area in which economy considerations constrain syntax. In section 6 we focus on the problem of how connectivity effects should be dealt with in absence of syntactic copies, pointing out that interpretive mechanisms alternative to the copy theory of traces are a last resort strategy. Section 7 concludes the paper.

2. Two Kinds of CLLD Sentences

What distinguishes the two CLLD constructions exemplified in (1)-(2) below is the kind of sentence initial XP: a DP in (1) and a PP in (2). These two constructions share two fundamental properties. First, the dislocated XP and the correspondent clitic must be in a local configuration (the clitic

cannot be in a strong island, as exemplified with an adjunct island in (3)-(4))
and, second, reconstruction effects with Principle C are attested (cf. (5)-(6)):

(1) Maria, Leo la incontra spesso
    Maria Leo her meets often
    'Maria, Leo often meets'
(2) In palestra, Leo (ci) va volentieri
    To the gym Leo there goes with pleasure
    'To the gym Leo likes to go'
(3) *Maria, ho visto Leo prima che la incontrasse
    Maria (I) have seen Leo before that (he) her meet(SUBJ)
(4) *In palestra, ho visto Leo prima che (ci) andasse
    To the gym (I) have seen Leo before that (he) there go(SUBJ)
(5) *Il libro di [Leo]$_i$, pro$_i$ l'ha letto volentieri
    The book of Leo (he) it has read with pleasure
(6) *A casa di [Leo]$_i$, pro$_i$ (ci) va volentieri
    To the house of Leo (he) there goes with pleasure

The presence of island effects and BT effects suggests an analysis in terms of
movement for both constructions, as, say, a case of topicalization out of a
clitic doubling (CD) configuration. However there are a number of properties
that make such an analysis not equally suitable for (1) and (2). Some
important ones are:

(7)   i. Non obligatoriness of the clitic with PPs
       ii. Lack of scope reconstruction with PPs
       iii. Absence of corresponding CD structure for PPs

As for property (7i), it has long been known that, while a sentence like (2)
is grammatical both with or without the clitic, in a sentence like (1) the
clitic must be present, or else severe ungrammaticality results.

The difference in scope pattern (property (7ii)) has to do with whether a
lower quantifier can have scope over the material in topic position or not. It
turns out that this is possible only over a dislocated DP. Scoping over a
dislocated PP appears to be impossible:

(8) Qualche compito di fonologia, Leo lo assegna a ogni studente ∀∃ or ∃∀
    Some phonology problem Leo it gives to every student
    'A phonology problem, Leo assigns to every student'

(9) In qualche cassetto, Leo ci tiene ogni carta importante ∃∀ but *∀∃
In some drawer, Leo there keeps every important paper[1]
'An important document Leo keeps in some drawer'

If we think of the topicalized material as moved, we have a puzzling situation. DPs are well behaved, in that they can be reconstructed both for purposes of BT (cf. the Principle C effects in (3)) and for scope. PPs, however, appear to be reconstructed only for BT-purposes; scope reconstruction appears to be impossible.

Let us now turn to property (7iii). In languages that have clear cut cases of (clause internal) CD, sentences like (1) typically do have a correspondent doubling configuration but sentences like (2) never do. There is no clitic doubling of locative PPs. The languages one has to look at to test this property are not the major Romance doubling languages (like Romanian and some varieties of Spanish), because these languages happen to lack locative clitics altogether. However, there are several Northern Italian dialects like Trentino where the generalization just given can be quite clearly observed. In Trentino, the accusative clitic can (and sometimes must) double the direct object (cf. (10)), but the locative clitic *ghe* (which corresponds to the Italian *ci*) never doubles a locative PP (cf. (11)):

(10) El *(me) vol mi
He me wants me
'He wants me'
(11) (*Ghe) vago volintiera a Roma
there (I) go with pleasure to Rome
(From Cordin (1993))

This strongly suggests that PP dislocation cannot be viewed as movement out of a doubling configuration, for the simple reason that PP doubling is just unattested to begin with (unlike its counterpart with DPs).

It is plain that the differences between DP and PP dislocation listed in (7) are hard or impossible to understand if their analysis is uniform. If, on the

---

[1] If the IP internal quantifier is a preverbal subject, the scope reconstruction reading is available also for PP dislocation:

i) In qualche cassetto, ogni ragazzo ci tiene la foto della fidanzata ∃∀ and ∀∃
In some drawer, every boy there keeps a picture of his girl-friend
'A picture of his girl friend, every boy keeps in some drawer'

We believe that there are various ways to address this issue. For the purposes of the present paper, it may suffice to note that the subject in examples like (i) can be shown to have an analysis where it too occurs in topic position. If that is the case, the "scope reconstruction" reading may result simply from the fact that two dislocated quantifiers are in a mutual c-commanding configuration and "reconstruction" is thus plainly irrelevant.

other hand, DP dislocation does involve movement, but PP dislocation does not, they fall readily into place. Let us see how.

3. A Mixed Analysis

As for the DP dislocation sentences exemplified by (1), we claim that an analysis via syntactic movement out of a CD configuration is indeed correct. Our analysis can be couched in different theories of CD. Mostly for concreteness, we assume here Torrego's (1992) proposal that the clitic and the double are initially found in a Spec-Head configuration in a "Big DP" phrase which is the real complement of the verb. We refer to Cecchetto (forthcoming) for details (and for an answer to Cinque's (1990) arguments against the movement analysis of CLLD). The bottom line of Cecchetto's proposal can be briefly summarized as follows. The double moves to the left peripheral position that, following Rizzi (1997), we take to be the Spec of a topic phrase within CP leaving a trace in the IP-internal position (more precisely, in the Spec position of the "Big DP" which in turn has moved to Spec, AgrOP for case reason). (12) is a schematic derivation for sentence (1) (for simplicity, we do not represent many irrelevant aspects, including the movement of the subject to Spec,IP and the movement of the verb to I°):

(12)   Maria, Leo la incontra

a [$_{TopicP}$ ... [$_{IP}$ Leo incontra [$_{AGRoP}$ ... [$_{VP}$ .... [$_{BIG DP}$ Maria la] ...]]]]

b [$_{TopicP}$ ... [$_{IP}$ Leo incontra [$_{AGRoP}$ [$_{BIG DP}$ Maria la]... [$_{VP}$ ... t$_{BIG DP}$]]]]

c [$_{TopicP}$ Maria [$_{IP}$ Leo la incontra [$_{AGRoP}$ [$_{BIG DP}$ t$_{Maria}$ t$_{la}$]... [$_{VP}$... t$_{BIG DP}$]]]]

As for the PP in (2), we assume, instead, that it is base generated in the Spec of a Topic Phrase in the immediate periphery of the clause in which its matching clitic is found. We assume that the verb and the clitic attached to it must move by LF to the head of the Topic phrase as only this movement can create the necessary Spec-Head configuration between the topic PP and the clitic that results in the coindexing between them. If the locative clitic is absent, it will be an element in the theta grid of the moved verb that is coindexed with the topic PP (assuming that locatives are optional arguments of motion verbs). Interestingly, this movement of the complex verb+clitic to the topic position is not an isolated phenomenon in Romance and, indeed, in other Romance varieties it takes place even in the overt syntax. For example, following Uriagereka's (1995) analysis, in Western Romance languages like Galician the complex verb+clitic overtly occupies what we call the Topic head (the head F in Uriagereka's terminology). So, for Italian, adopting an analysis which must be independently posited for other Romance languages. (13) gives a sample derivation for sentence (2):

(13)   In palestra, Leo (ci) va volentieri

a [$_{\text{TopicP}}$ In palestra   [$_{\text{IP}}$ Leo ci va ....   [$_{\text{VP}}$ ...   ]]]

b [$_{\text{TopicP}}$ In palestra ci va [$_{\text{IP}}$ Leo t$_{\text{V+cl}}$ [$_{\text{VP}}$...   ]]]

Our analysis implies that in a long-distance PP dislocation sentence like
(14), the PP must be generated in the topic position of the embedded clause
and is later moved to the topic position of the matrix clause (note that, as
shown by a sentence like (15), a dislocated PP can, in fact, occur in the
topic position of the embedded clause):

(14) In palestra, sono sicuro che Leo (ci) va volentieri
     To the gym (I) am sure that Leo there goes with pleasure
(15) Sono sicuro che, in palestra, Leo (ci) va volentieri
     (I) am sure that to the gym Leo there goes with pleasure
     'Going to the gym I am sure that Leo likes'

As far as semantics is concerned, the interpretation of (1), which involves
movement, is straightforward. The moved constituent is interpreted via its
copy as if it was in its base position (disregarding for simplicity possible
differences in presuppositions that might be associated with the topic
construction). The semantics of (2) requires, instead, forming a λ-abstract:

(16) A gym λt [Leo often goes to t]
     λP [∃x gym(x) ∧ P(x)] (λy [often goes in (Leo, y)])
     ∃x gym(x) ∧ λy [often goes in (Leo, y)] (x)
     ∃x gym(x) ∧ often goes in (Leo, x)

There is an aspect of this simple analysis that it is worth underscoring as it
will play an important role in the analysis of the scope reconstruction facts.
We are assuming that the variable associated with the pronoun (or the gap)
within IP is a variable over individuals (of type e). This seems plausible, as
the type of a pronoun is generally taken to be the one required to satisfy the
semantics of the verb. The indefinite $a\ gym$, on the other hand, being a
quantified DP will be of the semantic type of generalized quantifers, namely
$<\ <e,\ t>,\ t\ >$. This implies that the indefinite cannot be λ-converted in the
position of the variable associated with the clitic. That is, it cannot be
interpreted as if it was in situ. Thus, the only possible reading for a sentence
like (2) is the one given in (16). These assumptions on the semantics of PP
dislocation sentences are independently needed for standard cases of binding
such as (17):

(17) Every man believes that he is a genious

If the pronoun *he* in (17) could be of the type of generalized quantifiers, sentences such as (17) would be predicted to have a meaning paraphrasable as "every man believes that every man is a genious", contrary to fact. Thus, in our analysis of (2), we are simply following standard practice for the interpretation of pronouns.

4. Deriving the Properties of CLLD Structures

Let us now show how both similarities and differences between the two kind of CLLD constructions follow from the proposed analysis. Beginning with islands effects, we immediately see that they are expected to arise in both cases. In a sentence like (3), the dislocated DP, in order to reach the topic position, must escape its argumental position which is located within the adjunct island. In (4), the dislocated PP is generated in the embedded topic position (that is, within the adjunct clause) and a movement from this position to the topic position of the matrix clause triggers an island effect (cf. Iatridou (1990) for a similar account of island effects in CLLD).

Let us turn now to Principle C effects. The main point is that in both DP dislocation and PP dislocation chains are formed (albeit of a different kind) involving the base position of the dislocated phrase. In the case of DPs we have a canonical chain. In the case of PPs, the dislocated material generated in TopP ultimately winds up being coindexed (through Spec-Head agreement) with the relevant position in the verb's theta grid (or with the clitic, if it is present). Thus in both cases we have a natural basis from which to expect Principle C effects. Let us elaborate on the two relevant structures in turn, by means of concrete examples. In (5), the case involving "regular" movement, there is an IP-internal trace of the dislocated DP *il libro di Leo*. Assuming Chomsky's (1995) copy theory, this trace is a copy of the dislocated DP and contains (a copy of) the R-expression *Leo*. Hence, at LF we have an R-expression c-commanded by the null subject and a Principle C violation ensues through whatever mechanisms gives rise to similar violations in cases of *wh*-movement such as:

(18) Which claim that John$_i$ is a thief did he$_i$ resent the most

In the case of sentences like (6) there are, in principle, two ways to go. The first involves resorting to semantic techniques (arguably independently needed) that enable one to indirectly bind material in a displaced constituent from a lower position (see, e.g. Chierchia's (1995) "Dynamic Binding" approach or Sharvit's (1997) extension of the functional approach to *wh*-dependencies, among several options). This coupled with a version of Reinhart's Rule I (see Reinhart (1983) and Reinhart and Reuland (1993)) might suffice to derive the relevant effects. The second way to go is to exploit directly the information that chains (however formed) make available to us along the lines originally proposed in Barss (1986). In this paper we explore the second of these strategies, postponing the exploration of the first strategy to another occasion. The basic idea of Barss's proposal can be stated as follows. In a (possibly non regular) chain < XP_1, ..., XP_n> when a phrase YP c-commands a link XP_i of the chain, it counts for BT-purposes as if it c-commanded every link of the chain. This is a gross oversimplification but gives the gist of the proposal. Let us give a sketchy illustration of how Barss's proposal could work with example (6). In order to check the BT status of the DP *Leo* in this sentence, we work our way up the tree looking for potential antecedents. Since *Leo* is contained in the head of a chain, we very soon reach a position where we cannot go up any further. However, we are allowed to resume the computation from the foot of the relevant chain (the trace of the clitic *ci*). Any potential antecedent we find working our way up from the trace of *ci* counts as a potential antecedent for *Leo*[2].

There are obviously many important details that need to be attended to with extreme care in giving a formulation of the BT that exploits a definition of binding along the lines we have sketched, even though such a definition is conceptually fairly simple. There is no way that we can do justice to the complexity of the problems involved within the bounds of the present paper. However, in (20) we give a first version of the main parts of the formal definition of chain binding (crucially, the definition of CHAIN in (20iii)) subsumes the case of the non regular chain which we find in PP dislocation sentences).

(19) *The Binding Theory*
  A reflexive must be minimally bound
  A nonreflexive pronoun must be minimally free
  An R-expression must be free

(20) *Chain-Binding*
  i) α binds β relative to a chain accessibility sequence Δ iff α and β are coindexed and Δ connects β to α. α minimally binds β relative to Δ iff α binds β relative to Δ and for no Δ' and no α', Δ' connects β to α' and Δ' ⊆ Δ

  ii) Δ is a chain accessibility sequence that connects β to α iff Δ is a sequence of nodes <$β_1$......$β_n$> where (i) $β_1=β$; (ii) $β_n$=the mother of α and (iii) for each i, $1 \le i \le$ n, either $β_{i+1}$ immediately dominates $β_i$ or <$β_i$, $β_{i+1}$> are a link in a CHAIN

---

[2] If the prepositional clitic is not present, the CHAIN that triggers the Principle C effect is formed by the topic phrase and the θ-position in the verb grid (which is not filled by the clitic).

iii) A CHAIN $<\beta_1...\beta_n>$ is a sequence of nodes sharing the same Θ-role such that for any i, $1 \le i \le$ n, β_i c-commands and is coindexed with β_{i+1}

Summing up so far, we have argued that dislocation of DPs is a case of movement, while dislocation of PPs is a case of base generation in topic position, where the verb+clitic complex winds up forming a chain with the PP (through Spec-Head agreement and standard interpretive mechanisms). This accounts for the presence of island effects and Principle C effects in both constructions.

Let us now turn to the asymmetries between the two kinds of constructions. We will see that these too follow in a principled manner from our proposal. Beginning with the obligatoriness of the clitic with dislocated DPs (property (7i)), note that the accusative clitic is the head of the "Big DP" which is the input structure for sentences like (1). Heads must, of course, be realized. The locative clitic, on the other hand, is optional because the link between the topic and the rest of the sentence turns out to be a link between the topic and a θ-position in the verb grid that can but need not be overtly filled by the clitic.

The second main asymmetry concerns the different scope reconstruction pattern. It is easy to see that it too follows in a principled manner from our hypothesis. Consider, for example, sentences (8) and (9). In (8), we have a copy of the DP at LF. Hence, the dislocated quantificational DP at LF is, for all interpretative purposes, "back" in its original site. Hence, a lower quantifier, when present, can get scope over it via QR (or whatever subsumes its effects). In a sentence like (9), on the other hand, the dislocated quantificational PP has no copy in the correspondent IP-internal position. Hence, there is no way at LF for a lower quantifier to scope over it, assuming that QR is local and cannot cross over a topic phrase. Furthermore, the wide scope reading of the IP internal quantifier cannot be produced by an interpretive procedure either, under the assumption that the type of the clitic is determined by the type of the verb. Hence the only LF for (9) is (21a) and the only reading this gets is (21b).

(21) a. [In some drawer]$_i$ [every document]$_j$ [Leo keeps j in i]
b. $\exists x [drawer(x) \wedge \forall y [document(y) \rightarrow keeps(Leo, y, x)]]$

See (16) above for the derivation of (21b). Thus the observed scope facts could not be otherwise, under the present view.

Finally, the (non) availability of the corresponding CD structures follows in a completely transparent manner. PPs could not be obtained via movement out of a doubling configuration precisely because such configurations are not attested, given the different categorial status of DPs and PPs. Accusative clitics are D°'s; hence "Big DPs" can be generated using canonical principles of projection. An analogous doubling configuration involving prepositions cannot be created.

5. Further Consequences

Our approach has further welcome consequences that we will now discuss. The first consequence concerns Case Theory. One might wonder why DPs are moved and PPs are based generated in the topic position. Could things not turn out to be just the other way around? We think not and for principled reasons having to do with case. A dislocated DP must get structural case. This entails that such a DP *must* be generated in a IP-internal position in order to get case. Only after case-checking, it can be topicalized (note that, in case of CLLD, mechanisms of default case assignment are irrelevant, as shown by the fact that pronouns, when dislocated, carry a morphological case which varies as a function of their grammatical role and do *not* surface with a default case)[3]. A PP on the other hand can be directly inserted in topic position because it needs no (structural) case.

A further prediction of our approach concerns variable binding into a dislocated constituent from a position within the main clause. Consider sentences like (22) and (23) in which a referential element (such as a definite description) is dislocated:

(22) ? La casa che l_i'aveva ospitato, l'ho ridata a [ogni studente]$_i$
The house that him had hosted, (I) it have given again to each student
'In the apartment that he had already occupied, I put up every student'
(23) *Nella casa che l_i'aveva ospitato, ci ho risistemato [ogni studente]$_i$
In the house that him had hosted, (I) there have put again each student

A pronoun can marginally be bound by an IP internal quantifier when it occurs within a dislocated DP (cf. (22)). However, it cannot be bound by the same quantifier if it is found within a dislocated PP (cf. (23)). This contrast is just what we would predict. In (22) there is an IP internal copy of the dislocated DP. The quantifier undergoes QR reaching a position from which it c-commands the pronoun. This triggers a WCO effect, hence the (relatively slight) marginality of the bound variable reading. Contrast this

---

[3] Also note that a mechanism based on coindexing, like Chain-Binding, is not a plausible device for case checking, since two nominal expressions can be coindexed even if there is a mismatch between them in case features.

with (23) in which the PP has no IP-internal trace; hence scoping over it is tout court impossible[4].

A further important consequence concerns the dislocation of dative PPs, which we have not discussed so far. Consider:

(24) A Leo, Maria (gli) ha regalato un libro
      To Leo, Maria (to-him) has given a book
      'To Leo, Maria gave a book'

Datives are an interesting case because, as is often observed, they have an intermediate status between DPs and PPs. Since we have offered a movement analysis for DP dislocation and a base generation analysis for PP dislocation, a natural question is what happens in this intermediate case. A priori, one might think that two derivations for sentences like (24) are equally possible, one according to which datives are based generated in topic position and another where they are moved from within the clause. This is so for two reasons. On the one hand, CD configurations involving an indirect object are very common (while they are unattested for "true", i.e. non dative, PPs). So a "Big DP" source for datives must be available, making the movement strategy in principle viable. On the other hand, in languages in which indirect objects are PPs, the preposition that marks the dative DP must play a crucial role in case checking. Hence, case checking by the relevant preposition directly in topic position seems to be available. But then there should be no obstacle to the base generation option either. If this is so, what should we expect? A choice of this sort seems to be designed for economy considerations. Note, in fact, that both the base generation derivation and the movement one share the same enumeration (down to not only each lexical head but also the functional ones, like the head of TopP). Economy, then, should favour the base generation option. Of the two analyses available in principle for (24), the one with no movement is clearly more economical than the one with movement. If this is correct, we would expect dative PPs to pattern together with non dative PPs rather than with plain DPs[5]. This is the expectation. And it appears to be fully borne out. With respect to the empirical properties that differentiate dislocated PPs from

---

[4] It might be worth underscoring that the dislocated PP in (23), being referential, is of type e. Hence the semantics of this sentence is the following:

(i) $\lambda y \forall x [\text{student} (x) \rightarrow I \text{ put-up } x \text{ in } y] (\iota z[\text{house} (z) \wedge \text{had hosted} (z, x)])$

The standard semantics for abstraction prevents the quantifier $\forall x$ from binding into the ι term. Thinking procedurally, the ι-term could not undergo λ-conversion in (i), for otherwise a variable free before the conversion would wind up bound in the body of the λ-term. This is something the standard semantics for abstraction does not validate. Hence, there is just no way to get the pronoun *him* bound in (i) by *every student*.
[5] See Zubizzareta (1996) for a different analysis that nonetheless assumes that economy considerations constrain CLLD.

dislocated DPs, dative PPs clearly pattern with the former. For one thing, the dative clitic *gli* is always optional, as shown by (24). Moreover there clearly is no scope reconstruction (cf. (25)); and finally a pronoun in the dislocated dative PP cannot be bound by an IP internal quantifier (cf. (26)):

(25) A qualche professore, Leo (gli) ha assegnato ogni studente ∃∀ but *∀∃
    To some professor Leo to him has assigned every student
    'To one professor, Leo assigned every student'
(26) *Al professore che l$_i$'aveva messo in difficoltà, (gli) ho già presentato
    [ogni studente]$_i$
    To the professor that him had put in difficulties (I) to him have already
    introduced every student

So, the present analysis leads us to individuate a further area of grammar where economy considerations seem to play a crucial role.

6. The Copy Theory of Traces vs. Chain-Binding

It seems to be a fact that there are structures that display connectivity effects in the absence of syntactic movement. We have mentioned pseudoclefts, a well known case in point. Other structures of this sort have also been discussed in the literature (see. e.g. Chierchia (1995) on *if-then* conditionals). The case of CLLD is particularly interesting in this context. While dislocation of DPs is a canonical movement dependency, topicalization of PPs works differently. PPs are base generated in Spec of TopP, whose head (Topic°) gets eventually filled by the verb. Thus a chain is formed in sentences involving PPs dislocation. But it is not one that involves copying. Hence, in case of dislocated PPs, the presence of connectivity effects cannot be blamed on the presence of a copy (short of positing a downward copying rule). Something else seems to be called for. The line we are exploring here is based on chain binding, i.e. the idea that for binding theoretic purposes c-commanding the link of a chain tantamounts to c-commanding the whole chain. This gives rise to a certain redundancy between chain binding and the copy theory. The question that naturally arises in this connection is whether both devices are needed. Could the effects of the one not be reduced to the other? This is the question we would like to tentatively address in this section. As we just saw, doing away with chain binding in favour of the copy theory appears to be impossible, because connectivity effects are not restricted to chains created by movement. What about the other way around? Would it be possible to get by just with chain binding? For most purposes, it would appear to be so. In particular, chain binding is perfectly consistent with the minimalistic view that binding is an interface condition. There is, however, a set of facts, namely the so called "antireconstruction effects" (in a nutshell, overt movement bleeds Principle C, but only if the potentially offending R-expression is contained in an adjunct), that a simple minded appeal to chain binding gets wrong:

(27) *Which claim that John$_i$ was a thief did he$_i$ resent the most?
(28) Which claim that John$_i$ made did he$_i$ retract?

Building on Lebeaux's (1989) proposal, Chomsky (1995) accounts for this fact by assuming that adjuncts can be freely inserted before or after overt movement (while arguments must be inserted along with their heads) and that traces are copies. So, the relative clause in (28) can be inserted when the *wh*-expression has already reached the left peripheral position. As a consequence, the copy of the *wh*-expression in the base position contains no R-expression and no Principle C violation arises. This suggests that the copy theory is necessary and cannot be reduced to chain binding. It furthermore shows that the copy theory must take precedence over chain binding. Otherwise (28) would be ruled out, for *he* is a potential chain binder for the R-expression *John* in (28) as much as in (27). What emerges from these considerations is that chain binding must be a kind of last resort. One must assume that it applies only to chains that, not having been formed via movement, do not have copies through which one can compute binding relationships. With canonical chains BT conditions are checked by means of the relevant copies. Only when there are no copies to work with one resorts to chain binding (which, ultimately, is just an extended notion of c-command).

This approach makes an interesting and quite general prediction. Chains formed by movement display, as we see from (27)-(28) antireconstruction effects. However, since chain binding applies at the LF interface to chains that are not made up of copies, it will inherently be unable to see the adjunct/argument distinction. Hence chains not formed by movement are *not* expected to display antireconstruction effects. The sentences corresponding to (27) and (28) are expected to be equally ungrammatical. This expectation is borne out, e.g., in pseudoclefts:

(29) *What he$_i$ is is proud of John$_i$
(30) *What he$_i$ is is proud of a book that John$_i$ wrote

CLLD provides a further testing ground for this prediction which is even more challenging. Here we have two minimally different type of chains: the ones involving DPs, created by movement and the ones involving PPs not involving movement (of the canonical kind). DP chains should display argument/adjunct asymmetries and antireconstruction effects; PP-chains should not. The facts bear this out fully[6]:

(31) a. La scheda che Leo$_i$ ha preparato, pro$_i$ l'ha messa sulla nostra scrivania
The file that Leo has prepared (he) it has put on our desk
   b. *L'affermazione che Leo$_i$ e' un ladro, pro$_i$ la ha contestata con forza
The claim that Leo is a thief, (he) it has contested forcefully

(32) a. *Nella scheda che Leo$_i$ ha preparato, pro$_i$ ci ha messo i nostri CV
In the file that Leo has prepared (he) there has put our CVs
   b. *Nell'affermazione che Leo$_i$ e' un ladro pro$_i$ ci vede molta malevolenza
In the claim that Leo is a thief he sees much ill-will

Our approach reveals a further empirical property of PP dislocation which distinguishes it from DP dislocation. This receives a principled account within the framework adopted here.

7. Concluding Remarks

There seems to be strong evidence that CLLD is *not* a uniform structure. At least five properties differentiate dislocated DPs from dislocated PPs. They are: *i)* Obligatoriness vs. optionality of the clitic, *ii)* Scope reconstruction pattern, *iii)* Availability of a correspondent clitic doubling structure *iv)* Availability of the bound reading for a pronoun within a dislocated definite description and, finally, *v)* Presence versus absence of antireconstruction effects. We have argued that all these five differences can be derived from a simple hypothesis: CLLD of DPs is a straightforward case of movement out of a clitic doubling configuration, CLLD of PPs is a case of base generation of the topic. This hypothesis is virtually forced by the fact that DPs, but not PPs, need structural case.

   Our analysis of CLLD has important consequences. On the one side, it allows us to identify an area (the dislocation of datives) in which economy considerations constrain the choice between two derivations stemming from the same enumeration. Other general consequences have to do with the theory of reconstruction. A purely syntactic approach exclusively based on the copy theory of traces does not seem to be enough (short of positing an actual rule of reconstruction, in the form, e.g. of a downward copying rule at LF). Chains can be formed also through interpretative procedures and the result of this kind of chain formation seems to show connectivity/reconstruction effects. Hence an account which exploits a combination of syntactic and

---

[6] Although reasons of space do not allow us to give the full paradigm, we want to stress that dative PP's pattern with locative PP's and do not display argument/adjunct asymmetries and antireconstruction effects.

semantic devices seems to be called for. Here we have sketched one that exploits chain binding (viewed as a kind of last resort). Whether this ultimately turns out to be right or not, the data discussed here appears to be crucial in figuring out the architecture of Universal Grammar in so far as this aspect of the BT is concerned.

References

Barss, A. 1986. *Chains and Anaphoric Dependencies*, Doctoral dissertation, MIT
Boskovic. Z. 1997. Pseudocleft. *Studia Linguistica*, 51:3.235-277.
Cecchetto, C. forthcoming. Doubling Structures and Reconstruction. *Probus*
Chierchia G. 1995. *Dynamics of Meaning*. Chicago: The University of Chicago Press
Chomsky, N. 1995. *The Minimalistic Program*. Cambridge, Mass.: MIT Press
Cinque, G. 1990. *Types of A'-Dependencies*. Cambridge, Mass.: MIT Press
Cordin, P. 1993. Dative Clitics and Doubling in Trentino, in A. Belletti, ed., *Syntactic Theory and the Dialects of Italy*. Turin: Rosenberg and Sellier
Fox, D. forthcoming. Reconstruction, Binding Theory and the Interpretation of Chains. *Linguistic Inquiry*
Jacobson, P. 1994. Connectivity in Copular Sentences, in *Proceedings of SALT IV*, Cornell University, Ithaca
Heycock, C. 1995. Asymmetries in Reconstruction. *Linguistic Inquiry*, 26:4.547-570.
Heycock, C. and A. Kroch 1996. Pseudocleft Connectivity: Implications for the LF Interface Level. ms., University of Pennsylvania and University of Edinburgh
Higgins, R. 1973. *The pseudocleft construction in English*. Doctoral dissertation, MIT
Iatridou, S. 1990. Clitics and Islands Effects, ms., MIT
Lebeaux, D. 1989. *Language Acquisition and the Form of Grammar*. Doctoral Dissertation, UMass, Amherst
Reinhart, T. 1983. *Anaphora and Semantic Interpretation*. London: Croom Helm.
Reinhart, T. and E. Reuland 1993. Reflexivity. *Linguistic Inquiry* 24:4.657-720.
Rizzi, L. 1997. The Fine Structure of the Left Periphery, in L. Haegeman, ed. *Elements of Grammar: Handbook of Generative Syntax*. Dordrecht: Kluwer
Sharvit, Y. 1997. A Semantic Approach to Connectedness in Specificational Psuedoclefts, ms. University of Pennsylvania
Torrego, E. 1992. Case and Argument Structure, ms., UMass, Boston
Uriagereka, J. 1995. Aspects of the Syntax of Clitic Placement in Western Romance. *Linguistic Inquiry* 26:1.79-123.
Zubizarreta, M. L. 1996. Prosody, Focus and Word Order, ms., USC

Quantification Over Individuals and Events and the Syntax-Semantics Interface: The Case of the Existential Constructions

MARIE-HÉLÈNE CÔTÉ
Massachusetts Institute of Technology

1. Introduction[1]

Existential constructions are characterized cross-linguistically by a restriction on definite noun phrases. This restriction is standardly assumed to result from quantification over individuals, only indefinites being able to provide the right kind of variable. However, there are languages that escape the definiteness effect; Québec French (QU) is one of them.[2] An analysis of the syntactic and semantic properties of the QU existential construction, and a comparison with similar constructions in languages which display the definiteness effect, lead to two main results in the domain of quantification and the syntax-semantics interface. First, existential constructions may involve quantification over individual or event variables. Second, the facts suggest a strict correspondence between the type of quantification and the syntactic structure. Existential verbs take nominal complements in cases of quantification over individuals, and clausal complements in cases of quantification over events. This opposition is illustrated in particular by the contrast between QU and Haitian (HA) (section 2).

[1]Thanks to Michel DeGraff and Irene Heim for their support and comments, and to Noam Chomsky, Jon Nissenbaum and David Pesetsky. The Haitian data come from Michel; the Québec French judgments are from Jean-Pierre Gendreau-Hétu, Philippe Dansereau and myself. This research was partially supported by a grant from the SSHRC.

[2]Spoken French in general escapes this restriction, unlike the standard (written) variety. To keep the data as coherent as possible, I will restrict myself to the variety spoken in Québec.

These results shed light on a number of other constructions, in particular the English existential *there*-construction and certain complements of perception verbs in Romance. The analysis of these constructions is controversial, mainly because they appear to display characteristics of both nominal and clausal constituents. I show that, contrary to what has been suggested, complements in these constructions are nominal, not clausal. A structure involving the adjunction of a predicate to DP accounts for their syntactic properties as well as their eventive characteristics (section 3).

2. Existential Quantification and the Syntax-Semantics Interface

The existential constructions in QU and HA look identical: they both use an existential verb (*y a*[3]/*gen*) whose complement may contain what looks like a relative clause:

(1)   a.   Y a un gars qui est venu   (QU)
       b.   Gen yon nèg ki te vini   (HA)
             'There is a man who came'

A closer look at these constructions reveals, however, that they must be given quite different analyses. They differ on a number of syntactic and semantic properties (2.1), which leads to two main results regarding the variable involved in quantification and the relation between this variable and the syntactic structure (2.2).

In order to avoid any presupposition as to the structure of the sentences in (1), I will be using the following descriptive terms to refer to the two parts of the post-verbal sequence: the sequence introduced by *qui*/*ki* (*qui est venu*/*ki te vini*) is called the "predicative element" and the preceding nominal sequence (*un gars*/*yon nèg*) is called the "nominal element".

2.1 Properties of the Existential Construction in QU and HA
• *Restriction on definite DPs*: The most striking difference between HA and QU concerns the types of nominal elements tolerated in the existential construction. The definiteness restriction holds in HA (2b) but not in QU, where definite nominal elements can appear in the complement of *y a* (2a).

(2)   a.   Y a Jean qui est venu   (QU)
       b. * Gen Jan ki te vini   (HA)
             'There is J. who came'

• *Restriction on the type of predicate*: The availability of definite nominal elements in QU is constrained by the type of predicate in the predicative element. Unlike stage-level predicates (including stative ones), as in (2a),

---

[3]One must distinguish between spoken *y a* and written *il y a*, these constructions differing on various syntactic and semantic aspects (besides the absence of the expletive in the former).

individual-level predicates are incompatible with definite nominal elements:

(3)   * Y a Marie qui est intelligente/qui aime Montréal (no focus on *Marie*)
       'There is M. who is intelligent/who likes Montréal'

• *Interpretation*: Sentences such as (2a) do not assert the existence of an individual (Jean) but that of an event (Jean's coming). The distinction between an "eventive" and an "individual" reading of existential sentences can be illustrated with the contrast in English between (4c) and (4d). Intuitively (4c) asserts the existence of an individual - an employee - associated with a certain property - that of inspecting a building. The sentence in (4d), however, asserts the existence of an event of which the employee is a participant. What is to be noticed here is that the QU sentence in (4a) has both the individual and the eventive readings, and may correspond to (4c) or (4d), whereas the corresponding HA sentence in (4b) is compatible only with the individual interpretation.

(4)   a.   Y a un employé qui est après inspecter un édifice   (QU)
       b.   Gen yon anplwaye ki ap enspekte yon kay   (HA)
       c.   There is an employee who is inspecting a building
       d.   There is an employee inspecting a building

• *Extraction*: The constructions differ with respect to extraction possibilities out of the predicative element. Whereas *Wh*-extraction is totally excluded in HA (5), it is possible in QU, for arguments (6a-b) as well as adjuncts (6c-d).

(5)   a.   * Se kay la gen yon nèg ki te enspekte
            'This is the building there is a man who inspected'
       b.   * Kisa ki gen yon nèg ki te enspekte?
            'What is there a man who inspected?'

(6)   a.   V'là l'édifice qu'y a un gars qui a fait exploser   (argument)
            'This is the building that there is a man who blew up'
       b.   Qu'est-ce qu'y a un gars qui a fait exploser l'autre jour?   (arg.)
            'What is there a man who blew up the other day?'
       c.   C'est de même qu'y a un joueur qui s'est blessé   (adjunct)
            'It is like this that there is a player who hurt himself'
       d.   C'est comme ça qu'y a un invité qui s'est comporté hier   (adj.)
            'It is like that that there is a guest who behaved yesterday'

Facts related to quantifier scope support those on *wh*-extraction. In HA the predicative element acts as a barrier for quantifier scope. Thus an indefinite nominal element necessarily has wide scope over a universal quantifier inside the predicative element (7b). In QU, however, such a quantifier may easily have wide scope over an indefinite nominal element (7a).

(7)   a.   Y a un gars qui est après inspecter chaque édifice (QU)

                $\forall$y (édifice (y)) $\exists$x (gars (x)) [inspecter (x,y)] $\forall > \exists$

                $\exists$x (gars (x)) $\forall$y (édifice (y)) [inspecter (x,y)] $\exists > \forall$

    b.   Gen yon nèg ki ap enspekte chak kay   (HA) $*\forall > \exists$; $\exists > \forall$

        'There is a man who is inspecting every building'

These facts can be related to well-known generalizations regarding extraction. The predicative element in the *gen* construction has the same island properties as a relative clause. *Wh*-extraction out of relative clauses yields ungrammaticality (8), and a quantifier inside a relative clause cannot have wide scope over the head (9). Examples (5) and (7b) parallel (8) and (9). The structure of the complement of *gen* in (1) therefore seems to be transparent: it is a DP containing an embedded relative clause (10).

(8)   a.   * V'là l'édifice que j'ai rencontré un gars qui a inspecté (QU)

    b.   * Se kay la mwen kontre yon nèg ki te enspekte   (HA)

        'This is the building that I met a man who inspected'

(9)   a.   J'ai rencontré un gars qui a inspecté chaque édifice (QU) $*\forall > \exists$

    b.   Mwen kontre yon nèg ki te enspekte chak kay   (HA) $*\forall > \exists$

        'I met a man who inspected every building'

(10)   Gen [$_{DP}$ yon nèg [$_{CP}$ OP$_i$ ki t$_i$ te vini]]   (=1b)

It can be observed that the predicative element in QU does not behave like a relative clause (see (8)-(9) vs. (6)-(7a)). But we can go further in determining the status of the complement of *y a*. We know that extraction from non-*wh*-clausal complements is allowed for both arguments and adjuncts. This applies to full clauses (11) and to small clause complements of verbs like *consider* (12). *Wh*-complements (13) and adjuncts (14) behave differently in that they allow only argument extraction from them.

(11)   a.   V'là la fille que tu pensais que j'aimais   (arg.)

        'This is the girl that you thought I liked'

    b.   Comment ((est-ce) que) tu penses que j'ai rencontré Luc? (adj.)

        How do you think that I met L.?'

    c.   Comment ((est-ce) que) tu penses que tu t'es comporté? (adj.)

        'How do you think (that) you behaved?'

(12)   a.   Qu'est-ce que tu le considères apte à faire?   (arg.)

        'What do you consider him capable of doing?'

    b.   Combien de milles tu le considères capable de courir?   (adj.)

        'How many miles do you consider him capable of running?'

    c.   Comment tu le considères capable de se comporter?   (adj.)

        'How do you consider him capable of behaving?'

(13)   a.   (?) V'là la fille à qui tu veux savoir ce que j'ai donné   (arg.)
'This is the girl to whom you want to know what I gave'

          b.   * Comment ((est-ce) que) tu te demandais qui [s'était blessé t]?
'How were you wondering who hurt himself?'   (adj.)

          c.   *Comment ((est-ce) qu')il se demande si tu te comportes? (adj.)
'How does he wonder whether you behave?'

(14)   a.   V'là l'argent que t'as surpris Jean en train de voler   (arg.)
'This is the money that you caught J. steeling'

          b.   * De quelle manière ((est-ce) que) t'as surpris Jean [en train de voler de l'argent t]?   (adj.)
'In what manner did you catch J. steeling money?'

          c.   * Comment ((est-ce) qu')il l'a surpris en train de se comporter?
'How did he catch him behaving?'   (adj.)

The complement of *y a* in the QU existential construction does not display a contrast between argument and adjunct extraction. It therefore behaves like a non-*wh*-clausal complement. This suggests that the complement of *y a*, unlike that of *gen*, can be a non-*wh*-clause (whose internal structure will be made more precise in section 2.2):

(15)   Y a [$_{CLAUSE}$ un gars / Jean qui est venu]   (=1a, 2a)

However, these extraction possibilities - together with clausal complements - depend on the presence of a stage-level predicate. Individual-level ones are incompatible with *wh*- (16a) and scope-extraction (16b). So the predicative element behaves here like a relative clause, as in (10).

(16)   a.   * V'là l'édifice qu'y a un employé qui connaît
'This is the building that there is an employee who knows'

          b.   Y a un étudiant qui connaît chaque état américain   *∀>∃
'There is a student who knows every American state'

• *Asymmetry between subjects and objects*: So far we have only considered existential sentences in which the nominal element functions as the subject of the downstairs predicate. If the predicative element in (1) is a true relative clause, we expect not to find any asymmetry based on the function played by the nominal element with respect to the lower predicate. In cases where we suggest we are dealing with relative clauses - in HA and in QU with individual-level predicates - there seems to be no contrast whether the nominal element is or not a subject.

There is however a clear asymmetry between subjects and objects with stage-level predicates in QU. All the facts that are specific to the QU construction - definite DPs, eventive interpretation, extraction - only hold when the nominal element acts as the subject of the embedded predicate.

Otherwise the construction behaves like the HA one. The relevant facts are given in (17)-(19). Definite DPs are not allowed when they function as objects (17). The eventive interpretation is not available: unlike (18b), (18c) does not constitute a felicitous answer to (18a) (see also Lambrecht (1988) and Giry-Schneider (1988) for European French). The extraction of quantifiers and *wh*-arguments from the embedded clause is ungrammatical (19). Therefore we can consider that the predicative element is also a relative clause in complements of *y a* with non-subject nominal elements.[4]

(17)   * Y a Marie que j'ai appelée   (no focus on *Marie*)
        'There is M. who I called'

(18)   a. Qu'est-ce qui s'est passé à matin?
            'What happened this morning?'
        b. Y a Jean / un gars qui est venu
            'There is J. / a man who came'
        c. # Y a un gars que j'ai appelé
            'There is a man who I called'

(19)   a. * V'là le prof à qui (qu')y a un cadeau que Marie a donné
            'This is the man to whom (that) there is a gift that M. gave'
        b. Y a un devoir que chaque professeur lit   * ∀>∃
            'There is an assignment that every professor reads'

2.2 Quantification over Individuals and Events

We see that the QU and HA existential constructions display a number of properties which pattern together. The HA facts logically follow from an analysis in which individual variables get bound by an existential operator. Only indefinites can provide the appropriate variable, hence the exclusion of definite DPs. It is always the existence of the individual associated with the variable that is asserted, which explains the absence of an eventive interpretation. The presence of an individual variable suffices to license the construction, which does not depend on the nature of the embedded predicate.

---

[4]Another argument supports the structural distinction between the complement of *gen* and that of *y a*. A relative clause can never follow a non-restrictive relative (i). It is therefore predicted that such sequences are excluded in complements where the predicative element is a relative clause: those of *gen* (iii) and those of *y a* with individual-level predicates (iv) or non-subject nominal elements (v). But they are possible with stage-level predicates (ii), which confirms that the predicative element is not a relative clause in this case.
(i)   * J'ai parlé à l'employé, qui travaille pas aujourd'hui, qui a réparé ton auto
         'I spoke to the employee, who is not working today, who fixed your car'
(ii)   Y a un employé / Jean, qui travaille pas aujourd'hui, qui a réparé ton auto   (QU)
(iii)   * Gen yon anplwaye / Jan, ki pa ap travay jodi a, ki repare machin ou an   (HA)
         'There is an employee/J., who is not working today, who fixed your car'
(iv)   * Y a un employé, qui travaille pas aujourd'hui, qui est vraiment compétent
         'There is an employee, who is not working today, who is really competent'
(v)   * Y a un employé, qui travaille pas aujourd'hui, que j'ai félicité
         'There is an employee, who is not working today, who I congratulated'

The same analysis cannot apply to the existential construction in QU, which is characterized by the absence of the definiteness restriction (constrained by the type of predicate) and by the availability of an eventive interpretation. These properties naturally follow from the hypothesis that the existential operator can here quantify over event variables. Restrictions on existential quantification then apply to the whole event, and not to the individuals that participate in it. This explains the eventive reading of the construction, as well as the absence of a restriction on the kind of DPs that can appear in it. In order to account for the fact that only stage-level predicates are allowed, I adopt Kratzer's (1989) hypothesis that only those, and not individual-level ones, contain an event variable. Quantification over individuals remains possible when the necessary conditions hold. Sentences with stage-level predicates and indefinite nominal elements fulfill the requirements of both types of quantification; so the variable that is quantified over is here undetermined.

Syntactic tests, extraction in particular, also show that the complement of *gen*, as well as that of *y a* with individual-level predicates or non-subject nominal elements, is a DP containing a relative clause. This corresponds precisely to the contexts in which quantification necessarily involves individual variables. When quantification applies over events (with stage-level predicates and subjects) *y a* takes a clausal complement (15).

A correlation can then be established between the variable involved in quantification and the syntactic category of the complement of the existential verb. Quantification over events and clausal complements are indissociable phenomena, just like quantification over individuals and nominal complements. Let us assume that individual variables are associated syntactically with nominal projections, typically DPs, whereas event variables are associated with clausal projections. Let us further assume that quantification over a variable x involves government in the syntax by an operator of the projection corresponding to x, so that each type of quantification is associated with a distinct syntactic structure. If the verbs *gen* and *y a* contain an existential operator, it follows that they must take DP complements in cases of quantification over individuals and clausal complements in cases of quantification over events.[5]

2.3 Internal Structure of the Clausal Complement of *y a*
The analysis has left unexplained two issues in particular: the

---

[5]Other constructions in QU seem to be amenable to the same analysis as the one suggested for the existential construction, namely cleft (i), deictic (ii), and possessive (iii) constructions. These constructions are subject to the same subject-object asymmetry and to the restriction to stage-level predicates (see Côté (in preparation)).
(i)   C'est Marie qui est venue (pas Jean qui a appelé)
         'It is M. who came (not J. who called)'
(ii)   V'là Jean qui arrive
         'This is J. (who is) arriving'
(iii)   J'ai l'auto qui est en panne
         'I have the car (which is) out of order'

internal structure of the clausal complement of *y a*, and the subject-object asymmetry, which does not seem to naturally follow from quantification over events. I argue that the answer to the first question provides the key to both the extraction facts and the subject-object asymmetry.

Let us go back to the structure in (15). I suggest that the complement of *y a* - *Jean/un gars qui est venu* - is a clause whose subject is the nominal element and whose predicate is the predicative element. This clause thus contains a predicate of category CP headed by *qui*. I assume that the subject of this predicate is generated in Spec,CP, in line with the standard assumption for the underlying syntactic structure of subject-predicate relations. This structure thus corresponds to a CP small clause.[6]

An important question concerns the status of the subject of the CP predicate with respect to the embedded verb (*venu* in (15)). This subject is theta-marked, directly or indirectly, by the verb. Two possibilities then arise: 1. The subject DP is base-generated in Spec,CP and coindexed with an empty category in the subject position of the lower predicate (20a); 2. It is base-generated in this lower position and raised up to Spec,CP (20b).

(20)   a.   Y a [$_{CP}$ un gars$_i$ / Jean [$_{C'}$ qui [$_{IP}$ ec$_i$ est venu]]]   (=15)

b.   Y a [$_{CP}$ un gars$_i$ / Jean [$_{C'}$ qui [$_{IP}$ t$_i$ est venu]]]

Making a choice between these two options is not crucial here since both can account for the extraction facts and the subject-object asymmetry. We can use the idea that the subject position of a predicate is an argumental position. CP being here a predicate, its subject position in Spec,CP is an A-position (see Haïk (1985), Cinque (1995)), which is not a barrier to A'-movement. Both quantifiers and *wh*-elements can then cross the CP node without violating constraints on A'-movement. This accounts for the transparency of the construction illustrated in (6) and (7a).

In order to derive the subject-object asymmetry, the structure must be able to exclude the possibility that the subject of the CP predicate be linked to an element other than the subject of the lower predicate. Guasti (1993) adopts (20a) and suggests that the empty category in Spec,IP is *pro*. Capitalizing on the *que/qui* alternation, she posits that *pro* can be properly licensed by the agreeing complementizer *qui*, while *pro* in object position cannot be licensed by either the non-agreeing C *que* or the verb. Hence the subject-object asymmetry of the construction.

In a movement structure like (20b), the subject-object asymmetry can result from the combination of the argumental status of Spec,CP and Rizzi's (1990) Relativized Minimality. Movement to Spec,CP creates an A-chain. Movement of an object of the embedded verb to Spec,CP (whether from its VP-internal position or from AgrOP) is then always blocked since

---

[6]I abstract away here from the issue of the number of functional projections that may dominate this small clause (see the various contributions in Cardinaletti and Guasti (1995)).

Antecedent Government for the object trace cannot obtain: Spec,IP is a closer governor to this trace than Spec,CP. But movement of the subject from Spec,IP to Spec,CP obeys Relativized Minimality, the trace being head-governed by *qui* and antecedent-governed by the element in Spec,CP.[7]

3. Eventive Interpretation and Adjunction to DP

Clausal structures similar to the one I propose for the complement of *y a* have also been suggested for other constructions, in particular complements of perception verbs with pseudorelatives in Romance (21a) (Guasti (1993); Cinque (1995)), those with gerunds in English (21b) (Declerck (1982)), and the *there*-construction (21c) (Stowell (1978), (1981); Safir (1982)).

(21) a. J'ai vu Jean qui embrassait Marie   (Fr.)[8]
          'I saw J. (who was) kissing M.'
      b. I saw John kissing Mary
      c. There is a plane flying / in the garden

The clausal structure for the post-verbal sequences in (21) is motivated in particular by their eventive interpretation. What is perceived in (21a-b) is not simply the entity denoted by the nominal element (Jean/John), but the whole event expressed by the nominal and predicative elements (John's kissing Mary). Likewise in (21c), where it is not the existence of a plane, but that of an event involving a plane, that is asserted. However, several arguments, internal to the construction or derived from a comparison with the existential construction in QU, show that the complements in (21a) (in accordance with Labelle (1996)) (section 3.1) and (21c) (section 3.2) are not clausal. These verbs take DP complements, their syntactic and semantic properties stemming from a structure with adjunction of a predicate to DP.

3.1 Complements of Perception Verbs
Guasti (1993) and Cinque (1995) suggest that the complement in (21a) is (or can be) a CP small clause. The pseudorelative, they both claim, forms a CP predicate with a structure similar to the one I propose for (20):[9]

---

[7]One argument actually favors the structure in (20a) (despite the disadvantage that it involves referential *pro*, not normally licensed in French). The embedded verb does not agree in person with the subject in Spec,CP, but always carries third person agreement:
(i)   Y a vous-autres / moi qui a / *avez / *ai appelé
           'There is you (pl.) / me who has / have (2nd pl.) / have (1st sg.) called'
This is unexpected if *vous-autres* / *moi* goes through Spec,IP on its way to Spec,CP, since it should in this case trigger agreement on the verb in I.
[8]The examples in this section are compatible with spoken French in general, including QU. Notice however that the spoken varieties do not seem to differ from the standard/written one with respect to the phenomena that are relevant here.
[9]Cinque's and Guasti's analyses differ from mine on some aspects of the internal structure of the clause, but these are irrelevant to the present discussion.

(22)   J'ai vu [$_{CP}$ Jean [$_{C'}$ qui [$_{IP}$ embrassait Marie]]]

This structure (rather than one involving a nominal complement) is motivated by the eventive interpretation of these complements as well as by the fact that they can be pronominalized by a pronoun which normally stands for a clause (*ce/ça*) (23). This shows incidentally that the whole post-verbal sequence forms a constituent.

(23)   a.   Ce que j'ai vu, c'est Marie qui arrivait
               'What I saw, it is M. (who was) arriving'
         b.   Marie qui fume, j'ai jamais vu ça
               'M. (who is) smoking, I never saw that'

Guasti and Cinque also establish a correlation between clausal complements with predicate CPs (22) and standard CP complements (24a). Verbs compatible with the former also take the latter, both types of CP complements involving the same subcategorization rule. Moreover, the construction in (21a) displays the same subject-object asymmetry as the QU existential construction (24b).

(24)   a.   J'ai vu que Jean embrassait Marie
               'I saw that J. was kissing M.'
         b.   * J'ai vu Jean que Marie embrassait
               'I saw J. that M. was kissing'

Sentential pronouns are however not the only ones allowed when pronominalizing the complement: individual pronouns are also possible in Italian (25a), but not in French (25b). According to Cinque, the variation between sentential and individual pronouns in Italian signals structural ambiguity. Individual pronouns replace a DP and, alongside (22), Cinque proposes a structure in which the predicate CP (with a PRO subject in Spec,CP) is not a complement but is adjoined to DP. The logic of this argument then suggests that the structure (26) is available in Italian but not in French.[10]

(25)   a.   Gianni e Maria che ballano il tango, non li ho mai visti
               'G. and M. that dance the tango, them I never saw'(Cinque 1995)
         b.   * Marie qui fume, je l'ai jamais vue
               'M. who smoke, I never saw her'

(26)   Ho visto [$_{DP}$[$_{DP}$Gianni$_i$][$_{CP}$PRO$_i$ [$_{C'}$che [$_{IP}$correva a tutta velocità]]]]
         'I saw G. (who was) running at full speed'

---

[10]Cinque shows that the CP predicate can also be adjoined to VP. There is incidentally a class of verbs that accept only this structure (e.g. *surprendre* 'catch'). I put this structure aside since it does not appear to be problematic and does not interfere with the present analysis.

This analysis raises a number of problems. Counterexamples argue against the proposal that verbs compatible with the structure in (22) also take standard CP complements. Many verbs in French behave exactly like *voir* with respect to pseudorelatives (27a-b), but are incompatible with standard CPs (27c):[11]

(27) a. J'ai aperçu/entrevu/observé Jean qui courait
         'I saw/glimpsed at/observed J. (who was) running'
      b. Ce/*celui que j'ai aperçu/entrevu/observé, c'est Jean qui courait
         'What/the one I saw/glimpsed at/observed, it is J. running'
      c. * J'ai aperçu/entrevu/observé que Jean courait
         'I saw/glimpsed at/observed that J. was running'

Haïk (1985) concludes from the ungrammaticality of (27c) that the complement in (27a) cannot be a CP. But (27b) suggests, according to Cinque's analysis, that the structure with a DP complement is not available either. At this point we must give up one of the following hypotheses: either the connection betwen standard and small clause CP complements, or the idea that "sentential" pronouns always replace CPs or clauses.

A comparison with the QU existential construction provides us with an argument in favor of eliminating the clausal structure in (22), and consequently abandoning the necessary connection between the nature of the pronoun and the syntactic category it replaces. If complements of perception verbs had the same structure as those of *y a*, we would expect them to offer the same extraction possibilities. But *wh-* or scope-extraction from pseudorelatives is impossible (28), unlike in the QU existential construction. Pseudorelatives behave like adjuncts and unlike non-*wh*-clausal complements. The structure (26) with adjunction of the pseudorelative to DP then easily accounts for the island properties of the construction.

(28) a. * V'là la fille que j'ai vu Jean qui embrassait
         'This is the girl that I saw J. who was kissing'
      b. J'ai vu un gars qui inspectait chaque édifice $* \forall > \exists$
         'I saw a man (who was) inspecting every building'

Besides this argument against the structure in (22), the sub-categorization condition which relates the two types of CP complements (the standard one and the small clause one) seems to get support from complements of perception verb in English, illustrated in (21c). Contrary to what I argue for their Romance counterpart, a clausal structure really seems to be necessary for these complements. This structural distinction is motivated by two differences between the two constructions. First the English one is compatible with expletive subjects which never appear as

---

[11] See Rothenberg (1979) for a complete list of verbs whose complements are compatible with pseudorelatives in French.

objects (29a). Second both arguments and adjuncts can be extracted from the gerund predicate (29b-c), which suggests that this predicate is not an adjunct but a non-*wh*-clausal complement. This justifies a structure like (29d).

(29)   a.   I saw it raining
          b.   Which mountain did John see the moon rising over?   (arg.)
          c.   How badly did you see John behaving?   (adj.)
          d.   I saw [$_{VP}$ John [$_{V'}$ kissing Mary]]

What is to be observed here is the contrast between verbs like *see* and *watch*. Unlike *see*, *watch* does not take standard CP complements (30a). Crucially, it is also incompatible with the facts in (29a-c) which support the clausal structure in (29d) (30b-d).

(30)   a.   I saw / *watched that John was kissing Mary
          b.   */?? I watched it raining
          c.   (?) Who did John watch Peter kissing   (arg.)
          d.   * How badly did you watch John behaving?   (adj.)

The -*ing* predicate in (30b-d) behaves like an adjunct from which argument extraction is marginal and adjunct extraction ungrammatical. This suggests that *watch* accepts only the structure with adjunction of a predicate to the DP complement. Applying the same logic to verbs like *apercevoir* (see (27)) in French, we conclude that their complement cannot be a CP. And since these complements behave like those of *voir*, there is no reason for them to be assigned different structures. This parallels the extraction tests in (28).

If all (Romance) complements of perception verbs with pseudo-relatives are DPs, it remains to be explained why they get an eventive interpretation, and why they can be pronominalized by "sentential" pronouns. The CP (or VP in (29d), or PP in *I saw John with his mother*) that is adjoined to DP is a one-place predicate. The DP is an argument of type <e>. Combining the two saturates the predicate and we get a bare event. Hence the eventive reading and the corresponding use of appropriate pronouns to refer to events.

But some languages also resort to individual pronouns. Rather than accounting for this variation by the coexistence of distinct syntactic structures ((26) being the only possible one), I suggest that these two pronominalization strategies simply reflect the apparent mismatch between the syntactic category (DP) and the semantic interpretation (event) of the complement. Both a syntactic and a semantic agreement are possible. The former corresponds to the standard process of agreement with the head of the DP, hence the use of individual pronouns with number agreement. The latter uses the strategy outlined above of agreement with the event. The normal situation is for syntactic and semantic agreements to coincide, but adjunction to DP provides a crucial case where they do not.

3.2 The English *There*-Construction

The analysis involving adjunction of a predicate to DP allows us to take a different look at the *there*-construction. Since the English existential construction is, like the HA one, subject to the definiteness restriction (*There is the plane flying*), we can conclude that it involves quantification over individuals. The correspondence rule between the variable and the syntactic structure proposed above forces us to assume that the indefinite in (21c) heads a DP complement of *be*. This is already incompatible with analyses in which the nominal element is the subject of a small clause complement of *be* (Stowell (1978), (1981); Safir (1982)).[12] But the status of the predicative element following the indefinite (the coda) (*flying / in the garden*) remains to be determined. At least three options have been proposed:

(31) a. The XP coda is a complement of *be* independent of the DP (Milsark (1974))
b. The coda is inside the DP complement of *be* (Williams (1984))
c. The coda is adjoined to VP (McNally (1997))

The analyses (31a-b) are unsatisfying because they are incompatible with a number of syntactic tests that show that the coda can neither be a complement (or the predicate of a small clause), nor appear inside the indefinite DP. This is convincingly argued for in McNally (1997) and I will not go through her arguments here. Let us only mention that extraction from the coda behaves like extraction from adjuncts in displaying a contrast between arguments and adjuncts (McNally (1997: 68)):

(32) a. ? How many cookies have there been children baking? (arg.)
b. * How many miles a day are there people running? (adj.)

The question now concerns the element which the coda adjoins to. McNally suggests that it is adjoined to VP, like depictive adjuncts (e.g. *I ate the meat raw*). This option is in any case insufficient since some tests show that the nominal and predicative elements of the post-verbal sequence can form a constituent, which cannot be the case in McNally's structure. Unlike depictive adjuncts (34), the coda in the existential construction can be preposed (33a) or pronominalized (33b) together with the preceding DP.

(33) a. I asked John if there was a man in the room, and a man in the room John said there certainly was
b. What there is is a man drunk/hiding in the closet/under the bed

---

[12]The existential construction in Chamorro is subject to the definiteness restriction, which suggests that quantification applies over individuals. Moreover, complements of existential verbs containing a predicative element must be DPs and not clauses (Chung (1987)). This language therefore supports the correlation between the variable and the syntactic category of the complement.

(34)   a. * I asked John if he liked his coffee cold, and his coffee cold he
             indeed said he liked
         b. * What I drank was my coffee cold

The structure with predicate adjunction to DP can account for the facts in (33) as well as all those already considered by McNally. It also explains, unlike adjunction to VP, the eventive interpretation of the sentences in (21c). The structure in (26) thus seems to naturally apply to the *there*-construction, since it explains both its semantic (interpretation and definiteness restriction) and syntactic properties.[13]

(35)   There is [$_{DP}$ [$_{DP}$ a plane] [$_{VP}$ flying]]

4. Conclusion

This paper has tried to derive a number of significant results for the analysis of existential constructions and the syntax-semantics interface. Quantification in these constructions can apply over different variables, and the syntactic structure is determined by the variable involved: individual variables are associated with nominal projections, event variables with clausal projections. These conclusions allow us to take another look at certain constructions whose analyses have oscillated between a nominal and a clausal structure, in particular the *there*-construction and complements of perception verbs with pseudorelatives in Romance. The nominal structure seems to better account for the syntactic and semantic properties of these constructions, their eventive characteristics stemming from a structure involving predicate adjunction to DP. The eventive interpretation is therefore compatible with clausal as well as nominal configurations.

---

[13]Two other constructions can be cited for which the structure with adjunction to DP seems more appropriate than the standard analysis involving small clause constituents: subjects of copular sentences (i) (Safir (1983)) and complements of certain prepositions in absolute constructions (ii) (e.g. Ruwet (1979); Beukema (1984); McCawley (1983)). Pseudorelatives, subject to the subject-object asymmetry, can appear in French in these contexts.
(i)   Jean qui s'occupe du bébé est toujours un beau spectacle
         J. who takes care of the baby is always nice to see'
(ii)   Avec Jean qui est malade, la semaine va être dure
         'With J. (who is) sick, the week will be hard'
First the nominal structure avoids the stipulation that prepositions like *avec* take clausal complements. Second these constructions don't allow scope extraction from the CP predicate:
(iii)   Un gars qui inspecte chaque édifice est toujours du gaspillage   *∀>∃
         'A man who inspects every building is always wasting'
(iv)   Avec un gars qui inspecte chaque édifice, le campus est sécuritaire   *∀>∃
         'With a man who inspects every building, the campus is safe'
In copular sentences with a plural nominal element, verb agreement shows variation between singular and plural in languages such as Italian and English. This seems to be another illustration of the opposition between syntactic and semantic agreement: the singular corresponds to semantic agreement with the event, the plural to syntactic agreement with the head of DP (Kubo's (1993) purely syntactic analysis appears to be insufficient here). Interestingly French allows only semantic agreement (singular), as in complements of perception verbs with pseudorelatives.

References

Beukema, Frits. 1984. Small Clauses and Free Adjuncts, in Hans Bennis and W.U.S. van Lessen Kloeke, eds., *Linguistics in the Netherlands 1984*, 13-21. Dordrecht: Foris.

Cardinaletti, Anna and Maria Teresa Guasti, eds., 1995. *Small Clauses*. Syntax and Semantics 28. San Diego, Cal.: Academic Press.

Chung, Sandra. 1987. The Syntax of Chamorro Existential Sentences, in Eric J. Reuland and Alice G.B. ter Meulen, eds., *The Representation of (In)definiteness*, 191-225. Cambridge, Mass.: MIT Press.

Cinque, Guglielmo. 1995. The Pseudo-Relative and ACC-*ing* Constructions After Verbs of Perception, in *Italian syntax and Universal Grammar*, 244-275. Cambridge: Cambridge University Press.

Côté, Marie-Hélène. In preparation. On Certain Mismatches Between Syntax and Semantics. Ms. MIT.

Declerck, Renaat. 1982. The Triple Origin of Participial Perception Verb Complements. *Linguistic Analysis* 10. 1-26.

Giry-Schneider, Jacqueline. 1988. L'Interprétation événementielle des phrases en *Il y a*. *Linguisticae investigationes* XII. 85-100.

Guasti, Maria Teresa. 1993. *Causative and Perception Verbs: A Comparative Study*. Torino: Rosenberg & Sellier.

Haïk, Isabelle. 1985. *The Syntax of Operators*. Doctoral dissertation, MIT.

Kratzer, Angelika. 1989. Stage-Level and Individual-Level Predicates, in Emmon Bach, Angelika Kratzer and Barbara Partee, eds., *Papers on Quantification*. UMass Amherts Linguistics Dept.

Kubo, Miori. 1993. Are Subject Small Clauses Really Small Clauses?. *MITA working papers in psycholinguistics* 3. 93-115.

Labelle, Marie. 1996. Remarques sur les verbes de perception et la sous-catégorisation. *Recherches linguistiques de Vincennes* 25. 83-106.

Lambrecht, Knud. 1988. Presentational Cleft Constructions in Spoken French, in John Haiman and Sandra A. Thompson, eds.,*Clause Combining in Grammar and Discourse*, 135-179. Amsterdam: John Benjamins.

McCawley, James D. 1983. What's With *With*. *Language* 59. 271-287.

McNally, Louise. 1997. *A Semantics for the English Existential Construction*. New York: Garland.

Milsark, Gary L. 1974. *Existential Sentences in English*. Doctoral dissertation, MIT.

Rizzi, Luigi. 1990. *Relativized Minimality*. Cambridge, Mass.: MIT Press.

Rothenberg, Mira. 1979. Les Propositions relatives prédicatives et attributives: problème de linguistique française. *Bulletin de la société de linguistique de Paris* LXXIV. 351-395.

Ruwet, Nicolas. 1979. On an Absolute Construction in French. *Studies in French Linguistics* 1:3. 31-91.

Safir, Ken. 1982. *Syntactic Chains and the Definiteness Effect*. Doctoral dissertation, MIT.

Safir, Ken. 1983. On Small Clauses as Constituents. *Linguistic Inquiry* 14. 730-735

Stowell, Tim. 1978. What Was There Before There Was *There*?. *CLS* 14. 458-471

Stowell, Tim. 1981. *Origins of Phrase Structure*. Doctoral dissertation, MIT.

Williams, Edwin. 1984. *There*-Insertion. *Linguistic Inquiry* 15. 131-152.

Sublexical Modality and Linking Theory[1]

ANTHONY DAVIS & JEAN-PIERRE KOENIG

Cycorp Inc., Austin, TX & State University of New York at Buffalo

1 Introduction.

Theories of linking seek to minimize the amount of information that individual lexical entries must specify about the mapping between semantic roles and syntactic arguments. Approaches to linking vary in part according to the kind of lexical semantic representations that are assumed, with several relying on a hierarchy of thematic roles. Some recent influential proposals, in contrast, take lexical entailments as the sole basis for determinnng this mapping. In Dowty's (1991) and Wechsler's (1995b) models, for example, event types denoted by verbs entail the existence of certain kinds of participants, whose properties then determine the mapping.

In this paper we examine cases in which entailment-based theories of linking apparently fail, and argue that they can be maintained once we take *sublexical modality* into account in lexical semantic representations. We hypothesize that linking constraints are insensitive to the sublexical modality component of lexical entries, and depend only on information in a predicator's "situational core". By separating these two distinct types of

---

[1]The order of the authors' names is purely alphabetical; each contributed equally to this paper. Thanks to Cleo Condoravdi for useful discussion of the issues discussed in this paper and to Corinne Grimm for many helpful comments on a draft. Authors can be reached at davis@cyc.com and jpkoenig@acsu.buffalo.edu.

semantic information in lexical semantic representations, we can preserve the elegance of entailment-based theories of linking.

2 The problem.

2.1 The vagaries of entailments.

We first consider several families of semantically-related verbs displaying identical linking patterns. However, attempts within entailment-based linking theories to account for the identical linking within each family fail.

The ditransitive linking pattern in (1) is associated with a particular semantics— roughly, causing to possess (see Pinker (1989), Levin (1993), Goldberg(1995), among others).

(1)   Burns gave Smithers $10 for the dinner.

Entailments characterizing this semantics can be used in linking constraints. In a giving event there are of necessity at least three participants, playing different roles. One participant is entailed to causally initiate the action; it is realized as the subject. Another participant is entailed to receive something; it is realized as the first object. The third is entailed to come into the possession of the second; it is realized as the second object.

Unfortunately, these entailments (or similar ones used by Dowty (1991)) do not apply to similar ditransitive verbs. No entailment of an actual transfer of possession is present in (2), yet these verbs display the ditransitive linking pattern of *give*.

(2)   Burns sent/owed/promised/charged/denied Smithers $10 for the dinner.

By sending Smithers $10, Burns may intend that he receive it, but this is not entailed. If Burns owes or promises him $10, he certainly has not received it yet. Lastly, if Burns charges or denies him $10, again no transfer of possession has taken place, although Burns desires that Smithers does not have the $10. To account for the ditransitive linking pattern of all these verbs, we must either find a different set of entailments or postulate that their semantics are fundamentally the same as that of *give*, but contain some additional modifying elements.

This pattern is pervasive. Verbs denoting possession, perception, successfully performing an action, and successfully inducing another to perform an action also display linking patterns mimicked by related verbs that do not entail possession, perception, or the performance of any action, as seen in (3) - (6).

(3)   Bill had/received/lost/lacked/needed many books.

(4)   Sue perceived/noticed/overlooked/missed him.

(5)   Bill managed/tried/failed/neglected to read the books.

(6)   Sue forced/urged/forbade Bill to go.

Entailment-based theories of linking thus cannot invoke the simple conditions suggested by the semantics of verbs like *have*, *perceive*, *manage*, and *force* to account for the behavior of the wider sets of verbs above. Yet these theories have the virtue of solid semantic grounding, which we would like to preserve in an adequate linking theory.

2.2 Some previous attempts at a solution.

The issue we have raised has been partially addressed by others, but some aspects remain unresolved. One approach is to modify the entailments that linking is based on. Wechsler (1995b) suggests that the entailment responsible for linking the recipient to the first object is too strong; the first object might be merely the *intended* possessor of the second object rather than the actual possessor. This accounts nicely for *send* and for ditransitive forms of verbs such as *bake* and *write*. But it does not seem to apply to *owe*, *charge*, or *deny*, which will require other modifications of the basic entailments used in linking the arguments of *give*. Still other changes in entailments are needed for the verbs in (3)-(6). In brief, Wechsler's approach does not capture the intuitive parallelism between the series of verbs in (2) through (6); that is, the semantic relationship between *had* and *perceived* is similar to that between *received* and *noticed*; the semantic relationship between *managed* and *tried* is similar to that between *forced* and *urged*, and so forth.

The same shortcoming is evident in Goldberg (1995)'s approach, though she attacks the problem differently. She assumes argument structure patterns are each associated with a particular meaning. The central meaning of the ditransitive, for example, is X CAUSES Y TO RECEIVE Z. But the meaning of linking patterns is also extended by "polysemy links". For example, the ditransitive meaning is polysemously associated with the meaning 'the conditions of satisfaction imply X CAUSES Y TO RECEIVE Z' (p. 75). Goldberg does not explicitly extend this account to the parallel patterns for verbs of possession in (3), verbs of perception in (4), or the control verbs in (5) and (6). But, given her observation that similar polysemy links hold of resultatives, it is easy to extend her analysis to these other cases and say that each of the linking patterns exemplified in (3)-(6) displays the same polysemy links she discusses with respect to ditransitives. But, as we see it, there are three difficulties with Goldberg's solution.

First, why are these *particular* polysemy links recurrent in English and other languages? Do they form a natural class? We argue below that they do and to that extent, Goldberg's addition of individual polysemy links misses a generalization; her account does not provide an answer to the question of why *these* polysemy links rather than other possible ones are found again and again. Secondly, the polysemy account does not directly extend to the problem posed by the progressive illustrated in (7).

(7)   Sandra was giving Bob advice when she was interrupted.

In this sentence, no entailment that Bob (metaphorically) "received" advice is present. If we assume that linking is done at or above the word level, as Goldberg's constructional approach assumes (as far as we can tell), data such as (7) present a problem for her account. The sense in which a verb is polysemous between its progressive and, say, its past tense form is unclear; the polysemy analysis does not extend naturally to such cases. Thirdly, Goldberg's analysis would force us to say that a given linking pattern is polysemous between meanings *A* and *not A* so as to account for the identical linking of verbs such as *have* and *lack*, *perceive* and *miss*, or *force* and *forbid*. To our knowledge, such polysemy is rarely, if ever, attested. There seems to be little motivation for positing polysemy links in such cases.

3   Sublexical modalities.

A more fruitful and systematic approach to this problem is to introduce a modal component into the lexical entries of the verbs in (2)-(6) and propose that modal, negation, and aspectual operators modify a situational core within lexical entries. Although lexical entailments in this situational core do not necessarily hold in a verb's resultant meaning, they *always* hold with respect to a subset of the set of possible circumstances W. The relevant set is described in the italicized portion of (8b), (9b), (10b), or (11b).

(8)   a. Susan promised Brenda $10.
      b. 'Susan caused Brenda to have $10 *in all circumstances in which she honors her promises.*'

(9)   a. Susan lacked $10.
      b. 'Susan had $10 *in all circumstances which are not the circumstances in which Susan did not have $10.*'

(10)   a. Bill neglected to read the books.
       b. 'Bill did not read the books, but he did *in all circumstances in which he acts according to moral obligation.*'[2]

(11)   a. Sandra was giving him advice when she was interrupted.
       b. 'Sandra caused him to receive advice *in all the inertia circumstances.*'

A classification of some English verbs and their sublexical modalities is given in Table 1. "Modal" here includes negation and temporal operators (inchoative); "neutral" might be thought of as a possibility modal.

Some verbs involve more than one modality. Consider the verb *neglect*, as used in (10). To neglect to perform an action entails both that the action did not take place and that it ought to have taken place. The meaning of

---

[2] *Neglect* and all verbs followed by an asterisk in Table 1 are more complex. They involve both a negation and a necessity operator, without either one having scope over the other.

166 / Anthony Davis & Jean-Pierre Koenig

TABLE 1 A classification of verbs by their sublexical modality

neutral modal	positive modal	negative modal	necessity modal	inchoative modal	inchoative-negative modal
	have	lack	need	receive	lose
	perceive	miss	overlook*	notice	
send(?)	give	promise, owe, charge*			
try	manage	fail	neglect*		
	force	forbid	urge, persuade		

neglect thus includes both a negation and a necessity operator, neither of which has scope over the other.

In order to "sieve" the set of possible worlds and obtain the subset relevant to linking constraints, we require three kinds of operations, each of which is independently motivated semantically.[3]

We first need to determine the Modal Base of a sublexical modality operator (see Kratzer (1981) on the notion of modal base). Which subset of worlds is in the pool of worlds in which to check for a linking-relevant restricted entailment depends on the choice of Modal Base. The Modal Base for *need*, for example, is determined by its subject's referent's desires (that is, only those worlds that conform to his/her desires need be considered); the Modal Base for *neglect* is determined by moral obligations, and so forth. Secondly, we also need to define indirectly the meaning of verbs containing a negation operator. Again, such a definition of negative sublexical modal operators is independently motivated; it is common in dynamic approaches to meaning and in update semantics (see Heim (1983) or Chierchia (1995) among others). Finally, assuming for now that linking constraints are stated over words, we need to invoke *inertia* circumstances, following Dowty (1979): the set of circumstances is selected on the basis of the "natural" outcome of initiated (but possibly unfinished) events.

We summarize our proposal as to the lexical semantics of verbs in hypothesis 1 below, and turn to its role in solving our linking quandaries in the next section.

Hypothesis 1 *The meanings of verbs often include a sublexical modality component.*

---

[3]The "modality" component might also include sublexical temporal information (R. Oehrle, p.c. and Oehrle (1976)). See i. which is vague as to whether Bill had the job or not *prior* to the affair.

    i. The affair cost Bill his job.

    Due to lack of space, we do not directly discuss sublexical temporal "modal" structure in this paper.

1. *Like their superlexical counterparts (may, must . . .) sublexical modalities require the selection of a modal base.*

2. *The modal semantic structure comprises a list of operators that may, but need not, have scope over each other.*

3. *Each modal operator in the list of operators is classified as to the selection of modal base it induces.*

4 Sublexical modality 'transparency'.

4.1 Modally transparent linking.

Our second proposal— which we call the *Modal Transparency Hypothesis* (hereafter MTH)— is summarized in the following hypothesis (see section 4.2 for a refinement of this hypothesis).

Hypothesis 2 *[preliminary] Linking constraints are only sensitive to a verb's non-modal core-situational meaning, not to its (sublexical) modal modification.*

In this section we examine the implications of our two hypotheses for the architecture of lexical semantic representations. Although we implement our representations within HEAD-DRIVEN PHRASE STRUCTURE GRAMMAR (hereafter HPSG), the MTH can be incorporated into semantic representations and linking theories proposed within several current frameworks, provided their representation of the lexical semantics of verbs is rich enough. In particular, the conceptual structure representations of Pinker (1989), Jackendoff (1990), or Levin (1993) within a Principles and Parameters approach, the constructional approach of Goldberg (1995) or the Logical Form approach of Van Valin (1993) within Role and Reference grammar can easily be adapted to incorporate our observations, we believe. Approaches that take a "minimal" semantics as their basis for linking, though, such as those of Grimshaw (1990), Alsina (1996), and some others, will face difficulties in accommodating the data in (2)-(6). It is hard to see how they could account for the generalizations we cover in this section given the paucity of semantic information available in these frameworks for stating linking rules.

Technically, we factor the representation of the semantic content of predicators into two sets of properties, the SITUATIONAL-CORE and the MODAL-OPERATOR semantic structures. Each of these sets of properties is represented through an Attribute-Value structure within a TYPED FEATURE STRUCTURE architecture (see Carpenter (1992)). The SITUATIONAL-CORE structure represents the situation holding true in worlds within the modal base. For example, the situational cores of *give, send, owe*, and so on are all identical, representing 'cause to transfer possession'. Since entailments derived from situational-core semantic structures are the sole determinants of linking, we predict their common ditransitive linking pattern. (see Van Valin (1993) for an early proposal in this direction). The MODAL-OPERATOR structures consist of a list of partially scoped operators (see Copestake et al. (1997) for the technical details of partially scoped lists of semantic relations/operators in HPSG). Finally, the proper interaction of the two components is accomplished by structure-sharing (see tag ③ in (12), for instance). Readers not familiar with the formalism underlying Typed Feature Structures systems can think of such conumbered tags as identical variables in traditional First-Order Predicate Calculus.

To see this architecture in use, we now present the semantic representations of several verbs. We start with *need*. The Attribute-Value Matrix in (12) (hereafter AVM) represents the lexical semantics of *need* as a *have-rel* modified by a necessity modal operator. The diagram basically says that the meaning of *need* involves a relation of possession as well as a necessity operator whose state-of-affairs argument takes this possession relation as argument (see the tag ③).

(12)
$$
\begin{bmatrix}
\text{SIT-CORE}③ \begin{bmatrix} \textit{have-rel} \\ \text{ACTOR} \quad ① \\ \text{UNDERGOER}② \end{bmatrix} \\
\text{MOD-OP} \left\langle \begin{bmatrix} \textit{necess-op} \\ \text{SOA} \quad ③ \end{bmatrix} \right\rangle
\end{bmatrix}
$$

In (14) is a representation of the lexical semantics of *charge* in (13) as a *cause-possession-rel* whose embedded *have-rel* state-of-affairs is modified by a negation operator.

(13) She charged me $10.
       ①   ②   ④

The representation can be interpreted as: 'one entity causes another not to have a third.' *Charge* involves a second necessity modal operator as well, which modifies the causing event, assuming a modal base of worlds in which the causer's desires are fulfilled.

(14)
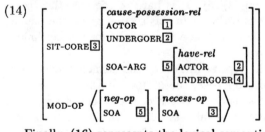

Finally, (16) represents the lexical semantics of *neglect* (in the sense of 'neglect to eat', as in (15)) as a *cause-act-rel* modified by a negation and necessity modal operator unscoped with respect to each other.

(15) She neglected to eat.
       ①   ③

(16)

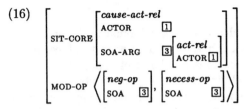

We now illustrate the use of this "factored" representation of the semantics of verbs in the statement of linking constraints. We cannot go into the details of our linking theory within HPSG in this paper and refer the reader to Koenig (1994), Davis (1996), and Davis and Koenig (1997) for details. Its fundamentals should be clear from our few examples, however. We first give the ACTOR to "subject" linking constraint in (17). This constraint is responsible for the mapping of actor-like arguments to the subjects of active verbs (the first element on the ARG-S list in HPSG generally corresponds to the subject of active verbs). Importantly, in accordance with the MTH, the MOD-OP semantic structure is left unspecified; the linking constraint encoded in the verb-class definition thus applies to verbs denoting relations that include an actor-like participant whatever sublexical modality is specified. The constraint thus applies to positive verbs of possession such as *have*, but also to modally modified verbs such as *need* or *lack*.

(17)

$$
\begin{bmatrix}
\text{CONTENT} & \begin{bmatrix} \text{NUCLEUS} & \begin{bmatrix} \text{SIT-CORE} & \begin{bmatrix} \textit{act-rel} \\ \text{ACTOR}\,\boxed{1} \end{bmatrix} \\ \text{MOD-OP} \end{bmatrix} \end{bmatrix} \\
\text{CAT} & \begin{bmatrix} \text{ARG-S}\langle \text{NP:}\boxed{1}, \dots \rangle \end{bmatrix}
\end{bmatrix}
$$

The English ditransitive verb class diagrammed in (18) illustrates the same point. Again, the definition leaves unspecified the modality operator values; it applies to any verb whose situational core denotes events of causing to possess (verbs whose core-situational semantics is of type *cause-possession-rel* and embedded state-of-affairs of type *have-rel*). Our strategy should be clear from these few examples: the entailments that ground linking constraints are those characteristic of particular core-situational relations (say, *have-rel*), irrespective of the modal operators also lexically encoded by the verb.

(18)

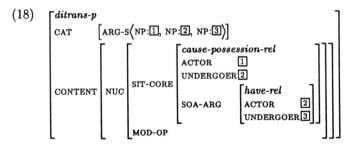

4.2 Apparent exceptions.

Although our proposal is independently motivated semantically and solves the basic problem we raised in section 2, some data seem troublesome for our second hypothesis. Here we examine two kinds of apparent violations of our second hypothesis, both relating to PP-complements of predicators. The first kind concerns PP complements headed by semantically meaningful prepositions, which appear in place of direct arguments in some verbs. In these cases the linking constraints for direct verbal arguments do not apply (or, more accurately, apply vacuously); these prepositions are responsible for a semantic contribution to the content of a VP, and the object of the PP is linked by the preposition rather than directly by the verb. The second set of cases concerns PP-complements headed by semantically "empty" prepositions. Here, we resort to a limited amount of stipulation of a verb's subcategorization. All of these PP-complements point to the need to limit the range of our Modal Transparency Hypothesis to linking of direct verbal arguments.

4.2.1 Semantically potent prepositions.

Let's compare first the verbs *give* and *take* in (19), and *persuade* and *dissuade* in (20).

(19) a. Helen gave a book to Bill.

b. Helen took a book from Bill.

(20) a. Burns persuaded Smithers to fire Simpson.

b. Burns dissuaded Smithers from firing Simpson.

The selection of *to* or *from* seems to depend on whether Bill has or does not have the book at the end, or whether Smithers actually fires Simpson, *contra* our Modal Transparency Hypothesis. Despite appearances, cases such as (19) do not contravene the MTH. We assume the analysis of semantically potent prepositions presented in Jackendoff (1983), Gawron (1986) and Wechsler (1995a). In particular, we assume with many others that prepositions such as *to* and *from* encode the path along which an object moves. Given this inherent semantics of directional PP's, we can model the data in (19) through a single caused motion verb class, represented in (21). This linking class applies to both *give* and *take* and specify that the path of motion is optionally encoded through a PP. The particular head of this PP need not be specified in the linking pattern; it follows from the inherent semantics of *to* and *from* and the kind of path semantically selected by *give* and *take* respectively. In other words, the distinction stems from the semantics of the prepositions which encode different portions of the path. Note that languages can differ as to the semantics of such prepositions. French *à* in (22), for example, can denote either goal-like or source-like paths, at least when combining with verbs denoting caused-motion relations. We end this brief discussion of caused-motion verbs by noting that

semantically potent prepositions constrain the situational core. As we will
see in the next subsection, the same is not true of idiosyncratic prepositions.

(21)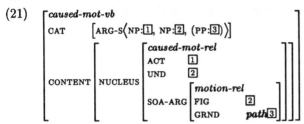

(22) a. Marie donnera   deux francs à   Paul.
        Marie give.FUT   two   francs to Paul
        'Marie will give two francs to Paul.'
     b. Marie prendra   deux francs à   Paul.
        Marie take.FUT   two   francs to Paul
        'Marie will take two francs from Paul.'

In the case of *dissuade, prevent,* and similar verbs, there is no physical
path to represent, and if *from* serves to denote a source it is a metaphorical
one. With these verbs *from* seems to contribute a negation operator to the
MOD-OP of the verb, rather than path information in the SIT-CORE. These
two verbs contrast with *forbid,* which does take an infinitive VP complement
like *force.* Thus the presence or absence of a *from*-PP may be a lexically-
specified fact about the subcategorizations of these verbs. This leads us to
the second set of cases, involving semantically empty prepositions, which
also are lexically specified.

4.2.2 Idiosyncratic prepositions.

The contrast between the verbs *give* and *deprive* is more challenging to our
MTH. The basic generalization is that the "theme" of 'negative' causative
verbs is realized as a PP headed by *of,* not as a second object (cf. also *rob
of, strip of* ...).

(23) a. Jean gave him a lift ticket.
     b. Jean deprived him of a lift ticket.

The analysis we propose for directional prepositions in the previous subsection cannot be adopted in this case. The prepositional phrase alternates
here with a direct object NP complement. We cannot posit a single linking
class covering both cases since the syntactic category of the linked elements
on the ARG-S lists of the two verbs differs. Moreover, we cannot leave
this category information unspecified and assume some Canonical Realization Principle is responsible for 'filling in' that information (see Pesetsky
(1982) or Langacker (1987)), since the presence of a PP-complement for the
"theme" of negative verbs seems to be an English-specific property (compare the ditransitive Swedish equivalent in (24)-(25) from Wechsler(1995b),

which allows passivization of either object). The *deprive* class may simply require an English-particular specification that an 'of' PP-complement realizes the "theme" role, rather than a second object.

(24) De   fråntog   honom   chefskapet.
they from-took   him   the headship
'They deprived him of the headship.'

(25) a. Han fråntogs   chefskapet.
he from-took-PASS the headship
'He was deprived of the headship.'

b. Chefskapet fråntogs   han.
the headship from-took-PASS he
'He was deprived of the headship.'

If our analysis is correct, we must slightly revise our Modal Transparency Hypothesis, since the linking properties of *deprive* do seem to require reference to a negative modal operator. Note that in contrast to semantically potent prepositions discussed earlier that constrain the situational core, idiosyncratic prepositions such as *of* in (23b) contribute constraints to the list of modal operators.

Hypothesis 2 (revised) *Linking constraints for direct Grammatical Functions are only sensitive to a verb's non-modal core-situational meaning, not to its (sublexical) modal modification.*

5   Conclusion.

This paper has made two claims.

1. The semantics of predicators often includes a sublexical modality component.

2. We can maintain an entailment-based grounding for linking constraints if we relativize entailments to a selected set of possible circumstances.

These two claims are logically independent, at least in isolation. But *if* the second one is correct (whether in the form of our MTH or otherwise), it bolsters our first claim given other natural assumptions about linguistic theory, such as Jackendoff (1983)'s Grammatical Constraint, according to which semantic representations that account for otherwise arbitrary syntactic and lexical generalizations are to be preferred, *ceteris paribus*. We would like to end this paper with two further questions which we intend to address in future work. First, we have restricted our data to English in this paper for lack of space. However, our analysis extends without difficulty to several languages, including French and Korean, and we are currently conducting a more widespread survey of languages. Secondly, are there differences between sublexical and superlexical modality? It is well-known that differences exist between some sublexical and superlexical negations (see Horn (1989)). Do these differences extend to cases of sublexical modal operators within monomorphemic words?

References

Alsina, Alex. 1996. *The role of argument structure in grammar.* Stanford: CSLI Publications.

Carpenter, Bob. 1992. *The Logic of Typed Feature Structures.* Cambridge: Cambridge University Press.

Chierchia, Gennaro. 1995. *The Dynamics of Meaning.* Chicago: Chicago University Press.

Copestake, Ann, Dan Flickinger, and Ivan A. Sag. 1997. Minimal Recursion Semantics: an introduction. Manuscript.

Davis, Anthony. 1996. *Lexical Semantics and Linking in the Hierarchical Lexicon.* Doctoral dissertation, Stanford University, Stanford.

Davis, Anthony, and Jean-Pierre Koenig. 1997. Linking as constraints on word classes in a hierarchical lexicon. Manuscript, State University of New York at Buffalo.

Dowty, David. 1979. *Word Meaning and Montague Grammar.* Dordrecht: Reidel.

Dowty, David. 1991. Thematic proto-roles and argument selection. *Language* 67:547–619.

Gawron, Jean Mark. 1986. Situations and Prepositions. *Linguistics and Philosophy* 9:327–382.

Goldberg, Adele. 1995. *Constructions: A Construction Grammar Approach to Argument Structure.* Chicago: Chicago University Press.

Grimshaw, Jane. 1990. *Argument structure.* Cambridge, Mass: MIT Press.

Heim, Irene. 1983. On the Projection Problem for Presuppositions. In *Proceedings of the Second West Coast Conference on Formal Linguistics,* ed. Daniel Flickinger et al. 114–125. Stanford: Stanford University Press.

Horn, Laurence. 1989. *A natural history of negation.* Chicago: Chicago University Press.

Jackendoff, Ray. 1983. *Semantics and Cognition.* Cambridge, Mass.: MIT Press.

Jackendoff, Ray. 1990. *Semantic Structures.* Cambridge: MIT Press.

Koenig, Jean-Pierre. 1994. *Lexical Underspecification and the Syntax/Semantics Interface.* Doctoral dissertation, University of California at Berkeley, Berkeley.

Kratzer, Angelika. 1981. The Notional Category of Modality. In *Words, Worlds, and Contexts,* ed. Hans-Jürgen Eikmeyer and Hannes Rieser. 38–74. Berlin: Walter de Gruyter.

Langacker, Ronald. 1987. *Foundations of Cognitive Grammar, vol.1.* Stanford: Stanford University Press.

Levin, Beth. 1993. *English Verb Classes and Alternations.* Chicago: Chicago University Press.

Oehrle, Richard. 1976. *The Grammatical Status of the English Dative Alternation.* Doctoral dissertation, MIT, Cambridge, Mass.

174 / ANTHONY DAVIS & JEAN-PIERRE KOENIG

Pesetzky, David. 1982. *Paths and Categories.* Doctoral dissertation, MIT, Cambridge, Mass.

Pinker, Steven. 1989. *Learnability and Cognition: the acquisition of argument structure.* Cambridge, Mass.: MIT Press.

Van Valin, Robert. 1993. A synopsis of Role and Reference Grammar. In *Advances in Role and Reference Grammar*, ed. Robert Van Valin. 1–164. Amsterdam: John Benjamins.

Wechsler, Stephen. 1995a. Preposition Selection Outside the Lexicon. In *Proceedings of WCCFL XIII*, ed. Raul Aranovich, William Byrne, Susanne Preuss, and Matha Senturia. 416–431. Stanford: CSLI Publications.

Wechsler, Stephen. 1995b. *The Semantic Basis of Argument Structure.* Stanford, CA: CSLI Publications.

Phonological Cohesion as a Reflex of Morphosyntactic Feature Chains

GORKA ELORDIETA

University of the Basque Country / Basque Center for Language Research
(LEHIA)

1. Introduction*

In this paper I show that there are phonological processes that cannot be accounted for by the different theories of phrasal and prosodic phonology. They are determined by syntactic relations holding among heads, not by prosodic factors. The syntactic relations are relations between the syntactic features realized by the heads intervening in these processes. These relations form feature chains (e.g., C-T, T-V, V-D), which are interpreted in the phonological component as phonological domains. The phenomena to be studied are Basque Vowel Assimilation and French liaison.

2. Basque Vowel Assimilation

In Lekeitio Basque the initial vowel of determiners and inflected auxiliaries assimilates optionally in fast or colloquial speech to the final vowel of preceding noun/adjective or verb, respectively. The examples in (1) and (2) illustrate the application of Vowel Assimilation (VA henceforth) in nominal and verbal contexts, respectively:

---

* The material presented in this paper is drawn from parts of my dissertation (Elordieta (1997)). I am very much indebted to Jean-Roger Vergnaud for invaluable input and ideas on the issues discussed here. I also want to thank the audience at WCCFL XVII for their feedback. All remaining errors are my own. This research was funded by a postdoctoral fellowship from the Department of Education, Universities and Research of the Basque Government.

175

(1) a. etxi-a   ~   etxii   b. gixon altú-ak   ~   gixon altúuk
house-det.sg.   man tall-det.pl.
'the house'   'the tall men'

    c. semí-en   ~   semíin   d. ortu-éta-n   ~   ortuútan
son-gen.pl.   orchard-det.pl.-ines.
'of the sons'   'in the orchards'

(2) a. erosi eban   ~   erosi iban   b. apurtu ében   ~   apurtu úben
buy infl   break infl
'(s)he bought it'   'they broke it'

    c. ostu ebasan   ~   ostu ubasan   d. asma ebésen   ~   asma abésen
steal infl   make up infl
'(s)he stole them'   'they made them up'

2.1 Restrictions on VA

In nominal contexts, VA cannot occur across two members of a compound or across two words, as shown in (3) and (4), respectively:

(3) a. soro-antza ~ *soro-óntza   b. buru-andi   ~   *buru-úndi
mad-look   head-big
'mad look'   'big-headed'

(4) a. etxe andiža ~ *etxe endiža   b. seru asula   ~   *seru usula
house big   sky blue

       In verbal contexts, VA is blocked between a main verb and a causative verb (cf. (5) below), between a verb and a modal particle that expresses epistemic attitudes of the speaker towards the events expressed in the sentence (cf. (6)), and between a verb and a subordinating conjunction or postposition (cf. (7)):

(5)   paga eraiñ neutzan   ~   *paga araiñ
pay caus infl
'I made him/her pay'

(6) a. ekarri ete dau   ~   *ekarri ite dau
bring dub. infl
'I wonder whether (s)he has brought it'

    b. atrapa ei   dózu   ~   *atrapa ai dózu
catch evid. infl
'It is being said that you have caught it'

(7) a. apurtu ezik ~ *apurtu uzik   b. erosi árte ~ *erosi írte
break unless   buy until

       In the next section I discuss the problems that the distribution of VA poses for different theories of phrasal and prosodic phonology proposed in the literature. In section 2.3 I present our alternative analysis to the problem.

2.2 Problems for theories of Prosodic Phonology

There are two different theories of postlexical phonology. The Direct Reference Theory (DRT) of Kaisse (1985) claims that domains of application of phonological processes between words are defined by c-command relationships and branching conditions applying to the words whose segments intervene in the process. According to the Prosodic Hierarchy Theory (PHT; cf. Nespor and Vogel (1986), Selkirk (1986), Hayes (1989)), on the other hand, each utterance has an independent prosodic structure, hierarchically organized in a finite set of universal prosodic constituents. According to original assumptions in the PHT, prosodic boundaries are inserted at the edges of syntactic heads and maximal projections, following certain parameters of prosodic structure formation. The prosodic constituents so formed may or may not coincide with syntactic constituents. Thus, prosodic structure is derived from syntactic structure but it is not isomorphic with it (i.e., a prosodic constituent may overlap two syntactic constituents, or split one syntactic constituent in two or more prosodic constituents). Phonological processes apply in domains defined by prosodic constituency, and not by syntactic constituency. In (8) an example of a prosodic structure tree is provided, with the prosodic constituents hierarchically organized (U = Utterance; IP = Intonational Phrase; PhP = Phonological Phrase; CG = Clitic Group; PWd = Prosodic Word):[1]

(8)

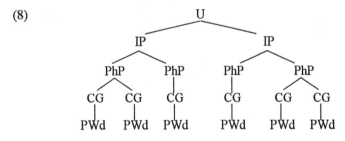

Since the predictions made by the DRT and the PHT depend on the assumptions on the syntactic structure of the utterance, it is necessary to present first the structure of the clause in Basque.

2.2.1 Syntactic structure

The structure of the clause in Basque I will be assuming is the following:

---

[1] The existence of the Clitic Group has been rejected by some authors (Inkelas 1990, Zec 1993, Selkirk 1996, among others). The structure in (8) is here maintained as it will be referenced later in this paper.

(9)

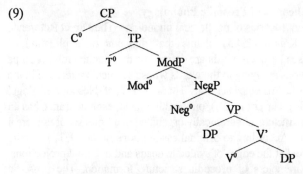

This structure allows a straightforward account of the linear order observed between the main verb, modal particles, inflected auxiliaries, and negation. In non-negative clauses, the main verb is immediately followed by the inflected auxiliary (cf. (10a) below). When a modal particle is present, it appears between the verb and the inflected auxiliary (cf. (10b)).

(10) a. etorri da   b. etorri ei   da
         come infl   come evid. infl

The sequence formed by the verb, modal particle and auxiliary, or negation, modal particle and auxiliary constitutes an unbreakable complex unit with a fixed word order. Observe the following examples:

(11) a. Nire laguna gaur goixian allaga ei da Lekitxora
         my friend today morning arrive evid infl Lekeitio-to
         'It is being said that my friend arrived in Lekeitio this morning'
     b. *Nire laguna gaur goixian allaga Lekitxora ei da
     c. *Nire laguna gaur goixian allaga ei Lekitxora da
     d. Nor allaga ete   da gaur goixian Lekitxora?
         who arrive dub   infl today morning Lekeitio-to
         'I wonder who arrived in Lekeitio this morning?'

(11a) shows the correct order in the sequence verb-modal particle-auxiliary. (11b,c) show that this sequence cannot be disrupted. (11d) illustrates an example of an interrogative clause, where the sequence verb-mod-aux is displaced to the left edge of the clause, most likely to C^0, since it immediately follows a wh-word which lies in Spec,CP. The sequence verb-mod-aux moves to C^0 as one constituent. This pattern is analyzed straightforwardly by positing incorporation of the verb onto the modal particle by left-adjoining to it, with subsequent raising of the complex unit to the position occupied by the auxiliary, which we assume is T^0. As for the reason for this movement, evidence is provided in Elordieta (1997) (following Ortiz de Urbina (1994), (1995)) that the inflected auxiliary in Basque is an affix that triggers the raising of the verb or negation to support it. Observe the diagram in (12), for instance:[2]

(12)

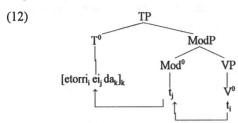

When a causative verb is involved, it appears between the main verb and the auxiliary (cf. (13a)). If a modal particle is present, the causative verb precedes it (cf. (13b)). (13c) illustrates an interrogative sentence with a causative verb, showing that the verbal complex appears as a unit on the left edge of the sentence:

(13) a. Joneri afari   guztia paga eraiñ dótze.
         Jon-to dinner all   pay   make infl
         'They made Jon pay the whole dinner'
     b. Joneri afari   guztia paga eraiñ ei   dótze
         Jon-to dinner all   pay   make evid infl
         'It is being said that they made Jon pay the whole dinner'
     c. Nori paga eraiñ dótze afari   guztia?
         whom pay make aux   dinner all
         'Who did they make pay the whole dinner?'

This pattern indicates that the verb incorporates to the causative, then to the modal particle, and finally to the auxiliary, in a head-to-head fashion, like in noncausative cases. The structure in (14) illustrates a sample of a derivation involving a causative verb:

(14)

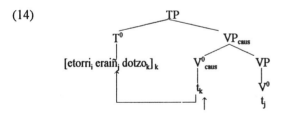

---

[2] Assuming a head-initial structure of the clause for Basque in (9) and left-adjunction of heads we derive the right order among heads and the dependency displayed by the auxiliary with respect to the verb and negation. For reasons of space limitation, the arguments will not be discussed in detail here; the reader is referred to Elordieta (1997). As pointed out there, our analysis would remain valid even if Basque were proven to be a true head-final language. The dependency displayed by the auxiliary and the complex unit it forms with the verb or negation and the modal particle would still have to be explained by positing raising of the verb or negation to T⁰.

Having established the main assumptions on the structure of the clause in Basque, we proceed to discuss the problems faced by the theories of phrasal and prosodic phonology in order to define the domain of application of VA in LB.

2.2.2 The DRT

In the DRT of Kaisse (1985), the application of postlexical rules between two elements *a* and *b* depends on the structural relationship of c-command existing between them. If our assumptions on the syntactic relationships among heads in Basque are correct, we must conclude that the DRT cannot make the correct predictions about the domain of occurrence of VA, since the same c-command relationships hold between a verb and an inflected auxiliary, where VA applies, as between a verb and a modal particle or a causative verb, where VA does not apply. The following are schematic representations of the structures obtaining from head movement by the verb:

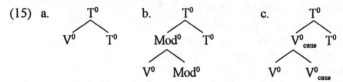

(15) a. T^0 / V^0 T^0 b. T^0 / Mod^0 T^0 / V^0 Mod^0 c. T^0 / V^0_{caus} T^0 / V^0 V^0_{caus}

2.2.3 The PHT

Within the PHT there are two models which differ in the way they view the creation of prosodic structure from syntactic structure, the Relation-Based Approach (Nespor and Vogel (1986), Hayes (1989)) and the End-Based Approach (Selkirk (1986)). The main problem both for the RBA and the EBA is that the domain of application of VA cannot be the Prosodic Word (PWd) or the Clitic Group (CG), because the verb and the inflected auxiliary may be stressed independently. The main criteria to define a PWd or CG is that it only contains a maximum of one primary stress:

(16)   ikusíko ebésen   ~ ikusíko obésen
        see-fut infl
        'they would see them'

The Phonological Phrase (PhP) cannot be the domain of VA either, because members of compound words are in one PhP, and VA does not apply across members of compounds (as in (3a, b): *soro-óntza, *buru-úndi). This indicates that the domain of application of VA does not correspond to a domain defined by prosodic considerations.

It can also be shown that the procedures to create prosodic constituents devised by the EBA cannot capture the correct domain of VA. According to this theory, prosodic constituents are delimited by boundaries that are inserted on the left or right edges of words and syntactic maximal projections. Which edge is chosen in each language depends on the particular parameter setting the language selects:

(17) (i) a. $]_{Word}$ b. $_{Word}[$
      (ii) a. $]_{Xmax}$ b. $_{Xmax}[$

The string delimited by two word boundaries defines a prosodic word, and the string delimited by two maximal projection boundaries defines a phonological phrase. Only words pertaining to lexical categories introduce boundaries on their edges; functional heads are invisible to prosodic boundary insertion (cf. Selkirk (1984)).

Let us see how this theory would fare in predicting the domain of VA. Boundaries inserted on the left edge of lexical words or each member of a compound word would correctly separate two lexical words in two different prosodic constituents, therefore predicting the absence of VA across two words or between two members of a compound:

(18) a. $[_N$ buru- $[_A$ andi   →   buru-ándi / *buru-úndi
          head- big
          'big-headed'
     b. $[_N$ lora $[_A$ ederra   →   lora ederra / *lora adarra
          flower   beautiful
          'beautiful flower'

Functional heads would not project boundaries to their left, and would therefore fall in the same prosodic constituent with the preceding lexical head. thus correctly predicting VA between a noun or adjective and a determiner, and between a verb and an inflected auxiliary (cf. (19)). But on the other hand, this theory would fail to recognize the differences among functional heads with respect to VA. Modal particles and subordinating conjunctions do not participate in VA, but this theory would assign them to the same prosodic constituent with the preceding word:

(19) a. $[_N$ umi - $_D$ a   →   umia ~ umii
          child det.sg.
     b. $[_V$ atrapa $_{Infl}$ eban   →   atrapa eban ~ atrapa aban
          catch   infl
          '(s)he caught it'

(20) a. $[_V$ leidu $_{Conj}$ ezik   →   leidu ezik ~ *leidu uzik
          read   unless
     b. $[_V$ ostu $_{Mod}$ ete $_{Infl}$ dábe   →   ostu ete dábe ~ *ostu ute dábe ?
          steal   dubit. infl

Clearly, then, an alternative theory is needed that may account for the domain of application of phonological phenomena such as VA. An alternative model is presented in the following section.

2.3 An analysis in terms of feature chains

The analysis I propose is based on the observation that the contexts where VA applies are composed of a lexical head and a functional head with inflectional features, i.e., a noun or adjective and a following determiner, in nominal contexts, and a verb and a following inflected auxiliary, in verbal contexts. This is a generalization that leads to the idea that there are some phonological phenomena that are sensitive to morphosyntactic relationships holding among syntactic heads, so that a close syntactic relationship is mapped or translated as a close degree of phonological cohesion in the phonological component. The close degree of morphosyntactic cohesion is defined in terms of sharing of syntactic features. As laid out in the minimalist framework of syntactic theory, syntactic heads contain sets of formal features, which have to be checked in order for the derivation to converge. The values of the features of one head are checked against the values of the same features of another head, and if they match, the derivation is convergent. Otherwise, the derivation is cancelled. The operation by which features are checked is called *Move* or *Attract F*: the set of formal features in one head are checked by triggering the raising of the formal features of a lower head. Features may move to the head position, or to the Spec position of the head triggering the movement, that is, to the checking domain of the higher head.

Thus, for instance, T has the feature [assign nominative Case], checked by the [nominative case] feature of the DP raising to Spec,TP. Also, T attracts a D feature to its Spec position, by virtue of the Extended Projection Principle (all clauses need a subject). Both the feature [nom] and the categorial feature [D] are present in the head D of the DP subject. The features [nom] and [D] raise to Spec,TP, together with the set of formal features of D, to check the feature specifications present in T. The following diagram illustrates this operation:

(21)

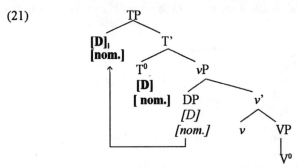

The features in italics represent the copies of the features that have been moved, which appear in boldface, the same as the features present in T. If movement is covert, it simply involves movement of features; the phonological material is spelled out in its in-situ position. If movement is triggered by a strong feature, however, movement is overt, and it involves raising of the whole category, including the phonological material.

T also has a categorial [V]-feature, which attracts the categorial feature of the verb, [V]. In turn, the verb also has tense features, which need to be checked with those features in T. In the tree diagram example in (22) we illustrate this relationship; the features [V] and [+past] (as an example of a tense feature) of the verb raise to T to check the same features in T:

(22)

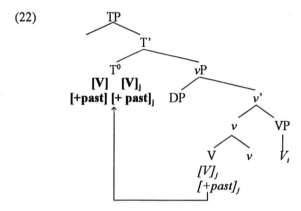

Additionally, the verb is specified for φ-features, present in the subject. The set of formal features of the subject raise to Spec,TP independently (cf. (21)), so the φ-features of the verb raise to T, to be checked with those of the subject:

(23)

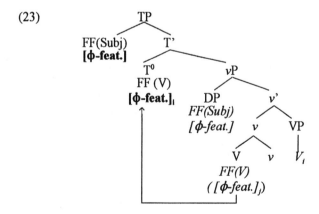

Other feature checking relationships are the one establishing between C and T. In interrogative clauses, C contains a feature[Q]. If T contains a *wh*-feature, C attracts this feature, to check its Q feature (cf. I→Q raising in Chomsky

(1995:290-1)).[3] Also, an object in a transitive clause is specified for the feature [accusative Case] as well as φ-features. The verb has the feature [assign accusative Case], and is also specified for the φ-features of the object. The checking of these features is done by raising the formal features of the object to Spec, *v*, an "outer" Spec position. The features are checked in the checking domain of *v*, where V has moved, forming the complex head $_v[V,v]$.

Feature checking takes place inside the DP as well. The head D has an N-feature,which attracts the categorial feature [N] of the head noun for checking. Again, if the N-feature in D is strong, it will trigger overt movement of the noun to D. Otherwise, the noun is spelled-out in its original position.

(24)

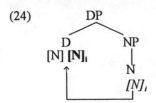

A preposition also assigns Case to its DP complement. Its Case feature needs to be checked by the Case feature of the DP, located in D. This is achieved by raising the formal features of D to {Spec,P}.

We propose that relations among features of the kind discussed above establish primitive morphosyntactic relationships that can be represented in the form of primitive chains or feature chains (cf. Zubizarreta and Vergnaud (in preparation)). These chains include the following:

(25)   C-T   T-V   T-D   V-D$_{Subj}$ V-D$_{Obj}$ D-N   P-D

The chain C-T expresses the attraction of T features by the complementizer, C; the checking of nominative case and the EPP is contained in T-D; V-D$_{Subj}$ represents the checking relation of the subject φ-features of V; V-D$_{Obj}$ represents the checking of accusative case and φ-features between a verb and its object; D-N is the relation of checking the categorial feature N and the φ-features of N by raising to D; P-D is the checking of case features in D and P. Our claim is that these chains are relevant in the phonological component as well. That is, these relationships are primitive entities that are subject to Full Interpretation at LF *and* PF. That is, these chains are relevant not only at LF but in the phonological component as well. The chains receive an interpretation as phonological constituents, units which may correspond to domains of occurrence of phonological processes. These domains are not derived by prosodic but

---

[3] See Chomsky (1995:290) for a suggestion that the feature satisfying the strong Q-feature of C might be a [V] feature.

morphosyntactic considerations. Thus, Basque VA applies between a noun and a determiner and between a lexical verb and verbal inflection; this indicates that the chains D-N and T-V are phonologically interpreted as the domain of VA. A schematic representation of this mapping between morphosyntactic feature chains and phonological constituency is provided in (26). Note that the phonological domain presents the reverse order of heads, reflecting the process of left adjunction by the incorporation of the noun and verb.[4] The examples in (27) illustrate these two contexts of application of VA:

(26)   D-N   ↔ $[N-D]_p$
        T-V   ↔ $[V-T]_p$

(27) a. $[umi-a]_p$ →   umia   ~   umii
         child-det.sg.

     b. $[ekarri\ eban]_p$ →   ekarri eban   ~   ekarri iban
         bring infl.

The contexts where VA does not apply are contexts were the heads do not participate in feature checking relationships with each other. That is, they do not form feature chains, and thus fall in different phonological domains. Members of compound nouns and two lexical words such as a noun and an adjective do not form feature chains:

(28) a. $[\ buru]_p$ - $[\ andi\ ]_p$ →   buru-ándi   ~   *buru-úndi
         head   big

     b. $[lora]_p$ $[ederra]_p$ →   lora ederra   ~   *lora adarra
         flower   beautiful

A verb does not form a feature chain with a modal particle, causative verb or subordinating conjunction. No features of the verb check features of these elements. These are contexts where VA does not apply:

(29) a. $[ekarri]_p$ $[ete]_p$ →   ekarri ete   ~   *ekarri ite
         bring   evid.

     b. [paga] [eraiñ]   →   paga eraiñ   →   *paga araiñ
         pay   caus.

     c. $[erosi]_p$ $[árren]_p$ →   erosi árren   ~   *erosi írren
         buy   despite

The validity of the theory we have proposed in this section is further demonstrated in the next section, where we analyze the domain of application of French liaison. Due to space limitations, this section will be more schematic than

---

[4] To be more specific, there is raising of NP to {Spec,D}, and the determiner is affixed to the last member of the NP (cf. Elordieta (1997):section 3.5 for discussion).

the one dedicated to Basque, but we hope it will suffice to show the advantages of our model. (For more detailed discussion, see Elordieta (1997).)

3. French liaison

Liaison refers to the pronunciation of latent word-final consonants before vowel-initial words. However, not all words with latent consonants make liaison with the same degree of frequency. Certain syntactic configurations are contexts of obligatory liaison, whereas others allow liaison optionally; finally, other syntactic configurations disallow liaison. We focus on the conversational or familiar style of speech in French (Style I), which is the most restrictive in liaison contexts. More formal or elevated styles of speech allow liaison to occur in more contexts, and there is little agreement on the facts. The contexts of application of liaison in Style I, however, are more consistently agreed upon by native speakers.[5]

Obligatory liaison is found between determiners, demonstratives, possessive adjectives, numerals or quantifiers and a following noun or adjective, between subject and object clitics and a following verb, and between a verb and a following subject or oblique clitic. Cf. (30), where '⌢' indicates liaison:

(30) a. les⌢amis
      'the friends'
   c. vingt-trois⌢oignons
      'twenty-three onions'

      b. nos⌢oppresseurs
      'our oppressors'
      d. Il vous⌢a donné la réponse.
      'He has given you the answer'

Liaison is frequent but not obligatory between monosyllabic prepositions, degree adverbs, auxiliaries or copulas and what follows:

(31) a. dans⌢une salle publique
      in   a   room public
   c. très⌢incommode
      very uncomfortable

      b. ont⌢acheté
      have bought
      d. est⌢insupportable
      is   unbearable

Liaison is rare between polysyllabic forms of the categories just mentioned (the symbol '/?' indicates low percentage of occurrence of liaison):

(32) a. pendant /? une semaine
      during one week
   c. assez /? intimes
      rather intimate

      b. avez /? étonné
      have   surprised
      d. seront /? impatientes
      will-be   impatient

Liaison is absent between two lexical words (indicated by '/' in (33)):

---

[5] The data are collected from Selkirk (1972) and from five native speakers of European French.

(33) a. des femmes / admirables   b.   les hommes / étaient fatigués.
          women   admirable   the men   were fatigued

Several proposals have been made to account for the domain of application of liaison. Some of them are reviewed here.

Using the End-based Approach, Selkirk (1986) argues that liaison applies obligatorily in a prosodic domain formed by placing a prosodic boundary at the right edge of each syntactic head. This domain is called the *Small Phonological Phrase*. That is, the end parameter setting chosen is]$_{Xhead}$ in French. Determiners, demonstratives, possessives, prepositions, auxiliary verbs and copulas are not heads, according to Selkirk, the same as prenominal adjectives and adverbs. Her analysis is exemplified by the following sentence:

(34) $_S[On_{VP}[[m'[a]]_{Aux}[souvent]_{AdvP}[amené]_V$ $_{PP}[[dans]_P[un][énorme]_{AP}[wagon]_N]_{NP}]]]]$
....]$_{Xhead}$ ....]$_{Xhead}$
(_____) (_____)

The problem with this analysis is that it cannot account for the differences among function words in degree of frequency of occurrence of liaison. Treating all function words alike, as invisible to prosodic boundary insertion (Selkirk (1984)), leads to the impossibility of capturing the distribution of liaison stated above.

De Jong (1990) acknowledged the existence of different degrees of frequency in the realization of liaison, depending on the grammatical category of the word whose final consonant was involved. He suggested that the difference between obligatory and optional liaison lies in the difference between 'real' function words and closed-category phrasal heads. 'Real' function words such as determiners, possessive pronouns, demonstratives, numerals and clitics are not heads of any kind, but specifiers or modifiers, whereas prepositions, auxiliaries, copulas are function words occupying the head position of a maximal projection (Prepositional Phrase and Verb Phrase, respectively). De Jong argues that the domain of obligatory liaison is the prosodic word, parsed from syntactic structure by picking out the right edge of every head. Since real function words are not heads, they will fall in the same prosodic word with an adjacent head. The domain of optional liaison would be the small phonological phrase (SPP), which is built inserting prosodic boundaries at the right end of every lexical head.

This analysis is still not satisfactory, because it assumes that determiners, possessive pronouns, numerals and quantifiers are specifiers or modifiers of some sort, not heads. However, for the past decade or so it has been standardly assumed in the syntactic theory De Jong adopts that these elements are heads, much like prepositions, copulas and auxiliaries. Therefore, this analysis cannot capture the different degrees of participation in liaison among functional heads.

The alternative analysis I propose is based on the theory of the mapping of feature chains as phonological domains explained in section 2.3. The feature chains in the lefthand column in (35) are interpreted as the phonological domains in the righthand column which are the domains of obligatory liaison:

(35)   D-N   ↔   [D N]
        Num-N   ↔   [Num N]
        V-D$_{Obj}$ ↔   [D V]
        V-D$_{Subj}$ ↔   [D V]   (or   T-D   ↔   [D T])

The chains D-N and Num-N represent the chains involving determiners, numerals and quantifiers and nouns (i.e., checking the categorial feature N and the φ-features of N by raising to D). The chain V-D$_{Obj}$ represents the checking of accusative case and φ-features between a verb and its object; V-D$_{Subj}$ represents the checking relation of the subject φ-features of V. Clitics are Ds, and hence they form part of the same phonological domain with verbs. Since the verb in French raises to T, the obligatory liaison between subject clitics and verbs could be interpreted as reflecting the feature chain T-D (checking of nominative case and the D-feature of T).

Degree modifiers do not form feature chains with following adjectives, because there is no feature checking relationship between them, and therefore they do not form domains of obligatory liaison. Copulas and auxiliaries are realizations of T-V chains themselves, i.e., they are verbs that raise to T, as their ability to appear apart from the main verb or the predicate attests (e.g., *Il a bien avancé* 'he has advanced well'):[6]

As for prepositions, I will assume that the chain P-D is not interpreted as a phonological constituent in French.

Before finishing the paper, an explanation should be provided for the frequent liaison occurring with monosyllabic forms of prepositions, degree modifiers, auxiliaries and copulas. Polysyllabic forms of these expressions make liaison only rarely. This behavior can be explained if we assume that these function words are clitics when they are monosyllabic. Monosyllabic function words often display clitic-like properties across languages, showing a close degree of phonological cohesion with adjacent heads. In the case of French, it could be suggested that cliticization forms a domain of optional application of liaison, possibly the clitic group. If this assumption is correct, it entails the conclusion that phonological domains defined prosodically and morphosyntactically may coexist in the grammar of a language, implying in turn that there may be two ways to derive phonological domains, by morphosyntactic relationships and by prosodic factors, and that languages may instantiate one or the other. I leave this issue open for further research.

---

[6] I consider the so-called auxiliary verbs of Basque as bundles of inflectional features (agreement, mood, tense). This bundle contains a root of an auxiliary verb, but it only surfaces as a vowel, and only one of the auxiliaries exists as an independent verb in modern Basque. I will treat them as features in T, rather than verbs.

4. Conclusion

In this paper I have demonstrated that there are phonological phenomena with domains of application that are directly sensitive to the morphosyntactic relationships holding between the morphemes containing the phonemes affected by the processes. The particular phenomena we have studied in this paper are Vowel Assimilation in Lekeitio Basque and French Liaison, that apply to phonemes appearing at the edges of morphemes or words in adjacency only when the morphemes are in a close degree of morphosyntactic cohesion. This cohesion is realized by the feature checking relationship holding between two syntactic heads. I proposed that the chains formed by feature checking relationships in syntax are also interpreted in the phonological component as phonological domains. I have shown that the theories of phonology-syntax interface developed so far are insufficient to account for the domains of application of processes of the sort presented in this paper. Further research will determine if and how prosodically defined entities may interact with the model proposed here.

References

Chomsky, Noam. 1995. *The minimalist program*. Cambridge, Mass.: MIT Press.

De Jong, Daan. 1990. The syntax-phonology interface and French liaison. *Linguistics* 28:57-88.

Elordieta, Gorka. 1997. *Morphosyntactic feature chains and phonological domains*. Doctoral dissertation, University of Southern California.

Hayes, Bruce. 1989. The prosodic hierarchy in meter, in Paul Kiparsky and Gilbert Youmans, eds., *Rhythm and Meter*, 201-260. San Diego: Academic Press.

Inkelas, Sharon. 1990. *Prosodic constituency in the lexicon*. New York: Garland Publishing.

Kaisse, Ellen. 1985. *Connected speech*. Orlando: Academic Press.

Nespor, Marina, and Irene Vogel. 1986. *Prosodic phonology*. Dordrecht: Foris.

Ortiz de Urbina, Jon. 1994. Verb-initial patterns in Basque and Breton. *Lingua* 94:125-153.

Ortiz de Urbina, Jon. 1995. Residual verb-second and verb-first in Basque, in Katalin E. Kiss, ed., *Discourse configurational languages*, 99-121. New York: Oxford University Press.

Selkirk, Elisabeth. 1972. The phrasal phonology of English and French. Doctoral dissertation, MIT.

Selkirk, Elisabeth. 1984. *Phonology and syntax: The relation between sound and structure*. Cambridge, Mass.: MIT Press.

Selkirk, Elisabeth. 1986. On derived domains in sentence phonology. *Phonology Yearbook* 3:371-405.

Selkirk, Elisabeth. 1995. The prosodic structure of function words.

Zec, Draga. 1993. Rule domains and phonological change. In *Phonetics and Phonology 4. Studies in lexical phonology*, ed. Sharon Hargus and Ellen Kaisse, 365-405. San Diego: Academic Press.

Zubizarreta, María Luisa, and Jean-Roger Vergnaud. In preparation. Primitive chains. Ms., University of Southern California.

Debuccalization with Preservation of Secondary Articulation

PAUL D. FALLON

Howard University

1. The Representation of Secondary Place

Recent work in feature geometry has seen a split between theories regarding the structure of secondary (or vowel-place) features.[1] Some work such as Sagey (1986) and Halle (1992, 1995) posits that secondary articulation features are structurally dependent upon primary place. For example, the feature [round] is a daughter of the Labial node, and [high], [low], and [back] are daughters of the Dorsal node, as shown in (1); articulator-free features, shown here as branching off the Root node for typographic reasons, are to be understood as additional daughters of the Root.

(1) Halle's Articulator-based Geometry

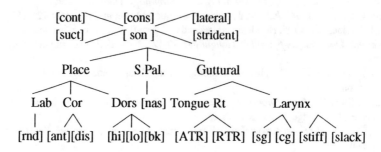

Other proposals such as Clements (1989, 1991), Herzallah (1990), Odden (1991), Hume (1992), Ní Chiosáin (1994), and Clements and Hume (1995)

---

1 I would like to thank David Odden, Elizabeth Hume, and Brian Joseph for comments made on Fallon (1998), from which this paper draws. I am also grateful to John Colarusso for providing data on Circassian, and for feedback from the audience of the 1996 LSA meeting (Fallon 1996).

hold that secondary place features are organized under a class node, often referred to as the Vocalic node, which is a sister to other consonantal place of articulation nodes. Work influenced by Clements divides the Vocalic node into V-Place, which describes secondary articulation for consonants, and primary place for vowels, and Aperture, which represents vowel height. This geometry is shown in (2):

(2) Clements and Hume's (1995) Constriction-based Feature Geometry

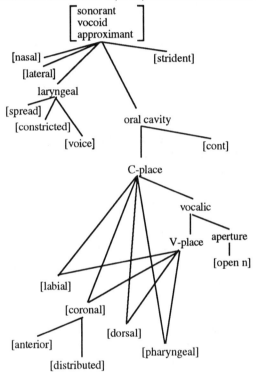

As Clements and Hume (1995:277) point out, the two models make different predictions regarding the behavior of vocoids. The model in (1) predicts that: (a) all vowels form a natural class with dorsal consonants; (b) the dorsal features [high, low, back] can function as single units in phonological rules, or all together, but not in a combination of two features spreading (though Halle (1995) has proposed that more than one terminal feature may spread in a phonological rule); (c) the dorsal consonants are opaque to rules spreading two or more vowel features (see also Steriade (1987)); and (d) all (supralaryngeal) consonants will be opaque to rules spreading lip rounding with one or more vowel features. In contrast, the constriction-based model (2) predicts that: (a) front vowels may form a natural class with coronal consonants, and back vowels, with dorsal consonants; (b) the V-place features, the aperture features, or both may function in phonological rules; (c) plain dorsal consonants will be transparent to rules spreading two or more vowel features; and (d) all plain consonants will be transparent to rules spreading lip rounding with one or more vowel features. Clements and Hume (1995) argue in detail to support their constriction-based model, using evidence for the independence of secondary articulation based on arguments from spreading. To their claims, I will add one more prediction, based upon evidence from delinking. The model in (1) predicts that deletion of Place will also delete secondary articulation, and that consonants with primary articulation and secondary articulation that is dependent upon that primary articulation will not preserve the secondary articulation should the primary place feature be delinked. The model in (2) predicts that loss of primary articulation does not necessarily entail loss of secondary articulation.

Evidence from Guddiri Hausa is offered which shows the preservation of secondary articulation (palatalization), but with debuccalization of oral dorsal articulation. This shows the inadequacy of the articulator-based model (1). Similar processes involving debuccalization with preservation of secondary articulation (diachronically in Circassian and synchronically in Irish) force a reconsideration of debuccalization as simply the delinking of Place, and some of the formalisms associated with this. Instead, based on the geometry in (2), Universal Grammar must permit at least three different parameters for debuccalization. Before examining them, I will review some of the different possibilities affecting secondary articulation.

2. Loss of Secondary Articulation

There are many phonological processes which may affect secondary articulation, including loss of secondary articulation, glide formation, and fusion.

First, a language may simply lose the secondary articulation. Mataco-Noctenes (Macro-Guaicuruan; Claesson (1994)) /kʷ/ is optionally delabialized in syllable-final position when preceded by a front vowel, e.g. /jikʷeh/ '(s)he goes for it' vs. [jik] '(s)he goes'.[2] The same type of change, though unrestricted, occurred in the development of Latin to French, e.g. Latin /kʷaːlis/ > Fr. /kɛl/ 'what, which'. The primary place features may

---

[2] In the spirit of Ladefoged (1990), all transcriptions conform where possible to the usage of the IPA.

also yield to the secondary places features so that a glide results: Proto-Oceanic *kʷ > w in Lenakel (Hume and Odden (1996), citing Rosenthall (1994)), and Proto-Uto-Aztecan *kʷ > w in Tubatulabal, Tarahumara, Guarijio, and in some conditions in Cahuilla, e.g. PUA *kʷasi 'tail' > /wasí/ in Tarahumara (Stubbs (1995)). Examples of both of these processes occurring in the same language may be found in Okrand (1989), who cites the changes between Proto-Costanoan (PC) *kʷ > Mutsun /k/ intervocalically, but *kʷ > /w/ preconsonantally:

(3) PC *ʔakʷ'es > /ʔak·es/ 'salt'
     PC *ʔakʷse > /ʔawse/ 'to salt'

Another relatively common change is a type of fusion, or what Clements (1989) terms 'tier promotion', in which V-place becomes C-place. In addition to the well-known examples in Indo-European (e.g. *kʷol-o > Greek polos 'pole'), and Romance (Latin quattuor > Rumanian patru 'four'), there are examples such as the development of Proto-Muskogean *kʷ to /b/ in Muskogean languages such as Choctaw, e.g. PM *jokʷala > Choctaw /obala/ 'behind' (Booker (1993)), and Proto-Uto-Aztecan (PUA) *kʷ to /b/ or /bʷ/ in many Sonoran languages, e.g. PUA *kʷis 'grasp, take' > Yaqui and Mayo /bʷise/ and Oʔodham /behi ~ behe/ 'get, take, acquire' (Stubbs (1995)).

There are at least two other possibilities involving secondary articulation: inertia and debuccalization. Inertia, a relatively uninteresting case, reflects lack of phonological change or alternation, e.g. PUA *kʷasa 'eagle' > Tubar /kʷasá/ 'large bird that fishes' (Stubbs (1995)), or Lillooet /s-qʷəm/ 'mountain' vs. /s-qʷə́m-qʷəm/ 'mountain range' (van Eijk (1985)). In debuccalization, a term coined by Hetzron (1972) and popularized by McCarthy (1988), an oral articulation is replaced by a glottal one. Within debuccalization, there are a few subtypes: secondary articulation is lost along with primary articulation, secondary articulation is preserved on another segment, or secondary articulation is preserved but primary articulation is glottalized.

One example of debuccalization with loss of secondary articulation is found in Kashaya, a Southern Pomo language (Buckley (1992)) which has several other debuccalization processes. Both plain and labialized uvulars debuccalize in syllable-final position. Obstruents preceding glottalized sonorants which are in onset position receive the feature [c.g.] in a process termed Glottal Transfer (4a) and (4c), while voiceless unaspirated stops are aspirated in coda position (4b). These processes feed uvular debuccalization:

(4) a. /kʰunuˑq-n̲o/→ kʰunuˑq'do → [kʰunuʔdo]
'they say it spoiled'
b. /ʰloqʷ-ʃe/ → hloqʷʰʃe → [lóhʃe]
'I wonder if it fell off'
c. /qaʃoˑqʷ-n̲o/→ qaʃoˑqʷ'do → [qaʃoʔdo]
'they say he's getting well'

Examples (4b) and (4c) show loss of both primary and secondary articulation in the debuccalization process (/qʷ/ → [h] or [ʔ]).

Sometimes, through an apparent process of fission, or simply transfer of secondary articulation, the secondary articulation survives on (or as) another segment, while the primary articulation debuccalizes. Such a process is found in Takelma, a Penutian language (Sapir (1922:44)). Before /x/, all velar stops (aspirated, labialized, voiceless, and ejective, and various combinations thereof) delete, except that the ejectives debuccalize to plain glottal stop. However, if a vowel follows /x/, labialization is transferred to that fricative to form /xʷ/. Example (3a) shows complete loss of the labialized pulmonic velar stop, while (3b) shows deletion of the most of the segment, but preservation of labialization on the velar fricative. The velar ejective is debuccalized to glottal stop in (3c), while debuccalization and labialization transfer are seen in (3d):

(5) a. /jẽkʷ-x-taʔ/ → [jẽxtaʔ] 'you will bite me'
b. /jẽkʷ-xinkʰ/ → [jẽxʷinkʰ] 'he will bite me'
c. /pa-tiník'-x/ → [pāatiníʔx] 'clouds spread out on high'
d. /lūkʷ'-xà/ → [lūʔxʷà] 'to trap'

Of greatest theoretical interest, however, and the central topic of this paper, is the preservation of secondary articulation and the loss of primary articulation through debuccalization, such that the result is a glottal stop or fricative with secondary articulation.

3. Debuccalization with preservation of secondary articulation

In Hausa, the Guddiri dialect has debuccalized the velar ejectives, which are preserved in the standard Kano dialect (Bagari (1982)). Debuccalization in initial position is shown in (6a), while medial position is shown in (6b):

(6)   Kananci   Guddiranci
a. k'eetaa   ʔeetaa   'wickedness'
   k'aunaa   ʔaunaa   'love'
   k'ootoo   ʔootoo   'feeding'

b. mak'ijii   maʔijii   'enemy'
    mak'ee   maʔee   'to cling'
    mak'alee   maʔalee   'to stick'
    ʃaak'u   ʃaaʔu   'suffocate'   (Bagari (1982:245))

The palatalized and labialized velar ejectives have also debuccalized in Guddiri, but have preserved their secondary articulation. Example (7a) shows the palatalized velars, and (7b), the labialized ones:

(7)   Kananci   Guddiranci
    a. kʲ'allee   ʔʲallee   'cloth'
        kʲ'afaa   ʔʲafaa   'a kind of bird'
        kʲ'ujaa   ʔʲujaa   'laziness'
    b. kʷ'aalaa   ʔʷaalaa   'to suffer'
        kʷ'alloo   ʔʷalloo   'ball'   (1982:246)

Halle has claimed that 'formally debuccalization renders the part of the feature tree that is dominated by the Place node invisible' (1995:14); in other words, Place is delinked, and features dominated by Place are delinked also. Articulator-based models cannot account for the preservation of palatalization on dorsals, since the feature characterizing palatalization, [-back], is dependent from Dorsal, and loss of Dorsal entails loss of [-back]. The constriction-based model, however, is perfectly suited to describing the change in Guddiri Hausa as the deletion of [dorsal] under C-place. A comparison of these models is shown below, where the failure of the articulator-based model can be seen in (8), in which delinking of Place yields the incorrect output, a plain glottal stop. (I adopt Kenstowicz's (1994) notation of the asterisk to indicate the major, or designated, articulator in lieu of the Sagey/Halle pointer arrow). In (9), if debuccalization may be viewed not only as delinking of C-place, but also individual place features, then the correct representation is derived. Even if the individual place feature Dorsal were delinked in (8), [-back] would still be erroneously deleted.

(8) Guddiranci Debuccalization in Articulator Geometry

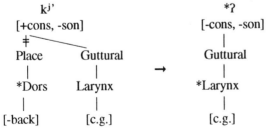

(9) Guddiri Debuccalization in Constriction Geometry

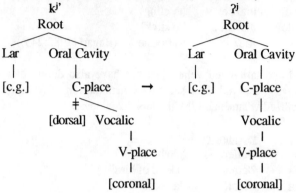

In sum, the Guddiri data demonstrate another shortcoming of the articulator-based model, and argue for the independence of primary and secondary articulation features. Data of this type also call into question Halle's (1995) account of debuccalization.

4. The Formalization of Debuccalization
4.1 Halle's Account of Debuccalization
Halle (1995:15-16) contains the most detailed formal account of debuccalization to date. Halle proposes redundancy rules (10a) and repairs (10b) and (10c):

(10)   a.   [-cont] → [+const gl]
              [+cont] → [+spread gl]
          b.   Upon debuccalization a segment becomes [-consonantal] and its AF [Articulator-Free] dependent features are deleted.
          c.   If the designated articulator is rendered inaccessible by the application of a rule, one of the articulators that remains accessible assumes the function of designated articulator. If no articulator remains accessible in a segment, the segment — but not its timing slot — is deleted.

The redundancy rules (10a) 'are implemented at an early stage in the derivation' and appear 'to hold of obstruents in many languages'. The repair rule (10b) converts the segment to a glide, and (c) eliminates the AF features except [-consonantal], 'since none of these can be stipulated in glides' (1995: 16).

4.2 Problems with Halle's Account

First, in terms of definitions, as mentioned above, Halle has claimed that 'debuccalization renders the part of the feature tree that is dominated by the Place node invisible'. As we have seen, debuccalization in Guddiri Hausa is not simply delinking of Place, but may also be of individual place features. I would also like to leave open the possibility of other types of debuccalization, such as delinking of Place, the Root node, and possibly the Oral Cavity node. I therefore propose the following revised definition of debuccalization:

(11)   Debuccalization is the loss of supraglottal articulation with retention of, or replacement by, a glottal gesture.

Second, Halle's redundancy rules (10a) are meant to capture the generalization that stops usually debuccalize to [ʔ], while fricatives debuccalize to [h] (Lass (1976)). Since Halle acknowledges that the redundancies hold of obstruents 'in many languages' he implies that these redundancies are not universal, which is indeed the case. In Kashaya, for example, a voiceless unaspirated uvular is aspirated in coda position, and then undergoes debuccalization to [h], not the predicted [ʔ] (see (4b) above). The Irish voiceless coronal stop, discussed below, debuccalizes to [h], as do pulmonic stops in Yucatec Maya (Straight (1976)). These are generally seen as the preservation of laryngeal features, which in some cases are implemented phonetically, not phonologically. I know of no exceptions to the generalization that (voiceless) fricatives (seen as redundantly specified for [spread glottis]) debuccalize to [h]; I have not found cases of ejective fricatives debuccalizing at all, let alone to [ʔ] (Fallon (1998)).

Third, in (10b) Halle claims that upon debuccalization, a segment becomes [-consonantal]. Halle's definition of [consonantal] is as follows:

(12) In producing a [+consonantal] phoneme, an articulator must make full or virtual contact with a stationary part of the vocal tract so as to create a cavity effectively closed at both ends; no such cavity must be created when [-consonantal] phonemes are produced. (1995:7).

He also notes that 'from an articulatory point of view [-sonorant] phonemes are a subset of [+consonantal] phonemes' (1995:7). There has been a complex debate on the status of glottals as glides or obstruents, but some researchers (Lass (1976), Besell (1992), Padgett (1991) inter al.) have argued that glottals are obstruents, and therefore [-sonorant], which by Halle's account means [+consonantal]. The glottal reflexes of uvular ejectives in

Circassian clearly act as [-sonorant], and thus this repair rule is not universal.

Correspondences between the Hakuči and Kabardian varieties of Circassian (Northwest Caucasian; Kuipers (1963), (1975)) suggest that Kabardian (and other varieties of Circassian) have debuccalized both the plain and rounded uvular ejectives, though as in Guddiri, labialization is preserved:

(13)   (data from Kuipers (1963:72))

Hakuči	Kabardian	
q'ɑ	ʔɑ	'hand'
qʷ'ɑ	ʔʷɑ	'speaking'

These correspondences led Kuipers (1975) to reconstruct plain and labialized uvular ejectives in Proto-Circassian (PC). Debuccalization is shown in (14) with reflexes from the West Circassian variety Bžedux; (14a) shows initial, and (14b), medial position.

(14)

	PC	Bžedux	Gloss
a.	*qʷ'ə	ʔʷə	'(cavity of the) mouth; orifice'
	*qʷ'a	ʔʷa	'pen, fold (for cattle)'
	*qʷ'əna	ʔʷəna	'nail'
b.	*naqʷ'ə	naʔʷə	'face'
	*pʰəqʷ'ə	pʰāʔʷə	'cap, hat'
	*ɬaqʷ'(a)	ɬāʔʷa	'to request'

Since labialization is preserved, the type of debuccalization must be individual place feature delinking. Although uvulars are commonly viewed as having branching [dorsal] and [pharyngeal] place (Elorrieta (1991)), which would entail two delinkings, I will adapt ideas discussed by Kenstowicz (1994) and based on proposals by McCarthy, to the constriction-based geometry of (2), in which the uvular stop will be represented with branching [dorsal] and [pharyngeal] under a Pharyngeal node, which is a sister node to Oral Place and Vocalic. The delinking would thus be represented as follows:

(15)

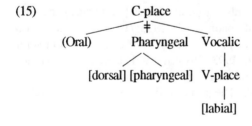

This representation allows us to preserve the prediction that individual place delinking will not affect more than one place of articulation (since otherwise two or more place features would need to be delinked). I know of no case in which debuccalization of say the labial /pʷ/ and velar /kʷ/ both become /ʔʷ/. However, as we saw in Guddiri Hausa, a single primary place Dorsal may debuccalize but retain more than one type of secondary articulation (labialization and palatalization).

In many Circassian varieties such as Bžedux, Abdax, and Kabardian, the debuccalized glottal stops clearly pattern as obstruents in inducing fortition of the second person verbal index. In Kabardian (Colarusso (1975), (1992), p.c., Fallon (1998)), the underlying form of the index is /w/, as shown in (16a). Before voiced stops, the glide undergoes fortition and becomes a voiced bilabial stop (16b), and before voiceless stops, it becomes a voiceless stop (16c). Before glottal stops, the glide also becomes a voiceless stop (16d). In contrast, the glides do not induce fortition (16e) (initial position is irrelevant):

(16)　a.　/ɸ-q'ə-w-a-d-ʁa-a-ɬaaʁʷ-aʁ-ç/ → [q'uwɛdʁɛɬàːʁʷáːç]
　　　　　'We showed it to you'

　　　b.　/sə-w-da-gʷə+ʃəʔa-aʁ-ç/ → [sɛbdogʷɪʃɛʔáːç]
　　　　　'I was joking with you'

　　　c.　/ɸ-q'ə-p-t-j-a-s-çə-aʁ-ç/ → [q'ɛpʰ.tʰeːs.çàːç]
　　　　　'I stole it from you'

　　　d.　/ɸ-q'ə-w-ʔʷə-a-w-ha/ → [q'ɛp.ʔʷɒ̀ː.hæ]
　　　　　'He is approaching you'

　　　e.　/w-j-aʁ-ç/ → [wujaːç]
　　　　　'You plastered it'

Since the glides /w, j/ may not occur as the second members of clusters, a biphonemic approach in which /ʔʷ/ is analyzed as /ʔw/ is improbable. There are also no glottalized sonorants, so a reanalysis as /w̰/ is also improbable, especially since spectrograms show that there is a stop gap, and not a laryngealized glide (Colarusso (1975)). Therefore, given the data above, I conclude that the Kabardian glottal stops are [-sonorant]. Since Halle (1992:210) excludes [-sonorant, -consonantal] on definitional grounds, we must accept the fact that at least some glottals pattern as obstruents, and revise Halle's definition of [consonantal] accordingly.

A fourth problem with Halle's account is also related to his view of [consonantal]. He proposes a constraint in which the designated articulator for [+consonantal] phonemes 'must be one of the three Place articulators, Labial, Dorsal or Coronal', while if the designated articulator is the Soft Palate, Tongue Root, or Larynx, the phoneme must be [-consonantal]

(1995:7). Recall that (10c) requires the designated articulator to shift to another ('accessible') articulator; in the case of debuccalization, it will be the Larynx. However, let us examine Irish debuccalization in order to illustrate this other problem.

Ní Chiosáin (1994) presents the following data from Irish, in which Coronals lenite (undergo debuccalization) in certain morphological environments. Note again that secondary articulation, palatalization, is preserved on the glottal. The plain coronals are shown in (17a), while the palatalized ones are shown in a variety of contexts in (17b-17d).

(17)   a.   tetʲiːn   'a cigarette'   mə hetʲiːn   'my cigarette'

              talə   'land'   mə halə   'my land'

              soləs   'light'   mə holəs   'my light'

              siːmʲ   'interest'   mə hiːmʲ   'my interest'

    b.   tʲinʲi   'a fire'   mə hʲinʲi   'my fire'

              sʲoːl   'sail'   mə hʲoːl   'my sail'

              sʲilʲiːnʲ   'a cherry'   mə hʲilʲiːnʲ   'my cherry'

    c.   sʲuːl   'to walk'   hʲuːl   'walked'

    d.   tʲoːrəntə 'limited'   roː hʲoːrəntə 'too limited'

              tʲuv/tʲuː 'thick'   roː hʲuv/hʲuː 'too thick'

In the articulator model, since palatalization is represented as [-back] under Dorsal, and Coronal is the designated articulator, the representation of /tʲ/ in Irish is as follows:

(18)

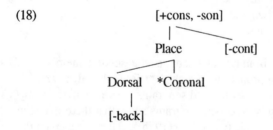

If we allow Halle's theory of debuccalization the possibility of delinking individual place features, and not simply Place, then Coronal would get delinked. The segment would lack a designated articulator, and so another accessible articulator would have to be assigned. The solution that Halle wants would be to assign Larynx under Guttural, since the debuccalized segment is glottal, yet why should new structure (Larynx) be inserted, while the Dorsal place feature is skipped over? The same would apply to the Guddiri data in (7b), in which Labial would remain a potentially accessible articulator after Dorsal deletes. Halle's theory needs a more principled basis on which to assign designated articulators when more than one is 'accessible'. The only explanation I believe Halle could offer is that since his version of debuccalization requires debuccalized segments to be [-consonantal], this feature specification is incompatible with designating Dorsal as the articulator, and so Larynx would have to be assigned the role. Nevertheless, the process in which new designated articulators are assigned must be more specific.

5. Other Types of Debuccalization

In this paper, I have presented evidence from three languages, Guddiri Hausa, Kabardian (and other Circassian languages), and Irish, that suggests a need to recognize a type of debuccalization in which primary place is deleted while secondary place is preserved. The evidence presented in (4) on Kashaya suggests the need to recognize another type of debuccalization in which secondary articulation is lost, but laryngeal features are preserved. In the constriction model, this would be represented as Oral Cavity delinking. Are there other types of debuccalization possible?

Lass (1976) suggested that just as schwa is often the 'reduction vowel', so too may glottal stop be the 'reduction stop', or a default stop. If a language were to debuccalize by delinking the root node, leaving only a timing slot, and if glottal stop were the default consonant, then this would suggest a third type of debuccalization. Several facts in English suggest that glottal stop may be the default. First, [ʔ] serves in careful speech as a marker of syllable boundaries when the second syllable is onsetless (Gimson and Cruttenden (1994:155)); it thus fills an otherwise empty onset position. Similarly, glottal stop may be inserted before any accented vowel to place emphasis on the word or morpheme. Secondly, glottal stop may be inserted before or coinciding with a voiceless stop or affricate in syllable-final position as a 'reinforcement of voiceless plosives' (Gimson and Cruttenden (1994)). Third, as is well known, voiceless stops may debuccalize to glottal stop in many dialects. Often overlooked, however, are dialects that debuccalize not only /t/ before syllabic nasals, as in *kitten*, but /d/ as well, in words like *couldn't*. This process entails an overriding of the feature specification for [voice] with [c.g.], something redundancy or default rules do not typically do. Thus I find it plausible that debuccalization in English is at the level of the root node, and not simply the Oral Cavity node.

The constriction model of feature geometry predicts the existence of a final type of debuccalization: delinking of C-place. This type of debuccalization is extremely difficult to test since the only difference between C-place delinking and Oral Cavity delinking hinges on the behavior of [continuant], a feature whose status on glottals is highly controversial

202 / PAUL D. FALLON

6. Conclusion

This paper has provided additional evidence for the independence of primary and secondary place features from delinking rules. We have seen in Guddiri Hausa, Circassian, and Irish that preservation of secondary place is still possible although primary articulation may be lost. Such facts force us to amend several of the proposals in Halle (1995) regarding debuccalization. Specifically, (1) his proposed redundancy rules, while common, are not universal; (2) debuccalization of segments does not automatically entail that they become glides, since evidence from Circassian showed the glottal stops pattern as obstruents; (3) the behavior of glottals as obstruents necessitates a revision of Halle's definition of [consonantal] (a feature which Hume and Odden (1996) argue should be abolished); (4) the basis for assigning designated articulators is currently vague when secondary place features are accessible; and finally (5) debuccalization cannot simply be seen as delinking of Place; instead, we must recognize at least Oral Cavity (or Place) delinking, and individual place feature delinking. The constriction-based model of feature geometry also suggests two other possible types of debuccalization: delinking of the Root node, and delinking of C-place, both of which need further empirical verification.

References

Bagari, Dauda M. 1982. Some Aspects of Guddiranci (The Guddiri Dialect of Hausa), In H. Jungraithmayr, ed., *The Chad Languages in the HamitoSemitic-Negritic Border Area*, 244-253. Berlin: Verlag von Dietrich Reimer.

Bessell, Nicola J. 1992. The Typological Status of /ʔ,h/. *Papers from the 28th Regional Meeting of the Chicago Linguistic Society 1992*, ed. by Costas Canakis et al., 56-71. Chicago: CLS.

Booker, Karen M. 1993. More on the Development of Proto-Muskogean *kʷ. *International Journal of American Linguistics* 59.405-415.

Buckley, Eugene. 1992. *Theoretical Aspects of Kashaya Phonology and Morphology*. Doctoral dissertation, University of California, Berkeley. (Published 1994 by CSLI).

Claesson, Kenneth. 1994. A Phonological Outline of Mataco-Noctenes. *International Journal of American Linguistics* 60.1-38.

Clements, George N. 1989. A Unified Set of Features for Consonants and vowels. Cornell University MS.

_____. 1991. Vowel height in Bantu languages. *Proceedings of the 17th meeting of the Berkeley Linguistics Society*, ed. by Kathleen Hubbard et al., 25-64. Berkeley, CA: Berkeley Linguistics Society.

_____ and Elizabeth V. Hume. 1995. The Internal Structure of Speech Sounds. In J. Goldsmith, ed., *The Handbook of Phonological Theory*, 245-306. Cambridge, Mass.: Blackwell Publishers.

Colarusso, John. 1975. *The Northwest Caucasian Languages: A Phonological Survey*. Doctoral dissertation, Harvard University. (Published 1988 by Garland).

_____. 1992. *A Grammar of the Kabardian Language*. Calgary: University of Calgary Press.

Elorrieta, Jabier. 1991. The Feature Specification of Uvulars. *WCCFL* 10.139-149. Stanford: CSLI Publications.

Fallon, Paul D. 1996. Three Parameters of Debuccalization. Paper presented at the 70th Annual Meeting of the Linguistic Society of America. Los Angeles.

_____. 1998. *The Synchronic and Diachronic Phonology of Ejectives*. Doctoral dissertation, The Ohio State University.

Gimson, A.C. and Alan Cruttenden. 1994. *Gimson's Pronunciation of English*, 5th edn. London: Edward Arnold.

Halle, Morris. 1992. Phonological Features. In W. Bright, ed., *Oxford International Encyclopedia of Linguistics*, vol. 3, 207-212. Oxford: Oxford University Press.

Halle, Morris. 1995. Feature Geometry and Feature Spreading. *Linguistic Inquiry* 26.1-46.

Herzallah, Rukayyah S. 1990. *Aspects of Palestinian Arabic Phonology: A Non-linear Approach*. Doctoral dissertation, Cornell University. (Published 1990 as *Working Papers of the Cornell Phonetics Laboratory* 4).

Hetzron, Robert. 1972. *Ethiopian Semitic: Studies in Classification*. Manchester, UK: Manchester University Press.

Hume, Elizabeth. 1992. *Front Vowels, Coronal Consonants and their Interaction in Nonlinear Phonology*. Doctoral dissertation, Cornell University. (Published 1994 by Garland).

_____ and David Odden. 1996. Reconsidering [consonantal]. *Phonology* 13.345-376.

Kenstowicz, Michael. 1994. *Phonology in Generative Grammar*. Cambridge, Mass.: Blackwell Publishers.

Kuipers, Aert H. 1963. Proto-Circassian Phonology: An Essay in Reconstruction. *Studia Caucasica* 1.56-92.

204 / PAUL D. FALLON

_____. 1975. *A Dictionary of Proto-Circassian Roots*. Lisse: Peter de Ridder Press.

Ladefoged, Peter. 1990. The Revised International Phonetic Alphabet. *Language* 66.550-552.

Lass, Roger. 1976. On the Phonological Characterization of [ʔ] and [h], in R. Lass, *English Phonology and Phonological Theory: Synchronic and Diachronic Studies*. Cambridge: Cambridge University Press.

McCarthy, John J. 1988. Feature Geometry and Dependency: A Review. *Phonetica* 43.84-108.

Ní Chiosáin, Máire. 1994. Irish Palatalisation and the Representation of Place Features. *Phonology* 11.89-106.

Odden, David. 1991. Vowel Geometry. *Phonology* 8.261-289.

Okrand, Marc. 1989. More on Karkin and Costanoan. *International Journal of American Linguistics* 55.254-258.

Padgett, Jaye. 1991. *Stricture in Feature Geometry*. Doctoral dissertation, University of Massachusetts, Amherst. (Published 1995 by CSLI).

Rosenthall, Sam. 1994. *Vowel/Glide Alternations in a Theory of Constraint Interaction*. Doctoral dissertation, University of Massachusetts, Amherst.

Sagey, Elizabeth Caroline. 1986. *The Representation of Features and Relations in Non-linear Phonology*. Doctoral dissertation, MIT. (Published 1990 by Garland).

Sapir, Edward. 1922. The Takelma Language of Southwestern Oregon. In F. Boas, ed., *Handbook of American Indian Languages, Part 2*, 1-296. Washington, DC: Government Printing Office.

Steriade, Donca. 1987. Locality Conditions and Feature Geometry. *NELS* 17.595-617. Amherst, Mass.: GLSA.

Straight, H. Stephen. 1976. *The Acquisition of Maya Phonology: Variation in Yucatec Child Language*. (Garland Studies in American Indian Linguistics). New York: Garland Publishing.

Stubbs, Brian Darrel. 1995. The Labial Labyrinth in Uto-Aztecan. *International Jorunal of American Linguistics* 61.396-422.

van Eijk, Jan. 1985. *The Lillooet Language: Phonology, Morphology, Syntax*. Doctoral dissertation, University of Amsterdam. (Published by the UBC Press).

Syntax of Negative Inversion in Non-Standard English

JOHN FOREMAN
University of California, Los Angeles

1. Introduction[1]

In their study of African American Vernacular English (AAVE), Labov et al. (1968) provide the first description of the phenomenon of Negative Inversion (NI), an example of which is given in (1):

(1)   Ain't nobody complainin' but you, man.
        "Nobody is complainin' but you."   (ex. 351, M, 16)[2]

---

[1] I would like to thank the WCCFL XVII attendees and the UCLA Syntax-Semantics group for all of their useful and interesting comments concerning this paper. I would also like to thank Javier Gutierrez-Rexach, Manuel Español-Echevarría, Ed Keenan and Tim Stowell for their helpful discussion of various points in this paper. Any errors that remain are solely the responsibility of the author.
[2] With each documented example, I cite the original work (i.e. Labov et al. (1968)), including page number and/or example number, if it is not clear from the surrounding text. In addition, if

NI sentences have the subject-Aux inverted word order of *yes/no* questions. However, they are interpreted as declarative sentences, as can be seen in the gloss of (1), and receive the falling intonation of a declarative. Labov et al. (1968) give two possible derivations for NI sentences. Some NI sentences they derive from underlying Existential sentences. Thus (1) would be related to *It ain't nobody complainin' but you man* where *it* is used as the Existential expletive pronoun in AAVE. (1) is then derived by deleting the dummy-*it* (or perhaps, *it* fails to be inserted). Other NI sentences they derive by raising the Aux over the subject and into what in modern terms would be C. In such an analysis, (1) would then be derived from *Nobody ain't complainin' but you, man* by having the Aux, *ain't*, raise over the subject into C.

This present paper will introduce new data from another non-standard variety of English spoken in western Texas. In contrast to Labov et al.'s study, my investigation of West Texas English (WTE) focuses more on native speaker judgements than on spontaneous speech production. I will compare this dialect to AAVE as described in Labov et al. (1968) and more recently in Sells et al. (1996) and argue that many NI sentences are not derived from Existentials or by Aux to C movement. Rather, I will establish that NI sentences are more closely related to such Standard English (SE) sentences as *Not just anybody can run for President* and *Not every student has finished the test*. Such sentences and their NI counterparts can best be accounted for by the introducing a second Negative Phrase (NegP$_2$) into the clause structure, in addition to the Negative Phrase (NegP$_1$) first proposed in Pollock (1989). This NegP$_2$ is located above AgrS-P and is the position into which both *not* in the SE sentences moves and *ain't* and other Aux's move in non-standard NI sentences.

2. West Texas English

After Labov et al.'s initial description of NI in AAVE, the phenomenon was also documented in other non-standard varieties of English. For example, Feagin (1979) confirms the existence of NI in Southern, rural, white speech in her investigation of Alabama English (AE).

The dialect presented in this paper, West Texas English (WTE), also exhibits the NI construction:

(2)   Ain't nobody doin' nothin' wrong.
         "Nobody's doing anything wrong."

---

it is available, I include biographical information such as the sex (M/F) and age of the speaker. All other non-standard English examples are based on judgements from my WTE consultants.

Sentence (2) has the NI characteristics of a question-like word order in which the Aux precedes the subject coupled with a declarative rather than an interrogative interpretation. It should be noted that, in fact, most NI sentences, (2) included, are, based on the surface word order alone, ambiguous between declaratives and interrogatives. That is, (2) and other NI sentences, could be read as a statement or a question. However, in speech, the intonational information will clearly disambiguate between these two possibilities.

The corresponding non-inverted word order can also be obtained:

(3)   Nobody ain't doin' nothin' wrong.
        "Nobody is doing anything wrong."

It is not true that all of the non-inverted forms of NI sentences are acceptable in WTE. Generally, if only the subject and the Aux bear negative morphology then speakers prefer the inverted word order:

(4)   a.   *None of the students ain't done their homework.
        b.   Ain't none of the students done their homework.

If further material bearing negative morphology is permitted in the clause, then its presence after the Aux can license the pre-verbal negative subject, making the non-inverted word order acceptable. The presence of *nothin'* in (3), then, is crucial to that sentence's acceptability. Compared with examples from Labov et al. (1968) and based on the discussion in Sells et al. (1996), this restriction on non-inverted sentences does not hold in AAVE.

Sentences (1)-(3) also display another feature, Negative Concord (NC), which is common among non-Standard English dialects. NC is the repetition of negative morphology at various points in a clause to indicate that the clause is negated. Sentence (4b) has two morphological instances of negation, *-n't* and *nobody*, (sentences (2) and (3) have three each), which can appear alone in other clauses as the sole indication of negation. In (4b) though, they are collectively interpreted as only a single instance of negation.

Although all three of the dialects under discussion exhibit both NI and NC, as Feagin (1979) documents, NC is not a necessary condition to license NI:

(5)   Dudn't anybody seem to understand...   (p. 215, ex. 73, F, 61)

Feagin found examples of this kind spoken by both upper and working class consultants. Such sentences are also accepted by my WTE consultants.

Comparing (2) and (3) above suggests that some element, such as the subject, *nobody*, or the Aux, *ain't*, is undergoing additional movement in at least one of these sentences. Either *ain't* is raising in (2) over the subject, but isn't in (3), or *nobody* undergoes more movement in (3) than in (2). As discussed below, both analyses have been proposed.

3. Previous Analyses

As noted above, Labov et al. (1968) provide two different syntactic derivations for NI sentences. One analysis derives NI sentences from underlying Existential sentences. To get the NI sentence the expletive pronoun is deleted (or perhaps a null expletive pronoun is inserted instead of an overt one). The second analysis for NI sentences generates them from sentences in which the subject moves up into its normal subject position (which here we are taking to be Spec of AgrS-P). The Aux then moves over the subject and into C. More recently, Sells et al. (1996) have proposed an analysis in which all NI sentences are derived with an unfilled Spec, AgRS-P. In such an analysis, the subject of the sentence remains in its original VP-internal position.

A question that arises with respect to Labov et al.'s (1968) analyses is why can the expletive be deleted in the Existential derivation and why can the Aux raise in the auxiliary inversion derivation. In particular, why should these processes be limited to negative sentences? As Sells et al. (1996) observe, positive correlates of the NI sentences above are not acceptable:

(6)   a.   *Is somethin' happenin'.
        b.   *Is everybody here.   (cf. (15) below)

In positive sentences, an expletive subject cannot be omitted nor can the Aux be raised over the subject (without forming a question).

Labov et al. (1968) do not discuss directly why the dummy subject cannot be left out of positive Existential sentences. However, to explain the Aux to C raising the idea of an 'affective' trigger is borrowed from Klima (1964). Presumably, this 'affective' trigger is also meant to allow expletive pronoun deletion.

Labov et al. (1968:285) describe NI sentences as being "emphatic, excited, and strongly affective" in character. Although NI sentences are often emphatic, it does not seem that such pragmatic features are enough to explain NI sentence structures.

As noted in Sells et al. (1996), if inversion is driven solely by some 'affective' component, it is unclear why the same emphatic trigger could not be applied to positive sentences as in (6). Surely statements about *somethin'* or *everybody* can play the same pragmatic roles as those about *nobody*.

In WTE, not all NI sentences are terribly emphatic in nature. As discussed below sometimes inversion is driven for scope reasons (when the subject is positive). Compare (7a) and (b) below:

(7)   a.   Ain't very many people read your book.
         b.   Not many people have read your book.

Furthermore, as noted above in Section 2, NI often occurs in WTE to allow Negative Concord between the Aux and subject. Therefore, many NI sentences are no more emphatic or 'affective' than are sentences containing Negative Concord. While NC may itself be emphatic in character, the 'affective' trigger for NC is not enough to force Aux raising:

(8)   a.   I ain't seen nobody today.
         b.   *Ain't I seen nobody today.

Thus, it seems the explanation of NI and its restriction to sentences containing a negative Aux will have to be syntactic rather than pragmatic in nature. The sections below will investigate how these analyses might be applied to WTE.

3.1 The Existential Analysis

For sentences involving a form of *be,* Labov et al. (1968) propose that the apparent inversion stems from a derivation from existential-*there* sentences. A sentence like *Ain't nothin' happenin'* would be derived from a sentence like *It ain't nothin' happenin'*. (*It* is used as the Existential pronoun in AAVE rather than *there* which is used in SE and WTE.) To obtain the NI word order, the expletive *it* is simply deleted.

Following Sells et al. (1996) and putting this analysis in modern terms, an NI sentence derived in such a fashion would have the following structure as in (a) and be derived from a structure as in(9b):

(9)   a. $[_{AGRS-P} \varnothing$ ain't $[_{VP}$ nothin' happenin']]
         b. $[_{AGRS-P}$ It ain't $[_{VP}$ nothin' happenin']]

On such an analysis, the structures of the WTE NI sentence in (2) and its corresponding non-inverted sentence, (3), would be:

(10)   a. $[_{AGRS-P} \varnothing$ ain't $[_{VP}$ nobody doin' $[_{DP}$ nothin' wrong]]]
         b. $[_{AGRS-P}$ Nobody ain't $[_{VP}$ doin' $[_{DP}$ nothin' wrong]]]

In the existential analysis, the NI subject in (11a) does not move out of its VP-internal position. The non-inverted word order in (11b) is generated by moving the subject up into the normal subject position, Spec, AgrS-P, over the Aux.

Labov et al. recognize that an existential analysis cannot account for all instances of NI because of sentences such as:[3]

(11)   a.   Don't nobody break up a fight.   (ex. 363, 12 years old)
            "Nobody breaks up fights."
        b.   Can't nobody beat 'em.   (ex. 367, 11 years old)
            "Nobody can beat them."

Since the above sentences do not contain a form of the verb *be* they cannot be derived from Existential sentences. The same is true for WTE as well.

WTE allows essentially any Aux which can bear negation to participate in this construction – *ain't* (which can stand for both *be+n't* as in (2) and perfective *have+n't* as in (7a)), *wudn't* (SE *wasn't*), *don't*, *didn't*, *won't*, *wouldn't*, *cain't* (WTE variation of *can't*), *couldn't*, *shouldn't* and *hadn't* as shown below:

(12)   a.   Wudn't no more than ten people allowed in at a time.
            "No more than ten people were allowed in at a time."
        b   Don't nobody live there.
            "Nobody lives there."
        c.   Didn't nowhere near a thousand people go to that concert.
            "Nowhere near a thousand people went to that concert."
        d.   Won't none of the students go to the party.
            "None of the students will go to the party."
        e.   Wouldn't no gentleman act like that.
            "A gentleman wouldn't act like that."
        f.   Cain't no dog but Ol' Blue do that trick.

---

[3] Although they propose a second solution, Labov et al. (1968) still need the Existential Analysis for such sentences as:

(i)   a.   Ain't no black Santa Claus.   (Sells et al. (1996), ex. 36)
       b.   Ain't nothin' you can do for 'em.   (Labov et al. (1968) ex. 358)

These sentences only allow an analysis in which an expletive subject pronoun has been omitted and they cannot be derived by additional Aux movement (whether it is Aux to C or NegP₂). This again raises the question of why the expletive pronoun can be omitted in negative Existentials but not positive ones. A question for which the answer remains unclear.

In WTE, there is variation among speakers on the acceptability of (ia). Some find it marginal, but none completely reject it. Sentence (ib) is generally accepted. This poses the same question for WTE as for AAVE as to why negative Existentials allow expletive deletion while positive Existentials do not.

"No dog but Ol' Blue can do that trick."
g.   Couldn't neither of 'em fit in the car.
     "Neither of them could fit in the car."
h.   Shouldn't nobody be allowed to act like that.
     "Nobody should be allowed to act like that
i.   Hadn't nary a soul set foot in that house, 'til Dave moved in
     "Not a soul had set foot in that house, until Dave moved in."

Note the lack of agreement between the Aux and subject, particularly in sentences (13a) and (13b). The loss of overt agreement only occurs with negative Aux's. Positive ones in WTE generally follow the agreement pattern of SE. The lack of overt agreement is not restricted to the realm of NI sentences, but extends to non-inverted sentences as well:

(13)   a.   We wudn't doin' nothin'.
       b.   He don't like nobody.

These sentences in (14) and in (8a) show that the lack of overt agreement does not affect the assignment of subjective Case, as it does in Belfast English (see Henry (1995)). The subject pronouns such as *I, we,* and *he,* which have distinct subjective forms are still licensed with negative Aux's, just as they are with modals which also don't show agreement morphology. This indicates then that subjective Case is still assigned in the presence of negative auxiliaries, even if it is not reflected in overt agreement on the Aux.

Other data, besides the NI with non-*be* Aux's, also indicate that the Existential analysis cannot account for all NI sentences. Even some NI sentences which contain an overt form of *be* in them cannot be accounted for in this manner.

For instance, Labov et al. describe NI sentences with positive subjects. Although both of their examples have *many* as the subject determiner, upon further investigation, it becomes clear that in WTE NI can occur with a range of positive subjects in addition to *many*:

(14)   a.   Didn't many people live there then.
       b.   Won't more than 5 people fit in that car.
       c.   Cain't all o' ya go at once.

Some of these positive subjects, however, cannot occur in existential *there* contexts. For example, subjects with universal determiners such as *every*, and with proportional determiners like *half*, can occur in NI constructions:

(15)   a.   Ain't every student here yet.
           b.   Didn't half the students do their homework.

but cannot occur in existential *there* contexts:

(16)   a.   *Was there every student in the garden?
                (Keenan (1996) ex. 45)
           b.   *Are there half the students outside?

Therefore, neither of the sentences in (15) including (15a) whose Aux is a form of *be* can be associated with existential *there* sentences.

     In addition to the above, there is further evidence that an Existential analysis, or indeed, any analysis relying on a VP-internal subject, such as in Sells et al. (1996), cannot account for all NI sentences. Tag questions provide evidence that (underlying) subjects of NI are in fact in the normal syntactic subject position, Spec, AgrS-P.

     If NI sentences are derived by eliminating expletive pronouns from Spec, AgrS-P, then we would expect the expletive to resurface in tag questions. However, tags of NI sentences show an agreement with the true subject of the NI sentence, instead of introducing a dummy pronoun:

(17)   a.   Ain't nobody doin' nothin' wrong, are they?
           b.   *Ain't nobody doin' nothin' wrong, is/are there/it?
           c.   Ain't no man gonna cheat on a woman like that, is he?
           d.   *Ain't no man gonna cheat on a woman like that, is there?

Sentences such as (17a) and (17c) indicate that the 'underlying' subjects of these NI sentences are in a position to serve as the antecedent for the tag pronoun. This is not true of 'underlying' subjects in Existential *there* sentences in SE:

(18)   There isn't anybody home, is there/(*are they)?

Furthermore, NI sentences which can only be analyzed as coming from Existential sentences, such as those discussed in footnote 3, show that in tag formation, the Existential pronoun can be recovered:

(19)   a.   Ain't no black Santa Clause   (Sells et al. (1996), ex. 36)
           b.   Ain't no black Santa Clause, is there?

For WTE speakers who find (19a) grammatical, they form the tag question with an overt Existential pronoun as seen in (19b). This clearly indicates that when NI sentences are derived from Existentials, the expletive pronoun is required in the tag questions. This is not the case for the sentences of (17) indicating that these sentences are not related to Existential ones.

A tag question only agrees with that element that is actually occupying the syntactic subject position in the surface string, and does not agree with any 'underlying' subjects that may be in a position other than surface subject position. Sentences like (17a) and (17c) indicate that in WTE that the 'underlying' subject does indeed occupy the surface subject position.

This counters the Existential Analysis which suggests that the NI word order is derived by the failure of the underlying subject to move up. The tag evidence instead indicates that the underlying subject has moved up to the subject position in both the non-inverted and inverted sentences.

Similar evidence holds for sentences without a *be* form of Aux:

(20)   I guess, cain't no man live forever, can he?

Again, this suggests that *no man* is in the surface subject position. This is not compatible then with any analysis, such as in Sells et al. (1996), which derives all NI sentences with the subject remaining in a VP-internal position in the surface string.

This argues then that the subject, *nobody* in (2) and (3), is undergoing the same amount of movement in an NI sentence, like (2), as it is in the corresponding non-inverted sentence, like (3). Therefore, the NI sentences must be arising from some other mechanism than failure of the underlying subject to raise. The other option then is that the Aux is moving higher in the NI sentences than in the non-NI ones.

3.2 The Aux-to-C Analysis
Labov et al. (1968) propose a different analysis for NI sentences which don't have an overt form of *be* in them, such as

(21)   a.   Cain't nobody do nothin' right.
         b.   Don't nobody like that.

They propose that the Aux undergoes additional movement, in a parallel fashion to questions. In modern terms, again following Sells et al. (1996), they propose that the Aux in NI is moving into the head of CP.

Although NI sentences have identical word order to questions, there are essential differences between the two. Negative questions don't require that negation move up to C with the modal:

(22)   a.   Won't John be going to the party?
         b.   Will John not be going to the party?

For NI sentences, however, negation must move with the modal:

(23) a. Won't none of the students go to the party.
      b. *Will none of the students not go to the party.
      c. *Will none of the students go to the party.

One possible explanation is that perhaps NI inversions are driven by a negative operator in C, just as question inversions are described as being driven by a question operator.

In fact, SE has a form of 'negative' inversion which can be analyzed in exactly this way. It behaves in a parallel fashion to *wh*-question formation. Some negative-like phrase, such as *scarcely, hardly, never, not often, seldom,* etc, raises to Spec, CP and the Aux raises into C:

(24) a. Not a word did he say.
      b. Rarely have I seen such insolence.

However, as Sells et al. (1996) observe, there is strong evidence that NI does not share the same structure as questions and SE 'negative' inversion. In all three non-standard dialects under discussion, there are examples of NI sentences in embedded structures with overt *that* complementizers:

(25) a. I know a way that can't nobody start a fight.
          (AAVE, Labov et al. ex. 370, 12)
      b. She told me that wasn't nobody gon run her out tonight.
          (AE, Feagin, p. 270, Female, 65)
      c. She loves the fact that don't nobody like her. (WTE/AAVE[4])

Subject-Aux inverted questions generally cannot appear in complement clauses with an overt *that*, particularly if it is a noun complement clause (cf. 25c). The same holds for the SE 'negative inversion' as can be seen in the following:

(26) a. ?*I know that not until he came to the U.S. did they decide to get married.
      b. *She loves the fact that never would he marry another.

The complementizer *that* is traditionally analyzed as occupying the head of CP to the exclusion of other material in that head position, including the raised auxiliaries of questions. The evidence of (26) indicates

---

[4] Janine Ekulona (p.c.) helped me work up this example and helped with establishing grammaticality judgements for it in AAVE.

then that although the negative Aux may be moving more in NI sentences than in non-inverted sentences, it is not moving into the head of CP.

A more substantial difference between WTE NI and questions and SE 'negative inversion' is which kinds of subjects the auxiliary is allowed to raise over. Both questions and SE 'negative inversion' allow the Aux to raise over Definite subjects:

(27)   a.   No sooner had Jack got in the shower than the phone rang.
            b.   Never would I do such a thing.
            c.   Are the teachers going to the party?
            d.   Isn't he here yet?

However, this is not the case for WTE NI. In NI sentences, the negative Aux cannot precede a Definite subject (Note crucially that the following sentences are bad on a declarative reading, but may be fine as questions.):

(28)   a.   *Ain't Jack doin' nothin' wrong.
            b.   *Wouldn't I do that.
            c.   *Didn't the teachers go to the party.

4. The NegP$_2$ Analysis

Indeed, it is not questions and SE 'negative inversion' which WTE NI most closely resembles. Instead, it patterns very much like SE *not*, which can appear before the subject in certain restricted contexts. Note the following parallels:

(29)   a.   Not many people went to the party.
            b.   Didn't many people go to the party.
            c.   Not everybody finished their homework.
            d.   Didn't everybody finish their homework.
            e.   Not more than three people will be allowed in at a time.
            f.   Won't more than three people be allowed in at a time.

In each of the above sentences in (29), both SE and WTE, the scope relations between negation and the quantified subject are unambiguous. In each, the negation must scope over the subject. This is not always the case when negation appears in its 'normal' verbal position as can be seen in such familiar examples as:

(30)   Everybody didn't go to the party.

Sentence (30) is ambiguous between the negation wide scope ("It is not the case that every person went to the party") and the negation narrow scope ("For all people, none went to the party.").

This suggests then that in the sentences of (32), the Aux (and SE *not*) are raising for scope reasons. This movement can be accounted for with a Negative Phrase above the subject position of these sentences, that is above AgrS-P. I label this NegP₂ to distinguish it from the NegP originally proposed in Pollock (1989).

It is this position in which *not* appears in the SE sentences of (29) and is the position to which the Negative Aux moves in NI structures. Thus, a sentence *Cain't nobody do that* would have the following structure:

(31)   [NEGP [NEG Cain't$_i$] [AGRS-P nobody t$_i$ [NEGP [NEG t$_i$] [VP do that]]]]

Here, the subject, *nobody* has raised out its VP internal position into the syntactic subject position, Spec, AgrS-P. The Negative Aux has then raised over it into the head of NegP.

This structure explains the ease with which NI sentences can occur with an overt *that* complementizer in an embedded clause, as seen in the sentences of (25). This structure also ensures that this inversion only takes place when the Aux bears negation and explains why there are no positive inversion sentences like those in (6).

Of course the restriction against Definite subjects in NI sentences still needs to be explained. Again, there is a parallel between the behavior of NI sentences and SE sentences with a pre-subject *not*:

(32)   a.   *Ain't Jack seen the baby yet.
        b.   *Not Jack has seen the baby yet.
        c.   *Won't the student answer the question.
        d.   *Not the student will answer the question.
        e.   *Cain't their dogs do that.
        f.   *Not their dogs can do that.

Kiss (1996) looking in part at just this kind of data in SE, provides an account of this asymmetry which is easily extended to the WTE sentences. She employs the Referential Projection (RefP) developed in Beghelli and Stowell (1997). They devise RefP as a high LF scope position for Definite DPs (and other Group-Denoting QPs which are referentially independent). Instead of using it as an LF position, Kiss (1996) introduces RefP as a surface position to which Definite DP subjects, among others, must overtly raise. In addition, as a surface position, RefP must be placed below CP instead of above it as in Beghelli and Stowell present it.

I place RefP above NegP₂ which is itself above AgrS-P. If Definite subjects are required to move up to RefP in the surface string (perhaps to check an Existential Feature after receiving Case) then the unacceptability of sentences like those in (32) can be explained. Definite subjects, such as *Jack, that student, John's dog, the ten mice, she, they,* etc. cannot appear below NegP$_2$, and thus cannot appear after *not* or *ain't,* because the Definite DPs must appear in RefP which is above NegP$_2$. Thus, as can be seen in the structure below, in the sentence *John cain't do that,* if the Definite subject *John* is required to move to RefP then *John* cannot appear below negation and the word order **Cain't John do that.* can not be derived:

(33)   [$_{REFP}$ John$_j$ [$_{NEGP}$ [$_{NEG}$ cain't$_i$] [$_{AGRS\text{-}P}$ t$_j$ [$_{AGRS}$ t$_i$] [$_{VP}$ do that]]]]

The only way that such a word order can be derived is if the Aux moves beyond NegP$_2$ into CP. But such a movement is only driven by other features, such as question operators, which will change the interpretation of the sentence.

Other DPs only raise as high as AgrS-P, and can therefore occur below *–n't* and under its scope, when the negative Aux moves to the head of NegP$_2$:

(34)   a.   [$_{NEGP}$ [$_{NEG}$ don't $_i$] [$_{AGRS\text{-}P}$ many people t$_i$ [$_{VP}$ know that]]]
        b.   [$_{AGRS\text{-}P}$ Many people [$_{AGRS}$ don't$_i$] [$_{NEGP}$ [$_{NEG}$ t$_i$] [$_{VP}$ know that]]]

The NegP in (34a) represents my NegP$_2$ while the NegP in (34b) is NegP$_1$. Kiss (1996) only has one NegP projection which is placed between AgrS-P and RefP. In contrast, I retain the original NegP projection below TP, which was first suggested in Pollock (1989). It seems necessary to continue to account for *do*-support facts, even with subjects that only need to raise as far as AgrS-P. Additionally, in both SE and WTE, both Negative Phrases can be filled:

(35)   a.   Ain't everybody NOT going to the party.
        b.   Not everybody ISN'T going to the party.

In such instances of multiple negative morphology, the WTE sentence has a double negative reading, instead of showing NC, as does the SE sentence.

Structures like those in (31) and (34) make certain predictions about Standard English. If SE pre-subject *not* is housed in NegP$_2$ then this suggests that strings such as *not many people, not everybody, not a single person,* etc. are not constituents. There is evidence that this is so. If these strings are indeed DP constituents then they should be able to appear wherever other DPs can, but they cannot. For instance, there is a very strong subject/object asymmetry (see Klima (1964)):

(36)   a.   Not everybody was interviewed today.
       b.   *I interviewed not everybody today.
       c.   I didn't interview everybody today.

(37)   a.   Not many people were amused that day.
       b.   *I amused not many people that day.
       c.   I didn't amuse many people that day.

This asymmetry is predicted by the structure given in (31). There is not a NegP immediately preceding the surface object position to house the *not* in (36b) and (37b). Therefore, a string such as *not everybody* could not occur in object position.

It might be argued that (36b) and (37b) are unacceptable because they contain a post-verbal negative element, *not*, although this element is part of the DP. After all sentences like *I saw nobody* are rather marked and literary in character. In Colloquial English, it is generally more natural to use the NPI, *anybody* with a pre-verbal *not*, instead of *nobody* alone in object position.

This cannot be the reason (36b) and (37b) are unacceptable. Even if negative DPs are not natural in SE object positions, in WTE and other dialects, strings *not everybody*, if they are constituents, should be licensed by another negative element higher in the clause due to NC. *No more than three people,* which does form a constituent, can be licensed is just this way:

(38)   I ain't seen no more than three people all day.

However, NC cannot license such strings as *not everybody, not a single person,* etc.:

(39)   a.   *I didn't interview not everybody.
       b.   *Didn't nobody see not many people.

Similarly, a constituent like *no more than three people* is licensed in the subject position of a NI sentence, but a string like *not everybody* is not:

(40)   a.   Didn't no more than three people come to the party.
       b.   *Didn't not everybody come to the party.
       c.   *Didn't not a single person come to my party.
       d.   *Didn't not more than three people come to the party.

These facts clearly indicate that strings like *not everybody, not many people, not more than three people,* etc. do not behave as though they form a constituent. Correctly, the structure presented in (34) does not treat these strings as constituents. Rather, it places *not* in its own projection, NegP$_2$, and not under the DP containing *every, many, more than,* etc. This structure does account for their behavior.

5. Conclusion

This paper presents evidence which confirms the claim of Labov et al. that NI sentences do indeed need two separate analyses. The Existential analysis is needed for such sentences as in (19). However, many NI sentences cannot be accounted for with this analysis and as Sells et al. (1996) show, Labov et al.'s (1968) second analysis is not quite accurate. I have argued for a proposal in which there is a second Negative Phrase above AgrS-P to which negative auxiliaries raise in NI constructions. I also provided cross-dialectal evidence that this is same position which houses pre-subject *not* in SE., as in the sentences of (29b, d, f).

References
Beghelli, Filippo and Tim Stowell. 1997. Distributivity and Negation: The Syntax of *Each* and *Every*, in A. Szabolcsi, ed., *Ways of Scope Taking.* Dordrecht: Kluwer.71-109.
Feagin, Crawford. 1979. *Variation and Change in Alabama English,* Washington D. C.: Georgetown University Press.
Henry, Alison. 1995. *Belfast English and Standard English.* Oxford University Press.
Keenan, Edward L. 1996. The Semantics of Determiners, in S. Lappin, ed., *The Handbook of Contemporary Semantic Theory.* Oxford: Blackwell. 41-63.
Kiss, Katalin É. 1996. Two subject Positions in English, *The Linguistic Review* 13.119-142.
Klima, Edward S. 1964. Negation in English, in J. A. Fodor and J. J. Katz, eds., *The Structure of Language.* Englewood Cliffs, N.J.: Prentice Hall. 119-210.
Labov, William, Paul Cohen, Clarence Robins, and John Lewis. 1968. *A Study of the Nonstandard English of Negro and Puerto Rican Speakers in New York City.* Final Report, Cooperative Research Project No. 3288, United States Office of Education.
Pollock, Jean-Yves. 1989. Verb Movement, UG and the Structure of IP, *Linguistic Inquiry* 20.365-424.
Sells, Peter, John Rickford, and Thomas Wasow. 1996. An Optimality Theoretic Approach to Variation in Negative Inversion in AAVE, *NLLT* 14.591-627.

The Double Access Reading and Complementizer Deletion in Italian

ALESSANDRA GIORGI & FABIO PIANESI
University of Bergamo/ ITC-IRST, Trento

1. Introduction

In this work we consider Sequence of Tense (henceforth SOT) phenomena in Italian and in particular the Double Access Reading (henceforth DAR). The main focus will be on the morphosyntactic properties which determine this interpretation.

We will argue that the DAR doesn't depend on either the mood or the tense of the subordinate predicate, i.e., the present indicative, as is often assumed in the literature on the topic. Rather, it is determined by the semantic and syntactic properties of the matrix predicate. It will be shown that the DAR is strongly related to another phenomenon of Italian, namely, Complementiser Deletion (henceforth CD. See Giorgi & Pianesi (1996), (1997a)). The generalisation we will illustrate is the following: if a syntactic structure allows CD, it does not allow DAR, and vice versa. Adopting the split-C analysis of CD we developed in previous work, we will propose that the DAR depends on the kind of complementiser introducing the subordinate clause.

Finally, we will extend the DAR analysis to tenses other than the present tense, and will argue that there are LF conditions preventing non-anaphoric tenses from appearing within the contexts created by a past tense matrix predicate.

2. The Double Access Reading

In English and Italian, but not in German, Russian or Japanese, for instance, a present tense verbal form embedded under a past tense receives a peculiar interpretation:

(1)   John said that Mary is pregnant.

Roughly speaking, for (1) to be true the pregnancy must hold both at the time of the utterance, *S*, and at the time of the saying, i.e., the *now* of the individual whose *dicta* are reported.[1]

Most scholars who analysed the DAR (see Abusch (1991), (1997), Ogihara (1995), von Stechow (1995), Heim (1994)) agreed in regarding the interpretative facts as involving a *de-re* construal of the embedded present tense. According to the theory developed by Lewis (1979) and further elaborated by Cresswell and von Stechow (1982), *de-re* attitudes involve: (a) an *acquaintance* relation connecting the self (the believer, the sayer, etc..) with the object of the attitude, namely, the *res*; in the cases at hand, the *res* consists of an interval (Abusch, von Stechow), or a state (Ogihara); (b) a semantic analysis of the embedded clause as corresponding to a property which is predicated of the *res*, as picked up by the acquaintance relation. Thus, Abusch (1997) assigns to (2a) the logical form in (2b):

(2)   a.   John believed that Mary is pregnant.
        b.   John Past believe $Pres_2$ [λ_2 Mary TNS_2 be pregnant]

In (2b), the embedded tense, $Pres_2$, is moved outside the embedded clause to an extensional position, leaving a trace, TNS_2, behind. Concerning the acquaintance relation, Abusch suggests that in (2a) the *self* (John) is related to the *res* (a temporal interval) by means of an acquaintance relation picking up the maximal interval at which Mary has a big belly. Furthermore, the meaning of the moved $Pres_2$ contributes the information that in the actual world such an interval overlaps the utterer's now. Hence (2b) states that (2a) is true iff John ascribes to a certain temporal interval, as presented to him by the acquaintance relation, the property of Mary's being pregnant at it.

Although it won't be possible to provide here an exhaustive discussion of the semantics of the DAR (see however Giorgi & Pianesi (1998)), let us briefly consider the role of the acquaintance relation in the intensional analysis of the DAR just presented. Lewis regards such a relation as basically perceptual. However, the very fact that an appropriate acquaintance relation always exists, or is available, is questionable (see Burge (1977), Higginbotham (1991)). Examples can actually be given in which the *res* involved in the DAR is a state for which no perceptual

---

[1]In this paper we will reserve the term *utterer's now*, also notated as *S*, for the time at which a sentence such as (1) is uttered. The time of the attitude (belief, saying, or whatever) will be called *self's time*.
In other languages, such as Japanese, German and Russian, (1) only implies that the pregnancy state holds at the self's time, with no implication with respect to the utterer's now. In this work, we will not investigate the SOT of these languages, but will focus on the principles ruling the DAR in English-like languages. It is however important to keep in mind such a cross-linguistic difference, since it shows that the DAR is not a universal property, but a language specific one.

evidence of any sort needs to be available, or needs to be known to the speaker/hearer, and yet the DAR is obligatory.

If this is correct, then we argue that a more appropriate account of the semantics of the DAR should avoid resorting to acquaintance relations, and, possibly, to an intensional analysis *tout court*. Crucially, it should be able to incorporate the insights about the morphosyntax of the DAR we are going to discuss.

3. Belief and Saying predicates

Let us illustrate the empirical evidence in Italian and English. We will consider separately the contexts created by *verba dicendi* — such as *say* — and those created by verbs such as *believe*, because, as will be seen, they exhibit different properties:

(3)   Gianni ha detto che Maria è incinta.
        Gianni said that Mary is pregnant. (DAR)

(4)   Gianni ha detto che Maria scrive/ sta scrivendo un libro.
        Gianni said that Maria writes/ is writing a book. (DAR)

In Italian these verbs select the indicative mood in the subordinate clause. In (3), where the subordinate clause contains a present tense stative predicate, the DAR is the only reading available. In (4) the subordinate clause contains an eventive predicate, *scrivere* (to write), and the DAR is again obligatory, both when the verb appears in the present form, and in the present progressive.

If the embedded verbal form is not a present tense, but a past form, e.g., an imperfect indicative, the interpretation is different:

(5)   Gianni ha detto che Maria era incinta.
        Gianni said that Maria was (IMPF) pregnant. (*DAR)

(6)   Gianni ha detto che Maria scriveva/ stava scrivendo un libro.
        Gianni said that Maria wrote (IMPF)/ was writing. (PROG IMPF) (*DAR)

The event denoted by the embedded predicate is interpreted either as simultaneous with the superordinate one (the simultaneous reading), or as past with respect to it (the shifted reading); importantly, it is never interpreted as simultaneous with the utterer's now. Therefore, there is no double access effect in these cases, because in (5) and (6) the only time relevant for interpreting the embedded event seems to be that of the superordinate event.[2]

---

[2]In Italian, shifted readings with the imperfect indicative depend on the availability of a contextually relevant time which the embedded eventuality can be located at. Therefore, both (5) and (6) cannot be uttered out-of-the-blue. This is an important property of the Italian imperfect indicative. In this work we will not consider the conditions under which the imperfect indicative is interpreted with respect to the matrix predicate, because they are not directly relevant for the present discussion. On the distribution and the properties of the imperfect see Delfitto & Bertinetto (1995), Giorgi & Pianesi (1997a), Ippolito (1997).

Belief predicates select the subjunctive mood in the embedded clause, even if, more or less marginally, they also allow for the indicative mood (see below; see also fn.11). Consider the following examples:

(7) a. Gianni credeva che Maria fosse incinta.
Gianni believed that Maria was pregnant. (IMPF SUBJ).

   b. Gianni credeva che Maria scrivesse/ stesse scrivendo un libro.
Gianni believed that Maria wrote (IMPF SUBJ) / was writing (IMPF SUBJ PROG) a book.

The SOT typical of the subjunctive mood is somewhat more rigid than the one found with the indicative, in that the choice of the embedded tense is not free. E.g., a present subjunctive cannot be embedded under a past tense, and the past (imperfect) subjunctive must be used:

(8) a. *Gianni credeva che Maria sia incinta.
Gianni believed that Maria is (PRES SUBJ) pregnant.

   b. *Gianni credeva che Maria scriva/ stia scrivendo un libro.
Gianni believed that Maria writes (PRES SUBJ)/ is writing(PRES SUBJ PROG) a book.

Therefore, in the contexts created by *credere* the DAR is *a fortiori* not available. Importantly, as noted above, for some speakers the indicative is (more or less) marginally acceptable with *credere*:

(9) a. ??Gianni credeva che Maria è incinta.
Gianni believed that Maria is (PRES IND) pregnant. (DAR)

   b. ??Gianni credeva che Maria scrive/ sta scrivendo un libro. (DAR)
Gianni believed that Maria writes (PRES IND)/ is writing (PRES IND PROG) a book.

(10) a. ??Gianni credeva che Maria era incinta.
Gianni believed that Maria was (IMPF IND) pregnant. (*DAR)

   b. ??Gianni credeva che Maria scriveva/ stava scrivendo un libro.
Gianni believed that Maria wrote (IMPF IND)/ was writing (IMPF IND PROG) a book. (*DAR)

As far as the indicative is acceptable, (9) and (10) exhibit the same pattern as (3) and (4), that is, the present tense obligatorily gives rise to the DAR, whereas the imperfect has the simultaneous or the shifted reading.

Let us consider now the distribution of the DAR in English.

(11) John said that Mary is pregnant. (DAR)

(12) *John said that Mary writes a letter.

The first difference between Italian and English is that in English the DAR is available with stative predicates. Sentence (12) is ungrammatical, contrasting with the corresponding Italian sentence, (4). Grammaticality is restored if a progressive form is used. In this case the DAR is again obligatory:

(13)   John said that Mary is writing a letter. (DAR)

In Italian, as seen above, both the present tense and the present progressive forms are available. The ungrammaticality of (12) is related to the impossibility for an English (non-progressive) present tense, eventive predicate to be interpreted continuously, i.e., as a progressive-like form:

(14)   a.   Mary is pregnant.
       b.   *Mary writes a letter.

We will not discuss here the reasons for such a difference.[3]

From the data discussed so far, a possible generalisation is that in Italian only indicative sentences have a real interpretable tense, and that the DAR can only be found in those cases. The subjunctive, on the contrary, can be argued to be a tenseless form. As a consequence, no temporal interpretation takes place in a subjunctive subordinate sentence. In what follows we will show that, although this intuition is partially correct, the subjunctive cannot be analysed as a tenseless form *tout court*. Rather, the presence/absence of a real temporal interpretation, hence of the DAR, is determined by the complementiser.

4. *Ipotizzare* (hypothesise) and related predicates.

As anticipated above, there are reasons to reject the hypothesis that a subjunctive is unable to give rise to the DAR, that is, that it behaves as a tenseless form. Indeed, there is a subclass of predicates which, though selecting the subjunctive mood in their subordinated clauses, exhibit different properties than predicates of the *credere* (believe) class. The relevant verbs are exemplified by *ipotizzare* (hypothesise), together with *suggerire* (suggest), *concludere* (conclude), and others. Consider the following examples, which contrast with (7a) and (8a):[4]

(15)   Gianni ha ipotizzato che Maria fosse incinta.
       Gianni hypothesised that Maria was (IMPF SUBJ) pregnant.

(16)   Gianni ha ipotizzato che Maria sia incinta.
       Gianni hypothesised that Maria is (PRES SUBJ) pregnant.[5]

Comparing (15) with (7b), we see that in both sentences a past subjunctive form is embedded under a past tense. Furthermore, in both cases the resulting sentence is grammatical and the tense of the subordinated event is interpreted as simultaneous with that of the matrix event. In this respect, the

---

[3]For a discussion of the factors determining these and other peculiarities of the English present tense with eventive predicates, both in subordinated and in matrix contexts, see Giorgi & Pianesi (1997a), (1997b).
[4]We thank Valentina Bianchi for bringing this fact to our attention during a talk delivered at Scuola Normale Superiore, Pisa, in 1997. We also thank the audience present at that talk for fruitful discussion and suggestions.
[5]The same judgement is obtained in our variant of Italian, i.e., central Italian, by using the simple past in the matrix clause:
(i)   Gianni ipotizzò che Maria sia incinta
      Gianni hypothesised (SIMPLE PAST) that Maria is (PRES SUBJ) pregnant
Many speakers, however, for independent reasons, reject the simple past *tout court*, i.e., they have the simple past only as a literary option in their systems. Therefore, we will not further consider this tense in this paper.

past subjunctive seems to behave as a sort of morphological tense agreement marker. However, *credere* (believe) and *ipotizzare* (hypothesise) differ when the embedded tense is a present subjunctive. The sentence with *credere* (believe) is ungrammatical, cf., (8a), whereas the one with *ipotizzare* (hypothesise) is perfectly acceptable and obligatorily yields the DAR. That is, the pregnancy of Maria in (16) must hold both at the utterance time, and at the time at which *Gianni* made the hypothesis, which is past with respect to *now*. The same considerations apply also when the embedded predicate is eventive:

(17)   Gianni ha ipotizzato che Maria scrivesse un libro.
         Gianni hypothesised that Maria wrote (PAST SUBJ) a book.

(18)   Gianni ha ipotizzato che Maria scriva/ stia scrivendo un libro.
         Gianni hypothesised that Maria writes (PRES SUBJ)/ (PRES PROG SUBJ) a book.

As in (16), also in (18) the DAR is obligatory, so that the writing of the book must overlap both the utterer's *now* and at the self's time.

The contrasting behaviour of *credere* (believe) and *ipotizzare* (hypothesise) corresponds to subtle differences of meaning. Most notably, in (18) *ipotizzare* not only describes an attitude of the subject, but also asserts that such an attitude was communicated by the subject itself. This is not what happens with the non-DAR version of *ipotizzare* in (17). In that case the verb simply reports an attitude of the subject, without entailing anything about his/her communicative behaviour. Similar considerations hold of predicates enforcing the DAR, e.g., *dire* (say), when compared with predicates rejecting it, such as *credere* (believe): the former always entail, more or less explicitly, a communicative behaviour by the subject, whereas the latter do not. Generalising, we can divide the relevant predicates into two classes, the first one including verbs of communicative behaviour, e.g., *dire* (say), and the second including verbs lacking such a component, e.g., *credere* (believe). Verbs belonging to the first class always enforce the DAR whereas verbs belonging to the second never do so. Finally, verbs such as *ipotizzare* (hypothesise) alternate between the two: their communicative behaviour component is in fact optional and corresponds to their ability of enforcing the DAR.[6]

Returning to our main topic, given the examples above, the hypothesis that the DAR is a property of the (present) indicative must be rejected. One could then claim that the DAR is a property of the present tense (independently of its mood) when embedded under a past tense, probably the most common proposal in the current literature on the topic. This claim seems *prima facie* correct, but the following problems then arise: Why should the present tense produce DAR effects? Which are the properties of a present-under-past configuration yielding the DAR? It seems to us that

---

[6]We thank James Higginbotham for discussion and suggestions on this point. He proposed (1998, MIT IAP lectures) a similar tripartite classification of this type of predicates in English: *say, believe,* and *guess.*

the answers available in the literature generally amount to taking the very fact to be explained as a primitive property of the present tense.[7]

5. On Complementiser Deletion

In Giorgi & Pianesi (1997a) we observed that there is a special pattern of Complementiser Deletion in Italian. As already discussed by Poletto (1995), CD is possible with the subjunctive, but not with the indicative. The presence of the subjunctive seems to be only a necessary condition, though not a sufficient one. For instance, a context introduced by the verb *credere* (believe) admits CD, but a context introduced by a factive verb such as *rammaricarsi* (regret) does not, in spite of the fact that they both require a subordinate subjunctive clause. Consider the following examples:

(19)   Crede (che) sia partito.
       He believes (that) he left (SUBJ).

(20)   Si rammarica *(che) sia partito.
       He regrets *(that) he left (SUBJ).

Belief predicates such as *pensare* (think) and *supporre* (suppose), and volitionals and desideratives such as *volere* (want), and *sperare* (hope), admit CD, whereas true factives, such as *rammaricarsi* (regret), do not. Predicates requiring a subordinate indicative never admit CD:[8]

(21)   Ha detto *(che) è partito.
       He said *(that) he left (IND).

This is true for *credere* (believe) too. Speakers who (marginally) allow an embedded indicative tense with *credere* (believe) judge CD as impossible:

(22)   ??Gianni crede *(che) è incinta.
       Gianni believes *(that) she is pregnant.

Consider, now, the following examples:

---

[7]This is true also of Abusch's (1997) proposal. She claims that, in intensional contexts, present tenses cannot be c-commanded by past tenses and formalises this statement within a system of transmitted temporal relations. Furthermore, it is such a syntactic constraints that forces the present tense to move outside the intensional context, yielding the LF reproduced in (2b).
In Abusch's system, as well as in Heim's (1994), the constraint, as such, is simply stipulated, that is, no explanation is provided. Empirically, such theories cannot provide an easy explanation for facts such as (i):
(i)   Mario believed that Carlo was saying that Maria is pregnant.
In British English the embedded present tense has the DAR. Furthermore, according to the view we are discussing, such an interpretive result is due to the movement of the tense to an extensional *de-re* position. Excluding that movement to a site within the first embedded clause suffices to escape the constraint, it must be concluded that the present tense moves to a position within the matrix clause. However, we know that this is not possible in British English, cf., (12). Thus, either the requirement on the nature of the landing site for the tense movement is relaxed, or the very idea that movement is triggered by the aforementioned constraint must be abandoned.
[8]The classification of verbs used in the text has been originally proposed by Hooper (1975). See also Giorgi & Pianesi (1997a) for a discussion of their properties with respect to mood selection.

(23)   Gianni crede (che) sia incinta/ stia scrivendo un libro.
       Gianni believes (that) she is (PRES SUBJ) pregnant/ is writing a book.

(24)   Gianni ha ipotizzato(che) fosse incinta/ stesse scrivendo un libro.
       Gianni hypothesised (that) she was (IMPF SUBJ) pregnant/was writing a book.

(25)   Gianni ha ipotizzato *(che) sia incinta/ stia scrivendo un libro.
       Gianni hypothesised *(that) she is (PRES SUBJ) pregnant/ is (PRES SUBJ) writing a book.

In examples (23) and (24) CD is possible, and the strict SOT is enforced, i.e., the subordinate sentence is interpreted as if it were tenseless, and the dependent event/state is interpreted as simultaneous with the superordinate one. In sentence (25), however, as illustrated above, the tense of the embedded subjunctive need not match that of the matrix predicate: the latter is a past form, whereas the subjunctive embedded predicate is a present tense. In this case, the DAR is obligatory, and, importantly, the complementiser cannot be dropped.

In Giorgi & Pianesi (1996), (1997a) we argued in favour of a split-C account of CD. We proposed that two complementisers are available in Italian: a higher complementiser, C, typically required by predicates selecting the indicative mood in the subordinate clause, and a lower complementiser, MOOD/AGR, occurring when the subjunctive mood is selected.[9]

In a sentence such as (25), *ipotizzare* (hypothesise) selects both the subjunctive mood, therefore MOOD/AGR, and the higher complementiser C. On the other hand, in sentences such as (23) and (24) *ipotizzare* simply selects the subjunctive, that is, MOOD/AGR. The complementiser C appearing with *ipotizzare* is the same complementiser found in subordinate indicative sentences. Therefore, we can conclude that there is a strict correlation between the DAR and the presence of the "high" complementiser C, independently of the mood of the embedded clause. Such a correlation can be expressed by means of the following generalisation:

(26)   DAR iff C

If (26) is true, then we expect the DAR to arise also with tenses other than the present tense. The presence of C, in fact, depends on the properties of the matrix predicate and not on the subordinate tense.

To test this prediction consider embedded future events.[10] In Italian, there are two ways of expressing an embedded future: the indicative future, and the perfect conditional. The latter, typically encodes the so-called future-in-the-past, that is, it locates the event in the future only with respect to the matrix event. The indicative future always locates the event after the

---

[9]MOOD/AGR is a category realising both ϕ-features and the feature *mood*. According to the theory developed in (Giorgi & Pianesi, 1997a) such features can either give rise to independent projections (by means of a process we called *feature scattering*), or produce a single projection (we dubbed this possibility the *syncretic* solution). These two possibilities account for CD in Italian.

[10]Consideration of the past tense is not directly revealing, due to independent reasons we have no space to discuss here.

utterance event/time, even in embedded clauses. Consider the following contrast:

(27) a. Mario ha detto che Carlo partirà.
          Mario said that Carlo will leave.

      b. Mario ha detto che Carlo sarebbe partito.
          Mario said that Carlo would leave.

The embedded future in (27a) can be argued to have the DAR. The point of the DAR analysis, in fact, is that the temporal location of the embedded event/state is computed not only with respect to the matrix event (local anchoring), but also with respect to the utterance even itself. This is what happens with (27a): the time of the leaving is crucially after the utterance time. The perfect conditional, cf., (27b), on the other hand, simply locates the embedded event after the matrix event, hence the DAR is absent.

It seems, therefore, that the DAR analysis can be generalised to tenses other than the present tense. If so, (26) crucially requires that CD phenomena do not arise in such cases. Consider the following examples:

(28) *Gianni credeva che tu partirai.
      Gianni believed that you will leave.

(29) Gianni credeva (che) tu saresti partito.
      Gianni believed (that) you would leave.

(30) Gianni ha detto *(che) tu saresti partito.
      Gianni said *(that) you would leave.

(31) Gianni ha detto *(che) tu partirai.
      Gianni said *(that) you will leave.

(32) Gianni ha ipotizzato (che) tu saresti partito.
      Gianni hypothesised (that) you would leave.

(33) Gianni ha ipotizzato *(che) tu partirai domani.
      Gianni hypothesised *(that) you will leave tomorrow.

All these examples comply with (26). As we know, *credere* admits CD and rejects C. Expectedly, the future indicative is impossible under such a verb and the perfect conditional is obligatory, cf., (28)-(29). On the other hand, a predicate such as *dire* (say) requires C. In these contexts, the future indicative is acceptable, CD is never allowed, and the DAR is obligatory, cf., (30)-(31). Finally, *ipotizzare*, with the relevant meaning discussed in §4, admits the future indicative. In this case, CD is impossible, and the embedded tense has the DAR, cf., the contrast between (32) and (33).[11]

---

[11]Notice that an indicative future can be embedded under a present tense *belief* predicate:
(i) Gianni crede che Mario partirà.
     Gianni believes that Mario will leave.
This is not surprising, since the indicative mood is usually acceptable in these contexts:
(ii) Gianni crede che Mario è intelligente.
      Gianni believes that Mario is(IND) intelligent..
Moreover, there is a contrast between (iiia) and (iiib):

6. On SOT in Italian

In §2 we suggested that belief verbs such as *credere* enforce a more rigid SOT than *verba dicendi*:

(34) a.   *Mario credeva che Carlo sia malato.
           Mario Believed that C. is (SUBJ) sick.

        b.   Mario credeva che Carlo fosse malato.
           Mario believed that Carlo was (IMPF SUBJ) sick.

        c.   Mario credeva che Carlo fosse partito.
           Mario believed that Carlo had (IMPF SUBJ) left.

        d.   *Mario credeva che Carlo partirà.
           Mario believed that Carlo will leave.

As exemplified by the data in (34), a past tense belief predicate only admits embedded imperfect (and pluperfect) subjunctives.[12] These verbal forms can be characterised as *tenseless*. Consider the following data:

(35)   Gianni credeva che Maria scrivesse una lettera.
        Gianni believed that Maria wrote (IMPF SUBJ) a letter.

(36)   Gianni credeva che Maria partisse domani.
        Gianni believed that Maria left (IMPF SUBJ) tomorrow.

(37)   Gianni credeva che Maria partisse ieri.
        Gianni believed that Maria left (IMPF SUBJ) yesterday.

In these examples, the event described by the subordinate predicate does not show a clear ordering pattern with respect to the local anchor (the matrix event). Thus, in (35) it can be simultaneous or in the past with respect to the matrix event. In (36) and (37), the temporal argument locates the event with respect to the utterance event, the location with respect to the matrix event being derivative and irrelevant.[13] Such a behaviour of the imperfect subjunctive clearly contrasts with that of tenses such as the present, the present perfect or the simple past (*passato remoto*):

(38)   Mario mi disse che Carlo se ne andò improvvisamente.
        Mario told me that Carlo suddenly left.

In (38) the embedded simple past (*passato remoto*) orders the leaving event in the past of the matrix event. In general, the contribution of a real *tensed* tense is a relation ordering the event with respect to the anchor. In matrix clauses, such an event is the utterance itself; in embedded clauses it is the

---

(iii) a.   Gianni crede (che) arrivi Paolo.
           Gianni believes (that) arrives (SUBJ) Paolo.
      b.   Gianni crede *(che) arriverà Paolo.
           Gianni believes (that) will arrive (IND) Paolo.

Therefore, even if the possibility of (i)-(ii) must be accounted for, (i) is not a counterexample to (26).

[12]The pluperfect subjunctive is the compound tense, appearing in (34c), formed by the imperfect subjunctive auxiliary and the past participle of the main verb.

[13]Thus, in (37) the embedded event follows the matrix event. In (38) it can either follow or precede it, according to the location of the latter.

matrix event/state (local anchor). On the other hand, (35)-(37) show that an embedded imperfect subjunctive does not contribute to the meaning of the sentence a relation ordering the event with respect to the local anchor. We understand the term *tenseless* in this sense: a morphological tense whose contribution to the meaning of the sentence does not correspond to an asserted relation between the event and the relevant anchor (see also von Stechow (1995)).

The data in (35)-(37) also show that the imperfect subjunctive is an anaphoric form, similar to the imperfect indicative. In other words, it requires the context to make available a suitable temporal location for the event it describes. Such a temporal location can coincide with (that of) the local anchor, as in the simultaneous interpretation of (35), or it can be provided by the temporal argument, as in (36)-(37). Finally, it can be provided by the discourse context, as in the shifted reading of (35). As expected, when such a temporal location is not available, a sentence with an embedded imperfect subjunctive is odd, as is the case with (39a) when uttered out-of-the-blue:

(39)   a.   #Maria crede che Carlo fosse malato.
       Maria believes that Carlo was (IMPF SUBJ) sick.

       b.   Riguardo a ieri, Maria crede che Carlo fosse malato.
       Concerning yesterday, Maria believes that Carlo was (IMPF SUBJ) sick.

Imperfect subjunctives, in fact, cannot be simultaneous with a present tense matrix tense. Given that the context does not make available any other temporal location, the anaphoric requirements of the imperfect are not satisfied in (39a). In these respects, (39a) contrasts with (39b), which is acceptable, even if uttered out-of-the-blue, because the sentence initial adverbial provides a suitable temporal location.[14]

From this discussion, we can conclude that, when a matrix *belief* verb appears in the past tense, only the imperfect subjunctive, an anaphoric form, is allowed in the subordinated clause. Consider now cases with present tense *belief* verbs:

(40)   Gianni crede che Mario sia malato/sia partito/partirà.
       Gianni believes that Mario is (PRES SUBJ) sick / has (PRES SUBJ) left / will leave.

(41)   Gianni crede che Mario mangiasse/fosse (già) partito.
       Gianni believes that Mario ate (IMPF SUBJ) / had (IMPF SUBJ) (already) left.

When *credere* appears in the present tense, all subjunctive tenses (including the tenseless and anaphoric imperfect subjunctive and the pluperfect) and the

---

[14]As should be clear from the discussion in the text, we prefer to keep the two properties discussed, *tenselessness* and *anaphoricity*, distinct. It is possible that, at least in some languages, there are tenseless form which are not anaphoric — perhaps infinite forms. However, we will not pursue this question here.

Higginbotham (1997, lectures delivered at the Scuola Normale Superiore, Pisa) developed a system in which the notion of anaphoricity is crucial in accounting for SOT phenomena in English. Our analysis owes much to his proposal.

future indicative are available in the embedded clause. In other words, with a matrix present tense there is no tense selection. A similar conclusion can be drawn when the matrix tense is the future:

(42)   Gianni crederà che Mario sia malato/sia partito/partirà.
         Gianni will believe that Mario is (PRES SUBJ) sick / has (PRES SUBJ) left / will leave.

(43)   Gianni crederà che Mario mangiasse/fosse (già) partito.
         Gianni will believe that Mario ate (IMPF SUBJ) / had (IMPF SUBJ) (already) left.

To conclude, we propose that when a *belief* matrix verb appears in the past tense only the anaphoric imperfect subjunctive tense is allowed in the embedded clause. When the matrix predicate has the present (or future) tense, there are no restrictions on the tense of the embedded verb.

7. Towards an explanation.

In the previous section we introduced the concepts of tenseless and anaphoric tenses. *Tenselessness* applies to tenses which do not contribute a relation between the event and the relevant anchor; *anaphoricity* applies to tenses which make the temporal location of their events referentially dependent on other linguistic expressions, both intra- and inter-sententially. We also established that the imperfect subjunctive exhibits both properties.[15] On the other hand, a *non-anaphoric* tense contributes to the interpretation of the sentence a relation between the event and the relevant anchor (in the sense of Enç (1987) and Giorgi & Pianesi (1997a)). Therefore, we can rephrase the conclusions of the previous section by saying that a non-anaphoric, anchored tense is ungrammatical when embedded under a past tense belief verb. Given that there are independent reasons for excluding embedded indexical tenses, this amounts to claiming that in Italian no tense contributing an asserted relation with the local anchor can be embedded under a past tense belief verb.

          The reasons for excluding the possibility of indexical tenses in subordinate clause is the following. We adopt an Interpreted Logical Form (ILF) approach to the semantics of so-called propositional attitudes, see Higginbotham (1991), Larson & Ludlow (1993), Larson & Segal (1996). Consider the following sentence:

(44)   Mario ha detto che Maria è incinta.
         Mario said that Maria is pregnant.

If tenses can be indexical in subordinate contexts, then upon computing the ILF of the embedded clause, the node dominating the indicative present tense is annotated with a relation between the relevant state (pregnancy) and the utterance, $s \approx u$. The truth conditions of the whole sentence would then dictate

---

[15]Some further discussion about the interplay between anaphoricity and tenselessness would be appropriate at this point. However, lack of space prevents us from delving into details. let us simply notice that an imperfect subjunctive, when embedded under a present tense, cannot be simultaneous with it, cf., (39a), nor can be located by a temporal argument after the local anchor. That is, although anaphoric, the imperfect maintains some kind of temporal dependency from the local anchor. For a more complete discussion, see Giorgi & Pianesi (1998).

that (44) is true iff the agent, *Mario*, said at some past time something which is *samesaying* with, or is *expressed* by the ILF of the embedded clause, Σ. On the other hand, Σ, because of the relation contributed by the tense, contains a reference to the utterance. But then, we argue, serious problems with the *samesaying* or the *express* relation arise. For under no reasonable understanding of such a relationship between Σ and *Mario's* original utterance can it be assumed that *Mario* uttered a sentence *expressed* by, or *samesaying* with an ILF containing the reference to someone else's utterance. Thence we conclude that mere indexical tenses, that is, non-anaphoric, indexically anchored tenses, are impossible in embedded contexts.[16]

What about *verba dicendi* with a past tense? According to the discussion in §2 and in §3, non-anaphoric tenses have the DAR in these cases. In the literature, this phenomenon has been argued to involve movement of the tense from its basic position to a clause external one (Abusch (1997), Ogihara (1995)). Although different explanations have been proposed for such a movement, they all share the idea that the tense, in its base position (within an intensional context) is ungrammatical. If this view is correct, we can further generalise the conclusions above in the following manner: an LF representation in which the matrix predicate appears in the past tense is ruled out if the tense of the complement clause is non-anaphoric. For the time being, we can explain this fact as the effect of a constraint applying to LF representations, in such a way that either the embedded tense is tenseless, or, if tensed, it must have moved to a position outside the subordinate clause. In the latter case, we argue, the resulting configuration gives rise to the DAR.

In (26) we proposed a generalisation stating that, in Italian, the DAR is available only in contexts where the higher complementiser, C, is realised. We are now in a position to explain such a generalisation by hypothesising that the role of C is both that of triggering tense movement and of enforcing the DAR. Thus, in a sentence such as (45a) the embedded tense covertly moves to the C selected by the *verbum dicendi*, yielding the LF representation in (45b):

---

[16] It is important to notice that such a result, which seems to capture a universal property, strongly relies on the choice of representing tenses as relations between events. As seen, for indexical tenses this amounts to having the utterance explicitly represented in the ILF of the embedded clause. Were we to analyse tenses as relations between times, the conclusion would not follow. In this case, in fact, an indexical tense would bring into the ILF a relation between the time of the event and the *utterance time*. Now, indexical reference to the utterance time is possible in embedded contexts:

(i)   Tre giorni fa Mario ha detto che Carlo oggi è a Roma.
        Three days ago Mario said that Carlo is in Rome today.

So, what accounts for the impossibility of mere indexical tenses in subordinate clauses is not reference to S, but reference to the very utterance u. To the extent that our conclusion is correct and captures a real universal property, it also provides strong evidence in favour of the view that tenses simply and directly order events.

(45) a. Mario ha detto che Maria è malata.
       Mario said that Maria is sick.
      b. [.....[..[$_C$ τ_i C] [$_{AgrP}$...T_i..]]]^{17}

We explain the DAR of structure such as (45b) by hypothesising, following Higginbotham (1991), that the ILF the interpretative axioms relate to the *verbum dicendi* is not built directly from the CP, but from the complement of C, that is, AgrP in (45b). Moreover, both the moved τ and its copy contribute to the interpretation, albeit in different manners. The former constrains the value assignment with respect to which the truth conditions for the ILF are computed, in such a way that the embedded event must overlap the utterance. The latter directly contributes to the ILF by establishing a relationship between the embedded event/state and its anchor (the matrix event/state).[18]

On the other hand, when the matrix predicate does not select for C, nothing forces the embedded tense to move outside the embedded context, and the sentence is ruled out:[19]

(46) *Mario credeva/temeva (che) Carlo sia malato/partirà.
      M. believed/feared that C. is sick/will leave.

Let us summarise our proposal. In (26) we stated a generalisation according to which, in Italian the DAR obtains only in contexts where the higher complementiser, C, is present. To explain the role of C, we observed that with a matrix *belief* predicate the past tense makes virtually all non-anaphoric embedded tenses unavailable. On the other hand, when the matrix predicate belongs to the class of *verba dicendi*, the same sentences are grammatical and have the DAR. To unify these two cases, we exploited suggestions available in the literature according to which the DAR involves movement of the embedded tense to an extensional position. Our conclusion was that, at LF, contexts created by matrix past tenses make non-anaphoric embedded tenses ungrammatical. Structures containing the latter can restore grammaticality by having the embedded tense move to C. The DAR, we argued, is a property of the resulting LF.

References

Abusch, D., (1991), "The Present under Past as a De Re Interpretation". In *Proceedings of WCCFL X*, Stanford University.

Abusch, D., (1997), "Sequence of Tense and Temporal De Re". In *Linguistics and Philosophy*

Burge, T., (1977), "Belief *De Re*". In *The Journal of Philosophy*, 74:338-361.

---

[17]In (45b) we represented covert movement of the temporal features, τ, of the embedded T by coindexing them with T itself. This is simply a notational device; actually, we interpret movement as feature copying.

[18]A more complete discussion of our semantics for the DAR can be found in Giorgi & Pianesi (1998).

[19]Sentences with a matrix future tense deserve a discussion which we cannot provide here. See Giorgi & Pianesi (1998).

Cresswell, M. & A. von Stechow, (1982), "De Re Belief Generalised". In *Linguistics and Philosophy*, 5:503-535.

Delfitto, D. & P.M. Bertinetto, (1995), "A Case Study in the Interaction of Aspect and Actionality: the Imperfect in Italian". In P.M. Bertinetto, V. Bianchi, J. Higginbotham & M. Squartini (eds.), *Temporal Reference, Aspect and Actionality*. Rosenberg & Sellier, Torino.

Enç, M., (1987), "Anchoring Conditions for Tense". In *Linguistic Inquiry*, 18: 633-657.

Giorgi, A. & F. Pianesi, (1996), "Verb Movement in Italian and Syncretic Categories", *Probus* 8, 137- 160.

Giorgi, A. & F. Pianesi, (1997a), *Tense and Aspect: from Semantics to Morphosyntax*. Oxford University Press, New York.

Giorgi, A. & F. Pianesi, (1997b), "Present Tense, Perfectivity and the Anchoring Conditions", in *Proceedings of IATL1997*, Bar Ilan University.

Giorgi, A. & F. Pianesi, (1998), "Sequence of Tense Phenomena in Italian: a Morphosyntactic Analysis". *ms.*, University of Bergamo, IRST, Trento

Heim, I., (1994), "Comments on Abusch's Theory of Tense". In H. Kamp (ed.), *Ellipsis, Tense and Questions*, Dyana-2 Esprit Basic Research Project 6852, Deliverable R2.2.B.

Higginbotham, J., (1991), "Belief and Logical Form". In *Mind & Language*, 6:344-369.

Higginbotham, J., (1994), Events and Aspect. *ms*. Somerville College, Oxford.

Hoekstra, E., (1992), *On the Parametrisation of Functional Projections in CP*. ms., Amsterdam.

Hooper, J.B., (1975), "On Assertive Predicates". In J.P. Kimball (ed.), *Syntax and Semantics*, Vol.4. Academic Press, New York.

Ippolito, M., (1997), unpublished MA Dissertation, Oxford University.

Larson, R. & P. Ludlow, (1993), "Interpreted Logical Forms". In *Synthese*, 95:305-355.

Larson, R. & G. Segal, (1996), *Knowledge of Meaning*. MIT Press.

Lewis, D., (1979), "Attitudes De Dicto and De Se". In *Philosophical Review*, 88:513-543.

Ogihara, T., (1995), "Double-Access Sentences and Reference to States". In *Natural Language Semantics*, 3:177-210.

Parsons, T., (1990), *Events in the Semantics of English*. MIT Press, Cambridge, MA.

Poletto, C., (1995), "Complementiser Deletion and Verb Movement in Italian". In *Working Papers in Linguistics*, University of Venice.

Rizzi, L., (1991), "Residual Verb Second and the Wh-Criterion". In *Technical Reports in Formal and Computational Linguistics*, Vol.2, University of Geneva.

von Stechow, A., (1995), "On the Proper Treatment of Tense". In *Proceedings of SALT 5*. University of Texas, Austin.

Vikner, S., (1994), "Finite Verb in Scandinavian Embedded Clause". In D. Lightfoot & N. Hornstein (eds.), *Verb Movement*. Cambridge University Press.

The Process Specific Nature of Weight: The Case of Contour Tone Restrictions

MATTHEW GORDON

University of California, Los Angeles

1. Introduction[*]

The goal of this paper is to explore the role of phonetics in phonology using syllable weight as a case study. In current theories of phonology, syllable weight is typically assumed to be a single phenomenon instantiated by a number of diverse phonological processes. In this paper, I will argue that, contra the established conception of weight, the cluster of properties associated with syllable weight actually are distinct and largely independent processes sensitive to different factors, many of them phonetic in nature. Weight-sensitive contour tone restrictions illustrate the process specific nature of syllable weight and the phonetic basis for many weight-based phenomena. It is argued in this paper that contour tone restrictions result from the phonetic requirement that tone be realized on a sonorant. Because this phonetic requirement is unique to tone among the weight-sensitive processes, it is predicted that phonological weight criteria for tone will be divergent from weight criteria for other weight-sensitive phenomena. This prediction is corroborated by an extensive cross-linguistic typology of syllable weight.

2. Background

2.1 Weight as a Phenomenon

It has long been known that many phonological phenomena treat certain syllable types as heavier than others (e.g. Jakobson (1931), Allen (1973), etc.). For example, primary stress in Latin (Allen (1973)) falls on the

[*] The author wishes to thank Bruce Hayes and Jie Zhang for comments on a draft of this paper. Thanks to audiences at the UCLA Phonology Seminar, at the 1998 annual meeting of the LSA, and at the 17th annual meeting of WCCFL for their comments and suggestions. Any remaining errors are my own responsibility. Also, thanks to Kristy Liang for being a subject for the Cantonese experiment and also for analyzing the Cantonese data, and to Alhaji Gimba for being a subject in the Hausa experiment.

penultimate syllable if it is either closed by a consonant(s) or contains a long vowel or diphthong (1a). If the penult does not meet any of these criteria, stress falls on the antepenultimate syllable (1b).

(1)   Latin stress
      a. kar.'pen.tum 'carriage', a.'mi:.kus 'friend'
      b. 'si.mi.le 'similar'

Thus in Latin, closed syllables (henceforth CVC) and syllables containing long vowels or diphthongs (both henceforth CVV) are "heavier" than open syllables containing a short vowel (henceforth CV).

    Stress is not the only weight-sensitive phenomenon; nor is the set of heavy syllables the same in every language. For example, consider restrictions on contour tones, the focus of this paper. In Kiowa (Watkins (1984)), contour tones are restricted to CVV and syllables closed by a sonorant (CVR) (2a). Contour tones may not occur on CV or on short-voweled syllables closed by an obstruent (CVO) (2b).

(2)   Kiowa contour tones (from Watkins 1984)
      a. kʰûːl 'pull off', hâ: 'arise' refl., kʰûltɔː 'pull off' future
      b. kʰút 'pull off' perfective (*kʰût), *kʰû

Thus, CVV and CVR are heavier than CV and CVO in Kiowa. This differs from Latin stress, where CVO is heavy. The determination of which syllables count as heavy and which as light for a given process in a given language will henceforth be referred to as the weight criterion for that process in that language. Thus, the weight criterion for stress in Latin is different from the weight criterion for contour tones in Kiowa.

    Other phenomena in addition to stress and contour tone restrictions have been linked to weight: minimal word requirements (McCarthy and Prince (1995)), metrical scansion (Hayes (1988)), compensatory lengthening (Hayes (1989)), reduplication (McCarthy and Prince), and syllable templatic restrictions such as prohibitions against long vowels in closed syllables (McCarthy and Prince). It is thus clear that syllable weight plays a very important role in phonology[1].

2.2 Assumptions about Weight
Current theories of weight are based on the assumption that weight criteria are uniform for different processes within the same language, but can vary from language to language. Latin provides an example of uniformity of weight criteria within a single language: both the metrical and stress systems treat CVV and CVC as heavy and CV as light (Mester (1994)). A comparison of Latin with Malayalam illustrates the parametrization of weight as a function of language: the stress system in Malayalam treats only CVV as heavy (Mohanan (1986)).

---

[1] An interesting aspect of weight which holds of virtually all weight-sensitive in all languages is that syllable onsets are weightless; the domain of weight is the rime of the syllable. Thus, wherever the onset consonant is included in abbreviations of syllable types in this paper, e.g. CVV, CVC, the reader should bear in mind that the presence or absence of the onset does not influence the weight pattern unless stated otherwise.

The assumptions of language internal uniformity of weight and language specific variation in weight criteria are particularly apparent in moraic theories of the syllable which are specifically designed to handle weight-sensitive phenomena (e.g. Hyman (1985, 1992), McCarthy and Prince (1995), Hayes (1989, 1995), etc.). For example, the fact that coda consonants may or may not contribute weight to a syllable is captured by Hayes' (1989) Weight-by-Position parameter. In languages where Weight-by-Position is operative (e.g. Latin), coda consonants receive their own mora; in other languages (e.g. Malayalam), codas do not link to their own mora. Crucially, this parameter is assumed to operate on a language-specific basis and not on a process-specific basis.

Current theories do not predict process specificity of weight criteria; thus, they do not predict different processes to have different weight criteria either within languages or across languages. Cross-linguistically, the number of languages which observe criterion X for process A is by default assumed by current theories to be equivalent to the number of languages which observe criterion X for process B. Language-internally, there is little provision for representing languages in which there is a mismatch of weight criteria between two (or more) processes. For example, in Khalkha Mongolian, Weight-by-Position appears to apply in the case of the minimal word, but not for the calculation of stress (Bosson 1964). Thus, if we conflate weight criteria for stress and the minimal word requirement, we are left with a three-way weight hierarchy (CVV > CVC > CV) which cannot be represented without additional apparatus not provided by the original theory. An increasing number of weight conflicts are becoming apparent as our data base expands (see, for example, Hyman (1992), Hayes (1995, ch.7)). While the problems encountered in the representation of these hierarchies are most acute in moraic theories, many of them are also faced by skeletal slot models of the syllable (e.g. Levin (1985)) despite the larger array of structures available to them (see Gordon (1998) for discussion).

Consideration of the process involved could potentially shed light on the nature of weight conflicts and, more generally, on the nature of weight. For example, if it turned out that the most common minimal word requirement treated both CVV and CVC as heavy and that the most common weight criterion for stress was CVV, the weight conflict in Khalkha between these two phenomena would not be at all surprising, unlike in current theories of weight in which Khalkha is predicted to be exceptional.

Given our current knowledge, the extent to which weight is a property of languages or of processes is unclear. Thus, we do not know whether weight tends to be more strongly uniform within languages or within processes. The theory of weight will differ substantially depending on the answer to these questions. This answer can only come from examining several weight sensitive phenomena in a large number of languages. This is done in the typology in section 3. First though, in section 2.3, we consider the basic ideas underlying the representation of contour tone restrictions in current models of weight.

2.3 The Representation of Contour Tone Restrictions

It is typically assumed that contour tones result from the combination of two level tones (e.g. Hyman (1985), Duanmu (1994a,b)). Thus, a rising tone results reflects the combination of a low tone followed by a high tone, while a falling tone is represented as a combination of a high tone followed by a low tone. Given the compositionality of contour tones, restrictions against contour tones are typically assumed to arise from a prohibition against associations between more than one tone and a single timing position (either skeletal slot or mora). Because a contour tone consists of two tones, it may require two timing positions on which to be realized, one for each element of the contour. For example, the Kiowa restriction against contour tones on CVO and CV follows if we assume that only sonorants are associated with weight bearing timing positions.

3. The Typology of Weight

A survey of six weight-sensitive phenomena in approximately 370 diverse languages was conducted in order to determine whether weight is more a function of language than of process or vice versa. The six phenomena examined were weight-sensitive stress, contour tone restrictions, metrics, syllable templatic restrictions, minimal word requirements and compensatory lengthening. The 370 languages were chosen according to their genetic diversity in order to yield a representative survey of cross-linguistic weight (see Gordon (1998) for details of the survey).

In sections 3.1-3.4, I present the results of the typology of weight for contour tone restrictions as it relates to weight criteria for other processes (see Gordon (1998) for discussion of the other weight-sensitive phenomena).

3.1 Universal Weight Hierarchies

106 languages in the survey possess contrastive tone, of which 31 possess weight-related restrictions on contour tones and a full range of syllable types (CV, CVO, CVR, CVV) which allows for disambiguation of weight criteria. These 31 languages observe an implicational hierarchy in terms of the ability of different syllable types to carry contour tones. This implicational hierarchy becomes clear if we consider the four basic patterns attested in languages which allow contour tones. In some languages (e.g. Somali), contour tones are limited to CVV. In other languages (e.g. Kiowa), contour tones are restricted to CVV and CVR[2]. In other languages (e.g. Hausa), contour tones may occur on any syllable other than CV, i.e. contour tones may occur on CVV, CVR, and CVO[3]. The final type of language allows contour tones on all syllable types, even CV. Languages of this last type, which appear to be quite rare, are less interesting for present purposes, since they lack restrictions on contour tones conditioned by syllable type. The four types of languages and the syllables which tolerate contour tones in each are summarized in tabular form in (3). "Yes" indicates that the given syllable type may carry a contour in the given language type, "No" indicates that it may not.

---

[2] One language in this group, Cantonese, displays somewhat exceptional behavior and will be discussed in detail in section 4.1.2..

[3] It will be argued in section 4.1.1 that this classification of these languages is rather misleading.

(3)   Patterns of contour tone restrictions

		Language Type			
		Type 1	Type 2	Type 3	Type 4
Syllable Type	CVV	Yes	Yes	Yes	Yes
	CVR	No	Yes	Yes	Yes
	CVO	No	No	Yes	Yes
	CV	No	No	No	Yes

Looking at table (3), an implicational hierarchy is apparent. If a language allows contour tones on CV, it also tolerates them on CVO, CVR, and CVV. If a language allows contours on CV and CVO, it also allows them on CVR and CVV. Finally, if a language tolerates contour tones on CV, CVO, and CVR, it also allows them on CVV. If we conflate these implicational statements, we are left with the hierarchy in (4) in which tolerance of contours on a given syllable type implies tolerance of contours on the syllable type(s) to its left.

(4)   Hierarchy of weight for tone

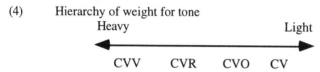

Heavy   Light

CVV   CVR   CVO   CV

3.2 The Lack of Language Internal Uniformity of Weight

If we look at languages which display at least one other weight-sensitive phenomenon in addition to weight-sensitive contour tone restrictions, we see that there is no tendency for different weight-sensitive phenomena to display the same weight criterion within the same language. This is shown in (5) which lists the number of languages with matched and mismatched weight criteria for a given phenomenon as compared to tone. Note that compensatory lengthening and syllable template restrictions are inherently deficient in the types of weight criteria which they have the potential to observe; they are thus excluded from (5) (see Gordon (1998) for discussion).

(5)   Matches and mismatches in weight (tone vs. other processes)

Tone vs.	Number of languages		
	Match	Mismatch	Not applic.
Stress	3	6	22
Metrics	2	3	26
Minimal Word	0	7	24

Despite the paucity of languages with another weight-sensitive process in addition to tone, (5) nevertheless indicates that there are more mismatches between weight for tone and weight for other phenomena than there are matches. Crucially, this is a rather unexpected finding given the assumption of standard theories that weight is a function of languages, but it may find an explanation in a theory of weight in which process specificity plays an important role.

3.3 The Process Specificity of Weight
In fact, the typology corroborates the hypothesis that weight is largely process specific; different processes display quite different distributions in their weight criteria. In (6), we see the number of languages displaying a given weight criterion for a given process[4].

(6)   Weight criteria for different weight-sensitive phenomena

		Process			
		Contour Tones	Stress	Metrics	Minimal Word
Heavy	CVV	18	37	0	20
Syllables	CVV, CVR	11	4	0	1
	CVV, CVC	2	28	17	81

Several interesting patterns are apparent in (6). I focus here on the comparison of weight criteria for contour tones with weight criteria for other processes (see Gordon 1998 for comparison for these other processes with each other). What is most striking is the extreme rarity of the CVV, CVR heavy criterion for all other processes *except* tone where it is relatively common. Conversely, the CVV, CVC heavy criterion, where CVC includes both CVR and CVO, is vanishingly rare for contour tones, but quite common for all other phenomena. The visibly different distribution of weight criteria for contour tones in comparison to other processes is confirmed statistically by a χ^2 analysis: tone vs. stress (p<.0001, $\chi^2 =$ 31.175), tone vs. metrics (p<.0001, $\chi^2 = 40.177$), tone vs. minimal word requirements (p<.0001, $\chi^2 = 66.599$).

The difference distribution of weight for different processes seen in (6) is quite unexpected in current theories of weight, as pointed out in 2.2. These theories thus do not account for several interesting findings in (6): the relative popularity of the CVV, CVR heavy criterion for contour tone restrictions and conversely its rarity for other processes, the rarity of the CVV, CVC heavy criterion for tone and conversely its popularity for other phenomena. Also left unexplained are other asymmetries apparent in (6) but which will not be discussed further in this paper (see Gordon (1998) for discussion): e.g. the absence of all criteria other than CVV, CVC heavy in metrical systems, the relative balance of the CVV heavy and the CVV, CVC heavy criterion for stress, and the predominance of the CVV, CVC heavy criterion for minimal word requirements.

3.4 The Distribution of Weight: A Summary
In summary, the typology of weight has yielded a number of interesting findings. First, we have seen that weight criteria for contour tone restrictions respect an implicational hierarchy with CVV at the top of the weight scale, followed in turn by CVR, CVO, and CV. Tolerance of

---

[4]Compensatory lengthening and syllable template restrictions are again omitted for reasons given above.

contour tones on a given syllable type implies tolerance of contours on syllable types which are higher in the hierarchy. Furthermore, the typology has provided evidence against the prediction made by current theories that weight is a property of languages. This evidence can be seen on at least two levels. First, weight criteria for multiple processes in the same language do not show any tendency toward uniformity. Second, the distribution of weight criteria differs markedly as a function of the process under consideration. These findings suggest that weight is less a function of language than of process. An adequate theory of weight should explain this fact and should explain the different weight patterns displayed by different processes. In the next section, we take a step toward explaining the process specific nature of weight focusing on contour tone restrictions.

4. A Phonetic Basis for Contour Tone Restrictions

One of the crucial results of the typological survey of weight in section 3 was the finding that weight criteria for contour tones show a much different distribution cross-linguistically than weight criteria for other weight-sensitive phenomena. In this section, we will see that this asymmetry finds an explanation in terms of the phonetic requirements of tone. Because these phonetic prerequisites are unique to tone among the weight-sensitive phenomena considered, the phonological asymmetry between weight for tone observed in section 3 is exactly what we would expect to find.

The physical correlate of tone is fundamental frequency which is only present in voiced segments. In fact, the property which defines a voicing contrast is the fundamental frequency: voiceless segments lack a fundamental, voiced segments have one. Thus, the only type of segment on which tone may be *directly* realized is a voiced one[5].

Crucially, the fundamental frequency profile of a segment or syllable (and hence its tonal profile) is cued not only by the fundamental frequency itself but also by other information. In particular, the presence of harmonics in the signal assists the recovery of the fundamental frequency. The reason for this is that harmonics occur at frequencies which are multiples of the fundamental frequency. Thus, a fundamental frequency of 200Hz will have harmonics at 400Hz, 600Hz, 800Hz, 1000Hz, and at 200Hz increments thereafter. The presence of harmonics greatly enhances the salience of the fundamental frequency, and can even allow for recovery of the tone when the fundamental itself has been extracted from the signal (see House (1990) and Moore (1995) for review of the relevant psychoacoustic literature).

While the relationship of harmonics to the fundamental in the frequency domain is the same for all segments (harmonics occur at multiples of the fundamental), voiced segments differ in terms of the number of harmonics present in their signal and the nature of the harmonics. Because vowels typically have the most energy at higher frequencies, they are also characterized by the greatest number of harmonics. Furthermore, because

---

[5]A voiceless segment does not inherently possess a fundamental frequency itself, although its laryngeal settings may influence the fundamental frequency of neighboring voiced segments, as demonstrated by the link between high tone and adjacent vowels in many languages. Influences of this sort are not strictly weight-sensitive and are thus not discussed here.

242 / Matthew Gordon

they are generally produced with a more open vocal tract than other voiced segments, vowels also have harmonics with the greatest acoustic intensity. Voiced sonorant consonants also possess a fairly rich and energetic harmonic structure relative to voiced obstruents, but typically do not possess as many or as intense harmonics as vowels. Nevertheless, the more crucial harmonics for the perception of the fundamental, the second through fourth (House (1990)), are typically present in sonorants.

In contrast to sonorants, obstruents provide either minimal or no cues to fundamental frequency. Voiceless consonants, including obstruents, do not have a fundamental. In voiced obstruents, harmonics above the fundamental typically have very little energy; furthermore, the fundamental itself is typically substantially less intense in obstruents in sonorants. The absence of a salient harmonic structure in obstruents and the low intensity of the fundamental frequency are due to the narrow constrictions associated with obstruents. In fact, the difficulty of recovering the fundamental frequency in obstruents, in conjunction with aerodynamic factors militating against voiced obstruents (see Maddieson (1997) for review), has phonological repercussions not only for tone but also for voicing contrasts in obstruents. Voiced obstruents are rare compared to both voiceless obstruents and voiced sonorants cross-linguistically, and voiced obstruents often devoice both historically and synchronically. Thus, voiced obstruents are inherently impoverished relative to voiced sonorants in terms of the salience of their fundamental frequency and their ability to carry tonal contrasts. We would thus expect voiced obstruents to contribute extremely little to the ability of a syllable to carry a contour tone or not. This fact, taken together with the inability of voiceless obstruents to carry tone, means that the class of obstruents considered as a whole is quite poorly suited to supporting tonal information.

The relative ability of different segment types to carry tone can be made more vivid by considering a narrow band spectrogram of different types of voiced segments (7). Voiceless segments are not included since they lack a fundamental and harmonic structure.

(7)

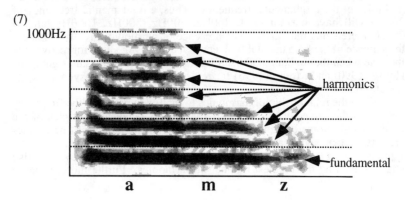

In (7) we see that the vowel has the greatest number of visible harmonics above the fundamental and also the most intense ones (as reflected in the darkness of the harmonics). The sonorant consonant also has a relatively rich harmonic structure and relatively intense harmonics, though the sonorant consonant's harmonics are fewer in number and less intense than the vowel's. Compared to both the vowel and sonorant, the voiced obstruent provides very little tonal information: there are no continuous harmonics visible above the fundamental and the fundamental itself is quite weak in terms of intensity.

The relative salience of tonal information realized on different segment types offers an explanation for the distribution of weight-sensitive contour tone restrictions discussed in section 3. Recall the implicational hierarchy of syllable types which may bear contour tones: CVV is heaviest, followed by CVR, followed by CVO, followed by CV. This hierarchy mirrors the phonetic hierarchy of tonal salience in (7) under the plausible assumption that contour tones require a longer duration to be realized than level tones. It is thus crucial that not only the initial portion of the rime but also the *latter* portion of the rime possess properties which will allow for recoverability of the tonal information. Thus, it is the second half of the long vowel in CVV and the coda consonant in CVR and CVO which serve to differentiate them from each other and from CV in terms of relative ability to carry a contour tone. The hierarchy of syllable types in (4) then reduces to a hierarchy of segment types able to carry the latter portion of the contour: V > R > O > Zero, (where the difference between O and zero is somewhat dubious; see the discussion on section 4.1). This hierarchy corresponds to the phonetic hierarchy of segments in (7) and also to the phonological hierarchy of syllable types in (4). Languages with weight-sensitive restrictions on contour tones draw different "cut-off" points along this hierarchy, as in (8).

(8)   Heavy   Light

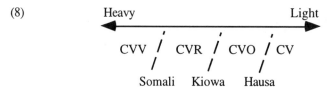

CVV / CVR / CVO / CV

Somali   Kiowa   Hausa

In any given language, contour tones are permitted on syllable types to the left of the line, but not on syllable types to the right of the line, reflecting the fact that syllable types further left on the continuum are phonetically better suited to carry a contour tone. Thus, the licensing of contour tones on a syllable which can better phonetically support a contour tone implies the licensing of contour tones on syllables which are phonetically less well suited to supporting a contour.

4.1 Apparent Exceptions
4.1.1 Hausa and Luganda
Positing a phonetic explanation for contour tone restrictions raises an interesting question about the two languages in the survey, Hausa and Luganda, which draw their cut-off point in (8) between CVO and CV. Assuming that obstruents are particularly ill-equipped to carry tonal information, there is then little reason to think that a CVO syllable would

be much, if any, better suited to carry a contour tone than CV. The Hausa and Luganda pattern is especially surprising when one considers the fact that many of the coda obstruents are voiceless and thus cannot carry tone at all.

In fact, as it turns out, phonetic data from Hausa which I have collected provide a solution to this puzzle. Measurements suggest that it is not the coda obstruent in CVO which makes CVO a better licenser of contours than CV, but rather it is the *vowel* in CVO which bears the burden of carrying the contour tone (9)[6]. Note that durations are in milliseconds.

(9)

	H	L	HL
V in CV	76	72	---
V in CVO	94	91	119
V in CVR	111	97	112
VV in CVV	234	230	237

Consider the data which demonstrates this. First, vowels in closed syllables are longer than vowels in open syllables. Although this is a typologically unusual pattern which runs contra to the general pattern of lengthening of vowels in open syllables (see Maddieson (1985)), it is also found in Japanese (Dalby and Port (1981)). Interestingly, both Hausa and Japanese share a structural property which is plausibly linked to closed syllable vowel lengthening: they either lack phonemic vowel length contrasts in closed syllables (Hausa), or assign them a highly marginal role in the phonology (Japanese). Because there is no length contrast, vowels can be longer in closed syllables without potentially jeopardizing the salience of a phonemic contrast in length. In open syllables where vowel length is contrastive, on the other hand, there is less room for subphonemic lengthening.

Because there is no phonemic vowel length in closed syllables, the vowel in CVO bearing a contour tone can lengthen to support the contour, since the obstruent itself provides little assistance in supporting tonal information. The data in (9) shows, in fact, that vowels in CVO syllables carrying contour tones are substantially longer than vowels carrying level tones in CVO. Strikingly, vowels in CVR and CVV syllables are *not* longer when they carry contour tones. This suggests that the vowel in CVO syllables carrying a contour tone is lengthening in order to aid in the realization of the contour, because the coda obstruent itself provides little assistance. Lengthening is not necessary in CVR and CVV, because the rime in these syllables consists entirely of sonorants which, for reasons enumerated earlier, are well suited to supporting tonal information.

Thus, despite initial appearances to the contrary, Hausa actually provides further evidence that it is really the duration of the sonorant portion of the rime which serves as the basis for determining syllable weight for tone. Thus, the presence of an obstruent does not itself contribute to the ability of a syllable to carry a contour tone. It is only when the presence of the obstruent allows for lengthening of the preceding vowel as in Hausa that CVO is better able to support a contour tone than CV. The Hausa pattern also suggests that the ability of a syllable to carry a contour tone is really a

---

[6] 1 speaker, 8 tokens for each rime + tone combination, vowels = /a/ and /i/, codas = /b/, /s/ and /n/.

property of the entire syllable and not merely a property of individual segments within the syllable summed together. It is the presence of the coda which licenses vowel lengthening in CVO syllables bearing a contour tone, but it is the vowel which actually carries the burden of realizing the tone[7].

It is interesting to note that Luganda, the other language in the survey which allows contours on CVO but not on CV, lacks phonemic vowel length in closed syllables, just like Hausa. Though I do not have any phonetic data on Luganda, it thus is plausible that, like Hausa, Luganda might display vowel lengthening in CVO syllables carrying a contour tone.

4.1.2 Cantonese

Cantonese is the only language in the survey which does not observe the implicational hierarchy in (4). The Cantonese tone facts are as follows (Kao (1971)). Contour tones are permitted on phonemic short vowels in open syllables (CV) and on syllables closed by a sonorant, whether they contain a short vowel (CVR) or a long vowel (CVVR). Contour tones, with a few scattered morphologically derived exceptions, do not occur on syllables closed by an obstruent, regardless of whether the vowel is short (CVO) or long (CVVO). Crucially, Cantonese lacks a vowel length distinction in open syllables. Also note that low, mid, and high level tones occur in obstruent closed syllables in Cantonese. Thus the restriction against contour tones in syllables closed by an obstruent is not a segmental effect.

Given these facts, Cantonese appears to be an exception in more than one way to the implicational hierarchy in (4). First, CV may bear a contour but CVO may not, a pattern which is the opposite of the Hausa type distribution. Second, both CV and CVR may bear a contour but CVVO may not, an apparent exception to the general pattern of CVV being heavier than both CV and CVR. Both of these patterns find a phonetic explanation in terms of language specific properties of Cantonese.

In (10), we see duration values (from data collected for this paper) of the vowel and the entire sonorous phase of the rime (i.e. everything except the obstruent closure, if present), the relevant portions of the syllable for assessing the ability of a syllable to carry a contour tone or not[8].

(10)	Rime Type (durations in milliseconds)				
	CV	CVO	CVR	CVVO	CVVR
Vowel	283	77	99	150	208
Sonorous phase	283	77	275	150	301

Interestingly, the three syllable types which can carry contours in Cantonese (CV, CVR, CVVR) are precisely those with the longest sonorant duration of the rime. The vowel in CV is quite long phonetically, much longer than

---

[7] A plausible hypothesis would be that in languages which allow contour tones on all syllable types, i.e. in languages without any weight-sensitive restrictions, not only would vowels in CVO syllables with contour tones be longer than vowels in CVO syllables with level tones, just as in Hausa, but also vowels in CV syllables with contour tones would be longer than vowels in CV syllables with level tones.

[8] Duration measurements are averaged over 8 tokens from one speaker. Rime types are /a, am, ap, aːm, aːp/; all are low-toned.

V in either CVR or CVO, or for that matter, than the phonemic long vowels in CVVR and CVVO[9]. The vowel in CV is also qualitatively quite similar to the long vowels in CVVR and CVVO which are more peripheral than the short vowels in CVO and CVR. Thus, although there is no phonemic contrast in length in open syllables, the vowel in CV is more accurately treated as a long vowel than as a short vowel, both in terms of quality and in terms of quantity. The assignment of the vowel in CV to the long category is also corroborated by the judgment of my consultant and also those of other authors (e.g. Kao (1971), also cf. Duanmu (1994b) on Mandarin). Presumably the length of the vowel in open syllables is a function of the more common cross-linguistic tendency for vowels to *lengthen* in open syllables (unlike the Hausa situation, see above) combined with a requirement that words be minimally a certain duration (cf. Duanmu (1994a). Most words are monosyllabic in Cantonese.

The long duration of the sonorous portion in CV relative to that in CVO and CVVO offers an explanation for why phonemic CV but not CVO and CVVO can carry a contour tone in Cantonese. Thus, the apparent opposite ordering in the relative weight of CV and CVO between Hausa and Cantonese stems from the same source: phonetic lengthening of the vowel in the heavier syllable type (CV in Cantonese and CVO in Hausa) due to independent language specific factors. In the case of Cantonese, the duration and quality of the vowel in phonemic CV warrants its treatment as CVV.

Furthermore, the second unexpected weight ranking in Cantonese, CVR ranked above CVVO, also has a phonetic explanation. The sonorous portion of CVVO is quite short relative to the sonorous portion of either CVR or CV.

4.2 Weight-Sensitive Tone: A Summary

In summary, we have seen that weight-sensitive restrictions on contour tones have a phonetic basis in terms of the ability of different syllable types to support a contour tone. Syllables containing a long vowel are best suited to license a contour tone due to the rich and intense harmonic structure of vowels. Hence, it is correctly predicted that many languages only allow contour tones on syllables containing a long vowel. Syllables closed by a sonorant also provide a good platform for realizing contour tones, though not as good as a long vowel. The relatively large number of languages which allow contours on both CVV and CVR thus also follows from phonetic considerations. Finally, CVO and CV syllables are basically equivalent in terms of their phonetic ability to carry contour tones. It follows that CVO and CV are treated identically by phonologies when it comes to contour tone restrictions. Apparent cases of exceptions to the phonetic motivations for tone restrictions (e.g. CVO and CV behaving differently from one another, and CVR but not CVVO carrying contours) are, upon closer evaluation, reducible to language specific phonetic patterns which provide further support for the phonetic basis of contour tone restrictions. Thus, the asymmetry between weight criteria for tone and

---

[9]Kao (1971) reports similar phonetic results in her study of Cantonese; however, vowel quality and coda consonant were not controlled for in her study, unlike in the present study.

weight criteria for other phenomena becomes even more striking, as does the case for process specificity of weight.

5. A Formal Analysis of Contour Tone Restrictions

Thus far, we have seen that weight-sensitive contour tone restrictions are grounded in phonetic considerations. In this section, I develop a formal analysis of these restrictions within an Optimality-Theoretic (OT) framework (Prince and Smolensky (1993)). The basic approach adopted here is similar to one adopted in much work within OT, that the ranking of constraints is governed to a large extent by phonetic scales (e.g. Prince and Smolensky (1993), Kenstowicz (1994), Jun (1995), etc.). The idea is that certain constraint rankings are universally impermissible, since they would contradict these phonetic scales. For example, consonants are never selected as syllable peaks preferentially over vowels, because consonants are less sonorous than vowels (Prince and Smolensky (1993)), where sonority is ultimately a function of phonetic properties. This is reflected in the constraint rankings: a constraint against vowel nuclei is never ranked above a constraint against consonant nuclei. Similarly, high vowels are never heavier than low vowels in stress systems, because high vowels are less sonorous than low vowels (Kenstowicz (1994)). The scale of sonority, which is correlated with a phonetic measurement of energy (Gordon (1998)), is reflected in constraint rankings: the constraint prohibiting stress on high vowels is in no language ranked above the constraint against stress on low vowels. By appealing to phonetic scales, the range of cross-linguistic variation in constraint ranking, and hence the range of grammars attested cross-linguistically, is greatly constrained.

Restrictions on contour tones can be formalized in terms of constraints which refer to elements in the weight hierarchy in (4). These constraints appear in (11). Note that for maximal transparency they are stated directly in terms of syllable types rather than features or timing positions.

(11) $^{*}\underset{V}{\overset{T\ T}{\vee}}$ $\quad$ $^{*}\underset{VO}{\overset{T\ T}{\vee}}$ $\quad$ $^{*}\underset{VR}{\overset{T\ T}{\vee}}$ $\quad$ $^{*}\underset{VV}{\overset{T\ T}{\vee}}$

The ranking of these constraints follows a (nearly, see below) universal hierarchy, with constraints to the left ranked ahead of those to the right; this ranking reflects the hierarchy in (4) and is phonetically grounded in terms of the relative ability of different syllable types to support contour tones.

The constraints in (11) conflict with faithfulness constraints requiring the preservation of underlying contour tones. By interleaving the relevant faithfulness constraint(s) with the constraints in (11) we get the four basic patterns of contour tone restrictions seen earlier in (3). This is illustrated in (12), where rankings are indicated by arrows from the higher ranked to the lower ranked constraint.

(12)   Faithfulness (Tone)

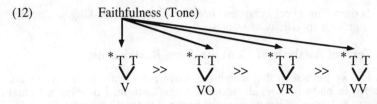

When Faithfulness outranks all four constraints on tone, we get a language which allows contour tones on all syllable types. If Faithfulness is ranked above the bottom three constraints on tone, we get a language which tolerates contours on all syllables except CV (e.g. Hausa). If Faithfulness outranks the bottom two tone constraints, the result is a language with contours on CVV and CVR (e.g. Kiowa). Finally, if Faithfulness is ranked above only the lowest ranked tone constraint, we get contours only on CVV (e.g. Somali). Cantonese requires modifications in the implicational hierarchy in (12); these modifications are correlated with language-specific phonetic factors, as shown in section 4.1.2. In Cantonese, all vowels in open syllables belong to the long vowel category. Furthermore, the relevant factor for contour tones in Cantonese is whether the syllable ends in an obstruent or not. Syllables ending in an obstruent cannot support a contour tone, unlike open syllables and syllables ending in a sonorant. Thus, the constraint against contour tones on VV must be subdivided into constraints sensitive to the presence or absence and type of coda consonant.

6. Conclusions

Weight criteria for contour tone restrictions are divergent from weight criteria for other weight-sensitive phenomena, suggesting that process specificity is an important ingredient in syllable weight. Once process specificity is incorporated into the formal analysis, the goal is then to find explanations for individual weight-sensitive processes. We have seen that one such phenomenon, contour tone restrictions, has a phonetic basis in terms of a syllable's overall sonority. Crucially, because the phonetic requirements motivating contour tone restrictions are different from those driving other weight-sensitive phenomena, it is correctly predicted that the phonology of weight for contour tones will be different from the phonology of weight for other weight-based processes. Languages which appear to contradict the phonetic basis for contour tone restrictions turn out, upon closer phonetic examination, to be only apparent exceptions which offer further support for the phonetically-driven nature of weight-sensitive tone and the process specificity of syllable weight.

References

Allen, W. Sidney. 1973. *Accent and rhythm*. Cambridge: Cambridge University Press.
Bosson, James E. 1964. *Modern Mongolian*. Uralic and Altaic Series 38. Bloomington: Indiana University.

Dalby, J and R. Port. 1981. Temporal Structures of Japanese: Segment, Mora, and Word. *Research in Phonetics*. Bloomington: Indiana University, Department of Linguistics.

Duanmu, San. 1994a. Against Contour Tone Units. *LI* 25(4).555-608.

Duanmu, San. 1994b. Syllabic Weight and Syllabic duration: A correlation between Phonology and Phonetics. *Phonology* 11.1-24.

Gordon, Matthew. 1998. *Syllable Weight: Phonetics, Phonology and Typology*. Doctoral dissertation, University of California, Los Angeles.

Hayes, Bruce. 1988. Metrics and Phonological Theory, in F. Newmeyer, ed., *Linguistics: The Cambridge Survey, vol. 2, Linguistic Theory: Extensions and Implications*. Cambridge: Cambridge University Press.

Hayes, Bruce. 1989. Compensatory lengthening in moraic phonology. *Linguistic Inquiry* 20. 253-306.

Hayes, Bruce. 1995. *Metrical Stress Theory: Principles and Case Studies*. Chicago: University of Chicago Press.

House, David. 1990. *Tonal Perception in Speech*. Lund: Lund Univ.Press.

Hyman, Larry. 1985. *A Theory of Phonological Weight*. Publications in Language Sciences 19. Dordrecht: Foris.

Hyman, Larry. 1992. Moraic Mismatches in Bantu. *Phonology* 9(2).255-266.

Jakobson, Roman. 1931. Die Betonung und ihre Rolle in der Wort- und Syntagma-Phonologie, in *Roman Jakobson, Selected Writings* I.117-136. The Hague: Mouton.

Jun, Jongho. 1996. Place Assimilation as the Result of Conflicting Perceptual and Articulatory Constraints, in J. Camacho, L. Choueiri and M. Watanabe, eds., *Proceedings of the 14th West Coast Conference on Formal Linguistics*, 221-38. Palo Alto: CSLI.

Kao, D. 1971. *Structure of the Syllable in Cantonese*. The Hague: Mouton

Kenstowicz, Michael. 1994. *Sonority-driven stress*. Ms. MIT. Available on Rutgers Optimality Network.

Levin, Juliette. 1985. *A Metrical Theory of Syllabicity*. Doctoral dissertation, MIT.

Maddieson, I. 1997. Phonetic Universals, in W. Hardcastle and J. Laver, eds. *Handbook of Phonetic Sciences*, 619-39. Cambridge: Blackwell.

Maddieson, Ian. 1985. Phonetic cues to syllabification, in V. Fromkin, ed.,*Phonetic Linguistics: Essays in Honor of Peter Ladefoged*, 203-21. Orlando: Academic Press.

McCarthy and Prince 1995. Prosodic Morphology, in J. Goldsmith, ed. *Handbook of Phonological Theory*, 318-66. Cambridge, MA: Blackwell.

Mester, Armin. 1994. The Quantitative Trochee in Latin. *NLLT* 12.1-61.

Mohanan, K.P. 1986. *The Theory of Lexical Phonology*. Dordrecht: Reidel.

Moore, Brian. 1995. *An Introduction to the Psychology of Hearing*. San Diego: Academic Press.

Prince, Alan and Smolensky, Paul .1993. *Optimality Theory: Constraint Interaction in Generative Grammar*. Ms. Rutgers University and University of Colorado at Boulder. Available on Rutgers Optimality Network.

Watkins, Laurel. 1984. *A Grammar of Kiowa*. Lincoln, Nebraska: University of Nebraska Press.

Group Indefinites

JAVIER GUTIÉRREZ-REXACH

Ohio State University

1. Bare Plurals vs. Indefinites

The most common view of the semantics of bare plurals and indefinites during the eighties (Kamp, 1981; Heim, 1982) conceived of these two types of expressions as uniformly contributing to LF free variables restricted by the nominal expression. In this view, bare plurals and indefinites receive their quantificational force indirectly, either when a c-commanding quantifier binds the variable they contribute to LF (Heim), or in the semantics, when the Discourse Representation Structure they occur in is interpreted or "embedded" in a model (Kamp). Since bare plurals and indefinites are in principle indistinguishable from the quantificational point of view, the differences in interpretation that may arise —generic vs. existential readings of bare plurals, or the contrast between specific and non-specific indefinites— have to be handled using additional operators —as in the case of generic readings— and via raising and reconstruction operations displacing the variable and its restriction from its original site (Diesing, 1992).

Recently, several authors have proposed what can be called a "neocarlsonian" approach to the interpretation of bare plurals (Chierchia 1997; Dobrovie Sorin, 1997; de Swart, 1997). In this view, and following some of Carlson's (1977) ideas, bare plurals and indefinites do not behave uniformly, and lexical type assignment and type-shifting mechanisms handle interpretive variation. Thus, from a cross-linguistic perspective, bare plurals and indefinites may be specified differently in the lexicon of different languages. Even within the same language, contrasting interpretations may be resolved using lexical devices. These contrasts in lexical specification are associated with a variety of type-shifting mechanisms (de Swart, 1997).

Chierchia (1997) formulates the Bare Noun Parameter, that attempts to capture the quantificational variability of bare nouns cross-linguistically. Bare plurals may be lexically specified as arguments —expressions of type e—, as predicates —expressions of type $< e, t >$—, or as both, as illustrated in the following table:

NP	NP	NP
$[+arg, -pred]$	$[-arg, +pred]$	$[+arg, +pred]$

In some languages, like Chinese, bare plurals are uniformly arguments, whereas in English they may be specified either as type e or type $< e, t >$ expressions. McNally (1995) convincingly argues that Romance bare plurals denote properties, i.e. they are expressions of type $< e, t >$, hence the unavailability of generic readings and other related effects. Treating bare plurals as arguments that syntactically incorporate into a verb requires a semantic correlate of the incorporation operation that combines the predicate with the bare plural. This semantic operation introduces the existential quantificational force in the semantic representation and consists in lifting the type of the verb from the type of a predicate to the type of an "incorporating verb." Let us call this operation *semantic incorporation* (Carlson, 1977; Van Geenhoven, 1995). If an expression P is an "incorporating (transitive) verb," then it denotes the function $\lambda Q \lambda y \exists x [P'(y, x) \wedge Q'(x)]$.

The lexical approach to the semantic of indefinites requires an association of two different semantic objects to indefinite expressions, corresponding to the characteristic distinction between referential and quantificational interpretations. Following Reinhart (1997) and Winter (1997), it can be proposed that indefinite expressions either (i) denote functions from properties to generalized quantifiers and are consequently subject to the Quantifier Raising operation, or (ii) denote choice functions.

Choice functions are taken to model the specific/referential readings of indefinites plus the intermediate readings of these expressions and are defined as follows:

(1) TYPE(f) = $<< e, t >, e >$
     CH = $\lambda f. \forall P_{<e,t>}[[P \neq \emptyset \to f(P) \in P] \wedge [P = \emptyset \to f(P) = \perp]]$

A choice function applies to a property and selects an individual from that property. Therefore, the interpretation of sentence (2a) according to the translation in (2b) may be paraphrased as "there is a choice function f selecting an individual from the set denoted by *man* and such that this individual is in the set denoted by *walk*."

(2)   a. A man is walking

    b. $\exists f[CH(f) \wedge walk'(f(man'))]$

2. A Third Class of Indefinites

In this paper and based on evidence from Spanish, the existence of a third class of indefinites which do not behave either as choice functions or as quantificational indefinite determiners of type $<< e,t >$ $,<< e,t >,t >>$ will be argued for. These indefinites will be called *group indefinites* as a result of their characteristic properties. In general, the existence of this class of indefinites provides further support for a lexicalist, type-driven and non-uniform approach to the semantics of indefinites.

There are two different indefinite determiners in Spanish: (i) *un* 'a/one' with its plural counterpart *unos* 'one-pl./a-pl.', and (ii) *algún* 'some', with plural *algunos* 'some-pl.' These determiners denote intersective (existential) functions (Keenan, 1987), where we say that a function $\mathbf{F} \in [\mathcal{P}(E) \rightarrow [\mathcal{P}(E) \rightarrow \{T, F\}]]$ is *intersective* iff it satisfies the following invariance condition: $\forall A, A', B, B' \subseteq E, A \cap B = A' \cap B'$ then $\mathbf{F}(A)(B) = \mathbf{F}(A)(B)$.

The standard definition of the plural determiners *unos* 'a-pl.' and *algunos* 'some-pl.' in type $<< e,t >, << e,t >,t >>$ would be as follows: $\mathbf{UNOS}(A)(B) = \mathbf{ALGUNOS}(A)(B) = 1$ iff $|A \cap B| \geq 2$. This definition predicts that *unos* 'a-pl' and *algunos* 'some-pl.' can occur in existential-*haber* constructions:

(3)   Hay   unos/algunos libros sobre la mesa
      there-are a-pl./some-pl. books on   the table

Nevertheless, there are several properties that contrast these two determiners systematically. First, a noun phrase headed by *unos* cannot occur as the subject of an individual-level predicate, whereas a noun phrase with *algunos* can, as shown in (4). Second, as observed by Villalta (1994), *unos N'* does not combine with the distributive predicates illustrated in (5).

(4)   a. *Unos/algunos atletas son inteligentes
        'Some athletes are intelligent'

    b. *Unas/algunas especies se extinguieron
       'Some species are extinct'

(5)   a. *Unos/algunos chicos se pusieron los   pantalones
        *a-pl./some-pl. boys SE put   their pants

       'Some boys put their pants on'

    b. *Unos/algunos estudiantes se dieron la vuelta
        *a-pl./some-pl. students   SE gave   the turn

       'Some students turned around'

Interestingly, the above restrictions on *unos* disappear when the determiner is contrastively focused (6). Similarly, the singular determiner *un* 'a' does not obey these restrictions, as shown in (7).

(6)   a. Unos estudiantes son inteligentes, otros no
        a-pl. students   are intelligent, others not

       'Some students are intelligent, others aren't'

    b. Unos chicos se pusieron los   pantalones, otros no
        a-pl. boys SE put   their pants,   others not

       'Some boys put their pants on, others didn't'

(7)   a. Un estudiante de física   es normalmente inteligente
        a   student   of physics is normally   intelligent

       'A student of physics is normally intelligent'

    b. Un chico se puso los pantalones
        a   boy SE put the pants

       'A boy put his pants on'

A third contrasting property is that the plural determiner *unos* only participates in group predication. It can combine with group level or collective predicates (8), but not with reflexives or reciprocals (9):

(8)   a. Unos soldados rodearon   la   ciudad
        a-pl. soldiers surrounded the city

       'A group of soldiers surrounded the city'

    b. Unos estudiantes se reunieron en el   pasillo
        a-pl. students   SE gathered in the corridor

       'Some students gathered in the corridor'

(9)   *Unas chicas se miraron a sí   mismas/una a la   otra
       *a-pl. girls SE looked to self same/one   to the other

'Some girls looked at themselves/at each other'

When the noun phrase headed by *unos* combines with a distributive predicate, it forces a group reading (10). Similarly, in (11) only the collectivizing modifier *entre todos* 'among all' is allowed. The presence of *cada uno* 'each one' would force distribution over students. Sentence (12) has only a collective reading: only one lifting takes place, i.e. a group of students lifted a table. [1]

(10)   Unos soldados se dieron la   vuelta
       a-pl. soldiers SE gave   the turn

'A group of soldiers turned around'

(11)   Unos estudiantes comieron una tarta *cada uno/entre   todos
       a-pl. students   ate   a   pie   *each one/among all

'Some students ate a pie *each/together'

(12)   Unos estudiantes levantaron una mesa
'Some students lifted a table'

Another important contrasting property between the plural determiners *unos* and *algunos* is that *unos* obeys what can be called a "no linking" constraint. In the following example, *unos de lingüística* 'a-pl. of linguistics' cannot be related to a discourse referent (a set of books) already present in discourse. In other words, it lacks a specific/partitive interpretation in the sense of Enç (1991). On the other hand, the only possible interpretation of *algunos de lingüística* 'some-pl. about linguistics' is the partitive one.

---

[1] A related piece of evidence is provided by the expression *veces* 'times,' which obligatorily triggers distribution over times. The adverbial *unas veces* 'a-pl. times' is ill-formed (ia), except when contrastively focused, as in (ib).

(i)   a. Algunas/*unas   veces no te apetece   trabajar
          some-fem.pl./*a-fem.pl. times not TE want-you work

       'Sometimes one does not want to work'

       b. Unas   veces no quieres,   otras sí
          a-fem.pl. times not want-you, others yes

       'Sometimes you want it, others you don't'

(13) Los libros de matemáticas están en el cajón, los de física debajo
      de la cama y hay ??unos/ algunos de lingüística sobre la mesa
      'Mathematics books are in the drawer, physics books are under
      the bed and there are some about linguistics over the table'

Pronominal determiners (Westerståhl, 1989) are those that can occur without an overt restriction. Pronominalization can be conceived
of as a type transition operation PRON (Gutiérrez Rexach, 1997a), [2]
raising a determiner expression to the type of a generalized quantifier
($<< e, t >, t >$). PRON accommodates a contextually provided restriction or context set C (Westerståhl, 1985) as the first argument of
the determiner, yielding the lifted quantifier function PRON($\mathbf{D}^C$) =
$\mathbf{D}$(C). Satisfaction of the "no linking" constraint by a determiner is incompatible with potential pronominal behaviour, because pronominalization involves linking to a contextually provided set. This treatment
of pronominalization straightforwardly predicts the fact that *unos* cannot occur as a pronominal determiner, in contrast to other determiners
such as *algunos* 'some-pl,' numerals, *muchos* 'many,' etc.

(14) Has   visto perros recientemente? Yo he   visto
      Have-you seen dogs   lately?   I   have seen
      tres/algunos/muchos/todos/*unos
      three/some-pl./many/all/*a-pl.

Finally, the noun phrase headed by *unos* may act as a predicate
and occur in a predicative position —after the copula *be*— in parallel
to bare plurals:

(15) Estos políticos   son idiotas/unos/*algunos/*los idiotas
      These politicians are idiots/a-pl./*some-pl./*the idiots

Again, this property may be explained as a result of the operation
BE (Partee, 1987) that lowers an expression of type $<< e, t >, t >$ to
type $< e, t >$. The question arises as to why this is possible in the
case of *unos* but not in the case of *algunos*. Additionally, there is a
difference between predication with a bare plural and predication with
unos N'. As observed above, *unos* induces group predication so the
most natural interpretation of (16) is 'these politicians are idiots *as a
whole*.'

(16) ??Los políticos   son siempre unos idiotas
      the   politicians are always a-pl. idiots

---

[2] In Gutiérrez Rexach (1997a) the operation is studied in the context of the
analysis of pronominal interrogative determiners.

The use of *unos N'* is also preferred as a way of expressing evaluative predication, as illustrated in (17).

(17) Estos estudiantes son unos normales
      these students   are a-pl. normal-pl.

'These students are really mediocre',
'These students are a mediocre bunch'

3. Group Quantifiers vs. Choice Functions

After considering the properties in the previous section, it seems obvious that a uniform treatment of indefinites is not tenable. Furthermore, the contrasts observed do not seem to be captured simply by a distinction between quantifiers and choice functions. I will claim that *algún* and *algunos* denote choice functions, and that *unos* does not denote a determiner in type $<< e,t >,<< e,t >,t >>$. Rather it denotes a determiner of a higher type. It is a group indefinite of type $<< e,t >,<<< e,t >,t >,t >>$.

In the box language of Discourse Representation Theory (Kamp and Reyle, 1993), the difference can be schematically characterized as follows: (i) group indefinites contribute a group discourse referent to the semantic representation, as shown in the Discourse Representation Structure (18a), whereas (ii) *algunos* contributes a choice function (18b). [3]

(18)   a.

X
$P^*(X)$
$Q^*(X)$

b.

f
$P(f(Q))$

In static terms, TYPE $(unos) = << e,t >,<<< e,t >,t >,t >>$, and the function denoted by this indefinite expression is as follows:

(19) $[\![unos]\!] = \lambda P_{<e,t>}\lambda Q_{<<e,t>,t>}.\exists X \subseteq P[|X| > 1 \wedge Q(X)]$

From (19), it follows that *unos (P)* is a quantificational determiner that carries an additional restriction: it necessarily combines with collective/group predicates. We say that a predicate Q is collective iff $[\![Q]\!] = \lambda X.Q(X) \wedge |X| > 1$. A collective predicate is only true of collections

---

[3] In Gutiérrez Rexach (1997b) a more restrictive DRT language without choice functions is assumed, and the relevant contrast is claimed to be the ability of *algunos* to trigger "box-splitting."

of individuals, i.e. sets of cardinality greater than 1. A group indefinite combines with a predicate that is not intrinsically collective only if the predicate is lifted to type $<< e, t >, t >$ through a group predication operator γ (Van der Does, 1992), where $\gamma = \lambda Q \lambda X.Q(X) \wedge |X| > 1$. Trivially, if a predicate Q is collective then $\gamma(Q) = Q$.

Dynamically speaking, the difference between bare plurals and NPs headed by *unos* is that *unos N'* introduces a group discourse referent and no access to its atoms is allowed. As a consequence, this type of discourse referent cannot combine with a predicative condition that requires distribution over the members of a discourse referent (Gutiérrez Rexach, 1997b). Bare plurals introduce a neutral discourse referent (Kamp and Reyle, 1993), and access to the atoms of this sort of discourse referent is not banned.

Bare plurals and group indefinites critically contrast in their ability to support plural anaphora in discourse. The predicative status of bare plurals makes anaphora support impossible, whereas the group discourse referent contributed by a group indefinite may serve as the antecedent of an anaphoric pronoun.

(20)   Pedro ha visto a unos estudiantes/*estudiantes y María también los ha visto
       'Pedro has seen some students/*students and María saw them too'

Plural group indefinites block distributive readings and combination with reflexives and reciprocals because the semantic operations of distribution and reflexivization require access to the atoms of the group. For example, consider a transitive relation $[\![R]\!]$ — i.e. the denotation of a predicate R such that $\text{TYPE}(R) = < e, < e, t >>$. Then, the operation of reflexivization REFL is defined as follows: $[\![REFL(R)]\!] = \lambda x.R(x, x)$. If we consider transitive predicates that are collective in one or more of its arguments, the situation does not change. Take a predicate R such that $\text{TYPE}(R) = << e, t >, << e, t >, t >>$. Then, $[\![REFL(R)]\!] = \lambda X.|X| = 1 \wedge R(X, X)$, so the property $[\![REFL(R)]\!]$ is not in the domain of the function $[\![unos(P)]\!]$.

The incompatibility with individual level predicates and categorical statements follows as a type mismatch. Individual-level predicates are generic polarity items (Chierchia, 1995). They only combine with expressions of type e (kinds), whereas categorical statements require strong (quantificational) subjects (Ladusaw, 1994; Gutiérrez Rexach, 1997b). Since *unos N'* is an expression of type $<<< e, t >, t >, t >$, it cannot apply to an individual-level expression.

The singular determiner *un* 'a' is a standard existential quantifier —TYPE $(un) = <<e,t>, <<e,t>,t>>$— denoting the function:

(21) $[\![un]\!] = \lambda P_{<e,t>}\lambda Q_{<e,t>}.\exists x[P(x) \wedge Q(x)]$

The quantifier *un(P)* may combine with distributive predicates, as shown in (7b), and with reflexive or reciprocal expressions. It can also combine with individual-level predicates and generics (7a). These facts strongly support the idea that *unos* is not just the pluralization of *un*, but rather a collectivization of this determiner.

4. Choice Function Indefinites

As advanced in the previous section, the plural determiner *algunos* 'some-pl.' introduces a choice function in the semantic representation. The only difference with its singular counterpart *algún* 'some' is that the individuals in the range of the choice function are plural individuals in the case of *algunos* and singular individuals in the case of *algún*.

(22) a. $[\![algunos]\!] =$
        $\lambda P_{<e,t>}\lambda Q_{<<e,t>,t>}.\exists f_{<<e,t>,<e,t>>}[CH(f) \wedge Q(f(P))]$

      b. $[\![\ algún\ ]\!] =$
        $\lambda P_{<e,t>}\lambda Q_{<e,t>}.\exists f_{<<e,t>,e>}[CH(f) \wedge Q(f(P))]$

In general, I will take choice functions to model the specificity and discourse linking properties of indefinites. The determiner *algunos*, in its specific or discourse linked reading, accommodates a context set. Restriction to context sets (Westerståhl, 1985) in the case of choice functions imposes an additional restriction on the choice function. The context set restricts the argument of the choice function, so that for any choice function f and property P, given a context set C, the value of f at P has to be in the intersection of P and C. The specific reading of *algunos N'* arises when the plural individual selected by the choice function after applying to $[\![N']\!]$ is also in a contextually provided set C. The definition of the context restricted indefinite is as follows:

(23) $\lambda P_{<e,t>}\lambda Q_{<<e,t>,t>}.\exists f_{<<e,t>,<e,t>>}[CH(f) \wedge Q(f(P \cap C))]$

The set C in (23) is the context set of the choice function. The context set can be considered a presupposition of the determiner (Zucchi, 1995; Von Fintel, 1994). Presuppositional determiners do not occur in existential *there* constructions. In this respect, *algunos* contrast with the overt partitive *algunos de los* 'some-pl. of the,' which is always restricted to a context set. Thus, *algunos* may occur in an existential construction (24a), but *algunos de los* may not (24b).

(24) a. Hay algunas rosas en el jardín
      there-are some roses in the garden

   b. *Hay algunas de las rosas en el jardín
      there-are some of the roses in the garden

The determiner *unos* never has a discourse linked interpretation
(25a), whereas *algunos* is ambiguous between the discourse linked or
specific reading and the non-specific reading (25b) in which no contextual restriction is imposed. *Algunos de los* is always discourse linked
(25c).

(25) a. Tengo unas   monedas en el   bolsillo
         have-I a-fem.pl. coins   in the pocket

      'I have some coins in my pocket'

   b. Tengo algunas   monedas en el   bolsillo
      have-I some-fem.pl. coins   in the pocket

      'I have some coins in my pocket' or 'Some of the coins are
      in my pocket'

   c. Tengo algunas   de las monedas en el   bolsillo
      have-I some-fem.pl. of the coins   in the pocket

      'Some of my coins/the previously mentioned coins are in
      my pocket'

Algunos and *algunos de los*, as defined in (23), do not impose any
restriction on the predicate they combine with. Thus, they can combine
with distributive predicates, as in (26).

(26) Algunos de los/ algunos niños se pusieron los pantalones
      some-pl. of the/ some-pl. boys SE put   the pants

      'Some of the boys/some boys put their pants on'

5. The Type of Focused Indefinites

In section two, it was observed that contrastive focus on the noun
phrase headed by *unos* has the effect of cancelling the properties of
this determiner related to collectivity. When the determiner *unos* is
focused, it is typically contrasted with the determiner *otros* 'others,' as
illustrated in the following example. In this case, *unos* can accommodate a contextually provided restriction.

(27)   De los libros que hablas   hay   unos sobre la   mesa y
       of the books that talk-you there-are a-pl. over the table and
       otros en el   cajón
       others in the drawer

       'With respect to the books that you are talking about, some are
       on the table and others in the drawer'

In Gutiérrez Rexach (1997b), it is proposed that *unos...otros* be
treated as a discontinuous determiner introducing a duplex condition
in a Discourse Representation Structure. This duplex condition is associated with a contrastive focus interpretation. The expression following
otros contributes the contrast. [4] Contrastive focus triggers lowering
of the indefinite to type *e* (Chierchia, 1997) and, as a consequence,
compatibility with individual-level predicates as illustrated in (28):

(28)   Unas especies se extinguieron, otras no
       a-pl. species SE extinct-past, others not

       'Some species are extinct, others are not'

It is interesting to compare the discontinuous determiner *unos* ...
otros 'some-pl. ... others' with *los unos ... los otros* 'the-pl. some-pl. ...
the-pl. others'. The discontinuous determiner *los unos ... los otros* satisfies the "no linking" constraint, as shown in (29), where a context set
of students cannot be accommodated as a restriction of *los unos*. The
contrast in the interpretation of the sentences in (30), is a by-product
of the different ability of these complex determiners to accommodate
a context set: *unos...otros* may accommodate a contextually provided
restriction, whereas *los unos...los otros* may not. [5]

(29)   Vino un grupo de estudiantes. Unos/*los   unos se
       Came a   group of students.   A-pl./*the-pl. a-pl. SE
       quedaron, otros/*los otros no
       stayed,   others/the others not

       'A group of students came. Some stayed. Others didn't'

---

[4] Syntactically, it might be claimed that the constitution of the discontinuous expression as a determiner takes place at LF through an operation such as absorption.

[5] Another property shared by *los unos...los otros* and *unos* is that the discontinuous determiner cannot co-occur with individual-level predicates either:

(i)   *Las   unas   especies se extinguieron, las   otras no
      the-fem.pl. a-fem.pl. species SE extinct-past, the-fem.pl. others not

(30)　a. Si hablas　con　policías,　unos te　diran　que cedas,
　　　　　If talk-you with policemen, a-pl. you will-tell that comply,
　　　　　otros　que　no
　　　　　others that not
　　　　　'If you talk to policemen, some of them will tell you to
　　　　　comply, others that you don't'

　　　　b. Si hablas　con　policías,　los　　unos te　diran　que
　　　　　If talk-you with policemen, the-pl. a-pl. you will-tell that
　　　　　cedas,　los　　otros que　no
　　　　　comply, the-pl. others that not
　　　　　'If you talk to policemen, some people will tell you to
　　　　　comply with them, others that you don't'

6. Scope and Indefinites

McNally (1995) and Laca (1996) observe that Spanish bare plurals always take narrow scope with respect to other operators in the same
clause. Indefinites (*unos, algunos*) take wide or narrow scope with respect to modal operators and negation, as shown in (31). The contrast
is explained by the fact that semantic incorporation forces narrow scope
of the existential quantifier it contributes to LF.

(31)　a. Pedro tiene que comprar libros/unos/algunos　libros
　　　　　Pedro has　that buy　　books/a-pl./some-pl. books
　　　　　'Pedro has to buy books/some books'
　　　　　(*BP > □; □ > BP; UNOS/ALGUNOS > □; □ >
　　　　　UNOS/ALGUNOS)

　　　　b. A la　reunión no　asistieron profesores/unos profesores/
　　　　　to the meeting not attended　professors/a-pl. professors/
　　　　　algunos　profesores
　　　　　some-pl. professors
　　　　　'No professor attended the meeting'
　　　　　(NO > BP; * BP > NO)
　　　　　'Some professors did not attend the meeting'
　　　　　(UNOS/ALGUNOS > NO; NO > UNOS/ALGUNOS)

Nevertheless, there is evidence that indefinites are not equal in their
scopal behavior. As stated in previous sections, *unos* does not allow distribution over the members of its restriction set. For example,
the presents cannot vary with the students in (32a) whereas in (32b)
presents may vary with students. The plural clitic *les* 'to them' forces

variation and distribution over the members of the doubled element (Gutiérrez Rexach, 1997c) and, as a consequence, is incompatible with *unos*, as shown in (32c).

(32)   a. Le dí   un regalo a unos estudiantes
            him gave-I a   present to a-pl. students

            'I gave a present to a group of students'

        b. Le dí   un regalo a algunos estudiantes
            him gave-I a   present to some-pl. students

            'I gave a present to some students'

        c. Les dí   un regalo a *unos/algunos estudiantes
            them gave-I a present to *a-pl./some-pl. students

            'I gave a present to some students'

Variation is allowed only when what varies is the group, so that there is not distribution over the members of the group. In the reading of (33a) in which *unos estudiantes* 'a-pl. students' has wide scope with respect to *cada mesa* 'each/every table,' there might be more than one table-lifting event, but every table has to be lifted by the same group of students. In the reading where *unos estudiantes* has narrow scope, different groups of students have to be involved in the lifting of different tables. The determiner *algunos* does not obey this restriction. As a consequence, in the reading of (33b) in which *algunos* scopes over *cada*, every student under consideration lifted all the tables. On the other hand, when *cada* has scope over *algunos*, there is one or more than one lifting for each table under consideration.

(33)   a. Unos estudiantes levantaron cada mesa
            a-pl. students   lifted   each table

        b. Algunos estudiantes levantaron cada mesa
            some-pl. students   lifted   each table

The pair-list reading of sentence (34) is characterized in Gutiérrez Rexach (1997a) as involving the formation of a polyadic quantifier in which the declarative and the interrogative quantifier undergo absorption. The reading consists in the pairing of members of the restriction sets of these two quantifiers. The critical fact for our purposes is that the presence of *unos* blocks the availability of the pair-list interpretation, as expected, whereas *algunos* or *algunos de los* do not.

(34)   ¿Qué niña vieron unos/algunos/algunos   de los niños?
        what girl saw   a-pl./some-pl./some-pl. of the boys

    'What girl did some boys see?'

Finally, there is an interesting interaction between conditionals and distributivity. The "double scope" effects observed by Reinhart (1997) and Winter (1997) can be derived from the differential semantics of indefinites. In (35a), the predicate *mueren* 'die-3p.pl.' cannot distribute over the members of the set denoted by *familiares* 'relatives'. Therefore, only one interpretation of the sentence is possible, namely, that I will inherit a fortune if all of my relatives in that group die. In sentence (35b), the predicate *mueren* may distribute over the set of relatives, so the sentence is ambiguous and it is possible that I inherit a fortune if only one of those relatives die.

(35) a. Si unos familiares míos mueren, heredaré   una fortuna
         if a-pl. relatives mine die,   inherit-will-I a fortune
         'If a group of my relatives die, I will inherit a fortune'

      b. Si algunos familiares mueren, heredaré   una fortuna
         if some-pl. relatives die,   inherit-will-I a fortune
         'If some relatives of mine die, I will inherit a fortune'

References

Carlson, Greg. 1977. *Reference to Kinds in English*. Doctoral dissertation, University of Massachusetts, Amherst.

Chierchia, Gennaro. 1995. Individual-Level Predicates as Inherent Generics, in G. Carlson and F. Pelletier, eds., *The Generic Book*. Chicago: Chicago University Press.

Chierchia, Gennaro. 1997. Partitives, Reference to Kinds and Semantic Variation. *Proceedings Semantics and Linguistics Theory (SALT)* VII.

Diesing, Molly. 1992. *Indefinites*. Cambridge, Mass.: MIT Press.

Dobrovie-Sorin, Carmen. 1997. Types of Predicates and the Representation of Existential Readings. *SALT* VII.

van der Does, Jaap. 1992. *Applied Quantifier Logics*. Doctoral dissertation, University of Amsterdam.

van Geenhoven, Veerle. 1995. *Semantic Incorporation and Indefinite Descriptions*. Doctoral dissertation. University of Tübingen.

Gutiérrez Rexach, Javier. 1997a. Questions and Generalized Quantifiers, in Anna Szabolcsi, ed., *Ways of Scope Taking*. Dordrecht: Kluwer Academic Publishers.

Gutiérrez Rexach, Javier. 1997b. Thetic/Categorial Predication and the Semantics of Existential Determiners, in R. Blight, ed., *Texas Linguistics Forum 38: The Syntax and Semantics of Predication*.

Gutiérrez Rexach, Javier. 1997c. *Quantification, Context Dependence and Generalized Minimalist Grammar.* Doctoral dissertation, UCLA.

Heim, Irene. 1982. *The Semantics of Definite and Indefinite Noun Phrases.* Doctoral dissertation, University of Massachusetts, Amherst.

Kamp, Hans. 1981. A Theory of Truth and Semantic Representation, in J. Groenendijk and M. Stokhof, eds., *Truth, Interpretation and Information.* Dordrecht: Foris. 1984.

Kamp, Hans and Uwe Reyle. 1993. *From Discourse to Logic.* Dordrecht: Kluwer Academic Publishers.

Keenan, Edward. 1987. On the Semantic Definition of 'Indefinite NP,' in E. Reuland and A. ter Meulen (eds.), *The Representation of (In)definiteness.* Cambridge, Mass.: MIT Press.

Laca, Brenda. 1996. Acerca de la Semántica de los Plurales Escuetos del Español, in I. Bosque, ed., *El Sustantivo sin Determinación.* Madrid, Visor Libros.

Ladusaw, William. 1994. Thetic and categorical, stage and individual, weak and strong. *Proceedings SALT IV.*

McNally, Luise. 1995. Bare Plurals in Spanish are Interpreted as Properties, in G. Morrill and D. Oehrle, eds., *Proceedings 1995 ESSLI Workshop on Formal Grammar.*

Partee, Barbara. 1987. Noun Phrase Interpretation and Type Shifting Principles, in J. Groenendijk et al., eds., *Studies in Discourse Representation Theory and the Theory of Generalized Quantifiers.* Dordrecht: Foris.

Reinhart, Tanya. 1997. Quantifier Scope: How Labor is Divided Between QR and Choice Functions. *Linguistics and Philosophy* 20.

de Swart, Henriette. 1997. Indefinites in a Type-Shifting Perspective, ms. Utrecht University.

Villalta, Elizabeth. 1994. Plural Indefinites in Spanish and Distributivity, ms., CNRS.

Westerståhl, Dag. 1985. Determiners and Context Sets, in J. van Benthem and A. ter Meulen, eds., *Generalized Quantifiers in Natural Language,* Dordrecht: Foris.

Westerståhl, Dag. 1989. Quantifiers in Formal and Natural Languages, in D. Gabbay and F. Guenthner, eds., *Handbook of Philosophical Logic,* Dordrecht: Reidel.

Winter, Yoad. 1997. Choice Functions and the Scopal Semantics of Indefinites. *Linguistics and Philosophy* 20.

Zucchi, Alessandro. 1995. The Ingredients of Definiteness and the Definiteness Effect. *Natural Language Semantics* 3.

Cross-linguistic Variation in the Compatibility of Negation and Imperatives*

CHUNG-HYE HAN
University of Pennsylvania

1. Introduction

Many works done on the syntax of imperatives in Romance and Slavic languages note that while some languages have negative imperatives, others do not, instead expressing prohibition through the use of suppletive subjunctives or infinitives (Joseph & Philippaki-Warburton (1987), Zanuttini (1991), Zanuttini (1994), Rivero (1994a), Rivero (1994b), Rivero & Terzi (1995), Zanuttini (1997)). This paper provides a novel account for the cross-linguistic variation in the compatibility of imperatives and negation. I argue that some languages rule out negative imperatives because the syntax derives a structure which maps onto an illegitimate semantic representation. This paper mainly considers data from Italian, Spanish, French, Modern Greek, Bulgarian, Serbo-Croatian, German and English.

In §2, I discuss the data and the issues they raise. In §3, I discuss previous studies that provide syntactic accounts of the relation between negation and imperatives. In §4, I discuss a puzzle concerning the non-availability of negative imperatives, which previous studies failed to take into account. In §5, I establish that C^0 is the locus of imperative operator which attracts the imperative verb. In §6, I propose that negative imperatives are ruled out because they have a syntactic configuration which maps onto a semantic representation that is simply uninterpretable. Under the proposed analysis, negative imperatives are ruled out by semantics and not syntax. In §7, I discuss and account for a potential counterexample to the proposed analysis posed by the existence of negative imperatives in Bulgarian and Serbo-Croatian. In §8,

---

*I thank Anthony Kroch for many valuable discussions on this topic. I also thank Robin Clark, Sabine Iatridou, Roumyana Izvorski, Eric Potsdam and Beatrice Santorini for helpful comments. I am also grateful to Alexis Dimitriadis, Luis López, Paola Merlo, Carmen Rio Rey, and Sandra Stjepanovic. Of course, all errors are mine.

I extend the proposed analysis to negative interrogatives.

2. Data and Issues

In Modern Greek and Spanish, imperatives are not compatible with negation. The prohibition is expressed through the use of subjunctives in Modern Greek and subjunctives or infinitives in Spanish.[1]

(1) Modern Greek

    a. * Mi grapse   to!   c. * Mi grapsete   to!
       Neg write-2sg.Imp it   Neg write-2pl.Imp it
       'Don't write it!'   'Don't write it!'

    b. (Na) mi to grapsis!   d. (Na) mi to grapsete!
       NA Neg it write-2sg.Subj   NA Neg it write-2pl.Subj
       'Don't write it!'   'Don't write it!'

(2) Spanish

    a. * No lee!   d. * No hablad!
       Neg read-2sg.Imp   not talk-2pl.Imp
       'Don't read!'   'Don't talk!'

    b. No leas!   e. No habléis!
       Neg read-2sg.Subj   not talk-2pl.Subj
       'Don't read!'   'Don't talk!'

    c. No leer!   f. No hablar!
       Neg read-Inf   not talk-Inf
       'Don't read!'   'Don't talk!'

In Italian, imperatives in the 2nd person singular cannot be negated, but imperatives in the 2nd person plural can be. The prohibition in the 2nd person singular is expressed through the use of suppletive infinitives.

(3) Italian

    a. ' * Non telefona le!   c. Telefonate le!
       Neg call-2sg.Imp her   call-2pl.Imp her
       'Don't call her!'   'Call her!'

    b. Non telefonare le!   d. Non telefonate le!
       Neg call-Inf   Neg call-2pl.Imp her
       'Don't call her!'   'Don't call her!'

[1] In Modern Greek, many imperative verbs in the 2nd person plural have the same forms as corresponding subjunctive verbs. One way to distinguish the two forms is through the use of pronominal clitics. In imperatives, clitics encliticize onto the verb, whereas in subjunctives, they procliticize.

Imperatives in the 2nd person singular have verbal forms unique to the imperative paradigm, whereas imperatives in the 2nd person plural have verbal forms morphologically identical to the corresponding indicative form. For this reason, Zanuttini (1991) refers to 2nd person singular imperatives as TRUE IMPERATIVES and 2nd person plural imperatives as SUPPLETIVE IMPERATIVES.[2] In French, German, Bulgarian, Serbo-Croatian and English, imperatives are compatible with negation.

(4) French

    a. Ne chante pas!
       Neg sing-2sg.Imp pas
       'Don't sing!'

    b. Ne chantez pas!
       Neg sing-2pl.Imp pas
       'Don't sing!'

(5) German

    a. Schreib nicht!
       write-2sg.Imp neg
       'Don't write!'

    b. Schreibt nicht!
       write-2pl.Imp neg
       'Don't write!'

(6) Bulgarian

    a. Ne četi!
       Neg read-2sg.Imp
       'Don't read!'

    b. Ne četete!
       Neg read-2pl.Imp
       'Don't read!'

(7) Serbo-Croatian

    a. Ne čitaj!
       Neg read-2sg.Imp
       'Don't read!'

    b. Ne čitajte!
       Neg read-2pl.Imp
       'Don't read!'

The data considered here raise the following issues.

- Why are imperatives compatible with negation in some languages but not in others?

- In languages like Italian, in which the imperative verbal paradigm has both true and suppletive imperative verbal forms, why are imperatives in the suppletive form compatible with negation, whereas true imperatives are not?

- Why do languages that do not allow negative imperatives choose infinitives or subjunctives as suppletive forms?

In this paper, I only address the first issue for lack of space. See Han (in prep.) for the discussion of the other issues.

---

[2] In Italian, although imperatives in the 2nd person plural have verbal forms morphologically identical to the corresponding indicative form, they do not have the syntax of indicatives. Pronominal clitics procliticize onto verbs in indicative sentences, but they encliticize in both affirmative and negative imperative sentences.

3. Previous Studies

3.1 Zanuttini (1991, 1994, 1997)

Zanuttini (1991, 1994, 1997) provides an account for Romance of the incompatibility of negation and true imperatives. Her basic claim is that imperatives are defective in that they lack a certain functional category required by a certain type of negation. Hence, languages with this type of negation do not have negative imperatives. Here, I discuss the version presented in Zanuttini (1991) in more detail (because it is the most straightforward and simplest version).

Zanuttini (1991) distinguishes between preverbal and postverbal negation in Romance: preverbal negation requires TP, whereas postverbal negation does not. She also argues that imperatives are tenseless and so do not project TP. Putting the two assumptions together, Zanuttini concludes that imperatives are incompatible with negation in languages that have preverbal negation (e.g., Italian, Spanish and Catalan).

Although Zanuttini's analysis works well for Romance, it does not easily extend to Balkan languages such as Modern Greek, Bulgarian, and Serbo-Croatian. These languages all have preverbal negation but differ in whether they allow negative imperatives: Modern Greek does not, whereas Bulgarian and Serbo-Croatian do. Given Zanuttini's analysis, one would have to argue that either the preverbal negation of Modern Greek requires TP but that of Bulgarian and Serbo-Croatian does not, or that TP is absent in the imperatives of Modern Greek but present in those of Bulgarian and Serbo-Croatian.

3.2 Rivero (1994), Rivero and Terzi (1995)

The accounts given in Rivero (1994) and Rivero and Terzi (1995) start from the assumption that Neg^0 projects to NegP in Modern Greek, Spanish, Bulgarian and Serbo-Croatian and that they share a phrase structure in which CP dominates NegP, which in turn dominates IP. Rivero and Terzi argue that in Spanish and Modern Greek (and potentially in Italian) the root C^0 hosts a strong imperative mood feature that must be checked by the verb before Spell-out requiring the imperative verb to move to C^0 overtly. The claim is that negative imperatives are unavailable in Modern Greek and Spanish because Neg^0 blocks imperative verb movement to C^0.

According to Rivero and Terzi, in Bulgarian and Serbo-Croatian, the strong imperative mood feature is located in I^0, rather than in C^0. This means that the imperative verb moves only up to I^0. Negative imperatives are available in these languages because imperative verbs do not cross Neg^0. According to Rivero and Terzi, C^0 cannot be the position associated with imperative force in these languages (or any other illocutionary force for that matter), because C^0 is reserved as the last-resort landing site for verb movement to rescue clause-initial clitics.

Rivero and Terzi's analysis is problematic in that it does not take into account the fact that negation in Spanish and Modern Greek have the morphosyntactic properties of clitics, which I discuss in more detail in §4. The issue does not arise for Bulgarian and Serbo-Croatian although the negation markers in these languages are also clitics.

4. A Puzzle Posed by the Clitic-like Nature of Negation

In negative sentences in Modern Greek, Spanish and Italian, negation always precedes the verb and nothing (except for clitics) can intervene between them. That is, negation has the morphosyntactic properties of clitics and it is treated as a unit with the verb in overt syntax. If a verb moves to C^0 in a certain construction in these languages, we expect the verb and negation to move as a unit in the negative counterpart. Hence, it is not surprising that the verb cannot move across Neg^0 in negative imperatives, under a system that assumes imperative verb movement to C^0 as in Rivero and Terzi's analysis.[3]

I observe that a real puzzle concerning the non-availability of negative imperatives comes from the fact that languages like Modern Greek, Spanish and Italian allow the verb and negation to move as a unit to C^0 in other types of sentences. For instance, in Italian Aux-to-Comp constructions, a participle or an infinitive (or, more marginally, a subjunctive) auxiliary inverts around a subject, as in (8a) (Rizzi (1982)). In a negative Aux-to-Comp construction, negation and the verb move to C^0 as a unit, as in (8b).

(8) Italian

    a.   Avendo Gianni fatto questo, ...
           having Gianni done this,   ...

    b.   Non avendo Gianni fatto questo, ...
           Neg having Gianni done this,   ...

In Spanish and Modern Greek, questions can be formed by moving the verb to C^0, resulting in subject-verb inversion. In negative questions, negation and the verb move to C^0 as a unit as well, as in (9).[4]

(9) a.   Ti   den edose o   Yannis stin Meri?
        what Neg gave the Yannis to   Meri
        'What didn't Yannis give to Meri?' (Modern Greek)

    b.   ¿Qué no le   dió Juan a María?
        What Neg to-her gave Juan to Maria
        'What didn't Juan give to Maria?' (Spanish)

Given Rivero and Terzi's analysis, examples in (8b) and (9) are expected to be ungrammatical. But this is not correct. Moreover, given the behavior of negation and the verb in Aux-to-Comp constructions in Italian and in questions in Spanish and Modern Greek, we expect Neg^0 and the verb to move to C^0 as a unit in negative imperatives as well. But this expectation is not borne

---

[3]I assume that clitic negation attaches to the verb in the overt syntax. That is, I am not assuming that cliticization of negation is a pure PF phenomena, where clitic negation attaches to the verb only at PF.

[4]I assume that Spanish allows verb movement to C^0 in some *wh*-questions (see Torrego (1984)). For Modern Greek, there is some controversy as to whether verb-movement to C^0 in questions exists at all (see Anagnostopoulou (1994)).

out. Then, the real puzzle (under the assumption that imperative verb moves to C^0) is why the construction in which Neg^0 and the imperative verb have moved to C^0 as a unit is ruled out in languages that allow verb movement to C^0 along with negation in other types of constructions.

5. The Locus of Imperative Operator: C^0

In this section, I establish that imperatives have CP structures and that C^0 is the locus of the imperative operator. I establish this indirectly by presenting various arguments from the literature that imperative verbs move to C^0 because C^0 hosts an imperative operator. The analysis that I will propose in §6 of the (non)-availability of negative imperatives relies on the result established here, which is based mainly on data from English, German, French, Spanish, Italian, and Modern Greek.

5.1 Subject Position
In German, when an imperative has an overt subject, the verb precedes the subject. In yes-no questions, the verb also precedes the subject.

(10) a. Schreib   Du den Aufsatz!
        write2sg.Imp you the paper
        'You write the paper.'

     b. Schreibst Du den Aufsatz?
        write   you the paper
        'Are you writing the paper?'

The fact that the verb must precede the subject in both imperatives and yes-no questions suggests that the verb in imperatives is located wherever the verb in yes-no questions is located: namely, in C^0.

In English, imperative verbs follow the subject in positive imperatives. But in imperatives with do-support, namely, negative imperatives and emphatic imperatives, the verb do precedes the subject.

(11) a. You open the door!

     b. Don't you talk back to me!

     c. Do at least some of you have a try. (Davies 1986:89)

This suggests that at least auxiliary do moves to C^0 in imperatives. Potsdam (1997) discusses various evidence for the claim that do and don't in imperatives are in C^0.[5]

5.2 Adverb Placement
Adverb placement in Italian imperatives suggests that imperative verbs move to a position quite high in the clausal structure. Zanuttini (1997) shows that imperative verbs obligatorily precede the adverbs pure and ben, which are particles of emphatic affirmation.

---

[5] I assume that in English imperative verbs in sentences without do-support move to C^0 at LF.

(12) a. Dagli   ben   una risposta!
       give-2sg.Imp-him indeed an answer
       'Do give him an answer!' (Zanuttini 1997:135)

     b. * Ben dagli una risposta! (Zanuttini 1997:135)

(13) a. Fallo   pure!
       do-2sg.Imp-it indeed
       'Go ahead and do it!' (Zanuttini 1997:135)

     b. * Pure fallo! (Zanuttini 1997:135)

According to Cinque (1996), *pure* and *ben* occur higher than TP. If so, then the fact that imperative verbs must precede these adverbs suggests that they move higher than the functional head that hosts tense features.

5.3 Clitic Placement

In French, Italian, Spanish and Modern Greek, a direct object clitic must follow the verb in imperatives, whereas it must precede the verb in other types of constructions, such as indicatives and subjunctives.

(14) French

    a. Faites   le!   b. * Le faites!
      do-2pl.Imp it   it do-2pl.Imp
      'Do it!   'Do it!

(15) Modern Greek

    a. Diavase   to!   b. * To diavase!
      read-2sg.Imp it   it read-2sg.Imp
      'Read it!'   'Read it!'

(16) Spanish

    a. Lée   lo!   b. * Lo lée!
      read-2sg.Imp it   it read-2sg.Imp
      'Read it!'   'Read it!'

(17) Italian

    a. Telefona   le!   b. * Le telefona!
      call-2sg.Imp her   her call-2sg.Imp
      'Call her!'   'Call her!'

According to Kayne (1994), a clitic adjoins to an empty head of a functional projection above I^0. In subjunctives and indicatives, the verb moves to I^0, resulting in clitic-verb order. Rooryck (1992), Rivero (1994b) and Rivero & Terzi (1995) take the verb-clitic order in imperatives to indicate that the imperative verb moves to C^0, bypassing the functional head to which the clitic is adjoined (adopting Kayne's analysis of the syntax of clitics).

5.4 Emphatic Commands

Under the assumption that imperative verbs move to C^0, this movement would be blocked if C^0 is already occupied by some other lexical element. Rivero (1994b) discusses such constructions in Spanish. In Spanish, emphatic commands are expressed with *que* and the subjunctive verb. Tellingly, the imperative is ruled out in this construction.

(18)   a.   Que escribáis!   b.   * Que escribid!
           that write-2pl.Pres.Subj   that write-2pl.Imp
           'You just write!'   'You just write!'
           (Rivero 1994b:99)   (Rivero 1994b:99)

The marker *que* is a complementizer in C^0 and it is being used with emphatic force. Since C^0 is already occupied by *que*, emphatic commands cannot co-occur with the imperative verb.

5.5 No Embedded Imperatives

As noted by Sadock & Zwicky (1985) and Palmer (1986), an imperative cannot occur as an embedded clause.

(19)   a.   * O Yannis se dietakse grapse.
          the Yannis you order-2sg write-2sg.Imp
          'Yannis ordered you to write.' (Modern Greek)

       b.   * Pido que dad-me el libro.
          ask that give-2sg.Imp-me the book
          'I ask that you give me the book.' (Spanish)

       c.   * Ti ordino (di/che) fallo!
          you order (of/that) do-2sg.Imp-it
          'I order you (of/that) do it!' (Italian)

       d.   * J'exige que tu chante.
          I-require that you sing-2sg.Imp
          I require that you sing.' (French)

       e.   * Hans schlägt-vor daß du den Aufsatz schreib(e).
          Hans suggests that you the paper write-2sg.Imp
          'Hans suggests that you write the paper.' (German)

Embedded clauses cannot express illocutionary force. If imperatives have an operator in C^0 that encodes directive force, it follows that imperatives cannot be embedded in and of itself. This fact does not show that imperative verbs move to C^0 but it is consistent with the claim that the locus of imperative operator that encodes directive force is in C^0.

6. Proposal

Before I present my analysis with respect to the cross-linguistic variation in the compatibility of negation and imperative, I note that the directive force contributed by the imperative mood cannot be negated. This is shown by the fact that negative imperatives only have reading in which the directive force has scope over the negation, never in which the negation has scope over the directive force.

(20)   Don't call!
        ≈ I order you not to call.
        ≉ I don't order you to call.

This fact is not specific to imperatives, but holds of interrogatives and statements as well. Just as the directive force of an imperative cannot be negated, neither can the question force of an interrogative nor the assertive force of a statement.

I propose an account of the cross-linguistic variation in the availability of negative imperatives based on the fact that the directive force cannot be negated and on the assumption that the imperative operator encoding the directive force is located in C^0.

The proposal is that negative imperatives are unavailable in some languages because they have syntactic configuration in which negation takes syntactic scope over the imperative operator in C^0. Such constructions are ruled out because they map onto a semantic representation in which the directive force ends up being negated. Such semantic representations are simply illegal. Under the proposed analysis, negative imperatives are ruled out by semantics and not syntax.

6.1 Languages without Negative Imperatives
Recall that negative imperatives are not available in Modern Greek, Spanish and Italian (in the 2nd person singular). In all three languages, sentential negation is expressed by a preverbal negation which has the status of a clitic on the verb. This means that the negative marker is treated as a unit with the verb in the overt syntax. Thus, in negative imperatives, we expect the negative marker and the verb to move to C^0 as a unit. However, if it did, the imperative operator would end up within the scope of negation. Consequently, the directive force would end up being negated, resulting in semantic uninterpretability.[6]

6.2 Languages with Negative Imperatives
Languages that have negative imperatives include English, French and German. In German, the verb in imperatives is also adjoined to C^0. But negation never forms a unit with the verb, and so it never ends up in C^0. Since Neg^0 stays low in the clause, it does not scope over the imperative operator in C^0.

In French, the imperative verb and the negative marker *ne* form a unit, and so when the imperative verb moves to C^0, *ne* also ends up there. Thus,

---

[6]I assume the definition of c-command given in Kayne (1994).

(1)   Definition of c-command (Kayne 1994)
       X c-commands Y iff X and Y are categories and X excludes Y (i.e., no segment of X dominates Y) and every category that dominates X dominates Y.

Under the definition of c-command in (1), when the negation and the verb adjoin to C^0, the negation c-commands C^0 but C^0 does not c-command negation. Thus, negation asymmetrically scopes over the imperative operator and the other scope possibility where the imperative operator scopes over negation is ruled out by the syntax.

the proposed analysis seems to predict incorrectly that imperatives should not be compatible with negation in French. However, closer look reveals why imperatives and negation are compatible in French after all. French forms sentential negation with *ne ... pas*, where *ne* is a proclitic on the verb. In informal registers, the negative clitic *ne* is not obligatory, indicating that *ne* is pleonastic and that sentential negation is expressed by *pas*. But then, the prediction is that negative imperatives are available in French: the imperative verb moves to C^0 with the pleonastic *ne*, and the true negation *pas* stays low in the clause. Hence, the negation does not take scope over the imperative force of C^0.

English has two types of negative imperatives: *do not* imperatives, as in *Do not call*, and *don't* imperatives, as in *Don't call*. The explanation for why *do not* imperatives are available is simple: *do* alone moves and adjoins to C^0, and *not* stays low in the clause. And so, negation does not take scope over the imperative operator of C^0.

In the case of *don't* imperatives, negation forms a unit with *do*. Moreover, as is evident from the order of *don't* and the subject in imperatives (e.g., *Don't you cry*), *don't* is in C^0. Just as in Spanish, Italian and Modern Greek, in *don't* imperatives, negation and the imperative verb form a unit and adjoin to C^0, the locus of imperative operator. However, unlike Spanish, Italian and Modern Greek, *don't* imperatives are ruled in. I argue that this can be explained with the assumption that *do* in imperatives is like the deontic modal verb *must*. In a negative deontic modal sentence in English, the deontic modal verb has scope over the negation.

(21)   John mustn't leave.
         ≈ It is obligatory for John not to leave. ($\Box\neg$)
         ≉ It is not obligatory for John to leave. ($\neg\Box$)

This means that the deontic modal verb, which takes scope over the entire sentence at LF or in semantic representation, passes the negation low in the representation, deriving the interpretation in which the deontic modal scopes over the negation. If *do* in *don't* imperatives is like the deontic modal verb *must*, then it, too, can also pass the negation low at LF or in semantic representation. In this representation, the negation does not take scope over the imperative operator, and so *don't* imperatives are not ruled out.

7. Apparent Counterexamples

In languages like Bulgarian and Serbo-Croatian, clitics encliticize onto the imperative verb, and yet negative imperatives are possible, as shown in (22) and (23).

(22)   Bulgarian

    a. Četi   ja!   b. Ne ja četi!
        read-2sg.Imp it   Neg it read-2sg.Imp
        'Read it!'   'Don't read it!'

(23)   Serbo-Croatian

    a. Čitaj   je!   b. Ne čitaj   je!
        read-2sg.Imp it   Neg read-2sg.Imp it.
        'Read it!'   'Don't read it!'

These facts appear to pose counterexamples to the analysis proposed here because they suggest that although the imperative verb moves to C^0, imperatives are compatible with negation.

But they are only apparent counterexamples because the imperative verb is not in C^0 on the surface. Following Rivero & Terzi (1995), I take the fact that clitics can appear preverbally in imperatives when they are not in a clause-initial position as evidence that the imperative verb is low in the clause. This is shown in (24).

(24) a.   Knjige im   čitajte!
            books to-them read-2pl.Imp
            'Read books to them!' (Serbo-Croatian)
            (Rivero and Terzi 1995, 17a)

     b.   Ela   i   mi kaži!
            come-2sg.Imp and me tell-2sg.Imp
            'Come and tell me!' (Bulgarian)
            (Hauge 1976, 5; cf. Rivero 1994, 35)

If imperative verbs do not move to C^0, then how can we explain the fact that clitics enclitize in some imperatives? An answer will be given in §7.2.

7.1 Imperative verb movement to C^0 at LF
Neither Bulgarian nor Serbo-Croatian allows embedded imperatives. This is consistent with the proposal that C^0 is occupied by an imperative operator.

(25) a.   * Ivan nastojava (ti)   govori.
            Ivan insists   (you) speak-2sg.Imp
            'Ivan insists that you speak.' (Bulgarian)

     b.   * Ivan insistira da je čitaj.
            Ivan insists   that it read-2sg.Imp
            'Ivan insists that you read it.' (Serbo-Croatian)

I therefore assume that Bulgarian and Serbo-Croatian imperatives also have an imperative operator in C^0, and I propose that the imperative verb moves and adjoins to C^0 at LF. But since morphological/phonological constraints do not apply at LF, the imperative verb can move alone stranding the clitic-like preverbal negation. Consequently, Neg^0 does not take scope over the imperative operator of C^0, and so negative imperatives are not ruled out.[7]

7.2 C^0 as the locus of illocutionary force operators
Recall that Rivero (1994b) and Rivero & Terzi (1995) argue that C^0 cannot host an operator which encodes directive or question force in Bulgarian and Serbo-Croatian. Their claim is that C^0 is the locus for last-resort verb movement to prevent clitics from occupying first position. This claim can be contradicted on two grounds:

---

[7]As Chomsky (1995), I assume that LF movement involves feature movement, where only necessary features are attracted by the target. Thus, the imperative operator in C^0 attracts the verbal feature, leaving behind other features.

(26) a.   It can be shown that verbs do not move to C^0 to prevent clitics from occurring in the first position.

b.   It can be shown that C^0 does indeed have something to do with encoding illocutionary forces.

If we adopt the account on participle-aux orders in Slavic given by Embick & Izvorski (1997), which is extended to verb-pronominal clitic orders, we can do away with the claim that C^0 is reserved for verb movement to prevent clitics from appearing in the first position. In Slavic, some sentences show participle-aux orders, as in (27).

(27)   Napísal som list.

written am letter

'I have written a letter.' (Slovak)

(Embick and Izvorski 1997:210)

According to Embick & Izvorski (1997), some auxiliaries in Slavic are like clitics. Thus, they cannot occur in a sentence-initial position. They propose that when clitic auxiliaries are stranded by the syntax in sentence-initial position, Morphological Merger (Marantz 1989) operates at a post-syntactic level to invert the stranded clitic auxiliary with an adjacent element, namely the participle, thus satisfying the clitic's need for a host and yielding participle-aux orders. Extending the account to verb-clitic orders, they argue that clause-initial clitics affix onto the adjacent verb at a post-syntactic level, eliminating the motivation for last-resort verb movement to C^0.

Assuming Embick and Izvorski's (1997) account, we immediately have an explanation for imperatives in which clitics have encliticized onto the imperative verb, as in (22a) and (23a): the clitics have affixed onto the verb in I^0 at a post-syntactic level. Also, clitics procliticize in negative imperatives in Bulgarian, as in (22b), because the presence of *ne* renders Morphological Merger unnecessary.[8]

We still need to explain why clitics enclitize in Serbo-Croatian negative imperatives, as shown in (23b). As pointed out by Rivero & Terzi (1995), in Serbo-Croatian, negation *ne* and the verb cannot be intervened by pronominal clitics. This is exemplified with indicative sentences as in (28).

(28)   Serbo-Croatian

a.   Ne čitate   je.   b.   * Ne je čitate.

Neg read-Pres.2pl it   Neg it read-Pres.2pl

'You are not reading it.'   'You are not reading it.'

---

[8]Macedonian imperatives potentially pose a problem. In Macedonian, clitics procliticize in finite clauses, but encliticize in non-finite clauses, where non-finite clauses include imperatives and gerunds (Tomić (1996), Legendre (to appear)). The clitic placement in imperatives suggests that the imperative verb is somewhere high in the clause. However, negative imperatives are available and pronominal clitics encliticize in negative imperatives just as in affirmative imperatives. This suggests that negation and the verb in negative imperatives are also located somewhere high in the clause. One possible explanation may be that non-finite verbs (including imperative verbs) are located in a functional head below Neg^0 but above I^0 on the surface, deriving (neg)-verb-clitic order. And then the imperative verb moves further to C^0 at LF.

Thus, the fact that clitics encliticize in negative imperatives in Serbo-Croatian is simply due to an independent constraint of the language.

The facts from questions in Bulgarian and Serbo-Croatian establish that C^0 does indeed have something to do with encoding illocutionary forces. In wh-questions, all wh-phrases undergo fronting.

(29) a. Koj kak udari Ivan?   b. Ko gdje spava?
         who how hit   Ivan   who where sleeps
         'Who hit Ivan how?'   'Who sleeps where?'
         (Bulgarian)   (Serbo-Croatian)

The structural position to which the wh-phrases move in wh-questions is generally argued to be [Spec, CP]. Then, the question relevant here is why the wh-phrases move to [Spec, CP] even when there is no clitic (either pronominal or auxiliary) to support. The obligatoriness of wh-movement in wh-questions suggests that C^0 is associated with an operator that encodes the illocutionary force of questions. Moreover, the Bulgarian particle li which occurs in yes-no questions is argued to be a complementizer in C^0 (Rivero (1993), Izvorski et al. (1997)). If these accounts are correct, then this is another case of C^0 hosting an operator that encodes illocutionary force.

Under the simplest theory, if C^0 is the locus of operator that encodes question illocutionary force in a language, it should also be the locus of the operator that encodes directive illocutionary force in that language. Under such a simple theory, the fact that a sentence cannot be both an imperative and an interrogative follows without any stipulation. Moreover, such a simple theory simplifies type theory in that operators with same semantic type associate with the same syntactic category.

8. Extension to Negative Interrogatives

The proposed analysis predicts that languages with verb movement to C^0 in questions and a clitic-like sentential negation should not have negative yes-no questions. We immediately realize that this prediction is not borne out.

(30) ¿No bebió Juan café?
       Neg drank Juan coffee
       'Didn't Juan drink coffee?' (Spanish)

As shown in (30), there are negative yes-no questions in which the verb and the negation occupy C^0 as a unit. I explain why such negative yes-no questions are available by appealing to the semantics of questions.

8.1 Negation in Yes-no-questions

Following Groenendijk & Stokhof (1985), I assume that a yes-no question denotes a partition that represents the possible answers: namely, the positive and the negative answer. An affirmative yes-no question and the corresponding negative yes-no question both denote the same partition because they both have the same set of possible answers. For instance, the question Does John drink? and Doesn't John drink? have the same set of possible answers: John drinks and John doesn't drink. They both denote the same partition in (31).

(31) $[\![Does\ John\ drink?]\!] \equiv [\![Doesn't\ John\ drink?]\!]$

John drinks
John doesn't drink

They differ in that while the negative question implicates that the speaker expects a positive answer, the affirmative question has no such implication.

Since the clitic-like negation in *yes-no* questions does not make a truth-conditionally relevant contribution to the denotation, we can assume that it is pleonastic. Thus, it does not negate the question force, and so negative *yes-no* questions are allowed.

8.2 A Prediction with respect to alternative questions
The analysis presented here makes a prediction with respect to alternative questions. The possible answers to an alternative question, such as *Did John drink coffee or tea?*, are *John drank coffee* and *John drank tea*. That is, an alternative question denotes a partition as in (32).

(32) $[\![Does\ John\ drink\ coffee\ or\ tea?]\!]$

John drank coffee
John drank tea

The negation in alternative questions is a true negation because it affects the denotation. Thus, the prediction is that alternative questions with negation in C^0 should not be available, whereas alternative questions with the negation low in the clause should be. This prediction is borne out in English.

(33) a. Didn't John drink coffee or tea?

b. Did John not drink coffee or tea?

The question in (33a) cannot have the alternative question reading in which the possible answers are *John didn't drink coffee* and *John didn't drink tea*. It can only be interpreted as a *yes-no* question in which the possible answers are *John drank coffee or tea* and *John didn't drink coffee or tea*. In contrast, the question in (33b) has both the alternative question reading and the *yes-no* question reading, as expected. The prediction with respect to alternative questions holds in other languages as well. See Han (in prep.) for more discussion on this issue.

9. Conclusion

I have proposed that a language does not allow negative imperatives if the syntax derives a structure in which the imperative operator ends up in the scope of negation. This is because such a syntactic structure maps onto a semantic representation in which the directive force is negated. This semantic representation is simply illegal. The proposed analysis has implications for the syntax to semantics mapping in imperatives. Given the proposed analysis, the cross-linguistic variation in the compatibility of negation and imperatives is another case that shows that the set of available syntactic structures in a language is restricted by the semantics.

References

ANAGNOSTOPOULOU, ELENA, 1994. *Clitic Dependencies in Modern Greek*. University of Salzburg dissertation.

CHOMSKY, NOAM. 1995. *The Minimalist Program*. Cambridge, Massachusetts; London, England: The MIT Press.

CINQUE, GUGLIELMO, 1996. Adverbs and the universal hierarchy of functional projections. Unpublished manuscript, University of Venice.

DAVIES, EIRLYS. 1986. *The English Imperative*. London; Sydney; Dover; Newhampshire: Croom Helm.

EMBICK, DAVID, & ROUMYANA IZVORSKI. 1997. Participle-auxiliary word orders in slavic. In *Annual Workshop on Formal Approaches to Slavic Linguistics: the Cornell Meeting 1995*, ed. by Natasha Kondrashova Wayles Brown, Ewa Dornisch & Draga Zec, volume 4, 210–239. Ann Arbor: Michigan Slavic Publications.

GROENENDIJK, JEROEN, & MARTIN STOKHOF, 1985. *Studies in the Semantics of Questions and the Pragmatics of Answers*. University of Amsterdam dissertation.

HAN, CHUNG-HYE, in prep. The Syntax and Semantics of Imperatives and Related Constructions. Ph.D Dissertation, University of Pennsylvania.

IZVORSKI, ROUMYANA, TRACY KING, & CATHERINE RUDIN. 1997. Against li-lowering in bulgarian. *Lingua* 102.187–194.

JOSEPH, BRIAN, & IRENE PHILIPPAKI-WARBURTON. 1987. *Modern Greek*. London: Croom Helm.

KAYNE, RICHARD. 1994. *The Antisymmetry of Syntax*, volume 25 of *Linguistic Inquiry Monograph*. Cambridge, Massachusetts; London, England: The MIT Press.

LEGENDRE, GERALDINE, to appear. Morphological and prosodic alignment at work: the case of south-slavic clitics. In *Proceedings of West Coast Conference in Formal Linguistics 17*.

MARANTZ, ALEC. 1989. Clitics and phrase structure. In *Alternative Conceptions of Phrase Structure*, ed. by M. Baltin & Anthony Kroch. Chicago: Chicago Press.

PALMER, FRANK ROBERT. 1986. *Mood and Modality*. Cambridge Textbooks in Linguistics. Cambridge: Cambridge University Press.

POTSDAM, ERIC, 1997. *Syntactic Issues in the English Imperative*. University of California at Sata Cruz dissertation.

RIVERO, MARIA-LUISA. 1993. Bulgarian and serbo-croatian yes-no questions: V^0 raising to -*li* vs. -*li* hopping. *Linguistic Inquiry* 24.567–575.

——. 1994a. Clause structure and v-movement in the languages of the balkans. *Natural Language and Linguistic Theory* 12.63–120.

——. 1994b. Negation, imperatives and wackernagel effects. *Rivista di Linguistica* 6.39–66.

——, & ARHONTO TERZI. 1995. Imperatives, v-movement and logical mood. *Journal of Linguistics* 31.301–332.

RIZZI, LUIGI. 1982. *Issues in Italian Syntax*. Dordrecht: Foris.

ROORYCK, JOHAN. 1992. Romance enclitic ordering and universal grammar. *The Linguistic Review* 9.219–250.

SADOCK, JERROLD M., & ARNOLD M. ZWICKY. 1985. Speech act distinctions in syntax. In *Language Typology and Syntactic Description*, ed. by Timothy Shopen, volume 1, 155–196. Cambridge: Cambridge University Press.

TOMIĆ, OLGA MIŠESKA. 1996. The balkan slavic clausal clitics. *Natural Language and Linguistic Theory* 14.811–872.

TORREGO, ESTHER. 1984. On inversion in spanish and some of its effects. *Linguistic Inquiry* 15.103–129.

ZANUTTINI, RAFFAELLA, 1991. *Syntactic Properties of Sentential negation. A Comparative Study of Romance Languages*. University of Pennsylvania dissertation.

——. 1994. Speculations on negative imperatives. *Rivista di Linguistica* 6.67–89.

——. 1997. *Negation and Clausal Structure: A Comparative Study of Romance Languages*. Oxford Studies in Comparative Syntax. New York, Oxford: Oxford University Press.

Temporal and Locative WH-Phrases and the Null P Incorporation*

TIEN-HSIN HSIN
University of Connecticut

1. Introduction

This study is an investigation on the categorial status of temporal and locative WH-Phrases. I will make two claims in this paper: First, temporal and locative WHs are accompanied by a null P; this idea is originally due to Huang (1982). Second, the null P incorporation can resolve the problem presented in Murasugi and Saito (1992) against Huang's (1982) null P hypothesis. This paper is organized as follows. In section 2 I review two important works in the literature on the issue of temporal and locative WHs: Huang (1982) and Murasugi and Saito (1992). In section 3 I will defend Huang's null P hypothesis based on empirical evidence. I argue in section 4 that the examples provided by Murasugi and Saito against Huang (1982) can be independently excluded by a process of null P incorporation. In section 5, I show that the null P incorporation is independently supported by the discussion in Anderson (1979). Some questions regarding null P incorporation and its further implementation are

---

* For helpful comments and discussions on the content of this paper I would like to thank Željko Bošković, Howard Lasnik and Diane Lillo-Martin, as well as the audience at University of Connecticut. Thanks are also due to Dave Braze and Masao Ochi for help in preparing the final version. Remaining errors are my own.

addressed in sections 6 and 7 respectively. A summary and concluding remarks are given in section 8.

2. Previous literature

2.1 Huang (1982)

One of the issues discussed in Huang (1982) is the categorial status of locative and temporal phrases. Huang observes that in Chinese when *nali* 'where' and *shemeshihou* 'when' move at LF, they behave like arguments rather than adjuncts. The following examples involve WH-in situ within complex NPs.

(1) a. ni   du guo   [NP [CP shei   xie   de] shu]
         you read-ASP   who   write DE book
         'You read the book who wrote?'
     b. *ni   du guo   [NP [CP Lisi weisheme xie   de] shu]
         you read-ASP   why   write DE book
         'You read the book that Lisi wrote why?'
     c. ni   du guo   [NP [CP Lisi shemeshihou /zai nali xie   de] shu]
         you read-ASP   when   at where write DE book
         'You read the book Lisi wrote when/where?'

The generalization is that argument WHs such as *shei* 'who' in (1a) can occur within an island, whereas adjunct WHs like *weisheme* 'why' in (1b) cannot. Huang argues that (1c) is well-formed because *nali* 'where' and *shemeshihou* 'when' appear in the categorial position of [PP P [NP ___], where the prepositions can be phonetically null. Thus, *nali* and *shemeshihou* are complements of the Ps and are on a par with *shei* 'who' in (1a) in being arguments. Huang, however, maintains that the PPs containing *nali* 'where' and *shemeshihou* 'when' are adjuncts.

The same point extends to English as well. The familiar argument/ adjunct asymmetry is shown in (2a) and (2b): while arguments can stay in situ, adjuncts can not. As the grammaticality of (2c) shows, *when* and *where* pattern as arguments (i.e. *what*) in this respect. This follows naturally under Huang's analysis, since, as shown in (3), *when* (or *where*) is a complement and thus an argument of the null P.

(2) a. Who bought what?
     b. *Who bought that book why/how?
     c. Who bought that book when/where?
(3) Who bought that book [PP [P e] when/where]

Under Huang's (1982) analysis, (2a) and (2b) have the LF representations in (4a) and (4b), respectively.

(4)   a.   [what$_j$, who$_i$]$_i$ t$_i$ bought t$_j$
        b.   *[why/how$_j$, who$_i$]$_i$ t$_i$ bought that book t$_j$?

The LF representation in (4a) satisfies the ECP, which requires that a non-pronominal empty category must be head governed or antecedent governed. The subject trace is antecedent-governed by COMP (via the Comp Indexing Mechanism of Aoun, Hornstein and Sportiche (1981)) and the object trace is head governed by the verb *bought*. In contrast, (4b) violates the ECP: although the subject trace is antecedent governed by the COMP, the adjunct trace is neither head nor antecedent governed.[1] The LF representation in (5) illustrates that the grammaticality of (2c) is due to the presence of the null P: the trace of *when/where* is head-governed by this P, satisfying the ECP. Since the subject trace is also governed by COMP, the ECP is satisfied in this example.

(5)   [when/where$_j$, who$_i$]$_i$ t$_i$ bought that book [$_{PP}$ [$_P$ e] t$_j$]

The argument status of *when* and *where* is further evidenced in the examples in (6a-b) in which *where* and *when* can be complements of overt prepositions. As a contrast, (6c-d) show that *why* and *how* can not appear in this position.

(6)   a.   [From where] did he come?
        b.   [Since when] have you been here?
        c.   *[For why] did he come?
        d.   *[By how] did he come?

In short, the data from Chinese and English demonstrate that Huang's null P hypothesis has a cross-linguistic applicability.

2.2 Murasugi and Saito (1992)

Recently, however, Murasugi and Saito (1992) argued against Huang's null P hypothesis. Their argument is based on examples in which *where* and *when* appear within NPs. Consider the following.

(7)   a.   Who read [$_{NP}$ the book on which shelf]?
        b.   *Who read [$_{NP}$ the book where]?
(8)   a.   Who won [$_{NP}$ the Olympics in which year]?
        b.   *Who won [$_{NP}$ the Olympics when]?

---

[1]Under the minimalist framework (cf. Chomsky (1995)), such notions as 'government' do not play a role. For an account under the current framework, see Bošković (in press).

The grammaticality of (7a) and (8a) is expected under Huang's (1982) analysis, because, as in (2a), the WH-phrases *which shelf* and *which year* are in complement positions. But the ungrammaticality of the (b) examples is not predicted under his analysis, for if the null P were present, the following structures for (7b) and (8b) should be possible. In (9) *where* and *when* are in complement positions as well, which means that the ECP should be satisfied here at LF in the same manner as in (7a) and (8a). Huang's analysis incorrectly predicts that (7b) and (8b) are grammatical,[2] contrary to the fact.

(9)   a.   *Who$_i$ t$_i$ read [$_{NP}$ the book [$_{PP}$ [$_P$ e] where]]?
      b.   *Who$_i$ t$_i$ won [$_{NP}$ the Olympics [$_{PP}$ [$_P$ e] when]]?

Murasugi and Saito (1992) argue that Huang's null P analysis is therefore untenable. Instead they claim that the ungrammaticality of (7b) and (8b) can be explained by assuming that temporal and locative phrases can have argument status in sentences but not in NPs. More precisely, they claim that temporal and locative phrases are arguments of INFL or the event predicate associated with V, and that they are pure adjuncts when they occur within NPs. This provides a simple account of the contrast in (7) and (8), assuming that there is no null P associated with *where* and *when*. Now let us reconsider (7), repeated as (10), under their analysis.

(10)   a.   Who$_i$ t$_i$ read [the book [$_{PP}$ on which shelf]]?
       b.   *Who$_i$ t$_i$ read [the book where]?

---

[2] The Chinese counterparts of (7b) and (8b) are in fact grammatical, indicating that the temporal/locative WHs in this language can occur within the NP, unlike in English.

(i)   a.   shei du-le   [$_{NP}$ nali   de   shu]?
           who read-ASP   where DE book
           'Who read [the book where]?'
      b.   shei yin-le   [$_{NP}$ shemeshihou de   ao-yun   (jin-pai)]?
           who win-ASP   when   DE   Olympics (gold-medal)
           'Who won [the Olympics when]?'

Those data may pose a problem for Murasugi and Saito (1992). But notice that there is a marker *de* obligatorily following *nali* 'where' and *shemeshihou* 'when' within the NP. I suggest that *de* is a preposition taking the temporal/locative WH as a complement (despite the fact that it follows the temporal/locative WH). More specifically, I assume that the temporal/locative WH, which originates as a complement of the P *de*, moves overtly to the specifier position of the PP headed by *de*.

(ii)   a.   shei du-le   [$_{NP}$ [$_{PP}$ nali$_i$ [$_{P'}$ de   t$_i$]] shu]?
            who read-ASP   where DE   book
       b.   shei yin-le   [$_{NP}$ [$_{PP}$ shemeshihou$_i$ [$_{P'}$ de   t$_i$]]   ao-yun   (jin-pai)]?
            who win-ASP   when   DE   Olympics (gold-medal)

If this is correct, then Chinese temporal/locative WHs in (i) are complements of the P *de* and are thus on a par with *which shelf* in (7a) and *which year* in (8a). Then, the Chinese data in (i) no longer pose a problem for Murasugi and Saito (1992).

In (10a), the WH-phrase *which shelf* is in the complement position of the P *on*. The ECP is then satisfied via head-government at LF.[3]

(11) [which shelf$_j$, who$_i$]$_i$ t$_i$ read [the book [PP on t$_j$]]?

In contrast, the ECP is violated in (10b) since, given that there is no null P, the trace of *where* is neither head-governed nor antecedent-governed if we assume that the object NP node blocks government and that the noun cannot head-govern t$_j$.[4]   According to Murasugi and Saito (1992), the ungrammaticality of (10b), with an LF representation as in (12), is due to extraction of the adjunct WH from the object NP, the same as in (13).

(12) [where$_j$ who$_i$]$_i$ t$_i$ read [the book t$_j$]?
(13) a. *[On which shelf]$_i$ did you read [NP the book t$_i$]?
      b. *[In which year]$_i$ did you win [NP the Olympics t$_i$]?

As for the example in (2c), repeated below, its grammaticality also follows straightforwardly under Murasugi and Saito's (1992) analysis. The trace left by LF WH-movement of *when* or *where* is properly governed by INFL (or the event predicate), thereby satisfying the ECP.

(14) Who bought that book when/where?

To summarize, examples such as (7b) and (8b) seem to provide evidence against Huang's null P hypothesis, hence Murasugi and Saito (1992) argue that we must dispense with the null P and analyze *where* and *when* as sentential arguments.

3. Problems

Although Murasugi and Saito's (1992) analysis is quite simple and attractive, there are some facts which lead us to question their conclusions. As also discussed in Huang (1982), where overt movement is concerned, *when* and *where* pattern not with arguments but with adjuncts. The Chinese data demonstrate that relativization of *nali* 'where' in (15b) and *shemeshihou*

---

[3] Although this involves extraction out of an adjunct (as the PP *on which shelf* is an adjunct within an NP), the Condition on Extraction Domain (CED), which prohibits an extraction out of a non-properly governed domain, is irrelevant because it constrains only overt movement (cf. Huang (1982)).

[4] Murasugi and Saito (1992) are not very clear about this part. It is true, as observed by Culicover and Rochemont (1992), that overt adjunct extraction from the object NP is prohibited in English (see (13)), suggesting that the object NP is a kind of barrier for adjunct movement (although it is a complement and hence is L-marked in the sense of Chomsky (1986)). See Murasugi and Saito (1992) and the references cited there for more discussion.

'when' in (15c) results in the same status as that of an adjunct *weisheme* 'why' in (15d).[5]

(15) a. ?zhe jiushi [NP [S wo xiang-zhidao [S ni   zai nali   mai t$_i$]]
          this is   I wonder   you at where buy
          de shu$_i$]
          DE book
          '?This is the book that I wondered where you bought.'
      b. *zhe jiushi [NP [S wo xiang-zhidao [S shei t$_i$ mai-le   shu]]
          this is   I wonder   who   buy-ASP book
          de difang$_i$]
          DE place
          '*This is the place where$_i$ I wondered [who bought the book t$_i$].'
      c. *zhe jiushi [NP [S wo xiang-zhidao [S shei t$_i$ mai-le   shu]]
          this is   I wonder   who   buy-ASP book
          de shihou$_i$]
          DE time
          '*This is the time when$_i$ I wondered [who bought the book t$_i$].'
      d. *zhe jiushi [NP [S wo xiang-zhidao [S shei t$_i$ mai-le   shu]]
          this is   I wonder   who   buy-ASP book
          de yuanyin$_i$]
          DE reason
          '*This is the reason why$_i$ I wondered [who bought the book t$_i$].'

The pattern is mirrored by the English data in (16).

(16) a. ?This is the book which$_i$ I wondered [where$_j$ you bought t$_i$ t$_j$].
      b. *This is the place where$_j$ I wondered [who$_i$ t$_i$ bought the book t$_j$]
      c. *This is the day when$_j$ I wondered [who$_i$ t$_i$ bought the book t$_j$]
      d. *This is the reason why$_j$ I wondered [who$_i$ t$_i$ bought the book t$_j$]

All the examples in (16) are degraded, since Subjacency is violated in each case. Still, (16b-d) are far worse than (16a). This is not expected if *when* and *where* are arguments of INFL (or the event predicate): (16a-c) should have the same status, and contrast with (16d), according to Murasugi and Saito's analysis. Huang's (1982) analysis, on the other hand, has the potential of accounting for the facts in (16). For example, (16b-c) have two possible structures under his analysis, depending on what category (PP or NP) moves across the WH-island.

---

[5]Unlike Huang (1982), who claims that (15a) is perfect, I find this example to have a marginal status due to a violation of WH-island condition.

(17) a. *This is the place [PP [P *e*] where]ⱼ I wondered [whoᵢ tᵢ bought the book tⱼ]

    b. *This is the day [PP [P *e*] when]ⱼ I wondered [whoᵢ tᵢ bought the book tⱼ]

(18) a. *This is the place [NP where]ⱼ I wondered [whoᵢ tᵢ bought the book [PP [P *e*] tⱼ]]

    b. *This is the day [NP when]ⱼ I wondered [whoᵢ tᵢ bought the book [PP [P *e*] tⱼ]]

Recall that under Huang's (1982) analysis, both temporal and locative PPs are adjuncts. Thus, the representations in (17), in which the whole PP moves, violate both Subjacency and the ECP. The representations in (18) show a derivation in which the NP *when/where* is moved. In addition to Subjacency, this derivation violates the CED. In either case, some constraint along with Subjacency is violated. Hence, the fact that (16b-c) are worse than (16a) is predicted under Huang's (1982) account, since (16a) violates only the WH-island Condition.

Therefore, Murasugi and Saito's (1992) claim that *when* and *where* are arguments of INFL (or the event predicate) faces some empirical problems. In contrast, Huang's (1982) analysis employing a null P is more adequate in handling cases like (16), which involve overt movement of *when* and *where*. I will thus assume that Huang's (1982) analysis is essentially correct, that is, *when* and *where* appear with a null P across languages,[6] and the locative and temporal PPs are adjuncts. But if this is the case, how do we account for data such as (7b) and (8b), which pose a problem for Huang's theory?

---

[6]The presence of the null P is independently motivated cross-linguistically, at least in the case of locative WHs. In Chinese and Japanese, for instance, adjunct locative phrases, including the WH-phrase corresponding to *where*, always require pre(post)positions.

(i) a. John *(zai) xuexiao yujian Mary
    John at school meet Mary
    'John met Mary at school.'

    b. John *(zai) nali yujian Mary
    John at where meet Mary
    'Where did John meet Mary?'

(ii) a. John-ga gakkoo*(-de) Mary-ni atta.
    John-NOM school-at Mary-DAT met
    'John met Mary at school.'

    b. John-ga doko*(-de) Mary-ni atta no.
    John-NOM where-at Mary-DAT met Q
    'Where did John meet Mary?.'

As the (b) examples indicate, Chinese *nali* and Japanese *doko* appear in the configuration [PP P [NP __]], consistent with Huang's (1982) analysis. Thus, the null hypothesis is that English *where* occurs in the same environment.

4. Solution: Null P incorporation

The solution I will pursue in this study involves null P incorporation. First notice that all the bad examples (such as (7b) and (8b)) which Murasugi and Saito (1992) provide as evidence against the null P hypothesis have one thing in common: *when* and *where* appear within NPs. Thus, if it is shown that *when* and *where* are excluded from NP-internal positions for independent reasons, then the problem for the null P analysis ceases to exist.

Following some general line of research as Ormazabal (1995) and Pesetsky (1995), I assume that null heads are affixal in nature and must incorporate into an appropriate head. More specifically, I propose the following.

(19)   Null P must incorporate into [-N] head.

I also assume some version of the Head Movement Constraint (HMC), which prohibits head movement from skipping a potential head position. With these assumptions in mind, let us consider the structure for (7b) under Huang's (1982) null P analysis.

(20)   *Who$_i$ t$_i$ read [$_{NP}$ the book [$_{PP}$ [$_P$ e] where]]?

The null P in (20) cannot incorporate into the closest head, namely, the N *book*, because this head is not [-N]. The null P cannot incorporate into the V, either, because of the presence of a closer head, the N *book*, or the D *the* if we assume the DP structure.

(21)   Who$_i$ t$_i$ read [$_{NP}$ the [$_N$ book] [$_{PP}$ [$_P$ e] where]]]?
        |_____*_____|

Thus the example in (7b) can be ruled out as a violation of the HMC. This in effect prevents *when* and *where* from appearing within the projection of N, assuming crucially that there is a null P with *when/where*. In contrast, examples such as (2c), in which *when* or *when* occurs outside the NPs allow the incorporation of the null P into the head V, which is [-N]. This is shown in (22b).

(22)   a.   Who$_i$ t$_i$ bought [$_{NP}$ the book] where?
        b.   Who$_i$ t$_i$ [$_{VP}$ [$_{V'}$ [$_V$ [$_P e$] [$_V$ bought]] that book]][$_{PP}$ [$_P$ t] where]]
                             |_____|

If this analysis is on the right track, then it eliminates the potential problem for Huang's (1982) null P analysis. However, one problem may arise.

Notice that, as illustrated in (23), this process involves lowering, which is generally excluded in the literature.

(23)

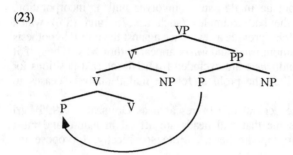

We will come back to this issue in section 6.

5. Independent support

Independent support for the conjecture in (19), namely that the target of the null P incorporation must be a [-N] head, comes from the discussion of P-reanalysis in Anderson (1979), assuming that P-reanalysis involves P incorporation. Anderson claims that prepositions can (occasionally) adjoin to adjacent verbs. But she shows that Ps cannot incorporate into adjacent nouns. One piece of evidence for her claim comes from examples involving Negative Polarity Item (NPI) licensing. Generally speaking, an NPI is licensed if it is in the scope of negation. Thus, (24b) is ungrammatical because the NP *few students* fails to c-command the NPI *anything*: the latter is not in the scope of the former.

(24) a. <u>Few</u> students said *anything* about it.
      b. *[Teachers [who teach <u>few</u> students]] said *anything* about it.

Given this, consider the following examples from Anderson (1979: 48).

(25) a. I refer to very <u>few</u> authors with *any* enthusiasm.
      b. *My reference to very <u>few</u> authors with *any* enthusiasm is typical.
      cf. My reference to very few authors with l's in their names is typical.
(26) a. He spoke to very <u>few</u> people about anything important.
      b. *His speeches to very <u>few</u> people about *anything* important were typical.
      cf. His speeches to very few people about politics were typical.

The (a) examples show that the NPI *any* is licensed when its licenser occurs within a PP. Yet, this does not mean that the PP node is irrelevant for calculating c-command, as the ungrammaticality of the (b) examples suggest. The crucial difference between (a) and (b) is the categorial status of the head of the projection in which the PP (with *few* in it) appears: it is V in (a) and is N in (b). On the basis of this contrast, Anderson suggests that the NPI is licensed in the (a) examples because of the reanalysis between V and P. As a result of this process, there is no longer a PP node to block the c-command of the NPI by *few (authors/people)*. In contrast, Anderson argues that the N-P reanalysis is impossible. This means that the NPIs *any(thing)* in the (b) examples are not licensed since *few* does not c-command them, hence the ungrammaticality of (b). Thus, our claim in (19) is independently motivated in this respect, assuming that P reanalysis involves null P incorporation

6. Further questions

Several questions arise concerning the proposed analysis of null P incorporation. First, as shown in (23), since we assume that the PP in question is adjoined to a projection of V, the null P incorporation seems to involve lowering, which is generally prohibited. There are a number of ways to deal with this problem. Here I will provide two possible solutions.

One is to assume that the null P incorporates into INFL instead, which I assume is [- N]. Then no lowering is involved in this process.

(27)   ... INFL [$_{VP}$ ...... [$_{PP}$ [$_P$ *e*] when/where]]
        |_____|

Another possibility is to assume the following.

(28)   a.   Null P incorporation takes place at LF.
        b.   V raises to INFL at LF in English (cf. Pollock (1989), Chomsky (1991)).

Under this hypothesis, the null P can incorporate into V after the latter has raised to INFL. There is no lowering involved in this derivation.

(29)   ... [V + INFL] [$_{VP}$ ... V$_t$ ...[$_{PP}$ [*e*] when/where]]]
        |_____|

Although both hypotheses solve the problem of lowering, for conceptual reasons, I will adopt the first approach, i.e., that the null P incorporates to INFL (overtly). Notice that the special property that distinguishes the null P from other overt prepositions such as *on* and *in* is the fact that it is phonologically null.[7] Following the line of reasoning in Pesetsky (1995: 196), that the zero affix must be moved to its host by PF, we may assume (30).

(30)   A Null P is a PF affix.

Given (30), then if null P incorporation takes place at LF, the PF requirement in (30) would not be satisfied, assuming that LF does not feed PF.

Another relevant question is the following: how does the incorporation apply if *when/where* appears in Spec of CP as in (31)?

(31)   Where did John go?

Based on the PF affix hypothesis I have adopted, I assume a derivation in which the null P incorporates into INFL before the whole PP moves to Spec of CP, as shown in (32).[8,9]

(32)   [$_{CP}$ [$_{PP}$ t$_j$ [$_{NP}$ where]]$_i$ [$_C$ [$_P$ e]$_j$ [$_C$ did] [$_{IP}$ John go t$_i$]]]?

To sum up this section, according to the present proposal, the null P is a PF affix which must incorporate into a [-N] head without violating the HMC. Our analysis of the null P incorporation is summarized as follows.

(33)   a.   Null P incorporation applies overtly.
        b.   Null P incorporates into V, but not into N.

---

[7]The grammaticality of examples in (i) indicates that overt prepositions such as *on* and *in* are not required to incorporate into [-N] head.

(i)   a.   Who read [$_{NP}$ the book [$_{PP}$ on which shelf]]?
        b.   Who won [$_{NP}$ the Olympics [$_{PP}$ in which year]]?

[8]Note that the trace left by the null P is not bound. If the effect of the Proper Binding Condition (Fiengo (1974)) is stated in derivational terms, we would be able to distinguish the case in (32) and other cases which involve lowering operations: only the latter violate the PBC derivationally.

[9]If we adopt the other hypothesis that null P incorporation takes place at LF, we may answer this question by assuming (i).

(i)   Movement is a copy & deletion process (cf. Chomsky (1981, 1993)).

Given this assumption, the S-structure representation of (31) is as shown in (ii)

(ii)   [$_{CP}$ [$_{PP}$ e [$_{NP}$ where]] did [$_{IP}$ John go [$_{PP}$ e [$_{NP}$ where]]]]?

Now notice that there are two instances of the null P, one in the specifier of CP and the other one in its original position (i.e. copy). Then, it is possible that this copy can incorporate into V at LF after the V raises to INFL.

7. Theoretical implementation

Our proposal of null P incorporation provides additional evidence for null head incorporation in general. For example, the contrast in (34) (cf. Ormazabal (1995)) shows that a null C is allowed if the CP which it heads is in the complement position of V, but not of N.

(34) a. John proved that/ø Mary is honest.
      b. John's proof that/*ø Mary is honest

This can be accounted for if we assume, following the claim in (35), that the null C is required to incorporate into a [-N] head.

(35) Null heads in general, being affixal, must incorporate into a [-N] head.

8. Summary and Conclusion

In this paper I examined Huang's (1982) and Murasugi and Saito's (1992) analyses concerning the grammatical status of locative and temporal WH phrases. Based on empirical evidence, I concluded, following Huang (1982), that temporal and locative WHs are accompanied by a null P. I demonstrated that null P incorporation resolves the problem presented in Murasugi and Saito (1992) against Huang's null P hypothesis, i.e. the fact that *when/where* cannot occur within NPs, unlike other temporal/locative phrases with overt prepositions. For the analysis of null P incorporation, I proposed that null P, being affixal in nature, must incorporate into a [-N] head. I showed that null P incorporation is supported by Anderson's (1972) proposal of reanalysis between P and V. Furthermore, I suggested that the analysis of null-P incorporation has the potential of being generalized to other null heads such as null C.

References

Anderson, Mona. 1979. *Noun Phrase Structure.* Doctoral dissertation, University of Connecticut.

Aoun, Joseph, Norbert Hornstein and Dominique Sportiche. 1981. Some Aspects of Wide Scope Quantification. *Journal of Linguistic Research* 1: 3.69-95.

Bošković, Željko. Sometimes in SpecCP, sometimes in-situ. In press, in Roger Martin, David Michaels, and Juan Uriagereka, eds., *Step by Step: Essays on Minimalism in Honor of Howard Lasnik.* Cambridge, Mass.: MIT Press.

Chomsky, Noam. 1981. *Lectures on Government and Binding*. Dodrecht: Foris.

Chomsky, Noam. 1986. *Barriers*. Cambridge, Mass.: MIT Press.

Chomsky, Noam. 1991. Some Notes on Economy of Derivation and Representation, in Robert Freidin, ed., *Principles and Parameters in Comparative Grammar*. Cambridge, Mass.: MIT Press, 417-454.

Chomsky, Noam. 1993. A Minimalist Program for Linguistic Theory, in Kenneth. Hale and Samuel Jay Keyser, eds., *The View From Building 20: Essays in Linguistics in Honor of Sylvain Bromberger*. Cambridge, Mass.: MIT Press, 1-52.

Chomsky, Noam. 1995. *Minimalist Program*. Cambridge, Mass.: MIT Press.

Culicover, Peter and Michael Rochemont. 1992. Adjunct Extraction From NP and the ECP. *Linguistic Inquiry* 23:496-501.

Fiengo, Robert. 1974. *Semantic Conditions on Surface Structure*. Doctoral dissertation, MIT.

Huang, Cheng-Teh James. 1982. *Logical Relations in Chinese and the Theory of Grammar*. Doctoral dissertation, MIT.

Murasugi, Keiko and Mamoru Saito. 1992. Quasi-Adjuncts as Sentential Arguments. *Proceedings of Western Conference on Linguistics* 5:251-264.

Ormazabal, Javier. 1995. *The Syntax of Complementation: On the Connection Between Syntactic Structure and Selection*. Doctoral dissertation, University of Connecticut.

Pesetsky, David. 1995 *Zero Syntax*. Cambridge, Mass.: MIT Press.

Pollock, Jean-Yves. 1989. Verb Movement, Universal Grammar, and the Structure of IP. *Linguistic Inquiry* 20:365-424.

The Role of Perceptibility in Consonant/Consonant Metathesis[*]

Ohio State University

1. Introduction

The focus of this paper is on consonant/consonant metathesis, the process whereby in certain languages, under certain conditions, consonants appear to switch positions with one another. Thus, in a string of sounds where we would expect the linear ordering of two consonants to be ...*xy*..., we find instead ...*yx*.... While less common than processes such as assimilation and deletion, regular synchronic C/C metathesis occurs in a wide range of languages, as the following representative examples illustrate. (For detailed discussion and additional data, the reader is referred to Hume 1997b).

(1) o **Obstruent/nasal,** e.g. Sidamo (Hudson 1975, 1995): a stem-final obstruent metathesizes with a following nasal, /hab+nemmo/ [hambémmo] 'we forget', /gud+nonni/ [gundónni] 'they finished', /it+noommo/ [intóommo] 'we have eaten', /has+nemmo/ [hansémmo] 'we look for', /duk+nanni/ [duŋkánni] 'they carry', /ag+no/ [aŋgó] 'let's drink'. Similar patterns are observed in Darasa, Gedeo, Hadiyya and Kambata with different, noncognate suffixes.

[*] This paper has benefitted from the input of a number of people including Mary Beckman, Osamu Fujimura, Ilse Lehiste, Keith Johnson, Robert Levine, Jennifer Muller, David Odden, Frederick Parkinson and Richard Wright. I am also grateful to Laurie Maynell, Robert Poletto and Frederick Parkinson for their research assistance.

e.g. Mutsun (Okrand 1977): metathesis is attested in the thematic suffix which shows the alternants [-mak] after consonants, [hu:s-mak] 'noses', [wimmah-mak] 'wing', [kahhay-mak] 'head louse', and [-kma] after vowels, [rukka-kma] 'house', [to:ʈe-kma] 'deer, meat', [čiri-kma] 'paternal aunt'. Note that in addition to final C/V metathesis, the order of the consonants is also reversed: in [-mak] the nasal precedes the velar, while in [-kma] the reverse order occurs.

o **Obstruent/liquid metathesis**, e.g. Elmolo (Zaborsky 1986), [tikir], [tírk-o] 'catfish, sg./pl.', [deker], [dérk-o] 'horn, sg./pl.', [mukul], [múlk-o] 'iron, sg./pl.'.

o **Stop/stop metathesis**, e.g. Kui (Winfield 1928): a suffix-initial labial stop typically follows the stem-final consonant, /gas+pa/ [gáspa] 'to hang onself', /mil+pa/ [mílpa] 'to turn over', /ūʈ+pa/ [ūʈpa] 'to give to drink'. However, when the stem-final consonant is a velar stop, the labial precedes the consonant, /bluk+pa/ [blúpka] 'to break down', /ag+ba/ [ábga] 'to be fitting'. A similar pattern is observed in Pengo (Burrow & Bhattacharya 1970).

o **Stop/fricative metathesis**, e.g. Modern Hebrew: the affix /t/ occurs to the right of a strident coronal, /hi+t+sarek/ [histarek] 'he combed his (own) hair', /hi+t+zaken/ [hizdaken] 'he grew old', /hi+t+šamer/ [hištamer] 'he preserved himself'; otherwise it precedes the stem-initial consonant, /hi+t+nakem/ [hitnakem] 'he took revenge', /hi+t+balet/ [hidbalet] 'he became prominent', /hi+t+kabel/ [hitkabel] 'it was accepted' (Bat-El 1988, 1989).
e.g. Faroese: a velar stop metathesizes with an adjacent coronal fricative just in case it is followed by another stop consonant (Jacobson & Matras 1961, Lockwood 1955, Rischel 1972), [frǿskor], [frǿkst] 'healthy, masc./neut.', [náskor], [nákst] 'impertinent, masc./neut.', [inskir], [iŋksti] 'to wish, pres.sg./past sg.'. A similar pattern is observed in Lithuanian (Kenstowicz 1972).

o **Nasal/liquid metathesis**, e.g. Old Spanish: the ordering of a nasal and liquid is reversed in the future and conditional forms of the verb (Martinez-Gil p.c., Wanner 1989), [poner], [porné] *[ponré] 'to put, inf./fut. 1st p.sg.', [tener], [terné] *[tenré] 'to have, inf./fut. 1st p.sg.'.
e.g. Chawchila: a nasal metathesizes with an adjacent lateral (Newman 1944), e.g. [patʈilin] 'body-louse', [cawa:ʔan patʈínl-i] '(he) shouted at the one with many body-lice'.

o **Pharyngeal fricative/C metathesis**, e.g. Rendille: the pharyngeal fricative switches with an adjacent consonant when preceded by the low vowel /a/ (Heine 1976, 1978, Oomen 1981, Sim 1981, Zaborsky 1986), [baħab], [babħ-o] *[baħbo] 'armpit, sing./plur.', [yaħar], [yarħ-a] *[yaħra] 'cough!, sing./plur.'

As the preceding examples illustrate, metathesis is not restricted to any one language family, nor does it involve a single segment type. Despite these differences, I will argue that the motivation behind these cases can be accounted for in a unified manner by drawing on linguistically natural phonetic and phonological considerations. A key goal of this paper, therefore, is to contribute to our understanding of *why* metathesis happens. A second objective is to provide evidence that consonant/consonant metathesis occurs as a regular synchronic process cross-linguistically and, thus, merits serious study.

2. Motivation

In attempting to account for why consonant/consonant metathesis occurs, previous accounts have often drawn on sonority considerations. For example, it has been proposed that metathesis serves to create a better syllable contact, whereby a coda is more sonorous than the following onset (Vennemann 1988). While able to describe cases of metathesis such as that observed in Elmolo, e.g. /tikir+o/ → [tirko] 'catfish sg./pl.', this approach makes incorrect predictions in the case of Mutsun where the output of metathesis positions an obstruent *before* a nasal, e.g. [rukka<u>km</u>a] 'house' *[rukka<u>mk</u>a], cf. hu:smak 'noses'. Further, no predictions are made for cases such as Kui where the sounds involved are of the same sonority grade, e.g. /ag+ba/ → [abga] 'to be fitting'. Drawing on sonority sequencing to account for metatheses involving tautosyllabic consonants is equally ill-fated. In Faroese, for example, the sonority contour is actually better in the ill-formed unmetathesized form, under the assumption that fricatives are more sonorous than stops, e.g. /fɛsk-t/ → [fɛkst] 'fresh, neut.sg.' *[fɛskt].

Relying on coda conditions as the motivation behind metathesis also runs into problems. Consider once again metathesis in Mutsun where the labial nasal consistently occurs in onset position in the metathesized variants, e.g. [rukka-km a] 'house', [hu:s-m ak] 'noses'. Positing a constraint which bars nasals from coda position fails, however, since nasals do occur as codas in the language, provided that they are not followed by another consonant, e.g. [sire:sum] 'with the heart', [re:ʈem] 'louse eggs'. Similar observations hold for Rendille with respect to the pharyngeal fricative; the pharyngeal is prohibited from coda position only when followed by another consonant, e.g. *[baħbo], [babħo] 'armpit', cf. [nabaħ] 'ear'. Consequently, reference to prosodic position alone is insufficient.

Alternatively, I would suggest that a unified account of these and many other cases of C/C metathesis is possible when the role of perceptibility is taken into account. That is, by metathesis, a perceptibly vulnerable consonant shifts to a context in which the phonetic cues to the sound's identification are more robust, thereby enhancing the consonant's auditory prominence and, in turn, strengthening syntagmatic and paradigmatic contrast among sounds in a given language.[1,2]   By perceptibly vulnerable, I refer to a consonant with comparatively weak segment internal and/or contextual cues to, e.g. place and/or manner of articulation. The occurrence of such consonants in syntagmatically or prosodically prominent contexts can yield more robust phonetic cues and hence, provide more information regarding their quality.

Prototypical examples of potentially vulnerable consonants include obstruent stops, labials, and nasals. As is well-known, obstruent stops depend heavily on contextual cues such as release burst and formant transitions for the identification of manner and place (see Wright (1996) and references therein). Thus, from a perceptibility perspective, the occurrence of stops in contexts in which these cues are present is to be preferred, e.g. prevocalic as opposed to preconsonantal position, or adjacent rather than nonadjacent to a vowel. Of interest is the observation that these are precisely the contexts in which stops surface by metathesis. In Faroese, for example, a stop shifts from interconsonantal position to postvocalic position, at the expense of fricative /s/, a sound with stronger internal cues to both place and manner, e.g. /frɑsk+t/ [frɑ́kst]'healthy, masc./neut.'. A similar pattern occurs in Hebrew although in this case the stop shifts to prevocalic position, also at the expense of a strident consonant, e.g. /hi+t+sarek/ [histarek] 'he combed his (own) hair'. And in Elmolo, Sidamo and other languages, stops shift to prevocalic position at the expense of nasals and liquids (see (1)).

Among stops, labials can be considered particularly vulnerable given inherently short vowel transitions and relatively weak bursts, as compared to coronals and velars.[3] As Ohala (1996:1720) states: "In the case of labial stops, [b] and [p], the amplitude of the burst may not be very great because these stops lack any resonating cavity downstream of their point of release." The shift of the labial stop from an unstressed to stressed position at the expense of a velar in Kui is therefore not surprising, given that prosodic prominence in the language results in greater duration of transitions into the labial, e.g. /lek+pa/ [lépka] 'to break'.[4]

---

[1]   While many cases of C/C metathesis can be understood as perceptually-driven, as shown in this paper, this does not rule out the possibility that metathesis may be motivated by other factors as well. See, for example, Hume (1997a) for discussion of metathesis in Dɛg which is argued to be motivated by articulatory timing considerations, and Hume (1997b) for related discussion.

[2]   Blevins & Garrett (1997) provide a different perceptually-driven account of certain types of diachronic C/V metathesis. See Hume (1997b) for detailed discussion and critique.

[3]   Jun (1995) claims that labial stops may be more robust than coronal stops based on the assumption that the gesture of the former is slower than the latter. If correct, this may suggest a potential conflict between acoustics and articulation for the labial in terms of robustness of place cues. The extent to which this conflict is manifested in the patterning of labials cross-linguistically remains a question for future research.

[4]   Stress in Kui is manifested as increased syllable duration (Winfield 1928). We speculate that the labial stop is released before [k] thus providing additional information concerning the consonant's place of articulation.

The vulnerability of nasals can be attributed to weak segment-internal cues for place (Wright 1996), and lowered amplitude of higher formants, due to the presence of formants as well as antiformants (Fant 1960, Johnson 1996). The most powerful cues to nasal place are contextual: frequency and durational information included in the vowel formant transition (Kurowsky & Blumstein 1984, Malécot 1956, Repp 1986). Examples of nasals involved in metathesis come from Mutsun where the labial nasal shifts to prevocalic position at the expense of a released velar stop (an epenthetic schwa may also occur between the stop and following sonorant, further strengthening the cues for the stop), e.g. čiri-k^{h}ma / čiri-k^{ə}ma *[čiri-mk^{h}a] 'paternal aunt'. And in Old Spanish and Chawchila, nasals shift to prosodically prominent contexts, at the expense of liquids (see (1)). More will be said about these cases below.

With this as a basis, consider the specific contexts to which a perceptibly vulnerable consonant shifts in metathesis. The most common landing site, as we would expect, appears to be prevocalic position (obstruent stops: Hebrew, Elmolo, Sidamo, Darasa, Gedeo, Hadiyya, Kambata; nasals: Old Spanish, Mutsun). Also observed are shifts to postvocalic, preconsonantal position, provided that the preceding vowel is *stressed* (obstruent stop: Kui, Faroese; nasal: Chawchila). Unattested, however, are cases in which a vulnerable consonant shifts from a stressed prevocalic position to an unstressed preconsonantal position; that is, from a more to a less salient context. Nor have cases been identified in which a perceptibly vulnerable consonant shifts to interconsonantal position.

3. Formal Account

These observations suggest that, all else being equal, prevocalic and post-stressed vowel positions are more favorable contexts for consonants than unstressed preconsonantal and interconsonantal positions. This is precisely what we expect when the potential cues to place and/or manner available in each of these contexts are taken into consideration, as outlined in very general terms in (2a, b). Briefly stated, there are more cues, including formant transitions, increased duration and amplitude, and release bursts prevocalically, available for the identification of consonants in the contexts, i.e. v́__c, c__v. These cues are either not present in the less harmonic contexts, or they are reduced.

(2)   *Cues (or lack thereof) to place and/or manner of articulation:*
    a.   v́__c: vowel formant transition, potential for increased
    duration/amplitude of phonetic cues due to prosodic prominence
            c__v: vowel formant transition, release burst for stop
    consonants, increased amplitude at onset of vowel, potential for
    increased duration/amplitude of phonetic cues if prosodically
    prominence

b. *c__c*: potential absence of formant transitions, potential absence of release bursts for stop consonants, compressed duration (masking) of phonetic cues

v̆__c: presence of vowel formant transition, potential lack of burst for stop consonants, compressed duration of phonetic cues, small modulation in signal

In the spirit of Archangeli & Pulleyblank (1994), Steriade (1995a,b, 1997), Jun (1995), Flemming (1995), among others, these observations are taken to provide the phonetic grounding for the Optimality theoretic constraints assumed in this work. The relevant constraints form part of the family of Avoid C/X constraints, stated in (3): avoid positioning a consonant in a context in which it is perceptually weak. It is important to note that while metathesis, by definition, involves two segments, only one constitutes the focus of Avoid C/X, that being the more perceptibly vulnerable consonant of the pair, given relevant segment internal and contextual cues.[5]

(3) AVOID C/X: Avoid positioning a consonant (C) in a context (X) in which it is perceptually weak.

Based on the observations regarding the distribution of cues laid out in (2), the following harmonic ranking of Avoid C/X constraints is proposed. Informally stated, from the point of view of perceptibility, it is worse for a consonant to occur interconsonantally or preconsonantally in an unstressed context than prevocalically or preconsonantally following a stressed vowel.[6]

(4) Harmonic ranking: *c/c__c, *c/v̆__c > *c/c__v, *c/v̆__c

Avoid C/X provides the motivation for metathesis. Its crucial ranking above LINEARITY (5) forces a change in the ordering of sounds. Informally stated, a violation of LINEARITY results when a mismatch in precedence relations occurs between an input and output.

---

[5] It is clearly beyond the scope of this paper to propose a hierarchy of sounds in terms of perceptibility, though such a ranking of sounds is clearly warranted. This hierarchy needs to be more than the sonority hierarchy in that contextual in addition to segmental internal properties of sounds must be taken into account. It seems, however, that further study of the patterning of sounds from a phonological perspective, as well as additional experimental phonetic work is needed before such a hierarchy can be firmly established.

[6] The ranking proposed in (4) is clearly simplified. Note only does this represent only a small number of possible Avoid C/X constraints, it may be the case that the proposed ranking is most relevant when cues to *place* of articulation are at issue. When the cues to manner of articulation are of concern, the ranking seems less clear at this point. For example, given anticipatory coarticulation of nasality on a vowel preceding a nasal consonant, it may be that the occurrence of a nasal in postvocalic position (stressed or unstressed) is to be preferred or at least equivalent to prevocalic position in terms of salience, when preserving or strengthening cues to *manner* of articulation is at issue. Similar observations would appear to be relevant for retroflexion (see Steriade (1995a)).

(5)   LINEARITY (McCarthy 1995; McCarthy & Prince, 1994, 1995; see also Hume, 1994, 1998): S_1 is consistent with the precedence structure of S_2, and vice versa.

Consider some of the predictions made by the interaction of the constraints in (4) with LINEARITY (see Hume (1997b) for further discussion and motivation). For example, given the ranking in (4), we predict a language in which *c/c__c and *c/v̌__c dominate LINEARITY and the remaining two contextual constraints. This is precisely what we find in Faroese where, it will be recalled, metathesis involves /k/ and /s/, e.g. /fɛsk-t/ → [fékst] *[féskt] *[fést] 'fresh, neut. sg.', shown in (6a). The focus of Avoid C/X is the stop, given the greater vulnerability of cues to place and manner in this context for the stop than for the fricative. Note that the crucial ranking of *c/c__c and *c/v̌__c above all others predicts that the stop will shift to postvocalic position only when that vowel is *stressed*. As shown in (6b), this prediction is borne out; when part of an unstressed syllable, the velar stop deletes, e.g. /føːrɪsk-t/ → [føːrɪst], *[føːrɪskt], *[føːrɪkst] 'Faroese, neut. sg.'. (The constraint MAX-C penalizes consonant deletion.)

(6)

(a)	I: fɛsk-t	*stop/ c__c	*stop/ v̌__c	MAX-C	*stop/ v́__c	LIN
	féskt	*!				
☞	fékst				*!	*
	fést		*!			
(b)	I: føːrɪsk-t					
	føːrɪskt	*!				
	føːrɪkst		*!			*
☞	føːrɪst			*!		

The shift of a vulnerable consonant from the context v̌ __c to prevocalic position is also predicted by the universal ranking posited in (4), a pattern supported by metathesis in Old Spanish, e.g. /poner-e/ → [porné] *[ponré]. With the nasal as the focus of the contextual constraint, the ranking *nasal/v̌ __c >> *nasal/c__v, LINEARITY correctly selects preservation of the nasal prevocalically, at the expense of the liquid.

Returning to the hierarchy in (4), it will be observed that no fixed ranking is imposed on the two most highly ranked constraints, nor on the two constraints at the bottom end of the scale. Thus, we predict that the constraints belonging to each pair may be ranked differently in different languages. For example, both *c/v́__c >> *c/c__v, (Linearity) as well as *c/c__v >> *c/v́__c, (Linearity) are possible rankings. Given the former, we predict a case in which a consonant shifts from stressed pre-consonantal position to prevocalic position. With the latter, on the other hand, a consonant shifts from prevocalic to stressed pre-consonantal position. Elmolo provides evidence for the first pattern, e.g. /tikir-o/ → [tírko] *[tíkro], accounted for by the ranking *stop/v̆__c >> *stop/c__v, LINEARITY. Evidence for the second comes from Kui and Chawchila. Recall that in Kui, a labial stop shifts from prevocalic position to stressed preconsonantal position, e.g. /ag+ba/ [ábga] 'to be fitting', a pattern accounted for by the ranking , *labial/c__v >> *labial/v̆__c, LINEARITY. Similarly, in Chawchila, a nasal consonant shifts, at the expense of a liquid, to stressed preconsonantal position, e.g. /paṭṭilin-i/ → [paṭṭínli] *[paṭṭílni], a pattern which emerges from the ranking *nasal/c__v >> *nasal/v̆__c, LINEARITY. Note that the shift of the nasal to the left of the liquid is exactly the opposite of that seen in Old Spanish. It is important to point out that sonority conditions alone are unable to predict these patterns. In fact, we would predict the two languages to behave in an identical manner. Conversely, this difference in patterning is exactly what we expect given the ranking of constraints outlined in (4); in both cases, the nasal shifts to a position of increased salience.

4. Resolving the Nasal/Obstruent Asymmetry

Drawing on information concerning both the inherent nature of a segment, as determined by internal cues, as well as contextual cues, provides a straightforward account of the observed asymmetry between metathesis in languages such as Mutsun and Sidamo. Recall that metathesis in Mutsun involves the thematic plural suffix, which shows two alternants: [-kma] and [-mak]. In addition to C/V metathesis (see Hume (1997b)), the ordering of the consonants is reversed: in [-kma], [k] precedes [m], while in [-mak], [m] precedes [k]. Note that in both cases, the nasal is positioned in prevocalic position, even when preceded by a stop. In Sidamo, on the other hand, the output of metathesis reveals a nasal followed by a homorganic obstruent, e.g. /hab+nemmo/ [hambémmo] 'we forget'. The problem then is this: while the output of metathesis in languages like Sidamo is nasal+obstruent, consistent with syllable contact considerations (Vennemann 1988), the exact opposite is observed in Mutsun.

Relevant to these patterns is the observation that in both languages nasal place is neutralized in preconsonantal position. In Mutsun, /m/ occurs most frequently in prevocalic position, either intervocalically or following a consonant. It rarely occurs in preconsonantal, postvocalic position except when followed by a homorganic consonant, e.g. [ṭaːkampi] 'bring', or as part of a geminate, e.g. [ṭamman] 'other side'. The limited distribution of /m/ in preconsonantal position is not limited to the labial nasal. Of the two other nasals in the language, the palatal nasal /ɲ/ never occurs in preconsonantal position, while the apical /n/ tends to assimilate in place of articulation to a following consonant. Hence, place contrasts among nasals are neutralized preconsonantally (yet maintained prevocalically and word-finally). Nasal place is also nondistinctive preconsonantally in Sidamo; nasals only occur as homorganic to a following obstruent or as part of a geminate. These observations motivate the contextual constraint in (7), assumed to be active in both languages: distinctive place in nasals is prohibited in preconsonantal position. (Recall that reference to coda position alone is insufficient since, as discussed above with regards to Mutsun, all nasals may occur in coda position provided that they are not followed by another consonant.)

(7) $*$nasal(place)/v__c

Consider next the nature of stop consonants in Mutsun and Sidamo. It is here, in particular, where the languages differ. Of crucial importance is the observation that in Mutsun, stops are aspirated and released in all positions. In fact, an excrescent vowel optionally occurs between a stop and a following sonorant, e.g. čiri-k^{h}ma / čiri-k^{ə}ma 'paternal aunt'. In Sidamo, on the other hand, released obstruents are only attested in prevocalic position. Since the release burst of a stop consonant provides crucial information regarding its place and manner, I assume, consistent with Padgett (1995), the harmonic ranking in (8). By taking into account the presence vs. absence of a release burst, this ranking presents a further refinement of the more general $*$stop constraint seen above. Informally stated, all else being equal, an unreleased stop is less harmonic in preconsonantal position than one which is released.

(8) $*$stop$_{unrel}$/v__c > $*$stop$_{rel}$/v__c   (Harmonic ranking)

This difference in the nature of stops in the two languages provides a straightforward account of the observed patterns. In Mutsun, where place contrasts among nasals are neutralized in preconsonantal position, while those of stop consonants are not, we may assume that the nasal is the more perceptibly vulnerable consonant. This leads to the ranking in (9) of the $*$nasal constraint above the released stop constraint. That is, it is worse for a nasal to occur preconsonantally than it is for a released stop to occur in this position, when place contrasts are at issue.

(9) Mutsun: ($*$stop$_{unrel}$/v__c), $*$nasal (pl)/v__c >> $*$stop$_{rel}$/v__c, Lin

I: relo + mak	$*$nasal(pl)/ v__c	$*$stop$_{rel}$ /v__c	LINEARITY
relomk^{h}a	*!		*
☞ relok^{h}ma		*	**

In Sidamo, on the other hand, distinctive place in both nasals and (unreleased) stops is disfavored in preconsonantal position. As a result, as shown in (10), no crucial ranking between the two contextual constraints is motivated.[7]

(10)   Sidamo: *stop$_{unrel}$/v__c, *nasal/v__c >> Lin, (*stop$_{rel}$/v__c)

I: duk+nanni	*stop$_{unrel}$/ v__c	*nasal(pl)/ v__c	LINEARITY
duknanni	*!		
dunkanni		*!	*
☞ duŋkanni V place			*

To conclude this section, it is important to emphasize that while a sonority-based account is unable to provide a unified account of the above patterns of metathesis, when the specific nature of the segments involved is taken into account, as determined by a segment's internal as well as contextual cues, the seemingly distinct patterns of Mutsun and Sidamo receive a straightforward account.

5. Boolean Disjunction and Metathesis

A further condition crucial to motivating many cases of metathesis involves contiguity of acoustically/auditorily similar consonants. For example, in Faroese metathesis the velar stop must be adjacent to another stop, e.g. /fɛs k-t/ [fɛkst]. Further, in Hebrew, metathesis only occurs when a coronal stop is contiguous to a coronal obstruent, e.g. [histakel]. In Chawchila and Old Spanish, as seen above, adjacent sonorant consonants are at issue. In Rendille, contiguity of the pharyngeal fricative with the pharyngeal vowel /a/ is a necessary condition, e.g. /baħab+o/ [babħo] *[baħbo]. And in Kui, metathesis only occurs between labial and velar stops, sounds classified by Jakobson, Fant and Halle (1952) by the acoustically-based feature [grave], referring to sounds with energy predominantly in the lower end of the spectrum.

Contiguity to an acoustically/auditorily similar segment adds to the perceptual vulnerability of a consonant, given the small modulation in the speech signal. This line of reasoning builds upon, most notably, Ohala (1992, 1993) and Kawasaki (1982), where it is claimed that sharper changes

---

[7]   Note that the ranking of *nasal(pl) above *stop$_{rel}$ in (9) is consistent with the ranking of place faithfulness constraints in Padgett (1995): faithfulness to obstruent place is universally ranked above faithfulness to nasal place. On the other hand, the lack of ranking between the two Avoid C/X constraints in (10) is in contrast to Padgett's proposal; for Padgett, faithfulness to obstruent place, produced with or without a release, is universally ranked above faithfulness to nasal place.

in the speech signal increase the salience of cues in the portion of the signal where the modulation takes place; the greater the magnitude of the modulation, the better a given signal is detected.

Phonological theory already provides the formal means of encoding this observation, in the form of OCP constraints. In the cases of metathesis under consideration, the OCP is defined on strictly adjacent segments, i.e. $*C_{[\alpha F]}/C_{[\alpha F]}$: root adjacent identical elements are prohibited.[8]

The role of the OCP in metathesis is exemplified by Rendille where, as noted above, the pharyngeal fricative metathesizes with a following consonant just in case it is preceded by /a/, e.g. *baħab, babħ-o *baħbo* 'armpit, sing./plur.'; *aħam, amħ-a *aħma* 'eat!, sing./plur.'; *yaħar, yarħ-a *yaħra* 'cough!, sing./plur.'. The shift of the pharyngeal from preconsonantal to prevocalic position at the expense of stops, nasals, and liquids is consistent with the patterns outlined above: the pharyngeal's vulnerability results from its contiguity to /a/, as well as its occurrence in preconsonantal position. That is, the pharyngeal may occur preconsonantally provided that it is not preceded by a pharyngeal vowel, e.g. [liħti] *[litħi] 'rock', cf. /baħb+o/ → [babħo] *[baħbo] 'armpit, pl.'. Further, it may occur adjacent to /a/ provided that it does not occur preconsonantally, e.g. [nabaħ] 'ear', [amħa] 'eat! plur.'. In other words, for metathesis to occur two conditions (constraints) must be violated: *phar/v__c and OCP[pharyngeal].

Crowhurst and Hewitt (1997) propose to account for such patterns by means of macro-constraints, comprised of two independent constraints, as illustrated by the relevant constraint for Rendille in (11) (see also, e.g. Smolensky (1997), Alderete (1997) on *local conjunction*). Following Crowhurst and Hewitt, a macro-constraint necessarily requires each coordinated constraint to share a common focus, which in this case is [pharyngeal]. A candidate passes a macro-constraint if it satisfies either of the coordinated constraints.

(11)   Macro-constraint: *phar/v__c $\vee^{phar}$ *[phar]/[phar]

The Rendille forms in tableau (12) serve to illustrate. In the first word, the unmetathesized candidate in (a) violates both parts of the macro-constraint since the pharyngeal occurs preconsonantally and is adjacent to /a/. In the metathesized form in (b), both conditions are satisfied, with only lower ranking LINEARITY violated. A similar situation occurs in the second word. Note that although candidate (d) incurs an OCP violation, this alone is not sufficient to rule it out. It wins out over candidate (c) which fatally violates the macro-constraint. The observation that a pharyngeal can occur preconsonantally when not adjacent to /a/ is illustrated in the third example where the unmetathesized candidate in (e) wins. And finally, contiguity of

---

[8]   The issue of whether or not OCP constraints are part of the family of Avoid C/X constraints remains an open question.

the pharyngeal consonant to /a/ is insufficient to rule out either candidates (g) or (h). The correct output is determined by LINEARITY, violated in (h).

(12)

i.		I: baħa b-o	*phar/v__c Vᵖʰᵃʳ	*[phar]/[phar]	LIN
	a.	bañ bo	(*)	*!	(*)	
☞	b.	babħ o				*
ii.		I: aħ am-a				
	c.	aħ ma	(*)	*!	(*)	
☞	d.	amħ a			(*)	*
iii.		I: liħ ti				
☞	e.	liħ ti	(*)			
	f.	lith i				*!
iv.		I: nabaħ				
☞	g.	nabaħ			(*)	
	h.	nabħ a			(*)	*!

Similar macro-constraints figure into the analyses of, among others, Faroese (*stop/c__c Vˢᵗᵒᵖ *[stop]/[stop]), Kui (*labial(grave)/c__v Vˡᵃᵇ *labial(grave)/velar(grave)),[9] and Hebrew (*[cor obst stop]/v__c Vᶜᵒʳ ˢᵗᵒᵖ *[cor obst stop]/[cor obst]). Since space limitations prevent us from illustrating these patterns, the reader is referred to Hume (1997b) for further discussion. Nonetheless, it is important to emphasize that the OCP condition in each of these cases is entirely consistent with the analysis of metathesis developed thus far. That is, contiguity to an acoustically/auditorily similar consonant contributes to the perceptual vulnerability of a given consonant, a key factor motivating metathesis.

6. Conclusion

To conclude, in this paper I have argued that in consonant/consonant metathesis, a perceptibly vulnerable consonant commonly shifts to a position where the cues to its identification are more robust. By drawing on segment-internal as well as contextual cues, a wide range of metatheses are accounted for in a phonetically natural and unified manner.

---

[9] I leave open the question of whether [grave] is the appropriate means of grouping labial and velar consonants together.

7. References

Alderete, John. 1997. Dissimilation as Local Conjunction. *NELS* 27. 17-32.

Archangeli, Diana and Douglas Pulleyblank. 1994. *Grounded Phonology*. Cambridge, Mass.: MIT Press.

Burrow, Thomas & S. Bhattacharya. 1970. *The Pengo Language*. London: Oxford University Press.

Bat-El, Outi. 1988. Remarks on Tier Conflation. *Linguistic Inquiry* 19 (3). 477-485.

Bat-El, Outi. 1989. *Phonology and Word Structure in Modern Hebrew*. PhD dissertation.UCLA.

Blevins, Juliette and Andrew Garrett. 1997. The Origin of Consonant-Vowel Metathesis. ms. University of Western Australia and University of California̓, Berkeley.

Blumstein, Sheila E. and Kenneth N. Stevens. 1979. Acoustic invariance in speech production: Evidence from measurements of the spectral characteristics of stop consonants. *Journal of the Acoustical Society of America* 66. 1001-1017.

Borden, Gloria and Katherine Harris. 1984. *Speech Science Primer: Physiology, Acoustics and Perception of Speech*. 2nd edition. Baltimore: Williams and Wilkins.

Crowhurst, Megan and Mark Hewitt. 1997. Boolean operations and constraint interactions in Optimality Theory. ms. UNC, Chapel Hill and Brandeis University.

Fant, Gunnar. 1960. *Acoustic Theory of Speech Production*. The Hague: Mouton.

Heine, Bernd. 1976. Notes on the Rendille Language. *Afrika und Ubersee* 59. 176-223.

Heine, Bernd. 1978. The Sam Languages. A History of Rendille, Boni and Somali. *Afroasiatic Linguistics* 6(2). 1-92.

Hudson, Grover. 1975. *Suppletion in the Representation of Alternations*. PhD dissertation. UCLA.

Hudson, Grover. 1995. Phonology of Ethiopian Languages. In John Goldsmith (ed.), *Handbook of Phonological Theory*. Oxford: Blackwell. 782-797.

Hume, Elizabeth, 1994. Metathesis in optimality theory. Paper presented to the Phonetics/Phonology Group, Department of Linguistics, Ohio State University.

Hume, Elizabeth. 1997a. Consonant Clusters and Articulatory Timing in Deg. ms. Ohio State University.

Hume, Elizabeth. 1997b. Towards an Explanation of Consonant/Consonant Metathesis. ms. Ohio State University.

Hume, Elizabeth. 1998. Metathesis in Phonological Theory: The Case of Leti. *Lingua* 104. 147-186.

Jacobsen, M.A. & C. Matras. 1961. *Førosysk-Donsk Ordabók*. Tørshavn: Føroya Fródskaparfelag.

Jakobson, Roman, Gunnar Fant and Morris Halle. 1952. *Preliminaries to Speech Analysis. The Distinctive Features and Their Correlates*. Cambridge, Mass.: MIT Press.

Johnson, Keith. 1996. *Acoustic and Auditory Phonetics*. Oxford: Blackwell.

Jun, Jongho. 1995. Place Assimilation as the Result of Conflicting Perceptual and Articulatory Constraints. *Proceedings of WCCFL 14*. 221-237.

Kawasaki, Haruko. 1982. *An Acoustical Basis for the Universal Constraints on Sound Sequences*. PhD dissertation. UC Berkeley.

Kenstowicz, Michael. 1972. *Lithuanian Phonology*. PhD dissertation. University of Illinois at Urbana-Champaign.

Kurowsky, K. and Blumstein, Sheila E. 1984. Perceptual Integration of the Murmur and Formant Transitions for Place of Articulation in Nasal Consonants. *Journal of the Acoustical Society of America* 76. 383-390.

Lockwood, William 1955. *An Introduction to Modern Faroese*. Copenhagen: Ejnar Munksgaard.

Malécot, André. 1956. Acoustic Cues for Nasal Consonants: An Experimental Study involving a Tape-slicing Technique. *Language* 32. 274-284.

McCarthy, John. 1995. Extensions of Faithfulness: Rotuman Revisited. ms. UMass, Amherst.

McCarthy, John and Alan Prince, 1993. Prosodic Morphology. ms. UMass, Amherst and Rutgers University.

McCarthy, John and Alan Prince, 1994. The Emergence of the Unmarked: Optimality in Prosodic Morphology. In Mercè Gonzàlez (ed.), *Proceedings of the North East Linguistic Society 24*, 333-379. Amherst, MA: Graduate Linguistic Student Association.

McCarthy, John and Alan Prince, 1995. Faithfulness and Reduplicative Identity. To appear in R. Kager, H. van der Hulst, W. Zonneveld (eds.), *Proceedings of the Utrecht Workshop on Prosodic Morphology*. The Hague: Mouton.

Newman, Stanley. 1944. *Yokuts Language of California*. New York: Viking Fund Publication in Anthropology, no.2.

Ohala, John, 1981. The Listener as a Source of Sound Change. In Masek, C.S., R.A. Hendrik, M. F. Miller (eds.), *Papers from the Parasession on Language and Behavior: Chicago Linguistics Society*. Chicago: CLS. 178-203.

Ohala, John. 1992. Alternatives to the Sonority Hierarchy for Explaining Segmental Sequential Constraints. *Papers from the Parasession on the Syllable: Chicago Linguistics Society*. Chicago: CLS. 319-338.

Ohala, John. 1993. Sound Change as Nature's Speech Perception Experiment. *Speech Communication* 13. 155-161.

Ohala, John. 1996. Speech Perception is Hearing Sounds, not Tongues. *Journal of the Acoustical Society of America* 99 (3). 1718-1725.

Okrand, Marc, 1977. *Mutsun Grammar*. PhD dissertation. University of California. Berkeley.

Oomen, Antoinette, 1981. Gender and Plurality in Rendille. *Afroasiatic Linguistics* 8(1), 35-75.

Padgett, Jaye. 1995. Partial Class Behavior and Nasal Place Assimilation. *Proceedings of the Arizona Phonology Conference: Workshop on Features in Optimality Theory.* Coyote Working Papers, University of Arizona, Tuscon, Arizona.

Prince, Alan & Paul Smolensky, 1993. Optimality Theory. ms. Rutgers University and the University of Colorado at Boulder.

Rischel, Jørgen. 1972. Consonant Reduction in Faroese Noncompound Wordforms. In E. Scherabon Firchow, K. Grimstad, N. Hasselmo and W. O'Neil (eds.), *Studies for Einar Haugen.* The Hague: Mouton.

Repp, Bruno. 1986. Perception of the [m]-[n] Distinction in CV Syllables. *Journal of the Acoustical Society of America* 79(6). 1987-1999.

Sim, Ronald J., 1981. Morphophonemics of the Verb in Rendille. *Afroasiatic Linguistics* 8(1), 1-33.

Smolensky, Paul. 1997. Constraint Interaction in Generative Grammar II: Local Conjunction or Random Rules in Universal Grammar. Talk presented at the Hopkins Optimality Theory Workshop/ University of Maryland Mayfest.

Steriade, Donca. 1995a. Licensing Retroflexion. ms. UCLA.

Steriade, Donca. 1995b. Positional Neutralization. ms. UCLA.

Steriade, Donca, 1997. Licensing Laryngeal Features. ms. UCLA.

Stevens, Kenneth and Sheila E. Blumstein. 1978. Invariant Cues for Place of Articulation in Stop Consonants. *Journal of the Acoustical Society of America* 64. 1358-1368.

Vennemann, Theo, 1988. *Preference Laws for Syllable Structure.* Berlin: Mouton de Gruyter.

Wang, W.S.-Y. 1959. Transition and Release as Perceptual Cues for Final Plosives. *Journal of Speech and Hearing Research* 3. 66-73.

Wanner, Dieter. 1989. On Metathesis in Diachrony. In Wiltshire, Caroline, R. Eraczyk, B. Music (eds.), *CLS 25: Papers from the 25th Annual Regional Meeting of the Chicago Linguistic Society.* Chicago: CLS.

Webb, Charlotte. 1974. *Metathesis.* PhD dissertation. University of Texas, Austin.

Winfield, W. W. 1928. *A Grammar of the Kui Language.* Calcutta: The Asiatic Society of Bengal.

Wright, Richard. 1996. *Consonant Clusters and Cue Preservation in Tsou.* PhD dissertation. UCLA.

Zaborsky, Andrzej, 1986. *The Morphology of Nominal Plural in the Cushitic Languages.* Institute für Afrikanistik und Agyptologie der Universität Wien. Wien.

Vowel Dynamics and Vowel Phonology[1]

KHALIL ISKAROUS

University of Illinois at Urbana-Champaign

1. Introduction

In this paper, I present evidence that a nearly universal asymmetry in vowel coalescence occurs as a result of the similarity in tongue motions between the alternants. The asymmetry concerns which sequences of vowels commonly coalesce, and which do not. A sequence of a high vowel followed by a low vowel, for instance [i] followed by [a], very rarely coalesces. In contrast, a low vowel followed by a high vowel, for instance [a] followed by [i] can coalesce to [e] (Casali (1996)). The question I address is why [e] alternates more commonly with [a]-[i] than with [i]-[a]. Using articulatory evidence from ultrasound imaging of tongue movement, I show that the tongue trajectory for the coalescence target is similar to the one for the sequence of a low vowel followed by a high vowel. For instance, both [a]-[i] and [e] have a frontward trajectory. On the other hand, the [i]-[a] sequence has a backward trajectory. The argument then is that the similarity in the tongue trajectories between the [a]-[i] sequence and [e] is the reason for their alternation and the fact that the [i]-[a] sequence does not alternate with [e] is due to the fact that their articulatory trajectories are in opposite directions. The phonological asymmetry therefore follows from the dynamic asymmetry. In sections 2 and 3, the asymmetry and previous accounts of it

[1] I would like to thank Jennifer Cole, Molly Homer, Jose Hualde, and Daniel Silverman for many discussions regarding this paper. And a special thanks to Leon Frizzell for allowing me to use the ultrasound equipment. All remaining errors are of course mine.

are discussed, and in sections 4 and 5, I present the argument and evidence for the dynamic articulatory account.

2. The Coalescence Asymmetry

Many strategies are used to resolve vowel hiatus. These strategies include diphthongization, glide formation, glide insertion, vowel elision, and coalescence. In coalescence, a sequence of two vowels is mapped to a single vowel different from the original two, whose features are a combination of the features of the original vowels. The specific qualities of the vowels involved in coalescence and the vowel resulting from it depend on language-specific properties such as the number of vowels in the system, syllable structure, and the presence of a length contrast in the language. These factors are discussed in the important typological study by Casali (1996), and in Schane (1987). But whichever specific vowels are involved, there is an asymmetry concerning the sequence of vowels that can undergo coalescence. If the first vowel is higher than the second, coalescence is very rarely a viable resolution strategy. Glide formation, glide insertion, or vowel elision are used in such cases. However, coalescence is a viable hiatus resolution strategy when the first vowel is lower than the second (Schane (1987); Casali (1996)). Table 1 shows an example of hiatus resolution strategies from Sanskrit (Schane (1987)).

Table 1: Sanskrit hiatus resolution strategies.

V2

		i	iː	u	uː	a	aː
	i	iː	iː	yu	yuː	ya	yaː
	iː	iː	iː	yu	yuː	ya	yaː
V1	u	wi	wiː	uː	uː	wa	waː
	uː	wi	wiː	uː	uː	wa	waː
	a	eː	eː	oː	oː	aː	aː
	aː	eː	eː	oː	oː	aː	aː

The double box shows the output of hiatus resolution for sequences of a low vowel followed by a high vowel. The output in these cases is a mid vowel with the frontness specification of the second vowel of the input sequence. Coalescence does not apply, however, to resolve the reverse sequences, as we see in the bold box. Sequencing therefore is an important factor in coalescence. In an extensive investigation of 92 languages, Casali (1996) finds few exceptions to this asymmetry.

3. Previous Accounts

Phonological accounts of this asymmetry stipulate either a representational difference between the sequences that may and may not undergo coalescence, or stipulate ranking of the constraints or rules to model the asymmetry. In this section I outline the analyses of Schane (1987) and Casali (1996), and motivate the need for a different kind of analysis.

To model hiatus resolution strategies, Schane (1987) utilizes the notion of *closure*, where two symbols fuse on a specific level. For instance, two V's could fuse into one on the CV-tier, or an /a/ and an /i/ can fuse into [e] on the segmental tier (assuming particle-theoretic notation as in (Schane 1984)). Figure 1, below, contains the rules and representations used to distinguish the glide formation that results from hiatus of the [i]-[a] (bold box in Table 1) from the coalescence that results from hiatus of [a]-[i] (double box in Table 1):

```
 σ  σ        σ         σ  σ   σ    σ
 |  |        |         |  |   / \  / \
 V  V  >     V         V  V > V V > V V
 |  |       / \        |  |   | |   \ /
 i  a      i   a       a  i   a i    e
```

Figure 1a. Glide Formation
[i]+[a] > [ya]

Figure 1b. Coalescence
[a]+[i] > [ai] > [e:]

In both cases, there is closure at the syllable tier, indicating that the original syllable count is reduced. Additionally, when the first vowel is high, there is closure, or fusion, on the CV-tier. The result is a (sonority) rising diphthong realized with an onglide. When the first vowel is low, on the other hand, closure occurs on the segmental tier only. However, the following question arises: why doesn't the closure on the CV-tier also occur in the case of (1b), yielding a glide in that case as well. Schane points out that the reason is that closure on the CV-tier abides by the universal sonority hierarchy principle as it applies to vowel sequences: "the left V may not be more sonorous than the right one" (Schane (1987:284)). This prevents CV-tier closure and eventual glide formation when the first vowel is low and the second vowel is high. What is not clear, however, is why segmental-tier closure doesn't also occur in (1a), when the first part of the diphthong is high and the second low. If this were to occur, both sequences would result in coalescence. In fact, earlier in his paper, Schane presents a case of the monophthongization of the (sonority) rising diphthong [ue] to [ö], operating on the structure in (2a), below, and yielding the structure in (2b).

```
        σ                σ
        |                |
        V                V
       / \               |
       u i               i
        a                u
                         a
  Figure 2a. [ue]    Figure 2b. [ö]
```

The coalescence of [i]-[a] to [e], therefore, does not seem to be incompatible with Schane's account. The typological distribution indicated by Casali's survey shows that coalescence of [i]-[a] to [e] is very rare. An account of the phonology of coalescence needs to reflect that.

The optimality-theoretic account of Casali (1996) captures the asymmetry by noting the fact that the target of coalescence has to receive a [-Hi] specification from the first vowel, and its other feature specifications from the second vowel. This is modeled by ranking faithfulness to the [-Hi] specification higher than faithfulness to [+Hi]. The sequential nature of the asymmetry is captured by specifying whether faithfulness is to a root or to an affix feature. For hiatus resulting from prefixation, for instance, faithfulness to a prefix feature [-Hi] is ranked higher than faithfulness to a root [+Hi] specification. The fact that asymmetric coalescence is much more common than symmetric coalescence is captured by a universal ranking of the constraints. However, in optimality theory, ranking is usually used to model variation, not lack of variation. One of the goals of a phonological theory is to allow us to understand the difference between variable and invariable sound patterns, and using the same theoretical device to account for both of them lessens our chance of understanding the difference. Invariable patterns may be revealing of some principle of linguistic computation, but they may also follow from the physical basis of speech. In the following sections I will argue that the coalescence asymmetry is of the second type.

4. Articulatory Evidence

In this section I argue that the asymmetry in vowel coalescence has an articulatory basis. Phonetic arguments depending on vowel statics, that is, the articulatory or acoustic steady states present in [a], [i], and [e], cannot explain why [e] alternates with [a]-[i] and not [i]-[a], since the same steady states are involved in both vocalic sequences. The solution to the problem lies in the dynamical nature of [e], [a]-[i], and [i]-[a]. What I show is that there is a dynamical similarity between the input and output of coalescence: [a]-[i] sequences and [e] involve the same frontward direction of tongue movement, while [i]-[a] sequences involve backing, the opposite of the movement involved in the mid vowel [e]. In other words, speech dynamics groups [a]-[i] sequences together with [e], and this group excludes [i]-[a] sequences. However this argument is available only if it can be empirically shown that mid vowels are indeed dynamical objects involving a fronting gesture. If [e] has a static target, it could be achieved either through a backing or a fronting gesture, depending on the segmental context. However, if it were inherently dynamic, then it would always be achieved with a fronting trajectory irrespective of the context. This would make it dynamically similar to the [a]-[i] sequence.

To demonstrate the dynamical nature of [e], ultrasound recordings of tongue movements of two native speakers of Korean and two native speakers of Spanish were made during the production of the mid vowel [e] in several different contexts. The subjects were all phonetically trained. These languages were chosen, because they are not reported to have diphthongized mid vowels. The data contain 18 Spanish and 14 Korean natural and nonsense words and phrases repeated three times each. The nonsense words respected each language's phonotactics. The imaging was done using an RT3600 GE ultrasound system with a 5 MHz transciever placed under the jaw about 5 cm posterior to the chin. In this procedure, the tongue is imaged from blade to about 2 cm above the hyoid bone at 30 frames per second. A marker is placed in the image of the tongue at a point where the closest constriction or excursion occurs for the [e]. This point was determined for each subject by trial and error by asking each subject to repeat [e] several times and determining the point of the tongue making the greatest excursion. The cursor is pointed in such a way that it is most sensitive to upward and frontward movements at that point, if any such movement is present. The motion mode of the ultrasound system then plots the changes in time of that point of the tongue. An example of the tongue image in one frame, with the cursor placed, is shown in Figure 3, below.

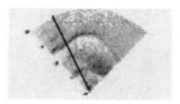

Figure 3. Tongue image with cursor placed.

5. Findings

The contexts chosen were the ones that would be predicted to be least hospitable to a minor raising and fronting gesture. The reason for this choice is that if the mid vowel [e] involves an active raising and fronting gesture, even in environments that do not favor such a gesture, then the vowel is truly dynamic. The most inhospitable environment is that of a falling and backing gesture. If the [e] were merely a static target, it would be simply interpolated through the backward-downward movement. If it is dynamic, on the other hand, we would see an active fronting-raising interruption of the backward-downward movement. The first context that was examined in the experiment, therefore, was [iBeBa] (where [B] is any labial). The labials were chosen to interrupt the vocalic sequence to make the examples from Korean as similar as possible to those in Spanish, while not making any intermediate requirements on the tongue. If the [e] is preceded by [i] and followed by [a], then the surrounding context requires the tongue to have an overall falling and backing trajectory as we see in Figure 4a, which shows schematically the movement in time of a point of the tongue going from [i] to [a]. If the [e] is static in nature, requiring the tongue to simply be in a certain place at some point during articulation, then we would expect that the [i]-[a] trajectory would accommodate the [e] by simply pausing at the static target for the [e] and then continuing to fall, as we see in Figure 4b, with the amount of time spent in the plateau dependent on the rate of speech. If on the other hand, [e] is a dynamical object, requiring an active raising and fronting gesture, we would expect that even during the general falling and backing trajectory from the [i] to the [a], that there would be a slight upward and frontward motion as in Figure 4c.

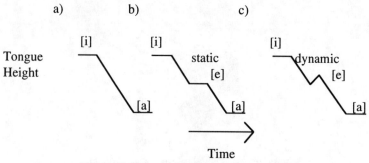

Figure 4. Schematic tongue motion for [i]-[a].

In Figure 5, below, we see the trajectories in time of the tongue for the 4 speakers pronouncing words containing the sequences [iBeBa]. The figures are labeled with the peaks due to [i], [e], and [a].

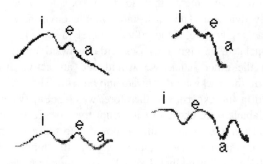

Figure 5. Trajectories in time of front tongue motion from examples with [iBeBa] for the 4 speakers. Top2 from Korean. Bottom 2 from Spanish.

The fact that a distinct peak is reached during the general downward and falling motion means that [e] involves an active upward and frontward movement, just like the sequence [a]-[i].

Another context inhospitable to [e] as an active motion is [KeK] (Where K is any velar). If the [e] were merely a static target, we might expect that the [e] would be simply interpolated during the downward motion of the tongue from the release of the initial [K]. The overall motion would be simply a downward motion followed by an upward motion of the tongue from back to tip as in Figure 6a. If an active motion is required for

[e], we would see a small upward and frontward motion superimposed on the overall downward and upward motion as we see in Figure 6b.

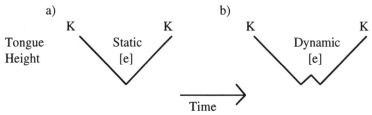

Figure 6. Schematic tongue motion for K-[e]-K.

The dynamic [e] is exactly what we see in Figure 7, showing examples from each subject of distinct peaks for the [e] in the [KeK] environment. I would like to emphasize here that this is not the trace of the point of the tongue that makes the velar constrictions. The trace of that point would look like (6a). The traces here are of the point that was seen to be most active in the achievement of the [e]. In each of the traces of that point, we see a passive raising due to movement in sympathy with the back of the tongue as it makes the velar closure, then an active raising and fronting for the [e], followed by another passive raising in sympathy with the back of the tongue for the second velar stop closure. This is consistent with a model of the tongue as a set of separate but interdependent articulators (Öhman 1965).

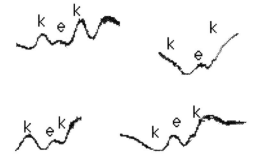

Figure 7. Trajectories in time of tongue front motion from examples containing [KeK] (K is any velar) for the 4 speakers. The first 2 are from Korean and the second 2 from Spanish.

The rest of the data show similar results with peaks for [e]. The only exceptions are the contexts where [e] is preceded by an alveolar and followed by a velar. In these two cases, there is no active raising of a point of the tongue intermediate between those points active in the alveolar and velar closure. This is of course not predicted, but investigation of data where other front vowels are between an alveolar and a velar showed similar results, with no appreciable fronting. Therefore there might be a special mechanism for accomplishing alveolar-vowel-velar syllables that masks the dynamic targets of the vowels. This will be investigated in further research.

6. Conclusion

To reiterate, the result of this research is that the coalescence asymmetry is a reflection of the asymmetry in vocalic trajectories. The [a]-[i] sequences and [e] have dynamic targets that are very similar in direction. This is why they alternate. The [i]-[a] sequences and [e] have opposite dynamic targets, and are therefore predicted not to alternate. Figure 8, below, shows schematically the dynamic classification of [i]-[a], [a]-[i], and [e]. Each trajectory in the figure shows the movement of some point of the tongue.

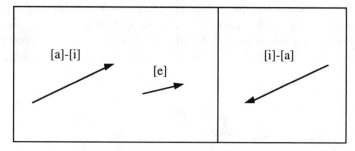

Figure 8. Dynamic patterning.

References
Casali, Roderic. 1996. *Resolving Hiatus*. Doctoral dissertation, UCLA.
Öhman, Sven. 1965. Coarticulation in VCV utterances: spectrographic measurements. *Journal of the Acoustical Society of America*. 39. 151-168.
Schane, Sanford. 1984. The fundamentals of particle phonology. *Phonology Yearbook*. 1. 129-155.
Schane, Sanford. 1987. The resolution of hiatus. *Papers from the 23rd annual regional meeting of the Chicago Linguistic Society*, Part Two, 279-290.

Focus without Variables: A Multi-Modal Analysis

GERHARD JÄGER

University of Pennsylvania

1. Introduction

It is an issue of ongoing controversy whether the information present at surface structure is sufficient for semantic interpretation or not. In the generative tradition the dominant position is that it is inevitable to enrich this structure with traces, indices etc. — devices that are to be interpreted like variables in logic — and that surface structure has to undergo certain syntactic transformations to get a suitable input for compositional interpretation.[1]

On the other hand, semanticists working in the tradition of Richard Montague (cf. Montague (1974)) usually assume that surface structure contains all information necessary for semantic interpretation. The Categorial tradition has strengthened this constraint by insisting that meaning composition can be done without essential reference to variable names as a kind of information that is not present at surface structure.[2]

Under the perspective of Occam's razor a surface compositional and variable free approach to semantics is certainly preferable, but the ultimate decision has to be made by comparing the empirical coverage of such theories with its competitors.

---

[1] See for instance von Stechow (1991) for a defense of this view.

[2] For the Combinatory branch of CG cf. Ades and Steedman (1982), Szabolcsi (1989), Jacobson (1997) among many others. Under the type logical perspective, the natural connection to a variable free semantics has been brought to attention by van Benthem (1983).

In this paper I will explore a certain phenomenon concerning the inter-action between ellipsis and focus that has been used as an argument (by Kratzer (1991), see also Pulman (1997)) that both the use of variables and of an intermediate level of representation are indispensable. I will present a surface compositional and variable free analysis. The techniques used are not new (the most important sources are Krifka (1992) and Jacobson (1997)), but the paper aims to show that integrating these concepts into multi-modal categorial grammar (cf. Carpenter (1997), Moortgat (1997), Morrill (1994)) results in a system that is more than just the sum of its parts.

Section 2 discusses the problem to be explored and Kratzer's proposal for it's solution. In section 3 the basic concepts of multi-modal categorial grammar are introduced. Section 4 and 5 are concerned with the treatment of ellipsis and of focus in this approach to grammar. Section 6 explicates the interaction of these modules.

2. The interaction of focus and ellipsis

Kratzer (1991) argues that the interpretation of focus requires semantic de-vices that make reference to names of variables. In a nutshell, the argument is the following. Rooth (1985) gives clear evidence that the non-local char-acter of focus interpretation cannot be modeled by means of LF movement, even if we assume that this operation exists. This is illustrated by his example (1):

(1) They only investigated the question whether you know the woman who chaired [the Zoning Board]$_F$

Only gets interpreted as an operator that takes the interpretation of *the Zoning Board* as one of its arguments. However, the focused constituent cannot become a syntactic sister of *only* at LF, since this would result in an island violation. Kratzer follows Rooth's conclusion that focus has to be interpreted *in situ*. Now consider Kratzer's (1991:830) example (2):

(2) I only went to [Tanglewood]$_F$ because you did.

From the considerations above it follows that *went to [Tanglewood]$_F$* is a constituent at the level which serves as input for interpretation. So no matter whether we adopt a theory of ellipsis interpretation that assumes copying of syntactic material or an identity of meaning approach, (2) should come out as synonymous with (3), but it doesn't.

(3) I only went to [Tanglewood]$_F$ because you went to [Tanglewood]$_F$.

The sentence (2) can be paraphrased as "The only place x such that I went to x because you went to x is Tanglewood". On the other hand, (3) can mean "The only pair of places $\langle x, y \rangle$ such that I went to x because you went to y is $\langle$Tanglewood, Tanglewood$\rangle$", which has different truth conditions.[3] Kratzer's proposal rests on the intuition that this is a difference between binding of two occurrences of the same variable versus simultaneous binding of two different variables. Technically, she assumes that each sign s has two interpretations, its ordinary meaning $\|s\|$ and its presupposition skeleton $\|s\|^p$. Each focus feature at S-structure comes with an index, and at this level, no two focus features share their index (the "novelty condition for F-indexing"). The presupposition skeleton of a constituent is obtained by interpreting the result of replacing all focused sub-constituents by the variable which bears the index of the respective focus feature. Both the ordinary meaning and the presupposition skeleton of a constituent *only VP* is obtained by applying the interpretation of *only* to both meaning components of its argument ($\|$only VP$\| = \|$only VP$\|^p = only'(\|$VP$\|)(\|$VP$\|^p)$). Crucially, the syncategorematic expression *only'* acts as an unselective operator that binds all free variables in its scope. Now due to the novelty condition, *only* binds two different variables in (3). In (2), ellipsis resolution preserves the focus index/variable name, and *only* binds two occurrences of the same variable.

While I agree with the basic intuition behind this approach — the focus sensitive operator in (2) discharges an assumption introduced by the overt focus, and it simultaneously discharges two assumptions in (3) corresponding to the two overt foci — I think that the implementation in terms of variables and a copy theory of ellipsis is not optimal. For one thing, the usage of variables requires abstract devices for managing variable names, since the latter do not correspond to observable phenomena. Kratzer employs the novelty condition for F-indexing here. However, it is crucial for her proposal that this constraint apply at S-structure, while the novelty condition for indefinites that was introduced in Heim (1982) is a constraint on the relation between a linguistic expression and its context of interpretation. So the theoretical status of Kratzer's condition is somewhat unclear.

More seriously, this approach predicts that every focused constituent is as-

---

[3] According to Krifka (1992), (3) cannot have this reading. I think it can; take the following parallel example:

(i)   A   You always make your electoral decision with a side-glance on me, either because you want to copy or because you want to defy me. 1992 you voted for Bush because I voted for Bush, and 1996 you voted for Dole because I voted for Clinton. Don't you have your own opinion?

        B   You are wrong. I didn't vote for Dole because you voted for Clinton. I only voted for BUSH because you voted for BUSH.

sociated with at most one operator. Krifka (1992:22) shows this to be wrong. His crucial example is:

(4) [At yesterday's party, people stayed with their first choice of drink. Bill only drank WINE, Sue only drank BEER, and]
John even only drank WATER$_F$

Here *water* is associated with *only* and *even* simultaneously. With the proviso that one constituent can bear more than one focus feature, this construction can be handled in Krifka's, but not in Kratzer's approach. On the other hand, Krifka's theory in its original formulation cannot account for the ellipsis examples. So the two theories have a different coverage, but they make identical predictions in constructions where both can be applied. Hence any extension of Krifka's theory to the ellipsis constructions would be preferable to either of the to approaches. In the next sections I will develop a compositional and variable free theory of ellipsis resolution which — in combination with Krifka's theory of focus — covers constructions like (2).

3. Multi-modal Categorial Grammar

3.1 The Lambek Calculus
Compositionality of Interpretation requires that each syntactic operation is accompanied by a corresponding operation on meanings. Categorial Grammar strengthens this idea by assuming that not only syntactic and semantic objects, but also syntactic and semantic operations form algebras, and that there is also a homomorphism from syntactic to semantic operations. In the type logical version of Categorial Grammar, the syntactic operations are taken to be theorems (valid sequents) of a logical calculus generated from a single axiom scheme by application of a small set of inference rules. Correspondingly, semantic operations are generated from a single combinatorial scheme by closure under certain operations.

Syntactic categories, i.e. formulas of the syntax logic in question, are recursively built from a finite set of atomic categories by means of the connectives "/" (rightward looking implication), "\" (leftward looking implication) and "•" (product). A *sequent* is a derivation $X \Rightarrow A$, where X is a string of formulas, and A is a formula. To transform such a logic into a full-blown grammar, two further ingredients have to be added, namely a set of designated categories (usually simply $\{S\}$), and an assignment of at least one category to each lexical item. A sequence of lexical items is recognized as a sentence by this grammar iff one of the designated categories can be derived from a sequent of corresponding categories. The simplest logic fitting into this framework is the associative Lambek Calculus **L** (Lambek (1958)). On the semantic side, there is a set of types which is the closure of a finite set of atomic types under the operations "→" (function space) and "∘" (Cartesian product). The homomorphism leading from categories to types is a straightforward generalization from the one in Montague's PTQ system, requiring that "\" and "/" be sent to "→" and"•" to "∘". The only basic semantic operations are the identity maps on the domain of each type. The meta-operations on semantic operations are most transparently defined as manipulations of polynomials in the simply typed λ-calculus (with product and projections). There is a one-one correspondence between inference rules and semantic meta-operations. Hence syntax and semantics can be presented simultaneously by augmenting the premises of the sequents in the Gentzen-style presentation with variables and the conclusions with polynomials over these variables. The axioms and rules of **L** are presented below.

(5)

$$\frac{}{x:A \Rightarrow x:A}^{[id]} \qquad \frac{X \Rightarrow t:A \qquad Y, x:A, Z \Rightarrow r:B}{Y, X, A \Rightarrow r_{[t/x]}}^{[Cut]}$$

$$\frac{X, x:A, y:B, Y \Rightarrow t:C}{X, z:A \bullet B, Y \Rightarrow t_{[(z)_0/x,(z)_1/y]}:C}^{[\bullet L]} \qquad \frac{X \Rightarrow t:A \qquad Y \Rightarrow r:B}{X, Y \Rightarrow \langle t, r \rangle : A \bullet B}^{[\bullet R]}$$

$$\frac{X \Rightarrow t:A \qquad Y, x:B, Z \Rightarrow r:C}{Y, y:B/A, X, Z \Rightarrow r_{[(yt)/x]}:C}^{[/L]} \qquad \frac{X, x:A \Rightarrow t:B}{X \Rightarrow \lambda x.t : B/A}^{[/R]}$$

$$\frac{X \Rightarrow t:A \qquad Y, x:B, Z \Rightarrow r:C}{Y, X, y:A \backslash B, Z \Rightarrow r_{[(yt)/x]}:C}^{[\backslash L]} \qquad \frac{x:A, X \Rightarrow t:B}{X \Rightarrow \lambda x.t : A \backslash B}^{[\backslash R]}$$

3.2 Multi-modality

The Lambek calculus is characterized by a very rigid resource management. In particular, it strongly depends on the linear order of premises, and every resource must be used exactly once. Natural language is more flexible in several respects. So we encounter word order variation, non-local crossing dependencies, the simultaneous use of the same resource in different local environments (for instance in parasitic gap constructions) and many more phenomena that cannot adequately be captured by the basic system. Yet relaxing the resource consciousness of **L** globally results in systems that are too coarse grained for linguistic purposes. These limitation can be overcome if a more flexible management can be made available locally. To this end, multi-modal Categorial Grammar extends the inventory of type forming connectives with a family of modal operators $\Diamond_i$ which are characterized by the logical rules below.[4] Premises are now bracketed sequences, i.e. labeled trees

---

[4]It is more in line with the properties of the basic connective of **L** to pair each $\Diamond_i$ with

of formulas. I assume that modalities don't have semantic impact, so the type corresponding to $\Diamond_i A$ is identical with the type corresponding to A.

$$(6) \quad \frac{X \Rightarrow t : A}{(X)^i \Rightarrow t : \Diamond_i A}{}^{[\Diamond_i L]} \qquad \frac{X, x : (A)^i, Y \Rightarrow t : B}{X, x : \Diamond_i A, Y \Rightarrow t : B}{}^{[\Diamond_i R]}$$

Now while we would lose important distinctions if we introduced additional axioms or rules like permutation as such to the calculus, we can relativize these non-standard operations to modal formulas. This move preserves the overall resource conscious and order sensitive character of **L** while allowing more flexibility in local domains.

4. Ellipsis and Contraction

One instance of the resource consciousness of **L** is the fact that in the meaning representation of a sentence, the meanings of the lexical items involved can each occur only once. This seems to be too restrictive if we turn our attention to anaphora and ellipsis. Consider a simple elliptic sentence like

(7)   a. John walked, and Bill did too

       b. $and'(walk'b)(walk'j)$

In its semantic representation, the meaning of the VP in the first conjunct occurs twice. There are several ways to deal with this fact. The source of this meaning duplication could be located in the lexical entry of *did*. For pronouns, such a strategy has been proposed in Szabolcsi (1989). However, this treatment only captures bound pronouns in the sense of Reinhart (1983). Since we want to maintain the option for a unified treatment of intra- and inter-sentential ellipses, this seems to be too narrow. Hence we are left with the need to allow duplicating meanings during syntactic composition. In a Lambek-style grammar, this amounts to enriching **L** with the structural rule of Contraction:

$$(8) \quad \frac{X, x : A, y : A, Y \Rightarrow t : B}{X, x : A, Y \Rightarrow t_{[x/y]} : B}{}^{[C]}$$

However, the unrestricted usage of Contraction would lead to a heavy over-generation. For instance, *John shows Mary* would be predicted to be a grammatical sentence with the meaning of *John shows Mary herself*. Therefore we have to impose constraints on the applicability of these rules to avoid such a

---

its dual $\Box_i^{\downarrow}$. For the sake of simplicity, I leave this out here. For a thorough discussion of the logical aspects of multi-modality see Moortgat (1997).

collapse. This can be done by employing multi-modality. Let us start with the intuition that anaphors are semantically incomplete expressions. To become complete, they have to be supplemented with an index (or pick up a discourse marker, whatever metaphor you prefer). To formalize this intuition in a categorial framework, we introduce a modal operator $\Diamond$, where $\Diamond A$ is intended to be the category of an index/discourse marker that was introduced by a sign of category A. An anaphoric pronoun hence should be assign the category $\Diamond N \setminus N$, since it behaves like a name if supplied with an nominal index. Since its meaning in a given context is just the meaning of the index, its lexical meaning is the identity function on individuals (ignoring matters of number and gender). Coindexing now amounts to identifying a "freely floating" index of category $\Diamond A$ with a sign of category A. This is captured by the following modally restricted version of Contraction:

$$(9) \quad \frac{X, x : A, y : \Diamond A, Y \Rightarrow t : B}{X, x : A, Y \Rightarrow t_{[x/y]} : B} \text{[C]}$$

The fact that a pronoun and its antecedent need not be adjacent can be captured by a restricted version of Permutation:

$$(10) \quad \frac{X, x : \Diamond A, y : B, Y \Rightarrow t : C}{X, y : B, x : \Diamond A, Y \Rightarrow t : C} \text{[P$\Diamond$]}$$

This proposal is very similar to the one made in Jacobson (1997), though there are important differences. According to her view, anaphors introduce an argument place of a special kind into the derivation. The category of a constituent that is of category A except that it has such an anaphoric argument place is A^N (corresponding to $\Diamond N \setminus A$ in the present account). The core of her proposal is the assumption that such a superscript can percolate up to larger constituents in a derivation, and that it can be discharged by merging it with a regular argument place.

Both assumptions are also captured in the present proposal. Percolation amounts to the fact that the following inference rule is derivable (A^B is to be read as an abbreviation for $\Diamond B \setminus A$):

$$(11) \quad \frac{x : A, y : B \Rightarrow t : C}{x : A, z : B^D \Rightarrow \lambda w.t_{[(zw)/y]} : C^D} \text{[Perc]}$$

In plain English: If an A and a B can be combined to a C, then an A and a B with a missing D can be combined to a C with a missing D. Merging of argument places is covered by the fact the the following sequent is derivable:

324 / GERHARD JÄGER

(12) $x : (A \setminus B)^A \Rightarrow \lambda y.xyy : A \setminus B$

Besides merging of argument places, the present proposal also admits another binding device that is not generally available in Jacobson's system. It says that if an A and a B can combine, then an A and a B with a missing A can also combine, by making a copy of the A and using it to fill the argument place indicated by the superscript. More precisely, the following inference rule is derivable too:

(13)
$$\frac{x : A, y : B \Rightarrow t : C}{x : A, z : B^A \Rightarrow t_{[(zx)/y]} : C} \text{ [Bind]}$$

The system is illustrated by the following sample derivation for (7). Note that function composition is derivable in the Lambek calculus; this together with Bind licenses the combination of *walks* with *and Bill does*.

(14)

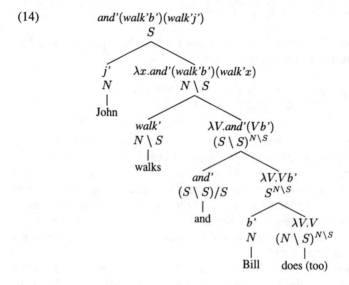

For a more thorough discussion of this approach to anaphors and ellipsis, the reader is referred to Jäger (to appear).

5. Krifka's theory of focus interpretation in a multi-modal setting

Krifka (1992) gives a compositional and variable free account of focus interpretation that is based on the concept of *structured meaning*. Constituents containing a focused sub-constituent have structured meanings, i.e. their meaning is an ordered pair consisting of a background part and a focus part (that can be structured meanings themselves). The focus part is just the "ordinary" meaning of the focused sub-constituent, while the background is a function from possible focus meanings to corresponding meanings of the whole constituent. The function of a focus morpheme is to put the meaning of its argument on a stack and to replace it by the identity function. It is worth noting that more than one focus morpheme can be attached to one and the same constituent. The motivation for this assumption comes from constructions such as (4). Both the focus part and the argument slot in the background part are passed on to larger constituents in the course of meaning composition. Crucially for the treatment of multiple foci, if both functor and argument in a local configuration contain a focus, they can be merged.

In what follows I will intermingle the illustration of this proposal with its incorporation into a type logical framework. Let us take a simple example like

(15) John only met SUE$_F$

The "ordinary" meaning of *Sue* is the individual Sue, represented by the constant s'.[5] Combining *Sue* with the focus morpheme gives us a structured meaning where the focus part is s' and the background part the identity function on individuals, i.e. the meaning of *Sue$_F$* is $\langle \lambda x.x, s' \rangle$.

The semantic type of this object is $(e \rightarrow e) \circ e$. Due to the strict category-to-type correspondence in Categorial Grammar, the category of *Sue$_F$* has to display the same structure. Which category would be adequate here? To answer this question, let us chose another perspective. The focus morpheme has two functions: it moves the meaning of the focused constituent to a store, and it replaces it with a hypothetical assumption. To bring this home in the present framework, we assume that both the store content and the hypothetical assumption(s) are marked by modalities. More concretely, we extend the system with two more modalities, $\triangle$ and ∇, where moving a sign of category A to the focus store results in a sign of category $\triangle A$, and a hypothetical assumption which replaces an A has category ∇A. Since the semantic type corresponding to a product type is always a structured meaning, we can employ the product connective to connect the background part and the focus part. So the syntactic category of *Sue$_F$* is $(N/\nabla N) \bullet \triangle N$. For simplicity's sake, I will treat the focus morpheme as a proclitic here. In the example, it then takes an N-argument from the right and returns an $(N/\nabla N) \bullet \triangle N$, so it should be assigned the category $((N/\nabla N) \bullet \triangle N)/N$ and the meaning $\lambda x.\langle \lambda y.y, x \rangle$ (the category of the focus morpheme in general is polymorphic

---

[5] Since Krifka uses a phrase structure grammar, he is forced to assign the type quantifier to proper nouns, which in turn complicates the definition of comparability of alternatives. Due to the flexibility of Categorial Grammar, we can avoid this "generalization to the worst case".

since not only names can be focused). More generally, a constituent of category A that contains a focused name will have the category $(A/\nabla N) \bullet \triangle N$. I will abbreviate this with A_N.

To combine Sue_F with *meet*, we function compose the meaning of the verb with the background part of its object and pass the content of the focus store unchanged. The result is $\langle \lambda y.meet'y, s' \rangle$. More generally, both ingredients introduced by focus can percolate up to larger constituents in a derivation. In other words, the following inference rule "Focus Percolation" should be valid:

$$(16) \quad \frac{X, x : A, Y \Rightarrow t : B}{X, y : A_C, Y \Rightarrow \langle \lambda z.t_{[((y)_0 z)/x]}, (y)_1 \rangle : B_C} \text{[FP]}$$

This rule becomes derivable if we assume that both modalities have restricted access to permutation,which is captured by the following two structural rules:

$$(17) \quad \text{a.} \quad \frac{X, x : A, y : \triangle B, Y \Rightarrow t : C}{X, y : \triangle B, x : A, Y \Rightarrow t : C} \text{[P$\triangle$]}$$

$$\text{b.} \quad \frac{X, x : \nabla A, y : B, Y \Rightarrow t : C}{X, y : B, x : \nabla B, Y \Rightarrow t : C} \text{[P∇]}$$

Since a transitive verb (category $N \backslash S/N$) and a name can combine to form a VP (category $N \backslash S$) via function application, in the presence of the above rule, *met* and Sue_F can combine to a sign of category $(N \backslash S)_N$ with the meaning given above.

Focus sensitive operators like *only* take a structured meaning as an argument and return an un-structured meaning. In our example, *only met Sue_F* is a VP and accordingly denotes a property which — since the lexical semantics of *only* is not at issue here — I will simply represent with $only'\langle \lambda y.meet'y, s' \rangle$. So the category of *only* is $(N \backslash S)/(N \backslash S)_N$ (again, lexical assignment is polymorphic since *only* can be associated with foci of different categories). This VP can finally be combined with the subject via function application, yielding finally the sentence meaning $only'\langle \lambda y.meet'y, s' \rangle j'$.

To deal with cases of multiple focus as in

(18) John only introduced BILL to SUE

Krifka assumes that two foci originating from different constituents can be merged. The corresponding inference rule is

(19)

$$\frac{x : A, y : B \Rightarrow t : B}{z : A_D, w : B_E \Rightarrow \langle \lambda v.t_{[((z)_0 v_0)/x,((w)_0(v)_1)/y]}, \langle (z)_1, (w)_1 \rangle \rangle : B_{(D \bullet E)}} \text{[M]}$$

For reasons of space, I refer the reader to Krifka's paper for discussion. In our multi-modal setting, this rule becomes derivable if we extend the grammar logic with the following two axioms:

(20)   a. $\triangle A \bullet \triangle B \Rightarrow \triangle(A \bullet B)$

   b. $\nabla(A \bullet B) \Rightarrow \nabla A \bullet \nabla B$

Finally it deserves to be stressed that the same constituent can be focused more than once, and that the result will be a recursively structured meaning. This is important for the analysis of (4). Here two focus morphemes are attached to the object *water*. This gives rise to the category $(N_N)_N$ and the doubly structured meaning $\langle \lambda x.\langle \lambda y.y, x \rangle, wt' \rangle$. *Only* decreases the embedding depth by one; so the meaning of *only drank water* here is a simply structured meaning, which serves as argument for *even*, and this returns the un-structured *even'*$\langle \lambda x.only'\langle drink', x \rangle, wt' \rangle$.

6. The interaction of the modules

Now let us return to our original example (2), repeated here in slightly modified form in (21).

(21) John only went to Tanglewood$_F$ because Bill did.

By employing Percolation (11) together with function application, we can derive the embedded clause to be a VP modifier which looks for a VP antecedent:

(22)   a. because Bill did.

   b.

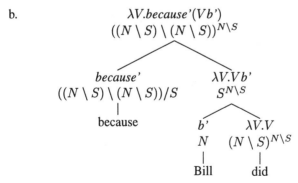

By means of the mechanisms described in the last section, we get the following derivation for the embedded VP:

(23)   a. went to Tanglewood$_F$

b.

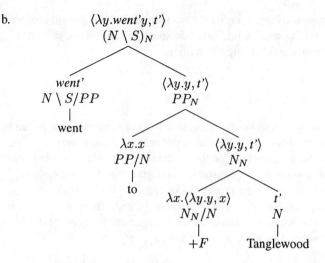

Every VP (category $N \setminus S$) can combine with a VP modifier (category $(N \setminus S) \setminus (N \setminus S)$) to a VP via function application. According to the "Bind" rule (13), we get the following local derivation with an arbitrary hypothetical VP:

(24) a. VP because Bill did

      b.

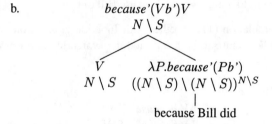

From this and the rule of "Focus Percolation" it follows that *went to Tanglewood* and *because Bill did* can combine in the following way:

(25) $\langle \lambda y.because'(went'yb')(went'y), t' \rangle$
                                    $(N \setminus S)_N$

        $\langle \lambda y.went'y, t' \rangle$ $\lambda V.because'(Vb')$
              $(N \setminus S)_N$ $((N \setminus S) \setminus (N \setminus S))^{N \setminus S}$

          went to Tanglewood$_F$ because Bill did

    The result can be combined with *only* and with *John* via functional application and yields the correct reading:

(26) $only'\langle\lambda y.because'(went'yb')(went'y),t'\rangle j'$

Informally, this derivation can be described in the following way: focusing has the effect of putting the content of *Tanglewood* on a stack and replacing it with a hypothetical assumption. The ellipsis resolution module operates on the background meaning of the antecedent VP *went to Tanglewood*, which contains this hypothesis. Ellipsis resolution hence has the effect of duplicating the background of the antecedent VP, including the assumption. This gives the effect of having two occurrences of the same variable. The focus sensitive operator *only* discharges the hypothetical assumption and simultaneously empties the focus stack. In sum, the effect of binding of multiple occurrences of a variable has been achieved by the interplay of the structured meaning approach to focus with the modeling of ellipsis resolution by means of Contraction.

This depends crucially on the fact that focusing is done prior to ellipsis resolution, and so it might be expected that reversing this order would result in the (impossible) multiple-focus reading. This derivation is blocked in the present analysis, however. To see why, observe that the category assignment $(N \setminus S)^{N\setminus S}$ to the VP anaphor *does* puts constraints on what may serve as an antecedent. Only a constituent from which category $N \setminus S$ can be derived can serve for this purpose.[6] This means that a VP containing a nominal focus like *went to Tanglewood$_F$* cannot antecede *does*, since it has category $(N \setminus S)_N$, and

(27) $(N \setminus S)_N \Rightarrow N \setminus S$

is not a valid sequent. Hence the derivation given above is — up to spurious ambiguities — the only one possible (provided the ellipsis has a sentence internal antecedent).

7. Conclusion and further research

This paper was intended mainly to illustrate two methodological points. First, it aimed to show that a surface compositional and variable free interpretation of ellipsis is possible also in non-trivial constructions like the interaction between VP ellipsis and focus. Second, it tried to demonstrate that the deductive

---

[6]The antecedent need not have this category itself. A prime example is

(i) John washed his car, and Bill did too

Here the constituent *washed his car* has category $(N \setminus S)^N$, i.e. a VP containing an unresolved pronoun. Since

(ii) $x : (N \setminus S)^N \Rightarrow \lambda y.xyy : N \setminus S$

is valid, this constituent can serve as antecedent of *did*, resulting in the sloppy reading of the sentence.

account to grammar that Type Logical Grammar is based on provides an adequate framework for integrating several proposals for a variable free semantics. The *tertium comparationis* is the fact that phenomena which motivate the use of variables — movement, anaphora, focus etc. — are uniformly formalized as involving hypothetical assumptions, while variable binding is re-analyzed as discharging of hypotheses. Modal operators serve to distinguish different instances of this general pattern.

Let me conclude with mentioning two features of the present proposal that deserve attention in further research. Although I remained as close as possible to Krifka's original proposal in the treatment of focus, the transfer from a phrase structure grammar to a categorial grammar has empirical impact. In the latter framework, the notion of a constituent is much more flexible, and accordingly, not only constituents in the traditional sense can be subject to focus assignment. This is certainly desirable — in fact, Steedman (1991) uses examples similar to the following as a major argument against the standard notion of constituency.

(28) I only claim that [MANY PEOPLE BELIEVE]$_F$ that Smith can solve the problem. I don't say that he really can.

On the other hand, since in the standard Lambek Grammar any substring of a sentence can be a constituent, this certainly leads to over-generation. This observation is in line with the current trend in Type Logical Grammar to explore calculi that re-impose hierarchical structure without assuming rigid tree structures. Motivation for this move comes from syntactic island constraints (cf. Morrill (1994)) and intonation structure (cf. Morrill (1994), Hendriks (1997)). It remains to be seen whether the different arguments in favor of cautious constituency will eventually coincide.

Finally it has to be mentioned that it is certainly an oversimplification to treat ellipsis and focus as two independent modules that only interact in quite marginal constructions. Quite the contrary, it is almost a commonplace wisdom that focus structure, intonation and ellipsis are intimately connected. Future research has to show how exactly this connection can be spelled out in a type logical perspective.

References

Ades, Anthony and Mark Steedman. 1982. On the Order of Words. *Linguistics and Philosophy* 4.517–558.

Carpenter, Bob. 1997. *Type-Logical Semantics*. MIT Press.

Heim, Irene. 1982. *The Semantics of Definite and Indefinite Noun Phrases*. Doctoral dissertation, University of Massachusetts Amherst.

Hendriks, Herman. 1997. The Logic of Tune. A Proof-Theoretic Analysis of Intonation, in J. M. G. Kruijff, G. V. Morrill and R. T. Oehrle, eds., *Formal Grammar 1997*. ESSLLI, Aix-en-Provence.

Jacobson, Pauline. 1997. Towards a Variable-free Semantics. ms., Brown University.

Jäger, Gerhard. 1998. A Multi-Modal Analysis of Anaphora and Ellipsis. to appear in *University of Pennsylvania Working Papers in Linguistics*. Philadelphia.

Kratzer, Angelika. 1991. The Representation of Focus, in A. v. Stechow and D. Wunderlich, eds., *Handbook Semantics*, de Gruyter, Berlin, New York.

Krifka, Manfred. 1992. A Compositional Semantics for Multiple Focus Constructions, in J. Jacobs, ed., *Informationsstruktur und Grammatik*, Linguistische Berichte, Sonderheft 4.

Lambek, Joachim. 1958. The Mathematics of Sentence Structure. *American Mathematical Monthly* 65.154–170.

Montague, Richard. 1974. *Formal Philosophy*. ed. by R. Thomason, Yale University Press, New Haven.

Moortgat, Michael. 1997. Categorial Type Logics. in J. v. Benthem and A. ter Meulen, eds., *Handbook of Logic and Language*. Elesvier, MIT Press.

Morrill, Glynn. 1994. *Type Logical Grammar*. Kluwer.

Pulman, Stephen G. 1997. Higher Order Unification and the Interpretation of Focus. *Linguistics and Philosophy* 20:1.73–115.

Reinhart, Tanya. 1983. *Anaphora and Semantic Interpretation*. Croom Helm.

Rooth, Mats. 1985. *Association with Focus*. Doctoral dissertation, University of Massachusetts Amherst.

Steedman, Mark. 1991. Structure and Intonation. *Language* 68.260–296.

Szabolcsi, Anna. 1989. Bound Variables in Syntax (Are There Any?). in R. Bartsch, J. v. Benthem and P. v. Emde Boas, eds., *Semantics and Contextual Expressions*. Foris.

van Benthem, Johan. 1983. The Semantics of Variety in Categorial Grammar. Report 83–29. Simom Fraser University Burnaby.

von Stechow, Arnim. 1991. Syntax und Semantik. in A. v. Stechow and D. Wunderlich, eds., *Handbook Semantics*, de Gruyter, Berlin, New York.

Sonority Constraints on Tonal Patterns

PING JIANG-KING

Chinese University of Hong Kong

1. Introduction[*]

One of the important roles sonority plays in segmental phonology is to regulate distributions of segments within and across syllable boundaries. Within a syllable, for example, certain consonant clusters like sp- and str- are allowed while others like *lp- and *nk- are disallowed in an onset position (Clements (1990), Rice (1992), Everett (1995)). Diphthongs with a falling sonority pattern are argued to be more preferred than with a rising sonority pattern (Jiang-King (1994), Rosenthall (1994)). Segments across syllable boundaries, on the other hand, also obey certain sonority constraints so that sequences with rising or equal sonority values are prohibited in certain languages (Clements (1990), Takano (1996)). In reduplications, sonority determines which segment gets copied and where a reduplicant can be located (Newman (1971), Bagemihl (1991), Carlson (1997)). The restrictions on segments within and across syllables are captured by the segmental sonority hierarchy (i.e., voiceless < voiced < nasal < liquid < glade < vowel) (Zec (1988), (1995)) and the peak/margin hierarchy of constraints within the framework of Optimality Theory (OT) (Prince & Smolensky (1993)). The ranking *P/t,k >> ... >> *P/l >> ... >> *P/i,u >> *P/e,o >> *P/a, thus, defines segmental markedness with respect to their suitability in occupying syllable positions.

[*] This research is partially supported by the Direct Grant for Research 96/97, 97/98 from the Chinese University of Hong Kong.

As for the segmental phonology, sonority also plays an important role in regulating tonal distributions within a syllable. Jiang-King (1996a), (1996b), (1997a), (1997b) argues that parallel to the segmental sonority hierarchy, the tonal sonority hierarchy, encoded in the constraint ranking: $*\mu_s/L >> *\mu_s/M >> *\mu_s/H$,[1] defines the well-formedness of tonal patterns and explains the markedness of tonal inventories cross-linguistically. In Fuqing (a Northern Min language spoken on the South coast of China), for example, sonority constraints prohibit linking a L tone to a head mora within a syllable, hence, the lack of rising contours in this langage.

In this article, I show that sonority constraints manifest themselves not only in tonal distributions cross-linguistically, but also in other phonological processes like child language acquisition, as well as brand names and personal names. Section 2 will investigate tonal inventories in 40 Chinese dialects, and explore the asymmetries exhibited in these dialects. Section 3 provides external evidence to show that these asymmetries observed in the 40 Chinese dialects are also found in child language acquisition, brand-naming and personal names. Section 4 proposes constraints capturing the asymmetries observed and demonstrates selection of optimal tonal inventories. I show that these asymmetries can be explained in terms of constraint ranking within the framework of Optimality Theory (McCarthy & Prince (1993), Prince & Smolensky (1993)). The conclusion is given in section 5.

2. Tonal Asymmetries in 40 Chinese Dialects

Chinese has 7 major dialectal groups: Northern group, Gan, Xiang, Wu, Min (including northern and southern Min), Yue and Hakka.[2] The dialects investigated in this paper range over all of these major groups. Data are from published dialect dictionaries (see the data sources in Appendix).

The data in (1) are arranged according to the tonal categories in traditional Chinese phonology. *Ping, Shang* and *Qu* are historical tonal categories representing level, rising and falling tones respectively. The *Ru* category refers to short tones in syllables with a stop coda. *Ying* and *Yang* are historically developed from voiceless and voiced onsets respectively. The data in (2) are arranged by the tonal patterns for ease of analysis.

---

[1] I assume the tonal features [±upper], [±raised] in Yip (1980), (1989) and Pulleybank (1986). However, I use H, M and L to represent high, mid and low tones respectively throughout this paper for convenience.

[2] Some scholars in China regroup Chinese dialects into 10 major dialectal areas with the addition of the Jin, Hui and Pinghua groups (Li (1989)). This new classification has not yet been widely accepted, however.

(1) Tonal categories in 40 Chinese dialects (listed by alphabetic order)

Name of dialects	# of tones	Ping Yin	Ping Yang	Shang Yin	Shang Yang	Qu Yin	Qu Yang	Ru Yin	Ru Yang
Beijing	4	ma^{55}妈	ma^{35}麻	ma^{214}马		ma^{51}骂			
Boshan	3	pɑ^{214}他		pɑ^{55}爬		pa^{31}怕			
Cantonese	9	fen$^{53/55}$分	fen^{21}坟	fen^{35}粉	fen^{13}愤	fen^{33}训	fen^{22}份	fet^{5}忽/fet^{3}发	fet^{2}佛
Changsha	6	pa^{33}巴	pa^{13}爬	pa^{41}把		pa^{55}霸	pa^{11}稗	pa^{24}爸	
Chengdu	4	ma^{44}妈	ma^{31}麻	ma^{53}马		ma^{13}骂			
Chongming	8	tæ^{55}耽	dæ^{24}谈	tʰæ^{424}坦	dæ^{242}淡	tæ^{33}旦	dæ^{313}但	pæʔ^{5}八	bæʔ^{2}拔
Danyang	6	pɑ^{33}巴	pɑ^{24}拜	pɑ^{55}摆		pɑ^{11}败		pɑʔ^{3}八	pɑʔ^{5}拔
Fuzhou	7	ki^{44}机	ki^{52}其	ki^{31}纪		kei^{213}记	kei^{242}忌	keiʔ^{23}急	kiʔ^{4}及
Fuqing	7	kuŋ^{53}公	kuŋ^{35}群	kuŋ^{33}滚		kuŋ^{21}贡	kuŋ^{41}郡	kuʔ^{22}谷	kuʔ^{5}掘
Guiyang	4	mi^{55}眯	mi^{31}迷	mi^{53}米		mi^{24}谜			
Haifeng	8	si^{33}诗	si^{55}时	si^{51}死	si^{24}是	si^{213}世	si^{21}示	sik^{2}失	sik^{42}蚀
Haikou	8	ka^{24}柑	ka^{21}衔	ka^{213}敢		ka^{35}教	ka^{33}咬	ka^{55}甲/kak^{5}角	kak^{3}芽
Hefei	5	kɔ^{212}高	tɕʰɤ^{55}前	xɔ^{24}好		kʰuE^{53}块		mɤʔ^{4}木	
Huojia	5	pa^{33}巴	pa^{31}拔	pa^{53}爸		pa^{13}霸		pʰeɪ^{33}拍	
Jiading	6	pu^{53}波	bu^{31}婆			pu^{34}布	mu^{13}母	kuA^{55}刮	bAʔ^{12}白
Jiangyong	7	pa^{44}睥	pa^{42}脾	pa^{35}比	pa^{13}婢	pa^{21}贝	pa^{33}鼻	pa^{5}笔	
Jinan	4	kɔ^{213}高	zɤ̃^{42}人	tuaɛ^{55}短		tɔ^{21}到			
Jinhua	7	lu^{33}噜	lu^{313}炉	lu^{535}鲁		lu^{55}怒	lu^{24}路	pɔʔ^{4}北	bɔʔ^{12}白
Lichuan	7	pʰu^{22}薄	pʰu^{35}菩	pʰu^{44}普		pʰu^{53}铺	pʰu^{13}部	tap^{3}插	tap^{5}杂
Liuzhou	5	so^{44}嗦	so^{31}索	so^{54}锁		so^{24}璅		so^{25}璅	

(1) Tonal categories in 40 Chinese dialects (cont.)

Dialect	n								
Loudi	5	mɔ⁴⁴妈	mɔ¹³抹	mɔ⁴²马		mɔ³⁵麦	mɔ¹¹骂		sa⁵涉
Luoyang	4	pa³³巴	pa³¹拔	pa⁵³把			pa⁴¹²霸		
Meixian	6	sa⁴⁴沙	sa¹¹蛇	sa³¹舍			sa⁵³射	sa¹匝	sa⁵涉
Nanchang	7	tʰan⁴²滩	tʰan²⁴谈	tʰan²¹³炭		tan³⁵担	tʰan¹¹淡	tʰaʔ⁵塔	tʰaʔ²踏
Nanjing	5	ma³¹妈	ma²⁴麻	ma¹¹马			ma⁴⁴骂	ma²⁵抹	
Shanghai	5	tɔ⁵³刀				to³⁴岛	do²³桃	tʰɔʔ⁵⁵托	dɔʔ¹²独
Suzhou	7	fɑ⁵⁵方	vɑ¹³房	fɑ⁵¹纺		fɑ⁴¹²放	vɑ³¹妄	fɑʔ⁵法	vɑʔ³罚
Taiyuan	5		ma¹¹麻	ma⁵³马			ma⁴⁵骂	faʔ²法	faʔ⁴⁴罚
Tianjin	4	21		44		24	42		
Wenzhou	8	na⁴⁴妈	ma³¹麻	ma⁴⁵马	ba³⁴罢	ma²²骂	po⁴²霸	ta³²³搭	da²¹²达
Wuhan	4	pa⁵⁵巴	pa²¹³八	pa⁴²把			pa³⁵霸		
Wulumuqi	3	pa⁴⁴巴	pa⁵¹八				pa²¹³霸		
Xiamen	7	pa⁵⁵巴	pa³⁵爬	pa⁵³饱		pa²¹霸	pa¹¹骂	pak¹¹腹	pak⁵⁵缚
Xi'an	4	ti²¹低	ti²⁴笛	ti⁵³底			ti⁴⁴第		
Xining	4	pa⁴⁴巴	pa²⁴拔	pa⁵³靶			pa²¹³罢		
Xinzhou	4	ma³¹³妈	ma³¹麻				ma⁵³骂	ma²²抹	
Yangzhou	5	pa¹¹巴	pa³⁵把			pa⁴²靶	pa⁵⁵爸	pa²⁴博	
Yinchuan	3	ma⁴⁴妈	ma⁵³麻				ma¹³骂		
Zhangping	6	po²⁴婆	po¹¹婆			po³¹宅	po²¹播	po⁵³薄	po⁵⁵博
Zhoushan	8	piŋ⁵³冰	biŋ²²瓶	piŋ³⁵饼	biŋ²⁴并	piŋ⁴⁴柄	biŋ¹³病	piŋ²⁵笔	biaʔ²¹²别

(2) Tonal patterns in 40 Chinese dialects (listed by an alphabetic order)

Name of Dialects	Level Tones			Falling Tones			Rising Tones			Complex Tones	
	H	M	L	HM	ML	HL	MH	LM	LH	concave	convex
Beijing	55					51	35			214	
Boshan	55				31					214	
Cantonese	55/5	33/3	22/2	53	21		35	13			
Changsha	55	33	11			41	24	13			
Chengdu	44			53	31			13			
Chongming	55/5	33/2					24			424/313	242
Danyang	55/5	33/3	11				24				
Fuzhou	44/4			52	31					213/23	242
Fuqing	44/5	33/22		53	21	41					
Guiyang	55			53	31		24				
Haifeng	55	33/2									
Haikou	55/5	33/3			21		35	24		213	
Hefei	55/4	33		53	21		34				
Huojia		33		53	31			13			
Jiading	55			53	31		34	13/12			
Jiangyong	44/5	33		42	21		35	13			
Jinan	55			42	21					213	
Jinhua	55/4	33					24	12		313/535	
Lichuan	44/5	22/3		53			35	13			
Liuzhou	44/5			54	31		24				

(2) Tonal patterns in 40 Chinese dialects (cont.)

Loudi	44			42			35	13			
Luoyang		33		53	31					412	
Meixian	44/5		11/1	53	31						
Nanchang	5		11/2	42			35	24		213	
Nanjing	44/5	22		53	32				14		
Shanghai	55			53			34	23/12			
Suzhou	55/5	3			31	51		13		412	
Tianjin	44			42	21		24				
Wenzhou	44	22		42	31		45	34		323/212	
Wuhan	55			42			35			213	
Wulumuqi	44					51				213	
Xiamen	55/55		11/11	53	21		35				
Xi'an	44			53	21		24			213	
Xining	44			53			24			313	
Xinzhou		2		53	31					213	
Xuzhou	55			53		51	35				
Yangzhou	55/4		11	42			35				
Yinchuan	44			53				13			
Zhangping	55		11	53	31/21		24				
Zhoushan	44/5	22		53			35	13/12	24		
Total occur:	37	18	9	28	23	6	26	16	2	16	2
Percentage:	92.5	45	22.5	70	57.5	15	65	40	5	40	5

The data in (1) show that different dialects have a different number of tones. Cantonese, for example, has 9 tones, while Yinchuan has only 3 tones. On the other hand, tones belonging to same categories have different contours. In Beijing dialect, for example, the tone in the *Yin Ping* category has the value 55, hence is a High level tone, whereas in Boshan, the tone in the same category has the value 214, hence is a low falling-rising tone.

Examining the data in (2), we observe that four frequent asymmetries exist cross-dialectally. First, High tone (H) occurs more frequently than Mid tone (M) and Low tone (L). Among 40 dialects investigated, 37 of them have H tone, but only 18 have M tone and 9 have L tone. Second, contour tones using full tonal space such as HL and LH occur much less frequently than tones using half tonal space such as HM, ML, LM and MH. Only two LH contour and six HL contours are found in the 40 dialects. Third, complex contour tones occur less frequently than simple contours. In particular, all 40 dialects have simple contour tones, but only 6 have complex contours. Fourth, within complex contours, concave tones occur more frequently than convex tones. We found only 2 dialects which have convex tones.

Tonal inventories in each dialect also exhibit asymmetrical distributions. First, dialects that have Low tone must also have High tone, but not vice versa. Second, dialects that have contour tones must also have level ones, but not vice versa. Third, dialects that have complex contour tones must also have simple contours, but not vice versa. The three pairs of distributional asymmetries found in different tones confirm the universals of tonal inventories claimed by Maddieson (1978).

3. Further evidence for tonal asymmetries

In this section, I provide further evidence supporting the existence of the tonal asymmetries observed in the 40 Chinese dialects. The first kind of evidence comes from lexical frequency. Zhang (1994) reports that among 60 disyllabic words with the syllable [wa] in Mandarin Chinese, the frequency of [wa] with H level tone is the highest, whereas that of [wa] including a L is the lowest. The second type of evidence comes from child language acquisition. It is reported that H tone is acquired earlier than other tonal categories in Mandarin-speaking children (Li & Thomson (1977)), Cantonese-speaking children (Tse (1978)), as well as Taiwanese-speaking children (King (1982)). The third type of evidence comes from personal names. It is reported that H tones in Cantonese are preferably used in personal names by Hong Kong Cantonese speakers (Fan & Ng (1993), Huang & Fan (1994)). The fourth type of evidence comes from brand names. Chan and Huang (1997) investigated 157 award-winning products with disyllabic names in Beijing city from 1979 to 1988, the majority of them had a H ending in both syllables. The tonal patterns in the disyllabic names of these products are given in (3):

(3)	Tone patterns	Frequency	Percentage	Ranking
	H-H	74	47.13	1
	L-H	40	25.48	2
	H-L	29	18.47	3
	L-L	14	8.91	4
	Total:	157	100	

The asymmetries exhibited in the four types of evidence and the findings from cross-dialectal comparison in the section 2 raise a number of questions: (i) why is the distribution of H tone more frequent than that of L tone? (ii) why are certain contour tones such as HL and LH more restrictive in occurrence than other contour categories, such as HM, ML, MH and LM? (iii) is there any universal principle that governs all tonal distributions in Chinese dialects, or in tonal languages in general? The answer to these questions will be given in section 4.

4. Optimality Account

4.1 Constraints on tonal asymmetries
The answer to the above questions lies in the constraint interaction within the framework of Optimality Theory (Prince & Smolensky (1993); McCarthy & Prince (1993); among others).

To account for the asymmetrical distributions between the level tones (i.e. H, M and L), the Tonal Sonority Hierarchy must be assumed, shown as in (4):

(4) Tonal sonority hierarchy (Jiang-King (1996a), (1996b)):
$$|H| > |M| > |L|$$

Parallel to the segmental sonority hierarchy, tones are also distinguished by their intrinsic sonority. That is, H tone is more sonorous than M tone, which in turn is more sonorous than L tone. Tonal sonority can be encoded into the Harmonic Tonal Alignment Schema in (5):

(5) Harmonic Tonal Alignment Schema (Jiang-King (1996a), (1996b)):
   a. $*\mu_S/[L] >> *\mu_S/[M] >> *\mu_S/[H]$ or
   b. $*\mu_S/[H] >> *\mu_S/[M] >> *\mu_S/[L]$

The harmonic ranking schema is universal. It can be interspersed by other constraints like faithfulness constraints, resulting in cross-linguistic variations. Precisely, for dialects in which L tone is absent, CORRESPOND$_{IO}$ must rank above the Harmonic Tonal Alignment Schema. The reverse ranking, on the contrary, gives tonal systems where all three level tones are permitted, such as in dialects like Cantonese.

To explain the asymmetry between the contour tones using half tonal space and the ones using the full tonal space, I extend the Grounding Conditions (Archangeli & Pulleyblank (1994)), which restrict the cooccurrence of segmental features, to the cooccurrence of tones, and propose a constraint in (6):

(6) Tonal Cooccurrence Constraint (Jiang-King (1996a), (1996b)):
   *H/L$^{\sigma}$: a H tone and a L tone cannot cooccur in the same syllable.

This constraint prohibits a cooccurrence of a H tone and a L tone in the same syllable, assuming that contour tones are a sequence of level tones. In particular, for dialects which disallow the full contours, the grounding constraint *H/L$^{\sigma}$ must rank above the CORRESPOND$_{IO}$. The reverse ranking yields tonal systems permitting the full contours like Mandarin.

4.2 Constraint rankings
In this section, I demonstrate how cross-dialectal asymmetries in tonal distributions, such as Yinchuan and Cantonese, which have the fewest and the most tones respectively among the Chinese dialects, can be accounted for by different rankings of the same set of constraints.

The tableaux in (7) shows how the ranking of Harmonic Tonal Alignment Schema with respect to the faithfulness CORRESPOND$_{IO}$ can successfully select the output tonal inventory for Yinchuan. First, we posit all kinds of possible inputs: H, M and L for level tones. Surprisingly, the optimal output is always the H tone since the faithfulness constraint CORRESPOND$_{IO}$ is dominated by the Harmonic Tonal Alignment Schema which have the internal rank by itself. In particular, the universal ranking *μ_S/[L]>>*μ_S/[M]>>*μ_S/[H] always select the H tone as the optimal output. Second, we give a full range of possible inputs for falling and rising tones. Again, the best outputs for falling and rising are always HM and MH respectively. The reason is that the undominated constraint *H/L$^{\sigma}$ rules out HL and LH as possible outputs. The remaining choice for falling is between HM and ML. Since the Tonal Alignment Schema, which has its internal ranking, in turn dominates CORRESPOND$_{IO}$. The optimal output, therefore, is always HM rather than ML, no matter what the inputs are. For the same reason, the best output for rising is always MH rather than LM.

(7) Constraint ranking for Yinchuan

Input	Output		Ranking			
		$*H/L^\sigma$, $*\mu_S/[L]$ >> $*\mu_S/[M]$ >> $*\mu_S/[H]$ >> CORSPND$_{IO}$				
(i)	a ☞ H				*	
/H/	b　 M			*!		*
	c　 L		*!			*
(ii)	a ☞ H				*	*
/M/	b　 M			*!		
	c　 L		*!		*	*
(iii)	a ☞ H				*	*
/L/	b　 M			*!		*
	L		*!			
(iv)	a ☞HM			*	*	
/HM/	b　ML		*!	*		*
	c　HL	*!	*!		*	*
(v)	a ☞HM			*	*	*
/ML/	b　ML		*!	*		
	c　HL	*!	*!		*	*
(vi)	a ☞HM			*	*	*
/HL/	b　ML		*!	*		*
	c　HL	*!	*!		*	
(vii)	a ☞MH			*	*	
/MH/	b　LM		*!	*		*
	c　LH	*!	*!		*	*
(viii)	a ☞MH			*	*	*
/LM/	b　LM		*!	*		
	c　LH	*!	*!		*	*
(ix)	a ☞MH			*	*	*
/LH/	b　LM		*!	*		*
	c　LH	*!	*!		*	

The tableau in (8) demonstrates the selection of the optimal outputs for Cantonese tonal inventory. All inputs in (8) are the same as in the tableau (7), the difference lies in the constraint ranking. First, the faithfulness CORRESPOND$_{IO}$ ranks above the Harmonic Tonal Alignment Schema which is not ranked by itself. Hence, the optimal outputs for level tones are always identical to the inputs. Second, the outputs for the falling and rising tones are also identical the their inputs except the HL and LH contours, since the Tonal cooccurrence constraint is undominated.

(8) Constraint ranking in Cantonese

Input		Output	Ranking $*H/L^{\sigma} \gg \text{CORSPND}_{IO} \gg *\mu_S/[L], \mu_S/[M], *\mu_S/[H]$				
			$*H/L^{\sigma}$	CORSPND_{IO}	$*\mu_S/[L]$	$\mu_S/[M]$	$*\mu_S/[H]$
(i)	a ☞	H					*
/H/	b	M		*!		*	
	c	L		*!	*		
(ii)	a	H		*!			*
/M/	b ☞	M				*	
	c	L		*!	*		
(iii)	a	H		*!			*
/L/	b	M		*!		*	
	c ☞	L			*		
(iv)	a ☞	HM				*	*
/HM/	b	ML		*!	*	*	
	c	HL	*!		*		*
(v)	a	HM		*!		*	*
/HL/	b ☞	ML			*	*	
	c	HL	*!		*		*
(vi)	a ☞	HM		*		*	*
/HL/	b ☞	ML		*	*	*	
	c	HL	*!		*		*
(vii)	a ☞	MH				*	*
/MH/	b	LM		*!	*	*	
	c	LH	*!		*		*
(viii)	a	MH		*!		*	*
/LM/	b ☞	LM			*	*	
	c	LH	*!		*		*
(ix)	a ☞	MH		*		*	*
/LH/	b ☞	LM		*	*	*	
	c	LH	*!		*		*

The different rankings for both Yinchuan and Cantonese are given in (9):

(9) Constraint rankings for Yinchuan and Cantonese

Dialects	Rankings
Yinchuan	$*H/L^{\sigma}, *\mu_S/[L] \gg *\mu_S/[M] \gg *\mu_S/[H] \gg \text{CORSPND}_{IO}$
Cantonese	$*H/L^{\sigma} \gg \text{CORSPND}_{IO} \gg *\mu_S/[L], *\mu_S/[M], *\mu_S/[H]$

5. Conclusion

I have shown in the above sections that tonal asymmetries exist not only in distributions in the 40 Chinese dialects, but also exist in child language acquisition, as well as in personal names and brand names. I further demonstrated that these asymmetries can be accounted for by the ranking among tonal markedness constraints (i.e., $*\mu_S/[L >> *\mu_S/[M]>> *\mu_S/[H])$ with respect to $*H/L^\sigma$ and CORSPND$_{IO}$ in the optimality theoretical framework. The dialectal variations can be achieved by different rankings of the same set of constraints.

References

Archangeli, Diana. and Douglas Pulleyblank. 1994. *Grounded Phonology.* Cambridge, Mass.: MIT Press.

Bagemihl, Bruce. 1991. Syllable structure in Bella Coola. *Linguistic Inquiry* 22:4.589-646.

Carlson, Katy. 1997. Sonority and reduplication in Nakanai and Nuxalk (Bella Coola). ROA-230.

Chan, Allan K.K. & Yue Yuan Huang. 1997. Brand naming in China: A linguistic approach. *Marketing Intelligence and Planning* 15:5.227-234.

Clements, George N. 1990. The role of the sonority cycle in core syllabification. in J. Kingston, and M. Beckman, eds., *Papers in Laboratory Phonology 1: Between the Grammar and Physics of Speech.* Cambridge: Cambridge University Press.

Everett, Daniel L. 1995. Quantity, sonority, and alignment constraints in Suruwahá and Banawáprosody. ms., University of Pittsburgh.

Fan, Kwou. & John S.J. Ng. 1993. A study of Cantonese names of Hong Kong youths: tonal pattern. Paper presented at the *4th International Conference on Cantonese and Other Yue Dialects.* Hong Kong.

Huang, Yue Yuan. & Kwou Fan. 1994. The grammar of Chinese personal names. Paper presented at the 3rd *International Conference on Chinese Linguistics.* Hong Kong.

Jiang-King, Ping 1994. An Optimality Account of Fuzhou Diphthongisation. *Proceedings of CLA.*

Jiang-King, Ping. 1996a. *An Optimality Account of Tone-Vowel Interaction in Northern Min.* Doctoral dissertation, University of British Columbia, Canada.

Jiang-King, Ping. 1996b. Tonal Sonority Hierarchy. Paper presented at the *Annual Research Forum,* Linguistic Society of Hong Kong, Chinese University of Hong Kong.

Jiang-King, Ping. 1997a. Sonority constraints on tonal patterns in Fuqing.

Paper presented in the *6th International Conference on Chinese Linguistics*, Leiden University.

Jiang-King, Ping. 1997b. An optimality account of tonal distributions in 26 Chinese dialects. in Enquan. Chen, ed., *Languages and Dialects in Modern China*. Beijing Language and Culture University Press.

King, Brian. 1982. Tone acquisition: some general observations. *Proceedings of Second International Conference on Child Language*.

Li, Charles N. and Sandra A. Thomson. 1977. The acquisition of tone in Mandarin-speaking children. *Journal of Child Language* 4.185-199.

Li, Rong. 1989. Languages and dialects in China [zhongguo de yuyan he fangyan]. *Fangyan* 3.161-167.

Maddieson, Ian. 1978. Universals of Tone. in Joseph H. Greenberg, et al., *Universals of Human Languages*, Vol. 2. Stanford University Press.

McCarthy, John and Allen Prince. 1993. *Prosodic Morphology I: Constraint interaction and satisfaction*. ms., University of Massachusetts Amherst, and Rutgers University.

Newman, Stanley. 1971. Bella Coola reduplication. *IJAL* 37.34-38.

Prince, Allen., and Paul. Smolensky 1993. *Optimality Theory: Constraint Interaction in Generative Grammar*. ms., Rutgers University, and University of Colorado Boulder.

Pulleyblank, Douglas. 1986. *Tone in Lexical Phonology*. Dordrecht: D. Reidel.

Rice, Keren D. 1992. On deriving sonority: a structural account of sonority relationships. *Phonology* 9.61-99.

Rosenthall, Samuel. 1994. *Vowel/Glide Alternation in a Theory of Constraint Interaction*. Doctoral dissertation, University of Massachusetts Amherst.

Takano, Michie. 1996. Coronal unmarkedness and sonority in Optimality Theory: the case of Ponapean. in Brian Agbayani, Kazue Takeda and Sze-Wing Tang, eds., *UCIA Working Papers in Linguistics I*.81-93.

Tse, Kwock-Ping John. 1978. Tone acquisition in Cantonese: a longitudinal case study. *Journal of Child Language* 5.191-214.

Yip, Moira. 1980. *The Tonal Phonology of Chinese*, Doctoral dissertation, MIT.

Yip, Moira. 1989. Contour Tones. *Phonology* 6.149-174.

Zec, Draga. 1988. *Sonority Constraints on Prosodic Structure*, Doctoral dissertation, Stanford University.

Zec, Draga. 1995. Sonority constraints on syllable structure. *Phonology* 2:1.85-130.

Zhang, Xi. 1994. Linguistic analysis of a sound change in Beijing dialect. Paper presented at the *Annual Meeting of Canadian Linguistic Association*, University of Calgary.

Appendix: Data sources

Beijing — Chen, Gang. et al. 1997. Modern *Beijing Dialect Dictionary*. Beijing: Yuwen Press.

Boshan — Qian, Zengyi. 1993. *Studies on Boshan dialect*. Beijing: Shehui Kexue Wenxian Press.

Cantonese — Rao, Binchai. et al. 1981. *Cantonese Dictionary*. Hong Kong: Shangwu Press.

Changsha — Bao, Houxing. et al. 1993. *Shangsha Dialect Dictionary*. Nanjing: Jiangsu Jiaoyu Press.

Chengdu — Luo, Yunxi. et al. 1981. *Chengdu Dialect Dictionary*. Chengdu: Sichuan Shehui Kexue Press.

Chongming — Zhang, Huiying. 1993. *Chongming Dialect Dictionary*. Nanjing: Jiangsu Jiaoyu Press.

Danyang — Cai, Guolu. 1995. *Danyang Dialect Dictionary*. Nanjing: Jiangsu Jiaoyu Press.

Fuzhou — Beijing University. (ed.) 1989. *Vocabularies of Chinese Dialects* (2nd edition). Wenzi Gaige Press.

Fuqing — Feng, Aizhen. 1993. *Studies on Fuqing Dialect*. Zhongguo Shehui Kexue Wenxian Press.

Guiyang — Wang, Ping. 1994. *Guiyang Dialect Dictionary*. Nanjing: Jiangsu Jiaoyu Press.

Haifeng — Yang, Bisheng. et al. 1996. *Studies on Haifeng Dialect*. Yuwen Press.

Haikou — Chen, Hongyun. 1996. *Haikou Dialect Dictionary*. Nanjing: Jiangsu Jiaoyu Press.

Hefei — Beijing University. (ed.) 1989. *Vocabularies of Chinese Dialects* (2nd edition). Wenzi Gaige Press.

Huojia — He, Wei. 1989. *Studies on Huojia Dialect*. Beijing: Shangwu Press.

Jiading — Tang, Zhenzhu. 1993. *Studies on Jiading Dialect*. Beijing: Shehui Kexue Wenxian Press.

Jiangyong — Huang, Xuezhen. 1993. *Studies on Jiangyong Dialect*. Beijing: Shehui Kexue Wenxian Press.

Jinan — Beijing University. (ed.) 1989. *Vocabularies of Chinese Dialects* (2nd edition). Wenzi Gaige Press.

Jinhua — Cao, Zhiyun. 1996. *Jinhua Dialect Dictionary*. Nanjing: Jiangsu Jiaoyu Press.

Lichuan — Yan, Shen. 1995. *Lichuan Dialect Dictionary*. Nanjing: Jiangsu Jiaoyu Press.

Liuzhou — Liu, Cunhan. 1995. *Liuzhou Dialect Dictionary*. Nanjing: Jiangsu Jiaoyu Press.

Loudi — Yan, Qinghui. and Liu, Lihua. 1994. *Loudi Dialect Dictionary*. Nanjing: Jiangsu Jiaoyu Press.

Appendix: Data sources (cont.)

Luoyang He, Wei. 1996. *Luoyang Dialect Dictionary*. Nanjing: Jiangsu Jiaoyu Press.
Meixian Huang, Xuezhen. 1995. *Meixian Dialect Dictionary*. Nanjing: Jiangsu Jiaoyu Press.
Nanchang Xuong, Zhenghui. 1994. *Nanchang Dialect Dictionary*. Nanjing: Jiangsu Jiaoyu Press.
Nanjing Liu, Danqing. 1995. *Nanjing Dialect Dictionary*. Nanjing: Jiangsu Jiaoyu Press.
Shanghai Xu. Baohua., Yang, Zhenzhu. 1991 *Vocabularies of Shanghai Dialect*. Shanghai Jiaoyu Press.
Suzhou Ye, Xianglin. 1993. *Suzhou Dialect Dictionary*. Nanjing: Jiangsu Jiaoyu Press.
Tianjin Beijing University. (ed.) 1995. *Chinese Dialects Vocabularies* (2nd edition). Yuwen Press.
Wenzhou Beijing University. (ed.) 1989. *Vocabularies of Chinese Dialects* (2nd edition). Wenzi Gaige Press.
Wuhan Zhu, Jiansong. 1995. *Wuhan Dialect Dictionary*. Nanjing: Jiangsu Jiaoyu Press.
Wulumuqi Zhou, Lei. 1995. *Wulumuqi Dialect Dictionary*. Nanjing: Jiangsu Jiaoyu Press.
Xiamen Zhou, Changji. 1993. *Xiamen Dialect Dictionary*. Nanjing: Jiangsu Jiaoyu Press.
Xi'an Wang, Junhu. 1996. *Xi'an Dialect Dictionary*. Nanjing: Jiangsu Jiaoyu Press.
Xining Zhang, Chengcai. 1994. *Xining Dialect Dictionary*. Nanjing: Jiangsu Jiaoyu Press.
Xinzhou Wen, Duanzheng. and Zhang, Guangmin. 1995. *Xinzhou Dialect Dictionary*. Nanjing: Jiangsu Jiaoyu Press.
Xuzhou Su, Xiaoqing. and Lu. Yonghong. 1996. *Xinzhou Dialect Dictionary*. Nanjing: Jiangsu Jiaoyu Press.
Yangzhou Wang, Shihua. and Huang, Jilin. 1996. *Yangzhou Dialect Dictionary*. Nanjing: Jiangsu Jiaoyu Press.
Yinchuan Li, Shuyan. and Zhang, Ansheng. 1996. *Yinchuan Dialect Dictionary*. Nanjing: Jiangsu Jiaoyu Press.
Zhangping Zhang, Zhenxing. 1992. *Studies on Zhangping Dialect*. Zhongguo Shehui Kexue Press.
Zhoushan Fang, Songxi. 1993. *Studies on Zhoushan Dialect*. Zhongguo Shehui Kexue Press.

The Argument-Predicate Distinction and the Non-Optionality of DO Clitic Doubling and Scrambling

DALINA KALLULLI
University of Durham

1. Introduction

Sportiche (1992) proposed that direct object clitic doubling (as in (1a,b)) and scrambling (as in (1c)) have a common basis, namely, the licensing of a property F, which he argues to be *specificity*.

(1) a. Albanian (Al): An-a **(e)** lexoi **libr-in** dje.
    b. Greek (Gr): I Anna **(to)** diavase **to vivlio** xtes.
             the Ann (it$_{cl}$) read-she the book yesterday
    c. German (Dt): Anna hat (**das Buch**) gestern (**das Buch)** gelesen.
             Anna has (the book) yesterday (the book) read
             'Ann read the book yesterday.'

The structure of both doubling and scrambling is argued to be the configuration in (2).

(2) $[_{ClaccP} XP^\wedge Cl_{acc}^0 [_{VP} V^0 [_{XP*} \dots]]]$

In (2), XP* must move by LF to the XP^ position. Movement is motivated by the Clitic Criterion, an analogue of Rizzi's (1991) Wh-Criterion. Further, movement of XP* to XP^ may occur overtly or covertly and both the head (Cl) and XP* may be overt or covert. By these parameters, among others, the following cases are predicted: Clitic doubling constructions (as in Romance and Balkan languages) arise when an overt XP* moves covertly with an overt Cl, and scrambling (in Germanic) arises when an overt XP* moves overtly with a covert Cl.

While the idea that the same syntactic configuration lies at the bottom of both clitic doubling and scrambling constructions is attractive theoretically, I argue that the property F, whose need to be licensed motivates the postulated maximal projections, is identified incorrectly by Sportiche. To show this, let us consider first some distributional facts for doubling and scrambling. It is well-known that the [±definite] feature of the DPs is not relevant for doubling and scrambling. In the examples in (1), the doubled and scrambled DPs are definite; the examples in (3) show that a-expressions, that is, indefinite DPs, may also be doubled and scrambled.[1]

(3) a. Al: Edhe An-a   arriti   t(-a)   botonte   një libër
          also   Ann-the managed to(-it$_{cl}$) publish   a book
          para se   të vdiste.
          before that to die
          'Even Anna managed to publish a book before she died'

    b. Gr: Akoma ke i Anna   katafere   na (to)   ekdosi   ena vivlio
          still and the Anna managed   to (it$_{cl}$) publish   a book
          prin   na pethani.
          before to die
          'Even Anna managed to publish a book before she died.'

    c. Dt: Ich habe (eine Zeitung) gestern (eine Zeitung) gelesen.
          I have (a newspaper) yesterday (a newspaper) read
          'I read a newspaper yesterday.'

---

[1]Example (3b) is a counterexample to the claim that DO clitic doubling in Greek is subject to definiteness (cf. Anagnostopoulou (1994)). As not all definites may be clitic doubled in Greek (cf. e.g. (4b)), Anagnostopoulou tries to relate direct object clitic doubling in this language to Heim's (1982) *Familiarity Condition*. Note, however, that this analysis is untenable in the face of doubling of indefinites unless Heim's crucial claim that all indefinites represent novel information is rejected. Anagnostopoulou acknowledges cases of doubling of indefinites but contends that doubling of indefinites is different from doubling of definites. I reject this contention. All other things equal, a uniform analysis for clitic doubling of both definite and indefinite DPs is of course more preferable. Such an analysis will be proposed in section 2.

The data in (4) show that even definite DPs cannot invariably be doubled and scrambled.

(4) a. Al: Nuk   shkoj   në këmbë,   (*e)   marr   autobus-in.
    b. Gr: Dhen pigheno me ta podhja, (*to) perno to leoforio.
        not   walk   with the feet,   it$_{cl}$ take   the bus
        'I don't walk, I take the bus to school.'
    c. Dt: Er sagte, daß er nicht zu Fuß in die Schule geht, sondern
        he said that he not on feet in the school walks, but
        daß er (*den Bus) immer (den Bus) nimmt.
        that he (*the bus) always (the bus) takes
        'He said that he doesn't walk to school but always takes the bus.'

The fact that the definite DPs in these examples cannot be doubled and scrambled is problematic for the specificity/presuppositionality/strength approaches to doubling and scrambling (cf. Sportiche (1992), Diesing (1992), de Hoop (1992), Anagnostopoulou (1994)) if we assume with Enç (1991) that all definites are specific/presuppositional/strong. While the claim that all definites are specific will be challenged (cf. section 3.4), there are indisputably specific/presuppositional/strong definites (and indefinites) that need not (and/or cannot) be doubled and scrambled (cf. (5)). Hence, doubling and scrambling emerge in these analyses as optional phenomena.

(5) A: What happened?
    B: a. Al: Jan-i   (#i)   hëngri fasule-t/   (#e) piu një birrë.
       b. Gr: O Yánnis (#ta)   éfaye   ta fasólia/ (#tin) ipje mia bira.
           the Yannis them$_{cl}$ ate   the beans/ her$_{cl}$ drank a beer$_{fem}$
           'Yannis ate the beans/drank a beer.'
       c. Dt: Hans hat heute das Thermometer/einen Teller zerbrochen.
           Hans has today the thermometer/a   plate broken
           'Hans broke the thermometer/a plate today.'
       d. Dt: #Hans hat das Thermometer/einen Teller heute zerbrochen.
           Hans has the thermometer/a plate today broken

In this paper, I show that neither doubling nor scrambling of direct object DPs induces specificity on these DPs. I argue instead that the locus of specificity is D, which for noun phrases[2] underlies argumenthood and that specificity effects in doubling and scrambling constructions are only epiphenomenal. Crucially, I claim that doubling and scrambling of direct object DPs unequivocally marks these DPs as [-Focus], which will be defined as an operator feature. There is no optionality.

---

[2]The term 'noun phrase', unlike 'DP' and 'NP', is used theory-neutrally throughout.

2. The Non-optionality of Clitic Doubling and Scrambling

2.1. Justifying [-Focus]

Informally, *focus* is viewed as the most informative part of an utterance. Hence, a definition of *focus* is sensitive to the speech act and varies according to it. For instance, the notion *information* or *information structure* for a question does not make sense unless defined as the type of answer expected. So, for *wh*-questions, *focus* is the variable represented by the *wh*-element; this also holds for *echo*-questions. For a *yes-no* question *focus* is either the assertion or the negation. *Focus* can also be an element which is contrasted. Finally, *focus* can be the item that fills in a slot in an information structure where other slots have already been filled. In this latter function, *focus* is close to the notion 'new information'. The complement of *focus* is *topic*. Following a long-established tradition in generative grammar, I assume that *focus* is a syntactic feature on phrases interpretable at both the LF and the PF interfaces as [+Focus] (cf. Jackendoff (1972), Rochemont (1986), Horvath (1986), Brody (1990)).

In view of the fact that a sentence may lack a topic (e.g. out-of-the-blue sentences) but will always have a focus, I assume that the [+Focus] feature is in fact the unmarked value in a markedness theory for natural language and that the [-[+Focus]] (i.e. [-Focus]) feature is the marked value. As such, derivational syntax renders it significant. I will argue that clitic doubling and scrambling are two of the means by which this feature gets licensed.

2.2. The Common Basis of Doubling and Scrambling

A variety of facts converges in showing that both doubling and scrambling of direct object DPs systematically yields ungrammaticality when these DPs are focus or part of the focus domain, that is, when they are marked [+Focus]. Some of these facts are outlined below.

If doubling and scrambling marks direct object DPs as [-Focus], doubling and scrambling of +*wh* direct objects should invariably yield ungrammaticality, assuming that +*wh*-elements are necessarily [+Focus] (cf. Rochemont (1986), Brody (1990)). This is indeed the case as shown by (6).

(6) a. Al: Kë/çfarë   (*e)   pe?
   b. Gr:Pjon/ti   (*ton/to)   idhes?
      [who/what]$_{acc}$ him/it$_{cl}$ saw-you
      'Who/what did you see?'
   c. Dt: Wem hat (*welche Frage)der Student (welche Frage) beantwortet?
      whom has which question the student which question answered
      'To whom did the student answer which question?'

In the examples under (7) the direct object is contained in the focus domain. Therefore it cannot be doubled. Nor can it scramble.[3]

(7) a. Al: An-a nuk (*i) zjeu   fasule-t, por (*i) hëngri fiq-të.
    b. Gr: I Anna dhen (*ta) mayirepse ta fasólia, alá (*ta) éfaye ta sika.
           the Ann not them$_{cl}$ boiled   the beans, but them$_{cl}$ ate the figs
           'Anna didn't [cook the beans]$_F$; she [ate the figs]$_F$.'
    c. Dt: Anna hat (*die Bohnen) nicht (die Bohnen) gekocht,
           Anna has (*the beans) not (the beans)   boiled
           sondern   sie hat die Feigen gegessen.
           but   she has the figs   eaten
           'Anna didn't [cook the beans]$_F$ but [ate the figs]$_F$.'[4]

Likewise, direct object DPs in out-of-the-blue sentences may be neither doubled in Albanian and Greek, nor scrambled in German (cf. e.g. (5)).

The data systematically reveal that doubling and scrambling of direct object DPs that are marked [+Focus] is disallowed. This is predicted under the hypothesis that direct object clitics license a(n operator) [-Focus] feature in the specifier of the phrases they head, which triggers movement in order to be checked off. Since the attracting feature is [-Focus], a (clitic doubled) [+Focus] DP would invariably cause the derivation to crash.

The examples in (8) show that doubling and scrambling of direct object DPs is obligatory in answers to yes-no questions.

(8) A: Did the Pope finally visit Tirana?
   B: a. (Dt) Der Papst hat (Tirana) noch immer nicht (#Tirana) besucht.
          the Pope has (Tirana) yet   always not (#Tirana) visited
      b. (Al) Pap-a ende nuk #(e) ka vizituar Tiran-ën.
          Pope-the yet not   it$_{cl}$ has visited Tirana-the
          'The Pope has not visited Tirana yet.'

This fact is straightforwardly accounted for under the hypothesis that doubling/scrambling of direct object DPs licenses a [-Focus] feature on these phrases, since direct object DPs in yes-no questions and answers to yes-no questions are outside of the focus domain (that is, they are not marked [+Focus]). Consequently, there is no feature clash between the clitic ([-Focus]) operator head and the doubled/scrambled DP in the specifier of

---

[3] I use square brackets followed by the subscript 'F' in the English translations of the examples to indicate focus domains.

[4] The sentences (7a,b) are OK also when the direct object (in the first conjunct) is clitic doubled, as is (7c) also when the direct object is scrambled, under an interpretation which can be rendered in English as: 'As for Anna and the beans, she didn't cook them, rather she ate the figs'. Under this interpretation, however, 'the beans' is unambiguosly outside the focus domain.

the CIP with respect to the feature [±Focus]. Note that the specificity/ presuppositionality/strength approaches to doubling and scrambling cannot account for the fact that doubling/scrambling of the direct object DPs in (8) (and generally in answers to yes-no questions) is obligatory, since *Tirana* as a name is referential specific also in the undoubled/unscrambled version.

While definite and indefinite DPs with overt determiners may be doubled and scrambled, bare indefinites cannot. For bare plurals this is shown in (9).[5] This also holds for count bare singulars (cf. (10a-c)).[6]

(9) a. Al: An-a nuk   (*i)   zjeu   fasule, por   (*i)   hëngri fiq.
    b. Gr: I Anna dhen   (*ta)   mayirepse fasólia, alá   (*ta)   éfaye sika.
        the Ann not   them$_{cl}$ boiled-she beans, but   them$_{cl}$ ate   figs
    c. Dt: Anna hat (*Bohnen) nicht   (Bohnen) gekocht,
        Anna has (*beans)   not   (beans)   boiled
        sondern sie hat Feigen gegessen.
        but   she has figs   eaten
        'Anna didn't [cook beans]$_F$ but [ate figs]$_F$.'

(10) a. Al: An-a   donte   t-(*a)   blente   fustan.
    b. Gr: I Anna ithele   na (*to)   aghorasi   forema.
        the Ann wanted   to-it$_{cl}$. buy   dress
        'Anna wanted to buy a dress.'
    c. Dt: Ich habe (*Zeitung) nicht/im Garten (Zeitung) gelesen.
        I   have (*newspaper) not/in the garden (newspaper) read
        'I have not read a paper'/'I have read a paper in the garden.'
vs. a'. Al: An-a   donte t-(a)   blente   **një** fustan.
    b'. Gr: I Anna   ithele na (to) aghorasi   **ena** forema
        the Ann   wanted to-it$_{cl}$ buy   **a** dress
        'Anna wanted to buy a dress.'
    c'. Dt: Ich habe (**eine Zeitung**) nicht/imGarten (**eine Zeitung**) glesen
        I   have (a newspaper) not/in the garden (a newspaper) read
        'I have not read a paper'/'I have read a paper in the garden.'

---

[5]In fact, this claim only holds for those bare plurals that receive an existential interpretation. This is explicated in section 3.3.

[6]As it happens, even closely-related languages differ with respect to the possibility of instantiating their direct objects by count bare singulars. Thus, while count bare singulars are virtually non-existent as direct objects in English, across Balkan and Mainland Scandinavian languages they may occur as direct objects of all predicates whose bare plural direct objects cannot get a generic interpretation but get an existential interpretation. In German, on the other hand, count bare singulars do occur as direct objects, but are much more restricted than in Balkan and Mainland Scandinavian. Note in this context that of all the languages mentioned above, only English disallows count bare singulars in predicate nominal position. Finally, note that count bare singulars are found also in English as objects of certain prepositions; e.g. *go to school/church/market; travel by train/plane* etc.

Let us consider first why bare singulars cannot be doubled/scrambled. To the extent that this question has been addressed at all, bare singulars have been treated as forming a complex predicate with the clausal predicate (cf. Haiden (1996)). However, the fact that bare singulars may be wh-moved shows that they are syntactic constituents. What a complex predicate is remains then only a vague idea in need of formalization.

(11) a. Al: Gazetë   ka-m · lexuar dje.
             newspaper have-I read yesterday
     b. Dt: Zeitung   habe   ich gestern gelesen.
             newspaper have   I yesterday read
             'It was a newspaper that I read yesterday.'

I propose that the impossibility of doubling and scrambling bare singulars is due to feature mismatch between the clitic head and the bare singular with respect to the D-feature. While clitics carry a D-feature, bare singulars are NPs that altogether lack a D-projection. That clitics carry a D-feature (alternatively: are specified in the lexicon as elements of category D^0 or are underlying determiners) is not surprising, in view of the fact that they originate from personal and demonstrative pronouns which are prototypical D-heads. This means that only DPs but not NPs may be doubled and scrambled since the [-D] feature of the latter will clash with the [+D] feature on the clitic head, thus causing the derivation not to converge.

My claim that bare singulars are NPs that lack a D-projection seems to run counter to Longobardi's (1994) claim that only DPs but not NPs may function as arguments, his idea being that bare noun objects have a morphologically null D-head. In what follows, I will argue that there is evidence that legitimizes the claim that bare singulars lack a D-projection.

First, note that bare singulars occur only as predicate nominals and as direct objects. Further, bare singulars do not occur as direct objects of any predicate but only of those predicates whose bare plural direct objects cannot get a generic (in the sense: *kind-denoting*) reading. I suggest that the factors that govern the distribution of bare singulars are semantic. However, on the assumption that a given syntactic construction cannot be systematically ambiguous, my basic working hypothesis is that semantic interpretations for noun phrases are fundamentally dependent on their internal structure. From this perspective, I crucially claim that whereas DPs may be either arguments or predicates, depending on whether they denote individuals or properties, NPs invariably denote properties; they are LF predicates, not variables or restricted quantifiers. Consequently, doubling/ scrambling does not apply to them.

The distinction between individual vs. property-denotation is in fact what clarifies the distinction specific vs. non-specific for nouns.

3. Specificity, Individuation, Argumenthood

3.1. The Meaning of Bare Singulars

The a-expressions *një fustan* in (10a') and *ena forema* in (10b') may denote:

(12)a. some particular dress that Ann has seen on some display
    b. some particular kind of dress (eg. some *Dior* (vs. *Chanel*) dress)
    c. some/any object which classifies as a dress; i.e. any dress at all

With respect to specificity, the (12a) and (12b) readings are both specific readings. Only the (12c) reading is non-specific.[7]

Importantly, the bare singulars *fustan* in (10a) and *forema* in (10b) cannot refer to some particular dress or to some particular kind of dress. Thus, the bare singulars in (10a,b) may not receive specific interpretations. What Ann is interested in (in (10a,b)), is some individual or other which embodies a certain property, namely that of being [+dress]. The identity of the item that Ann wants, beyond its being [+dress], is irrelevant here. Assuming that properties do not exist outside individuals, that is, that properties are not ontological primitives, Ann is interested in some individual or other that has the property [+dress]. But each individual that has the property [+dress], has in addition other properties, at least one, that make it distinct from other individuals that have the same property, namely, [+dress]. The very existence of distinct individuals possessing the same basic property which makes them be regarded as members of the same class is due to the existence of at least one distinct property. Being a distinct individual itself is a property. These other properties of individuals, beyond the property [+dress], are not only irrelevant to Ann in (10a,b), but indeed unable to be expressed by the bare singulars here. The bare singulars in (10a,b) do not and indeed cannot denote individuals but properties. The meaning of (10a) and (10b) may be given as in (13).

(13) Ann wants to engage/is interested in dress-buying.

It is then my contention that while direct object a-expressions may denote individuals, direct object bare singulars may not. The distinction between properties and individuals may be represented as in (14).

---

[7]Note that the referential/attributive dichotomy divides the three readings in (12) in a different manner: (12a) is referential, while (12b,c) are attributive. This is so because only in (12a) has Ann established a direct relationship with some particular haecceitas. This is not the case in (12b); any Dior dress is sufficient for Ann under the reading in (12b). Yet, the indefinite noun phrase in (12b) receives a specific interpretation, because Ann is not interested in any dress; she wants a specific *type* of dress, namely, a Dior one, but obviously she does not mind as to what particular sample (e.g. concerning colour, cut, production year, etc.) she gets.

(14) **P vs. P $\cap$ p$_i$**
(where 'P' is the fundamental property that identifies individuals as members of the same class and 'p' is a property that does not contradict 'P')

It is by now a well-established claim in the semantic literature that specific readings are presuppositional and non-specific readings are not so (cf. Ioup (1977), Enç (1991), Diesing (1992)). The hypothesis that bare singulars are property-denoting expressions, that is, predicates, can account for the fact that they are not presuppositional by assuming that presupposition is about saturated structures, that is, about individuals (and propositions), not about properties. It follows then that specificity involves individuation; individual-denoting expressions are always specific, irrespective of the fact that they may be used referentially or attributively. Since arguments are saturated structures, noun phrase arguments denote individuals, that is, are specific. Given that direct objects may be instantiated by bare singulars, it follows that direct objects may be predicates. Adopting the formalization (cf. Dobrovie-Sorin and Laca (1996)) for existential bare plurals, it may be stated that direct object bare singulars are predicates that restrict an existentially bound argument variable that enters the LF representation as the place-holder of the theta-slot of the clausal predicate. The clausal predicate may then be translated as an open formula whose open positions are bound by existential quantification, as given in (15b) for (15a):

(15) a. Dt: Ich lese Zeitung.
      I   read newspaper
    b. $\lambda x_1 \ [\exists \ (x_1 \ read \ x_2 \ at \ e^\wedge \ Zeitung \ (x_2))] \ (ICH_1)$

3.2. The Scopal Behaviour of Bare Singulars
Bare singulars invariably take (existential) narrow scope in the presence of other scopal items in the sentence. Thus, (16a), unlike its English translation, has only the reading in (16b) but lacks the reading in (16c):

(16) a. Al: Nuk dua   biçikletë.
          not   want-I bicycle
          'I don't want a bicycle.'
    b.   It is not the case that I want a bicycle.
    c.   #There is a bicycle that I don't want.

In this respect, bare singulars differ both from definite descriptions and a-expressions which may though need not take wide scope. This scopal property of bare singulars reminds one of Carlson's (1977) observation for the English bare plural in non-generic contexts. He accounts for this by suggesting that the existential force of the bare plural comes from a source external to the bare plural itself, namely from the verb. I adopt this proposal also for the bare singulars.

3.3. On the Relation of Count Bare Singulars to Bare Plurals

My proposal as to why (existential)[8] bare plurals may not be doubled/scrambled rests on the claim that generically and existentially interpreted bare plurals differ with respect to the D-feature. While generic bare plurals are DPs with a morphologically null D, existential bare plurals are NPs that altogether lack a D-projection. Consequently, generic and existential bare plurals differ with respect to the specificity feature: generic bare plurals are [+specific] (i.e. individual-denoting), whereas existential bare plurals are [-specific] (i.e. property-denoting).

What does it mean for generic bare plurals to be individual-denoting? It means that generic bare plurals denote kinds (in non-quantified contexts) or (in quantified contexts) instantiations of kinds via (quantified) individuals. This means that generic bare plurals are either constants or variables depending on whether they name a kind or in (quantified contexts) denote instantiations of it. I claim that existential bare plurals, on the other hand, denote properties (cf. also Laca (1990)). As such, they are not constants or variables but predicates. Above I argued that bare singulars, as well, denote properties. What is then the difference between bare singulars and existential bare plurals given that all languages that have bare singulars also have existential bare plurals? I contend that the difference between bare singulars and existential bare plurals has to do with event reference. While the meaning of a sentence containing a bare singular like the one in (17a) can be rendered as in (18a) or (18b), the meaning of the minimally different, (17b) containing a(n existential) bare plural instead of the bare singular, can be rendered either as in (18a) as in (18b), not as in (18a).

(17) Dt: a. Eva will Zeitung lesen.
         Eva wants newspaper read
         'Eva wants to read a newspaper.'
      b. Eva will Zeitungen lesen.
         Eva wants newspapers read
         'Eva wants to read newspapers.'

(18) a. Eva wants to engage in newspaper reading for (at least) once.
     b. Eva wants to engage in newspaper reading several times.

---

[8]In Balkan languages, like in Romance and unlike in Germanic, bare plurals may receive only an existential interpretation, whereas generic readings are in these languages incompatible with bare plurals. Generic readings in Balkan (and Romance) languages require an overt determiner, namely, the definite determiner for plural noun phrases and either the definite or the indefinite determiner for singular noun phrases.

Thus, (17a) can though need not be synonymous with (17b), whereas (17b), unlike (17a), can only mean that Eva might engage in several events of newspaper reading. Strictly speaking, there is no *small* event in which a person can read more than one newspaper at a time. Thus, I claim that existential bare plurals are the plural counterparts of bare singulars. On one hand, the fact that bare singulars occur as direct objects of only those predicates whose bare plural direct objects cannot get a generic interpretation (unless in the scope of overt or non-overt adverbs of quantification) supports this claim. On the other hand, however, the reverse does not hold across all the languages that have bare singular objects. German is a case in point. However, in view of the fact that the meaning of bare singulars is a subset of the meaning of a-expressions (cf. section 3.1) and since they also share the meaning of existential bare plurals, it is reasonable to try to relate the lack of (one-to-one) distributional parallelism between bare singulars and existential bare plurals within and across languages to economy considerations.

If existential bare plurals are the plural counterparts of bare singulars, they should have the same clausal distribution, among other things. At first sight, this is counterevidenced by constructions like (19).

(19) Dt: Studenten   lärmen   auf der Straße.
       students   make noise   in the street
       'Students are making noise in the street.'[9]

I claim, however, that *Studenten* in (19) under its existential interpretation is a predicate nominal in the Spec of CP (possibly derived from a cleft construction), as given in (20).

(20) [$_{CP}$ Studenten lärmen$_j$ [$_{IP}$ [$_{VP}$t$_j$ [$_{PP}$ auf der Straße]] t$_j$]]

Interestingly, Hellan (1986) observes that in Norwegian, adjective phrases (APs) used predicatively agree in number and gender with their subject. In (21a,b), however, they do not. If the bare nouns in (21a,b) were really the subjects, such constructions would represent genuine counterexamples to the theory of agreement. I suggest that *bil/biler* 'car/cars' in (21a,b) are not in subject position but in Spec of CP and that (21a,b) are derived from constructions like the ones given in (21c) or its variant (21d).

---

[9]It is well-known that simple present in German can have both an episodic and a generic meaning. Here I am concerned with the existential reading of the bare plural only. Hence the given English translation.

(21) Norwegian: a. Bil   er   dyr-t.   (Hellan 1986:95)
              $car_{s,masc}$ is   expensive-s, neut
         b. Bil-er   er   dyr-t.   (Hellan 1986:95)
              car-$s_{p, masc}$ is   expensive-s, neut
         c. Bil/biler   er   dyr-t   å   ha.
              car/cars   is   expensive-s, neut   to   have
              'To have a car/cars is expensive.'
         d. Å   ha   bil/biler   er   dyr-t.
              to   have   car/cars   is   expensive
              'To have a car/cars is expensive.'

3.4. Definite Expressions and the Argument-Predicate Distinction
Consider now the example in (22):

(22) I shall kiss the first woman to enter this room.

The definite expression in (22) also is specific though it may have both a referential and an attributive reading depending on whether or not the speaker knows beforehand who the first woman to enter the room will be. In other words, the definite expression in (22) may denote either a particular individual in relation to the speaker, or a particular type of individual namely, the type of 'first woman to enter the room' vs. the type of 'second woman to enter the room' or the type of 'no woman to enter the room'. The type of 'first woman to enter the room' is an individual with respect to the concept/property *woman*. So, independently of whether the definite expression is intended to refer or not, it is specific (cf. also Enç (1991)).

The question, however, arises as to whether definite noun phrases in direct object position can ever be predicates, that is, denote properties (like bare singulars and a-expressions on non-specific reading). I believe they can. Examples that come to mind are definite object noun phrases in set expressions like: *take the bus* in (23), *play the violin* in (24).[10]

(23) I like to take the bus.

(24) Ben has played the violin beautifully at times.

The definite expression *the bus* in (23) may have both a referential-specific and an attributive-specific reading (as paraphrased in (25a,b)), but it also has a non-specific reading, as paraphrased in (25c). Likewise, *the violin* in (24b) also has a non-specific reading which may be paraphrased as in (26).

---

[10]Definite expressions in some locative phrases (e.g., *I am going to the airport/to the doctor's/to the shore/to the hospital*) have a predicative reading, as well. Note that these are not generic: *The only time I went to Texas I took the plane.*

(25) a. There is a bus-vehicle, always the very same, that I like to take.
   b. There is a bus-line that I like to take.
   c. I like to travel by bus (I don't like to walk/drive/take the train/fly)

(26) Ben is a talented violin-player.

The fact that not only indefinite expressions but also definite expressions may have both a specific and non-specific reading constitutes a counterexample to the claim that all definites are specific (cf. Enç (1991)). It suggests that the class of definite expressions is far from homogeneous semantically (cf. also Vergnaud and Zubizarreta (1992)). Note, however, that both a-expressions and definite expressions may only be interpreted non-specifically when they occur as predicate nominals or as direct objects (or objects of certain prepositions), but not when they occur as subjects and datives. (That subjects and datives invariably denote individuals when they are instantiated by noun phrases, should not be a matter of controversy in a framework like *Principles and Parameters*.[11])

The fact that bare singulars are synonymous with a-expressions on their non-specific reading only, suggests that a-expressions are potential designators of either properties or individuals, that is, a-expressions may be predicates or variables. However, postulating that a-expressions are intrinsically ambiguous between a specific (read: individual-denoting) and a non-specific (read: property-denoting) interpretation cannot explain in any principled manner why: (i) a-expressions occurring as subjects and datives lack a non-specific (i.e. property-denoting) interpretation; (ii) the ambiguity specific vs. non-specific for a-expressions arises only when they occur as direct objects of certain predicates (e.g. *want, buy, draw, hunt, smoke, find, own,* etc.) but not of certain others (e.g. *love, hate, respect, adore,* etc.) These facts can be ·accounted for if we assume that many though not all natural language predicates of type $<e,<e,t>>$ (e.g. *buy*) can be raised to type $<<e,t>,<e,t>>$ (cf. Zimmerman (1993)), meaning (27):

(27) $\lambda P \; \lambda x \; \exists y \; [P(y) \; \& \; BUY \; (x,y)]$
   (with dynamic existential quantifier $\exists y$ which can be applied to a predicative noun of type $<e,t>$).

In addition, we need to assume that the dual nature of a-expressions is due to their lexical underspecification with respect to specificity (i.e. individual vs. property-denotation). Hence they can oscillate between type $<e>$ and

---

[11]In the *Principles and Parameters* framework the subjects of examples like: *Being wise/To be wise is crazy* or *Being crazy is crazy* (examples from Chierchia (1985:418)) are clausal syntactically and propositional semantically (cf. Koster and May (1982)).

<e,t>. But in view of the fact that many definite noun phrases as well, may be interpreted non-specifically/predicatively when objects of verbs and prepositions, we need to assume that also the-expressions are underspecified with respect to individual vs. property-denotation and can therefore oscillate between type <e> and <e,t>. To generalize, we may then state that while NPs are unambiguously type <e>, DPs may be of type <e> or <e,t>.

De Hoop (1997) gives the example in (28) to support her claim that even 'predicate modifier' definites may scramble optionally.

(28) Dutch: a. omdat ik altijd om drie uur   de bus neem
                because I always at three o'clock the bus take
             b. omdat ik de bus altijd om drie uur   neem
                because I the bus always at three o'clock take
                'because I always take the bus at three o'clock.'

De Hoop's argument rests on the implication that (28a) and (28b) have the same (set of) interpretations. This is, however, incorrect. While (29b) is a valid paraphrase for both (28a,b), (29a) is a valid paraphrase for (28a) only.

(29) a. because as for me, I always engage in bus-taking at three o'clock.
     b. because as for me and the bus, I always take it at three o'clock.

Contrary to de Hoop, I argue that predicate definites (de Hoop's 'predicate modifier' definites) may never scramble and that the scrambled in (28b) is not a 'predicate modifier', as it can be in (28a), but an argument variable. In other words, it is specific, though it is not necessarily referential as it does not have to refer to a certain bus-vehicle. (*De bus* in (28b) denotes some bus or other of some bus-line or other that is regularly at a certain stop at a certain time, viz. three o'clock; it is therefore clearly presuppositional.) Since specificity is a property of arguments not of predicates, *de bus* in (28b) is an argument not a predicate as it can (though it need not) be in (28a). Hence the unavailability of the reading in (29a) for (28b).

4. Conclusion

Definite noun phrases and a-expressions are semantically and syntactically non-homogeneous. They are not always syntactic arguments when objects of verbs (and prepositions) but may translate both as arguments or as predicates at LF depending on whether the clausal predicate selects an individual (type <e>) or a property (type <e,t>) as its internal argument (cf. also van Geenhoven (1996) for indefinites). The type shifting mechanism (cf. Partee (1987)) allows for this duality. This creates the illusion that scrambling/doubling of definites and a-expressions is optional. In fact, scrambled/doubled objects are always syntactic arguments. Since argument noun phrases are always specific (read: individual-denoting), specificity effects will be observed in scrambling constructions. Non-scrambled/non-doubled objects may but need not be arguments.

References

Anagnostopoulou, Elena. 1994. On the Representation of Clitic Doubling in Modern Greek. *EUROTYP Working Papers*, Theme Group 8, 5:1-66.

Brody, Michael. 1990. Some remarks on the focus field in Hungarian. UCL *Working Papers in Linguistics* 2:201-225.

Carlson, Gregory. 1977. *Reference to Kinds in English*. Doctoral dissertation., University of Massachusetts, Amherst.

Chierchia, Gennaro. 1985. Formal Semantics and the Grammar of Predication. *Linguistic Inquiry* 16:417-43.

Diesing, Molly. 1992. *Indefinites*. Cambridge, Mass.: MIT Press.

Dobrovie-Sorin, Carmen and Brenda Laca. 1996. *Generic Bare NPs*. Manuscript, Université Paris 7 and Université de Strasbourg.

Enç, Mürvet. 1991. The Semantics of Specificity. *Linguistic Inquiry* 22:1-25.

Geenhoven van, Veerle. 1996. *Semantic Incorporation and Indefinite Descriptions: Semantic and Syntactic Aspects of Noun Incorporation in West Greenlandic*. Doctoral dissertation, Universität Tübingen.

Haiden. Martin. 1996. The aspect of short scrambling. *Wiener Linguistische Gazette* 57-59:121-145.

Heim, Irene. 1982. *The Semantics of Definite and Indefinite Noun Phrases*. Doctoral dissertation., University of Massachusetts, Amherst.

Hellan, Lars. 1986. The headedness of NPs in Norwegian. In P. Muysken and H. van Riemsdijk, eds., *Features and Projections*. Dordrecht: Foris.

Hoop de, Helen. 1992. Case Configuration and Noun Phrase Interpretation. *Groningen Dissertations in Linguistics*.

Hoop de, Helen. 1997. Optional scrambling and predication. Paper presented at the Texas Linguistics Society conference "The Syntax and Semantics of Predication", Austin, March 13-15.

Horvath, Julia. 1986. *FOCUS in the Theory of Grammar and the Syntax of Hungarian*. Dordrecht: Foris.

Ioup, Georgette. 1977. Specificity and the interpretation of quantifiers. *Linguistics and Philosophy* 1:233-245.

Jackendoff, Ray. 1972. *Semantic Interpretation in Generative Grammar*. Cambridge, Mass.: MIT Press.

Koster, Jan and Robert May. 1982. On the Constituency of Infinitives. *Language* 58:116-143.

Laca, Brenda. 1990. Generic objects: some more pieces of the puzzle.*Lingua* 81:25-46.

Longobardi, Giuseppe. 1994. Reference and proper names: a theory of N-movement in syntax and logical form. *Linguistics and Philosophy* 25: 609-669.

Partee, Barbara. 1987. Noun Phrase Interpretation and Type-Shifting Principles. In J. Groenendijk, D. de Jongh and M. Stockhof, eds., *Studies in Discourse Representation Theory and the Theory of Generalized Quantifiers*. Dordrecht: Foris.

Rizzi, Luigi. 1991. Residual Verb Second and the Wh-criterion. *Technical Reports in Formal and Computational Linguistics* 2, University of Geneva.

Rochemont, Michael. 1986. *Focus in Generative Grammar*. Amsterdam: John Benjamins.

Sportiche, Dominique. 1992. *Clitic Constructions*. Manuscript, UCLA.

Vergnaud, Jean-Roger and Maria Luisa Zubizarreta. 1992. The Definite Determiner and the Inalianable Construction in French and English. *Linguistic Inquiry* 23:595-652.

Zimmerman, Ede. 1993. On the proper treatment of opacity in certain verbs. *Natural Language Semantics* 1:149-179.

Object Drop and Discourse Accessibility[*]

FRANK KELLER & MARIA LAPATA

University of Edinburgh

1. Introduction

Object drop constructions are attested in several languages despite the absence of overt verb-object agreement (Cole 1987; Huang 1995). It has been claimed that languages vary crosslinguistically in the conditions licensing object drop: European and Brazilian Portuguese (Farrell 1990; Raposo 1986) and Quiteño Spanish (Suñer and Yépez 1988) license null objects only for definite NPs (cf. (1), (2)), whereas European Spanish (Campos 1986), Modern Greek (Dimitriadis 1994a,b; Giannakidou and Merchant 1997) and Bulgarian (Dimitriadis 1994a) license object drop only for indefinite NPs (cf. (3), (4)).

(1)   Quem é   que viu   **o filme**? O Manel viu   Ø.
        who   was-3sg that saw-3sg the film   the Manel saw-3sg Ø
        'Who saw the film? Manel saw it.'   (Raposo 1986: 377)

(2)   Cuándo quieres que te   mande **las tarjetas**? Puedes mandarme Ø
        when   want-2sg that you send-1sg the cards   can-2sg send me   Ø
        mañana?
        tomorrow?
        'When do you want me to send you the cards? Can you send them
        to me tomorrow?'   (Suñer and Yépez 1988: 513)

[*]Both authors have contributed equally, the names appear in alphabetical order.

    The following people have provided comments on earlier versions of this paper: Theodora Alexopolou, Ash Asudeh, Possidonia Gontijo, Vasilios Karaiskos, Jonas Kuhn, Alex Lascarides, Line Mikkelsen, Renata Vieira. These comments, as well as the support of ESRC Postgraduate Research Studentships to both authors, are gratefully acknowledged.

(3)   Compraste **café**? Si compré   Ø.
        bought-2sg coffee yes bought-1sg Ø
        'Did you buy coffee? Yes, I bought some.'   (Campos 1986: 354)

(4)   Nosiš   li **palto**? Nosja   Ø.
        wear-2sg Q coat   wear-1sg Ø
        'Do you wear a coat? I wear one.'   (Dimitriadis 1994a: 159)

Using evidence from Modern Greek (MG), we argue against the view that object drop can be explained in terms of definiteness. Instead, we claim that the anaphoric status of the object determines whether it can be dropped or not. We conjecture that the discourse accessibility of the antecedent NP licenses null objects and show that object drop in MG is sensitive to the distinction between object and kind anaphora (McGivern 1995, 1997). On the basis of this distinction, we explain under which conditions object drop is triggered in MG. We provide a formalisation of this analysis within the framework of Discourse Representation Theory (DRT, Kamp and Reyle 1993) using DRT's notion of discourse accessibility and anaphoric linking.

2. Object Drop and Definiteness

2.1. The Empty Clitic Account
Dimitriadis (1994a,b) uses examples like the ones in (5) to motivate the claim that indefinite object pronouns in MG can be dropped, while definite ones have to be overt. Dimitriadis (1994a,b) does not attempt to give a definition of definiteness and it seems that he uses a syntactic rather than a semantic definition which reduces definiteness to the presence or absence of a definite article. Note that Dimitriadis (1994a,b) exemplifies object drop in MG using question/answer pairs only (cf. (5)). We use declarative discourses instead, so as to factor out possible focus effects that might arise in question/answer contexts.

(5)   a.   Vrike   o Kostas **kerasia**? *Ta/Ø vrike.
             found-3sg the Kostas cherries   CL/Ø found-3sg
             'Did Kostas find cherries? He found some.'

        b.   Eferes   **to vivlio**? To/*Ø efera.
             brought-2sg the book   CL/Ø brought-1sg
             'Did you bring the book? I brought it.'   (Dimitriadis 1994b)

Dimitriadis (1994a,b) claims that the null object is a "special" object pronoun, i.e., an empty, clitic-like indefinite pronoun, and predicts that clitics and null objects are in complementary distribution. Dimitriadis (1994b), however, does not explain why in a sentence like (6a) the indefinite NP *enan antra* 'a man', similar to the definite NP *ton antra* 'the man' in (6b), does not license object drop. The discourse in (6a) is felicitous only if an overt clitic is present as the object of the verb *filisa* 'kissed'. Another set of counterexamples concerns sentences with generic/habitual readings. In (7a) the definite

NP *ta kerasia* 'the cherries', similar to the indefinite NP *kerasia* 'cherries' in (7b), licenses object drop; the object of the verb *agorasa* 'bought' cannot be cliticized but has to be dropped.

(6)   a.   Gnorisa **enan antra**. Ton/*Ø filisa.
              met-1sg a   man   CL/Ø   kissed-1sg
              'I met a man. I kissed him.'

        b.   Ida   **ton antra**. Ton/*Ø filisa.
              saw-1sg the man   CL/Ø   kissed-1sg
              'I saw the man. I kissed him.'

(7)   a.   **Ta kerasia** ine   igiina. Htes   *Ta/Ø agorasa.
              the cherries be-3sg healthy yesterday CL/Ø bought-1sg
              'Cherries are healthy. Yesterday I bought some.'

        b.   Troo   **kerasia** sihna. Htes   *Ta/Ø agorasa.
              eat-1sg cherries often   yesterday CL/Ø bought-1sg
              'I eat cherries often. Yesterday I bought some.'

Furthermore, Dimitriadis (1994a,b) does not consider examples like (8) and (9) where both the clitic and the null object are admissible, depending on the interpretation of the antecedent NP: in (8a) the clitic refers to the set of cherries which were bought and which the speaker wanted to eat, whereas in (8b) the dropped object refers to cherries as a kind. In (9a) the clitic refers to the set of ten cherries which the speaker eats and buys every day, whereas in (9b) the null object refers to cherries as a kind.

(8)   a.   Agorase   **kerasia**. Ithela   na   ta fao.
              bought-3sg cherries   wanted-1sg SUBJ CL eat-1sg
              'He/she bought cherries. I wanted to eat them.'

        b.   Agorase   **kerasia**. Ithela   na   Ø fao.
              bought-3sg cherries   wanted-1sg SUBJ Ø eat-1sg
              'He/she bought cherries. I wanted to eat some.'

(9)   a.   Troo   **deka kerasia** tin imera. Ta agorazo kathe proi.
              eat-1sg ten   cherries the day   CL buy-1sg every morning
              'I eat ten cherries a day. I buy them every morning.'

        b.   Troo   **deka kerasia** tin imera. Ø agorazo kathe proi.
              eat-1sg ten   cherries the day   Ø buy-1sg every morning
              'I eat ten cherries a day. I buy some every morning.'

2.2. The LF-Copying Account

Giannakidou and Merchant (1997) argue that null objects in MG are indefinite pronouns semantically licensed by weak antecedent NPs (in the sense of Milsark 1979). They suggest that null objects are interpreted via an LF copying mechanism: the dropped object is a copy of an antecedent weak NP and therefore disjoint from it.

Giannakidou and Merchant (1997) treat object drop as an instance of NP-ellipsis. In order to explain why strong NPs cannot be ellided, they assume, following Lobeck (1995), that only XPs identified by strong functional heads can be ellided (i.e., IP, VP, NP). They conjecture that strong determiners occur outside the NP projection and consequently are strong NPs unavailable for copying and thus for licensing object drop.

This account fails to explain why the weak NP *enan antra* 'a man' in (6a) does not license object drop but an overt clitic instead. Giannakidou and Merchant (1997) cannot account for the generic sentences in (7) either. They would, wrongly, predict that the strong NP *ta kerasia* 'cherries' in (7a) has to license an overt clitic. The examples in (9) are also problematic for their account: the weak NP *deka kerasia* 'ten cherries' can license either a clitic (cf. (9a)) or a null object (cf. (9b)), contrary to the assumption that weak NPs license only null objects.[1]

There are also a number of conceptual problems with reducing object drop to NP ellipsis. One would expect the phenomenon to apply to all types of NPs. However, as the authors observe themselves, NP-ellipsis seems to hold only for one type of NPs, i.e., weak NPs. On syntactic grounds the authors do not give any motivation as to why strong determiners occur outside the NP projection. Furthermore, under the assumption that strong NPs cannot be ellided, one cannot explain why VPs containing strong NPs as objects undergo VP ellipsis. We would expect the behaviour of strong NPs to be uniform across all types of ellipsis. Finally, if we claim that object drop is in fact NP ellipsis, we would expect the antecedent weak NP in examples like (8) and (9) to license the null objects only (cf. (8b), (9b)) and could not predict the occurrence of an overt clitic (cf. (8a), (9a)). The fact that object drop in these examples alternates with clitics depending on the interpretation of the antecedent NP is evidence against an ellipsis account.

3. Anaphoric Linking, Accessibility, and Kind Anaphora

3.1. Accessibility Constraints

Discourse Representation Theory puts forward an account of anaphora resolution based on anaphoric linking. An anaphor is anaphorically linked to its antecedent by equating the referent of the anaphor and the referent of the antecedent. As a consequence, the two referents have to be interpreted as coreferential. Anaphoric linking is only possible if the antecedent is accessible from the anaphor, where accessibility is defined as in (10):

---

[1] Giannakidou and Merchant (1997) assume that in the default case the dropped object is referentially disjoint from its antecedent. This means that the dropped object in (9b), being a copy of its antecedent NP *deka kerasia* 'ten cherries', introduces a new set of ten cherries. However, we were not able to reproduce this judgement with our informants.

(10)   **Accessibility**
Let K be a DRS, **x** a discourse referent and γ a DRS-condition.
We say that **x** is *accessible from* γ *in* K iff there are $K_1 \leq K$ and
$K_2 \leq K_1$ such that **x** belongs to U_{K_1} and γ belongs to Con_{K_2}.

(Kamp and Reyle 1993: 120)

Here, U_K denotes the set of discourse referents in the discourse representation
structure (DRS) K, Con_K denotes the set of DRS-conditions in K, and $\leq$ is
the subordination (intuitively, nesting) relation on DRSs.

The crucial observation for our account is that object drop correlates
with anaphoric linking: in (5b), (6), (8a), and (9a), the object clitic is anaphorically linked to (and thus co-referential with) the antecedent NP. In (5a), (7),
(8b), and (9b), however, no anaphoric link (co-referentiality) is established.
Note that in (5a), the antecedent NP is part of a question, while in (7), it receives a generic/kind interpretation. In both cases, the antecedent NP is not
accessible from the anaphor, and object drop is obligatory.

The properties of cliticized and dropped objects can be summarized
as follows:

(11)

dropped object (5a), (7), (8b), (9b)	**overt object clitic** (5b), (6), (8a), (9a)
not co-referential with an- tecedent NP	co-referential with antecedent NP
not anaphorically linked to an- tecedent NP	linked to antecedent NP (stan- dard anaphor)
antecedent inaccessible (ge- neric/kind reading)	antecedent accessible (object reading)

This observation about the relation between accessibility (manifested as
anaphoric linking) and object drop can be formulated in the form of the following generalization:[2]

(12)   **Constraint on Object Drop**
An object pronoun has to be overt if it is anaphorically linked to its
antecedent, otherwise it can be dropped.

Note that the antecedent NP can be familiar (and thus definite, as in (5b)
and (6b)) or new (and thus indefinite, as in (6a)). If we adopt a familiarity-
based approach to definites (e.g., based on Heim 1983), then familiarity and
accessibility are orthogonal, and object drop is only sensitive to the latter.

Crosslinguistically, the constraint in (12) predicts that languages
classified as allowing indefinite object drop in the literature (European Span-

---

[2]Here and in the following, we refer to the dropped element as a pronoun. This is
merely for terminological convenience, and should not be taken to make any theoretical claims (e.g., that the dropped element is a *pro* in the sense of Government and
Binding Theory).

ish and Bulgarian) should pattern with MG. For languages classified as allowing definite object drop (Quiteño Spanish, European and Brazilian Portuguese), we expect the inverse of the constraint in (12), i.e., an object pronoun has to be overt if it is not anaphorically linked to its antecedent, otherwise it can be dropped. This predication is born out with respect to Brazilian Portuguese, as we will show in section 4.

3.2. Object Drop and Kind Anaphora

In the last section, we argued that overt object pronouns (clitics) have an accessible antecedent, while dropped objects do not. Intuitively, however, dropped objects also establish some kind of anaphoric relationship to an antecedent NP. This relationship is weaker than the co-referential relationship that holds between an overt clitic and its antecedent: the dropped object seems to refer only to the kind denoted by the antecedent NP. For instance, the dropped object in (5a), (7), (8b), and (9b) is assigned a partitive reading, i.e., it denotes an instance of the substance or the kind referred to by its antecedent NP. This instance can be either a group or an individual (represented by a group referent **X** or an individual referent **x** in DRT). Note that in English, the corresponding kind-denoting anaphor has to be realized overtly, viz., as *some* or *one*.

Going a step further, we can hypothesize that a dropped object *does* actually have an accessible antecedent, viz., the kind introduced by its antecedent. This can be implemented by introducing referents for kinds, which are independently motivated for the analysis of generics in DRT, as argued for by McGivern (1995, 1997). McGivern assumes that certain NPs (e.g., bare plurals) introduce kind referents (denoted as $\mathcal{X}$ in DRT), which are anchored in the topmost DRS, and thus are universally accessible. This is motivated by examples like (13), where the kind introduced by *spiders* can be referred to anaphorically.

(13)   a.   I killed spiders last night. They are ugly creatures.

         b.   Spiders are ugly creatures. They have invaded my bathroom.

                                               (McGivern 1997)

Our approach to object drop relies on the fact that a kind referent (k-referent) is universally accessible, while an object referent (o-referent) can be embedded in a subordinate DRS, which might make it inaccessible.

     To illustrate this consider (14), the DRS for the first sentence of (6a):

(14)
$$\begin{array}{|l|}
\hline
\text{i x} \\
\hline
\text{man(x)} \\
\text{met(i,x)} \\
\hline
\end{array}$$

Here, the referent **x** introduced by *enan antra* 'a man' is accessible, as it is not embedded in a sub-DRS introduced by negation, quantificational structures, or intensional contexts. The anaphor *ton* 'him' in the second sentence of (6a) then introduces an o-referent **y**, which can be anaphorically liked to **x**, resulting in the following DRS:

(15)

> i x y
>
> man(x)
> met(i,x)
> kissed(i,y)
> y = x

Now consider (16), the DRS for the first sentence of (7a). Here, the antecedent NP *ta kerasia* 'the cherries' receives a generic interpretation, which is represented in DRT (following McGivern 1995, 1997) as a quantificational structure: there is a kind $\mathcal{X}$ called cherries and for every instance **x** of this kind, it is typically the case that **x** is healthy. Note that the k-referent $\mathcal{X}$ is introduced in the topmost DRS, while the o-referent **x** is located in the restrictor of the quantificational structure.

(16)

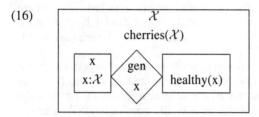

The next sentence of (7a) introduces an empty object pronoun, whose representation we assume to be (17). To paraphrase, an empty object pronoun introduces a new o-referent η and a new k-referent $\mathcal{Y}$, along with the condition that η is an instance of $\mathcal{Y}$, and that $\mathcal{Y}$ has to be resolved to an existing k-referent.

> Note that the o-referent can be either an individual referent or a group referent (as is the case in (18)). This is implemented in (17) by the use of an underspecified o-referent η (Kamp and Reyle 1993: 335), which can be disambiguated into either an individual referent or a group referent.

(17)

> $\eta\ \mathcal{Y}$
>
> $\eta{:}\mathcal{Y}$
> $\mathcal{Y} = ?$

Now consider (18), the DRS for (7a) after anaphora resolution:

(18)

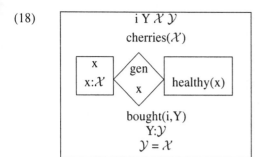

$$\begin{array}{|c|}
\hline
i\ Y\ \mathcal{X}\ \mathcal{Y} \\
\text{cherries}(\mathcal{X}) \\[2pt]
\boxed{x \mid x{:}\mathcal{X}} \;\diamondsuit\!\!\!\!\begin{array}{c}\text{gen}\\ x\end{array}\!\!\!\!\diamondsuit\; \boxed{\text{healthy}(x)} \\[2pt]
\text{bought}(i,Y) \\
Y{:}\mathcal{Y} \\
\mathcal{Y} = \mathcal{X} \\
\hline
\end{array}$$

The empty object introduces the referent **Y**, which is the argument of *agorasa* 'bought', and the anaphoric referent $\mathcal{Y}$, which can be resolved to $\mathcal{X}$, the k-referent introduced by *ta kerasia* 'the cherries'. (Note that **x** is not accessible for $\mathcal{Y}$, and therefore does not play a role in resolving $\mathcal{Y}$.)

To summarize, our claim is that object drop in MG is sensitive to the distinction between object and kind anaphora. This leads to the following reformulation of the generalization in (12):

(19)   **Constraint on Object Drop**
An object pronoun has to be overt if it introduces an o-anaphor, it can be dropped if it introduces a k-anaphor.

3.3. Predictions

The generalization in (19) makes a number of predictions about when object drop can occur. In particular, it predicts that there are cases where either the overt or the dropped pronoun should be licensed, as some contexts provide both an o-antecedent and a k-antecedent. We illustrate this with respect to negation and intensional verbs.

Negation creates a subordinate DRS that contains the DRS-conditions introduced by the negated phrase. All referents inside this subordinate DRS are inaccessible from superordinate DRSs. As an example, consider the DRS in (21) that represents the discourse in (20). The o-referent **X** introduced by *kerasia* 'cherries' is embedded in a sub-DRS, and thus inaccessible from the top DRS. However, *kerasia* 'cherries' also introduces a k-referent $\mathcal{X}$ (referring to cherries in general), which is located in the topmost DRS. Hence $\mathcal{X}$ is accessible to the k-referent $\mathcal{Y}$ introduced by the empty pronoun. This explains why a clitic is disallowed in (20), while object drop is possible.

(20)   Den agorase **kerasia**, ala ithela   na   *ta/Ø fao.
       Not bought-3sg cherries but wanted-1sg SUBJ CL/Ø eat-1sg
       'He/she didn't buy cherries but I wanted to eat some.'

(21)

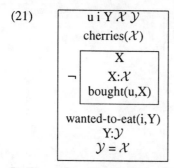

In (8), on the other hand, the first sentence of the discourse is unnegated, and therefore both the o-referent and the k-referent introduced by *kerasia* 'cherries' are accessible. This results in an ambiguity: either a dropped object or an overt object clitic is possible in the next sentence, referring to cherries as a kind, or to the cherries that were bought, respectively. As an illustration, consider (22). In (22a), the DRS corresponding to (8a), the object clitic introduces an o-referent **Y** which can be anaphorically linked to **X**, the o-referent already established for the cherries. This is possible because **X** is not embedded under negation and hence is accessible from **Y**. In (22b) then, the DRS corresponding to (8b), the dropped object pronoun is resolved exactly like in (21), i.e., by anaphorically linking it to the k-referent $\mathcal{X}$.

(22)　　a.

$$\boxed{\begin{array}{c} \text{u i X Y } \mathcal{X} \\[4pt] \text{cherries}(\mathcal{X}) \\ X{:}\mathcal{X} \\ \text{bought}(u,X) \\ \text{wanted-to-eat}(i,Y) \\ Y = X \end{array}}$$

　　　　b.

$$\boxed{\begin{array}{c} \text{u i X Y } \mathcal{X}\,\mathcal{Y} \\[4pt] \text{cherries}(\mathcal{X}) \\ X{:}\mathcal{X} \\ \text{bought}(u,X) \\ \text{wanted-to-eat}(i,Y) \\ Y{:}\mathcal{Y} \\ \mathcal{Y} = \mathcal{X} \end{array}}$$

Another interesting case is intensional verbs. Consider (23a), which contains the extensional verb *hano* 'lose', the argument of which introduces an o-referent, which can be picked up by a clitic in the next sentence. No k-referent is available, therefore no object drop is possible.

In (23b), on the other hand, *psahno* 'look for' is ambiguous between an extensional and an intensional reading. The intensional reading provides a k-referent (referring to the kind looked for), but makes the o-referent introduced by *ena isitirio* 'a ticket' inaccessible, as it is embedded in a sub-DRS representing the propositional attitude (Kamp 1990). The extensional reading of *psahno* 'look for' provides an accessible o-referent, just like in (23a). Therefore, we predict an ambiguity between the object clitic and object drop, which is born out.

(23)   a.   Ehasa **ena isitiro** gia to theatro. Telika to/*∅ vrika.
            lost-1sg a   ticket for the theater finally CL/∅ found-1sg
            'I lost a ticket for the theatre. Finally, I found it.'

       b.   Epsahna   **ena isitiro** gia to theatro. Telika to/∅ vrika.
            looking-for-1sg a   ticket for the theater finally CL/∅ found-1sg
            'I was looking for a ticket for the theatre. Finally, I found it/one.'

Other interesting cases are the discourses in (24), which at first glance seem to be counterexamples to our account:

(24)   a.   **Ta kerasia** ine   igiina, ala ta/*∅ miso.
            the cherries be-3pl healthy, but CL/∅ hate-1sg
            'Cherries are healthy, but I hate them.'

       b.   Troo   **kerasia** sihna, ala ta/*∅ miso.
            eat-1sg cherries often, but CL/∅ hate-1sg
            'I eat cherries often, but I hate them.'

The NP *ta kerasia* 'the cherries' in the first sentence of (24) is generic, but nevertheless, an overt clitic can be used to refer to it. Note however, that the sentences in (24) are analogous to the discourse in (13a) in that the clitic acts as a kind anaphor, i.e., it refers to the kind introduced by the antecedent. A dropped object, in contrast, receives a partitive reading, i.e., it refers to an instance of the kind denoted by its antecedent NP, not the kind proper. This point can be illustrated by comparing the lexical entry for a dropped object in (17) with the lexical entry for a clitic in (25a): the clitic only introduces a k-referent and a co-referentiality condition; it does not introduce an extra o-referent that is an instance of the k-referent. (Note that the lexical entry for a kind-denoting clitic in (25a) is exactly parallel to the one for an object-denoting clitic in (25b); no additional assumptions are required.)

(25)   a. $\boxed{\begin{array}{l} y \\ y = ? \end{array}}$

       b. $\boxed{\begin{array}{l} \eta \\ \eta = ? \end{array}}$

4. Crosslinguistics

The account outlined in the previous sections predicts that languages exhibiting object drop are parametrized in that they license object drop only for k-anaphora or only for o-anaphora. More specifically, in Bulgarian and European Spanish, similar to MG, the dropped object is a k-anaphor, whereas in European and Brazilian Portuguese and Quiteño Spanish the dropped object is an o-anaphor. In the latter case one would expect the inverse of the constraint on object drop in (19): an object pronoun has to be overt if it introduces a k-anaphor, it can be dropped if it introduces an o-anaphor.

The prediction seems to be born out in the Brazilian Portuguese (BP) examples given in (26)–(29). In (26) the empty object co-refers with the o-referent introduced by the NPs *um homem* 'a man' and *o homem* 'the man' and object drop is licensed. In (27) the object of the verb *comprei* 'bought' cannot be dropped but has to be overtly realized. As the empty object is an o-anaphor, it cannot co-refer with the k-referent introduced by the NP *cerejas* 'cherries' and object drop is not licensed.

(26) a. Encontrei **um homem** e beijei Ø.
          met-1sg a man and kissed-1sg Ø
          'I met a man and I kissed him.'

      b. Vi **o homem** e beijei Ø.
          saw-1sg the man and kissed-1sg Ø
          'I saw the man and I kissed him.'

(27) a. **Cerejas** são saudàveis e ontem comprei algumas/*Ø.
          cherries be-3sg healthy and yesterday bought-1sg some/Ø
          'Cherries are healthy and yesterday I bought some.'

      b. Como **cerejas** frequentemente e ontem comprei
          eat-1sg cherries often and yesterday bought-1sg
          algumas/*Ø.
          some/Ø
          'I eat cherries often and yesterday I bought some.'

In (28a) the NP *cerejas* 'cherries' introduces an o-referent which is embedded under negation and hence inaccessible, and a k-referent which is globally accessible. Object drop is not licensed, since an empty object cannot co-refer with a k-referent in BP. Instead, reference to cherries as a kind has to be lexically realized via the pronoun *algumas* 'some'. Note that in (28b) both the o-referent and the k-referent introduced by *cerejas* 'cherries' are accessible and both the overt pronoun and the dropped object are possible.

(28) a. Não comprou **cerejas** mas queria comer algumas/*Ø.
          not bought-3sg cherries but wanted-1sg eat some/Ø
          'He didn't buy cherries but I wanted to eat some.'

      b. Comprou **as cerejas** por que queria comer algumas/Ø.
          bought-3sg the cherries because wanted-1sg eat some/Ø
          'He bought cherries because I wanted to eat some/them.'

Finally, in (29a) the object of the extensional verb *perdere* 'lose' introduces an o-referent and object drop is possible. On the other hand the verb *procurar* 'look for' in (29b) can be ambiguous between an extensional and intensional reading introducing an o-referent in the first case and a k-referent in the latter. Similar to MG, this ambiguity is born out in BP. Note, however, that BP is different from MG in that the overt pronoun *um* 'one' co-refers with the k-referent introduced in the antecedent sentence, whereas the empty object is co-refers with the o-referent.

(29) a. Perdi **um ingresso** para o teatro e finalmente encontrei Ø.
          lost-1sg a ticket for the theatre and finally found-1sg Ø
          'I lost a ticket for the theatre and finally I found it.'

      b. Estava procurando **um ingresso** para o teatro e finalmente,
          was-1sg look-for-1sg a ticket for the theater and finally
          encontrei um/Ø.
          found-1sg one/Ø
          'I was looking for a ticket for the theatre and finally I found one/it.'

5. Conclusions

In this paper, we argued against an account of object drop based on definiteness (as put forward by Dimitriadis 1994a,b) or in terms of LF copying (as proposed by Giannakidou and Merchant 1997). Using Modern Greek as a test case, we demonstrated that object drop cannot be reduced to purely syntactic factors, but depends on discourse conditions such as the accessibility of an antecedent for the dropped object.

More specifically, we demonstrated that object drop in Modern Greek is sensitive to the distinction between object and kind anaphora, a dichotomy that is independently motivated for the analysis of generics as proposed by McGivern (1995, 1997). We arrived at the generalization that an object pronoun has to be overt if it introduces an object-anaphor, while it can be dropped if it introduces a kind-anaphor. This generalization correctly predicts the behavior of object drop with respect to negation and intensional contexts, and can be formalized in DRT without requiring the introduction of additional formal machinery.

Concerning the crosslinguistics of object drop, we predicted that there should be languages that are the inverse of Modern Greek in that they require an object pronoun to be overt if it introduces a kind-anaphor, and allow it to be dropped if it introduces an object-anaphor. We demonstrated that this predication is born out for Brazilian Portuguese, which is the mirror image of Modern Greek in this sense.

References

Campos, Héctor. 1986. Indefinite Object Drop. *Linguistic Inquiry* 17.354–359.
Cole, Peter. 1987. Null Objects in Universal Grammar. *Linguistic Inquiry* 18.597–612.
Dimitriadis, Alexis. 1994a. Clitics and Island-Insensitive Object Drop. In James H. Yoon, ed., *Proceedings of the 5th Annual Conference of the Formal Linguistics*

Society of Mid-America, Studies in the Linguistic Sciences 24.1/2, 153–170. Department of Linguistics, University of Illinois, Urbana-Champaign.

Dimitriadis, Alexis. 1994b. Clitics and Object Drop in Modern Greek. In Chris Giordano and Daniel Ardron, eds., *Papers from the 6th Student Conference in Linguistics*, MIT Working Papers in Linguistics 23. Department of Linguistics, Massachusetts Institute of Technology, Cambridge, MA.

Farrell, Patrick. 1990. Null Objects in Brazilian Portuguese. *Natural Language and Linguistic Theory* 8.325–346.

Giannakidou, Anastasia and Jason Merchant. 1997. On the Interpretation of Null Indefinite Objects in Greek. In G. Veloudis and M. Karali, eds., *Studies in Greek Linguistics* 17, 290–303. Aristotle University, Thessaloniki.

Heim, Irene. 1983. File Change Semantics and the Familiarity Theory of Definiteness. In Rainer Bäuerle, Christoph Schwarze and Arnim von Stechow, eds., *Meaning, Use, and Interpretation of Language*, 164–189. Berlin: de Gruyter.

Huang, Yan. 1995. On Null Subjects and Null Objects in Generative Grammar. *Linguistics* 33.1081–1123.

Kamp, Hans. 1990. Prolegomena to a Structural Theory of Belief and Other Attitudes. In C. Anthony Anderson and Joseph Owens, eds., *Propositional Attitudes: The Role of Content in Logic, Language, and Mind*, CSLI Lecture Notes 20, 27–90. Stanford, CA: CSLI Publications.

Kamp, Hans and Uwe Reyle. 1993. *From Discourse to Logic: Introduction to Modeltheoretic Semantics of Natural Language, Formal Logic and Discourse Representation Theory*. Dordrecht: Kluwer.

Lobeck, Anne. 1995. *On Ellipsis*. Oxford: Oxford University Press.

McGivern, Patrick. 1995. *Representing Generics in DRT*. Master's thesis, Centre for Cognitive Science, University of Edinburgh.

McGivern, Patrick. 1997. Representing Generic Bare Plurals in DRT. In Harry Bunt, Leen Kievit, Reinhard Muskens and Margriet Verlinden, eds., *Proceedings of the 2nd International Workshop on Computational Semantics*. Tilburg.

Milsark, Gary L. 1979. *Existential Sentences in English*. New York: Garland.

Raposo, Eduardo. 1986. On the Null Object in European Portuguese. In Osvaldo Jaeggli and Carmen Silva-Corvalán, eds., *Studies in Romance Linguistics*, 373–390. Dordrecht: Foris.

Suñer, Margarita and Maria Yépez. 1988. Null Definite Objects in Quiteño. *Linguistic Inquiry* 19.511–519.

Local Dependencies in Comparative Deletion

CHRISTOPHER KENNEDY

Northwestern University

1. Comparative Deletion

The focus of this paper is the derivation and interpretation of comparative deletion (CD) in English. Comparative deletion constructions include comparatives in which the comparative clause (the complement of *than* or *as*, henceforth the 'c-clause') contains some clausal material, but is "missing" an adjectival, adverbial or nominal constituent, as illustrated by (1)-(3), (4)-(5), and (6)-(7), respectively (see Bresnan (1975) for general discussion of this phenomenon).

(1)   Jupiter is more massive than Saturn is __.
(2)   A neutron star is less dense than a black hole is __.
(3)   The mission wasn't as successful as we expected it to be __.
(4)   Light travels more quickly than sound travels __.
(5)   Jones drives as carelessly as Smith flies __.
(6)   Jones saw more stars than Smith saw __.
(7)   Uranus has fewer rings than Saturn has __.

Comparative deletion constructions contrast with examples of comparative subdeletion, like (8)-(10), in which only a degree word is "missing" (see Bresnan (1975), Grimshaw (1987), Corver (1993), Izvorski (1995)).

(8)   The space telescope is longer than it is (*that/very/2 meters) wide.
(9)   Jones drives as carelessly as Smith drives (*so/quite/too) carefully.
(10)   Jones saw more stars than Smith saw (*two/many/few) planets.

The traditional analysis of CD derives examples like (1)-(7) from underlying representations that are structurally parallel to the corresponding subdeletion constructions in (8)-(10) (Lees (1961), Chomsky (1965, 1977), Bresnan (1973, 1975), Napoli (1983), von Stechow (1984), Heim (1985), McCawley (1988), Moltmann (1992a), Izvorski (1995), Hazout (1995)). For example, adjectival CD constructions like (1)-(3) are assigned underlying representations along the lines of (11)-(13), where the boldfaced material is left unpronounced in the surface forms in accord with principles of ellipsis.

(11)   Jupiter is more massive than Saturn is **massive**.
(12)   A neutron star is less dense than a black hole is **dense**.
(13)   The mission wasn't as successful as we expected it to be **successful**

This analysis has two very compelling aspects. First, nothing special needs to be said about CD; instead, it can be viewed as an instance of a more general ellipsis operation in English that targets adjectival (and other) predicates, as in (14) (see Napoli (1983)).

(14)   Jupiter is massive, and Saturn is __ too.

Second, this analysis supports a very straightforward mapping between structure and interpretation, given a few apparently well-motivated assumptions. The first, which captures the dependency between comparative morpheme and c-clause marker (*more/less ... than* vs. *as ... as*), is that the comparative morpheme and the c-clause are a constituent at the level of interpretation (see e.g. Chomsky (1965), Bresnan (1973), Jackendoff (1977), McCawley (1988)). The second, based on facts like (15)-(17), which show that the c-clause is sensitive to syntactic islands (enclosed in brackets), is that the c-clause is a type of *wh*-construction in which a null operator binds a position inside the elided adjectival constituent (Chomsky (1977); see Bresnan (1975) for an alternative analysis, however).

(15)   a.   Mercury is closer to the sun than I thought it was.
        b.   *Mercury is closer to the sun than I knew [who said it was].
(16)   a.   Hale-Bopp was brighter than Karl claimed it would be.
        b.   *Hale-Bopp was brighter than [Karl's claim that it would be].
(17)   a.   The solar flares were more energetic than the sunspots were.
        b.   *The solar flares were more energetic than we were amazed [when the sunspots were].

Given these two assumptions, the derivation and interpretation of

CD can be characterized as follows. The constituent headed by the comparative morpheme raises out of AP at LF, leaving behind a constituent of the appropriate syntactic type to supply the value of the elided material in the c-clause. In particular, this constituent contains an empty category that can be bound by the null operator in the c-clause, as shown by (18), the LF of (1) on this analysis.[1]

(18)   [more than [Op$_x$ Saturn is [$_{AP}$ e$_x$ massive]]]$_x$ [Jupiter is [$_{AP}$ e$_x$ massive]]

This syntactic representation can be mapped onto an interpretation in which the comparative introduces quantification over degrees (either existential quantification, as in e.g. Hellan (1981), Heim (1985), Lerner and Pinkal (1995), and Gawron (1995), or universal quantification, as in Cresswell (1976), Moltmann (1992a), and Hendriks (1995)), and gradable adjectives like *massive, energetic,* and *bright* denote relations between objects and degrees (Seuren (1973), Cresswell (1976), von Stechow (1984), etc.). For example, in Heim's (1985) analysis, the LF in (18) is assigned the interpretation in (19), whose truth conditions can be paraphrased as follows: for some degree d such that d exceeds the degree to which Saturn is massive, Jupiter's mass equals d.

(19) $\exists d[d > \iota d'.massive(Saturn, d')][massive(Jupiter,d)]$

In its core respects, this analysis of CD is the same as the standard analysis of antecedent-contained VP-deletion constructions like (20), which has the LF in (21) and the interpretation in (22) (see Sag (1976), Larson and May (1990), Fiengo and May (1994), Kennedy (1997b)).

(20)   Jones saw every meteorite Smith did.
(21)   [every Op$_x$ meteorite Smith did [$_{VP}$ saw e$_x$]]$_x$ [Jones [$_{VP}$ saw e$_x$]]
(22) $\forall x[meteorite(x)$ & $saw(Smith,x)][saw(Jones,x)]$

The goal of this paper is to show that this analysis of CD, compelling as it appears to be, is fundamentally incorrect. In particular, the missing constituent in CD cannot be analyzed as the target of an ellipsis operation. Two arguments will be presented in favor of this claim, the first empirical, the second more theory-internal. Focusing on examples

---

[1]I will assume here that elided material in comparatives is recovered by a copying operation at LF, though this is not crucial. See Kennedy and Merchant (1997) for arguments that this must be the case, however.

involving adjectival predicates, such as (1)-(3), I will start out by showing that the interpretation of the missing material in CD shows a local dependency not observed in true ellipsis constructions; specifically, the missing material in the c-clause must receive its interpretation from the adjective that heads the comparative predicate. I will then show that a syntactic analysis of the adjectival projection in which the adjective projects extended functional structure headed by degree morphology – an analysis which is independently supported by a range of empirical and theoretical considerations (see Abney (1987), Corver (1990, 1997), Grimshaw (1991)) – is incompatible with an ellipsis analysis of CD. I will conclude by presenting an alternative analysis of CD in which the missing constituent is the target of a movement operation, rather than ellipsis. Specifically, I will claim that the null operator in the c-clause directly binds an empty category corresponding to the predicate rather than a (degree) position inside AP, as in the standard analysis outlined above. I will demonstrate that this alternative analysis is both compatible with the syntax of extended projection, and, when coupled with the right semantic analysis, derives the local dependencies in comparative deletion.

2. Two Problems for an Ellipsis Analysis

2.1 Local Dependencies in Comparative Deletion
A well-known characteristic of ellipsis is that the antecedent of an elided expression must be found in some local segment of discourse, but it need not immediately precede the ellipsis site. This characteristic is illustrated by the second sentence in (23), which can have either the interpretation in (24a) or the one in (24b), depending on which VP in the first sentence is taken to be the antecedent for the elided VP in the second.

(23) Smith said she would launch the rocket before she ate her lunch. I don't know if she has yet.

(24) a. I don't know if she has **launched the rocket** yet.
      b. I don't know if she has **eaten her lunch** yet.

Examples of antecedent-contained VP-deletion display the same sort of interpretive variability, as shown by (25), in which the second conjunct can have either the interpretation in (26a) or the one in (26b).

(25) Smith saw every alien I did, and she met every alien Jones did.

(26) a. ... she met every alien Jones **met**.
      b. ... she met every alien Jones **saw**.

That (25) is ambiguous is unsurprising: according to the standard analysis of ACD, the LF of this sentence should be (27), in which case both VP$_1$ and VP$_2$ are potential antecedents for the elided VP in the second conjunct.

(27)   [every alien I did __][Smith [$_{VP1}$ saw e]] and [every alien Jones did __][she [$_{VP2}$ met e]]

Although readings in which the closer, "local" VP provides the antecedent seem to be preferred in neutral contexts, the "nonlocal" reading can be brought out by constructing examples in which the local reading is in some way anomalous, as in (28).

(28)   Jones didn't meet all the aliens he wanted to, but I bet he liked the ones he did.

The local interpretation of the elided VP in (28) corresponds to a tautology (*I bet he liked the ones he liked*); as a result, the nonlocal reading (*I bet he liked the ones he met*) emerges quite clearly.

If CD involves ellipsis, then it should give rise to the same ambiguity as VP-deletion in contexts that include more than one potential antecedent for the elided constituent. Surprisingly, however, this expectation is not realized. The second conjunct in (29), for example, is *not* ambiguous: the interpretation of the missing adjectival constituent must be recovered locally, as in (30a); the nonlocal interpretation paraphrased in (30b) is unavailable.

(29)   This spaceship is wider than Smith's spaceship is, but it's not longer than hers is.
(30)   a.   This spaceship is not longer than Smith's spaceship is **long**.
         b.   *This spaceship is not longer than Smith's spaceship is **wide**.

The absence of an ambiguity in (29) is completely unexpected if CD is derived in the same way as ACD. According to this analysis, the LF of (29) should be (31), which is structurally parallel to (27), and both AP$_1$ and AP$_2$ should be potential sources for the missing AP in the second conjunct.

(31)   [er than Smith's is __][this ship is [$_{AP1}$ e wide]] but [er than hers is __][it's not [$_{AP2}$ e long]]

The impossibility of the nonlocal reading in (29) cannot be blamed on contextual factors (or lack thereof). Even when we construct examples which strongly prefer a nonlocal reading (analogous to (28) above), the relevant interpretation remains unavailable:

(32)   #Now that the remodeling has been completed, the space station is longer than it used to be, and it's even wider than it is.

(33)   #The spaceship is longer than it used to be, and now it's as wide as it is, too.

The oddity of (32) and (33) is due to the fact that the local interpretations are contradictory (*the space station is even wider than it is wide*) and tautological (*the spaceship is not as wide as it is wide*), respectively. In contrast, the nonlocal interpretations, paraphrased in (34) and (35), make perfectly reasonable claims (and moreover correspond to grammatical sentences), but are nevertheless unavailable.

(34)   The space station is even wider than it is long.

(35)   The spaceship is as wide as it is long.

The descriptive generalization that emerges from these facts is that the interpretation of the "missing" adjective in CD must be recovered locally, from the adjective that heads the entire comparative construction. If CD and ACD constructions are derived in the same way, however, this local dependency is completely unexpected. This problem is independent of the analysis of ellipsis – whether it involves syntactic identity at LF (as in e.g. Hazout (1995)) or recovery of meaning (as in e.g. Gawron (1995)). Any analysis that attempts to analyze CD in terms of more general principles of ellipsis in English will fail to derive the interpretive contrast between comparative deletion and VP-deletion illustrated by these facts.

2.2   The DegP Hypothesis and Problems of Identity

Recent work on the syntax of the adjectival projection has challenged some of the traditional assumptions discussed in section 1, in particular, the hypothesis that the comparative morpheme and comparative clause form a constituent exclusive of the adjective. This work claims instead that adjectives, like nouns and verbs, project extended functional structure, which in the case of adjectives is headed by degree morphology (see Abney (1987) and Corver (1990, 1997) for extensive empirical evidence in support of this analysis; see Grimshaw (1991) for more meta-theoretical arguments). For example, the structure of a typical predicative comparative such as (36) in this analysis is (37), where the *than*-constituent is a selected adjunct.[2]

---

[2]Alternatively, the *than*-constituent could be a second complement of Deg^0, resulting in a ternary-branching structure (as in Abney (1987)). The question of which structure is the correct one is independent of the current discussion.

(36)   Jupiter is more massive than Saturn is.

(37)

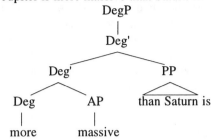

Like the traditional syntactic analysis, the DegP analysis also supports a straightforward interpretation, provided we slightly modify our assumptions about the interpretation of gradable adjectives and comparatives. Specifically, as shown in Kennedy (1997a), we need to adopt a model in which gradable adjectives denote functions from objects to degrees (rather than relations between objects and degrees, as standardly assumed; cf. Bartsch and Vennemann (1973)) and comparatives denote properties of individuals characterized as relations between degrees, rather than expressions that quantify over degrees. With these modified assumptions, the compositional interpretation of structures like (37) is simple and direct. The semantics of the comparative morpheme *er/more* is given in (38) (*less* and *as* have similar analyses, with an appropriate change in ordering relation), where G is a gradable adjective meaning (a function from objects to degrees), d is a degree, and x is an individual.

(38) $[_{Deg} \text{er/more}] = \lambda G \lambda d \lambda x [G(x) > d]$

Assuming that the comparative clause is interpreted as a definite description of a (maximal) degree (Russell (1905), von Stechow (1984), Rullmann (1995), Kennedy (1997d)), the interpretation of DegP is (39): the property of having a degree of mass that exceeds that of Saturn.

(39) $\lambda x[massive(x) > \iota d[massive(Saturn) = d]]$

Predicating this expression of the subject gives the expression in (40) whose truth-conditions can be paraphrased as follows: the degree to which Jupiter is massive exceeds the degree to which Saturn is massive.

(40) $massive(Jupiter) > \iota d[massive(Saturn) = d]$

An important part of this analysis is that the comparative clause is interpreted as a description of a degree.[3] A question that needs to be answered is how this interpretation is derived: where does the adjective meaning in the description come from? In other words, what is the analysis of comparative deletion in the context of the DegP analysis of the adjectival projection? The simplest solution would be to adopt a slightly modified version of the traditional answer to this question and say that CD involves some kind of "DegP ellipsis" in the c-clause. The Logical Form of an example like (41) would be (42), where the null operator binds a degree variable inside DegP (e.g., the position occupied by the measure phrase in a sentence like *Benny is 4 feet tall*).

(41)   Pluto is [$_{DegP}$ colder than [Mercury is]]
(42)   Pluto is [$_{DegP}$ colder than [Op$_x$ Mercury is [$_{DegP}$ e$_x$ cold]]]

The problem with this approach is that (42) is not a possible LF for (41), given standard assumptions about identity in ellipsis. As observed in section 1, CD involves antecedent-containment. As a result, in order to eliminate the infinite regress problem and license ellipsis, a constituent containing the elided material must raise out of DegP at LF. Assuming that the c-clause is the constituent that moves (the argument is the same if the entire *than*-constituent moves), the LF of (41) is not (42), but rather (43).

(43)   [Op$_x$ Mercury is [$_{DegP}$ **colder than e$_x$**]][Pluto is [$_{DegP}$ colder than e$_x$]]

Since ellipsis requires identity, the recovered DegP in (43) must include the comparative morphology on the matrix DegP. As a result, (43) maps onto an interpretation with the wrong truth conditions for the comparative. Assuming as above that the c-clause denotes a definite description of a (maximal) degree, the interpretation of the c-clause in (43) should be something like "the maximal degree d such that Mercury is colder than d". Even if we allow for the possibility that there is such a degree (and if scales

---

[3]Although I claimed above that the c-clause denotes a definite description of a degree, the basic approach to the semantics of DegP presented here is also compatible with an analysis of the c-clause as a restriction on a universal quantifier, as in e.g. Lerner and Pinkal (1995) and Gawron (1995) (though see Kennedy (1997d) for arguments against this analysis). The interpretation of (36) would be something like (i): for every degree *d* such that Saturn is *d*-massive, Jupiter is more massive than *d*.

(i) $\forall d[Saturn\ is\ d\text{-}massive][massive(Jupiter) > d]$

are dense (Bierwisch (1989), Kennedy (1997c)), there isn't, with the result that the c-clause should fail to denote), we incorrectly predict that (41) would be true in a context in which Pluto and Mercury are cold to the same degree, since the comparative would require only that Pluto be colder than the highest degree d such that Mercury is colder than d.

An alternative analysis, which would appear to avoid the problem of incorrectly recovering degree morphology, would be to say that CD targets only AP. That CD must in some cases target at least DegP, however, is shown by an example like (44), which can have the interpretation in (45).

(44)   Poseidon wants the ocean to be 40 degrees colder than Zeus does.

(45)   Poseidon wants the ocean to be 40 degrees colder than Zeus wants
        it to be.

In order to derive the interpretation in (45), the missing material in the c-clause receives its interpretation from the VP headed by *want*. Since this VP includes the comparative DegP, an ellipsis analysis of CD would have to maintain that there is some mechanism for "ignoring" the comparative morphology (as well the measure phrase) in the antecedent, otherwise (44) would run into the same problems as (41). This mechanism would be have to be restricted to comparatives only, however: in other contexts, recovery of an elided comparative DegP *must* include comparative morphology and measure phrases. This is shown by an example like (46), which has only the interpretation in (47)a, not the one in (47)b, in which the comparative morpheme and measure phrase in the antecedent are ignored.

(46)   Mercury is 60 million miles closer to the sun than Earth, and
        Venus is, too.

(47)   a. ...Venus is 60 million miles closer to the sun than Earth, too.
        b. *...Venus is close to the sun, too.

The conclusion to be drawn from this discussion is that in order to maintain both an ellipsis analysis of comparative deletion and the DegP syntactic analysis of the adjectival projection, it would be necessary to weaken the constraints on identity in ellipsis in comparatives to a degree which does not hold for ellipsis of DegP constituents in other constructions (such as (46)). Since the local dependency facts discussed in section 2.1 raised independent empirical problems for an ellipsis analysis of CD, the broader conclusion to be drawn is that an alternative to an ellipsis analysis of CD should be sought. In the next section, I will introduce just such an alternative analysis, which both avoids the problems of identity outlined here and derives the local dependency facts discussed in section 2.1.

3. A Movement Analysis of Comparative Deletion

My goal in this section is to show that the problems for the traditional analysis discussed in section 2 can be resolved by adopting an analysis in which the missing DegP constituent in comparative deletion is analyzed not as the target of an ellipsis operation, but rather as the target of movement: the operator in the comparative clause directly binds a DegP position, rather than a degree position within DegP, as in the traditional analysis (see Moltmann (1992b); see also Bresnan (1973)). In other words, the "missing" material in CD constructions is an empty category throughout the derivation, not an ellipsis site whose content is recovered at LF. (48)-(50) illustrate the LFs of examples (1)-(3) (which are identical to the surface representations) on this analysis.

(48)   Jupiter is more massive than [Op$_x$ Saturn is e$_x$]
(49)   A neutron star is less dense than [Op$_x$ a black hole is e$_x$]
(50)   The mission wasn't as successful as [Op$_x$ we expected it to be e$_x$]

This analysis clearly avoids the problems discussed in section 2.2: if no ellipsis is involved in the recovery of DegP content in CD, then the problem of introduction of unwanted comparative morphology into the interpretation of the comparative clause disappears. More importantly, this analysis also provides a means of deriving the local dependency facts discussed in section 2.1.

The first thing to observe about the LFs (48)-(50) is that they are "deficient" in a very specific way: there are no adjectives in the comparative clauses. According to the semantics for DegP outlined in section 2.2, the c-clause introduces a definite description of a degree which is supplied as one of the arguments of the ordering relation denoted by the comparative morpheme (the other argument is the degree derived by applying the adjective that heads the comparative construction to the subject). For example, the interpretation of the c-clause in (48) should be "the (maximal) degree to which Saturn is massive". But if there is no occurrence of the adjective *massive* in the LF to supply the adjective meaning in this description, where does this meaning come from?

The answer that I will pursue here, building on the empirical observations in section 2.1, is that this missing adjective meaning comes from the adjective that heads the comparative DegP, and, crucially, that it is supplied to the c-clause as part of the compositional semantics of comparatives. This type of approach was first adopted by Klein (1980) in a GPSG framework, who analyzed the missing material in CD as an empty category licensed by a SLASH feature (see Gazdar, Klein, Pullum, and Sag (1985); Klein's analysis was later recast in GB terms (and slightly modified) in Larson (1988)).[4] What has not been noticed before is that this analysis derives the local dependency facts presented in section 2.1 (since the facts themselves have not been previously discussed)

The proposal can be implemented in the framework outlined in section 2.2 by assuming that the interpretation of the c-clause in CD constructions is not a definite description of a degree, but rather a function from a gradable adjective meaning to a definite description of a degree. This hypothesis can be formalized by assigning the comparative operator the semantic analysis in (51), where C corresponds to the interpretation of C'.

(51) $[_{DegP} Op] = \lambda C \lambda G(\iota dC(\lambda x[G(x) = d]))$

Applying this to (48) gives (52) as the interpretation of the c-clause: a function from an adjective meaning G to the degree to which Saturn is G.

(52) $\lambda G(\iota d[G(Saturn) = d]))$

We then need to revise the interpretation rule for the comparative morpheme as shown in (53), so that it not only applies the function denoted by the adjective that heads the comparative DegP to the subject, deriving one of the degrees that stand in the comparison relation, but also supplies this function as the argument to the comparative clause.

(53) $[_{Deg} er/more] = \lambda G \lambda D \lambda x[G(x) > D(G)]$

This gives (54a) as the interpretation of DegP in (48); lambda-conversion derives (54b), which is equivalent to (39) above: the comparative DegP denotes the property of having a degree of mass that exceeds that of Saturn.

(54)   a. $\lambda x[massive(x) > \lambda G(\iota d[G(Saturn) = d]))(massive)]$
        b. $\lambda x[massive(x) > \iota d[massive (Saturn) = d]]$

This analysis thus provides a descriptively adequate semantics for CD (see Kennedy (1997a) for more detailed discussion of other types of comparatives); it's most important empirical consequence is that it also

---

[4]Klein's analysis of the meaning of gradable adjectives and the semantics of comparatives is quite different from the one proposed here, however. Klein analyzes gradable adjectives as vague predicates (McConnell-Ginet (1973), Kamp (1975)) and comparatives in terms of conjunction and negation (Seuren (1973)). See Kennedy (1997a) for arguments against a vague predicate analysis of the meaning of gradable adjectives.

derives the local dependency facts. Since the interpretation of the adjective that heads the comparative is supplied as the argument to the c-clause as part of the compositional interpretation of DegP, the fact that the "missing" adjective must have the same interpretation follows. More generally, this result shows that an analysis of comparative deletion in terms of DegP movement, originally adopted to satisfy the constraints imposed by the syntax of the extended adjectival projection, supports an explanation of a set of facts that constitute a puzzle for the traditional ellipsis analysis of CD.

4. The Emergence of an Ambiguity

Example (29), repeated below as (55), demonstrated that the missing adjective in CD must receive its interpretation locally: (55) has only the reading in (56a), the reading in (56b) is impossible.

(55)   This spaceship is wider than Smith's spaceship is, but it's not longer than hers is.
(56)   a.   This spaceship is not longer than Smith's spaceship is **long**.
        b.   *This spaceship is not longer than Smith's spaceship is **wide**.

According to the analysis of CD presented in the previous section, the absence of an ambiguity in (29) is due to the compositional semantics of comparatives, which requires the adjective that heads DegP to be supplied as the value of the missing adjective in the c-clause. It comes as quite a surprise, then, that the ambiguity we would expect to see in (55) if CD involved ellipsis actually surfaces in sentences in which the first conjunct involves *subdeletion* rather than CD. (57), for example, quite clearly has the both the local interpretation in (58a) and the nonlocal reading in (58b).

(57)   This spaceship is wider than Jones' ship is long, and it's also wider than Smith's ship is.
(58)   a.   This spaceship is also wider than Smith's ship is **wide**.
        b.   This spaceship is also wider than Smith's ship is **long**.

In fact, the ambiguity of sentences like (57) is completely consistent with the analysis of CD proposed in section 3. Since structures that involve movement of a null operator from DegP position and structures that involve DegP ellipsis are string identical, the second conjunct in (57) is *ambiguous* between an analysis as a CD construction and a subdeletion construction in which DegP has been elided under identity with the DegP in the first conjunct. The two analyses are shown in (59a) (the CD construction, which corresponds to the local reading) and (59b) (the elided subdeletion construction, which corresponds to the nonlocal reading).

(59)   a.   ... it's also wider than [Op$_x$ Smith's ship is e$_x$]
          b.   ... it's also wider than [Smith's ship is [$_{DegP}$ **long**]]

More generally, the analysis of CD as DegP movement predicts that nonlocal interpretations should arise *only* in contexts such as (57), in which the local discourse includes a subdeletion construction. Even though the second conjunct in the unambiguous (55) could in principle be analyzed as an ellipsis construction, since the first conjunct also involves CD, an ellipsis analysis would be structurally (and interpretively) nondistinct from a non-ellipsis, DegP movement analysis: both would have LFs in which a DegP empty category is bound by the null operator.

5. Conclusion

The primary conclusion of this paper, supported by both empirical and theoretical considerations, is that comparative deletion cannot be analyzed in terms of ellipsis of an adjectival (DegP) constituent; instead, it must be analyzed in terms of movement of that constituent. This claim does not mean that comparatives never involve some kind of ellipsis–examples in which a constituent larger than DegP, such as (44) above, presumably involve DegP movement *plus* VP-deletion (see Kennedy and Merchant (1997)). It means only that the mechanisms responsible for the phonological elimination, and ultimate interpretation, of adjectival material in CD fall within the domain of syntactic movement operations, rather than the domain of ellipsis licensing and resolution. This in turn implies that these domains have distinct properties, raising important questions for theories that seek to unify them (see e.g. Chomsky (1995:202-3)).

A final consequence of the analysis presented here is that comparative deletion and comparative subdeletion are distinguished in two ways. Not only do they differ in syntactic derivation (a conclusion reached for independent reasons in Grimshaw (1987) and Corver (1993); see Izvorski (1995) for the opposite view, however), they also have different compositional interpretations (though not different truth conditions; see Kennedy (1997a)): since the c-clause in subdeletion contains an adjective, it can be directly interpreted as a definite description of a degree (see Larson (1988:22) for similar remarks in the context of a Klein-style analysis). Whether this second distinction is justified should be a question for future work.

References

Abney, Steven. 1987. *The English Noun Phrase in its Sentential Aspect.* Doctoral dissertation, MIT.

Bartsch, Renate and Theo Vennemann. 1973. *Semantic Structures: A Study in* the Relation between Syntax and Semantics. Frankfurt: Athenäum Verlag.

Bierwisch, Manfred. 1989. The Semantics of Gradation, in Bierwisch, M. and E. Lang eds., *Dimensional Adjectives*. Berlin: Springer-Verlag.

Bresnan, Joan. 1973. Syntax of the Comparative Clause Construction in English. *Linguistic Inquiry* 4:3.275-343.

Bresnan, Joan. 1975. Comparative Deletion and Constraints on Transformations. *Linguistic Analysis* 1.25-74.

Chomsky, Noam. 1965. *Aspects of the Theory of Syntax*. Cambridge, Mass.: MIT Press.

Chomsky, Noam. 1977. On Wh-movement, in P. Culicover, T. Wasow, and A. Akmajian eds., *Formal Syntax*. New York: Academic Press.

Chomsky, Noam. 1995.*The Minimalist Program*. Cambridge, Mass.: MIT Press.

Corver, Norbert. 1990. *The Syntax of Left Branch Constructions*. Doctoral dissertation, Tilburg University.

Corver, Norbert. 1993. A Note on Subcomparatives. *Linguistic Inquiry* 24:4.773-781.

Corver, Norbert. 1997. *Much*-support as a Last Resort. *Linguistic Inquiry* 28:1.119-164.

Cresswell, Max. J. 1976. The Semantics of Eegree, in B. Partee ed., *Montague Grammar*. New York: Academic Press.

Fiengo, Robert and Robert May. 1994. *Indices and Identity*. Cambridge, Mass.: MIT Press.

Gawron, Jean-Mark. 1995. Comparatives, Superlatives, and Resolution. *Linguistics & Philosophy* 18.333-380.

Gazdar, Gerald, Ewan Klein, Geoffry Pullum and Ivan Sag. 1985. *General-ized Phrase Structure Grammar*. Cambridge, Mass.: Harvard University Press.

Grimshaw, Jane. 1987. Subdeletion. *Linguistic Inquiry* 18:4.659-669.

Grimshaw, Jane. 1991. Extended Projection. Ms., Brandeis University.

Hazout, Ilan. 1995. Comparative Ellipsis and Logical Form. *Natural Language and Linguistic Theory* 13:1.1-37.

Heim, Irene. 1985. Notes on Comparatives and Related Matters. Ms., University of Texas, Austin.

Hellan, Lars. 1981. *Towards an Integrated Analysis of Comparatives*. Tübingen: Narr.

Hendriks, Petra. 1995. *Comparatives and Categorial Grammar*. Doctoral dissertation, University of Groningen.

Izvorski, Roumyana. 1995. A Solution to the Subcomparative Paradox, in Camacho, J., L. Chouieri and M. Watanabe eds., *The Proceedings of WCCFL 14*. Stanford: CSLI Publications.

Jackendoff, Ray. 1977. *X-bar Syntax*. Cambridge, Mass.: MIT Press.

Kamp, Hans. 1975. Two Theories of Adjectives. In Keenan, E. ed. *Formal Semantics of Natural Language*. Cambridge: CUP.

Kennedy, Christopher. 1997a. *Projecting the Adjective: The Syntax and*

Semantics of Gradability and Comparison. Doctoral dissertation, University of California, Santa Cruz.

Kennedy, Christopher. 1997b. Antecedent-contained Deletion and the Syntax of Quantification. *Linguistic Inquiry* 28:4.662-688.

Kennedy, Christopher. 1997c. Comparison and Polar Opposition, in Lawson, A. ed., *The Proceedings of SALT 7*. Ithaca: CLC Publications.

Kennedy, Christopher. 1997d. On the Quantificational Force of the Comparative Clause, in Avrutin, S. and D. Jonas eds., *Proceedings of ESCOL '97*. Ithaca: CLC Publications.

Kennedy, Christopher and Jason Merchant. 1997. Attributive Comparatives and Bound Ellipsis. Linguistics Research Center report LRC-97-03, University of California, Santa Cruz.

Klein, Ewan. 1980. A Semantics for Positive and Comparative Adjectives. *Linguistics & Philosophy* 4:1.1-45.

Larson, Richard. 1988. Scope and Comparatives. *Linguistics & Philosophy* 11:1.1-26.

Larson, Richard and Robert May. 1990. Antecedent Containment or Vacuous Movement: Reply to Baltin. *Linguistic Inquiry* 21:1.103-122.

Lees, Robert. 1961. Grammatical Analysis of the English Comparative Construction. *Word* 17:2.171-185.

Lerner, Jean-Yves and Manfred Pinkal. 1995. Comparative Ellipsis and Variable Binding. Computerlinguistik an der Universität des Saarlandes Report No. 64.

May, Robert. 1985. *Logical Form.* Cambridge, Mass.: MIT Press.

McCawley, James. 1988. *The Syntactic Phenomena of English.* Chicago: University of Chicago Press.

McConnell-Ginet, Sally. 1973. *Comparative Constructions in English: A Syntactic and Semantic Analysis.* Doctoral dissertation, University of Rochester.

Moltmann, Fredeirike. 1992a. *Coordination and Comparatives.* Doctoral dissertatioin, MIT.

Moltmann, Friederike. 1992b. The Empty Element in Comparatives, in *The Proceedings of NELS 23*. GLSA Publications, Amherst, Mass.

Napoli, Donna Jo. 1983. Comparative Ellipsis: A Phrase Structure Analysis. *Linguistic Inquiry* 14:4.675-694.

Rullmann, Hotze. 1995. *Maximality in the Semantics of WH-Constructions.* Doctoral dissertatioin, University of Massachusetts, Amherst.

Russell, Bertrand. 1905. On Denoting. *Mind* 14.479-493.

Sag, Ivan. 1976. *Deletion and Logical Form.* Doctoral dissertation, MIT.

Seuren, Pieter. 1973. The Comparative. In F. Kiefer and N. Ruwet eds., *Generative Grammar in Europe.* Dordrecht: Riedel.

von Stechow, Arnim. 1984. Comparing Semantic Theories of Comparison. *Journal of Semantics* 3:1.1-77.

Transitive Expletive Constructions

OLAF KOENEMAN & AD NEELEMAN

Utrecht University & University College London

1. Introduction

This paper addresses the question whether clausal architecture is universal. If there is evidence for a particular functional projection in some languages but not in others, should that projection be assumed universally, or is it the case that different languages may have different clause structures? This question is a difficult one, because it is unclear which empirical predictions distinguish structure that is absent from structure that is not used, at least not in overt syntax. Nevertheless we present an argument in this paper against the universal base hypothesis and in favour of what one may call flexible syntax. The latter approach seems to provide the most straightforward account of the distribution of transitive expletive constructions (henceforth TECs) across languages.

1.1 The Issue
Some languages have expletive constructions with transitive verbs, while such constructions are absent in other languages. The contrast is illustrated in (1) for Icelandic and Danish respectively (see also Jonas and Bobaljik (1993), Bobaljik (1995), Thráinsson (1996), Vikner (1990, 1995) and Bobaljik and Jonas (1996)).

(1) a. Það hafa margir jólasveinar borðað búðing   Icelandic
         there have many Santa Clauses eaten pudding

b.   *Der har nogen spist et æble   Danish
       there has someone eaten an apple

This is not to say that Danish lacks expletive constructions altogether. The example in (2), with an ergative verb, is grammatical.

(2)   Der er kommet en dreng   Danish
            there is come a boy

One might want to argue that generating a TEC is possible in Icelandic, since this language has independent V to I movement, an operation which Danish lacks (see section 4 and Vikner (1990, 1995)). If TECs were licensed by an overtly realized I-position, however, one would expect English and French to have these constructions as well, contrary to fact:

(3) a.   *Il a un homme mangé une pomme   French
         there has a man eaten an apple
    b.   *There a man ate an apple   English

Thus, what seems to make Icelandic special is that it has both verb second (V2) and V to I. Only if a language has both movements do TECs become possible, a generalization already noted by Vikner (1990, 1995).

1.2 A Short Outline of the Proposal

The purpose of this paper is to derive Vikner's generalization. We will argue that it follows from predication theory (see Williams (1980) and subsequent work) in conjunction with two, not completely new, claims. These are presented here as (4) and (5).

(4)   *Claim 1*
      Expletives mark the head of a subject chain

(5)   *Claim 2*
      Nothing can be moved to a position in which it can be generated

It is implied by (4) that an expletive marks a position to which a subject moves at LF. This leaves two possibilities. Either the expletive is inserted in a subject position itself (cf. 6a)) or it is generated higher, for instance in spec-CP (cf. (6b)). In the latter case, the associate will have to occupy a subject position at some stage in the derivation. (The outer brackets in (6) indicate the domain in which the subject can be inserted.)

(6) a.   [expletive-DP ... [$_{VP}$ ... t$_{DP}$ ...]]   (LF)
     b.   expletive-DP ... [t$_{DP}$ ... [VP]]   (LF)

According to predication theory, there is no fixed subject position. Rather, predicates must find their subject somewhere within their m-command domain. Suppose, now, that a DP is generated within this domain and moves to a position still within this domain (cf 7a). Then this movement will be excluded by (5). On a par with (7a), suppose we insert both a subject and an expletive within VP's m-command domain (cf. (7b)). Then (5) will also exclude this structure, since at LF the subject again moves from and to a position within VP's m-command domain.

(7) a.   *[DP ... t$_{DP}$ [$_{VP}$ ...]]
     b.   *[expletive-DP ... t$_{DP}$ ... [VP] ...]   (LF)

If a language has one functional projection dominating VP in declarative clauses, the specifier of this projection is within VP's m-command domain. Hence, expletive insertion is blocked if a subject is already present (cf. (7b)). If, on the other hand a language has two functional projections dominating VP, it becomes possible to generate the expletive in a position outside VP's m-command domain (cf. (8)). Movement of the subject to this position is not ruled out by (5): If DP is generated outside of the predicational domain, it cannot be interpreted as a subject of VP.

(8)   expletive-DP [t$_{DP}$ [$_{VP}$ ... [VP] ...]]

Hence, the possibility of generating a TEC hinges on the number of functional projections present in declarative clauses.

In section 2 we will outline the basics of predication theory. In section 3 we will elaborate on our second claim (cf. (5)). Section 4 will explicate our ideas on flexible syntax and it will be shown that these ideas make it possible to empirically test our proposal in a straightforward manner. The data that support our predictions will be presented in section 5.

2. Predication Theory

Williams (1980, etc.) argues that subjects are external arguments. Associated with each lexical head is a thematic grid that may contain one or more internal Θ-roles, which are assigned within the head's m-command domain, as well as an external Θ-role, which is inherited by the head's maximal projection and subsequently assigned within this category's m-command domain. Subjects, then, are literally external arguments; they are not dominated by the category that Θ-marks them:

(9)   [DP ... XP]

Given this assumption, let us now see where predication theory allows for the generation of subjects. In principle, two positions are available. The subject may appear adjoined to VP, as in (10a), or in the specifier position of the first functional projection dominating VP, as in (10b).

(10) a.   [$_{VP}$ DP [$_{VP}$ ... V ...]
       b.   [$_{FP}$ DP F [$_{VP}$ ... V ...]]

In (10a), the category VP does not dominate DP; only one of its segments does. Hence, DP occurs external to the category VP and can be interpreted as VP's subject. In (10b) the m-command domain of VP is FP and this node again dominates DP. Hence, a predication relation can be established.

What predication theory blocks is generation of subjects in a functional projection that does not immediately dominate VP. In (11), VP's m-command domain is FP$_1$ and DP does not appear within this domain. Therefore, no predication relation between DP and VP can be established.

(11)   *[$_{FP-2}$ DP F-2 [$_{FP-1}$ F-1 [$_{VP}$ ... V ...]]]

Second, it may be possible to realize the subject in more than one position, but it is not possible to generate more than one subject, since there is only one external theta role. A structure like (12), in which both DPs are subjects, is ruled out.

(12)   *[$_{FP}$ DP F [$_{VP}$ DP [$_{VP}$ ... V ...]]]

So, VP must find a unique subject within its m-command domain to which it assigns the external Θ-role.

We will assume that VP always enters into a predication relation with an external argument. Note that if subjects are defined thematically, namely as external arguments that saturate the external role of VP, the question is how to analyze NP-raising. The standard analysis is that the argument of an unaccusative verb receives the internal Θ-role in object position. If so, what triggers raising? And how can VP enter into a predication relation when the verb's single Θ-role is already saturated? We will assume that derived subjects are still thematic subjects entering into a predication relation with

VP. More specifically, we propose that traces of NP movement are interpreted as variables that are bound by a lambda operator. This operator is introduced at the VP-level. Consequently, the interpretation of (13a) looks like (13b) (cf. Kitagawa (1989) and Chierchia (1995)).

(13) a. $[_{VP} \ V \ t]$
     b. $\lambda x \ [_{VP} \ ... \ (x) \ ... \ ]$

The intuition that this analysis expresses is that, from a semantic point of view, there is a similarity between VPs with an unsaturated thematic function and VPs that contain a trace of NP movement: Both contain a 'gap' that makes it possible for VP to function as predicate. Since NP raising is only partly relevant for the analysis of TECs that we propose, we refer the reader to Koeneman & Neeleman (1998) for technical details. The consequences of this analysis for the distribution of unaccusative expletive constructions can be found in footnote 3.

3. Unmotivated Movement

We will adopt the by now standard assumption that every movement is triggered. One way of stating this is to say that the head of a movement chain $\{\alpha, t_\alpha\}$ must have at least one function, F, which cannot be satisfied by the tail of the chain:

(14) α ... t_α
          F

If this is the defining property of triggers, one would expect a further requirement to hold as well: Something must motivate the presence of a trace. Like the head, the tail of a movement chain must have at least one function, F', which cannot be satisfied by its head (cf. (15)). In the absence of F', the trace is not licensed.

(15) α ... t_α
          F   F'

One consequence of the condition just proposed is that no element can be moved to a position in which it could have been base-generated: (15) has the same effect as our second claim above (cf. (5)), which is hereby replaced.

Recall that predication theory allows the subject to be generated in any position m-commanded by VP. If there is no fixed subject position, one may expect movement of the subject within VP's m-command domain to be possible. However, if the subject were to move from a VP-adjoined position to the first specifier c-commanding it, as in (16), a structure would result in which no motivation for the presence of a trace obtains. The Θ-role assigned to tail of the chain could also have been assigned to its head, and hence the structure is ruled out by economy of movement.

(16)   *[$_{FP}$ DP F [$_{VP}$ t$_{DP}$ [$_{VP}$ ... V ...]]]

Suppose now that spec-FP contains an expletive. In that case, it is impossible to have a subject adjoined to VP (cf. (17)). At LF, this subject moves and adjoins to the expletive in spec-FP, thereby leaving a trace. Although this trace can receive a Θ-role, so can the head of the chain: In the position adjoined to the expletive, DP is still within VP's m-command domain.

(17)   *[$_{FP}$ expletive F [$_{VP}$ DP [$_{VP}$ ... V ...]]]

Hence, there is again no unique function that the trace performs. Consequently, (17) is ruled out by economy, just like the structure in (16), since it involves an unmotivated movement.

Note that nothing excludes a subject from moving to a position outside of VP's m-command domain. Suppose, for instance, that two projections dominate VP and that the subject moves from spec-FP$_1$ to spec-FP$_2$.

(18)   [$_{FP-2}$ DP F-2 [$_{FP-1}$ t$_{DP}$ F-1 [$_{VP}$ ... V ...]]]

In this case the trace is licensed, since it is necessarily present in order to receive VP's external Θ-role. This function cannot be performed by DP in spec-FP$_2$ since it lies outside VP's m-command domain. The consequence is now that it should be possible to generate an expletive in spec-FP$_2$.

(19)   [$_{FP-2}$ expletive F-2 [$_{FP-1}$ DP F-1 [$_{VP}$ ... V ...]]]

At LF DP moves to the expletive, but here this movement is from a position within VP's m-command domain to a position outside of it. This implies that the presence of a trace in spec-FP$_1$ is sufficiently motivated: It is engaged in a predication relation with VP and the head of the relevant movement chain is not able to do the same.

In sum, the ban on unmotivated movement, in conjunction with predication theory, blocks movement of the subject within VP's predicational domain, but not movement of the subject to a position outside of this domain. The effect is that expletives and subjects can only cooccur if two functional projections dominate VP. Only then will movement of the associate to the expletive leave a trace that performs a unique function. If TECs can only be generated if two projections dominate VP, the question is what determines the size of the functional domain across languages. We will argue next that overt verb movement provides the proper diagnostic.

4. Minimal Projection

Whether or not TECs are available depends on the number of functional projections that a language has: It must at least have two. Common practice has it that the functional architecture of clauses is fixed, built up from a universal set of nonlexical heads (C, AgrS, T and AgrO), which need not be filled by lexical material. Hence, structure is introduced for which in many languages no evidence can be found. Moreover, if the distribution of TECs depends on properties of the functional domain, the universal base hypothesis would at first sight predict that all languages allow for TECs, contrary to fact. In order to circumvent this prediction, additional assumptions must be introduced that will inactivate at least part of the postulated structure. Such an approach seems rather artificial to us: Why would one postulate structure only to nullify it later?

What we will alternatively assume, then, is a principle of minimal projection according to which each functional shell must contain a (trace of a) lexical head prior to spell out (compare Grimshaw (1995)). To be more precise, an extra projection on top of VP can be generated in two ways. The most straightforward one involves an overt functional head (for instance, a complementizer or a modality or aspect marker), which is taken from the lexicon and merged with VP. Another option is to extend the tree by head movement. This second case requires some discussion.

It is usually asserted that if an element α is attached to a node ß by movement, it is ß that projects. However, we can see no valid independent reason for ruling out projection of α across the board (see van Riemsdijk (1987), Ackema et al. (1993) and Koeneman (1997) for further discussion). In fact, if a verb is attached to the top-node of its own projection line, where it projects again, the resulting structure exactly matches the structure assigned to a functional projection hosting verb movement:[1]

---

[1] This analysis makes crucial use of 'self-attachment', an option which is blocked in Chomsky (1995). Since the top node is ambiguously a projection of the right or the left node, the structure crashes. The ban on self-attachment thus hinges on the stipulation that the computational system cannot handle such ambiguity. We will alternatively assume that the top

(20) $[_{VP} \ldots [_{V'} \; V \; [_{VP} \ldots [_{V'} \; t_V \ldots \;]]]]$

So, what happens in (20) is that the verb moves out of VP and merges again with its own projection. The result of this operation is a second, functional, VP, projected from the moved verb. Given this system, it will be clear that if no verb movement takes place, no functional projection is present either (modulo functional projections derived through direct insertion). Thus, verb movement is indicative of the availability of functional structure.

The exact characterization of the *function* of extra structure does not immediately bear on the core of the proposal. What is crucial for the distribution of TECs is variation in the *number* of functional projections across languages, and the fact that this number coincides with the number of verb movements and heads inserted.[2]

In short, we have turned our theoretical claim into a strong empirical one. TECs only occur in clauses where the verb moves twice. In the next section we will see that this proposal seems to make the correct prediction cross-linguistically and even language-internally.[3]

5. Explaining Vikner's Generalization

Let us now turn to the predictions made by our proposal and consider the functional structure of languages other than English. With the exception of

---

node will automatically be analyzed as a projection of the moved verb. If it were analyzed as a projection of the right node, VP would dominate two head positions (namely the verb and the trace of the verb) and the structure would crash.

[2] For ease of presentation we will continue to use CP and IP as descriptive terms below, even though such labels have no theoretical content in the system of projection described here.

[3] Recall that, according to predication theory, subjects should occur within VP's m-command domain, that is adjoined to VP or in the specifier of the projection immediately dominating VP. If an expletive marks the head of a subject chain, it should be able to occur in these two positions as well, namely in unaccusative contexts. The object will then move to the position marked by the expletive at LF.

(i)   a. $[_{VP}$ expletive $[_{VP} \ldots V \; DP \ldots]]$
        b. $[_{FP}$ expletive F $[_{VP} \ldots V \; DP \ldots]]$

This analysis has the following consequence for the distribution of expletive constructions across languages. Although we predict that TECs only occur in languages with two functional projections dominating VP, expletive constructions with unaccusative predicates should, at least in principle, be able to occur in all languages, irrespective of the number of functional projections generated. As far as we know, this is correct: At least, all languages without TECs that are discussed in this paper allow for unaccusative expletive constructions (see also Vikner (1990, 1995)).

English, all Germanic languages have V2. The finite verb always occurs in second position; if another element than the subject is topicalized, subject-verb inversion is obligatory. This basic fact is illustrated by the examples in (21).

(21) a. [_CP Bókina keypti [Jón ekki]]   Icelandic
       books bought John not
    b. [_CP Dos bukh shik [ikh avek]]   Yiddish
       the book send I away
    c. [_CP Boken köpte [Ulf inte]]   Swedish
       books bought Ulf not
    d. [_CP Denne film har [børnene set]]   Danish
       this film have the children seen

V2 is analyzed as the result of two movement operations. The first fronts the verb and thus creates a functional projection; the second places some XP in sentence-initial position, presumably in the specifier of the projection headed by the moved verb. These sentences therefore provide evidence for the existence of at least one functional projection on top of VP.

There is a typological split between Icelandic and Yiddish on the one hand, and Mainland Scandinavian on the other. It can be shown that the first two have a second verb movement operation, known as V to I. This operation is absent in Mainland Scandinavian as can be directly observed in embedded clauses, where no V2 occurs. Here the finite verb follows adverbials that mark the left edge of VP, suggesting that it does not leave its base position.

(22) a. [_CP at [_VP Peter [_VP **ofte** havde læst den]]]   Danish
       that Peter often had read it
    b. [_CP att [_VP Jan [_VP **ofta** kysser Maria]]]   Swedish
       that Jan often kisses Maria

In Icelandic and Yiddish, V2 also occurs in embedded contexts, but not in certain embedded questions (see Vikner (1990, 1995)). Examples are given in (23a) for Icelandic and (23b) for Yiddish.

(23) a. * ... [_CP af hverju [_CP í herberginu hefur [kyrin staðið]]]
       I know not why in the room has the cow stood
    a'. ... [_CP af hverju [kýrin hefur (**oft**) staðið í herberginu]]
       I know not why the cow has stood in the room

b.   * ... [$_{CP}$ ven [$_{CP}$ in tsimer iz [di ku geshtanen]]]
I know not when in the room has the cow stood

b'.   * ... [$_{CP}$ ven [di ku iz (**oyfn**) geshtanen in tsimer]]
I know not when the cow has stood in the room

If these WH-elements block V2 for some reason, these environments provide us with a means of testing whether independent V to I occurs. If it does, we expect the finite verb to precede VP-adverbials, in contrast to what could be observed in Mainland Scandinavian. As can be observed in (23a') and (23b'), this is indeed what we find if an adverbial is inserted.

So, in addition to V2, Icelandic and Yiddish have a second verb movement, which gives evidence for the presence of a functional projection between VP and what is usually called CP. Given the system of functional projection described in the previous section, this entails that Mainland Scandinavian has one functional projection on top of VP (say, CP), while Icelandic and Yiddish have two (say, CP and IP). Hence, we straightforwardly account for the fact that Icelandic (cf. (25a)) and Yiddish (cf. 25b) have TECs, whereas Swedish (cf. (25c)) and Danish (cf. (25d)) lack these constructions.[4]

(25) a.   [$_{CP}$ Það hafa [$_{IP}$ margir jólasveinar [$_{VP}$ borðað búðing]]]
there have many Santa Clauses eaten pudding

      b.   [$_{CP}$ Es hot [$_{IP}$ imitser [$_{VP}$ gegesn an epl]]]
there has someone eaten an apple

      c.   *[$_{CP}$ Det har [$_{VP}$ någon [$_{VP}$ ätit ett äpple]]]
there has someone eaten an apple

      d.   *[$_{CP}$ Der har [$_{VP}$ nogen [$_{VP}$ spist et æble]]]
there has someone eaten an apple

The ungrammaticality of (25c,d) originates in the fact that VP's predicational domain consists of the entire clause. This domain contains both an expletive and a subject, which implies that raising of the latter will leave an unmotivated trace. In the grammatical representations in (25a,b), on the other hand, VP's predicational domain includes IP but not CP, so that the expletive can be inserted outside this domain. Hence, trace left by movement

---

[4] As is well known, the specifier of a complementizer like *that* tolerates only a limited set of elements, namely syntactic operators and their traces. Whatever is responsible for this restriction also precludes insertion of expletives in the specifier position of a complementizer. Thus, insertion of expletives in spec-CP is allowed as long as the projection is not headed by a complementizer.

of the subject is motivated by the Θ-role it receives from VP.

On the basis of the data presented so far, one may conjecture that V to I is a sufficient condition for having TECs. There is at least one language, however, showing that this hypothesis must be incorrect, namely French. Example (26a) shows that French lacks V2. Example (26b) shows that the finite verb must precede the VP-adverbial, indicating that it has moved from its base position.

(26) a. *[$_{CP}$ Souvent embrasse [$_{IP}$ Jean t [$_{VP}$ t Marie]]]
          often kisses John Mary

      b. [$_{IP}$ Jean embrasse [$_{VP}$ **souvent** t Marie]]
          John kisses often Mary

Therefore, we have evidence for only one functional projection, namely IP, which allows expletive insertion. Our theory now correctly predicts that TECs are ungrammatical in French (cf. (27a)). Like in Mainland Scandinavian, the predicational domain is the entire clause and expletives and subjects may not cooccur here.

(27)   *[$_{IP}$ Il a [$_{VP}$ un homme [$_{VP}$ mangé une pomme]]]
          there has a man eaten an apple

So, it cannot be the presence of IP that licenses TECs, as French illustrates (the same point can be made on the basis of English). It cannot be the presence of CP either because of Mainland Scandinavian. Only if both projections are present is it possible to generate TECs. This follows straightforwardly from our analysis, which does not refer to any particular piece of structure but rather to the overall architecture of the functional domain: At least two projections are required.

A language that corroborates our analysis in an interesting way is Faroese. This language has V2 in main clauses only: It is an asymmetric V2 language, as (28) shows.

(28) a. [$_{CP}$ Í morgin fer [Maria tíðliga á føtur]]
          Tomorrow will Mary get-up early

      b. *Jón ivast í [$_{CP}$ um $_{CP}$ í morgin fer [Maria tíðliga á føtur]]]
          John doubts on that tomorrow will Mary get-up early

Jonas (1995) argues that within Faroese there is a split between a dialect that has V to I and a dialect that does not. This can be observed in embedded clauses, where, as said, V2 fails to apply. In one dialect, the finite verb precedes VP-adverbials, while in the other it follows them. Of these two dialects, usually referred to as Faroese 1 and Faroese 2, only the former provides evidence for two functional projections:

(29) a. Taþ var ovæntaþ [$_{CP}$ at [$_{IP}$ dreingirnir voru [$_{VP}$ **als ikki**
  ósamdir]]]   F1
  it was unexpected that boys-the were at-all not disagreed

   b. Taþ var ovæntaþ [$_{CP}$ at [$_{VP}$ dreingirnir [$_{VP}$ **als ikki** voru
  ósamdir]]]   F2
  it was unexpected that boys-the at-all not were disagreed

It is hence predicted that only Faroese I has TECs. According to Jonas (1995) and Bobaljik and Jonas (1996), this is correct: Only speakers that accept (29a) accept TECs.

(30) a. [$_{CP}$ Tað bygdu [$_{IP}$ nakrir íslendingar [$_{VP}$ *t* hús i Havn]]]   F1
  there built some Icelanders houses in Torshavn

   b. *[$_{CP}$ Tað bygdu [$_{VP}$ nakrir íslendingar [$_{VP}$ *t* hús i Havn]]]   F2
  there built some Icelanders houses in Torshavn

We further expect that languages with asymmetric V2 and V to I can have TECs in main clauses only. In such languages, an expletive can be inserted outside VP's predicational domain, but only if a second functional projection is derived. This prediction is confirmed by German, as we will now show. In German, V2 is a root phenomenon (like in Faroese):

(31) a. [$_{CP}$ Dieses Buch hat [Hans nicht gelesen]]
  This book has Hans not read

   b. [$_{CP}$ dass [$_{CP}$ dieses Buch hat [Hans nicht gelesen]]]
  I believe that this book has Hans not read

Since German is an OV language, it is not immediately apparent from surface order whether it has V to I or not. If IP is head-final, this movement will be rightward and therefore string-vacuous. Nevertheless, contrasts between German and Afrikaans, another OV language, suggest that the former has V to I, while the latter does not.

   Like German, Afrikaans is an OV language with V2:

(32) a. [$_{CP}$ In hierdie jaar sal [daar verandering kom]]
  in this year will there change come

b. [$_{CP}$ Tot almal se verbazing word [die meubels betyds afgelewer]]
to everyone his surprise were the furniture on time delivered

Now, as the data in (33a,a') show, Afrikaans has a productive process of PP extraposition, which is VP-bound (see Ponelis (1977)). This process is absent in German; in as far as speakers accept a PP following the main verb (cf. (33b)), that PP must be heavy or heavily stressed (Anke Lüdeling and Dirk Bury, p.c.). This is not required in Afrikaans, a conclusion confirmed by the findings of Steyn (1996). The contrast between German and Afrikaans follows immediately if only in German the verb moves rightward, out of VP.

(33) a. [$_{CP}$ Ek sal [$_{VP}$ die advokaat <in sy kiesafdeling> help <in sy kiesafdeling>]]
I will the lawyer in his electoral-district help in his electoral-district

b. [$_{CP}$ Dass [$_{IP}$ er [$_{VP}$ Zucker <beim Bäcker> t$_v$ <beim Bäcker>] kauft]], is ungewöhnlich
that he sugar at-the baker's buys is strange

b'. ??[$_{CP}$ Dass [$_{IP}$ er [$_{VP}$ Zucker t$_v$] kauft] beim Bäcker], ist ungewöhnlich
that he sugar buys at-the baker's is strange

Moreover, several authors have argued that rich verbal inflection triggers V to I. According to definitions of rich agreement proposed by Rohrbacher (1994) and Koeneman (1997), the German paradigm contains enough distinctions to trigger V to I, in contrast to the paradigm of Afrikaans, which has undergone a severe process of deflection. Again, this supports the conclusion that the verb moves out of VP in German, but not in Afrikaans.

We conclude that German has V to I and asymmetric V2, while Afrikaans lacks V to I. Hence, an expletive can be inserted outside VP's predicational domain in German main clauses, owing to the verb moving twice. This allows for TECs. In embedded clauses, there is only one functional projection between the complementizer phrase and VP, so that expletives must be inserted within VP's predicational domain. Hence, TECs are excluded in embedded clauses. Both predictions are correct:

(34) a. [$_{CP}$ Es hat [$_{IP}$ jemand [$_{VP}$ einen Apfel gegessen]]]
there has someone an apple eaten

b. *[$_{CP}$ dass [$_{IP}$ es [$_{VP}$ jemand [$_{VP}$ einen Apfel gegessen hat]]]]
that there someone an apple eaten has

As expected, TECs are ungrammatical in Afrikaans, because only one functional projection, derived by V2, is present (cf. (35a)).

(35)   *[$_{CP}$ Daar het [$_{VP}$ baie mense [$_{VP}$ baie bier gedrink]]]
         there have many people much beer drunk

Finally, recall that Icelandic and Yiddish are symmetric V2 languages. This means that embedded clauses have two functional projections between the complementizer and VP. Consequently, expletives can be inserted outside VP's predicational domain, not only in main but also in embedded clauses. As a result, it is correctly predicted that embedded TECs are acceptable in Icelandic (cf. (36a)) and Yiddish (cf. (36b)), in contrast to German:[5]

(36) a.   að [$_{CP}$ það mundi [$_{IP}$ einhver [$_{VP}$ hafa borðað þetta epli]]]]]
          that there would someone have eaten this apple
     b.   az [$_{CP}$ es volt [$_{IP}$ imitser [$_{VP}$ gevolt esn der epl]]]]]
          that there will someone would eat an apple

7. Conclusion

In this paper we have argued that the distribution of TECs follows from the theory of predication in interaction with independently motivated verb movement parameters. Our main claim is that TECs are allowed if the expletive can be generated outside VP's predicational domain, a possibility dependent on the functional structure of a language. More in particular, TECs only occur in clauses containing both CP and IP. This simple condition captures most of the data discussed in recent analyses (see Jonas and Bobaljik (1993), Bobaljik (1995), Thráinsson (1996), Vikner (1990, 1995) and Bobaljik and Jonas (1996)). Assuming that overt verb movement is indicative of available structure, we derive Vikner's (1995) generalization, which says that only languages with V2 and V to I have TECs. Under the universal base hypothesis more assumptions need to be made.

The empirical consequences are as follows. Icelandic and Yiddish are symmetric V2 languages with V to I; they therefore have TECs in main and embedded clauses. Faroese is a V2 language of which one dialect has V to I, while the other does not. As expected, only the former dialect allows

---

[5] There are a number of further issues concerning the distribution of expletives in languages with V to I. In perhaps all these languages expletives are banned from occurring in spec-IP. In Koeneman & Neeleman (1998) we show that this can be derived from a particular formulation of the V to I parameter.

TECs. German is an asymmetric V2 language with V to I; hence it allows TECs in main clauses only. Mainland Scandinavian and Afrikaans are V2 languages without V to I; they consequently do not allow TECs at all. This is true of French as well, which is a language with V to I but without V2.

References

Ackema, Peter, Ad Neeleman and Fred Weerman. 1993. Deriving Functional Projections, in *Proceedings of NELS* 23, Volume I: Clause Structure, GSLA, Amherst, 17-31.

Bobaljik, Jonathan. 1995. *Morphosyntax: The Syntax of Verbal Inflection*. Doctoral dissertation, MIT.

Bobaljik, Jonathan and Dianne Jonas. 1996. Subject Positions and the Roles of TP. *Linguistic Inquiry* 27.195-236.

Chierchia, Gennaro. 1995. Individual-Level Predicates as Inherent Generics', in G. Carlson and F. Pelleties, eds. *The Generic Book*, University of Chicago Press, Chicago, pp. 176-233.

Chomsky, Noam. 1995. *The Minimalist Program*, MIT Press, Cambridge.

Grimshaw, Jane. 1995. Projection, Heads and Optimality. *Linguistic Inquiry* 28.373-422.

Jonas, Dianne. 1995. *Clausal Structure and Verbal Syntax of Scandinavian and English*. Doctoral dissertation, Harvard University.

Jonas, Dianne and Jonathan Bobaljik. 1993. Specs for Subjects: The Role of TP in Icelandic, in J. Bobaljik and C. Philips, eds., *Papers on Case and Agreement I: MIT Working Papers in Linguistics* 18.59-98.

Kitagawa, Yoshihisa. 1989. Deriving and Copying Predication, in *Proceedings of NELS* 19.270-300.

Koeneman, Olaf. 1997. On V to I movement and Flexible Syntax, in Cambier-Langeveld, T., J. Costa, R. Goedemans & R. van de Vijver, eds., *Proceedings of ConSOLE* 5. SOLE, Leiden University, 183-198.

Koeneman, Olaf & Ad Neeleman. 1998. Transitive Expletive Constructions in Flexible Syntax, UiL OTS Working Paper, Utrecht University.

Ponelis, Fritz. 1977. *Afrikaanse Sintaksis*. Van Schaik, Goodwood.

Riemsdijk, Henk van. 1989. Movement and Regeneration, in P. Benincà, ed., *Dialect Variation and the Theory of Grammar; Proceedings of the GLOW Workshop in Venice*, Foris, Dordrecht.

Rohrbacher, Bernhard. 1994. *The Germanic Languages and the Full Paradigm: A Theory of V to I Raising*. Doctoral dissertation, University of Massachusetts.

Steyn, Emma. 1996. Extraposition of Prepositional Phrases in German as a Foreign Language. *Deutchunterricht im Südlichen Afrika* 27.26-34.

Thráinsson, Höskuldur. 1996. On the Non-Universality of Functional Categories, in W. Ambraham, S.D. Epstein, H. Thráinsson and C.J.W. Zwart, eds., *Minimal Ideas*. John Benjamins, Amsterdam.

Vikner, Sten. 1990. *Verb Movement and the Licensing of NP Positions in the Germanic Languages*. Doctoral dissertation, University of Geneva.

Vikner, Sten. 1995. *Verb Movement and Expletive Subjects in the Germanic Languages*. Oxford University Press, Oxford.

Williams, Edwin. 1980. Predication. *Linguistic Inquiry* 11.203-238.

Williams, Edwin. 1981. Argument Structure and Morphology. *The Linguistic Review* 1.81-114.

Williams, Edwin. 1989. The Anaphoric Nature of Θ-Roles. *Linguistic Inquiry* 20.425-456.

Williams, Edwin. 1994. *Thematic Structure in Syntax*. MIT Press, Cambridge.

Projection and Bounding in Possessor Raising*

Idan Landau

Massachusetts Institute of Technology

1. Introduction

The question of how argument structure interfaces with syntactic projection is at the center of intensive research in linguistic theories. Within this research program, the question of what counts as an argument of a predicate becomes urgent. "Borderline" cases, sometimes called "semi-arguments", are therefore of special interest: Elements that behave in some respects as arguments and in others as adjuncts. The case study of this paper, possessive datives (1), is a notorious example of this class of cases:[1]

(1) Hebrew
   a. Rina kilkela *le-Gil* et ha-ša'on.
      Rina spoiled to-Gil Acc. the-watch
      'Rina spoiled Gil's watch'

   French
   b. J'ai coupé les cheveux *à Pierre*.
      I cut the hair to-Pierre
      'I cut Pierre's hair'

---

* I am grateful to the following people for providing me with data on French and Spanish: Marie-Hélène Côté, Caterina Donati, Monica Santa-Maria Somohano and Philippe Schlenker.
[1] A distinct pragmatic feature of PDC, which the English glosses fail to convey, is that the possessor is somehow *affected* by the action denoted by the verb.

Spanish
c. Les revisé los informes *a los estudiantes*.
to-them I-revised the reports to the students
'I revised the students' reports'

Possessive datives, or more neutrally, non-genitive possessive arguments, have been extensively studied in a variety of languages, under different theoretical frameworks (Roldán (1972); Guéron (1985); Borer and Grodzinsky (1986); Cheng and Ritter (1987); Yoon (1990); Branchadell (1992); Kempchinsky (1992); Keach and Rochemont (1992); Shibatani (1994)). The classical puzzle posed by the possessive dative construction (PDC) can be stated as in (2):

(2)   *The Classical Puzzle of Possessive Datives*:
        An argument in the clause (the possessor) derives its *semantic* role from another argument (the possessee), but its *syntactic* behavior from the predicate. What is the possessor dative an argument of?

There are two major schools of thought on the argumenthood of the possessor dative (PD). They are briefly summarized in (3):

(3) a. The possessor dative is an argument of the verb (e.g., BENEFACTIVE). The possessive interpretation arises through binding of an anaphoric element in the possessee. The explanatory burden is carried by θ-theory.

   b. The possessor dative is an argument of the possessee. Its misleading syntax is due to syntactic raising to a position typically occupied by verbal arguments. The explanatory burden is carried by theories of movement and projection.

In this paper I argue for a possessor *raising* analysis of PDC, which falls naturally under (3b). In particular, I argue that PD is generated inside the possessed DP and raises to a VP-internal position by syntactic movement. The data base consists mainly of Hebrew examples, with occasional reference to similar phenomena in French and Spanish.

2. Basic Properties of PDC

The first property of PDC is that PD is interpreted as the possessor or creator/author of another DP in the sentence. Crucially, PD cannot be interpreted as the object/theme of the possessee. This contrasts with the genitive construction, as illustrated in (4):

(4)   a.   Gil   higdil   et   ha-tmuna šel Rina.
               Gil enlarged Acc. the-picture of Rina
               'Gil enlarged Rina's picture' [Rina = possessor/creator/theme]

        b.   Gil   higdil   le-Rina et ha-tmuna.
               Gil enlarged to-Rina Acc. the-picture
               'Gil enlarged Rina's picture' [Rina ≠ theme]

This suggests a requirement that PD be interpreted as the "subject" of the possessed DP. This requirement has a natural account in terms of the internal structure of DP's, to be articulated below.

    Secondly, the possessee cannot be an external argument of the verb, an insight due to Borer and Grodzinsky (1986):

(5)   a.   ha-kelev ne'elam le-Rina.
               the-dog disappeared to-Rina
               'Rina's dog disappeared'

        b. * ha-kelev hitrocec le-Rina
               the-dog ran around to-Rina
               ('Rina's dog ran around')

Thus, B&G argue, PD serves as an unaccusative diagnostic for Hebrew (see Guéron (1985) for similar observations for French). The prohibition against linking PD with an external argument follows, according to B&G, from the fact that PD must c-command the possessee or its trace at S-Structure. While the c-command condition turns out to be necessary, I will argue that it is far from being sufficient.

    Thirdly, as just observed, the possessor must c-command the possessee (or its trace). To see this, consider the following pair:

(6)   a.   Gil nika le-Rina et ha-xulca / et ha-xulca le-Rina.
               Gil cleaned to-Rina Acc. the-shirt / Acc. the-shirt to-Rina
               'Gil cleaned the shirt for Rina'

        b.   Gil lixlex le-Rina et ha-xulca / # et ha-xulca le-Rina.
               Gil dirtied to-Rina Acc. the-shirt / Acc. the-shirt to-Rina
               'Gil dirtied Rina's shirt'

In (6a) DAT is a BENEFACTIVE, whereas in (6b) it is a possessor. Note now that switching from V-DAT-ACC to V-ACC-DAT has no interpretive effect on the former, but destroys the possessive reading in the latter. Since no alternative interpretation is available for (6b), it is deviant with DAT following ACC.[2]

Fourthly, PDC obeys strict locality conditions. Thus, the possessor and the possesse must be clausemate (7), and furthermore, cannot be separated by more than one DP projection (8):

(7) a. Jean semble lui avoir lavé les cheveux.
         John seems him-DAT to-have washed the hair
         'John seems to have washed his hair'

     b. * Jean lui semble avoir lavé les cheveux.
                                              (Guéron (1985): ex.18)

(8) a. Gil harag le-Rina et ha-gur šel ha-kalba.
         Gil killed to-Rina Acc. the-puppy of the-dog (Fem.)
         'Gil killed the dog's puppy which belongs to Rina'

     b. Gil harag le-Rina et ha-ima šel ha-gur.
         Gil killed to-Rina Acc. the-mother of the-puppy
         'Gil killed the puppy's mother which belongs to Rina'

Notice that in (8a) Rina need only own (or at least, hold in her possession) the puppy, not its mother, whereas the opposite holds in (8b).

In the following section I outline the possessor raising analysis. I then show how it naturally accounts for the above properties, as well as deriving novel generalizations concerning the interaction of PDC with various syntactic phenomena, such as variable binding, extraction, control and agentivity.

3. Possessor Raising: A Movement Analysis

The discussion of PDC has so far yielded the following properties:

(9) a. PD must be interpreted as possessor/creator, not object/theme.
     b. The possessed DP cannot be an external argument.
     c. PD must c-command the possessed DP (or its trace).
     d. Possessive interpretation is constrained by locality.

---

[2] V-ACC-DAT is acceptable in PDC only if DAT is phonologically heavy, suggesting rightwards heavy-shift.

I would like to argue that the simplest, and most adequate explanation for the cluster of properties in (9) is a case-driven movement analysis, summarized in (10) and illustrated in (11):

(10)   a.   The possessor is generated in a caseless Spec position within the possessee.

          b.   It is generated with dative case features.

          c.   It then raises to check its case features with V.

Following Hale and Keyser (1993), Chomsky (1995) and Kratzer (1996), I assume that an external argument (AGENT or CAUSER) is introduced by a designated verbal head v with some causative force. The derivation of PDC will be as follows:

(11)   Possessor Raising

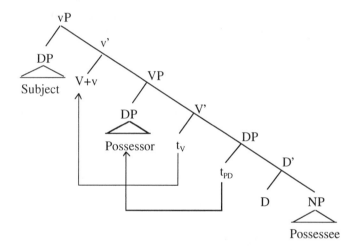

Possessor-raising analyses have been proposed in the past for a variety of constructions (Kubo (1990); Keach and Rochemont (1992); Ura (1996)). Curiously enough, the core studies on PDC, focusing mainly on Romance, have consistently taken every possible path except the movement analysis (Guéron (1985), (1991); Borer and Grodzinsky (1986); Cheng and Ritter (1987); Branchadell (1992); Shibatani (1994)). As we proceed I will point out data that are problematic for the latter alternatives.

    Consider now how (11) derives the properties in (9). For possessor raising to violate (9a), it should be possible to generate a dative-marked theme inside a DP and then raise it outside. Assuming themes are generated as complements to their heads (whether V or N), this would entail that a dative DP is generated as a sister to N and then raises to check its case in the verbal domain.

However this scenario runs counter what we know about case assignment in Hebrew nominals. In particular, the complement domain (in the sense of Chomsky (1995)) of N *is* a proper domain for licensing of dative case, (e.g., *ha-mixtav le-Rina* 'the letter to Rina') But if so, raising a dative-marked complement out of DP to check its case with V would violate Last Resort (Chomsky (1995)). Therefore, PD cannot be generated in a complement position.

As for (9b), the ban on possessor raising out of an external argument, this would follow from minimalist assumptions concerning feature checking. Consider again the structure in (11). In order for PD to raise out of the external argument - the topmost [Spec,vP] - there must be yet a higher verbal position, in the inflectional domain, to check dative case; otherwise, PD would have to lower, an excluded option. By assumption, there is no potential checker of dative case outside of VP; hence raising of PD would not be case-driven, violating Last Resort.

Property (9c) follows automatically from the definition of chains: the c-command condition simply reflects the fact that lowering is disallowed. As to property (9d), it is easy to see that the domain of possessor-raising is identical to the domain of NP-movement. The categories DP and IP contain subjects, hence block any NP-movement out of them. Since possessor raising is nothing more than NP-movement, it is constrained to apply within these domains.

The raising analysis has three important consequences, which crucially distinguish PDC from DOC (double object construction):

(12) Consequences of Possessor Raising:

    a.   The DO contains an empty category in PDC but not in DOC.
    b.   That empty category is a *trace* - PD is *not* an argument of V.
    c.   The landing site, [Spec,VP], is a position projected by V.

In the following sections I argue that there is independent evidence for each and every ingredient in (12).

4. Establishing the Movement Analysis

4.1 ∃ec in the Possessee
The possessor raising analysis attributes to PDC a structure quite distinct from that of superficially similar constructions like the double-object

construction. Thus, the accusative argument in the surface string V-DAT-ACC contains an empty category in PDC but not in DOC. The presence of that trace should be detectable by standard tests; to the extent that these tests yield contrasts between PDC and DOC, the possessor raising analysis is supported.

Empty categories in the syntax behave like variables in the semantics. As such, they may be bound by quantificational DP's. We therefore expect quantifier binding into an argument to be possible by a dative QP which is a possessor but not a GOAL or BENEFACTIVE:

(13) a. Gil lixlex le-kol yalda$_1$ et t$_1$ ha-xulca haxi yafa.
          Gil dirtied to-every girl Acc. the-shirt the-most pretty
          'Gil dirtied every girl's prettiest shirt'

      b. # Gil natan le-kol yalda et ha-xulca haxi yafa.
          Gil gave to-every girl Acc. the-shirt the-most pretty
          ('Gil gave every girl the prettiest shirt')

      c. Gil natan le-kol yalda$_1$ et ha-xulca haxi yafa šela$_1$.
          Gil gave to-every girl Acc. the-shirt the-most pretty her
          'Gil gave every girl her prettiest shirt'

The oddness of (13b) is directly related to the clash between the quantifier, which requires multiple assignments, and the definite description, which requires uniqueness.[3] This can be seen in (13c), where adding an overt (pronoun) variable renders the sentence grammatical.

Consider next the implications of the empty category assumption for possible categorial choices of the possessee. When the latter is a DP, either bare or embedded in a PP, there is a potential base position for the possessor, namely [Spec,DP]. However, if the possessee is expressed as an adverb, no such position exists. This explains the surprising contrast between (14b,c):

(14) a. ha-sid mitkalef le-Rina$_1$ [$_{PP}$ ba- [$_{DP}$ t$_1$ salon u-ve-xadar ha-šena]].
          the-paint peels to-Rina in-the-living-room and-in-the-bedroom.
          'The paint peels off in Rina's living-room and bedroom'

---

[3] (13b) can be saved by a type-reading of "the prettiest shirt". However notice that under this reading as well there is no binding relation with the quantifier: Values of "girls" do not determine values of tokens of "the prettiest shirt". Moreover, no type-reading is forced in (13a).

b. [_PP_ be- [_DP_ t_i eyze xadarim] ha-sid mitkalef le-Rina_i?
    in-which rooms the-paint peels to-Rina
    'In which of Rina's rooms does the paint peel off?'

c. * [_AdvP_ eyfo] ha-sid mitkalef le-Rina?
   where the-paint peels to-Rina
   ('where (of Rina's) does the paint peel off?')

Notice that there is nothing wrong with combining a *where*-question with PDC as such:

(15) eyfo ha-or mitkalef le-Rina?
      where the-skin peels-off to-Rina
      'Where does Rina's skin peel off?'

Rather, the problem with (14c) is that there is no syntactic way to generate a possessor inside an AdvP, thus leaving the dative DP uninterpretable; by contrast, in (15) the dative is associated with the (unaccusative) subject DP, which may contain an empty category in its Spec position (an option which yields pragmatic oddness in (14c)).

4.2 ec = *trace*

Having established the existence of an empty category inside the possessee, we are in a position to pose the question - what kind of an empty category is it. Given standard assumptions of the Principles and Parameters approach, the answer can be either of the following four candidates: (i) trace, (ii) PRO, (iii) null anaphor, (iv) *pro*. The latter option in fact was never proposed (a PD-bound *pro* would violate Condition B), so the choice narrows down to (i)-(iii). In this section I argue for option (i) and against the (ii)-(iii); in particular, I show that certain distributional facts about PDC are only compatible with - indeed, follow from - the trace analysis and not with any other analysis.

The most straightforward evidence for the trace analysis is the observation that possessor raising is sensitive to islands. Thus, although LOCATIVE, SOURCE, and INSTRUMENTAL PP's do not in general block possessor raising from the prepositional object (16), typical adjunct PP's (expressing cause, purpose, etc.) do so (17):

(16) a.   Gil yašav le-Rina ba-mitbax.   [LOCATIVE]
            Gil   sat to-Rina in-the-kitchen
            'Gil sat in Rina's kitchen'

b. Gil ganav le-Rina me-ha-tik.   [SOURCE]
    Gil stole to-Rina from-the-bag
    'Gil stole (something) from Rina's bag'

c. Gil hitkaleax le-Rina im ha-sabon.   [INSTRUMENTAL]
    Gil bathed   to-Rina with the-soap
    'Gil took a shower with Rina's soap'

(17) a. * Gil pitpet le-Rina biglal ha-hofa'a.   [CAUSE]
         Gil chatted to-Rina because the-performance
         ('Gil chatted because of Rina's performance')

b. * Gil hitkaleax le-Rina bli ha-sabon.   [cf. (16c)]
    Gil bathed to-Rina without the-soap
    ('Gil took a shower without Rina's soap')

e. * Gil azav le-Rina lamrot ha-'iyumim
    Gil left to-Rina despite the-threats
    ('Gil left despite Rina's threats')

The emerging generalization is: All and only argumental PP's are compatible with PDC.[4] Under the assumption that arguments are L-marked and adjuncts are not (Chomsky (1986)), the contrastive pattern observed above follows from the possessor raising analysis: Arguments are transparent to extraction, adjuncts are opaque.

Notice that accounts of PDC which do not assume movement cannot appeal to the L-marking analysis. Consequently, theories of PRO/pro/anaphor-binding cannot rule out PDC with adjunct PP's without recourse to some extra machinery: While these PP's create islands for extraction, they are transparent to binding of non-trace empty categories.

---

[4] The sole exception to this generalization is SUBJECT-MATTER PP's, which block possessor raising:

i. * Gil ifyen le-Rina et ha-hitnahagut.
    Gil characterized to-Rina Acc. the-behavior
    ('Gil characterized Rina's behavior')

ii. * Gil hitbases le-Rina al ha-netunim.
    Gil based-himself to-Rina on the-data
    ('Gil based himself on Rina's data')

These verbs may involve an additional, implicit argument, of which the overt SM-argument is predicated. If so, they will fall under the cases discussed in section 5. For lack of space I leave this as a suggestion for future research.

If PD raises to its surface position from a possessee-internal position, then, given standard assumptions on θ-marking, it is not an argument of the verb. Thus, failure at argumenthood tests provides additional, independent support for the raising analysis. One such test comes from the interaction of PDC with control into purpose clauses.

It is well-known that obligatory control is restricted to thematic configurations (Chomsky (1981); Manzini (1983)). Without going into the details of how controller choice is determined, a minimal necessary requirement seems to be the following (Nishigauchi (1984)):

(18) In the environment [... X ...Y ... [$_S$ PRO to VP...]], X may control PRO only if:

   i)   X and S are co-arguments, or:
   ii) X and Y are co-arguments, S is predicated of Y.

Control into infinitival complements falls under (18i), while control into purpose clauses (predicated of the THEME argument) falls under (18ii). Observe now that both types are fully compatible with dative controllers:

(19) a. Gil himlic le-Rina$_1$ [PRO$_1$ lir'ot rofe].
          Gil recommended to-Rina PRO to-see doctor
          'Gil recommended to Rina to see a doctor'

      b. Gil natan la-Rina$_1$ [taklitim [PRO$_1$ lenagen ba-msiba]].
          Gil gave to-Rina records PRO to-play at-the-party
          'Gil gave Rina records to play at the party'

However, minimally changing the DOC in (19b) (where the goal-DAT is selected by V) to PDC (where the possessor-DAT is *not* selected by V) - results in ungrammaticality:

(20) * Gil sarat la-Rina$_1$ [taklitim [PRO$_1$ lenagen ba-msiba]].
          Gil scratched to-Rina records PRO to-play at-the-party
          ('Gil scratched Rina's records to play at the party')

Crucially, when the infinitive is an argument (complement) of the Possessee - PD *can* control PRO (via trace); hence, there is nothing intrinsic about possessors which bars them from entering control relations, rather it is their thematic (un-)relatedness to the infinitival that matters:

(21) Gil haras le-Rina$_i$ et [$_{DP}$ t$_i$ ha-sikuy [PRO$_i$ lizkot be-acma ba-taxarut]].
      Gil ruined to-Rina Acc the-chance PRO to-win in-herself in-the-contest
      'Gil ruined Rina's chances to win the contest by herself'

The island-sensitivity and the control incompatibility of PDC follow straightforwardly from the possessor raising analysis, providing direct support for (12c).

5. Possessor Raising and Argument Structure

The last ingredient of the analysis, (12d), predicts that if the verb chooses to project an argument in [Spec,VP], that should block possessor raising into that position. Such cases are expected to arise with *non*-agentive verbs, selecting *two* internal arguments and no light-verb projection. The predicted generalization, novel as far as I can tell, is the following:

(22) Dyadic non-agentive verbs are incompatible with PDC.

(22) is illustrated below with three different verb classes.

5.1 Experiencer Verbs
Consider the following examples:

(23) a. * Gil ahav le-Rina et ha-tisroket.
         Gil loved to-Rina Acc the-hairstyle
         ('Gil loved Rina's hairstyle')

      b. * Gil hitpale le-Rina al ha-ma'amar.
         Gil was-puzzled to-Rina about the-article.
         ('Gil was puzzled at Rina's article')

Why should experiencer verbs be incompatible with PDC? According to our analysis, these verbs do not project an AGENT, hence the EXPERIENCER argument is projected VP-internally, in the specifier position of VP. This leaves no room for PD to raise to, resulting in sharp ungrammaticality.

This result is significant, because the behavior of this class of verbs in PDC is standardly attributed to the so-called "theme affectedness" condition on the construction (see Cheng and Ritter (1987); Yoon (1990); Branchadell (1992); Shibatani (1994)). Under this story, what rules out (23) is the fact that the THEME is "unaffected" in it.

The thesis of "theme-affectedness" is, I believe, empirically false. In fact, as the data in (24) makes clear, PDC occurs quite freely with "unaffected" objects:

(24) a. Gil madad le-Rina et ha-salon.
Gil measured to-Rina Acc. the-living-room
'Gil measured Rina's living-room'

b. ha-sapar hiš'ir le-Rina et ha-tisroket kmo še-hi.
the-barber left to-Rina Acc. the-haistyle as that-it
'The barber left Rina's hairstyle as it is'

c. Gil histakel le-Rina al ha-kova.
Gil look-at to-Rina on the-hat
'Gil looked at Rina's hat'

d. Je lui ai photographié les pieds.
I to-her photographed the feet
'I photographed her feet'

The examples in (24) have one thing in common with other grammatical cases of transitive PDC discussed above; in all of them the subject is agentive, even though the theme is "unaffected". If it were the latter factor that determined their status, rather than the former, they should have patterned with (23), contrary to fact.

5.2 Subject-Goal Verbs
A second type of non-agentive dyadic verbs which are incompatible with PDC are subject-goal verbs:

(25) a. * ha-misrad kibel le-Rina et ha-mixtav.
the-office received to-Rina Acc. the-letter
('Rina's office received the letter'/'The office received Rina's letter'

b. * Le bureau lui a reçu la lettre.
the office to-her received the letter
('The office received her letter' / 'Her office received the letter')

Both the GOAL and the THEME are internal arguments; thus the two argumental positions within the VP - complement and specifier - are occupied. Given that *receive* is non-agentive, no vP level is projectable. The ungrammaticality of (25) follows, with no further stipulations.

5.3 Stative Location Verbs

Further contrasts suggest that agentivity plays a less direct role in PDC than that proposed in (22). Consider the following minimal pair:

(26) a. * šney xadarim hexilu le-Rina et ha-rahitim.
two rooms contained to-Rina Acc. the-furniture
('Two rooms contained Rina's furniture';
'Two of Rina's rooms contained the furniture')

b. ha-rahitim tafsu le-Rina šney xadarim.
the-furniture catch to-Rina two rooms
'The furniture took up two of Rina's rooms'

The contrast in (26), which is extremely sharp for Hebrew speakers, refutes the claim that PDC is only found with "action verbs" (Roldán (1972); Cheng and Ritter (1987); Branchadell (1992); Shibatani (1994)). The verb *tafas* 'take, occupy' in (26b) is a stative verb par excellence, perfectly compatible with PDC (the contrast is in fact replicated in the very languages for which this claim has been made - French and Spanish).

The verbs *contain* and (the stative) *take/fill* differ in that although both are non-agentive statives, *take/fill* does have an (additional) agentive entry, whereas *contain* does not.[5] We thus modify (22) as follows:

(27) PDC is incompatible with transitives lacking an agentive entry.

Suppose that the availability of an agentive entry for V licenses projection of the light-verb v in all instances of V (perhaps as a result of lexical economization). What distinguishes the agentive entry of V from its non-agentive one is simply that v projects a specifier in the former but not in the latter. Thus the non-agentive *take* projects the structure $[_{v'}$ v $[_{vP}$ THEME $[_{v'}$ V LOCATION $]]]$. Notice that a potenial landing site is available for possessor raising, namely [Spec,vP], precisely because the agent is not projected. The ban on movement into θ-position is respected since in this particular construction [Spec, vP] is *not* a θ-position. As for the ungrammatical (26a), the lack of an agentive entry for *contain* makes the "v-less" structure the only one available. Possessor raising is consequently ruled out.

The facts surveyed in this section thus provide strong support for the possessor raising analysis, and in particular, the claim that PD raises to a

---

[5] Other stative verbs that pattern with *tafas* 'occupy': *hekif* 'surround', *histir* 'cover', *xasam* 'block', *tala* 'hang'. All of them have independent agentive entries.

position projected by the verb. For comparison, consider the model proposed in Borer and Grodzinsky (1986), where PD is argued to be linkable to an internal argument but not to an external one. This model would fail to rule out any of the ungrammatical examples discussed in this section, since all of them involve possession of a VP-internal argument.[6]

Conclusion

The basic thesis this paper argues for is the possessor raising thesis: That is the claim that possessive dative constructions are derived by movement of the possessor DP from a position internal to the possessed DP. The minimal assumption made with regard to that movement is that it is case-driven. A wide variety of properties follows, syntactic and semantic: Obligatoriness of possessive construal, strict locality, exclusion of external arguments as PD-hosts, c-command effects, extraction asymmetries, interaction with control and with various argument structures. Most of these properties are hard, if not impossible to capture within alternative analyses which only posit an empty category within the possessed DP, concentrating their theoretical thrust on the thematic properties of PDC.

References

Borer, Hagit, and Yosef Grodzinsky. 1986. Syntactic Cliticization and Lexical Cliticization: The Case of Hebrew Dative Clitics, in H. Borer (ed.), *Syntax and Semantics 19*, New York: Academic Press, 175-217.

Branchadell, Albert. 1992. *A Study of Lexical and Non-Lexical Datives.* Doctoral Dissertation, Universitat Autonoma de Barcelona.

Cheng, Lisa Lai-Shen and Elizabeth Ritter. 1987. A Small Clause Analysis of Inalienable Possession in Mandarin and French. *NELS* 18, 65-78.

Chomsky, Noam. 1981. *Lectures on Government and Binding.* Foris, Dordrech

---

[6] The proposed account implies that strictly Larsonian shells do not exist, at least not for triadic verbs like *put*. Otherwise, possessor raising would be predicted to fail there for the same reason, namely competition over [Spec,VP] - but it doesn't:

i.   Gil sam le-Rina xol ba-kisim.
       Gil put to-Rina sand in-the-pockets
       'Gil put sand in Rina's pockets'

I therefore assume, with Hale and Keyser (1993), that such constructions involve two-place prepositions, placing the direct object in [Spec,PP]. The designtaed position for possessor raising - [Spec,VP] - is thus made available.

Chomsky, Noam. 1986. *Barriers*. MIT Press, Cambridge, MA.

Chomsky, Noam. 1995. *The Minimalist Program*. MIT Press, Cambridge, MA.

Guéron, Jacqueline. 1985. Inalienable Possession, PRO-Inclusion and Lexical Chains, in Obehauer, H. -G., Jean Yves Pollock and Jacqueline Guéron (eds.), *Grammatical Representations*. Foris, Dordrecht.

Hale, Ken and Samuel Jay Keyser. 1993. On Argument Structure and The Lexical Expression of Syntactic Relations, in Hale, Ken and Samuel Jay Keyser (eds.), *The View From Building 20*. MIT Press, Cambridge, MA.

Keach, Camillia N. and Michael Rochemont. 1992. On the Syntax of Possessor Raising in Swahili. *Studies in African Linguistics* 23:1, 81-106.

Kempchinsky, Paula. 1992. The Spanish Possessive Dative Construction: θ-Role Assignment and Proper Government, in Paul Hirschbuhler (ed.), *Linguistic Symposium on Romance Languages* 20, 135-149.

Kratzer, Angelika. 1996. Severing the External Argument From Its Verb, in J. Rooyck & L. Zaring (eds.), *Phrase Structure and the Lexicon*, Dordrecht: Kluwer, 109-137.

Kubo, Miori. 1990. Japanese Passives. Ms, MIT.

Manzini, Rita. 1983. On Control and Control Theory. *Linguistic Inquiry* 14, 421-446.

Nishigauchi, Taisuke. 1984. Control and the Thematic Domain. *Language*, 60, 215-250.

Shibatani, Masayoshi. 1994. An Integrational Approach To Possessor Raising, Ethical Datives and Adversative Passives. *BLS* 20, 461-485.

Ura, Hiroyuki. 1996. *Multiple Feature Checking: A Theory of Grammatical Function Splitting*. Doctoral Dissertation, MIT.

Yoon, James, Hye-Suk. 1990. Theta Theory and the Grammar of Inalienable Possession Constructions. *NELS* 20, 502-516.

Ellipsis Resolution in Comparatives & the Right Periphery of DP

WINFRIED LECHNER
University of Massachusetts, Amherst

1. Introduction

Since Bresnan (1973), a consensus has emerged in the generative literature that the rules of grammar contributing to comparative formation minimally have to include the process of Comparative Deletion ('CD'). CD is defined as an obligatory operation which removes the gradable property expression from within the comparative clause:

(1)   Mary knows younger authors than Peter knows ⌂
       (⌂$_{CD}$ = d-young authors)
(2)   *Mary knows younger authors than Peter knows young authors

    The present paper investigates the syntactic and semantic properties of CD, and tries to answer three questions: First, at which level of representation is CD identified? Should the CD-site be assumed to be present already in the syntactic representation (for instance at LF), or should the ellipsis be restored in semantics? Second, what is the fine-grained structure and interpretation of attributively modified NP-comparatives such as the object *younger than Peter knows* in (1)? Third, which exact mechanism is responsible for the recovery of the empty gradable property in comparatives? These questions will be addressed in turn in sections 2 to 4. Section 5 finally discusses empirical extensions of the theory to be presented.

2. Semantic Approaches towards CD-Resolution

In two recent studies, Kennedy (1997) and Lerner & Pinkal (1995) propose to treat CD as a manifestation of semantic ellipsis, which is identified in the semantic component. According to L & P, the content of CD in NP-comparatives is recovered by means of a discourse anaphoric mechanism, which resembles the one that governs the distribution of *one*-anaphora. The silent categories in (3a) and (3b) would consequently be identified by the same - or similar - principles:

(3) a. Mary knows a younger author than Peter knows △
     b. Mary knows a young author and Peter knows one, too △
         (△ = d-young author)

In essence, their account rests on the assumption that a context variable P_o built into the denotation of the empty comparative operator takes up the reference of a gradable property, and is λ-converted into the appropriate position in the course of the semantic computation. For the comparative complement of (3)a, this yields the informal representation (4)a, which results in (4)b after the context variable has been instantiated by *young author*:

(4) a. (than) $\exists y[P_o(d)(y)$ & know (y)(Peter)]
     b. (than) $\exists y[$**young author** (d)(y) & know (y)(Peter)]

An idea similar in spirit is defended in Kennedy (1997), who also adopts a semantic approach towards CD, but does not employ the help of context variables. To begin with, he points to the fact that the content of the CD-site is always determined locally, unlike other kinds of semantic ellipsis, notably VP-deletion (Williams (1977): 102). The empty node inside the comparative clause in (5) is e.g. unequivocally interpreted as *d-long*, a gradable property that is provided by the matrix predicate of the second conjunct, and cannot be recovered at a distance by the property *d-wide* in the first conjunct:

(5) The table is wider than this rug is, but this rug is longer
     than the desk is △
     (△ = d-long/*△ = d-wide)   (Kennedy (1997): 154)

CD contrasts in this respect with VP-deletion, which is more permissive w.r.t. the locality conditions on ellipsis, as shown by the ambiguity of (6) below:

(6) Marcus read every book I did and I bought every book Charles did △
     (△ = bought/△ = read)   (Kennedy (1997): 154)

In developing an account for this asymmetry between CD and VP-ellipsis, Kennedy adopts L & P's suggestion to let the recovery of the content of CD be mediated by the empty comparative operator. However, instead of opting for a solution in terms of discourse identification, he capitalizes on the fact that OP and the antecedent of the CD-site are in a local relation at LF ((7b)):

(7) a. Syntax: Mary is younger than Peter is Δ_{CD}
     b. LF: Mary is **younger** [than [$_{CP}$ **OP$_i$** Peter is **t$_{i, <e,t>}$**]]

According to Kennedy, the comparative operator binds the trace of a Degree Phrase (Abney (1987), Corver (1993)), which corresponds to an expression of the type of an individual property. This higher-type variable (t$_i$ in (7b)) serves as a place holder into which the AP-denotation of the local antecedent is λ-converted in semantics, once the comparative complement has been combined with the denotation of the comparative AP *younger* (t$_i$ is translated as variable 'G' in (8); 'AB' stands for 'absolute'; see Kennedy (1997) for further details):

(8) [younger]([[than [$_{CP}$ OP$_i$ Peter is **t$_{i, <e,t>}$**]]]) =
     = λQλx[MORE(young(x))(Q(young))](λG[max(λd[AB(**G**(Peter))(d)])])
     = λx[MORE(young(x))(λG[max(λd[AB(**G**(Peter))(d)])(**young**)])]
     = λx[MORE(young(x))(max(λd[AB(**young**(Peter))(d)]))]

Recapitulating briefly, in both L & P's and Kennedy's theory of CD, the ellipsis site is recovered at a late stage in the derivation, that is, in the semantic component. We are therefore led to expect that principles that operate on purely syntactic representations (overt syntax and LF) are blind to the content of CD. In the next section, I will demonstrate that this prognosis is incorrect, and that one should therefore seek an alternative analysis of CD.

3. Identification of CD in Syntax

3.1. Evidence from Binding Theory
The first argument supporting the view that the CD-site is restored prior to semantics comes from disjoint reference effects. In order to establish this point, it will be necessary to turn to a brief discussion of two competing analyses of the variable size of the CD-site in predicative constructions first.

If the comparative adjective is transitive, CD may affect either the adjectival head alone, or erase the adjective along with its complement:

(9) a. Mary is prouder of John than Bill is of Sally
         (Δ = d-proud)
     b. Mary is prouder of John than Bill is Δ
         (Δ = d-proud of John)

The question that arises in this context is whether the PP in (9b) has been suppressed by a deletion process separate from CD, or whether it has been elided along with the adjective. For if the second option can be shown to obtain, the properties of an elided PP represent a heuristic tool for the detection of more general properties of CD.

Paradigm (9) is reminiscent of one that shows up in contexts of sentential conjunction. In coordinate structures, deletion can be either restricted to the adjective, exemplified by Pseudogapping in (10a), or may affect the adjectival predicate and its argument, as in the 'VP'-ellipsis (10b):

(10) a.   Mary is proud of John and Bill is of Sally
      b.   Mary is proud of John and Bill is, too

Following Lasnik's (1995) treatment of Pseudogapping, I assume that the difference between (10a) and (10b) does not lie so much in the size of ellipsis, but rather in the presence of an additional movement step in the derivation of (10a) (Johnson (1997), Jayaseelan (1990)). While (10b) constitutes a simple case of VP-deletion, the object PP in (10a) moves out of the containing VP (and AP) prior to elision, yielding the appearance of A°-deletion:

(11) a.   Mary is proud of John and Bill is [$_{VP}$ [$_{AP}$ proud of Sally]]
      b.   Mary is proud of John and Bill is [$_{PP}$ of Sally]$_i$ [$_{VP}$ [$_{AP}$ proud t$_i$]]
      c.   Mary is proud of John and Bill is [$_{PP}$ of Sally]$_i$ △
           (△ = [$_{VP}$ [$_{AP}$ proud t$_i$]])

We can now employ the same strategy in the derivation of the comparative (9a): In an initial step, the object PP is evacuated out of the AP, followed by application of CD, which targets the whole AP-node:

(12) a.   Mary is prouder of John than Bill is [$_{AP}$ proud of Sally]
      b.   Mary is prouder of John than Bill is [$_{PP}$ of Sally]$_i$ [$_{AP}$ proud t$_i$]
      c.   Mary is prouder of John than Bill is [$_{PP}$ of Sally]$_i$ △$_{CD}$
           (△$_{CD}$ = [$_{AP}$ proud t$_i$])

That is, the categories affected by CD in (9a) and (9b) are of the same size; in both cases it is an AP that has been removed from the respective surface strings. It follows that the PP object that is elided along with the adjectival head in (9b) is also contained in the CD-site, and not erased by some additional operation.

Consider in this light example (13):

(13)   Mary is prouder of John$_i$ than he$_{*i/j}$ is $\Diamond$[1]
        ($\Diamond$ = d-proud of John)

(13) does not possess a reading in which *John* and the pronominal subject of the comparative clause corefer, indicating that the PP *of John* resides inside the c-command domain of the pronoun already at LF, triggering a Principle C violation.[2] Since the object PP is part of the CD site, we are moreover led to the conclusion that the CD-site *d-proud of John* has been restored already as early as during the syntactic computation.

Binding Theory and the behavior of reciprocals also provide a second argument in support of a syntactic account of CD resolution. As demonstrated by the examples under (14), the subject of the comparative can sloppily bind an anaphor or a reciprocal contained within the CD-site:

(14)   a.   Mary is prouder of herself than Sally is $\Diamond$
             ($\Diamond$ = d-proud of herself)
       b.   The girls are prouder of each other than the boys are $\Diamond$
             ($\Diamond$ = d-proud of each other)

Again, this observation serves as a diagnostic that the anaphors in (14) - and therefore also the AP's containing them - are already reconstructed at LF.[3]

3.2. Coordinate Structure Constraint

The third and final piece of evidence in favor of a syntactic approach towards CD-resolution stems from overt extraction. Observe first that extraction out

---

[1] (13) improves if the pronoun is focused, a behavior typical of Principle C (Reinhart (1983)).

[2] The same conclusion is reached if Principle C is assumed to constitute an innate interface strategy (Reinhart (1983, 1995); Reinhart & Grodinzky (1993)). According to Reinhart's (1995: 51) 'Interface Rule I', the LF-representation of (i)a, which employs a bound variable, is more economical than - and therefore preferred over - the LF of (i)b, which includes an overt name:
    (i)   a.   He$_i$ touched himself$_i$
           b.   *He$_i$ touched Max$_i$
If it is not possible to establish the structural context for variable binding, as in (ii), Rule I licenses coreference between names and pronouns:
    (ii)   The bear near Max$_i$ touched him$_i$
Crucially, Rule I evaluates competing LF-representations, and not semantic formulas. Thus, the comparison set for (13) will have to include a representation in which the name (and consequently the containing AP) have been reconstructed into the CD-site already at LF.

[3] The point can be strengthened, if an LF-cliticization analysis of reflexives and reciprocals is adopted, according to which the anaphor covertly raises to its antecedent (Chomsky (1995), Heim, Lasnik & May (1991), Lebeaux (1985)). Since movement presupposes the existence of a syntactic target, these accounts require that the anaphor be syntactically present already at LF.

of the object position of a transitive positive adjective, as in (15a), as well as simultaneous movement of the AP-complement out of the matrix and the comparative clause, as in (15b), leads to well-formed structures:

(15) a. a person **that**$_i$ Mary is proud of **t**$_i$
b. a person **that**$_i$ Mary is [more proud of **t**$_i$] than Peter is ⌂
(⌂ = d-proud of **t**$_i$)

However, if movement targets the adjectival complement in the matrix clause alone, the result surface string is deviant:

(16) *a person **that**$_i$ Mary is [more proud of **t**$_i$] than Peter is ⌂ of John
(⌂ = d-proud of **t**$_i$)

Compare now the contrast between (15b) and (16) to the one which sets apart the coordinate structure (17a) from (17b).

(17) a. a person **OP**$_i$ that Mary is [proud of **t**$_i$] and Peter is ⌂, too
b. *a person **OP**$_i$ that Mary is [proud of **t**$_i$] and Peter is ⌂ of John
(⌂ = proud of **t**)

Let me assume that comparatives are subject to the Coordinate Structure Constraint ('CSC') much in the same way that coordination is.[4] Then, the unacceptability of (16)[5] and (17b) receive a uniform explanation and can be reduced to a reflex of the more general ban on asymmetric extraction. Notice furthermore that examples that militate against the CSC are fully interpretable. The common noun of (16) denotes *the set of individuals x, such that there is a degree d such that Mary is d-proud of x and d is greater than the maximal degree d' to which Peter is proud of John* (assuming von Stechow's (1984) comparative semantics in terms of maximality). Thus, the CSC arguably represents a condition that poses restrictions on syntactic derivations, and not on semantic representations. It follows that violations of

---

[4] See also Napoli (1983: 687f), who observes that the CSC holds for NP-comparatives:
(i) a. *Who did you see [more pictures of t] than (you read) books about Ronald Reagan
b. *Who did you see more pictures of Nancy Reagan than (you read) [books about t]
c. Nancy Reagan, I've seen [more pictures of t] than I've read [books about t]
On coordinate-like properties of comparatives vd. Corver (1994), Lechner (1998a), Pinkham (1982).

[5] Some speakers judge (16) to be marginally acceptable, acknowledging though a clear contrast between (16) and (15b). This might be attributed to the fact that comparatives meet the (poorly understood) conditions which rescue CSC-violations in English examples such as *What did you go to the store and buy* (Culicover (1972), Culicover & Jackendoff (1997), Goldsmith (1985); Williams (1994)). Note incidentally that e.g. the German equivalent of (16) is strictly ungrammatical, correlating with the observation that German does not license exemptions from the CSC.

the CSC have to be computed in syntax, and the conclusion that the CD-site in the ill-formed structure (16) has been reconstructed prior to semantics becomes inescapable. The sensitivity of comparatives to the CSC therefore constitutes a further piece of evidence in favor of the view that the CD-site is restored as early as in the syntactic component.

This concluded the argumentation in favor of syntactic CD-resolution. Next, I will turn to a discussion of the syntax of NP-comparatives, proceeding from there to the presentation of an alternative account of CD.

4. Towards a New Theory of CD

4.1. The Representation of NP-Comparatives
The current section focuses on the fine-grained structural relations between the DP, the AP-modifier and comparative marking in NP-comparatives such as the object in (1), repeated below as (18):

(18)   Mary knows younger authors than Peter knows

In developing an account of NP-comparatives, I will diverge from standard assumptions about the degree and DP-internal modifier system that can be found in the literature in two respects. First, I will advocate a new account of the relation between the comparative clause and the AP it is associated with. Second, it will be argued that the standard analysis of attributive modification should be reevaluated in the light of internally complex NP's such as (1).

To begin with, I will adopt the functional AP-hypothesis, which holds that each AP is embedded under a functional Deg(ree)P(hrase) (Abney (1987), Bresnan (1973), Corver (1993, 1997)). Prior studies that have considered comparatives from the perspective of the DegP-hypothesis have assigned to simple predicative comparatives such as (19a) the factorization (19b), in which the AP and the *than*-XP are both generated as daughters of a recursive Deg'-node (Corver (1993), Kennedy (1997), Merchant & Kennedy (1997)).

(19)   a.   Mary is younger than Peter
       b.   .... [$_{DegP}$ [$_{Deg'}$ [$_{Deg'}$ Deg° [$_{AP}$ younger]] [than-XP]]

Contrary to the positions taken in the literature, I would however like to suggest that the *than*-XP serves as a complement to Deg° and that the AP originates in SpecDegP as the external argument of the degree head:[6]

---

[6]Thus, the *than*-XP is effectively treated as an internal argument, which can under certain

(20)　[$_{DegP}$ [$_{AP}$ younger] [$_{Deg'}$ Deg°$_{[+comparative]}$ [$_{than-XP}$ than Peter]]]

One immediate consequence of the parse in (20) is that AP and Deg° are in a Spec-Head configuration. Comparative morphology can therefore be base-generated directly on the adjectival head, and checked on the AP by a suitable [+comparative] feature in Deg° (Chomsky 1995).[7]

Consider at this point once again NP-comparatives such as (18) and their analysis under the DegP-hypothesis. If one were to follow the standard assumption that prenominal modifiers are adjuncts to NP, the whole DegP - the string *younger than Peter knows* in (18) - would have to be left-adjoined at the NP-level, resulting in the illicit surface serialization given under (21):

(21)　[$_{NP}$ [$_{DegP}$ [$_{AP}$ younger] [$_{Deg'}$ Deg°$_{[+comp]}$ [$_{than-XP}$ than Peter ...]]] [$_{NP}$ authors]]

Thus, NP-comparatives reveal the limitations of the traditional NP-adjunction analysis, which fails to capture word-order correctly.

In principle, there are two ways to reconcile the DegP-hypothesis with the actually observed serialization. On the one hand, one could invoke obligatory extraposition, shifting the *than*-XP in (21) to the right-periphery of the DP. As it turns out, however, this option can be shown to empirically untenable. Right-ward shift of the *than*-XP would violate the locality constraints which are generally thought to restrict extraposition (Ross (1976), Lechner (1998a)). On the other side - and this is the line I would eventually like to pursue - it is possible to take the data above as an argument against the traditional NP-adjunction analysis of prenominal modification.

The alternative account for prenominal attributes that I will advocate here is modeled after Abney (1987), and combines a non-endocentric structure for the DP with the DegP-hypothesis. For Abney, prenominal AP-modifiers are selected by D°, and take the head noun they modify as a complement (vd. Berman (1973)). According to present assumptions, AP is embedded under DegP. Substituting 'DegP' for 'AP', we arrive at a phrase structure for NP-comparatives, in which DegP no longer originates as an adjunct to NP, but is generated as a complement of DP, as in (22):

---

conditions be contextually recovered (cf. *Mary is younger*), much in the same way that the complement of a transitive predicate such as *eat* can (cf. *Mary eats*).

[7]In periphrastic comparatives, the degree marker *mehr/*'more' arguably moves from Deg° into a higher functional projection, marked 'QP' in (i)b (see Corver (1997) on the distinction between DegP and QP; a similar phrasal architecture was independently proposed by Izvorski (1995)):

(i)　a.　Mary is more interesting than Peter

　　　b.　....[$_{QP}$ more$_1$ [$_{DegP}$ [$_{AP}$ interesting][$_{Deg'}$ t$_1$ [$_{than-XP}$ than Peter]]]]

(22)

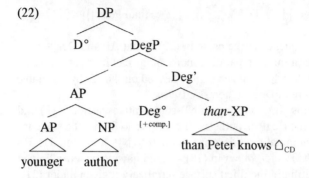

A first consequence of (22) is that the *than*-phrase originates now to the right of the head noun, in compliance with the observed surface word-order. Second, the higher AP node (*younger authors*) c-commands the CD-site, an aspect that will turn out to be crucial in the alternative account of CD to be presented in the next section.[8]

4.2. The AP-Raising Analysis of CD

Notice that adopting the parse (22) entails that both the AP in the comparative complement and the AP modifying the item of comparison reside in the specifier positions of a DegP. Both DegP's are moreover contained in a uniformly right-branching tree, resulting in a configuration in which the CD-site is c-commanded by its antecedent. Thus, the relation between the CD-site and its antecedent satisfies the structural conditions on chain-formation. I would like to propose now that the category removed by CD is indeed a trace, or more precisely a copy of the antecedent left by AP-movement from the lower SpecDegP into the higher SpecDegP. This leads to the AP-Raising analysis of CD, which is stated in (23):

(23)   **AP-RAISING HYPOTHESIS:** Comparative Deletion consists in AP-Raising from the comparative clause into the matrix clause.

Applying (23) to example (18) consequently results in the tree diagram given

---

[8]Further evidence for the right-branching DP structure in (22) comes from bounding theory (Lechner (1998b)) and the observation that the precedence relations of the terminals in the tree directly translate into c-command. A DP-internal quantificational modifier may e.g. bind a pronoun contained within the subject of the *than*-XP (Lechner (1998a)):

(i)   weil Maria einen kritischeren Artikel über [jeden der Autoren]ᵢ als seinᵢ Manager △ schrieb
       since M.   a   more critical article about each of the authors than his manager △ wrote
       (△ = wrote a d-critical article about t)
       "since Mary wrote a more critical article about each of the authors than his manager"

under (24):[9]

(24)   a.   Mary knows younger authors than Peter knows
       b.

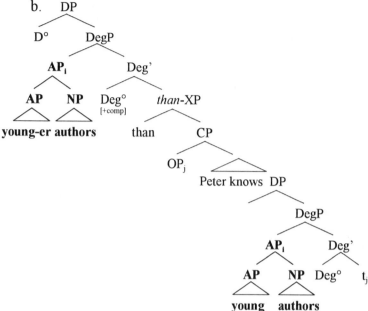

AP-Raising in (24) is triggered by the need to eliminate the [+comparative] feature of Deg° in the higher DegP, and complies in this respect with the well-established generalization in the Minimalist Program that movement processes are motivated by morphological properties of heads (Chomsky (1995)). Given that a [+comparative] on the matrix Deg° counts as an uninterpretable feature, failure of AP-Raising results in a structure in which the matrix Deg°[+comp] winds up with an unchecked feature, causing the derivation to crash.

The tree (24) reveals a second essential aspect of the AP-Raising analysis. Unlike in other instances of movement, we need to ensure that in comparative formation both copies of the dislocated AP are preserved at LF. Whereas it is characteristic of regular chains that all but one chain members are deleted at LF, both the higher and the lower AP-copy in (24) are

---

[9]The comparative operator (OP) binds a degree trace which serves as a complement to a semantically vacuous Deg° inside the comparative clause. Since Deg° is semantically empty, the AP is translated in its positive form (*d-young authors*), and not as a comparative. Note on the side that the analysis naturally carries over to predicative comparatives.

submitted to semantic interpretation. This difference between ordinary movement and AP-Raising falls out from conditions on interpretability. Failure to delete all but a single chain link in an XP-movement chain that is footed in an argument position results e.g. in an uninterpretable structure, because the resulting derivation contains an argument which is not linked to a predicate, in violation of Full Interpretation. The situation is significantly different with AP-Raising. In (24), the semantic interface conditions dictate that none of the copies of the AP may be deleted. Otherwise, either the matrix or the comparative clause would end up without an internal argument.[10]

The AP-Raising hypothesis (23) entails three direct consequences. First, it contributes to an understanding why the AP in the matrix clause displays comparative marking (*young-er authors*), while the standard of comparison is restored in its positive form *young authors* (vd. e.g. Moltmann (1992)). In the present system, this follows from the fact that comparative morphology and semantics are exclusively encoded in the higher $Deg^{\circ}_{[+comp.]}$.

Second, the fact that the elliptical constituent in comparatives is related to its antecedent by movement - taken together with the traditional constraints on extraction - accounts for Kennedy's observation that CD operates locally (vd. example (5)).

Third, the AP-Raising theory of CD has immediate repercussions on the analysis of the reconstruction and CSC effects introduced in section 3. In comparatives, the AP is base-generated inside the comparative clause, and we therefore expect its content to be visible to the principles of Binding Theory and the CSC in syntax. Consider to this effect e.g. once again the Principle C violation in (13), repeated below under (25), and its underlying source:

(25) a. Mary is prouder of John$_i$ than he$_{*i/j}$ is $\triangle$
          ($\triangle$ = d-proud of John)
      b. Mary is [$_{DegP}$ [$_{AP}$ prouder of John]] than **he** is [$_{DegP}$ [$_{AP}$ proud of **John**]]

In (25b), the pronoun c-commands the name inside the lower AP-copy already in syntax, deriving the attested disjoint reference effect.

Section 5 provides further empirical support for AP-Raising, and demonstrates that the AP-Raising hypothesis successfully captures two asymmetries between pre- and postnominally modified NP-comparatives, that prove as a litmus test for any theory of CD.

---

[10]Technically, this ban on deletion can be achieved by taking AP-Raising to be an instance of movement without chain-formation. For further discussion, empirical evidence in defense of AP-Raising and the semantic rules for comparatives see Lechner (1998a).

5. Pre- vs. Postnominal Asymmetries

The AP-Raising hypothesis as its stands makes a number of empirical predictions about the distribution and properties of NP-comparatives, two of which will be discussed in this ultimate section.

5.1. The CD-Site *can* be Small

Bresnan (1973) and Stanley (1969) observed that the interpretation of NP-comparatives is sensitive to DP-internal word order. While (26a) entails that my mother is a man, (26b) can be uttered felicitously without such an implication:

(26)　a.　#She met a younger man than my mother
　　　　　　($\triangle$ = (is a) d-young man)
　　　　b.　She met a man younger than my mother
　　　　　　($\triangle$ = (is) d-young)

This asymmetry is standardly attributed to variation in the size of the respective CD-sites. In the classic analysis of Bresnan (1973), the CD-site is assumed to correspond in size to the sister node of the *than*-XP. In the prenominal construction, the *than*-XP adjoins to the NP, as illustrated by (26)a', and the ellipsis is restored as a modified common noun (bold face). Low attachment - as in (26)b' - leads to the postnominal construction, in which CD targets a constituent no larger than an AP.

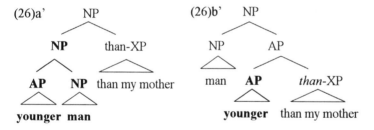

Crucially, Bresnan allows the *than*-XP to adjoin at different nodes, depending upon serialization. But if the deliberations of section 3 are on the right track, there are good reasons to believe that the *than*-XP is invariably attached lowest within the DP, and Bresnan's account for the pre- vs. postnominal asymmetry (26) can consequently not be maintained.

　　　Let us examine at this point how the AP-Raising hypothesis fares w.r.t. (26), restricting the attention to the prenominal structure (26)a first. As shown by the parse for (26)a given under (27), *young man* originates in the comparative complement, from where it moves into the higher SpecDegP.

This (trivially) forces the CD-site to be restored as *young man*:

(27)

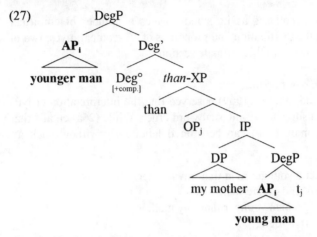

The analysis of the postnominal construction (26)b proceeds equally straightforward.

(28)

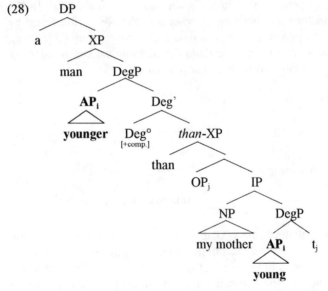

As illustrated by (28) above, the underlying source of the comparative in (26b) is a predicative clause headed by the AP *young*. AP-Raising therefore targets the AP only, and the postnominal DegP is subsequently combined with the head noun.[11]

What is important for present purposes is the observation that the two serializations and their respective interpretations correspond to the two possible base-generated stuctures inside the comparative clause that the current theory allows AP-Raising to operate on. SpecDegP may either host an AP that modifies an NP, or an AP alone, which predicates of the subject of the *than*-XP. These different base-generated structures directly translate into two different word-order patterns for the matrix DP.

5.2. The CD-Site *can* be Small

The second pre- vs. postnominal asymmetry to be considered here stems again from Bresnan (1973). Whereas the contrast (26) demonstrated that the CD-site of a postnominal comparative *can* be small, example (29) attests to the fact that the ellipsis may not remove a constituent larger than an AP.

(29)   She met a man younger than Mary △
    a.   △ = (is) d-young
    b.   *△ = met a d-young man

In (29), the CD-site *has* to small, the sentence lacks a 'wide', VP-elliptical reading, which is manifest exclusively in prenominal NP-comparatives:

(30)   She met a younger man than my mother △
    a.   △ = (is) d-young
    b.   △ = met a d-young men

Again, this follows straightforwardly from current assumptions. In the postnominal construction, it is only an AP which is raised into the higher SpecDegP. SpecDegP of the comparative clause in (29) therefore also has to be occupied by an AP. But the selectional restrictions induced by the main predicate inside the comparative clause require that the verb take a DP-object - and not a bare AP - as an internal argument. Thus, the wide reading (29b) is unavailable for the same reason for which its underlying source (31a) is deviant:

(31)   a.   *She met a man younger than Mary met young
    b.   *... a man [$_{DegP}$ [$_{AP}$ younger] than [$_{CP}$ Mary met [$_{DegP}$ [$_{AP}$ **young**]]]]

The AP-Raising hypothesis correctly leads us to expect that in the

---

[11]I will remain agnostic as to the syntactic structure of the nexus between the DegP and the NP in the postnominal modifier. The present proposal is compatible with a variety of assumptions, such as right-adjunction, as in (28), or low embedding (following Haider (1995), Kayne (1994)).

postnominal construction, the main predicate of the *than*-XP is realized as an AP, efficiently blocking the wide construal of the ellipsis.[12]

6. Conclusion

I have argued that CD is not the product of ellipsis, but derives from overt movement of an AP from the comparative into the matrix clause. The AP-Raising analysis adequately accounts for the locality restrictions on CD, reconstruction effects into the comparative clause, and the impact of word-order variaton on the size of the CD-site. Furthermore, evidence in favor of a new structure for prenominally modified NP's was supplied which supports the assumption of a right-branching extended projection of the DP.

References

Abney, Stephen. 1987. *The English NP in its Sentential Aspect.* Doctoral Dissertation, MIT.

Berman, Arlene. 1973. *Adjectives and Adjective Complement Constructions in English.* Doctoral Dissertation, Harvard University.

Bresnan, Joan. 1973. Syntax of the Comparative Clause Construction in English. *Linguistic Inquiry* 4:3. 275-343.

Chomsky, Noam. 1986. *Knowledge of Language.* New York: Praeger.

Chomsky, Noam. 1995. *The Minimalist Program.* Cambridge, Mass.: MIT-Press.

Corver, Norbert. 1993. *Functional Categories, Phrase Structure and Word Order within the Adjectical System.* Ms., University of Tilburg.

Corver, Norbert. 1994. A Note on Subcomparatives.*Linguistic Inquiry* 25:4. 773-781.

Corver, Norbert. 1997. *Much*-Support as a Last Resort. *Linguistic Inquiry* 28:1. 119-165.

Culicover, Peter. 1972. OM-Sentences. *Foundations of Linguistics* 8. 199-236

Culicover, Peter & Ray Jackendoff. 1997. Semantic Subordination Despite Syntactic Coordination. *Linguistic Inquiry* 28:2. 195-219.

Goldsmith, John. 1985. A principled exception to the Coordinate Structure Constraint. *Proceedings of CLS 21.* 133-143.

Grodinsky, Yosef & Tanya Reinhart. 1993. The Innateness of Binding and Coreference. *Linguistic Inquiry* 24:1. 69-101.

Haider, Hubert. 1993. *Deutsche Syntax - Generativ.* Tübingen: Gunter Narr.

Haider, Hubert. 1995. *Extraposition.* Ms., University of Stuttgart.

Heim, Irene, Howard Lasnik & Robert May. 1991. Reciprocity and Plurality. *Linguistic Inquiry* 22:1. 63-101.

Izvorski, Ruoumi. 1995. A DP-Shell for Comparatives. *Proceeding of CONSOLE* III.

Jayaseelan, K.A. 1990. Incomplete VP Deletion and Gapping. *Linguistic Analysis* 20:1-2. 64-81.

Johnson, Kyle. 1997. *When Verb Phrases go Missing.* Ms., Umass/Amherst.

---

[12]Furthermore, as pointed out by B.Partee (pc), postnominal comparatives are - correctly - predicted to be well-formed whenever independent syntactic considerations license a bare AP-predicate inside the comparative clause:

    (i)   She met a man more intelligent than I consider him △   (△ = d-intelligent)

Kayne, Richard. 1994. *The Antisymmetry of Syntax.* Cambridge, Mass.: MIT-Press.

Kennedy, Christopher. 1997. *Projecting the Adjective: The Syntax and Semantics of Gradability and Comparison.* Doctoral Dissertation, UCSC.

Kennedy, Christopher & Jason Merchant. 1997. Attributive Comparatives and Bound Ellipsis. *Linguistics Research Center Report* LRC-97-03. Santa Cruz: UCSC.

Lasnik, Howard. 1995. A Note on Pseudogapping, in R. Pensalfini and H. Ura, eds., *Papers on Minimalist Syntax,* MITWIPL. Cambridge, Mass.: MIT.

Lechner, Winfried. 1988a. *The AP-Raising Analysis of Comparative Deletion.* Ms., Umass/Amherst.

Lechner, Winfried. 1988b. Phrasal Comparatives and DP-Structure. *Proceedings of NELS 28.*

Lerner, Jan & Manfred Pinkal. 1995. Comparative Ellipsis and Variable Binding. *Proceedings of SALT V.* 222-236.

Moltmann, Friederike. 1992. *Coordination and Comparatives.* Doctoral Dissertation, MIT.

Napoli, Donna Jo. 1983. Comparative Ellipsis: A Phrase Structure Account. *Linguistic Inquiry* 14:4. 675-694.

Pinkham, Jessie. 1982. *The Formation of Comparative Clauses in French and English,* reprinted as Pinkham (1985), New York: Garland.

Reinhart, Tanya. 1983. *Anaphora and Semantic Interpretation.* Croom-Helm, Chicago University Press.

Reinhart, Tanya. 1995. *Interface Strategies.* OTS Working Papers, Utrecht University.

Stanley, Richard 1969. The English Comparative Adjective Construction, in R. Binnick et al., eds., *Papers from the 5th Regional Meeting of the Chicago Linguistics Society.* Chicago: University of Chicago.

von Stechow, Arnim. 1984. Comparing Semantic Theories of Comparison. *Journal of Semantics* 3. 1-77.

Williams, Edwin. 1994. *Thematic Structure in Syntax.* Cambridge, Mass.: MIT-Press.

Williams, Edwin. 1977. Discourse and Logical Form. *Linguistic Inquiry* 8:1. 101-141.

Morphological and Prosodic Alignment at Work: The Case of South-Slavic Clitics*

Géraldine Legendre

Johns Hopkins University

1. Introduction

Closely related Bulgarian (B) and Macedonian (M) share a basic inventory of clausal clitics. This includes auxiliary clitics, pronominal clitics, a negative particle and a yes-no question particle, some of which are given in (1).

(1) Clausal Clitics: *go* 'it-accusative'; *ti* 'you-dative'; *mu* 'him-dative'; *ne* 'negative'; *li* 'Q particle'; B *sŭm*/M *sum* 'be-1sg'; B *šte*/M *ḱe* 'future'.

B and M clitics share a number of properties. Auxiliary and pronominal clitics are syntactically inactive, compared to their non-clitic counterparts -- as argued in Legendre (1998, in press). Second-position effects are detectable in both null-subject languages. Yet, two clitics systematically evade second-position effects: *ne* and *šte/ḱe*. Stressed clitics are possible in both languages. Finally, prosodic constraints play a role in both languages as well: *li* cannot precede the first stressed word. Stressed syllables/clitics are represented in uppercase.

A closer look, however, reveals a markedly different distribution.

(2) B   a. poKAzax *mu go.*
           '(I) showed it to him'
       b. *ne MU go* POkazax.
           '(I) didn't show it to him'

       e. VIŽdal *li go e?*
           'Has (he) seen him?'
       f. *ne ŠTE li go* VIŽdaš?
           'Will (you) not see him?'

* Special thanks go to Olga Tomić and Marina Todorova for their help with the Macedonian and Bulgarian data and to Loren Billings and Paul Smolensky for comments and discussion. The usual disclaimers apply.

436

c. *šte s ŭm* PROčel.
    '(I) will read'
d. *ne ŠTE s ŭm* PROčel.
    '(I) will have read'

g. *šte go* VIŽdaš *li*?
    'Will (you) see him?'
h. *ne MU li* IZpratix KNIgata?
    'Didn't (I) send him the book?'

As shown in (2), the B perfect auxiliary *s ŭm* and pronominal clitics *mu go* cluster in second position (P2), regardless of context. B *ne* and *šte* can serve as hosts for P2 clitics which then precede the verb rather than follow it. B *ne* and *li* may not be stressed. Any clitic immediately following *ne* must be stressed (Hauge (1976)). B *ne* systematically affects the prosody, yielding two stress domains. Finally, in the absence of a focused element, B *li* must immediately follow the first stressed element, verbal head or clitic (Hauge (1976)).

(3) M   a. *ti go* DAde.
            '(He) gave it to you'
        b. *ne ti GO* dade.
            '(He) did not give it to you'
        c. NAjaden *sum*.
            '(I) have come'
        d. *NE sum* NAjaden.
            '(I) have not come'
        e. *sum ti go* KAzal.
            '(I) have told it to you'
        f. *ne sum ti GO* kazal.
            '(I) have not told it to you'

        g. *ti go* DAde *li*?
            'Did (he) give it to you?'
        h. *ne ti GO* dade *li*?
            'Didn't (he) give it to you?'
        i. NAjaden *li sum*?
            'Am (I) fed (=full)?'
        j. *NE sum li* NAjaden?
            'Ain't (I) fed?'
        k. dajTE *mu go*!
            'Give it to him!'
        l. *ne* davajTE *mu go*!
            'Don't give it to him!'

In M, however, the perfect auxiliary and pronominal clitics cluster in pre-verbal position in some contexts, in post-verbal position in others. Like in B, M *ne* (and *ke*) can serve as hosts for P2 clitics. Yet, encliticization persists in negative imperatives. M *li* is the only clitic that cannot be stressed. But unlike in B, M *ne* can be stressed and M clitics following *ne* need not be stressed. Nor does the presence of *ne* systematically result in two stress domains in M, though it sometimes does (e.g. 3b vs. 3d). Finally, M *li* does not necessarily immediately follow the first stressed element either, though it sometimes does (e.g. 3h vs. 3j).

This descriptive summary highlights the complex nature of clitic distribution in the two languages. I shall argue here that a comparatively simple account of this distribution in terms of a small set of universal constraints is possible if these constraints are assumed to be violable within and re-rankable across languages.

2. The Role of Morphology

In recent work (Legendre (1997, 1998, in press)), I have argued that Balkan clausal clitics are not syntactic elements subject to syntactic constraints; rather they are PF realizations of functional features attached to verbal nodes in the syntax. In other words, following Anderson (1992), I take clitics to be phrasal affixes or morphological categories.

In Optimality Theory (OT, Prince and Smolensky (1993)), morphology is grounded in universal alignment constraints. One important job of morphology is to align bound affixes with the edge of a particular domain. Because affixes typically occur in a sequence, alignment constraints must be individualized. Thus alignment is a universal schema (Align (αCat, E(dge); βCat, E(dge); McCarthy and Prince (1993a,b)) which yields families of constraints.

OT's theory of morphology can be straightforwardly extended to phrasal affixes or clitics (See also Anderson (1996)). Alignment immediately explains why clitics, like bound affixes, cluster. It is simply because they compete for the same position. Given several features which all seek to be aligned with the same (say, left) edge of a single domain, the ranking of individualized alignment constraints predicts their respective order of PF realization. This approach naturally captures the fact that clitics do not get re-ordered within a given language based on context, even in languages with fairly free word order such as B and M. The OT implementation is as follows: clitics are subject to a set of individualized EDGEMOST(F) constraints which align the left edge of the PF realization of [F] with the left edge of a particular domain D.

The second most important property of clitics pertains to where they cluster. In our terms, clustering results from the interaction of EDGEMOST(F) with another (negative) alignment constraint called NONINITIAL(F). The latter requires that any feature [F] be realized in a non-initial position in a domain D.

In OT terms, two constraints always yield two possible rankings. Assuming the domain D to be identifiable with null-subject clauses like (2)-(3) for the moment, consider the consequences of the two rankings. If NONINITIAL(F) outranks EDGEMOST(F), [F] is realized in P2. That is, [F] is realized as close as possible to the left edge of the domain D without violating NONINITIAL(F). If, on the other hand, EDGEMOST(F) outranks NONINITIAL(F), [F] is realized domain-initially (i.e. P1). That is, it is more important for [F] to be realized in P1 than to satisfy NONINITIAL(F).

2.1 Bulgarian
Both rankings are in fact found within B, for different instantiations of [F].

(4) a. poKAzax *mu go*.   c. *šte s*$\check{u}$*m* PROčel.
      '(I) showed it to him'   '(I) will read'
     b. *ne MU go* POkazax.   d. *ne ŠTE s*$\check{u}$*m* PROčel.
      '(I) didn't show it to him'   '(I) will have read'

As shown in (4), some B clitics are P2 clitics (perfect auxiliary and object pronouns) while others are P1 clitics (negative particle and future auxiliary.) This distribution straightforwardly follows from a ranking in which some EDGEMOST(F) constraints outrank NONINITIAL(F) while other EDGEMOST(F) constraints are outranked by NONINITIAL(F). The competition is formalized in T1.

T1. BULGARIAN PARTICIPLES[1]

I: [fut] [perf]	E(FUT)	NIN(F)	E(PERF)
☞ a. [v' šte sŭm pročel knigata]		⊛	⊛
b. [pročel šte sŭm knigata]	*!		**
c. [šte pročel sŭm knigata]		*	**!

Consider what the domain of these alignment constraints is, turning to EDGEMOST first. Note that šte and ne satisfy EDGEMOST, despite the fact that they do not carry stress. The fact that a P2 clitic can be hosted by a phonologically weak element is evidence that the left edge requirement is not prosodic in nature. Rather it pertains to a phrase structure constituent. The precise characterization of this syntactic constituent largely depends on one's assumptions about clausal structure. A central concept in OT is economy, including economy of structure (Legendre et al. (1995, 1998)). Under the VP-internal subject hypothesis this means that a simple clause need not involve more than a VP. Another relevant assumption concerns null subjects. If null subjects do not exist -- as proposed in Grimshaw and Samek-Lodovici (1995) -- then a subjectless clause is a V'.

Empirical evidence for a V' domain comes from sentences containing an overt subject.

(5) B   Az šte sŭm pročel knigata.
         I fut perf read book-the
         'I will have read the book'

As (5) shows, the domain-initial clitic šte follows rather than precedes the overt subject, az. This shows that the domain is V' rather than VP. Otherwise, šte would precede az.

Consider next the fact that EDGEMOST(F) is a gradient constraint. That is, violations of EDGEMOST(F) increase as [F] is realized further away from the left edge of V'. As T1 shows, EDGEMOST(PERF) is fatal to candidate (c) because of

[1] All tableaux incorporate standard OT conventions: ☞ = optimal candidate; * = individual violations of a given constraint; *! = fatal violations; ⊛ = violations incurred by optimal candidates. Leftmost constraints = highest ranked; rightmost constraints = lowest ranked. The input (I) consists of lexical items and their propositional structure, plus functional features like [perfect], [negation], etc. In the interest of space, only the best candidates for a given input are being considered.

its gradiency. Degree of violation of EDGEMOST(F) could in principle be measured in terms of morphological or prosodic units. As it turns out, both are relevant to B and M.

Note that a non-stressed clitic like *ne, šte* may serve as host for auxiliary and pronominal clitics, as shown in (2-3). This means that degree of violation of EDGEMOST(F) for these clitics is measured in terms of the number of morphemes that separate the PF realization of [F] from the left edge of V'. As we will see later, it is Prosodic Words that count for *li*.Thus EDGEMOST(F) is clearly an interface constraint, connecting on the one hand the morphology to the syntax and the morphology to the prosody, on the other.

Finally, consider the domain of NONINITIAL(F). Simple sentences offer no evidence for a prosodic or phrase structure characterization because the two domains are conflated. Complex sentences, however, show that the relevant domain is the Intonational Phrase.

(6) B   Knigata, Penka *ja*   *e*   dala na Petko.   (Tomić (1996))
       book-the Penka it-acc be-3 given to Petko
       'As for the book, Penka gave it to Petko'

Note that the fronted topicalized object in (6) is separated by an intonational break from the rest of the sentence. Note also that no word-order change affects the subject, the verb, and the clitics. For the purpose of counting second position, it is as if the topicalized NP doesn't exist. This follows if the domain of NONINITIAL(F) is the Intonational Phrase.[2]

2.2 Macedonian

In M, clitics precede finite verbs (7a,b) while they follow non-finite structures -- such as predicative and presentative constructions (7c,d).

(7) M   a. *Ti go* dade.   c. Mil *si mi*.
          '(He) gave it to you'   '(You) are dear to me'
       b. *Ke* dojdam.   d. Ene *go* čovekot.
          will come   here him man-the
          '(I) will come'   'Here is the man'

In Legendre (in press), I argue that the core M pattern is a verb-second (V2) pattern. This can be interpreted in terms of the constraints proposed above if NONINITIAL is decomposed into two alignment constraints: NONINITIAL(T) -- where T stands for tense/finiteness -- and NONINITIAL(F) for all remaining

---

[2] See additional evidence in Tagalog (Legendre (1998)) and Serbo-Croatian (Radanović-Kocić (1996)).

features. V2 in (7a,b) results from NONINITIAL(T) outranking (>>) EDGEMOST(T).

Clitics, however, follow non-finite verbs/predicates, as shown in (7c,d). This suggests that M clitics favor P2 as well: NONINITIAL(F) >> EDGEMOST(F). The outcome is a competition for P2. If present in the input, [T] prevails with the result that [T] is realized on the verb in P2 while clitics are not (7a,b). This reveals the relative ranking of the constraints pertaining to [T] and those pertaining to other features: NONINITIAL(T) >> NONINITIAL(F). That is, NONINITIAL(F) will be violated in order for NONINITIAL(T) to be satisfied. Clitics appear in P1 because the P2 requirement on [T] outweighs that of other features.[3] This is formally represented in T2.

T2. MACEDONIAN FINITE VERBS

I: [dat] [acc] [T]	NIN(T)	NIN(F)	E(DAT)	E(ACC)
☞ a. [$_V$, *ti go* dade]		⊛		⊛
b. [dade *ti go*]	*!		*	**
c. [ti dade go]		*		**!

Of particular interest in M are the deviations from the core pattern, exemplified in (8). (8a) contains an *l*-participle while (8b) contains a past participle usually referred to as a verbal adjective. Both (8a,b) are non-finite -- see Legendre (in press) for evidence. The only difference is that *l*-participles carry an evidentiality feature/suffix -*l* conveying an unwitnessed event.

(8) M   a. *Sum ti go* kazal.   b. Najaden *sum*.
        '(I) have told it to you'   '(I) am fed'

Note that clitic auxiliaries like *si, sum* are special from the perspective of the present feature-based approach. They instantiate two separate features, [perfect] and [T]. Suppose that M [perf] is basically like B [fut], that is, it is a P1 clitic in an otherwise P2-clitic language. In terms of constraint ranking, this means that EDGEMOST(PERF) outranks NONINITIAL(F). This leads to a conflict: on the one hand, *sum* seeks P1 because it instantiates [perf]; on the other, *sum* seeks P2 because it instantiates [T].

This conflict can be resolved by ranking EDGEMOST(PERF) equally with NONINITIAL(T) -- see the dotted separations in tableaux T3-T5. As a consequence, EDGEMOST(PERF) and NONINITIAL(T) violations cancel out and the optimal candidate is determined by lower ranked constraints.

---

[3] In B, the distribution of clitics is not sensitive to finiteness. This means that NONINITIAL(T) is low-ranked in B.

In the case of verbal and predicate adjectives, the next constraint on the hierarchy is NonInitial(F), which precludes clitics in P1. There is one way and one way only to satisfy it: by encliticization. This is shown in T3.

T3. Macedonian verbal adjectives

I: [T] [perf]	E(Perf)	NIn(T)	NIn(F)
☞ a. [$_{V'}$ najaden *sum*]	⊛		
b. [*sum* najaden]		*	*!

In the case of *l*-participles, all elements carry at least one feature, hence NonInitial(F) is violated by all candidates, as shown in T4.

T4. Macedonian *l*-participles

I: [T][perf][dat][acc][ev]	E(Perf)	NIn(T)	NIn(F)	E(Dat)	E(Acc)	E(Ev)
☞ a. [$_{V'}$ *sum ti go* kazal]		⊛	⊛	⊛	⊛⊛	⊛⊛⊛
b. [*ti go sum* kazal]	*!*		*		*	***
c. [kazal *sum ti go*]	*		*	**!	***	
d. [*sum* kazal *ti go*]		*	*	**!	***	*
e. [*sum ti* kazal *go*]		*	*	*	***!	**

The optimal candidate in T4 is the one which minimizes violations of lower-ranked constraints, hence the one in which the dative clitic is in P2 and the accusative clitic in P3: candidate (a).

Negation in M is interesting because it affects the position of clitics, in a superficially non-systematic way. Enclitics surface as proclitics in participle and predicative constructions but they remain as verbal enclitics in imperatives.

(9) M   a. Najaden *sum*.   c. *Ne sum* najaden.
        '(I) am fed'   '(I) am not fed'
    b. Mil *si mi*.   d. *Ne si mi* mil.
        '(You) are dear to me'   '(You) are not dear to me'

(10) M   a. Daj *mu go*!   b. *Ne* davajte *mu go*!
        'Give it to him!'   'Don't give it to me!'

In fact, both patterns naturally follow from the present analysis. Given a high-ranking of Edgemost(neg), all candidates violate NonInitial(F).

T5. MACEDONIAN NEGATIVE VERBAL ADJECTIVES

I: [neg] [T] [perf]	E(N)	E(PERF)	NIN(T)	NIN(F)
a. [*ne* dojden *sum*]		**!		*
☞ b. [*ne sum* dojden]		⊛		⊛

The decision falls to EDGEMOST(PERF) in T5, which favors realizing [perf] as close as possible to the edge but not quite at the edge, hence in P2.

In the case of imperatives -- argued to be finite in Legendre (in press)--, the decision falls to EDGEMOST(IMP) in a parallel fashion, under the assumption that EDGEMOST(IMP) occupies the same relative ranking as EDGEMOST(PERF). But because [imp] is also a word-level affix, it results in the verb seeking P2.

T6. MACEDONIAN NEGATIVE IMPERATIVES

I:[neg] [T][imp][dat][acc]	E(N)	E(IMP)	NIN(T)	NIN(F)	E(DAT)	E(ACC)
☞a. [*ne* davajte *mu go*]		⊛		⊛	⊛⊛	⊛⊛⊛
b. [*ne mu go* davajte]		*!**		*	*	**

To summarize the discussion of M, all features favor P2. The outcome of the competition depends on which features compete for a given input.

Note that the position of clitics under the present analysis results from morphological alignment with V'. But some clitics carry stress, as illustrated in (2)-(3). Hence, it is imperative to investigate next the role of prosody in B and M.

3. The Role of Prosody

3.1. Bulgarian

That B *ne* and *li* obey prosodic constraints has been known since Hauge (1976)[4]. I shall argue below that the prosodic parsing of B clitics is as in (11), where curly brackets {} are used to represent Prosodic Words (PrWds).

(11) B a. *Šte go* {$_{PrWd}$ VIŽdas}.
      '(You) will see him'
   b. {$_{PrWd}$ *Ne ŠTE*} *go* {$_{PrWd}$ VIŽdas}.
      '(You) will not see him'

Clitics, unlike lexical heads, are in general stressless. In our terms, this follows from a constraint, PARSE(F, PRPH), which requires them to be parsed directly in

---

[4] Working within a standard transformational approach, Hauge states that '*ne* always moves its stress over to the following word, also when this word is a clitic'(p. 18) and '*li* is placed immediately to the right of the first stressed element within the verb constituent' (p. 20).

the higher unit of prosodic structure called Prosodic Phrase (PrPh). Hence, they are not parsed into PrWd and receive no word-level stress. Lexical Heads, on the other hand, are assumed to be left-aligned in the PrWd they head (Selkirk (1995)): ALIGN(LEXHEAD, L; PRWD, L).

Obviously, at least some B clitics do get parsed into a PrWd in a negative context, as (11b) above shows. Stress on the future clitic *ŠTE*, I propose, results from the interaction of two constraints. One is PARSE(F, PRPH) which both *ne* and *šte* violate. In light of Hauge's generalization, the other constraint pertains to *ne*. It can be stated as another instantiation of prosodic alignment: ALIGN(NEG, R; PRWDHD, L). That is, [neg] is right-aligned with the left edge of the head of PrWd or stressed syllable.[5] Finally, these prosodic constraints interact with a general constraint on economy of prosodic structure ,*PRWD, a member of the *STRUCTURE constraint family proposed in Prince and Smolensky (1993:25).

The resulting competition is formalized in the double tableau T7, with the positive context at the top and the negative context at the bottom.

T7. PROSODY OF BULGARIAN *NE*

	A(N)	A(LEXHD)	P(F, PRPH)	*PRWD
☞ a. [$_V$, *šte go* {VÍŽdas}]				⊗
b. [{*šte go* VÍŽdas}]		*!*	**	*
c. [{*ŠTE go*} {VÍŽdas}]			*!*	**
☞ d. [{*ne ŠTE*} *go* {VÍŽdas}]			⊗⊗	⊗⊗
e. [{*ne ŠTE go*} {VÍŽdas}]			***!	**
f. [{*ne ŠTE*} {*go* VÍŽdas}]		*!	***	**
g. [{*NE šte*} *go* {VÍŽdas}]	*!		**	**

In the presence of *ne* (bottom competition), the two highest-ranked constraints -- A-R(NEG) and A-L(LEXHD) -- can both be satisfied if the sequence is parsed into two prosodic words and *go* is not parsed within the second PrWd (candidates (d) and (e)). This, in turn, suggests that *PRWD is relatively low-ranked in B. In T7 then, the decision falls to PARSE(F, PRPH) which favors parsing the clitic *go* outside of either PrWd.

Recall Hauge's generalization according to which *li* must immediately follow the first stressed element. In our terms, *immediately* is the consequence of ALIGN(Q, L; PRWD, R) while *after the first stressed element* is the consequence of EDGEMOST(Q). But here is the twist: while the EDGEMOST constraints governing other P2 clitics are evaluated on the basis of the number of morphemes

---

[5] The alignment constraint on *ne* refers to alignment with the PrWd Head in B but with PrWd in M. As far as I can tell, this is the simplest way of capturing the fact that B *ne*, unlike its M counterpart, may never be stressed.

that separate them from the left edge of V', the EDGEMOST constraint governing *li* is evaluated on the basis on the number of PrWds that separate it from the left edge of V'. This is shown in T8.[6]

If the units relevant to violations of EDGEMOST(Q) were the same as those of EDGEMOST(ACC), then candidate (b) would win the top competition -- *li* is closer to the left edge of V' in terms of morphemes (two) than candidate (a) (three). In terms of PrWds, however, *li* is equally close to the left edge of V'in candidates (a) and (b). As T8 shows, the decision falls to lower-ranked EDGEMOST(ACC) which favors realizing [acc] in P2. Note that the relative ranking EDGEMOST(Q) >> EDGEMOST(ACC) is independently supported by the competition between candidates (f) and (g).[7]

T8. PROSODY OF BULGARIAN *LI*

	A(Q)	P(F, PrPh)	*PRWD	E (Q)	E (FUT)	E (ACC)
☞ a. [ᵥ' *šte go* {VIŽdas} *li*]			⊛	⊛		⊛
b. [*šte* {VIŽdas} *li go*]			*	*		*!**
c. [*šte li go* {VIŽdas}]	*!**		*			**
d. [*šte go li* {VIŽdas}]	*!*		*			*
e. [*go šte* {VIŽdas} *li*]			*	*	*!	
☞ f.[{*ne ŠTE*} *li go* {VIŽdas}]		⊛⊛	⊛⊛	⊛	⊛	⊛⊛⊛
g.[{*ne ŠTE*} *go* {VIŽdas} *li*]		**	**	**!	*	**
h. [{*ne šte li go* VIŽdas}]	*!**	****	*		*	***
i.[{*ne GO*} *li šte* {VIŽdas}]		**	**	*	**!*	*

3.2 Macedonian

With respect to prosody, M differs from B in two important respects. One is its stress system. While B has lexical word stress, M has antepenultimate stress (AP), a fairly unusual system discussed in Franks (1987). Though AP ultimately results from the interaction of several constraints (Prince and Smolensky (1993)), I will treat it here as a single constraint 'AP' because I am only interested in the interaction between stress and the alignment constraints pertaining to clitics.

M also differs from B with respect to the prosody of *ne*. The data is organized into subpatterns, labelled A , B, C , etc. in (12). The prosodic bracketing reflects the outcome of optimization.

---

[6] Constraints A(N) and A(LexHd) are omitted in T8 for space considerations. They do not affect the outcome of the competitions though they are fatal to other candidates omitted in T8.

[7] If EDGEMOST(ACC) outranked EDGEMOST(Q), then candidate (f) would lose to (g): two violations of EDGEMOST(ACC) for (g) vs. three for (f).

(12) Macedonian Stress Patterns   (*AP = AP is violated)

Pattern A	*AP	**Pattern B**	AP
a. *ti go* {DAde}		a. {*ne ti GO* dade}	
b. *sum ti go* {KAzal}		b. {*ne sum ti GO* kazal}	

Pattern C	AP	**Pattern D**	AP
a. {dajTE *mu go!*}		a. {*ne* davajTE *mu go!*}	
b. {doNEsi *go!*}		b. {*ne* doneSUvaj *go!*}	

Pattern E	*AP	**Pattern F**	
a. {TATko} *mi e*		a. {*NE*} *mi e* {TATko} *AP	
b. {NAjaden} *sum*		b. {*NE*} *sum* {NAjaden} AP	

In the absence of *ne*, the sequence of clitics and its host carries one word-level stress (e.g. patterns A, C, E). In the presence of *ne*, however, patterns B and D carry one stress while pattern F carries two. This suggests that *PRWD is higher-ranked in M than B: it is violated only in a subset of cases.

Looking briefly at the patterns in (12), one may observe some broad effects of AP. In some cases it results in stressed clitics (pattern B); in other cases it results in movable stress on the root, depending on the number of enclitics present (as is the case with imperatives in patterns C and D).

But note the complexity of the stress pattern. Note first that satisfaction of AP does not correlate with either encliticization or procliticization. That is, AP is satisfied in some patterns of encliticization (C, D), but violated in others (E). With respect to procliticization, AP is satisfied in (B) and (Fb) but violated in (A, Fa). Nor does satisfaction of AP correlate with either presence or absence of *ne*: AP is satisfied in some negative patterns (B, D) but violated in others (Fa). Finally, AP is satisfied in some positive patterns (C) but violated in others (A, E).

The OT approach, however, allows us to make sense of this complexity in a straightforward fashion. First, the alignment constraint on *ne* is clearly high-ranked in M, based on (B,D). This, in turn, results in parsing *ne* within the PrWd headed by the verb, allowing AP to be satisfied. As a consequence, P(F,PrPh) is violated. In the absence of *ne*, however, AP is violated but P(F,PrPh) is satisfied, as (A) shows. This suggests that P(F,PrPh) outranks AP.

Consider next the two encliticization cases in (C) and (E). Suppose that there is another alignment constraint at work whose effects were undetectable in B: ALIGN(PRPH, R; PRWD, R). It aligns the right edge of PrPh with the right edge of PrWd. This constraint is in fact satisfied in every case where AP is satisfied, including B, C, D, and F. It's clearly violated in pattern E, however. Otherwise

AP would prevail (clitics encliticize to their host in E).[8]

The explanation of M patterns C and D is simple: M clitics are parsed within PrWd rather than PrPh becasue it makes the right alignment of PrPh and PrWd possible. This is turn shows that P(F,PrPh) can be violated within M, despite the fact that it often is satisfied, as shown in Patterns A ,E, and F. This explanation in formalized in T9. Note that A(NEG) -- omitted for space considerations -- is satisfied by all candidates.

T9. PROSODY OF MACEDONIAN IMPERATIVES (Patterns C and D)

	*PRWD	A(PRPH, PRWD)	P(F, PRPH)	AP	A(LEXHD)
☞a. {dajTE *mu go*}	⊛		⊛⊛		
b. {DAJte} *mu go*	*	*!		*	
☞c. { *ne* davajTE *mu go*}	⊛		⊛⊛⊛		⊛
d. {*NE*} {davajTE *mu go*}	**!		***	**	
e. {*NE*} {davajTE} *mu go*	**!	*	*	****	
f. {*ne* davajTE} *mu go*	*	*!	*	**	*
g. {*ne* DAvajte} *mu go*	*	*!	*		*

Turning to patterns A and B, clitics are parsed outside of PrWd in positive contexts as expected, given P(F, PHPR). They are, however, parsed within PrWd in the presence of *ne* because *ne*'s requirement to be parsed within PrWd outweighs the general constraint on parsing clitics outside of PrWd. The formal competition is displayed in T10. Note that A-R(PrPh,PrWd) -- omitted for space considerations -- is satisfied by all candidates.

T10. PROSODY OF MACEDONIAN L-PARTICIPLES (Patterns A and B)

	A(N)	*PRWD	P(F,PRPH)	AP	A(LEXHD)
a. {*sum ti GO* kazal}		*	*!**		***
b. *sum ti* {*GO* kazal}		*	*!		*
☞ c. *sum ti go* {KAzal}		⊛		⊛	
☞ d.{*ne sum ti GO* kazal}		⊛	⊛⊛⊛⊛		⊛⊛⊛⊛
e. *ne sum ti* {*GO* kazal}	*!	*	*		*
f. {*NE*} {*sum ti GO* kazal}		**!	****	**	***
g. {*NE*} *sum ti* {*GO* kazal}		**!	**	**	*
h. {*NE sum ti*} {*GO* kazal}		**!	****		*
i. {*ne SUM ti go*}{KAzal}		**!	****	*	

---

[8] Note that ALIGN(PRPH, R; PRWD, R), while generally satified in M, is systematically violated by *li* in positive B contexts. This suggests that its relative ranking in B is low.

What remains to be explained is the odd pattern of past participles (patterns E and F).[9] Clearly, *PRWD is doubly violated in negative verbal adjectives. This suggests that there is a higher-ranked constraint at work which is not present in other verbal forms. Note that the pattern is limited to forms that are verbal, but in a limited sense. In fact, these past participles are typically referred to in the Slavic literature as *verbal adjectives*. This is because they share several fundamental properties of adjectives. They are inflected for gender and number and they are the only participles that can function as attributes (Lunt (1952)). The third person copula can never be omitted with adjectives including verbal adjectives while its homophonous perfect counterpart must be omitted with *l*-participles (which can never function as attributes).

Thus, I propose that there are additional alignment constraints on [+N] categories: predicative adjectives and nouns as well as verbal adjectives. One, ALIGN(+N, L; PRWD, L) requires alignment of the left edge of a [+N] Lexical Head with the left edge of PrWd. The other, ALIGN(+N, R;PRWD, R) requires alignment of the right edge of a [+N] Lexical Head with the right edge of PrWd. Together, these two constraints have the effect that [+N] categories form their own PrWd. This shows that the prosody is sensitive to features, including [neg], [Q], and [+N].

As T11 shows, in the absence of *ne*, oprimal M verbal adjectives violate a constraint otherwise satisfied: A-R(PrPh,PrWD).

T11. PROSODY OF MACEDONIAN VERBAL ADJECTIVES (PATTERNS E AND F)[10]

	A-L(+N)	A-R(+N)	*PRWD	A(PRPH, PRWD)	P(F, PRPH)
☞ a. {NAjaden} *sum*			⊛	⊛	
b. {naJAden *sum*}		*!	*		*
c. {NAjaden *sum*}		*!	*		*
d.{*NE sum*}{NAjaden}			**		**!
☞ e.{*NE*}*sum*{NAjaden}			⊛⊛		⊛
f. {*ne sum* NAjaden}	*!*		*		**

I have omitted *li* from the M discussion simply because its behavior is completely regular. The interaction of A-L(Q) and EDGEMOST(Q) results in *li* being placed immediately after the first PrWd. In the case of M, this means, for example, the pattern in (13). In B, however, this means the pattern in (14).

---

[9] Pattern F is omitted in Franks' (1987) discussion of M prosody.

[10] Note that candidates (c), (d), and (e) also violate low-ranked AP, omitted for space considerations.

(13) M   a. *Sum ti go* {KAzal} *li?*   b. {*Ne sum ti GO* kazal} *li?*
          'Have (I) told it to you?'   'Haven't (I) told it to you?'

(14) B   a. {izPRAtix} *li mu* {knigata}?   b. {*ne MU* } *li* {izPRAtix}...?
          'Did (I) send him the book?'   'Didn't (I) send him ...?'

Leaving aside the morphological alignment of other clitics which provides the input to the prosody, my proposal is that the difference results from different constraint rankings in M and B. Of particular relevance to B is the high-ranking of A-L(LexHd), which together with P(F,PrPh), result in a default parsing of clitics outside of PrWd. The marked case in B is *ne*. In M, on the other hand, the default parsing of clitics is inside PrWd. Interestingly enough, the present analysis reveals that this state of affairs is not due to AP-- since AP is lower ranked than P(F,PrPh). Rather, the default parsing of M clitics within the PrWd results from a stronger aversion for building prosodic structure and a stronger desire to right-align PrPhs with PrWds. Crucially, the constraints are the same. This means that the distribution relies on constraint re-ranking. The rankings of M and B prosodic constraints are given in (15).

(15) Rankings of Prosodic Constraints:
     a. M: A-L(Q) >> A-L(NEG) >> A-L(+N, PRWD), A-R(+N, PRWD) >>
     *PRWD >> A-R(PRPH,PRWD >> P(F, PRPH) >> AP >> A-L(LEXHD)

     b. B: A-L(Q), A-R(NEG) >> A-L(LEXHD) >> P(F, PRPH) >> *PRWD >>
     A-R(PRPH,PRWD)

4. Conclusion

To sum up, this paper has argued that the complex distribution of clausal clitics in B and M is greatly simplified if (a) it is viewed as the product of both morphological and prosodic alignment and (b) the relevant constraints bear different weight in the two languages, as OT leads us to expect. The immediate consequence of this approach is that all constraints are assumed to be violable. As the reader may verify, an impressive number of constraints -- those which receive a ⊛ mark in any B or M tableau -- are indeed violated by optimal candidates.

References
Anderson, Stephen R. 1992. *A-Morphous Morphology*. Cambridge University Press.
Anderson, Stephen R. 1996. How to Put your Clitics in their Place. *The Linguistic Review* 13, 165-191.
Grimshaw, Jane and Vieri Samek-Lodovici. 1995. Optimal Subjects. In J. Beckman, L.

Walsh Dickey, and S. Urbanczyk (eds.), *Papers in Optimality Theory*, GLSA, UMass, 589-605.

Franks, Steven L. 1987. Regular and Irregular Stress in Macedonian. *International Journal of Slavic Linguistics and Poetics* 35-36, 93-142.

Hauge, Kjetil R. 1976. *The Word Order of Predicate Clitics in Bulgarian*. Meddelelser No. 10. University of Oslo.

Legendre, Géraldine. 1997. Optimal Romanian Clitics: A Cross-linguistic Perspective. Johns Hopkins University Technical Report JHU-CogSci-97-9.

Legendre, Géraldine. 1998 . Morphological and Prosodic Alignment of Bulgarian Clitics. In J. Dekkers, F. van der Leeuw, and J. van de Weijer (eds.), *Optimality Theory: Syntax, Phonology, and Acquisition*. Oxford University Press.

Legendre, Géraldine. In press. Second Position Clitics in a V2 Language: Conflict Resolution in Macedonian. *Proceedings of the 1997 ESCOL Meeting*, Yale University.

Legendre, Géraldine, Colin Wilson, Paul Smolensky, Kristin Homer, and William Raymond. 1995. Optimality and Wh-Extraction. In J. Beckman, L. Walsh Dickey, and S. Urbanczyk (eds.), *Papers in Optimality Theory*, GLSA, UMass, 607-636.

Legendre, Géraldine, Paul Smolensky, and Colin Wilson. 1998. When is Less More? Faithfulness and Minimal Links in Wh-Chains. In P. Barbarosa, D. Fox, P. Hagstrom, M. McGinnis, and D. Pesetsky (eds), *Is the Best Good Enough? Optimality and Competition in Syntax*. MIT Press. 249-289.

Lunt, Horace G. 1952. *A Grammar of the Macedonian Literary Language*. Skopje.

McCarthy, John and Alan Prince. 1993a. *Prosodic Morphology I; Constraint Interaction and Satisfaction*. To appear, MIT Press.

McCarthy, John and Alan Prince. 1993b. Generalized Alignment. *Yearbook of Morphology*, 79-153.

Prince, Alan and Paul Smolensky. 1993. *Optimality Theory: Constraint Interaction in Generative Grammar*. Ms. Rutgers University and University of Colorado. To appear in MIT Press.

Radanović-Kocić, Vesna. 1996. The Placement of Serbo-Croatian Clitics: A prosodic Approach. In A.L. Halpern and A.M. Zwicky (eds.), *Approaching Second: Second Position Clitics and Related Phenomena*. CSLI Publications.

Selkirk, Elizabeth. 1995. The Prosodic Structure of Function Words. In J. Beckman, L. Walsh Dickey, and S. Urbanczyk (eds.), *Papers in Optimality Theory*, GLSA, UMass, 439-469.

Tomić, Olga M. 1996. The Balkan Slavic Clausal Clitics. *NLLT* 14, 811-72.

Derived Environment Effects in OT

ANNA ŁUBOWICZ

University of Massachusetts, Amherst

1. Introduction[*]

The theory of Lexical Phonology limits cyclic rule application to derived environments which are created by either morpheme concatenation or prior rule application. This restriction to derived environments is achieved by imposing a Strict Cycle Condition on rule application (Chomsky (1965); Kean (1974); Mascaró (1976); Kiparsky (1982); Rubach (1984)):

(1) Strict Cycle Condition (Kiparsky 1982: 4)
    a. Cyclic rules apply only to derived representations.
    b. *Definition:* A representation ϕ is derived w.r.t. rule R in cycle j iff ϕ meets the structural analysis of R by virtue of a combination of morphemes introduced in cycle j or the application of a phonological rule in cycle j.

This paper shows how these derived environment effects can be understood within the Optimality Theory framework (OT) by making use of local conjunction (Smolensky (1993), (1995), (1997)). By conjoining a markedness constraint with a faithfulness constraint, the markedness

[*] I am grateful to Christina Bethin, Ellen Kaisse, Alan Prince, Douglas Pulleyblank, Curt Rice, Jerzy Rubach, and Lisa Selkirk for valuable comments on this article, and especially to John McCarthy for extensive discussion of the theory and constant encouragement. Thanks also to the UMass phonology grant group members, as well as to the participants of the Fall 1997 MIT-UMass Phonology Workshop. This work was supported by the National Science Foundation under grant SBR-9420424. It is an abbreviated version of Łubowicz (1998).

constraint is active, causing a phonological process, only when the faithfulness constraint is violated. I will argue that this proposal captures all legitimate effects of the Strict Cycle Condition.

The interaction of Velar Palatalization and Spirantization in Polish (Rubach (1984)) provides an example of an environment derived by prior rule application. In Polish, velars turn into postalveolars before front vocoids (see (2a)). In the very same environment, however, as (2b) shows, a voiced velar *g* also spirantizes and so turns into a voiced postalveolar fricative *ž*. But not all voiced postalveolar affricates *ǰ* spirantize in Polish. In particular, underlying *ǰ* makes it faithfully to the surface (see (2c)).

(2) Interaction of First Velar Palatalization and Spirantization in Polish (Rubach (1984))

a. First Velar Palatalization: /k, g, x/ → [č, ǰ, š]/ _ [-cons, -back]

kro[k]+i+ć	→ kro[č]+y+ć	'to step'
kro[k]+ĭk+ĭ	→ kro[č]+ek (dim)	'step'
stra[x]+i+ć	→ stra[š]+y+ć	'to frighten'

b. Spirantization of *ǰ* derived from *g* by Palatalization:

wa[g]+i+ć	→ wa[ž]+y+ć	'to weigh'
dron[g]+ĭk+ĭ	→ dron[ž]+ek (dim)	'pole'
śnie[g]+ĭc+a	→ śnie[ž]+yc+a	'snow-storm'

c. No Spirantization of underlying voiced postalveolar affricates *ǰ*:

bry[ǰ]+ĭk+ĭ	→ bry[ǰ]+ek (dim)	'bridge'
ban[ǰ]+o	→ ban[ǰ]+o	'banjo'
[ǰ]em+ĭ	→ [ǰ]em	'jam'

The Polish data pose a question of why the same affricates behave differently in (2b) and (2c). Only derived *ǰ*'s spirantize. Rubach (1984) proposes that Spirantization in Polish is subject to the Strict Cycle Condition (SCC); it is restricted to apply only in a derived environment which is created by the application of a prior rule, First Velar Palatalization. Hence, *ǰ* spirantizes if and only if Palatalization has taken place. This is illustrated in (3):

(3) SCC Account of Polish (Rubach (1984))

	a. *derived ǰ*	b. *underlying ǰ*
UNDERLYING FORM	wa[g]+i+ć	bry[ǰ]+ĭk+ɨ̵
VELAR PALATALIZATION	wa[ǰ]+i+ć	does not apply
SPIRANTIZATION	wa[ž]+i+ć	blocked by SCC
Other rules	wa[ž]+y+ć	bry[ǰ]+ek

In OT (Prince and Smolensky (1993)) the Polish case is problematic. As I will show in detail below, any constraint ranking that permits the affricate *ǰ* at the surface will do so regardless of its source, underlying or derived. Since *ǰ* is permitted in output forms of Polish, the markedness constraint against *ǰ* must be low-ranked. Because this markedness constraint is low-ranked, the output form in (3a) is expected to have the affricate *ǰ* and not the actual fricative *ž*.

As for faithfulness, output *ǰ* would violate only one faithfulness constraint (i.e., 'no palatalization'). In comparison, the actual output form with *ž* violates not only 'no palatalization', but also an additional faithfulness constraint - 'no spirantization'. So the actual output form in (3a) incurs a double violation of faithfulness. For faithfulness reasons therefore, it should never occur in Polish.

This paper offers an explanation of what forces this seemingly unmotivated double faithfulness violation. The main idea is that an otherwise low-ranked markedness constraint is activated when faithfulness is violated. In Polish, for instance, the markedness constraint against the affricate *ǰ* is activated only in segments that undergo palatalization. Therefore, only 'derived' *ǰ*'s are ruled out. This activation of a markedness constraint by the violation of a faithfulness constraint is accomplished by locally conjoining the two constraints. Generally speaking, a constraint formed by local conjunction (LC) is violated if and only if all of its conjuncts are violated within a certain domain (Smolensky (1993) et seq.). The role of the domain is crucial to the concept of LC, and will have important implications below.[1]

The remainder of this paper is organized as follows. Section 2 presents schematically the rule-based approach to environments derived by prior rule application and shows why this type of derived environment effect is problematic for OT. Section 3 develops a novel account of this type of derived environment effect by making use of LC. The LC account is illustrated with Polish Spirantization in Section 4. Section 5 applies the LC

---

[1] LC has been employed previously for the analysis of a number of phonological phenomena. Due to space limitations I do not list all the references (but see Łubowicz (1998)).

account to cases of environments derived by morpheme concatenation. Section 6 compares entailments of the LC account with two alternative accounts of derived environment effects, the original SCC, and Kiparsky's (1993) underspecification account. Section 7 contains the summary.

2. ABC's of Phonologically-Derived Environments

This section begins by explaining rule interaction in cases of environments derived by prior rule application, called phonologically-derived environments (§2.1). It later shows why derived environments of this type are problematic for OT (§2.2).

2.1 Serial Rule Interaction

Let's begin with some observations about the Polish example (similarly for Slovak (Rubach (1993)), Hebrew (Prince (1975))). As we saw in (3), in Polish the voiced velar *g* palatalizes to the affricate $\acute{j}$ and then spirantizes to the fricative *ž* (therefore, $g \rightarrow \acute{j} \rightarrow \check{z}$), but underlying $\acute{j}$'s are not affected. Significantly and typically, the intermediate $\acute{j}$ step is featurally more similar to the input *g* than the output *ž* is to the input *g*, and the $\acute{j} \rightarrow \check{z}$ process is context-free.

Generalizing, we can describe cases of phonologically-derived environments schematically as a language L' in which there are two rules, a rule changing A to B following D (RULE 1: A→B/D_), and a context-free rule changing B to C (RULE 2: B→C). RULE 2 is resticted by the SCC to apply only in a derived environment which is created by the application of RULE 1.

Therefore, in case of an underlying /B/, RULE 2 does not apply, and so *B* makes it to the surface. But in case of an underlying /A/, both rules apply and so underlying /A/ changes to surface *C* (shown in (4)).

(4) Schematically L'

	a. *derived B*	b. *underlying B*
UNDERLYING FORM	DA	DB
RULE 1: A→B/D_	DB	does not apply
RULE 2: B→C (context-free)	DC	blocked by SCC

The /A/ to *C* mapping that we observe in (4a) is shown in (5).

(5) Observed mapping

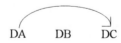

DA   DB   DC

This /A/ to C mapping presents a problem for OT. As I will show in detail below, it is not clear what compels the /A/ to C mapping, since the /A/ to B mapping is more faithful and B is a possible output in L'.

2.2 OT Parallelism

In OT, instead of serial rule ordering, outputs are accounted for by the interaction of two families of constraints: markedness and faithfulness. Therefore, the first step to solve the puzzle of L' is to determine the language-particular constraint rankings.

Since DA is ruled out in L' (see (4a)), the markedness constraint disfavoring DA (written *DA) must outrank the faithfulness constraint prohibiting the change from /A/ to C (written $F(A{\rightarrow}C)$). With the opposite ranking, DA would freely occur in L'. Also, since B exists in L' (see (4b)), the faithfulness constraint against the change from /B/ to C ($F(B{\rightarrow}C)$) must compel violation of the markedness constraint ruling out B (*B). In this way, B outputs are allowed in L'. The rankings are given in (6).

(6) Constraints in L'
      DA is ruled out: *DA >> $F(A{\rightarrow}C)$
      B exists: $F(B{\rightarrow}C)$ >> *B

But due to the low rank of *B, the expected output form in (4a) is B and not the actual output C. In other words, there is nothing to stop B from surfacing as an output in L'.

To put the matter differently, the actual /A/$\rightarrow$$C$ mapping is problematic, because it violates two faithfulness constraints: $F(A{\rightarrow}B)$ and $F(B{\rightarrow}C)$. But there is a more harmonic unintended mapping in L', namely /A/$\rightarrow$$B$, which violates only one faithfulness constraint, $F(A{\rightarrow}B)$. This is shown in (7).

(7) Faithfulness Violation

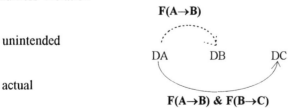

                                            $F(A{\rightarrow}B)$

unintended

                           DA   DB   DC

actual

                              $F(A{\rightarrow}B)$ & $F(B{\rightarrow}C)$

So the actual /A/$\rightarrow$$C$ mapping is less harmonic, because it incurs a double violation of faithfulness. The challenge for OT, therefore, is to explain why the less harmonic mapping is taking place in L'.

To illustrate what I have just noted, I will now show that the constraint rankings in (6) choose the wrong mapping as optimal:

(8) /DA/ in the input - wrong result

/DA/	*DA >> F(A→B) , F(B→C)			F(B→C) >> *B	
	*DA	F(A→B)	F(B→C)	F(B→C)	*B
a. DA	*!				
b. ☞DB		*			*
c. ☞DC		*	!*!	!*!	

The faithful parse, candidate (a), is ruled out due to *DA. Candidate (c), the actual mapping, fails on faithfulness. Candidate (b), the unintended mapping (indicated by ☞), emerges as optimal. It fares better on faithfulness than its competitor (c), as it violates only one faithfulness constraint, F(A→B). It violates the markedness constraint *B, but *B cannot rule it out, as it is low-ranked. So how is candidate (c) optimal?

3. The Proposal: Local Conjunction [M & F]$_{Seg}$

To choose the candidate with double violation of faithfulness as optimal, the force of the additional faithfulness violation that it incurs, F(B→C), must be rendered irrelevant. Intuitively, it seems that the low-ranked markedness constraint *B is activated if and only if there is a change from A to B. This is the case when B is not already in the input.

This activation of the markedness constraint *B by the violation of the faithfulness constraint F(A→B) is achieved by locally conjoining them. The domain for LC of these constraints is the segment which violates F(A→B), namely segment A. In other words, the markedness constraint (*B) and the faithfulness constraint (F(A→B)) cannot be violated together within the same segment. (The conjoined constraint has nothing to say about violation of its two conjuncts within different segments.) The locally conjoined constraint is ranked above F(B→C), so that it nullifies its force:

(9)   [*B & F(A→B)]$_{Seg}$ >> F(B→C) >> *B

In other words, the markedness constraint *B is low-ranked, but its conjunction with the faithfulness constraint F(A→B) is high-ranked. Consequently, *B is only relevant when there is a change from A to B, that is, when the faithfulness constraint (F(A→B)) is violated.

When /A/ is in the input, as shown in (10), *B is activated by the violation of F(A→B). Thus the conjoined constraint favors the less faithful mapping /DA/→*DC* over the more faithful one /DA/→*DB*.

(10) /A/ in the input

/DA/	[*B & F(A→B)]$_{Seg}$	F(B→C)
a. DB	*!	
b. ☞ DC		*

Yet, when /B/ is in the input, there is no change from A to B, so F(A→B) is not violated, and therefore the conjoined constraint has no force. In this case the faithfulness constraint F(B→C), which outranks *B, is decisive, and so the faithful parse *DB* comes out as optimal.

(11) /B/ in the input

/DB/	[*B & F(A→B)]$_{Seg}$	F(B→C)	*B
a. DC	√	*!	
b. ☞ DB	√		*

Consequently, as illustrated in (12), the mapping /DA/→*DC* is forced by the locally conjoined constraint:

(12) The Role of [*B & F(A→B)]$_{Seg}$

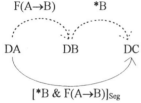

DA   DB   DC

[*B & F(A→B)]$_{Seg}$

The conjoined constraint compels the otherwise problematic double faithfulness violation. Thus there is no *B* in the output unless it is already present in the input. The ranking that has been established is in (13):

(13) Ranking for L'

*DA   [*B & F(A→B)]$_{Seg}$

F(A→B)   F(B→C)

*B

Generalizing, *B is only relevant when F(A→B) is violated, and this is so when *B* is not in the input. That is the effect of local conjunction.

4. Application: Spirantization in Polish

In this section the LC proposal is applied to the Polish example introduced in §1. From an OT perspective, spirantization in Polish takes place only when IDENT(anterior) is violated. Otherwise, the voiced postalveolar affricate ǰ is faithfully parsed in the output form. Since there are ǰ's at the surface, the markedness constraint against them (*ǰ) must be ranked below a faithfulness constraint against spirantization:

(14)   IDENT(continuant) >> *ǰ [2]
        (Velar Palatalization itself is subject to a morphologically-derived environment and is discussed in §5).

This constraint ranking, when faced with the input /rog+ek/, wrongly chooses as optimal the candidate that incurs a lesser violation of faithfulness, that is, the one with a voiced postalveolar *affricate* in the output form *(*roǰek)*. The candidate with a voiced postalveolar *fricative* (*rožek*) is wrongly ruled out, because it diverges from the input in both place and manner of articulation.

(15) /g/ in the input - wrong result

/rog+ek/[3]	IDENT(ant)[4] ,	IDENT(cont)	IDENT(cont) >>	*ǰ
a. ☞ roǰek	*			*
b. ☞ rožek	*	!*!	!*!	

Why then is *rožek* (with palatalization and spirantization) optimal?
        To choose the candidate that incurs a double violation of faithfulness as optimal, I propose that the markedness constraint against voiced postalveolar affricates (*ǰ) is activated only when IDENT(anterior) is violated. This activation of the markedness constraint by the violation of a faithfulness constraint is accomplished by locally conjoining them within the domain of a segment:

(16)   [*ǰ & IDENT(anterior)]$_{Seg}$ >> IDENT(continuant) >> *ǰ

---

[2] I follow Rubach (1992) in assuming that Polish affricates are strident stops: [-cont, strident].

[3] This is a simplified input form. According to Rubach (1984), the input is /-g+ïk+ɫ/.

[4] In standard Feature Geometry accounts (Sagey (1986), Steriade (1986)) only coronals are specified for [anterior]. The analysis in the text presupposes that IDENT(anterior) is violated even when an input segment is not specified for [anterior].

Because of this conjunction of constraints ranked above IDENT(continuant), there are no surface ǰ's except those already present in the input. The relevant tableaux are given in (17).

(17) Illustration

   a. /g/ in the input

/rog+ek/		[*ǰ & IDENT(ant)]$_{Seg}$	IDENT(cont)	*ǰ
a.	roǰek	*!		*
b. ☞	rožek		*	

   b. /ǰ/ in the input

/banǰ+o/		[*ǰ & IDENT(ant)]$_{Seg}$	IDENT(cont)	*ǰ
a. ☞	banǰo	√		*
b.	banžo	√	*!	

As a result, the markedness constraint *ǰ emerges via local conjunction with a faithfulness constraint, the violation of which is incurred when ǰ is not in the input.

(18)

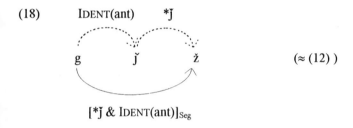

The local conjunction of *ǰ and IDENT(anterior) compels the otherwise problematic double faithfulness violation. The optimal candidate with the fricative ž violates both IDENT(anterior) and IDENT(continuant).

5. LC Account of Morphologically-Derived Environments

So far I have argued that local conjunction accounts for phonologically-derived environments. In this section I extend the LC account to cases of derived environments by morpheme concatenation. I observe that cases of morphologically-derived environments always lead to violation of stem:syllable anchoring. Therefore, I propose that this violation of anchoring activates the relevant markedness constraint.

5.1 Rule-based Account

In this section I give a rule-based account of SCC effects with morphologically-derived environments. As an example I use First Velar Palatalization from Polish (after Rubach (1984)).

As we saw in (2), First Velar Palatalization turns velars into postalveolars before front vocoids. But there is no Palatalization when the trigger and target belong to the same morpheme:

(19) No Velar Palatalization in tautomorphemic sequences

[ke]lner	'waiter'	[k'i]siel	'jelly'
a[ge]nt	'agent'	[g'i]ps	'plaster'
[x'i]storia	'history'	[xe]tera	'shrew' (person)

Rubach (1984) postulates that First Velar Palatalization is a cyclic rule and therefore subject to the SCC; it is restricted to apply only across a morpheme boundary. This is shown schematically in (20).

(20) The Role of SCC (Rubach (1984))

Cycle 1	xemik	
	blocked by SCC	VELAR PALATALIZATION
Cycle 2	xemik+ĭk	WFR: dimin.
	xemič+ĭk	VELAR PALATALIZATION
	xem'ič+ek	Other rules

Consequently, Velar Palatalization is allowed to apply only when the trigger and target of the process are heteromorphemic, that is after word formation rules on cycle two.

5.2 OT Account

The fact that a process is restricted to apply only across a morpheme boundary initially seems problematic for OT. Since there are instances of velars that do not palatalize before front vowels, the markedness constraint calling for palatalization, PAL, must be ranked below a faithfulness constraint militating against a change in anteriority, IDENT(anterior).

(21)   IDENT(anterior) >> PAL

But with this ranking, there should be no palatalization whatsoever.

To force palatalization when the target of the process is input stem final, I note that the addition of a palatalizing suffix always results in violation of stem:syllable anchoring. Since the palatalizing suffix starts with a vowel, the final consonant of the stem becomes the onset of the syllable contributed by the palatalizing suffix. Therefore, the rightmost segment of the input stem does not coincide with the right edge of the syllable in the output. This is illustrated in (22).

(22) Violation of stem : syllable anchoring.

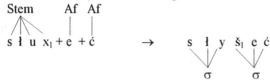

I propose that this violation of stem:syllable anchoring activates the markedness constraint demanding palatalization. Consequently, only input stem final segments may undergo palatalization.

Formally, the constraint calling for palatalization is locally conjoined with the constraint guarding stem:syllable anchoring. The relevant anchoring constraint is given in (23) and the ranking is in (24).

(23)   R-ANCHOR (Stem; σ) - the rightmost segment of a stem in the input has a correspondent at the right edge of a syllable in the output.[5]

(24)   [PAL & R-ANCHOR(Stem;σ)]$_{\text{AdjacentSegments}}$ >> IDENT(ant) >> PAL

The two constraints are conjoined within the domain of adjacent segments. Therefore, only a segment that violates stem:syllable anchoring undergoes palatalization when followed by a front vowel. There is no palatalization of a segment that vacuously satisfies anchoring, such as tautomorphemically. This is illustrated in (25).

(25) The Role of LC
a. Palatalization heteromorphemically

/[xemik$_1$]$_{\text{Stem}}$ + ek/	[PAL & R-ANCHOR]$_{\text{AdjSeg}}$	IDENT(ant)
a. ☞ xe.mi.č$_1$ek.		*
b. xe.mi.k$_1$ek.	*!	

---

[5] Anchoring is a type of position specific faithfulness constraint replacing the MCat:PCat Alignment constraints of McCarthy and Prince (1993) (see McCarthy and Prince (1995), McCarthy (to appear)).

b. No palatalization monomorphemically

/[x₁emik]Stem /⁶	[PAL & R-ANCHOR]AdjSeg	IDENT(ant)	PAL
a. ☞ x₁e.mik.	√		*
b. š₁e.mik.	√	*!	

The locally conjoined constraint is only relevant when the palatalizing segment is stem final (as in (25a)). Otherwise, the conjoined constraint has no force, and so lower-ranked constraints are decisive (shown in (25b)).[7]

The LC account of morphologically-derived environments shows in what way faithfulness between morphological and prosodic categories activates a phonological process.

6. Comparison with Previous Approaches

This section compares predictions made by three alternative accounts of non-derived environment blocking (NDEB) effects: the original SCC account (Mascaró (1976), Kiparsky (1982)), an underspecification account (Kiparsky (1993)), and the LC account developed in this work. The predictions of these accounts are compared with respect to five basic claims made by the SCC.

- **Derived environment effects and the cycle.** The original SCC equates NDEB with cyclicity. But the underspecification model of Kiparsky (1993) and the LC account presented in this work make no necessary connection between cyclicity and NDEB. In fact, subsequent work (reviewed by Kiparsky) has rejected the cyclic basis for NDEB.

- **Two types of derived environment effects.** Under the SCC the two distinct types of derived environment, phonological and morphological, are always united. This implies that a rule subject to the first type of derived environment will be subject to the second type, if evidence is available. Unlike the SCC, the underspecification model and the LC account make no necessary connection between the two types of derived environment. In fact, it has not been proved that there exists a rule subject to both types of derived environment effects. (Two apparent cases, Finnish assibilation and Sanskrit *ruki* (Kiparsky (1973), (1982)), are analyzed differently in Hammond (1992)).

---

⁶ According to Rubach (1984), the full underlying form is: /xemik+ɨ/

⁷ I take it that the stem is a recursive category. A consequence of this view is that there can be strict cycle effects among suffixes, because every right suffix edge is a stem boundary:
(26) [[[pies]stemek₁]stemek]stem → pie.se.č₁ek. 'dog' (double dim)

- **Morphologically-derived environments.** The SCC predicts that all cyclic rules are blocked in morphologically simplex environments. The underspecification account predicts that only structure-building rules can show effects of morphological NDEB. LC makes no connection with cyclicity or structure-building. Rather, it makes two novel predictions. First, it predicts that the trigger and target of a process that is resticted to apply across a morpheme boundary are adjacent. This follows from the requirement that constraints be conjoined in some local domain. Secondly, it predicts that morphologically-derived environments will always involve violation of stem:syllable anchoring. Both predictions turn out to be true of all Palatalization processes in Slavic (Rubach (1984)); Polish Iotation (Rubach (1984), Rubach & Booij (1990)); Affrication in Korean (Kiparsky (1993)). Apparent counterexamples can be analyzed differently (Anderson (1969), Kiparsky (1993), Łubowicz (1998), Myers (1987)).

- **Prior rule altering the context.** According to the SCC and the underspecification model, a phonologically-derived environment can arise by a prior rule either targeting the segment or altering its context (see Mascaró (1976)). The LC account, on the contrary, predicts no derived environment effects when the prior rule targets the context. (In the LC account, the structure of the double faithfulness loop is restricted by the locality condition on constraint conjunction. Since the domain for LC is a segment, the LC account predicts no derived-environment effects when the faithfulness and markedness constraints are violated within different segments.) In fact, the cases of a derived environment by a prior rule altering the environment are regarded as problematic, as shown in Hammond (1992).

- **Vacuous rule application.** Under the SCC, a derived environment can arise by vacuous rule application (Mascaró (1976)). In the LC account and in the underspecification account, however, the derived environment cannot arise by vacuous rule application. (In the LC account the particular markedness constraint is activated by a violation of the relevant faithfulness constraint. In the case of vacuous rule application, however, there is no violation of faithfulness, and so there is no way to activate the markedness constraint. As a result, the markedness constraint is satisfied vacuously and local conjunction has no force.) In fact, the apparent cases of vacuously derived environment can be analyzed differently (see Kiparsky (1993)).

To conclude, the predictions of the LC account differ radically from the original SCC, but are very similar to the underspecification model of Kiparsky (1993). This similarity holds even though the LC account and the underspecification account are based on very different theoretical premises. Thus, one can conclude that work on NDEB virtually since Kiparsky (1982) consistently supports the results achieved by local conjunction.

7. Summary

In this paper I have argued that local conjunction of a markedness and faithfulness constraint enables OT to handle all cases of derived environment effects. A markedness constraint is low-ranked in the particular grammar, whereas its conjunction with a faithfulness constraint is high-ranked. Violation of the faithfulness constraint thus activates the markedness constraint. This accounts for both phonologically- and morphologically-derived environment effects.

References
Anderson, Stephen. 1969. An outline of the phonology of Modern Icelandic vowels. *Foundations of Language* 5. 53-72.

Chomsky, Noam. 1965. *Aspects of the Theory of Syntax*. Cambridge, Mass.: MIT Press.

Hammond, Michael. 1992. Deriving the Strict Cycle Condition, in J. Denton, G. Chan and C. Canakis, eds., *CLS 28: Parasession on the Cycle in Linguistic Theory*. Chicago: CLS. 126-140.

Kiparsky, Paul. 1982. *Explanation in Phonology*. Dordrecht: Foris Publications.

Kiparsky, Paul. 1993. Blocking in Non-derived Environments, in S. Hargus and E. Kaisse, eds., *Studies in Lexical Phonology*. San Diego: Academic Press. 277-313.

Łubowicz, Anna. 1998. Derived Environment Effects in OT, ms., University of Massachusetts, Amherst. [Rutgers Optimality Archive #239.]

Mascaró, Joan. 1976. *Catalan Phonology and the Phonological Cycle*. Doctoral dissertation, MIT.

McCarthy, John. Faithfulness and Prosodic Circumscription. To appear, in J. Dekkers, F. van der Leeuw, and J. van de Weijer, eds., *The Pointing Finger: Conceptual Studies in Optimality Theory*. Amsterdam: HIL.

McCarthy, John and Alan Prince. 1993. *Prosodic Morphology I: Constraint Interaction and Satisfaction*, ms., University of Massachusetts, Amherst, and Rutgers University. [To appear, Cambridge, Mass.: MIT Press.]

McCarthy, John and Alan Prince. 1995. Faithfulness and Reduplicative Identity, in Beckman et al., eds., *University of Massachusetts Occasional Papers in Linguistics 18: Papers in Optimality Theory*. University of Massachusetts, Amherst: GLSA. 249-384.

Myers, Scott. 1987. Vowel shortening in English. *Natural Language and Linguistic Theory* 5. 485-518.

Prince, Alan. 1975. *The Phonology and Morphology of Tiberian Hebrew*. Doctoral dissertation, MIT.

Prince, Alan and Paul Smolensky. 1993. *Optimality Theory: Constraint Interaction in Generative Grammar*, ms., Rutgers University, New Brunswick, and University of Colorado, Boulder. [To appear, Cambridge, Mass.: MIT Press.]

Rubach, Jerzy. 1984. *Cyclic and Lexical Phonology: The Structure of Polish*. Dordrecht: Foris Publications.

Rubach, Jerzy. 1992. Affricates as strident stops in Polish. *Linguistic Inquiry* 25. 119-143.

Rubach, Jerzy. 1993. *The Lexical Phonology of Slovak*. New York: Oxford University Press Inc.

Rubach, Jerzy and Geert Booij. 1990. Syllable Structure Assignment in Polish. *Phonology* 7.1. 121-58.

Sagey, Elizabeth. 1986. *The representation of features and relations in nonlinear phonology*. Doctoral dissertation, MIT.

Smolensky, Paul. 1993. Harmony, markedness, and phonological activity. Paper presented at Rutgers Optimality Workshop-1, Rutgers University, New Brunswick, NJ, October 1993. [Rutgers Optimality Archive #87.]

Smolensky, Paul. 1995. On the internal structure of the constraint component of UG. Colloquium presented at UCLA, April 7, 1995. [Rutgers Optimality Archive #86.]

Smolensky, Paul. 1997. Constraint interaction in generative grammar II: Local Conjunction, or Random rules in Universal Grammar. Talk presented at Hopkins Optimality Theory Workshop/Maryland Mayfest '97. Baltimore: MD.

Steriade, Donca. 1986. A note on the feature coronal, ms., MIT.

Tense and Aspect Parallelism in Antecedent Contained Deletions*

AYUMI MATSUO

University of Connecticut

1. Introduction

Fiengo and May (1994) and Fox (1995) have observed that there is an effect of structural parallelism in VP-ellipsis constructions regarding pronoun indices and a quantifier scope. This paper adds to these findings by Fiengo and May, and Fox; I argue that there is also a parallelism effect in tense and aspect in ACD constructions.

In what follows, the details regarding ACD will be examined. However, the parallelism discussed by Fiengo and May, and Fox will first be summarized. Consider (1), in which Fiengo and May propose that there is a parallelism effect regarding indices. In other words, in (1), we see the parallelism between *Max's sister* and *Oscar's sister*:

(1)   Max's sister said that he₁ saw his₁ mother and Oscar₂'s sister did, too. (Fiengo and May (1994))
        a.   Max₁'s sister said that he₁ saw his₁ mother and
             Oscar₂'s sister [said he₁ saw his₁ mother].--strict reading

---

* I would like to thank Howard Lasnik, Zeljko Boškovic, and Myriam Uribe-Extebarria for their comments and discussions. Also, I would like to thank the organizers of WCCFL XVII for giving me a chance to present this work and the audience of WCCFL XVII, especially Hamida Demirdache and Chris Kennedy for their insightful comments. I am grateful to Nigel Duffield, Kimary Shahin and Elise Springer for their help with the manuscript.

b. Max$_1$'s sister said that he$_1$ saw his$_1$ mother and
   Oscar$_2$'s sister [said he$_2$ saw his$_2$ mother].--sloppy reading
c. Max$_1$'s sister said that he$_1$ saw his$_1$ mother and
   Oscar$_2$'s sister [said he$_1$ saw his$_2$ mother].--mixed reading

Fiengo and May claim that (1) is several ways ambiguous. It can have a strict reading as in (1a), a sloppy reading as in (1b) and a mixed reading as in (1c). The expressions in the brackets represent how *did* is interpreted. They propose that there is an interesting contrast in a sentence such as (2), which does not involve a structural parallelism. In (2), the first conjunct has *Max* as its subject instead of *Max's sister*. They propose this is the reason why the indices cannot be assigned as specified in (2c) even though (1c) is grammatical with the same indices as in (2c). In (2), the mixed reading represented in (2c) is not available.

(2)   Max$_1$ said he$_1$ saw his$_1$ mother and Oscar$_2$'s sister did, too.
        (Fiengo and May (1994))
        a. Max$_1$ said he$_1$ saw his$_1$ mother and
           Oscar$_2$'s sister [said he$_1$ saw his$_1$ brother].--strict reading
        b. Max$_1$ said he$_1$ saw his$_1$ mother and
           Oscar$_2$'s sister [said he$_2$ saw his$_2$ brother].--sloppy reading
        c. *Max$_1$ said he$_1$ saw his$_1$ mother and
           Oscar$_2$'s sister [said he$_1$ saw his$_2$ mother].--mixed reading

Fox (1995b) extends this idea from Fiengo and May to apply to scopal ambiguities, as in examples (3) and (4):

(3)   Some boy admires every teacher and some girl does, too.
        (∃>∀; ∀>∃)
(4)   Some boy admires every teacher and Mary does, too.
        (∃>∀; *∀>∃)

The parallelism is satisfied in (3); both the first and the second conjuncts have *some* plus NP as their subject but that is not the case in (4). In (4), the second conjunct has *Mary* as a subject instead of *some* plus NP. Fox proposes that (3) is ambiguous; *some* can take wide scope over *every* and *every* can take narrow scope. On the other hand, (4) is unambiguous and there is only one reading; i.e., that in which *some* takes wide scope over *every*.

2.   Tense   Parallelism   in   Antecedent   Contained Deletions

May (1985) raises the issue of an infinite regression problem in an ACD example like (5); namely, in (5), the VP, *suspected everyone*

Angleton did [e] is copied in the null VP after *did*, [e], at LF. Since the copied VP also contains *[e]*, it will bring about an infinite regression.

(5)   Dulles suspected everyone Angleton did [e].

May proposes that the quantifier phrase, *everyone Angleton did*, raises in (5) and the null VP after *did* copies *suspected* and the trace of the quantifier phrase. Hence, no infinite regression problem arises. There have been differing proposals as to where this movement occurs; this issue will be re-addressed in section 3.

   In ACD examples like this, I propose a similar kind of parallelism effect is observed regarding Tense and Aspect in ACD sentences such as (6) and (7):

(6)   *?John read the same books that Mary will [e].
(7)   John read the same books that Mary did [e].
(8)   John read the same books that Mary will read. (non-ACD)
(9)   Mary read the books and Fred will the magazine. (pseudo-gapping)
(10)   Mary read the books and Fred will, too. (VP-ellipsis)

(6) has a Tense mismatch in verbs; the former verb is in Past Tense and the latter is in Future Tense. This kind of intolerance in Tense mismatch is only observed in ACD sentences and not in sentences with non-ACD as in (8), pseudo-gapping as in (9) or VP-ellipsis as in (10). We have to note that the Tense and Aspect Parallelism that I discuss here is more restricted than the scopal and indices Parallelism that I summarized. So, (8): *John read the same books that Mary will read* , which is a non-ACD example that contrasts with (6), is grammatical with Past in the matrix clause and Future in the embedded clause. Also, (9): *Mary read the books and Fred will the magazine*, the pseudo-gapping example, is good with the Past tense in the first conjunct and the future tense in the second conjunct. Finally, (10): *Mary read the books and Fred will, too*, a VP-ellipsis is also good with different Tenses.

   I suggest a way to account for the Tense mismatch problem seen in (6) by recourse to an LF-copying analysis. As part of this account, I propose that when a VP is copied in [e], the temporal variable (proposed by Stowell (1993)) that is in a VP is also copied, and that this temporal variable plays a role in deciding if the Tense is matched or not.

2.1 Syntax of Tense by Stowell (1993)
Before we discuss what is copied and what rules out the ACD examples with Tense Parallelism, let me briefly talk about the analysis that I am adopting. Stowell (1993) proposes that there are two phrases (ZPs, time phrases) in a syntactic structure, which refer to the Utterance Time and the

Event Time, respectively. Stowell's proposed structure for 'John ran', which includes two ZPs, is shown in (11).

(11)

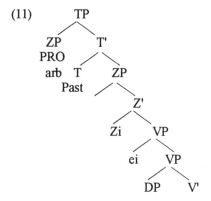

Past Tense under T requires the Event Time, namely, the time of John's running, to precede the Utterance Time that is denoted by the ZP in TP-Spec. What is important here is there is a variable in VP that is co-indexed with the lower event ZP. This variable is, according to Stowell, compatible with the event variable proposed by Carlson (1977). This variable serves to convey to a VP the information at which time that event takes place; I propose that it is doing important work in Tense Parallelism in ACDs. With this much in mind, let us return to (6) and (7) with ACDs which have Tense mismatches.

2.2 LF-copying and Tense Parallelism

The following examples confirm that there is a strong requirement in Tense Parallelism in ACDs. Let us first look at the examples as in (6) and (7), repeated here as (12) and (13) with some new examples to investigate what kind of pattern exists:

(12)   *?John read the same books that Mary will.
(13)   John read the same books that Mary did.
(14)   *? John read the same books that Mary does.
(15)   John reads the same books that Mary does.
(16)   *? John reads the same books that Mary did.

The examples that we have seen exhibit the following patterns:

(17)   Present...Present (cf. (15))
        Past...Past   (cf. (13))
        Future...Future

(18)   *Past...Present   (cf. (14))
         *Past...Future   (cf. (12))
         *Present...Future
         *Present...Past

The grammatical example in (13) has an LF representation as in (19):

(19)   John [$_{ZP}$ [$_{ZP_i}$ Past [$_{VP}$ [e_i read the same books that
                 UT ET   ET (e>u)
         [$_{ZP}$ [$_{ZP_i}$ Past Mary did [$_{VP}$ [e_i]
         ET (e>u)   ET(e>u)

In (19), the matrix event-ZP refers to a point that is Past with respect to the Utterance Time and it binds a temporal variable within a VP that is represented as e_i. When a VP is copied, this temporal variable is also copied after *did*. This variable does not conflict with the Past Tense of *did* and this copying operation is perfectly possible in (19). Unlike (13), (12) has an LF representation as in (20):

(20)   *? John [$_{ZP}$ [$_{ZP_i}$ Past [$_{VP}$ [e_i read the same books that
                 UT ET   ET (e>u)
         [$_{ZP}$ [$_{ZP_i}$ Future Mary will [$_{VP}$ [e_i]
         ET (u>e)   ET(e>u)

Example (20) has a matrix event-ZP that refers to a point that is Past with respect to the Utterance Time, and when its variable is copied, it brings about a contradiction with the Future Tense in *will*. The Future Tense in an embedded clause calls for the Event Time to follow the Utterance Time namely, (u>e). However, as we have already noted, the variable in the copied VP is past, so a tense mismatch arises. Let us next look at one more example, which involves Past and Present Tense as in (14), repeated here as (21). After the VP is copied, the LF representation for (14/21) is as seen in (22):

(21)   *? John read the same books that Mary does.
(22)   *? John [$_{ZP}$ [$_{ZP_i}$ Past [$_{VP}$ [e_i read the same books that
                 UT ET   ET (e>u)
         [$_{ZP}$ [$_{ZP_i}$ Present Mary does [$_{VP}$ [e_i]
         ET (u=e)   ET(e>u)

The sentence in (22) has a variable in VP that refers to a point that is past with respect to the Utterance Time, and when its variable is copied, it bring about a contradiction with the Present Tense in *does*. The Present Tense calls for the Event Time that refers to the same point as the Utterance time but it is not the Tense that the variable in the copied VP has.

Uribe-Extebarria (1994) proposes that *will* calls for the Event Time to follow the Utterance Time but *would* calls for an event time to be past. So, if that is right, (12) should improve its grammaticality when *will* is changed to *would* as in (23) and it is exactly what happens. Just for reference, we can illustrate that (23) has an LF representation as in (24):

(23)   John read the same books that Mary would.

(24)   John [$_{ZP}$ [$_{ZPi}$ Past [$_{VP}$ [e_i read the same books that
            UT ET   ET (e>u)
     [$_{ZP}$ [$_{ZPi}$ Present Mary would [$_{VP}$ [e_i]
     ET (u>e)   ET(e>u)

Let me discuss one more point regarding Tense Parallelism before I move to Aspect Parallelism. This discussion involves the cases where the Future Tense appears in the matrix clause as in (25) and (26):

(25)   John will read the same books that Mary did.
(26)   John will read the same books that Mary does.

It seems a little puzzling that (25) and (26) do not call for any Tense Parallelism. When the matrix clause has Past and the relative clause has Future Tense, it seems degraded but when the order is reversed as in (25), it seems better. Boskovic (p.c.) suggests it must be because *will* takes a verb *read* that contains no Tense information—that is, it takes something bare, and it is true that we do not see any inflection in *read* in (26). Since *read* in (25) and (22) is bare and contains no Tense information, it can be copied after *did* or *does*, yielding no conflict with the Past Tense in *did* or Present tense in *does*. However, when the order is reversed as in (12), repeated here as (27), this is not true.

(27)   *?John read the same books that Mary will [e].

Since *will* in an embedded clause in (27) cannot take any verb with a variable that carries information on Past or Present, (27) is degraded. Let us next move to the Aspect Parallelism in ACDs.

3.   Aspect Parallelism in ACDs

We see a similar parallelism effect with respect to Aspect. First, I will summarize the basics of the syntax of Present Perfect that I will be using here.

Following Stowell (1993), Brugger (1996), Demirdache & Uribe-Extebarria (hereafter D&E) (1997) and Travis (1996), I assume that Aspect takes two time-denoting phrases as arguments. D&E propose that Aspect takes a reference time (AST-T) as its external argument and an event time as its internal argument; they claim that the phrase structure of Tense and Aspect is as follows:

(28)

```
            TP
          /    \
        UT      T'
              /    \
            T      AspP
                 /     \
             AST-T      Asp'
                      /     \
                   Asp       VP
                 /     \
               ET       VP                    (1997;3)
```

3.1 McCawley's (1971) Analysis of the Present Perfect in Telic and Atelic Verbs

McCawley (1971) claims that atelic verbs are ambiguous when they appear in the Present Perfect—unlike telic verbs, which are unambiguous.

(29) The Present Perfect of an atelic verb   McCawley (1971)
      1. "indicates that a state of affairs prevails throughout some interval stretching from the past into the present" when it appears with certain adverbials such as *for_ times* or *since--* (look at (30)).
      2. it does not indicate a state of affairs stretching into the present when it does not appear with these adverbials as in (31):

Following McCawley (1971)'s claim, D&E show that atelic verbs are ambiguous in (30) and (31):

Atelic
(30)   Max has slept for two hours. (now—i.e., he is still sleeping) (D&E 1997;10)
(31)   Max has slept. (he is no longer sleeping at UT-T) (D&E 1997;10)

The Present Perfect in (30) has an adverbial, *for two* hours; hence, the event of Max's sleeping is stretched into the present. The equivalent without any adverbial in (31) does not allow the event to stretch into the present. On the other hand, for telic verbs, "the Present Perfect indicates that the direct effect of a past event still continues" (D&E 1997;10). So, (32) means that John is still here at the Utterance Time even without any adverbials:

Telic
(32)   John has arrived. (indicates persistence of the result of John's arriving, i.e., that John is still here.)

3.2 Aspect Parallelism and LF-Copying
We now consider the different interpretations of the Present Perfect in ACD constructions.

Atelic
(33)   Max has slept in the same bed that Mary has.
         --Max and Mary are no longer sleeping at the Utterance Time
(34)   Max has lived in Vancouver for 3 years in the same house that Mary has.
         a.   Max and Mary are still living in Vancouver.
         b.   * Max is living in Vancouver but Mary is not living in Vancouver.
(35)   Max has lived in Vancouver in the same house that Mary has for 3 years.
         a.   Max and Mary are still living in Vancouver.
         b.   *Max is not living in Vancouver but Mary is living in Vancouver.

In examples (33)-(35), the atelic verbs: *sleep* and *live* are in the Present Perfect form. In (33), *slept* can only have the interpretation in (31); namely, Max and Mary are no longer sleeping at the Utterance Time. In (34) and (35), both Max and Mary have to be living in Vancouver at the Utterance Time. In (34), the matrix clause has the adverbial phrase: *for 3 years* which enforces the interpretation in (30), but the embedded clause does not have the adverbial phrase. The opposite is true in (35); namely, the embedded clause has the adverbial phrase but the matrix clause does not. Still, in both cases, there is no way for the verbs without the adverbial phrase to have an interpretation like (31) where the event has not stretched into the Utterance Time— namely, Mary (for (34)) or Max (for (35)) does not live in Vancouver any longer—so both (34b) and (35b) are not available for (34) and (35).

Unlike ACD constructions, other VP-ellipsis examples do not demonstrate the same kind of intolerance for Aspect mismatch, and a similar fact was previously pointed out with respect to Tense mismatch. Consider the following examples.

(36)   Max has lived in Vancouver and Mary has in Seattle for 3 years. (pseudo-gapping)
         a.   Max is not living in Vancouver but Mary is still living in Seattle.

(37)   Max has lived in Vancouver and Mary has too, for 3 years.
         (VP-ellipsis)
         a.   Max is not living in Vancouver but Mary is still living in
              Vancouver.
(38)   Max has slept in this bed and Mary has in that bed for 3 hours.
         (pseudo-gapping)
         a.   Max is not sleeping in this bed but Mary is sleeping in that
              bed.
(39)   Max has slept in this bed and Mary has too, for 3 hours.
         (VP-ellipsis)
         a.   Max is not sleeping in this bed but Mary is sleeping.

In these examples, the second verb can have a different interpretation from the first verb despite the fact that both are in the Present Perfect form. For (36) and (37), there is a reading where Max is not living in Vancouver any longer but Mary is still living in Seattle (for (36)) or Vancouver (for (37)). (38) and (39) are similar examples with a different predicate. These contrast with the ACD examples that we looked at in (34) and (35), where both first and second verbs in the Present Perfect form must exhibit the same interpretation—either the one where a state of affairs is stretched into the present or the one where a state of affairs has stopped sometime before the present. Let us consider how we can account for this.

D&E propose that the continuative perfect as in (30) has a syntactic structure as follows:

(40)

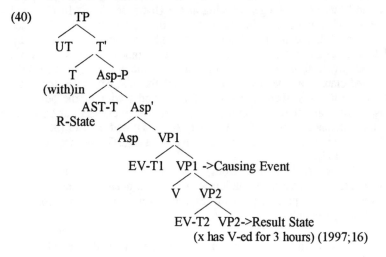

VP2 has a role in deciding whether an event has been completed or is still continuing at the Utterance Time. Having this structure in mind, let us look over the ACD Aspect mismatch case in (41):

(41)   Max has lived in Vancouver for 3 years in the same house as Mary
         has.

Example (41) has a reading where "Max and Mary have lived in the same
house and they are still living there". If we assume that *lived* in the matrix
clause has a AST-T that states that "Max has lived in the house and this
state is stretched into the present" and if this information in AST-T is
copied in [e] after *has* in the relative clause, then there is no way for AST-T
to have the interpretation where "Mary is not living there at the Utterance
Time".

4. LF-copying or PF-deletion?

We have been looking at Tense and Aspect Parallelism and we found that
this parallelism is only observed in ACDs and not in non-ACD, VP-
ellipsis and pseudo-gapping constructions. This indicates that there is
something other than PF-deletion going on in ACD. Let us go back to a
pseudo-gapping examples like (42). (42) allows Aspect interpretation to
differ between the first and the second verbs:

(42)   Max has [$_{VP2}$ lived in Vancouver and Mary has [$_{VP2}$ in Seattle for
         3 years. R state-Max is not in Vancouver   R state-Mary is in
         Seattle

Suppose that the first verb *lived* has a resultative AST-T that indicates that
"Max is not in Vancouver any longer" and the second verb *lived* has a
resultative AST-T that says that "Mary is still living in Seattle"   If
pseudo-gapping is a PF-operation as Lasnik argues, the second verb *lived*
can be clided at PF even if AST-T of the second verb has a different
resultative interpretation from that of the first verb.   The different
interpretations of the Present Perfect Tense are not reflected in phonology.
The PF-interface does not distinguish this semantic difference, so the second
VP can be elided under identity in the phonological component to the first
VP, *lived t*, thus we know why different interpretations of the Present Perfect
form in (42) is possible.
         As we saw in the Introduction, there was an infinite regress
problem with ACDs and we need to move an object from a VP so that it
will not be contained in the antecedent. There are two competing ideas
about the point at which this movement occurs.

(43)   Covert movement of Object NPs
         Agbayani (1995), Hornstein (1994), Kennedy (1997), May (1985)-
         only LF copying

(44)   Overt movement of Object NPs
         Takahashi (1993)-both PF-deletion or LF-copying are possible

In conclusion, based on the fact that it is the LF interface that is sensitive to semantic interpretation and it should be the LF interface that can see an operator-variable relationship, I claim that ACD sentences, at least those shown above, are produced by an LF-copying operation of a VP that already contains Tense and Aspect information. This leads us to the idea that if we take (43) to be plausible, ACDs are made only with LF-copying; but if we take (44) to be plausible, then we will conclude that ACDs can be made by both PF-deletion and LF-copying, except for examples that call for Tense and Aspect Parallelism, which must be constructed by way of LF-copying.

4. References

Agbayani, B. 1995. Interpretation of Noun Phrases and Feature Licensing. Ms., University of California at Irvine.

Baltin, M. 1987. Do Antecedent Contained Deletions Exist? *Linguistic Inquiry* 18: 579-595.

Bouton, M. 1970. Antecedent-Contained Pro-Forms. *Papers from the sixth Regional Meeting of Chicago Linguistic Society*, 154-167.

Brugger, G. 1996. The Temporal Representation of Present Perfect Types. Ms., UCLA and University of Vienna.

Carlson, G. 1977. *Reference to Kinds in English*. Ph.D. dissertation University of Massachusetts, Amherst.

Chomsky, N. 1995. *The Minimalist Program*. MIT Press: Cambridge, Mass.

Demirdache H. & M. Uribe-Etxebarria. 1997. Towards a Unified Theory of Tense and Aspect, a talk given at the University of Connecticut.

Demirdache H. & M. Uribe-Etxebarria. To appear. The Primitives of Temporal Relations. In D. Michaels, R. Martin and J. Uriagereka (eds.), *Essays in Honor of Howard Lasnik,* MIT Press, Cambridge, Mass.

Diesing, M. 1992. *Indefinites*. MIT Press, Cambridge, Mass.

Fox, D. 1995a. Condition C effects and ACD. In H.Ura and R. Pensalfini (eds.), *Papers on Minimalist Syntax*. MITWPL 27: 105-119, Cambridge, Mass.

Fox, D. 1995b. Economy and Scope. *Natural Language Semantics* 3: 283-341.

Fiengo, R., and R. May. 1994. *Indices and Identity*. MIT Press, Cambridge, Mass.

Hornstein, N. 1994. An Argument for Minimalism: The Case of Antecedent Contained Deletion. *Linguistic Inquiry* 25: 455-480.

Hornstein, N. 1995. *Logical Form: From GB to Minimalism.* Basil Blackwell: Cambridge, Mass.

Kennedy, C. 1997. Antecedent-Contained Deletion and the Syntax of Quantification. *Linguistic Inquiry 28*: 662-688.

Lasnik, H. 1995. A Note on Pseudogapping. *The MIT Working Paper in Linguistics 27*: 143-163. MITWPL, Cambridge, Mass.

Lasnik, H. In press. Pseudogapping Puzzles. In M.Darnell, E. Moravscik, F. Newmeyer, M. Noonan, and K. Wheatley (eds.) *Functionalism and Formalism in Linguistics*, Volume 1 (SLCS 41). John Benjamins Publishing Co.

Lasnik, H. In press. On Feature Strength: Three Minimalism Approaches to Overt Movement. *Linguistic Inquiry.*

McCawley, J. 1981. They Syntax and Semantics of English Relative Clauses. *Lingua 53*: 99-149.

Oku, S. 1996. On Remnant Aux Structure. Ms. University of Connecticut.

Stowell, T. 1993. Syntax of Tense. Ms., UCLA.

Takahashi, D. 1993. On Antecedent-Contained Deletion. Ms. University of Connecticut.

Travis, L. 1991. Derived Objects, Inner Aspect, and the Structure of VP. presented at NELS, University of Delaware.

Uribe-Echevarria, M. 1994. *Interface Licensing Conditions on Negative Polarity Items: A Theory of Polarity and Tense Interactions*, Doctoral Dissertation. University of Connecticut.

Williams, E. 1976. Discourse and Logical Form. *Linguistic Inquiry 8*: 101-139.

E-type A′-traces under Sluicing

JASON MERCHANT

University of California, Santa Cruz

One of the most puzzling aspects of the investigation of elliptical structures has been the fact that the interpretation of an ellipsis site seems to be able to deviate from the interpretation of its antecedent. The working hypothesis of most researchers has been that the interpretations are in fact identical at the relevant level of structure (as in the classic Sag-Williams analysis of 'sloppy' identity facts). This paper uncovers another aspect of the 'deviance from identity' that is attested in ellipsis, under sluicing, and argues that certain problems that arise for the standard accounts of sluicing can be resolved if syntactic variables (A'-traces) are allowed to form an equivalence class with pronominals under ellipsis. These 'pronominal' variables can be interpreted using an E-type strategy.

Section 1 presents a very brief review of the main relevant points of the account of sluicing assumed here, section 2 introduces and explains the problem, and section 3 offers my solution.

Parts of this paper have benefited from comments from audiences at WCCFL17 in Vancouver, the 71st LSA in Chicago, and talks in Groningen, Thessaloniki, Berlin, Leiden, and Utrecht. Thanks especially to Anastasia Giannakidou, Chris Kennedy, and Jim McCloskey for detailed discussion.

1   Background on sluicing

Sluicing is an IP-level elliptical phenomenon first discussed (and named) in Ross 1969, and subsequently investigated by a number of researchers (Rosen 1976, Levin 1982, Chao 1987, Lobeck 1991, 1995, Ginzburg 1992, Chung Ladusaw and McCloskey [CLM] 1995, Reinhart 1995, Ramos-Santacruz 1996, Romero 1997, among others). (1) collapses a number of examples. The structure for the embedded interrogative clause prior to LF is given in (2) (see especially Chao 1987, Lobeck 1995, and Merchant 1996 for support for this structure).

(1)   a.   Jack bought a flag, but I don't know where/how/why/
        when/for who(m)/on what day.
        b.   Mark baked a cake for someone—guess for who!

(2)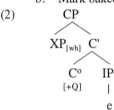

The general analytical question posed by the interpretation of (2) is that posed by all elliptical constructions—how do we get something from nothing? I will follow CLM's answer here in assuming that the interpretation is generated by 'recycling' an IP present in the discourse. Specifically, the null IP is replaced at LF by means of an operation of IP-copy (see also Reinhart 1991 and Hazout 1995), the clause-level equivalent to VP-copy assumed in many approaches to VP-ellipsis. (I will sidestep the issue of deletion vs. reconstruction/copying approaches to ellipsis here, and follow CLM in assuming a copying account for ease of exposition, though nothing rests on this; see especially Winkler 1997 for a recent comparison.) IP-copy will yield the LFs in (3) and (4), corresponding to (1a) type examples with adjunct wh-phrases and (1b) type with arguments, respectively.

(3)   ... [CP where/how/... [IP Jack bought a flag]]

(4)   ... [CP for who [IP Mark baked a cake for someone]]

        The question of how to associate the wh-phrases with an appropriate bindee internal to the elliptical IP is the property of sluicing that has occupied most researchers, but since the solution to this is orthogonal to the problem I will present below, I will not discuss it further here.

2   The problem: A'-traces under sluicing

The problem, given IP-copy or its equivalent mechanism in a PF-deletion or higher-order unification approach, arises quite simply: IPs which contain A'-traces are themselves licit targets of IP-copy.   Such IPs can provide the necessary antecedent IP to resolve a sluice.   Constructed examples are given in (5), and some attested ones are in (6)-(8).

(5)   a.   The report details what IBM did and why.
       b.   Who did the suspect call and when?
       c.   We know which families bought houses on this block, but we don't know which (houses), yet.
       d.   It was clear which families had mowed their lawns, but we can only guess with which brands of lawnmower.
       e.   The judge had records of which divers had been searching the wreck, but not of how long.
       f.   The hospital spokeswoman told us which patients had died, but she wouldn't say when.
       g.   The Guiness Book records how long some alligators can hold their breaths, but not which (ones).
       h.   Though Abby eventually told us who she saw that night, she never revealed where.

(6)   a.   That's a gazebo. But I don't know who built it or why. [overheard conversation]
       b.   A ride-along with an officer shows who gets ticketed, and why. [SJ Mercury News 8/9/96]
       c.   A chronology was the first step in piecing together what had happened—which had to precede figuring out why.   [K.S. Robinson Green Mars p. 222]
       d.   They didn't have any clear idea of what they were going to try to do, or why. [K.S. Robinson Green Mars p. 535]
       e.   What's proposed and why. [SJ Mercury News headline 11/28/96]

(7)   a.   [The Smart Toilet] is a paperless device that not only accommodates calls of nature, but also 'knows' who's using it and how. [SJ Mercury News 8/6/96]
       b.   What interveners are able to 'get out of the way', and how? [Szabolcsi & Zwarts 1993: 14]
       c.   Investigators want to know who is supplying the drugs—and how—since Kevorkian's medical license was suspended in 1991. [SJ Mercury News 8/17/96]

(8) a. [The police asked] who'd seen him last and where. [D. Tartt
         The Secret History p. 294]
     b. But R.C. Lahoti, a High Court judge appointed to lead the
         investigation of the accident, must decide who will decode the
         recorders and where. [SJ Mercury News 11/30/96]
     c. He only wanted to know whom they had met, and where. [K.S.
         Robinson Red Mars p. 515]

Even multiple wh-phrases may be in the antecedent IP:

(9) a. We need to know who saw what, and when.
     b. [He] makes no empirical claims concerning what domain will be
         opaque for what relations, [or] why. [Szabolcsi & Zwarts 1993
         fn. 4]
     c. You know exactly who will laugh at which particular kind of
         joke, and for how long. [slightly altered ex. from L. de Bernières
         Corelli's Mandolin p. 33]

Traces of QRed constituents in the antecedent IP can also give rise to the
same effect.

(10) a. The suspect phoned everyone on this list, but we don't know
         when.
     b. Most gangs will be at the rumble, though it's not clear why.
     c. Every boy scout helped, though most didn't know why.
     d. (Only a) Few boats looked for survivors, though it's not clear
         why.
     e. At least five guerrillas survived the raids, but no-one could figure
         out how.
     f   The duke hid exactly six of the jewels, and even Holmes didn't
         know where.

After IP-copy, we will have the representative LFs in (11), where the
material in bold has been copied in. These LFs have the glaring defect that
the wh-trace in the second conjunct, which has been copied along internal to
the IP, is now unbound. Under normal circumstances we'd expect an
unbound trace to give rise to spectacular ungrammaticality—but these
examples show that it doesn't.

(11) a. ... [$_{CP}$ what$_1$ [$_{IP}$ IBM did t$_1$]] and [$_{CP}$ why [$_{IP}$ **IBM did t$_1$**]]
     b. [$_{CP}$ who$_2$ did [$_{IP}$ the suspect call t$_2$]] and [$_{CP}$ when [$_{IP}$ **the suspect call t$_2$**]]

I suggest that the key to explaining these examples' acceptability is the fact
that they have interpretations parallel to the sentences in (12), which contain

overt pronouns anaphoric to preceding non-c-commanding wh-phrases, but no ellipsis.

(12) a. The report details what₁ IBM did and why IBM did it₁.
   b. Who₂ did the suspect call and when did the suspect call him₂?
   c. Most gangs₃ will be at the rumble, though it's not clear why they₃'ll be there.
   d. Every boy scout₄ helped, though most₅ didn't know why they₄/₅ helped.

While no analysis has ever been proposed for sentences like those in (5)-(10), ones like those in (12a,b) were discussed in Bolinger's seminal 1978 paper and more recently in Comorovski 1996. Comorovski only mentions them in passing, since her main interests lie elsewhere, and attributes the possibility of an anaphoric link of the observed kind to the existential presuppositions of wh-questions. Whether or not this is the correct approach to the feasibility of such anaphoric links in the first place, this observation obviously doesn't solve the problem raised by the elliptical sentences in (5)-(10).

Note especially that none of these examples is plausibly the result of some novel, mysterious application of across-the-board (ATB) movement of the first wh-phrase out of both conjuncts. Such an ATB account would obviously run into numerous problem (phrase-structural, to begin with, as well as island violations); in addition, there are many examples which are not coordinate structures of the kind necessary for ATB extraction (see the appendix for additional examples).

3   The solution: Vehicle change and E-type pronouns

The solution I will suggest in effect assimilates sluices to their nonelided counterparts above. I propose that the LFs of copied IPs like those in (11) are in fact fully parallel in the relevant respects to the LFs of sentences like (12)—specifically, that wh-traces (and traces of QR) can be treated as equivalent to pronouns under this kind of ellipsis (namely, when not bound by another operator). Fiengo and May 1994 propose and defend a mechanism for capturing exactly this kind of syntactic sleight of hand: vehicle change (see also van den Wyngaerd and Zwart 1991, Brody 1995, Giannakidou and Merchant 1998, Kennedy 1997, Merchant and Kennedy to appear). Vehicle change in essence defines certain equivalence classes under ellipsis; this is given in its general form in (13). For our purposes, the relevant instantiation of vehicle change is the one given schematically in (14), which states that nonpronominals may be treated as pronominals under ellipsis. Specifically, a variable like a wh-trace can be treated as a pronominal—its 'pronominal correlate', in Fiengo and May's term, as in (15).

(13) *Vehicle change* (Fiengo and May 1994:218ff.)
      Nominals can be treated as nondistinct with respect to their pronominal status under ellipsis.

(14) [-pronominal] $=_e$ [+pronominal]   (where $=_e$ means 'forms an equivalence class under ellipsis with')

(15) [-a, -p] (variable or name) $=_e$ [-a, +p] (*pronominal correlate* $= {}^pe$)

Fiengo and May take pains to argue that vehicle change is syntactic, and has syntactic effects, and is not simply relevant at some more abstract level of semantic equivalence (as in property-anaphora treatments of ellipsis). They show that the pronominal correlates of names and wh-traces under VP-ellipsis do not trigger Principle C violations, do trigger Principle B, and do not respect islands, all of which they assume are syntactic phenomena. Though their discussion is limited exclusively to VP-ellipsis, the first and third of these properties can be observed under sluicing as well.

3.1   *Vehicle change under sluicing*

Let us begin with the Binding Theory effect, namely the disappearance of Principle C effects. (16) presents a standard case of a Principle C violation with a name. If the trace of a moved wh-phrase is copied under a co-indexed c-commanding pronoun as in (17a), however, no deviance arises, contrary to naive expectation, since featurally names and wh-traces are indistinct. Vehicle change, however, can convert the trace into its pronominal correlate, as in the LF given in (17b), in which the variable t_4 is realized as its pronominal correlate ${}^pe_4$; ${}^pc_4$, being [+pronominal], is no longer subject to Principle C.

(16) *The detectives wanted to know whether they$_3$ knew why Sue hated the Thompsons$_3$.

(17) a.   The detectives wanted to know who$_4$ [Sue hated t_4] and whether they$_4$ knew why.
      b.   ... they$_4$ knew why [**Sue hated ${}^pe_4$**]

Principle B is not testable, since in sluicing an entire IP is elided, so no example with a clause-mate c-commanding pronoun can be constructed.

Second, we find that the normal binding relation between a wh-phrase and its bound trace, which is constrained by islands, is relaxed under this type of sluicing as well. In other words, the pronominal correlate of a reconstructed trace can find its antecedent outside of an island. This is indeed trivially true under sluicing, since sluicing involves wh-islands to begin with, but even embedding the CP immediately dominating the sluiced IP inside another island does not affect the status of these examples. Again, normal binding could not be expected to hold in the first place, since the wh-phrase does not even c-command the pronominal correlate.

The following example is structured as follows. The (a) example is simply a control, showing the ungrammaticality of extraction from the island (here, a subject; see the appendix for this kind of sluice inside 24 other kinds of islands as well). The (b) example shows that a wh-link into a non-elided IP is impossible. The (c) example gives a version with no ellipsis, but with a pronoun linked to the wh-antecedent. This link from a pronominal element is what makes the sluiced version in the (d) example (and those in the appendix) grammatical, as its LF in (e) shows.

(18) subject island

    a. *Which crime$_4$ did the FBI admit that <solving t$_4$> will prove difficult?

    b. *The FBI knows which truck$_4$ was rented, but <figuring out from where t$_4$ was rented> has proven difficult.

    c. The FBI knows which truck$_4$ was rented, but <figuring out from where it$_4$ was rented> has proven difficult.

    d. The FBI knows which truck$_4$ was rented, but <figuring out from where> has proven difficult.

    e. ... figuring out from where [^{P}e$_4$ **was rented**] has proven difficult.

3.2   *Interpreting the result of vehicle change: E-type wh-traces*

An account of the anaphoric link between the pronominal correlate and its antecedent must distinguish them from regular bound wh-traces or bound pronouns. Once the syntactic mechanism of vehicle change has played its role, the semantics can treat these pronominal correlates exactly as it does their overt pronominal counterparts. These are essentially a subspecies of donkey pronouns: anaphoric on a preceding quantificational expression, yet not bound by it.

Let us take as our working example (19a) and its associated LF after vehicle change, and its unelided counterpart in (20):

(19) a. Which suspect did Abby call, and when?

    b. [$_{CP}$ which suspect$_2$ did [$_{IP}$ Abby call t$_2$]] and [$_{CP}$ when [$_{IP}$ **Abby call** ^{P}e$_2$]]

(20) Which suspect did Abby call, and when did she call him?

The pronominal correlate is indistinguishable for purposes of interpretation from the pronoun in (20); both are interpreted as donkey pronouns. For simplicity, I will assume a functional analysis of donkey pronouns as E-type pronouns, following essentially Lappin and Francez 1994 (see also Heim 1990, Neale 1990, and Chierchia 1995; see Tomioka 1994 for VP-ellipsis). Nothing hinges on the particulars of this analysis of donkey anaphora, and I will return to the dynamic binding approach in section 3.3.

(21) $[\![{}^{P}\mathbf{e}]\!] = f(x)$

Using a Karttunen-style semantics for questions, the interpretation of the conjoined questions will be that in (22).

(22) $[\![(19b)]\!] = \lambda p[\exists x.\mathbf{suspect}(x) \wedge {}^{\vee}p \wedge p = {}^{\wedge}[\mathbf{call}(\mathbf{abby}, x)]] \wedge$
       $\lambda p[\exists t \wedge {}^{\vee}p \wedge p = {}^{\wedge}[\mathbf{call}(\mathbf{abby}, f(x), \mathbf{at}\ t)]]$

This formula is interesting because it makes clear that the interpretation of the antecedent IP (here, ${}^{\wedge}[\mathbf{call}(\mathbf{abby}, x)]$) is not identical to that of the elliptical IP, even ignoring the results of the binding association necessary to interpret the wh-XP (without this, we have ${}^{\wedge}[\mathbf{call}(\mathbf{abby}, f(x)]$). This shows that a purely semantic account of ellipsis would have to countenance a deviance from identity at that level as well; here, a bound pronoun translates as a variable, while an E-type pronoun as a function.
       Note that the conjunction in (22) is not trivial (as Bolinger 1978 suggests)—(19a) does not mean what a multiple question does:

(23)   Which suspect did Abby call when?

       If this is the correct analysis of the semantics of these expressions, we might expect to find them giving rise to effects prototypically associated with donkey anaphora, specifically in 'proportion problem' (after Kadmon 1987) environments. To the extent that such proportion problem effects can be discovered under sluicing, we have extremely suggestive supporting evidence for the treatment proposed here.
       In fact, these effects *can* be observed with sluicing, once the interaction of sluicing with quantificational variability effects (QVE) is brought into play (see Berman 1991, Lahiri 1991, and Ginzburg 1995 for discussions of QVE). Briefly, interrogative clauses embedded under certain predicates give rise to readings in which a quantificational adverb quantifies not over instances of the matrix predicate as expected, but rather over, loosely speaking, answers to the embedded question (the open sentence derived by lambda-abstracting over the wh-trace, in a Karttunen-style semantics). Thus (24a) has a reading given by (24b).

(24)   a. The sergeant {usually/for the most part} knows who has guard duty.
       b. $\mathbf{MOST}_x$ ($\mathbf{has\text{-}guard\text{-}duty}(x)$) [$\mathbf{know}(\mathbf{the\text{-}sergeant}, \mathbf{that}\ x$
          $\mathbf{has\ guard\ duty})$]

Though this aspect of sluicing has never been investigated, it is unsurprising that QVEs arise in sluicing contexts as well. Thus the sluice in (25) shows the same ambiguity that (24a) did, as expected.

(25)   Someone from Company D always has guard duty. The sergeant usually knows who.

Likewise, conjoined embedded interrogatives display QVE:

(26)   The sergeant mostly knows who has guard duty and who has KP.

Although the interpretation of conjoined interrogatives has not been the subject of much investigation in the literature (though see Bolinger 1978 for some initial observations), I will assume that nothing special need be said beyond the semantics of coordination. For our purposes, it is enough to note that (26) has a reading which can be rendered by (27), where the open questions are conjoined in the restriction of the quantificational adverb.

(27) $MOST_{x,y}$ (**has-guard-duty**(x) ∧ **has-KP**(y)) [**know(the-sergeant, that** x **has guard duty** ∧ **that** y **has KP**)]

That is, in QVE under conjunction, there is quantification over n-tuples (here pairs).

It will come as no surprise, then, that QVE is retained under sluicing with traces in antecedent IP:

(28)   The sergeant {usually, for the most part} knows who has guard duty, and when.

Though this has a symmetric reading[1], the most interesting property for our purposes is the availability of an asymmetric reading. Indeed, in (28), the subject asymmetric reading is highly preferred. Under this reading, the proportion problem emerges; (28) will be true in the situation sketched in (29):

---

[1]   This is reminiscent of the interpretation of QVE in multiple questions (mentioned in Berman 1991:209-210); a full exploration of these parallels will have to be postponed to future work, however. Here I note only that the interpretation of (28) in the text can be distinguished from that of an embedded multiple question like (i), which highly favors the symmetric reading given in (ii) (some speakers cannot get the asymmetric reading at all).

(i)   The sergeant usually knows who has guard duty when.
(ii) $MOST_{x,t}$ (**has-guard-duty**(x, at t)) [**know(the-sergeant, that** x **has guard duty at** t)]

Here quantification is over pairs of individuals and times. This is expected if all wh-phrases in multiple questions move to SpecCP at LF, where they all form the restriction of the quantificational adverb. The asymmetric readings discussed in the text for conjoined CPs seem to be available mostly when there is an donkey pronoun present in the second conjunct. This recalls the triggering influence of donkey pronouns in the standard examples as well, noted by Bäuerle and Egli 1985, though in neither case does the presence of such pronominals absolutely preclude other readings.

Again, these partial equivalences should presumably be derived from the correct account of the contribution of conjunction to the restriction in such environments.

(29)   Sergeant knows that: Private A has guard duty Mon.
                                   Private B has guard duty Tues.
                                   Private C has guard duty Wed.
       Sergeant is unaware that: Private D has guard duty Thur, Fri, Sat,
                                   and Sun.

In this situation, however, the symmetric interpretation, where quantification is over pairs of individuals and times, will predict (28) to be false. Instead, the correct interpretation of (28) under the subject asymmetric reading is given in (30), where quantification is over individuals alone.

(30) $MOST_x$ (**has-guard-duty**(x)) [**know**(**the-sergeant, when** x **has guard duty**)]

Here, the wh-phrase of the second conjunct remains in the nuclear scope of the quantifier.

Thus, there is considerable evidence that the approach advocated here is correct in its essentials, namely that these pronominal correlates are interpreted as E-type pronouns.

3.3   Eliminating vehicle change?

Having come this far, let us step back from the analysis presented and ask a more fundamental question: What is vehicle change? At this point in our understanding of the relevant phenomena, it is simply a stipulation—a bit of syntactic sleight of hand to get the right result, without any theory of why things can vary as observed, or why they are restricted to just this way. A more skeptical reader might say that it is little more than an artifact of a too slavish reliance on syntactic phrase markers. (It is indeed Fiengo and May 1994's factotum for mysteries: they put it to 13 different uses between pp. 219-230.)

Although space precludes a full working out of an alternative, I would like to sketch another view of the above phenomenon which relies on a dynamic binding approach to donkey anaphora (Groenendijk and Stokhof 1991, Chierchia 1995). Under this approach, dynamic definitions of ∃ and ∧ allow the existential to bind variables outside its scope, and the occurrence of the variable x in the second conjunct in (31)—the translation of (19a)—would be licitly bound by the quantifier ∃x in the first conjunct.

(31) $\lambda p[\exists x.\textbf{suspect}(x) \wedge {}^\vee p \wedge p = {}^\wedge[\textbf{call}(\textbf{abby}, x)]] \wedge$
       $\lambda p[\exists t \wedge {}^\vee p \wedge p = {}^\wedge[\textbf{call}(\textbf{abby}, x, \textbf{at } t)]]$

Of course, it will have to be established that it is not pernicious to allow dynamic conjunction with dynamic ∃ to scope through λ–operators, since these operators are generally static. However, some sort of scopal mechanism of this sort will be necessary in any case for examples like (32), where a regular indefinite scopes into a second question.

(32)   Where can I a buy a paper around here, and how much will it cost?

Under this approach to wh-traces under sluicing, a strict identity at a semantic level of interpretation (modulo the addition of a bindee for the sluiced wh-phrase) can be established, since the second conjunct will simply contain the same variable as the first conjunct does ($^\wedge$[**call(abby**, x)]).

The dynamic binding approach can be implemented just as successfully if we adopt the choice function analysis of indefinites (and sluicing) proposed by Reinhart 1995, 1997, and Winter 1997). Under this analysis, a wh-trace consists of the restriction and a choice function variable, as in the LF for (19a) given in (33).

(33)   [$_{CP}$ which suspect$_2$ did [$_{IP}$ Abby call f_2(suspect)]] and
       [$_{CP}$ when [$_{IP}$ **Abby call** f_2**(suspect)**]]

Now it is the choice function variable f that is the beneficiary of dynamic binding, as in (34).

(34) $\lambda p[\exists f.CH(f) \wedge {}^\vee p \wedge p = {}^\wedge[\textbf{call(abby}, f(\textbf{suspect}))]] \wedge$
       $\lambda p[\exists t \wedge {}^\vee p \wedge p = {}^\wedge[\textbf{call(abby}, f(\textbf{suspect}), \text{at } t)]]$

Neither of these alternatives needs recourse to any mechanism like vehicle change, if the appropriate level for establishing equivalences for elliptical identity is semantic (for (31)) or LF (for (33)), since the relevant parts of the respective structures are truly identical. This does not show, of course, that vehicle change can be dispensed with in general, but it does make clear that vehicle change, in this case at least, is required only under one (widespread) view of the necessary components for resolution of ellipsis: syntactic phrase markers of a particular sort.

4   Conclusions

The investigation of the behavior of A'-traces under sluicing has provided evidence for a number of conclusions. First, I argued that these wh-traces form an equivalence class with their pronominal correlates under sluicing, an extension of the notion introduced in Fiengo and May 1994 to capture a wide array of deviancies from identity long known to hold under VP-ellipsis. This equivalence class behavior was captured formally by the syntactic mechanism of vehicle change. The fact that these A'-traces are pronominals at LF explains the absence of effects associated with standard variables, namely that Principle C effects and island-sensitivity are voided. I further gave an interpretation of these pronominal correlates as E-type pronouns anaphoric on wh-phrases, parallel to E-type pronouns anaphoric on other non-binding quantifiers investigated in the literature on donkey anaphora, and showed a parallel to other donkey anaphora in giving rise to proportion problem effects. Finally, I speculated on an alternative using dynamic binding and showed how this approach obviates the need for vehicle change to establish the requisite semantic identity, bringing these facts into line with the classic analyses of 'deviance from identity' under ellipsis.

Appendix: A quick tour of some other islands (adapted from Postal 1996):

(35) finite embedded interrogative clauses

We knew who the FBI had arrested, but we forgot to find out \<when\>.

(36) nonfinite embedded interrogative clauses

They told me who to call, but they didn't tell me \<when\>.

(37) complements of head nouns

Which books are being hidden, and do you believe \<the claim that the librarian knows where\>?

(38) conjuncts

We discovered which capacitors Mark had disabled, and that Lucy knew about it but \<didn't reveal why\>.

(39) nonfinite adjuncts

Who did Bob confess he had robbed \<without admitting where\>?

(40) finite adjuncts

What did Bob try to fix \<before he knew how\>?

(41) restrictive relative clauses

It was obvious which capacitors were to be connected, but I couldn't find anyone \<who knew where\>.

(42) embedded exclamatory clauses

I know what Mark bought, I just can't believe \<for how little money\>!

(43) right dislocated phrases

He explained which pieces were there, though he tried to avoid it, \<our question about why\>.

(44) non-wh nonrestrictive

We found out who Moriarty spoke to, though Holmes, \<and I'm sure he even knew when\>, said it wasn't enough.

(45) extraposed PPs

We were told which traps had been set off, and rewards were offered \<for figuring out when\>

(46) the finite complement of *so*

Which Pharaoh built the Sphinx? I don't know, but Mark will— he's so smart \<that he'll probably even know in which year\>.

(47)   left-extracted constituents
       Mark knew what he had lost, though <how>, he couldn't imagine.

(48)   exceptive phrases
       We knew everything about which items had been stolen <except how>.

(49)   the pivot of pseudoclefts
       It's easy to see what was stolen—what is difficult is <to figure out how>.

(50)   predicate nominals/clauses
       Who had left was obvious—the problem is <the question when>.
       Who had left was obvious—the problem is <that we don't know when>.

(51)   *namely* and *that is* constituents
       Although she figured out who Jack bribed, Charlene still said she was unsuccessful, that is, <that she hadn't been able to discover with how much money>.

(52)   the nonfinite complements of *too/enough*
       Mark told us what he found, but was too astute <to tell us where>.

(53)   the nonfinite complements of object-raising triggers
       Mark told us what he found, but was hard <to persuade to tell us where>.

(54)   *as* parentheticals
       What Frank had hidden was known, but, <as finding out where showed>, it wasn't easy to get him to reveal details of his crime.

(55)   relative-like nonrestrictive clauses
       We need to find out what they filmed, and talk to Arthur, <who will know how.>

(56)   the relative clause-like part of clefts
       We all knew who Lucy had had dinner with, but it was only Bert <who knew where>.

(57)   either piece of *the more ... the more* comparatives
       We knew what kind of house Mark was planning to build, but the more <we started to realize where>, the more horrified we became.

(58)   comparative clauses
       Mark told more people who he had seen <than he told where>.

References

Bäuerle, R., and Urs Egli. 1985. Anapher, Nominalphrase und Eselssätze. Papier 105 des Sonderforschungsbereichs 99: Univ. Konstanz.

Berman, Steven. 1991. The semantics of open sentences. PhD thesis, UMass Amherst.

Bolinger, Dwight. 1978. Asking more than one thing at a time. In Hiz (ed.), *Questions*. Pp. 107-150.

Brody, Michael. 1995. *Lexico-logical form: A radically minimalist theory*. MIT Press: Cambridge.

Chao, Wynn. 1987. On ellipsis. PhD thesis, UMass: Amherst . Published 1988 by Garland.

Chierchia, Gennaro. 1995. *Dynamics of meaning*. UChicago Press: Chicago.

Chung, Ladusaw, and McCloskey. 1995. Sluicing and logical form. *Natural Language Semantics* **3**:239-282.

Comorovski, Ileana. 1996. *Interrogative phrases and the syntax-semantics interface*. Kluwer: Dordrecht.

Fiengo, Robert, and Robert May. 1994. *Indices and identity*. MIT Press: Cambridge.

Giannakidou, Anastasia, and Jason Merchant. 1998. Reverse sluicing in English and Greek. *The Linguistic Review*.

Ginzburg, Jonathan. 1992. Questions, queries, and facts: A semantics and pragmatics for interrogatives. PhD thesis, Stanford.

Ginzburg, Jonathan. 1995. The quantificational variability effect (QVE) to some extent defused and generalized. In Beckman (ed.), NELS **25**.

Groenendijk, Jeroen, and Martin Stokhof. 1991. Dynamic predicate logic. *Linguistics and Philosophy* **14**: 39-100.

Hazout, Ilan. 1995. Comparative ellipsis and Logical Form. *NLLT* **13**:1-37.

Heim, Irene. 1990. E-type pronouns and donkey anaphora. *Linguistics and Philosophy* **13**:137-177.

Kadmon, Nirit. 1987. On unique and non-unique reference and asymmetric quantification. PhD thesis, UMass Amherst.

Kennedy, Chris. 1997. VP deletion and 'nonparasitic' gaps. *LI* **28**.4.

Kennedy, Chris, and Jason Merchant. To appear. Attributive comparatives and the syntax of ellipsis. In F. Corblin et al. (eds.) *Proceedings of CSSP2*. Peter Lang: Paris.

Lahiri, Utpal. 1991. Embedded interrogatives and the predicates that embed them. PhD thesis, MIT.

Lappin, Shalom and Nissim Francez. 1994. E-type pronouns, i-sums, and donkey anaphora. *Linguistics and Philosophy* **17**:391-428.

Levin, Lori. 1982. Sluicing: A lexical interpretation procedure. In Bresnan (ed.), *The mental representation of grammatical relations*. Pp. 590-654. MIT Press: Cambridge.

Lobeck, Anne. 1991. The phrase structure of ellipsis. In Rothstein (ed.), *Perspectives on phrase structure*. Pp. 81-103. Acad. Press: San Diego.

Lobeck, Anne. 1995. *Ellipsis*. Oxford Univ. Press: Oxford.

Merchant, Jason. 1996. The hidden structure of the sluice: Evidence from German. Ms., UCSC.

Neale, Stephen. 1990. *Descriptions*. MIT Press: Cambridge.

Postal, Paul. 1996. The characterization of constituents as islands. Paper presented at WECOL, UCSC.

Ramos-Santacruz, Milagrosa. 1996. On the nature of discourse ellipsis: Evidence from sluicing. Paper presented at the LSA annual meeting.

Reinhart, Tanya. 1991. Elliptic conjunctions—Non-quantificational LF. In Kasher, (ed.), *The Chomskyan turn*. Pp. 360-384. Blackwell: Oxford.

Reinhart, Tanya. 1995. Interface strategies. OTS-WP-TL-95-002. Utrecht.

Reinhart, Tanya. 1997. Quantifier cope: How labor is divided between QR and choice functions. *Linguistics and Philosophy* **20**: 335-397.

Romero, Maribel. 1997. Recoverability conditions for sluicing. *Proceedings of CSSP1*: Paris.

Ross, John. 1969. Guess who? In Binnick et al. (eds.), *CLS* **5**:252-286.

Rosen, Carol. 1976. Guess what about? In Ford et al. (eds.), *NELS* **6**:205-211.

Szabolcsi, Anna, and Frans Zwarts. 1993. Weak islands and algebraic semantics for scope taking. *Natural Language Semantics* **1**:235- 284.

Tomioka, Satoshi. 1994. Focus, ellipsis, and pronominal interpretation. Ms., UMass Amherst.

Webber, Bonnie. 1978. A formal approach to discourse anaphora. Harvard PhD thesis.

Winkler, Susanne. 1997. Ellipsis and information structure in English and German: The phonological reduction hypothesis. Arbeitspapiere des SFB 340, Nr. 121.

Winter, Yoad. 1997. Choice functions and the scopal semantics of indefinites. *Linguistics and Philosophy* **20**: 399-467.

van den Wyngaerd, Guido, and Jan-Wouter Zwart. 1991. Reconstruction and vehicle change. In F. Drijkoningen and A. van Kemenade (eds.), *Linguistics in the Netherlands,* Pp. 151-160.

How Children Cope with Scope

JULIEN MUSOLINO
University of Maryland

1. Introduction

This paper reports the findings of an interconnected set of experiments designed to assess children's knowledge of the semantics of quantification and scope. The primary focus is on the interaction of negation and quantified noun phrases (QNPs). It is well-known that in English negation is capable of entering into scopal relations with quantified expressions (Jackendoff (1972), Lasnik (1979), Horn (1989)), as the following examples illustrate.

(1) Every student didn't solve the problem.
(2) The students didn't solve every problem.
(3) The students didn't solve two problems.
(4) The students didn't solve some problems.

Example (1) is ambiguous. On one interpretation, it can be paraphrased as meaning that every student is such that he didn't solve the problem; in other words, none of the students solved the problem. In this case, *every* is interpreted outside the scope of negation (Every > not). The other interpretation of (1) can be paraphrased as 'not every student solved the problem'. Here, *every* is interpreted in the scope of negation (not > every). In the example in (2), *every* must be interpreted in the scope of negation (not > every). In other words, (2) must mean that not all the problems were solved[1]. (3) is ambiguous. On one interpretation it can be paraphrased as 'the number of problems that were solved is not two'. In this case, the phrase 'two problems' is interpreted in the scope of negation (not > two). (3) could also mean that two problems are such that they didn't get solved; in which case the phrase 'two problems' takes wide scope over negation (two > not). Finally, in (4) the phrase 'some problems' must be interpreted outside the scope of negation (some > not). (4) must mean that some problems are such that they didn't get solved.

From the point of view of a child acquiring English, the different interpretive options illustrated in (1)-(4) recast the problem of generalization in language acquisition (Baker (1979), Pinker (1989), Crain & Fodor (1987)). Essentially, for the learner, the problem amounts to finding a reasonable compromise between undergeneralization and overgeneralization. As Pinker (1989, p. 6) remarks, "...children cannot simply stick with the exact sentences they hear, because they must generalize to the infinite language of their community". On the other hand, he adds that "if the child entertains a grammar generating a superset of the target language, ... no amount of positive evidence can strictly falsify the guess." (p 6.). At the heart of this dilemma lies the fact that, as Crain and Fodor (1987) observe, "The generalizations that natural languages exhibit are partial generalizations only" (p.36). This property can be easily seen in the examples above: the interpretation of quantified expressions with respect to negation is sometimes based on the surface order of these elements, as in (2), sometimes on the reverse of the surface order, as in (4), and sometimes on a combination of these two options as in (1) and (3). Consequently, a child generalizing on the basis of (2) where the QNP must be interpreted in the scope of negation would undergeneralize with respect to (3), where the QNP can also be interpreted outside the scope of negation and misgeneralize with respect to (4) where the QNP must be interpreted outside the scope of negation. A child generalizing on the basis of (3) where both scope options are available would overgeneralize with respect to (2) where only one scope option is available, etc. In short, the complexity of the facts surrounding the interaction of negation and QNPs raises the possibility that children could entertain erroneous hypotheses and therefore reach invalid conclusions unless the hypothesis space is constrained in some way. The observation that all language learners ultimately reach similar conclusions, presumably without negative (syntactic or semantic) evidence, lends credence to the conclusion that innately specified linguistic constraints may be operative in the acquisition of semantic knowledge. If so, it is reasonable to expect children

---

[1] Assuming, of course, that the set of problems is different from the null set.

to adhere to such constraints early in the course of language development.

In what follows we will explore through a series of experimental investigations the extent to which these expectations are met; that is, how well children navigate through this maze of interpretive options, what routes they follow and how conservative or adventurous they are in the hypotheses they formulate. Our study is based on four experiments testing children's interpretations of sentences such as (1)-(4) above. All the experiments are based on the Truth Value Judgment Task methodology of Crain and McKee (1985) and Crain and Thornton (1998). Each experiment corresponds to a different section. Section 2 deals with sentence (2), section 3 with sentence (1), section 4 with sentence (3) and section 5 with sentence (4). Section 6 discusses the results of this series of experiments. Finally, in section 7, a conclusion is offered.

2. Experiment 1: comprehension of *every* and negation: the object case

In this experiment, children's interpretation of sentences like (5) was tested using a Truth Value Judgment Task. In the Truth Value Judgment Task, short stories are acted out with toys and props by one experimenter. The stories are watched by the child and a puppet, Kermit the Frog, played by a second experimenter. After each story, Kermit the Frog says what he thinks happened in the story. The child is asked to indicate whether Kermit's description of the story is correct or not. If the child thinks that Kermit is correct then she pretends to feed him something tasty, like a slice of pizza. If the child thinks that Kermit's description of the story is not correct, she pretends to feed him something less tasty, like a leaf of lettuce, to remind him to pay closer attention. Whenever Kermit says the wrong thing, the child is encouraged to tell him 'what really happened' in the story. This technique allows us to make sure that the child's response is based on her adequate understanding of the story.

(5) The smurf didn't buy every orange.
   a. $\neg \forall(x)$ [orange $(x) \rightarrow$ smurf bought (x)]
   b. $* \forall(x) \neg$ [orange, $(x) \rightarrow$ smurf bought (x)]

For adults, the only possible interpretation of *every* with respect to negation is the narrow scope reading. That is, *every* must be interpreted in the scope of negation to give the 'not all' reading. In other words, (5) must mean that not all the oranges were bought by the smurf. What (5) cannot mean (assuming that the set of oranges is not null) is that the smurf bought none of the oranges. This interpretation would correspond to a reading where *every* has wide scope over negation.

The research question was to determine whether children are aware that in a sentence like (5), only the narrow scope reading of *every* is possible. The strategy of the Truth Value Judgment Task was to place children in an experimental situation where both the narrow scope and the wide scope reading of *every* with respect to negation are under consideration, the former being true in the context of the story while the latter is false. Children who have access to the narrow scope reading of *every* should therefore accept a statement of the form 'The character didn't V every NP' in this situation. If, on the other hand, children only have access to the wide scope reading of *every*, they should reject that statement.

Participants. The subjects were 20 children ranging in age between 3;11 and 6;0 (mean 4;10). Prior to the experiment, children had been familiarized with the task both in groups and individually.

Materials and procedures. The protocols for the stories typically involved a main character and two sets of three objects with respect to which the main character was to perform an action such as eating, buying, cleaning etc. In a first round of activity, the main character considers performing the action with respect to one set of objects but upon reflection, decides not to do so. He then performs the action with respect to one of the objects of the second set but not the two others. In the end, therefore, a sentence of the form 'the character didn't V every Y' is true.

In one story for example, a smurf decides to go to the grocery store to buy some apples. He examines the three apples in the store to see if he can buy them. The first two have big bruises and the third one has a worm inside. The smurf then decides that he is not going to buy any apples. Instead, he considers buying some oranges. There are three oranges in the store and the smurf starts examining them. The first one is big and firm and he decides to buy it. The second one is not firm enough and the third one is too small so the smurf decides not to buy them. The puppet's description of the story is *The smurf didn't buy every orange*. In this situation, it is felicitous to say 'YES', because the negation of the sentence was under consideration. That is, if the outcome had been different, it would not have been true that the smurf didn't buy every orange; he could also not have bought the first orange and in this case, not buy any oranges. The context of the story also falsified the wide scope reading of *every* over negation; i.e. the interpretation where it is taken to mean that none of the oranges were bought. Indeed, it is not true that the smurf didn't buy any oranges since he actually bought one. Therefore, a child who could only assign the wide scope interpretation should have responded 'NO' to the puppet's statement that the smurf didn't buy every orange.

The complete experimental package in this experiment (as well as all the others) contained a total of four test stories all based on the logic of the story described above. Three control stories were also used to make sure that children could say 'YES' and 'NO' when it is appropriate. The control stories were of equal complexity as the test stories and they were administered after each test trial. Usually, if a child answered 'YES' to a test story, the following control story was chosen to elicit a 'NO' from the child.

Results. Out of 20 children, 18 accepted the 'not all' interpretation of sentences like (5) 94 % of the time. Two children rejected the 'not all' interpretation on all the trials. These results show that children correctly interpret *every* with respect to negation when the former occurs in object position of a negated clause.

3. Experiment 2: comprehension of *every* and negation: the subject case

This experiment was design to test children's comprehension of sentences like (6). (6) is ambiguous between a reading where *every* takes scope over negation or vice-versa. In the former case, the sentence can be paraphrased as 'No horse jumped over the fence' while in the latter it would mean that not all the horses jumped over the fence.

(6) Every horse didn't jump over the fence.
    a. $\forall(x) \neg [\text{horse}(x) \rightarrow \text{jumped over the fence}(x)]$
    b. $\neg \forall(x) [\text{horse}(x) \rightarrow \text{jumped over the fence}(x)]$

The research question was to determine whether children have access to the interpretation where negation takes scope over the universal quantifier, i.e. the 'not all' interpretation. Children were placed in an experimental situation where both the narrow scope and the wide scope reading of (6) were available, the latter being false and the former true in the context of the story. If children have access to the interpretation where negation takes scope over *every*, they should accept the statement 'Every horse didn't jump over the fence' in this situation. On the other hand, if children only have access to the interpretation where *every* takes scope over negation, they should reject that statement.

498 / JULIEN MUSOLINO

Participants. The participants were 20 English speaking children ranging in age between 4;0 and 7;3 (mean 5;11). Prior to the experiment, children had been familiarized with the task both in group and individually.

Materials and procedures. The protocol for the stories typically involved three characters and an action to be performed with respect to different objects. In a first round of activity, all three characters fail to perform the action with respect to the first object. In a second round of activity, two of the characters, but not the third one perform the action with respect to the second object. In the end, therefore, a sentence of the type "Every character didn't VP" is true of the action performed with respect to the second object since not all of the characters performed that action.

In one story, for example, three horses decide to jump over various obstacles to test their skills. First they consider jumping over a barn. They start running towards it but as they get closer, they realize that the barn is too tall for them to jump over. The horses then decide to jump over a fence, which would be easier than jumping over the barn. The first horse jumps over the fence and so does the second one. The third horse considers jumping but remembers that he hurt his leg the day before and decides that it should rest. The third horse thus decides not to jump over the fence. The puppet's description of the story is 'Every horse didn't jump over the fence'. In this situation, it is felicitous to say 'YES', since, although it was their initial intention, not all of the horses ended up jumping over the fence. Therefore, a child who could assign the narrow scope interpretation should respond 'YES' to the puppet's statement that every horse didn't jump over the fence. The context of the story also falsified the wide scope reading of *every* over negation since it is not true that every horse is such that it didn't jump. In other words, it is not true that none of the horses jumped over the fence, since two of them did. Therefore, a child who could only assign the wide scope interpretation should respond 'NO' to the puppet's statement.

Results. Out of 20 children, 18 rejected the puppet's statement, that is the interpretation where negation takes scope over *every* in an example like (6), 100 % of the time. When asked 'what really happened' all the children gave the wide scope reading as an explanation; that is, they said that the puppet was wrong because two horses did jump over the fence. Two children aged 6;11 and 7;3 accepted the puppet's statement 75 % of the time.

Adult control We tested a group of adult native speakers of English on the basis of a videotaped version of the stories which were presented to the children. All subjects accepted the 'not all' reading, allowing negation to take scope over *every*, 100% of the time.

These results indicate that until the age of about seven, the children tested are not aware of the fact that negation can take scope over a universally quantified expression in subject position.

4. Experiment 3: comprehension of *two* and negation

This experiment was designed to test children's comprehension of sentences like (7) where *two* occurs in the scope of negation. For adult speakers, (7) is ambiguous. On one interpretation, it can be paraphrased as 'the number of slices of pizza that Cookie Monster ate is not two'. In this case, 'two slices of pizza' is interpreted in the scope of negation (neg > two). On the other interpretation, (7) can be paraphrased as 'There are two slices of pizza that Cookie Monster didn't eat'. In this case, the phrase 'two slices of pizza' takes wide scope over negation (two > neg).

(7) Cookie Monster didn't eat two slices of pizza.
    a. $\exists$ (two x), (slice of pizza, x) $\land \neg$ (Cookie Monster eat x)
    b. $\neg \exists$ (two x), (slice of pizza, x) $\land$ (Cookie Monster eat x)

The research question was to determine whether children have access to the interpretation of (7) where the phrase 'two slices of pizza' has wide scope over negation (two > neg). The strategy was to place children in an experimental situation where both the narrow and wide scope reading of 'two slices of pizza' were available, the former being false and the latter true in the context of the story. If children have access to the wide scope interpretation of 'two slices of pizza' they should accept a statement of the form in (7) in such a context. On the other hand, if children only have access to the narrow scope interpretation of 'two slices of pizza', they should reject (7) in the same context.

Participants. The participants were 20 English speaking children ranging in age between 3;11 and 6;1 (mean 4;10). Prior to the experiment, children had been familiarized with the task both in group and individually.

Material and procedures The protocols for the stories typically involved one main character and an action to be performed with respect to four objects or other characters. The main character would successfully perform the action with respect to two of the objects or characters but crucially, he would fail to perform the action with respect to the two other objects or characters. In the end, therefore, a sentence of the form 'The character didn't V two N' is true.

In one story, for example, Cookie Monster's friend the troll, who heard of Cookie Monster's reputation as a great eater, brings him four big slices of pizza and challenges him to eat them all. Cookie Monster takes up the challenge and starts eating the pizza. He eats the first two slices only to realize that he is too full to even touch the two others. The puppet's description of the story is 'Cookie Monster didn't eat two slices of pizza'. In this situation, it is felicitous to say 'YES', because the negation of the sentence was under consideration. That is, if the outcome had been different, it would not have been true that Cookie Monster didn't eat two slices of pizza, he could also have eaten all the slices. The context of the story also falsified the narrow scope reading of *two* with respect to negation; i.e. the interpretation where it is taken to mean that two is not the number of slices of pizza that Cookie Monster ate. Indeed, it is not true that the number of slices of pizza that Cookie Monster ate is different from two: Cookie Monster actually ate exactly two slices. Therefore, a child who could only assign the narrow scope interpretation should have responded 'NO' to the puppet's statement that 'Cookie Monster didn't eat two slices of pizza'.

Results Out of 20 children, 9 rejected the puppet's statements, i.e. sentences like (7), 94 % of the time. 10 children accepted the puppet's statements 90% of the time. One child rejected the puppet's statements on the first two trials and accepted them on the last two. In order to determine whether this split could be caused by age, we divided the 20 children into two groups of 10, according to age. In the first group, G1, the 'older' group, the ages range between 6;1 and 4;8 (mean 5;5) and in G2, the 'younger' group, the ages range between 4;5 and 3;11(mean 4;3). We found that while the children in G1 accepted the puppet's statements 72,5 % of the time, the children in G2 only accepted the puppet's statements 27,5 % of the time. This result suggests that the split among children is caused by age.

Adult control We tested a group of adult native speakers of English on the basis of a videotaped version of the stories which were presented to the children. All subjects accepted the wide scope reading of examples like (7) 100% of the time.

5. Experiment 4: comprehension of *some* and negation

The purpose of this experiment was to test children's comprehension of sentences like (8) where *some/someone* occurs in the scope of negation. For adults, the phrase 'someone/some guys' must be assigned wide scope with respect to negation; that is, (8) must mean that there is/are someone/some guys that the detective didn't find. (8) cannot be taken to mean that the detective didn't find anyone/any guys.

(8) The detective didn't find someone/some guys.
    a.   ∃(x), (guy, x) ∧ ¬ (Detective find x)
    b.   * ¬∃(x), (guy, x) ∧ (Detective find x)

The research question was to determine whether children would correctly interpret 'someone/some' guys outside the scope of negation or rather (incorrectly) interpret it where it occurs syntactically, that is in the scope of negation. The strategy was to place children in an experimental situation where the narrow scope and the wide scope reading of an example like (8) are both available, the former reading being false and the latter true in the context of the story. If children correctly interpret *someone/some* with respect to negation, then they should accept a statement of the form in (8) in this situation. On the other hand, if children take (8) to mean 'John didn't see any students' thus incorrectly interpreting *some* in the scope of negation, they should reject a statement of the same form in that situation.

Participants. The subjects were 30 children ranging in age between 3;10 and 6;6 (mean 5;1). Prior to the experiment, all children had been familiarized with the task both in groups and individually.

Material and procedures. The protocols for the stories involved a set of characters and a specific action to be performed by a main character and accomplished with respect to some object(s) or other character(s). In a first round of activity, the main character failed to accomplish the action altogether. In a second round of activity, he accomplished the action with respect to some object(s) or character(s) but crucially failed to accomplish it for a specific object(s) or character(s). In the end, therefore, a sentence of the form 'the character didn't V someone/something/some N' is true.

    In one story, for example, a detective and his two friends decide to play hide and seek. While the detective has his eyes covered, one of the characters hides behind a tree and the other one hides under the seat of a covered wagon. After inspecting the tree, the covered wagon and a third hiding place without success, the detective reflects that his friends are really well hidden. He nonetheless refuses to give up and inspects the hiding places again, this time more carefully. The detective successfully spots the character hidden behind the tree but misses the one hidden inside the covered wagon again. The puppet's description of the story is *The detective didn't find someone*. In this situation, it is felicitous to say 'YES', i.e. to assign wide scope to *someone*, because the negation of the sentence was under consideration. That is, if the outcome had been different, it would not have been true that the detective didn't find someone; the detective could also have missed the character hidden behind the tree and in this case, not find anyone. The context of the story also falsified the narrow scope reading of *someone*; i.e. the interpretation where it is taken to mean *anyone*. Indeed, it is not true that the detective didn't find anyone since he found the character hiding behind the tree. Therefore, a child who could assign only the narrow scope interpretation should have responded 'NO' to the puppet's statement that the detective didn't find someone. Notice also that the last event mentioned in the experiment is the detective failing to find the character hiding under the seat of the covered wagon. The wide scope interpretation should, therefore, be readily available.

Results. Out of 30 children, 14 rejected the puppet's statements, that is the wide scope interpretation of *some/something* under negation, 87.5 % of the time. When asked 'what really happened' in the story, these children gave the narrow scope interpretation. In other words, in the case of the detective story, they said that the puppet was wrong because the detective found someone: the character hidden behind the tree. 13 children accepted the puppet's statements 90 % of the time and 3 children accepted the puppet's statement on 2 trials and rejected it on the 2 others.

In order to determine whether this split could be due age, we divided the 30 children into two groups of 15, according to age. In the first group, G1, the ages range between 6;6 and 5;2 (mean 5;7). In the second group, G2, the ages range between 5;2 and 3;10 (mean 4;7). We found that while chilldren in G1 accepted the puppet's statements 65 % of the time, children in G2 only accepted the puppet's statements 35 % of the time. This result suggests that the split observed among children is caused by age.

Adult control a group of adult speakers of English was tested on the basis of a videotaped version of the stories presented to the children. In all stories, all adults accepted the wide scope reading of *some* over negation 100% of the time.

6. Discussion

We started with the paradigm below which illustrates different ways in which negation and QNPs can interact in terms of scope. Our research question has been to determine the extent to which children acquiring English are aware of these different interpretive options. In order to address this issue, we tested experimentally children's interpretation of each of the sentences in (1)-(4).

(1) Every student didn't solve the problem.
(2) The students didn't solve every problem.
(3) The students didn't solve two problems.
(4) The students didn't solve some problems.

Our finding is that by and large, children do not interpret sentences containing negation and QNPs the way adult speakers do. Specifically, experiment 2 showed that children do not allow negation to scope over *every* in an example like (1); experiment 3 showed that younger children do not allow phrases like 'two problems' to take wide scope over negation in (2); and, finally, experiment 4 showed that younger children incorrectly interpret *some* in the scope of negation in (4).

These findings raise two questions: (a) what drives children to formulate interpretative hypotheses which are different from those of adults ? (b) how do children eventually arrive at the adult system of interpretation ? The remainder of this paper is devoted to addressing these questions. Regarding the first one, the experimental findings presented here suggest the following descriptive generalization: children's initial interpretion of sentences containing negation and QNPs is isomorphic to the overt form of these sentences. In other words, if a QNP occurs in the scope[2] of negation in overt syntax it is semantically interpreted in the scope of negation. Conversely, if a QNP occurs outside the scope of negation in overt syntax, it is semantically interpreted outside the scope of negation. Specifically, in (2) where *every* occurs in the scope of negation in overt syntax, we saw that children correctly assign the *not > every* reading. In (1), where *every* takes scope over negation in overt syntax, we saw that children, unlike adults, fail to assign the reverse scope reading, i.e. the *not > every* reading; but instead, that they access the isomorphic *every > not* reading. In (3), where *two* occurs in the scope of negation in overt syntax, we saw that younger

---

[2] Note here that "Y occurs in the scope of X" can either be read as "Y occurs in the c-command domain of X" or "Y occurs to the right of X". In order to tease these two definitions apart, we would need cases where the c-command relations between the QNPs and negation do not systematically coincide with their linear arrangement.

children, unlike adults, fail to assign the reverse scope reading, i.e. the *two* > *not* reading; but instead, that they access the isomorphic *not* > *two* reading. Finally, in (4), younger children are misled by the fact that *some* occurs in the scope of negation in overt syntax which is where they (incorrectly) interpret it (i.e., *not* > *some*), unlike adults for whom *some* must be interpreted outside the scope of negation (i.e. *some* > *not*).

Apart from the case of (4), where children access an interpretation not available in the adult grammar[3], in the two other cases where their interpretations differ from those of adults, children are restricted to a subset of the interpretive options available to adults. In 'Every horse didn't jump over the fence' *every horse* can either receive a narrow scope or a wide scope interpretation with respect to negation in the adult grammar while for children only one of these two options seems to be initially possible. In a similar vein, for adults, 'Cookie Monster didn't eat two slices of pizza' is ambiguous between a wide scope and a narrow scope reading of the phrase 'two slices of pizza' with respect to negation whereas for younger children only the narrow scope interpretation is available. In these cases, the task that children face in order to move to the adult system of interpretation is relatively straightforward. They simply need to add an extra interpretation in addition to what their grammar can already generate. That is, for sentences like 'Every horse didn't jump over the fence', children need to learn that in addition to the wide scope reading of *every horse,* there exists another reading where negation takes scope over *every*; i.e. the 'not all' reading. For sentences like 'Cookie Monster didn't eat two slices of pizza', children need to learn that in addition to the narrow scope reading of 'two slices of pizza' with respect to negation, there is also a wide scope reading. In each case, such learning can take place on the basis of positive evidence. All children would need to be exposed to, in principle, are situations where examples like (1) and (3) are uttered in narrow and wide scope contexts respectively.

The results from experiment 4 pose a potential learnability problem. When *some* occurs in the scope of negation, younger children interpret it as though it meant *any*, an option not available in the adult grammar. This raises the following question: how do children manage to expunge from their grammar this incorrect interpretive option on the basis of positive evidence only ? A possible solution to this problem is offered by Musolino (1998b) who argues that *some* and *any* are allomorphs (Klima (1964)) and

---

[3] In fact, in cases of metalinguistic negation (Horn 1989) it is possible for *some* to be interpreted in the scope of negation. For example, as a reply to a statement like 'John had some beans', one may say 'he didn't have some beans, he had some rice'. In this special case, however, what is being negated or denied is the first speaker's assertion that John had some beans. At any rate, such cases are irrelevant to our purposes since children in our experiment were not responding to previous statements containing *some*.

that children initially lack knowledge of this fact. When children come to realize that *some* and *any* are morphologically related, a version of the Uniqueness Principle (Wexler and Cullicover (1980)) forces them to the conclusion that both allomorphs cannot be interpreted in the same way under negation. Consequently children are led to revise their initial hypothesis that *some* means *any* under negation (for a more detailed version of this account see Musolino (1998b, Chapter 4)). If this approach is along the right track, the learnability problem disappears.

7. Conclusion

This paper reports the results of an experimental study designed to investigate the way in which children interpret sentences containing negation and QNPs. The main finding is that children around the age of 5 do not interpret such sentences the way adults speakers do. Specifically, children's initial interpretive hypotheses regarding the relative interpretation of negation and QNPs are systematically based on the position occupied by these elements in overt syntax; hence the notion of isomorphism at the syntax-semantics interface. This, of course, only represents a descriptive generalization regarding the nature of children's early interpretive hypotheses. In other words, we have addressed the question *how* children's interpretations differ from those of adults. The next step in this research project is to determine *why* children's interpretations differ from those of adults as well as the extent to which the observation of isomorphism extends to other scope related phenomena. These issues, although not addressed here, are discussed in detail in Musolino (1998b).

References

Baker, Lee 1979. 'Syntactic Theory and the Projection Problem' *Linguistic Inquiry* 10, 533-581.
Bellugi, Ursula 1967. 'The acquisition of the system of negation in children's speech'. Ph.D. dissertation. Cambridge, Mass.: Harvard University.
Chomsky, Noam 1995. *The Minimalist Program*, MIT press, Cambridge MA.
Clark, Eve 1987. 'The principle of contrast: a constraint on language acquisition'. In B. McWhinney (eds.) *Mechanisms of language acquisition*. Lawrence Erlbaum Associates, Hillsdale.
Crain, Stephen and Fodor Janet 1987. 'Simplicity and generality of rules in language acqusition' in B. MacWhinney, ed. *Mechanisms of language acquisition.*

Crain, Stephen and Cecile McKee. 1985. 'The Acquisition of Structural Restrictions on Anaphora', in S. Berman, J.-W. Choe, and J. McDonough, eds., *Proceedings of the Northeastern Linguistic Society*, GLSA, Amherst, Massachusetts.

Crain, Stephen and Rosalind Thornton (in press) *Investigations in Universal Grammar: A Guide to Reasearch on the Acquisition of Syntax and Semantics,* The MIT Press, Cambridge, Massachusetts.

Horn, Larry 1989. *A natural history of negation.* University of Chicago Press, Chicago.

Jackendoff, Ray 1972. *Semantic Interpretation in Generative Grammar*, MIT Press.

Klima, Edward 1964. 'Negation in English.' In J.A. Fodor and J.J Katz (eds.) *The structure of language.* Prentice Hall, Englewood Cliffs.

Lasnik, Howard 1972. 'Analyses of negation in English' Doctoral dissertation, MIT.

Musolino, Julien 1998a. 'Not any child can deal with *some'* Proceedings of the 1997 Boston University Conference on Language Development.

Musolino, Julien 1998b 'Universal Grammar and the acquisition of semantic knowledge: a experimental investigation into the acquisition of quantifier-negation interaction in English' Doctoral Dissertation, University of Maryland at College Park.

O'Leary, Carrie 1994. 'Children's Awareness of Polarity Sensitivity' M.A. thesis, University of Connecticut.

O'Leary, Carrie and Stephen Crain 1994. 'Negative polarity items (a positive result) positive polarity items (a negative result)'. Paper presented at the 1994 Boston University Conference on Language Developement.

Pinker, Stephen 1989. *Learnability and cognition: The acquisition of argument structure,* MIT Press.

Wal van der, Sjoukje 1996. *Negative Polarity Items & Negation, Tandem Acquisition.* Groningen Dissertations in Linguistics 17, Groningen, The Netherlands.

Wexler, Kenneth and Peter Culicover 1980. *Formal principles of language acquisition.* Cambridge, MA: MIT Press.

Derived Predicates and the Interpretation of Parasitic Gaps*

JON NISSENBAUM

Massachusetts Institute of Technology

1. Introduction

This paper provides empirical support for the claim that predication created by syntactic movement plays a role in syntactic computation. The proposal that every movement operation creates a predicate abstract over the target of movement was suggested by Heim and Kratzer (1998) in order to simplify the semantic component of the grammar. I show that it also has empirical consequences. Specifically, I demonstrate that well-known properties of Parasitic Gap (PG) constructions can be derived in a principled way from the proposal. Further, I present evidence for a previously unnoticed property of PGs inside subject NPs: they are licensed only if the subject undergoes reconstruction. I show that this property follows as well from the analysis.

The paradigm (1) illustrates three characteristic properties of PGs:
•*PGs cannot be licensed by covert movement,* as shown in (1h);
•*they obey an anti-c-command condition* (1c); and
•*they are not licensed by A-movement to subject position* (1d).

(1) a. Which book did John look for _ in order to buy _ ?
     b. *Who looked for which book in order to buy _ ?
     c. *Which book did John buy _ for the man who wanted _ ?
     d. *A book was pulled _ off the shelf in order (for me) to buy _

I will show that these properties can be explained on the basis of the Heim/ Kratzer proposal, without recourse to stipulated conditions such as a requirement that PGs are licensed at s-structure, or by A-bar movement alone, or by ad hoc rules such as Chain Composition.

Building on the empty-operator analysis of Chomsky (1986), I propose that PG structures are licensed by exactly the same interpretive mechanism that licenses other null operator constructions. Specifically, I

---
* I am very grateful to Danny Fox and Martin Hackl for the countless hours they spent helping me develop the ideas in this paper. Special thanks are also due to Noam Chomsky, Michel DeGraff, Irene Heim and David Pesetsky for extremely helpful discussion and criticism, as well as to Rajesh Bhatt, Ken Hale, Sabine Iatridou, Orin Percus, Gina Rendon, Uli Sauerland, and the participants of the Spring 1997 generals workshop and the LF reading group at MIT.

argue that the constituent containing a PG (like other null operator constructions) is interpreted as a one-place predicate (type $<e,t>$). If this predicate is to compose with the VP by a standard composition rule of predicate modification, then the latter must also be interpreted as a one-place predicate. I argue that an intermediate step of wh-movement in the main clause turns the VP into a derived predicate (by the Heim/Kratzer proposal), allowing composition with the adjoined constituent containing a PG. The resulting interpretation of the VP-plus-adjunct is that of a (conjoined) predicate, which can compose with the intermediate trace by standard Function Application. In this sense, the PG is in no way parasitic on wh-movement to Spec,CP, but rather is licensed solely by the intermediate trace.

The basic insight of the analysis is that the VP becomes a derived predicate by intermediate movement of the wh-phrase, and as such is able to compose by Predicate Modification with an adjunct in which a null operator binds a PG. Crucially, I will show that such an adjunct must merge *after* intermediate wh-movement to the VP (countercyclically). If merger of the adjunct *precedes* movement, then predicate modification will fail for type reasons: intermediate movement will form the predicate abstract over *both* the VP and the adjunct, too high to allow their composition.

The paper is organized as follows: section two gives the analysis in detail and demonstrates that the basic properties of PG constructions seen in (1) follow from it. A consequence will be that A-movement can in principle license PGs. Section three addresses subject PGs. A surprising prediction is shown: subjects with PGs will undergo obligatory reconstruction. The correctness of this prediction is supported by a variety of tests.

2. The analysis: movement and derived predication

2.1 Three assumptions about the syntax of Parasitic Gaps

The analysis rests on three non-innocent (but independently supported) assumptions about the syntax of PG constructions:

• PGs are bound by a null operator

Chomsky (1986) argued that PGs are bound not by the wh-phrase that binds the licensing gap (as in (2a)), but by a phonetically empty operator (2b).

(2) a.   [Which book]$_1$ did John [$_{VP}$[$_{VP}$ look for t$_1$] [in order to buy t$_1$]]

 b.   [Which book]$_1$ did John [$_{VP}$[$_{VP}$look for t$_1$][Wh$_2$ in order to buy t$_2$]]

Other constructions that have been analyzed to have the across-the-board structure of (2a) differ from PG constructions in important respects. The claim that PGs are bound independently of the licensing gap predicts binding and reconstruction asymmetries (unlike ATB constructions), and there is ample evidence that such asymmetries exist.[1] For the purposes of this paper, we will simply take the null operator hypothesis as given.

---

[1] For a summary of Chomsky's arguments for the structure (2b), as well as further evidence, see Nissenbaum (1998). Cf. Munn (1992).

• Adjuncts which contain PGs are VP-adjuncts

The second assumption that is crucial for the analysis is that the relevant adjuncts are adjoined to VP, rather than internal to a right-branching VP. The kinds of adjuncts that typically host PGs are those headed by temporal prepositions *(before, after, while)*, rationale clauses *(in order to..., because...)*, and participial adjuncts headed by *without.* Arguments against a right-branching structure for such adjuncts are given in Nissenbaum (1998).

• Wh-movement leaves an intermediate trace at the VP

The third crucial assumption about the syntax of PG constructions is that the wh-movement that licenses a PG leaves an intermediate trace at the level of the VP, a position local to the attachment site of VP-adjuncts. Fox (forthcoming) gives compelling arguments that wh-movement passes through an intermediate position between the surface subject position and the highest internal argument of the VP. The copy of this intermediate movement is always unpronounced in English, but Fox shows that its presence at LF can be detected by means of a correlation between Condition C and variable binding reconstruction effects.

Taking these three independently motivated assumptions together, we may consider the structure (3) to reflect the basic syntactic properties of PG constructions and use it as the basis for an examination of the mechanisms involved in licensing PGs.

(3)

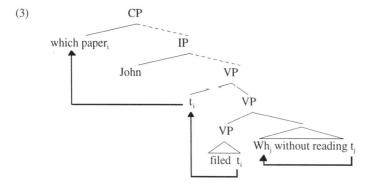

2.2 The interpretation of PG constructions

Given the structure (3), it is not obvious how the PG receives the right interpretation, or for that matter how the adjunct is supposed to compose with the main clause. Intuitively, we know that the PG is interpreted as "the same" as the licensing gap; "the paper that John filed without reading" refers to a single book which has the property that John filed it without reading it. The immediate goal is to account for this interpretation. The account will, in turn, explain the properties in (1) and make several important predictions.

The following fairly standard assumptions about semantic composition enter into the analysis.

§ VP adjuncts have the semantics of conjunction with VP

It is standard to assume that in addition to a basic composition rule of Function Application, the interpretive component of the grammar makes use of a rule that semantically conjoins two phrases. As already noted, a sentence like *John filed the paper without reading it* has a natural paraphrase as the conjunction *John filed the paper and he didn't read it.* Formally, we can spell this out by saying that the VP (with a VP-internal subject) and the adjunct are both propositional cores, with semantic type <t>. their truth conditions are stated roughly in (4a) and (4b) respectively, with g taken as a variable assignment function and t_{subj} the subject trace. Their composition is then determined by the rule of semantic conjunction, yielding the denotation (4c). (Assume that PRO in the adjunct is a bound pronoun, anaphoric on the subject.)[2]

(4) a. $[\![\ [_{VP}\ t_{subj.}\ \text{filed the paper}]\ ]\!]^g$ = 1 iff $g(t_{subj})$ filed the paper

b. $[\![\ [\text{without PRO reading it}]\ ]\!]^g$ = 1 iff $\neg\ \big(g(\text{PRO})\ \text{read}\ g(\text{it})\big)$

c. $[\![\ [_{VP}[_{VP}\ t_{subj.}\ \text{filed the paper}][\text{without PRO reading it}]]\ ]\!]^g$
$= 1$ iff $g(t_{subj})$ filed the paper $\&\ \neg\ \big(g(\text{PRO})\ \text{read}\ g(\text{it})\big)$

§ Null Operator Structures are predicates

Other constructions which have been argued to have null operators have the semantics of predicates: the operator binds a gap and turns the clause where it takes scope into a function of type <e,t>. In relative clauses the wh-operator may be either null or overt, but in both cases the interpretation is the same: they are CPs that compose with NPs by predicate modification. Thus, "a cat that is grey" expresses the same meaning as "a grey cat":

(5)

$= \lambda x.x$ is a cat $\&$ x is grey

Given this general method of interpreting null operator structures, an adjunct like (4b) with a gap bound by an operator would interpreted as in (6), roughly, "the set of objects that PRO didn't read":

(6) $[\![\ [\text{Op}_x[\text{without PRO reading}\ t_x]]\ ]\!]^g = \lambda x.\ \neg\big(g(\text{PRO})\ \text{read}\ x\big)$

§ Every link in a chain is interpreted

Two-membered chains have a straightforward interpretation: the head binds the tail. What about three-membered chains like the one in (3)? It is sometimes assumed in the syntactic literature that intermediate traces delete

---

[2] The denotations in (4) are simplified for ease of presentation. For a more detailed analysis making use of Davidsonian event variables (as well as a treatment of more complicated adjuncts), see Nissenbaum (1998). There it is assumed that VPs and adjuncts are both predicates of events, and compose by predicate modification. The basic idea — that they semantically conjoin — is the same.

and that LF representations consequently contain only two-membered chains.[3] However, it is a rather simple matter to extend the semantic rule that interprets chains (a rule of predicate abstraction) to structures with intermediate traces: each link higher than the tail binds the one immediately below it. The effect of such a rule is illustrated schematically below:

(7)   ⟦ [Wh-phrase[... t' ...[filed t]] ⟧ = Wh-phrase[λx....t$_x$[λy...[filed t$_y$]]]

The semantic rule of predicate abstraction that is required treats all instances of movement, including the intermediate step in (7), alike. Each step of movement is interpreted as the sister of a lambda abstract, hence as the binder of its trace. The interpretation of multi-link chains is identical to that of simple chains where the intermediate traces have deleted, so there is no obvious reason to assume that intermediate traces must delete. If (3) correctly reflects the structure of PG sentences, then the presence of the intermediate trace in the LF is crucial, as is shown in the next subsection.

2.3 How VPs compose with Null Operator structures

Recall that ordinary VP adjuncts (with no PG) compose with VPs by an interpretive rule that semantically conjoins two proposition-denoting sisters (type <t>). But an adjunct with a PG is *not* a proposition — the null operator that binds the gap turns it into a predicate of type <e,t>, as noted above. If a VP is a proposition, and an adjunct with a PG (i.e. a null operator structure) is a predicate, there is no straightforward semantic rule by which they could compose.

However, given the rule of predicate abstraction which is needed independently for interpreting chains, then the VP is *also* interpreted as a predicate — provided, crucially, that the intermediate trace is present at LF. That is, the presence of the intermediate trace *forces* the VP to be interpreted as a lambda abstract. So as long as there is an intermediate trace for them to compose with, the VP and the adjunct can semantically conjoin by the same rule of predicate modification that conjoins relative clauses and NPs. The resulting conjoined predicate composes with the intermediate trace by standard function application, yielding a VP of type <t>.

(8)

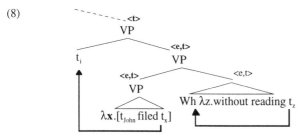

One important loose end remains to be tied up. The rule of predicate abstraction needs to be formulated so as to guarantee that only the *lowest* VP segment becomes a lambda abstract. Otherwise (if both lower segments were to be interpreted as a single lambda abstract), then the lowest

---

[3] For instance, by Lasnik and Saito (1984).

VP would still not be of the right semantic type to compose with the adjunct. This outcome is illustrated in (8'):

(8') *

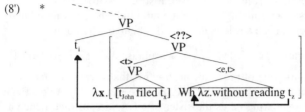

How can we guarantee that the rule of predicate abstraction yields (8) instead of (8')? Clearly the simplest way of formulating the predicate abstraction rule would be to say that the *sister* of the moved constituent becomes a predicate abstract. But such a formulation would yield the unwanted (8').

It turns out, however, that the simplest formulation will work, if we adopt exactly the version that was proposed by Heim and Kratzer (1998).

2.4 Movement creates derived predicates *in the syntax*

Heim and Kratzer proposed that the work done by the predicate abstraction rule is divided into a syntactic and a semantic component. Specifically, they proposed that every syntactic movement operation introduces a predicate abstract to the target of movement *during the course of the syntactic computation.* The output of a syntactic movement thus looks like the structure (9a) rather than the more standard (9b).

(9) a.   b.

This proposal allowed Heim and Kratzer to greatly simplify the semantic component: the binding relation that holds between the two links in the chain is read directly off the LF.

2.5 Countercyclic adjunction

Note that the Heim-Kratzer proposal appears to guarantee exactly the wrong result, namely it would yield the structure (8') rather than (8). However, this appearance is misleading. The assumption that movement creates predicate abstracts allows a derivational solution to the problem, since a predicate that is created derivationally might in principle be eligible for subsequent syntactic operations. The type mismatch in (8') need not arise, if the adjunct merges at a point in the derivation where the predicate abstract over the VP has already been formed.[4] Consider the structure at three successive stages of the derivation:

---

[4] This assumes that some operations do not need to obey the cycle. Lebeaux proposed that countercyclic merger of relative clauses is possible, to explain the absence of Condition C effects within a copy theory of movment. See also Sauerland (1998) for another empirical argument in favor of the Heim/Kratzer proposal.

(10) a. 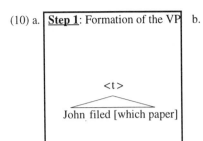 b.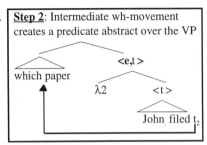

The first two steps, shown in (10a-b), are the construction of the VP (without the adjunct), and then wh-movement of the wh-phrase to the intermediate VP-level position (using rule (9a)). Prior to the movement, the VP is a proposition (type <t>). The intermediate wh-movement creates a predicate abstract over the VP, turning it into a predicate (type <e,t>).

Recall that the interpretability problem of (8') stemmed from the fact that the adjunct, a predicate, needed to compose with another predicate. But *after* the intermediate wh-movement of Step 2, there is a suitable node to which the adjunct clause can adjoin (and ultimately compose by Predicate Modification) — the predicate abstract formed by the movement itself. The third step, illustrated in (10c), is the merger of the adjunct with the newly derived predicate. Crucially, merger is to a position *immediately below* the root, to the sister node of the moved wh-phrase, a node that did not exist until it was created by the movement.

c.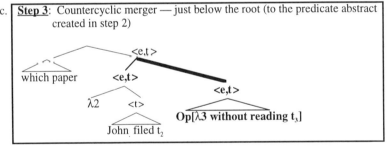

The wh-phrase ultimately raises to Spec,CP of the matrix clause, leaving a trace at the VP-level. Interpretation of the resulting structure is now straightforward. The VP and the adjunct, both being predicates, compose at LF by Predicate Modification. This conjoined predicate, whose denotation is stated in (11a), is the right semantic type to compose with the trace (a variable of type <e>) by Function Application. The result of that composition in turn denotes a proposition (11b).

(11) a. $[\![\, [_{VP}[_{VP}\lambda 2 \text{John filed } t_2][\text{Op}\,\lambda 3 \text{ without PRO reading } t_3]] \,]\!]^g$
   $= \lambda y. \text{John filed } y \ \& \ \neg(g(\text{PRO}) \text{ read } y)$

   b. $[\![[_{VP}t \ [_{VP}[_{VP}\lambda 2 \text{John filed } t_2][\text{Op}\,\lambda 3 \text{ without PRO reading } t_3]]] \,]\!]^g$
   $= 1 \text{ iff John filed } g(t) \ \& \ \neg(g(\text{PRO}) \text{ read } g(t))$

514 / JON NISSENBAUM

To summarize, in order to guarantee an LF like (8) rather than (8'), two components are needed: (i) the intermediate wh-trace is the sister of a predicate abstract, and (ii) merger of the adjunct may be countercyclic — it may merge to the predicate abstract over the VP after the latter is formed. An adjunct with a PG crucially *must* merge counter-cyclically (step 3). If merger in (10) had been cyclic (i.e., before the intermediate wh-movement), then the wh-movement would have formed its predicate abstract over *both* the VP and the adjunct — too high to allow their composition.

2.6 Results of the analysis

•Covert movements don't license PGs

It follows automatically that movements after spellout will not license adjuncts containing PGs, since such adjuncts must crucially merge to a predicate abstract that does not exist before movement. If the adjunct were to merge before the licensing movement, then the predicate abstract would be *formed over a constituent containing both VP and adjunct,* too high to allow their composition. On the other hand, an adjunct that merges after a covert movement (post-spellout) could not be pronounced, assuming a Y-model of the grammar.

•Anti-c-command condition

The analysis also derives the anti-c-command condition as an automatic consequence. Since the null operator phrase must merge to a predicate derived by movement, it follows both that the trace of the licensing movement cannot c-command the PG, and that the null-operator-containing phrase itself will end up c-commanding the trace of the original movement.

•Subject A-movements don't license PGs

It is also a trivial result of this theory that A-movement under passivization, or A-movement of a VP-internal subject, will not license a PG, under the well-motivated assumption that there is no intermediate A-movement step that would put such a phrase in a position to license an adjunct with a PG. If A-movement to a VP-position is case-driven, it is an accusative case position. If, on the other hand, subjects *adjoined* to VP as a first step, further movement (to IP) would constitute improper movement.

•A Further Prediction: short A-movement (of objects) *does* license PGs

The analysis predicts that cases of overt A-movement to the VP level should license PGs. This prediction is amply borne out by short scrambling in German, Dutch and Hindi. As noted by Webelhuth (1989), Mahajan (1990) and Deprez (1989), short scrambling in these languages displays all the hallmark properties of A-movement, yet it also licenses PGs. This fact has been considered paradoxical in the literature. But under the account proposed here the "paradox" evaporates, because the stipulation that PGs are solely an A-bar-movement property has been dispensed with. The puzzle is resolved unequivocally: short scrambling in these languages is A-movement. It is local to VP, so it licenses PGs as predicted.

3. Parasitic Gaps inside subjects

So far, we have only addressed PGs contained in VP adjuncts. But as is well known, PGs are licensed in subjects as well ((12a) is from Kayne 1983):

(12) a.   John's a guy that [people who talk to _] usually end up liking _
     b.   Johns' the guy that we invited because [everyone who talks to _]
         is likely to appreciate _

Under the analysis proposed in the previous section, the licensing of subject PGs would follow in essentially the same way as the licensing of adjuncts with PGs — *if* such subjects were interpreted in their base position at LF.

3.1 Licensing of subject NPs in the VP-internal position

The crucial step in the analysis is the "sandwiching" of the PG adjunct in between the intermediate trace and the predicate abstract created by its movement. In principle, *any* VP-level constituent containing a PG could be licensed in the same manner, assuming that its semantic type is suitable for composition with the abstract over the VP (type <e,t>). In other words, this same intermediate trace could in principle license VP-internal PG subjects as well as adjuncts, provided that (i) the subject could merge countercyclically to the derived predicate formed by the intermediate movement, and (ii) the subject's semantic type allows it to compose with the derived predicate.

    Assume, then, that subjects containing PGs are allowed to merge countercyclically. As noted, the analysis forces this consequence. The constituent with the PG needs to be the *sister* of the predicate abstract of the licensing movement, and if it were to merge cyclically, then the predicate abstract would be too high (over the node *dominating* the PG constituent).[5]

    The next thing to establish about PG subjects is their semantic type. We might begin with a consideration of bare plural subject NPs, since subject PGs quite often involve bare plurals. Assume that bare plural NPs are predicates of type <e,t>, suitable for composing with V' by Predicate Modification. Thus, the NP in (13a) composes with V' (13b) to form (13c), both of whose open positions may be bound by existential closure.

(13) a. $[\![$ *people who talk to John* $]\!]^g = \lambda x.\text{people}(x)$ & x talk to John
     b. $[\![$ *like him* $]\!]^g = \lambda x.x$ like g(him)
     c. $[\![$ *[people who talk to John][like him]* $]\!]^g$
                           $= \lambda x.\text{people}(x)$ & x talk to John & x like g(him)

If bare plurals could compose with V' by PM in the ordinary case, as above, then a bare plural with a PG would be a *two*-place predicate of type <e,<e,t>> in virtue of the operator binding the PG, as in (14). Hence composition with V' should be impossible.

---

[5] The countercyclic operation is not unprecedented. In addition to Lebeaux's proposal for NP adjuncts (see footnote 4), Richards (1997) proposes de-coupling the cycle from the Extension Condition: the first instance of wh-movement must extend the tree, but subsequent movements tuck the mover into a position just below the previously moved phrase. We might similarly redefine the cycle so as to permit merger of a phrase to the node immediately below the root just in case the preceding operation resulted in a recomputation of the semantic (or, possibly, phonetic) properties of this node.

(14) $[\![OP_y[people\ who\ talk\ to\ t_y]]\!]^g = \lambda y.\lambda x.people(x)\ \&\ x\ talk\ to\ y$

As noted above, however, there is a way for the grammar to allow the constituent in (14) compose with V': the same way as for adjuncts. After an intermediate licensing movement forms a predicate abstract (in this case over V'), the subject merges countercyclically to the predicate abstract:

(15)

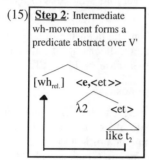

Step 2: Intermediate wh-movement forms a predicate abstract over V'

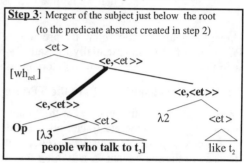

Step 3: Merger of the subject just below the root (to the predicate abstract created in step 2)

Just as before, the node immediately below the root in (15a) is exactly the right semantic type to allow composition with the subject NP by the rule PM (15b). The resulting denotation, also a two-place predicate, composes with the intermediate trace by Function Application. The remaining open position is then bound externally (by an existential or generic operator).

Thus, the theory allows bare plural subject NPs with PGs to be interpreted in their base position, on the assumption that bare plurals have the same semantic type as V' and that countercyclic merger is allowed.[6]

3.2 Licensing is *only* possible in the base position

But *are* PG subjects interpreted in their base position at LF? It turns out that they must be. This is an unavoidable consequence of the theory, because it arises from the claim that the constituent with a PG must "sandwich" between some previously moved element and its derived predicate. (Its sister must be the lambda abstract of a licensing movement.) But given the crucial assumption that movement creates derived predicates, a subject containing a PG would, by raising, create its own predicate abstract over the one already formed by the licensing wh-movement — so its sister can *in principle* never be the lambda abstract of the licensing movement. A raised subject (or for that matter any raised constituent) containing a PG would therefore never be able to compose with its sister.[7]

Thus, the theory predicts that a subject NP can contain a PG *only if it is interpreted in its base position*. The rest of this section will show that, indeed, subjects with PGs yield reconstruction effects in every instance.

---

[6] An added complication is introduced when we consider PGs inside quantifier phrases. Generalized quantifiers do not compose with their sisters by Predicate Modification, but rather by Function Application. This problem turns out to be fairly easy to resolve, if we allow a natural extension and redefinition of Heim and Kratzer's basic composition rules as a single recursive operation, as proposed in Nissenbaum (1998).

[7] For a demonstration that this is the case, see Nissenbaum (1998), section 4.1.3. What is actually shown there is that even under stipulated conditions that would allow Predicate Modification, the resulting LF would always yield a Strong Crossover violation.

3.3 The prediction confirmed: subject PGs must reconstruct

(a) Variable binding from the raised position

If subject QPs need to reconstruct in order to license a PG, then we would expect a variable that can only be bound from the raised position to create a conflict with a PG in the subject. This expectation is borne out in (16). (16a) is an acceptable instance of a PG contained in a QP that has undergone surface A-movement over the raising predicate *appear*. (16b) is the test case: the PG becomes unacceptable when the QP subject containing it needs to bind a variable from the raised position. (16c) is a further control, showing that the QP is able to bind a variable from its raised position if it doesn't contain a PG. (Example (16d) shows that binding by a PG subject is no problem if the variable can be bound from the reconstructed position)

(16) a.   Sue's the kind of person that [everyone who talks to _] appears to my colleagues to like _ .

     b.   *Sue's the kind of person that [everyone who talks to _]$_i$ appears to his$_i$ colleagues to like _ .

     c.   Sue's the kind of person that [everyone I know]$_i$ appears to his$_i$ colleagues to like _ .

     d.   *cf. Sue's the kind of person that [everyone who talks to _]$_i$ appears to want his$_i$ colleagues to meet _.*

(b) Condition C violations resulting from reconstruction

Obligatory reconstruction should also create Condition C effects.[8] (17)-(18) bear out this prediction. The (a) examples are the control cases, with the r-expression and the co-indexed pronoun positioned such that reconstruction would not violate condition C. The test cases are the (b) sentences, and as predicted they are very much degraded in acceptability. The (c) sentences are identical to those in (b) except that the pronoun is embedded so as not to c-command the reconstructed r-expression, providing a further control to show that Condition C is the relevant factor.

(17) a.   Mary's the one that [his$_i$ constant criticism of _] seemed to John$_i$ to have (finally) upset _ .

     b.   *Mary's the one that [John's$_i$ constant criticism of _] seemed to him$_i$ to have (finally) upset _ .

     c.   Mary's the one that [John's$_i$ constant criticism of _] seemed to [his$_i$ mother] to have upset _ .

(18) a.   That's the kind of film that [people who recommend _ to her$_i$] usually strike Mary$_i$ as liking _ for the wrong reasons

     b.   *That's the kind of film that [people who recommend _ to Mary$_i$] usually strike her$_i$ as liking _ for the wrong reasons

     c.   That's the kind of film that [people who recommend _ to Mary$_i$] usually strike [her$_i$ husband] as liking _ for the wrong reasons

---

[8] On the assumption that binding conditions are sensitive to scope reconstruction, as expected under Chomsky (1993), and argued for empirically by Fox (forthcoming) and Romero (1997).

(c) Scope interactions with modals

The first two tests were grammaticality judgment paradigms. The examples in (19)-(20) make use of ambiguities created by QP subjects and modal verbs. Ordinarily such sentences are ambiguous between a meaning where the surface scope relation is preserved, and an inverse scope interpretation resulting from optional subject reconstruction. (19a) illustrates the ambiguity by means of two disambiguating follow-up clauses. (19a) may be felicitously followed up by (i) in a context where *anyone* from the department would be sufficient to achieve the desired result, whereas professors from other departments would not sufficiently draw attendance if they taught the topic. This is the interpretation that results from subject reconstruction below *needs*; the interpretation can be paraphrased as "It needs to be the case that someone from our department teaches the topic..."

(19) a. This is the topic that someone in our department needs to teach...

      (i) ... if we want people to show up   *(subject takes narrow scope)*

      (ii)... if the guy ever wants tenure   *(subject takes wide scope)*

If, on the other hand, (19a) is followed up by (ii), the sentence is disambiguated toward a wide scope reading for the subject. With this meaning, the sentence cannot be paraphrased as above, but only as "There's someone in our department such that he needs to teach this topic..."

A parasitic gap in the subject disambiguates such sentences, allowing only the narrow scope reading:[9]

(19) b. This is the topic that someone who's (just) written about _ needs to teach _ (if we want people to show up).

   c. *This is the topic that someone who's (just) written about _ needs to teach _ (if the guy ever wants tenure)

The same logic is used in (20). (20a) has two versions. Disambiguating follow-up sentences are provided, and in addition each of the two interpretations for the sentence comes with a characteristic intonation pattern, very crudely reflected by upper- and lower-case letters. The narrow scope (i) states that "it must happen that no one leaves," and the wide scope (ii) merely asserts that there is no particular individual who must leave.

(20) a. (i) No one must LEAVE. (If anyone does, there will be a severe penalty)   *(narrow scope)*

     (ii) NO one MUST leave. (But everyone should feel free to)

                                                              (wide scope)

It is important to note that the narrow scope reading of (20a) is the more marked reading. It is therefore all the more surprising that this is the only

---

[9] The contrast in (19) is not due to the so-called "specific" interpretation of the indefinite in (19c). If we further embed the indefinite under the scope of a universal quantifier, as in (i)-(ii), the indefinite in (ii) can lose its specific character yet the contrast remains:

(i)   This is the topic that every dean thinks someone who's (just) written about _ needs to teach _ (if we want people to show up).

(ii) *This is the topic that every dean thinks someone who's (just) written about _ needs to teach _ (if the guy ever wants tenure)

reading that is available when a PG is put in the subject, as shown by the contrast between (b) and (c). This is so no matter what intonation pattern is used. Once again, the facts provide striking support for the prediction that subject PGs are licensed only under reconstruction.

(20) b. John's the guy who no one that insulted _ must talk to _ (or he'll be really upset)   *(narrow)*

c. #John's the guy who NO one that insulted _ MUST talk to _
(but everyone should feel free to)   *(wide)*

(d) Interactions with other scope-bearing predicates
The same test as above can be replicated with other kinds of predicates besides modal auxiliaries. The indefinite subject of (21) can take either narrow or wide scope with respect to *likely*. The narrow scope version (21a) is felicitous in a context where *you* refers to an individual who is an inside candidate for the job (and thus has a good chance at getting it). The wide scope (21b) is only felicitous in a context where *you* is not an inside candidate (and thus has a poor chance). Here, as in (24), the two meanings have characteristic pronunciations (indicated crudely by capital letters).

(21) a. That's the job that you've got a decent shot at _ because an inside candidate is LIKEly to get _   *(Presumption: "you" are an inside candidate)*

b. That's the job that you shouldn't even bother with _ because an INSIDE CANdidate is likely to get _   *("You" are not an inside candidate)*

Again, using the condition set up in (21), we can test the reconstruction hypothesis by putting a parasitic gap inside the QP. And as the hypothesis predicts, the sentence is disambiguated in favor of narrow scope reading:

(22) a. That's the job that you've got a decent shot at _ because an inside candidate for _ is LIKEly to get _

b. *That's the job that you shouldn't even bother with _ because an INSIDE CANdidate for _ is likely to get _

3.4 A note on PGs in bare plural subjects
It is sometimes claimed, contrary to what is argued here, that bare plural subjects do not reconstruct in generic environments. Diesing (1992) and Kratzer (1989) proposed a correlation between interpretation of bare plurals and their structural position at LF: reconstructed bare plurals are interpreted existentially, while VP-external bare plurals are interpreted generically (by Diesing's Mapping Hypothesis). Obviously, this hypothesis is incompatible with the claim that subject NPs containing PGs must reconstruct, given the fact that subject PGs are often found in generic bare plurals.
        The Diesing/Kratzer account is apparently given strong support by examples such as (23)-(24). A-movement of (existentially interpreted) bare plurals (23) doesn't allow variable binding (A-movement generally allows binding from the raised position in these environments (23d)). When the bare plurals are interpreted generically rather than existentially as in (24), however, variable binding from the raised position is perfectly acceptable.

(23) a. *Chimps seem to their caretakers to be in the room
    b. *Chimps strike their caretakers as being in the room
    c. *Chimps are expected by their caretakers to be in the room
    d. *cf. Several chimps seem to their caretakers to be in the room*

(24) a. Chimps always seem to their caretakers to be in the room/smart
    b. Chimps often strike their caretakers as being in the room/smart
    c. Chimps are usually expected by their caretakers to be in the room

       However, (25) casts doubt on the Diesing/Kratzer account. While the unacceptability of the examples in (25a) are fully expected (since the variables are not in the scope of their binders) the acceptability of the (25b) examples comes as a complete surprise.

(25) a. *It seems to their caretakers that chimps are in the room
       *It strikes their caretakers that chimps are intelligent

    b. It always seems to their caretakers that chimps are in the room
       It often strikes their caretakers that chimps are intelligent

No current theory (to my knowledge) predicts a covert movement of the bare plural in (25b) to license the pronoun. Diesing and Kratzer do not predict that this should even be necessary: the embedded clauses allow a generic operator to license the bare plurals in their surface position, so covert raising is not forced. If covert raising is simply allowed (to bind the pronoun), then the unacceptability of (25a) is unexplained.

       Whatever is going on in (25b) to make them acceptable, it is clear that they are not grossly different in interpretation from the examples in (24). Therefore, to the extent that an alternative analysis is warranted for (25b) which licenses the pronouns in some manner other than binding by the NP, it is reasonable to suppose that such an analysis also allows the pronouns in (24) to get an interpretation other than as bound by the NP. It is then far from obvious that (24) supports the Diesing/Kratzer claim that bare plurals don't reconstruct in generic sentences. And we have already seen evidence (e.g. 18) that bare plurals do reconstruct, if they contain PGs.

4. Conclusions

This paper showed empirical consequences of Heim and Kratzer's proposal that the semantic reflex of constituent movement is encoded directly in the syntactic derivation. The evidence in support of their proposal was provided by an analysis of parasitic gap constructions. The analysis accounts in a non-stipulative way for three of the characteristic properties of the construction: the requirement for licensing by an overt movement, the failure of subject A-movement to license PGs, and the anti-c-command condition. A prediction was made that A-movement can, in principle, license PGs, and it was suggested that short scrambling represents such a case. Furthermore, a previously unnoticed property of PGs was shown to follow from the analysis, namely that PGs in subjects can be licensed only if the subject undergoes reconstruction at LF. An array of evidence was presented to show that this prediction is correct. Most available alternative accounts of PG licensing require stipulations that the construction is licensed at s-structure and that the licensing movement is limited to A-bar movement. No available alternative theory predicts the subject reconstruction property; the HPSG/connectedness family of theories (Kayne 1983, Sag 1983), and Steedman (1997), as well as Richards (1997) all predict that subject NPs should be able to host PGs as long as the subject c-commands the licensing gap.

The major consequence of the analysis, in addition to the support it provides to the Heim/Kratzer proposal, is that it argues in favor of the Y-model of the grammar; the explanation for lack of PG licensing by covert movements rests on the assumption that operations after spellout cannot be reflected in the phonetic form. Finally, the discovery of reconstruction effects for PG subjects has fairly broad implications for the theory of reconstruction and the analysis of bare plurals.

References

Chomsky, Noam (1986), *Barriers,* MIT Press.
Chomsky, Noam (1993), "A Minimalist Program for Linguistic Theory," in K. Hale & S. J. Keyser, eds., *The View From Building 20: Essays in Honor of Sylvain Bromberger,* MIT Press.
Deprez, Vivienne (1989), *On the Typology of Syntactic Positions and the Nature of Chains.* PhD Dissertation, MIT. Distributed by MITWPL.
Diesing, Molly (1992), *Indefinites,* MIT Press.
Engdahl, Elizabeth (1983), "Parasitic Gaps," in *Linguistics and Philosophy* 6, 5-34.
Fox, Danny (1995), "Economy and Scope," in *Natural Language Semantics* 3.3, 283-341.
Fox, Danny (forthcoming), "Reconstruction, Binding Theory, and the Interpretation of Chains," to appear in *Linguistic Inquiry.*
Heim, Irene, and Angelika Kratzer (1998), *Semantics and Generative Grammar,* Blackwell.
Kayne, Richard (1983), "Connectedness," in *Linguistic Inquiry* 14.2, 223-220.
Kratzer, Angelika (1988), "Stage-Level and Individual-Level Predicates," in G. Carlson and F. J. Pelletier, *The Generic Book,* Univ. of Chicago Press (1995).
Lasnik, Howard, and Mamoro Saito (1984), *Move α,* MIT Press.
Lebeaux, David (1988), *Language Acquisition and the Form of the Grammar,* PhD dissertation, UMass. Distributed by GLSA.
Mahajan, Anoop (1989), *The A/A-bar Distinction and Movement Theory.* PhD dissertation, MIT. Distributed by MITWPL.
Munn, Alan (1992), "A Null Operator Analysis of ATB Gaps," in *The Linguistic Review* 9.1, 1-26.
Nissenbaum, Jon (1998), "Movement and Derived Predicates: Evidence from Parasitic Gaps," in *The Interpretive Tract,* MITWPL 25, 247-295.
Pesetsky, David (1995), *Zero Syntax,* MIT Press.
Richards, Norvin (1997), *What moves where when in which language?* PhD dissertation, MIT. Distributed by MITWPL.
Romero, Maribel (1998), "The Correlation between Scope Reconstruction and Connectivity Effects," in *The Proceedings of the 16th West Coast Conference on Formal Linguistics,* CSLI.
Sag, Ivan (1983), "On Parasitic Gaps," in *Linguistics and Philosophy* 6, 35-45.
Sauerland, Uli (1998), "Plurals, Derived Predicates and Reciprocals," in *The Interpretive Tract,* MITWPL 25, 177-204.
Steedman, Mark (1997), *Surface Structure and Interpretation,* MIT Press.
Webelhuth, Gert (1989), *Syntactic Saturation Phenomena and the Modern Germanic Languages.* PhD dissertation, University of Massachusetts, Amherst. Distributed by GLSA.

Some Instructions for the Worldly[1]

ORIN PERCUS

University of Massachusetts, Amherst

1. A little puzzle.

For most theoretical descendants of Heim 1982, sentences like (1) and (2) are predicted to be identical in logical form and interpretation. (1) contains a determiner quantifier (*every*). (2) contains an adverbial quantifier with the same force (*always*) and an indefinite. Their purported logical form roughly conforms to the sketch in (3), which contains two instances of an individual variable and a quantifier which in this case ranges over individuals.

(1) Every good semanticist is a good syntactician as well.
(2) A good semanticist is always a good syntactician as well.
(3) EVERY$_x$ [x [good semanticist]] [x is a good syntactician]

    If sentences like (1) and (2) really *are* indistinguishable at logical form, then we should expect them to make exactly the same contribution to sentences in which they are embedded. But they don't. That's the puzzle.

    Compare (4) and (5a). (4) and (5a) differ only with respect to their antecedents. The antecedent in (4) is a sentence with a determiner quantifier, the antecedent in (5a) is a parallel sentence with an adverbial quantifier and an indefinite. (4) makes a sensible if disputable claim. It asks us to consider what the world would be like if those people who are semanticists as things stand now were not semanticists but rather syntacticians. (5a) is just ridiculous. It asks us to consider worlds that contain people who are simultaneously semanticists and not semanticists.

---

[1] This paper benefited from remarks by Kai von Fintel, Irene Heim, Bernhard Schwarz, and especially Angelika Kratzer.

CONTEXT OF EMBEDDING: ANTECEDENT OF COUNTERFACTUALS
(RESTRICTION OF MODAL OPERATOR).

(4) If *every semanticist was a syntactician instead,* a lot more would get
done in our field.

(5) a. ?? If *a semanticist was always a syntactician instead,* a lot more
would get done in our field.
(cf. b. If a semanticist was always a syntactician as well, a lot more would
get done in our field.)

The same pattern occurs in other intensional contexts.[2] One way
of looking at the pattern is that the sentences differ with respect to who
they allow a nominal predicate to describe. In the cases with determiners,
we can use the predicate that restricts the determiner – *semanticist, solid
state physicist, visiting assistant professor* – to talk about individuals who
have that property as things stand now, irrespective of whether these
individuals have that property in worlds the intensional context takes us to.
In the cases with adverbial quantifiers, we can't. If John knows that
visiting assistant professors are not tenured, for example, it is quite
reasonable to claim (8); here, we are talking about individuals who *we* take
to be visiting assistant professors. It is quite *un*reasonable to claim (9a);
here, we must talk about individuals who *John* takes to be visiting assistant
professors.

CONTEXT OF EMBEDDING: SCOPE OF MODAL OPERATOR.

(6) Imagine that the field of physics vanished last century and that every
physicist we know got his degree in linguistics instead. Probably,
every solid state physicist would have gotten his degree in semantics.

(7) a. Imagine that the field of physics vanished last century and that
every physicist we know got his degree in linguistics instead. ??
Probably, *a solid state physicist would have always gotten his degree
in semantics.*
(cf. b. Imagine that every physicist we know got a degree in linguistics
before he pursued physics. Probably, a solid state physicist would
have always gotten his first degree in semantics.)

---

[2] The (b) examples are controls to insure that there are no independent problems incurred by the
presence of an adverbial quantifier and indefinite. Make sure these examples are good for you
before examining the contrast between the determiner quantifier sentence and the parallel
adverbial quantifier sentence.

CONTEXT OF EMBEDDING: SCOPE OF ATTITUDE.

(8) John is mistaken about the rank of some of our instructors. In particular, he has concluded that *every visiting assistant professor here is tenured.*

(9) a. John is mistaken about the rank of some of our instructors. # In particular, he has concluded that *a visiting assistant professor here is always tenured.*

(cf. b. John is mistaken about the household status of some of our instructors. In particular, he has concluded that a visiting assistant professor here is always married.)

This paper has a modest goal: to solve the little puzzle.

2. A big agenda.

It also has a more ambitious goal.

It is frequently assumed that the representation that serves as input to semantic interpretation contains elements that function as variables over possible worlds. As far as their interpretation goes, these elements are no different from pronouns. To give an illustration: a sentence like (10a) has a structure like (10b) that contains two silent pronouns, w_1 and w_2, that take worlds as their values rather than individuals. This structure also contains two operators (λw_1 and λw_2); these are interpreted as abstracting over the positions occupied by these pronouns. On the basis of this structure, the rules of semantic interpretation determine that the sentence accurately characterizes a world under the conditions in (10c). The basic informational contribution of the sentence is a proposition, a function from worlds to truth values.

(10) a. Mary thinks that John is Canadian.

b.

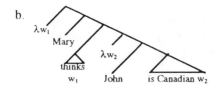

c. (10a) is true in a world w iff in all worlds w' consistent with Mary's thoughts in w, John[3] is Canadian in w'.

---

[3] More precisely (in view of the discussion to come): *John or a counterpart of his.*

Why assume that there are silent world pronouns? Why assume that expressions of natural language are like expressions of (at least) two-sorted logics? First, the assumption is interesting. It allows us to say that language builds propositions in the same way that it builds derived predicates. The building blocks are pronouns and operators that abstract over positions occupied by pronouns. Second, we have to adopt something a lot *like* this assumption no matter what! Cresswell 1990 and others have argued forcefully that, if we want any kind of possible worlds semantics for modality in natural language, we must conclude that natural language has the expressive power of a langage with explicit quantification over worlds.

We just saw that, in intensional contexts, predicates like *semanticist* can be used to talk about individuals who *we* take to be semanticists, or about individuals who are semanticists in the worlds the intensional context introduces. In the former case, the predicate has a *transparent use*. In the latter case, the predicate has an *opaque use*.[4] World pronouns give us a simple way of distinguishing between transparent and opaque uses of predicates. The idea is this. When one uses a predicate transparently, one assigns a different structure to the sentence than when one uses a predicate opaquely. The two structures differ in the indexing of a world pronoun.

Consider for instance the sentence in (11). We can take (11) to be true given either of the scenarios in (12). When we judge (11) to be true on scenario (12a), we understand the predicate *professor* to be used transparently. When we judge (11) to be true on scenario (12b), we understand the predicate *professor* to be used opaquely.

(11) John thinks that every professor is asleep.

(12) a. *Scenario 1*: Everyone has fallen asleep at the linguistics department faculty meeting. John looks in through the window, and mistakes the slumped and snoring bodies for those of overworked students.
b. *Scenario 2*: Everyone has fallen asleep at the student meeting. John looks in through the window and shakes his head. Being under the misapprehension that the meeting is a faculty meeting, he has concluded that the entire faculty has collapsed from exhaustion.

The idea now is that (11) is ambiguous. When it is true given (12a), it has one representation. When it is true given (12b), it has another. For

---

[4] The use of the terms *transparency* and *opacity* here is a distorted reflection of the original use of the terms by Whitehead and Russell, and by Quine.

concreteness, say that a noun like *professor* (or *semanticist*) selects for a world argument and yields a predicate that is true of an individual if he is a professor *in that world*. Then, when we use *professor* transparently, the world pronoun that the noun selects for is coindexed with the higher λw abstractor – it is non-locally bound ((13a)). When we use *professor* opaquely, this world pronoun is coindexed with the lower λw abstractor – it is locally bound ((13b)).

(13) a. [λw_1 [John thinks w_1 [λw_2[every w_1 professor] is asleep w_1]]]
 b. [λw_1 [John thinks w_1 [λw_2[every w_2 professor] is asleep w_1]]]

The rules of semantic interpretation will determine that (13a) is true in a world *w* iff in all worlds *w'* consistent with John's thoughts in w, every professor in *w* is asleep in *w'*. Accordingly, if we use (13a) to make a claim about the actual world, we will be making a claim about individuals who are professors in the actual world. (13b), on the other hand, will be true in w iff in all worlds *w'* consistent with John's thoughts in w, every professor in *w'* is asleep in *w'*. So in using (13b) to make a claim about the actual world, we will *not* be making a claim about actual professors.

The core of our little puzzle was that sometimes a predicate cannot have a transparent use. If it is the indexing of a world pronoun that determines the transparency of a predicate, then what this amounts to is that certain indexings for world pronouns are just impossible. This is not a real surprise: we are used to the fact that pronouns that take individuals as values are constrained in what values they can take. After all, this is what Binding Theory is about. But we don't have a Binding Theory for world pronouns. It looks as though we need one. The big agenda behind the little puzzle is to contribute to this enterprise.[5]

3. Plot.

In what follows, I will motivate a simple Binding Theory for world pronouns, needed independently of the curious facts in (4)-(9). On the basis of this simple Binding Theory, we will be able to draw conclusions

[5] I am neglecting temporal expressions in this paper, but I could have made analogous remarks about silent time interval pronouns. Enc 1986 was the first to raise the question of whether we need a Binding Theory for world and time pronouns; Enc thought not. Musan 1995 showed that there are constraints on the indexing of time pronouns, and suggested that there may be parallel constraints on the indexing of world pronouns. This capsule summary is metaphorical. These authors' perspectives on the data were different from the one I am presenting here.

about what kind of theory of indefinites we need to explain the facts in (4)-(9). I will close by observing that there is a theory of the right kind on the market.

4. Assumptions.

Throughout, I will be asuming that the input to semantic interpretation is a *logical form* in the style of Heim and Kratzer 1998. Logical forms are trees that may be embellished by objects functioning as variable abstractors. (10b) was an example. I will depart from my earlier discussion in that I will adopt a *situation*-based approach (cf. Kratzer 1989). Situations are parts of (Lewis-style) worlds. So the pronouns I have been talking about are not world pronouns, but situation pronouns. Cross out all instances of "world pronoun" and replace them with "situation pronoun." There are no sortal restrictions to worlds.

I will be assuming that DPs and VPs contain positions that are occupied by situation pronouns. I will depart from my earlier exposition in that I will *not* assume that situation pronouns are arguments (hence sisters) of nominal predicates like *semanticist* or *professor*. I will simply not take a position on where the situation pronouns are. I *will* take it for granted that the value of the pronoun affects the meaning of the DP or VP in certain ways. For instance, I will leave the structure of definite descriptions like *the loser* and *my brother* largely unanalyzed, and just accept that they have a semantics of the kind in (14).[6] With some exceptions, I will also leave VPs unanalyzed and just accept that they have a semantics of the kind in (15). It is important to note that the semantics of VPs, unlike the semantics of definite descriptions, makes reference to *counterparts.*[7]

(14) a. $[[_{DP}[\text{the loser } s_1]]]^g$ = the unique individual who lost the unique game in the situation $g(1)$, undefined if there is none
   b. $[[_{DP}[\text{my brother } s_1]]]^g$ = the unique individual in the situation $g(1)$ who is my brother, undefined if there is none.

---

[6] Similarly for quantifiers like *every good semanticist*: $[[_{DP}[\text{every good semanticist } s_1]]]^g(P) = 1$ iff for every individual x in $g(1)$, if x is a good semanticist, then $P(x) = 1$. Note that (14b) is simplified: really, it should talk about the brother of my counterpart in the world of $g(1)$.

[7] If you are a reader who prefers to imagine that individuals exist across worlds, then you can safely rewrite the VP entries for yourself and erase every instance of "some counterpart of." If you are a reader for whom counterparts make sense, here is a warning. This particular assumption of mine about VPs, together with the assumption that VPs contain a single situation position, will subtly shape the theory I will develop.

(15) a. $[[_{VP}[\text{sneezes } s_1]]]^g(x) = 1$ iff *some counterpart of x* is located in g(1) and sneezes for the entire temporal duration of g(1).

b. $[[_{VP}[\text{won the game } s_1]]]^g(x) = 1$ iff *some counterpart of x* is located in g(1) and won the unique game in g(1).

I will assume that adverbial quantifiers, modals and attitude verbs all quantify over situations. They select for predicates of situations, and for some other things as well. Even if these arguments are not pronounced, they are present at logical form. (They are realized as silent pronouns, and accordingly they depend on an assignment for their semantic value.) Sample lexical entries for *would* and *thought* are:

(16) a. $[[\text{would}]]^g (R)(s)(p_s)(q_s) = 1$ iff for every s' accessible by R from s, if $p_s(s') = 1$ then $q_s(s') = 1$.

b. $[[\text{think}]]^g (s)(p_s)(x) = 1$ iff for every s' accessible by B_x from s, $p_s(s') = 1.$ [8] (I will further abbreviate this as: ... *for every s' "consistent with x's beliefs in s"* ...)

And take note. I will assume that adverbial quantifiers select for a *situation* as well as two predicates of situations, and quantify over *parts of that situation*. This will be of importance in the discussion to come.

(17) $[[\text{always}]]^g (s)(p_s)(q_s) = 1$ iff for every s' that *is part of s*, if $p_s(s') = 1$, then $q_s(s') = 1$.

These last assumptions mean that a sentence like (18a) could have the logical form in (18b). In (18b), three abstractors over situation positions are present. The bottom one, λs_3, creates the predicate of situations that serves as the last argument of *always*. It abstracts over the position occupied by the pronoun that shares its index, the situation pronoun s_3. The middle one, λs_2, creates the predicate of situations that serves as the last argument of *thinks*. The top one, λs_1, makes the sentence into a predicate of situations, or in other words a proposition. *P* is the implicit second argument of *always*. This logical form will receive the interpretation in (18c).[9]

---

[8] This entry is obviously simplified. For expository convenience I have ignored among other things the fact that the semantics of VPs makes reference to counterparts.

[9] A terminological note: in a case like (18b), where a pronoun (e.g. s_3) is coindexed with the situation abstractor below a quantifier (e.g. with λs_3, below *always*), I will sometimes speak of the pronoun as being *bound* by the situation abstractor (s_3 *is bound by* λs_3) and I will sometimes speak of it as being *bound* by the quantifier (s_3 *is bound by* always). This is sloppy but convenient.

(18) a. Mary thinks that John always sneezes.

b.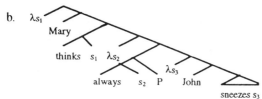

c. (18a) is true in s iff every s* "consistent with Mary's beliefs in s" has the property that, for every $s**$ that is part of s*, if $[[P]]^g(s**) = 1$, then John has a counterpart who sneezes at $s**$.

5. A "binding theory" for situation pronouns.

I will now daringly motivate a simple binding theory for situation pronouns on the basis of two sentences.

Consider first (19a). (19a) can have logical forms of the kind schematized in (19b). In these logical forms, two situation abstractors are present, one at the top of the main clause (λs_1) and one at the top of the embedded clause (λs_2). Also, three situation pronouns are present, one that is sister to *thinks*, one in the definite description *my brother* and one in the VP *is Canadian*. Let's consider the latter two situation pronouns. In principle, any one of these pronouns could be coindexed with any one of the λs abstractors -- I have given the pronouns the labels S and T in (19b), treating S and T as variables over $\{s_1, s_2\}$. Now, (if we restrict ourselves to indexings that do not result in vacuous abstraction,) are all of these indexings really possible?

(19) a. Mary thinks that my brother is Canadian.

b.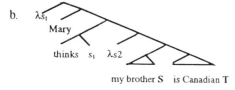

No. It is possible to give the description's pronoun the index of the higher abstractor λs_1 and the VP pronoun the index of the lower abstractor λs_2. (This yields a "transparent reading" for *my brother* and an "opaque reading" for *is Canadian*.) It is also possible to give both pronouns the index of the lower abstractor (yielding an "opaque reading" for both predicates). What is *not* possible is to give the VP pronoun the index of the higher abstractor (or, in other words, to use *is Canadian* transparently). To see this, notice that if this indexing were possible, we would permit (19a) to have the logical form in (20a), which is interpreted as in (20b). Accordingly, we would take (19a) to truly describe the world if the person who John thinks is my brother happens to be Canadian. But we don't. We unhesitantly judge the sentence to be *false* given the scenario in (20c).

(20) a. $[\lambda s_1 [\text{ John thinks } s_1 [\lambda s_2 [\text{my brother } s_2] \text{ is Canadian } s_1]]]$

    b. (20a) is true in s iff for every s* "consistent with John's beliefs in s," the unique individual in s* who is my brother has a counterpart who is Canadian in s.

    c. *Scenario*: John mistakes Pierre, a Canadian, for my brother. Knowing that I am American, he naturally concludes that Pierre too is American.

    The conclusion:

(21) **Generalization X**: The situation pronoun in a VP must be coindexed with the nearest abstractor over situations.[10]

This is our first binding principle.

    Now consider a sentence like (22a). Logical forms for sentences like (22a) contain one more situation pronoun than our previous logical forms did. This is because *always* selects for a situation. Let's look at a particular class of logical forms that are in principle available for (22a). This class is schematized in (22b). In logical forms of the kind in (22b), the situation pronoun in *my brother* is coindexed with the abstractor below *thinks* (so *my brother* gets an "opaque reading"). Also, the situation pronoun in *lost the game* is bound by *always*, so Generalization X is satisfied. What I am interested in is this. Once these indexings are established, what indexings are available for the situation that the adverbial quantifier selects for? In principle, the pronoun I have labelled T in (22b) could be coindexed with λs_1 or with λs_2. Are both of these indexings really possible?

(22) a. Mary thinks that my brother always lost the game.

---

[10]   By the "nearest" abstractor, I mean the lowest one that c-commands the pronoun.

b.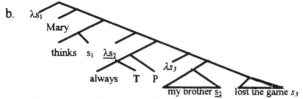

Again, no. It *is* possible to give this situation pronoun the index of the lower abstractor λs_2. You would assign this logical form when using the sentence to claim that poor deluded Mary -- who falsely believes that you have a brother and also falsely believes that there was a series of games being played – has convinced herself that your brother lost each of those games. Or I would assign this logical form when using the sentence to claim that Mary – who falsely believes that Pierre is my brother and also misunderstands the rules of the game we were playing – takes Pierre to have lost each time when in fact Pierre won each time. In these cases, because the situation argument of *always* is coindexed with the abstractor below *thinks*, *always* quantifies over parts of situations *consistent with Mary's thoughts* rather than parts of *actual* situations. On the assumption that P is a predicate that holds of game-playing situations, *always* quantifies over game-playing situations according to Mary's thoughts rather than actual game-playing situations.[11] But it is not possible to give the situation pronoun that is sister to *always* the index of the *higher* abstractor λs_1. This logical form would be interpreted as in (23a). Accordingly, we would take (22a) to be true whenever the person who Mary thinks is my brother happens to have lost each of the *actual* games that were played. We don't. We unhesitatingly judge the sentence to be false in scenario (23b).

(23) a. (22a) is true in s iff every s* "consistent with Mary's beliefs in s" has the property that, for every *s'* that is part of s, if s' is a (relevant) game-playing situation, then the unique individual who is my brother in s* has a counterpart who lost the game in s'.

b. *Scenario*: Mary, who correctly takes Allon to be my brother, is unaware of the fact that Allon and I played a series of games. It so happens that Allon lost all of those games.

---

[11] The logical form will be interpreted as in (i):

(i) (22a) is true in s iff every s* "consistent with Mary's beliefs in s" has the property that, for every *s*** that is part of s*, if s** is a (relevant) game-playing situation, then the unique individual who is my brother in s* (has a counterpart who) lost the game in s**.

The conclusion:

(24) **Generalization Y**: The situation pronoun that is sister to an adverbial quantifier must be coindexed with the nearest abstractor over situations.

Or in other words, adverbial quantifiers must range over parts of the situations that the nearest quantifier over situations ranges over. This is the second binding principle.

6. A definite resemblance.

With our mini-Binding Theory, we can already account for quite a range of facts. In particular, we can explain what is going wrong in (25a)-(27a), which by a remarkable coincidence look very much like our original examples with indefinites.

CONTEXT OF EMBEDDING: ANTECEDENT OF COUNTERFACTUALS (RESTRICTION OF MODAL OPERATOR).
(25) Last semester, not one class went by without some student trying to embarrass me by asking me a tough question.
   a. ?? If the student had always been a professor, I would have turned into a real bundle of nerves.
(cf. b. If the student had always been a semanticist, I would have turned into a real bundle of nerves.)

CONTEXT OF EMBEDDING: SCOPE OF MODAL OPERATOR.
(26) The course of the game was absolutely random.
   a. ?? It could easily have happened that the loser always won.
(cf. b. It could easily have happened that the loser always started out winning.)

CONTEXT OF EMBEDDING: SCOPE OF ATTITUDE VERB.
(27) John could never remember the rules of the game we were playing. He was continually under the impression that the person who ended up with the largest number of points was the winner, when in fact that person was the loser. As a result,
   a. ?? John thought that the loser had always won the game.
(cf. b. John thought that the loser had always been an excellent sport.)

Once again, it looks as though these sentences ask us to entertain impossible or atypical states of affairs. But why? In particular, why can't we use (25a) to talk about people who were students in the *actual* course of events? Why can't we use (27a) to talk about people who *we* take to be losers?

To answer this, let's ask first what we are doing when we evaluate these sentences. For a start, the context is guiding us to a particular *kind* of representation, one where *always* binds the situation pronoun in the description *the student* or *the loser*. The context makes salient a set of situations in the evaluation world, and corresponding sets of situations in alternate worlds that the modals/attitudes take us to (situations of a student trying to embarrass me, games). The context also makes salient a set of individuals, where each individual is associated with a different situation (obnoxious students, losers). Recall that expressions like $[_{DP}$ *the loser s* $]$ are used to talk about the *unique* loser of the *unique* game in the situation that is the value of the situation pronoun *s*. Well, there is no *single* salient student or loser (or game) in the evaluation world or the alternate worlds, but there is a salient student or loser *per situation*. We are therefore led to a logical form where *always*, which ranges over situations in the actual worlds or in the alternate worlds, binds the situation pronoun in the description.

So why can't we use (25a) to talk about alternative ways the world might have been in which those people who were students in my class got stripped of their student identity and endowed with professorships? Once *always* binds the situation pronoun in *the student*, *always* has got to range over actual rather than counterfactual situations in order for the description to talk about an *actual* student. And the logical form that permits this, the one in (28), violates binding generalizations X and Y both.

(28)

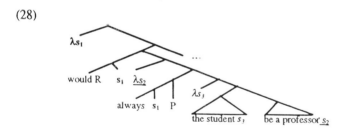

For space reasons, I won't treat (26) and (27) here, but parallel remarks apply.[12]

So here is the full story. In sentences like (25)-(27), we are led to a particular kind of logical form. Some aspects of this logical form are that

---

[12] In fact, more serious problems arise in these cases. I can't go into them here, but just try to draw a logical form for (27a) (parallel to the one in (22b)) that expresses that John thought that in each game the person who *we* take to be the loser won.

the adverbial quantifier is directly below the modal/attitude verb and that the adverbial quantifier binds the situation pronoun in the description. Now, once we have a logical form with these properties, the binding generalizations prevent us from filling it out in such a way that we interpret the description as selecting an individual in the utterance world. Why? In order for the description to contain a variable bound by the adverbial quantifier *and* select an individual in the utterance world, the adverbial quantifier must range over situations in the utterance world. This incurs a violation of Generalization Y because of the structure of the sentence. The adverbial quantifier is directly below a modal, and therefore is not allowed to range over situations in the utterance world. Moreover, we imagine that (25)-(27) talk about impossible states of affairs. Why? Generalization X is responsible for this. Since the verb is in the immediate scope of the adverbial quantifier, Generalization X forces the situation pronoun in the verb phrase to be bound by the adverbial quantifier, and consequently coindexed with the situation pronoun in the description.

Our mini-Binding Theory makes further predictions. Here is one. Suppose we change our examples so that the adverbial quantifier can appear *above* the modal at logical form. Suppose that as before we are led to a logical form in which the adverbial quantifier binds the description's situation pronoun. Then we should not run into the same kinds of problems. Since the adverbial quantifier is no longer directly below the modal, Generalization Y will allow the description to select an individual in the utterance world. And, since the verb is no longer in the immediate scope of the adverbial quantifier, Generalization X will not force the situation pronoun in the verb phrase to be coindexed with the situation pronoun in the description. This prediction seems right. (25*)-(27*) (near-)minimally contrast with (25)-(27). Given the same context, they can express the kinds of claims that (25)-(27) cannot – sensible claims about students and losers in the utterance world. The salient difference between the two sets of sentences is that (25*)-(27*) allow logical forms in which the adverbial quantifier appears above the modal.[13] (I give in (29) the logical form that we appear to assign to (27*). The logical forms for (25*) and (26*) are parallel.)

(25*) Had the student been a professor, I would have turned into a real bundle of nerves.
(26*) It was always the case that the loser could just as easily have won.
(27*) As a result, John always thought that the loser had won the game.

---

[13] I assume that (25*) contains a covert *always*. This claim can be defended.

(29)

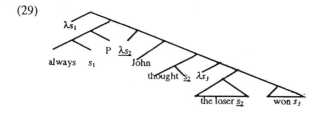

Here is something else our theory leads us to expect. If in (25)-(27) it was really the context that did us in – by suggesting a logical form where the adverbial quantifier binds the description's situation pronoun – then a different context should improve the examples. And in fact, if we adjust our context so that it contains a *single* loser, sentences like (27) don't seem so bad anymore. (30) indicates this. (Evidently, we assign to the italicized sentence in (30) a logical form like (22b), except that T is replaced by s_2 and the description's situation pronoun by s_1.)

(30) When we played last Saturday, the same person lost every single game. Everyone felt sorry for him. Everyone but John, that is. Later, we found out why. John was under the impression that the person who ended up with the largest number of points was the winner, when in fact that person was the loser. So *John had concluded that the loser had always won the game.*

7. Back to the puzzle.

We set out to account for the oddness of certain sentences with adverbial quantifiers and *indefinite* descriptions – sentences such as (5a), where the adverbial quantifier (*always*) appears below a modal at logical form. We have now seen how to account for the oddness of certain sentences with *definite* descriptions – sentences such as (25a), where again *always* appears below a modal at logical form.

(5) a. ?? If a semanticist was always a syntactician instead, a lot more would get done in our field.
(25) a. ?? If the student had always been a professor, I would have felt even more intimidated.

The implication for our original sentences is clear. The indefinite cases should be ruled out in just the way the definite cases are.

Recall how the oddness of (25a) arises. To begin with, *the student* contains a situation pronoun, and the semantics of *the student* determines that the description picks out a student in the situation that is this pronoun's value. Now, the logical form that we entertain for (25a) is one where the adverbial quantifier binds the description's situation pronoun. On the basis of the logical form, the Binding Theory determines that the description's situation pronoun is coindexed with the situation pronoun in the verb phrase – and thus that the sentence talks about individuals who are simultaneously students and professors. What does it mean to say that (5a) suffers from the same problem as (25a)? Among other things: that, in (5a) as in (25a), the description (*a semanticist*) contains a situation pronoun whose value determines whether we are talking about actual semanticists; and that, in (5a) as in (25a), the adverbial quantifier binds the description's situation pronoun. It looks as though we need a theory of indefinites from which these things follow.

I know of one such theory. Percus 1997 argues that indefinite descriptions are like definite descriptions in that they contain a situation pronoun, and gives a semantics to indefinites just like the semantics that we have been giving to definites. (I give a sample in (31).) Percus suggests that indefinites and definites differ at a level of fine detail that we have been ignoring here in our logical forms. More importantly, Percus' analysis supports the idea that, in sentences like (5a), the adverbial quantifier binds the description's situation pronoun. Percus shows that, if the adverbial binds the description's situation pronoun in sentences like (2), our pragmatic competence will guarantee that we take a sentence like (2) to express what a sentence like (1) expresses. Our little puzzle seems to lead us to this bigger picture.

(31) $[[$ a s_1 semanticist$]]^g$ = the unique semanticist in $g(1)$; undefined if there is none.

References
Cresswell, M.J. 1990. *Entities and Indices*. Dordrecht: Kluwer.
Enc, M. 1986. *Tense without Scope*. PhD diss., USC.
Heim, I. 1982. *The Semantics of Definite and Indefinite Noun Phrases*. PhD diss., University of Massachusetts at Amherst.
Heim, I. and A. Kratzer. 1998. *Semantics in Generative Grammar*. London: Blackwell.
Kratzer, A. 1989. An Investigation of the Lumps of Thought. *Linguistics and Philosophy* 12, 607-653.
Musan, R. 1995. *On the Temporal Interpretation of Noun Phrases*. PhD diss.,MIT.
Percus, O. 1997. *Aspects of A*. PhD diss., MIT.

Two Classes of Cognate Objects[*]

Asya Pereltsvaig

McGill University

1. Introduction

In this paper I investigate cognate objects (CO) in different languages. Some illustrative examples from English and French are given in (1a) and (1b) respectively.

(1)   a. Dan smiled a happy smile.

      b.   Jean-Pierre   a   dansé une grande danse.
                   Jean-Pierre   has danced a   grand   dance.
                   'Jean-Pierre danced a grand dance.'

Linguists who deal with COs treat them uniformly as either arguments of the verb (Massam, 1990; Hale & Keyser, 1993; Lefebvre, 1994; Macfarland, 1995; Mittwoch, 1997) or adjuncts (Zubizarreta, 1987; Jones, 1988; Moltmann, 1989). However, a closer look at COs in less familiar languages

[*] My special thanks to Anita Mittwoch, Talke Macfarland, Diane Massam and all the participants in the Syntax Project at McGill University, the Adverbial Workshop in Halle and WCCFL XVII for helpful discussions of the issues related to this paper and to Edit Doron, Yael Ziv, Miriam Engelhardt, Eyal Hurvitz and Irit Meir for providing judgments for Hebrew sentences. I am also grateful to Hoa Pham for the Vietnamese data, to O.T. Stewart for Edo data and Ileana Paul for Malagasy data.

shows that neither of these analyses can account for differences in syntactic and semantic behavior of COs. Therefore, I propose to distinguish between two types of COs: argument COs and adverbial COs. In this paper, I provide evidence for the distinction on the basis of data from Russian, Hebrew, Vietnamese and Edo[1] (section 2) and give a structural analysis of adverbial COs (section 3).

2. Two types of COs

2.1. Distribution across predicate types
In languages investigated in this paper, COs can occur with a wide range of predicates. For example, in Hebrew they can occur with unergatives (2), transitives (3), passives (4), ditransitives (5), unaccusatives (6), psych verbs (7), adjectival predicates (8), stative verbs (9) and individual-level predicates (10)[2].

(2)   Dani   xijex xijux same'ax.
        Danny smiled smile happy
        'Danny smiled a happy smile.'

(3)   Hezinu oto hazana melaxutit.
        they-fed him feeding artificial
        'They fed him artificially.'   (from Mittwoch, 1997, (24a))

(4)   Ha-toca'ot nivdeku   bdika   jesodit.
        The-results were-examined examination thorough
        'The results were examined a thorough examination.'

(5)   Hu šalax lanu mixtav šlixa   bilti axrait.
        He sent to-us letter   sending non responsible
        'He sent us a letter in an irresponsible way.'

(6)   Hu nafal nefila kaša.
        He fell falling hard
        'He had a heavy fall.'   (from Mittwoch, 1997, (22b))

(7) a. Ani poxedet mi-klavim (paxad mavet).
        I   fear   from-dogs fear   death
        'I fear dogs (with a deadly fear).'

---

[1] Edo is a Kwa language spoken in Nigeria.

[2] There exists a fair amount of variation between speakers with respect to the distribution of COs in Hebrew. I base the present discussion on fairly liberal judgments and a collection of attested examples from Mittwoch (1997).

    b.   Klavim mafxidim oti (paxad mavet).
           Dogs   frighten me fear   death
           'Dogs give me a deadly fright.'

(8)   Hu axrai   axrajut   eljona...
           he responsible responsibility supreme
           'He has supreme responsibility .'   (from Mittwoch, 1997, (23a))

(9)   Hu mevin ota havana muxletet.
           He understands her understanding complete
           'He understands her completely.'

(10)   Ein hu mofi'a hofa'a taxbirit ba-mišpat.
           not it appears appearance syntactic in-the-sentence
           'It does not appear syntactically in the sentence.' (from Mittwoch,
                1997, (22d))

The same wide distribution of COs across various predicate types is true in
Russian, Vietnamese and Edo. This fact is problematic for the hypothesis
that COs are (internal) arguments of the verbs. First, they are not selected by
the predicate they appear with. Moreover, they can appear with predicates
whose internal argument position is occupied by a thematic argument (such
as transitive and unaccusative verbs) and those that do not have internal
arguments in principle (such as adjectival predicates).

     A closer examination reveals that COs of (some) unergative verbs
(Type B) behave differently from those that occur with other types of
predicates (Type A)[3]. In what follows, I illustrate these differences
providing evidence for the distinction between the two types of COs. The
same data are also intended to show that Type A COs behave as adverbials
rather that as arguments.

2.2. Referentiality Related Properties
First of all, Type A COs cannot occur with strong determiners (in contrast
with Type B COs). This is illustrated in (11) for Vietnamese (from Pham,
1996).

(11)   a.   * Ti phebinh toi **tung** su phebinh gaygat.
                  Ti criticize me every CL criticism sharp
                  'Ti criticized me every sharp criticism.'
        b.   Hien gap **tung** gap.
                  Hien pick every pick
                  'Hien picked every pick.'

---

[3] English and French COs are all of Type B. For fuller discussion of COs in these languages
see Macfarland (1995).

The same is true in Hebrew and Edo. In Russian the range of determiners that are possible within CO phrase is limited to possessives (even cardinal numerals are excluded).

(12) a. * Ulybnis'   dvumja ulybkami / etoj ulybkoj / kazhdoj ulybkoj.
          Smile:imp two   smiles   this smile   every   smile
          'Smile two smiles / this smile / every smile.'

    b. Ulybnis'   ulybkoju svojej ...   (from a child song)
          Smile:imp smile   own
          'Smile your own smile...'

The incompatibility with strong determiners is one of the characteristic properties of predicative nominals (see Doron, 1986).

In addition, Type A COs do not create scope ambiguities, as illustrated by Hebrew examples from Mittwoch (1997).

(13) a. Ha- rofe   biker   xole   japani   šeš pe'amim.
          The-doctor visited patient Japanese 6   times
          'The doctor visited a Japanese patient 6 times.'

    b. Ha- rofe   biker   xole   japani   šiša bikurim.
          The-doctor visited patient Japanese 6   visits
          'The doctor visited a Japanese patient 6 visits.'

The sentence in (13a) is ambiguous: either the doctor visited the same Japanese patient 6 times or he made 6 visits to different Japanese patients. The (13b) sentence is non-ambiguous: it has to be the same Japanese patient for all 6 visits. This shows that COs (unlike frequentative adverbials) cannot be scoped out of their surface position. As argued in Williams (1994), the requirement to be interpreted in situ is another distinctive property of predicative NPs.

Another related property of Type A COs is that they cannot be pronominalized. This is illustrated with a Hebrew example in (14) and is also true in Russian and Edo.

(14) a. Jakov kar'a et   ha-sefer kria   jesodit.
          Jacob read ACC the-book reading thorough
          'Jacob read the book thoroughly.'

    b. * Jakov kar'a et   ha-sefer ota / hi / ze.
          Jacob read ACC the-book her / she / it
          'Jacob read the book it [= thorough reading].'

Yet another property of Type A COs is that they do not delimit the event denoted by the main predicate (as internal arguments/direct objects do). As the Hebrew example in (15) shows, an addition of a CO in (15b) does not change the aspectual properties of the predicate.

(15) a. Dani   kar'a sfarim be-mešex / * be-xameš dakot.
         Danny read books   during /   in-five   minutes
         'Danny read books for / in five minutes.'

   b. Dani kar'a sfarim kri'a yesodit be-mešex / * be-xameš dakot.
       Danny read books reading thorough during / in-five   minutes
       'Danny read books thoroughly for / in five minutes.'

2.3. Syntactic Properties

In addition to the referentiality-related properties discussed above, Type A COs exhibit syntactic behavior different from that of Type B COs. For example, Type A COs cannot be passivized (as illustrated with a Vietnamese example in (16))[4].

(16) a. * Mot su kinhtrong dacbiet duoc (Hien) kinhtrong
          a   CL respect   special PASS (Hien) respect
          'A special respect was respected (by Hien).'

   b. Mot gap duoc (Hien) gap
       a   pick PASS (Hien) pick
       'A pick was picked (by Hien).'

Likewise, Type A COs cannot be extracted by A'-movement, as shown for Hebrew in (17) and (18).

(17) Relativization
     * Ha- kri'a   še- Dani kar'a et   ha- sefer hajta jesodit.
       The-reading that-Danny read ACC the-book was   thorough
       'The reading that Danny read the book was thorough.'

(18) a. Cleft
     * Zu hajta kri'a   jesodit še- Dani kar'a et   ha- sefer.
       That was reading thorough that-Danny read ACC the-book
       'It was a thorough reading that Danny read the book.'

   b. Pseudo-cleft
     * Ma   še- Dani kar'a et   ha- sefer hajta kri'a   jesodit.
       What that-Danny read ACC the-book was   reading thorough
       'What Danny read the book was a thorough reading.'

---

[4] Type A COs cannot be passivized in Hebrew or Russian either. I omit the relevant examples for the sake of space. There is no relevant data for Edo because there are no passives in that languages.

In addition, Type A COs are questioned by *How?*, not *What?* (as illustrated for Vietnamese). The same is true of Hebrew, Russian and Edo.

(19) a. *Hien kinhthrong cha cai gi? b. Ti bo cai gi?
Hien respect her-father did what Ti bundle did what
'What did Hien respect her father?' 'What did Ti bundle?'

Moreover, Type A COs can be coordinated with manner adverbs, but not with direct objects. I illustrate this with the Hebrew example in (20).

(20) a. Hu kar'a et ha-sefer kria yesodit ve-leat.
he read:pst ACC the-book reading thorough and-slowly
'He read the book thoroughly and slowly.'

    b. * Hu kar'a et ha-sefer ve-kria yesodit.
he read:pst ACC the-book and-reading thorough
'He read the book and thoroughly.'

2.4. Language-Specific Properties

In addition to the cross-linguistically valid properties discussed above, there are some more language specific properties that distinguish between the two types of COs. First, in languages that have rich morphological case marking on full DPs, Type A COs bear adverbial case (for instance, Instrumental in Russian (21) and Locative in Malagasy (22)). In contrast, Type B COs bear Accusative case.

(21) a. On ljubil eje strastnoj ljubovju.
he loved her passionate:**instr** love:**instr**
'He loved her passionately.'

    b. Sdelal delo - guljaj smelo. (Russian proverb)
did work:**acc** have-fun:imper freely
'The work finished, you can have fun.'

(22) Mihomehy ampikakakahana koto.
laugh:prs **loc**:chuckle Kutu
'Kutu laughs a chuckle.'

In addition, Genitive of Negation in Russian does not apply to Type A COs.

(23) a. * On bol'še ne ljubil eje strastnoj ljubovi.
he more not loved her passionate:gen love:gen
'He didn't love her passionately anymore.'

    b. On bol'še šutok ne šutil.
he more jokes:gen not joked
'He didn't joke anymore.'

Furthermore, in some languages, Type A COs can be distinguished from Type B COs by their morphological form. Thus, in Hebrew the two types of COs can be distinguished (in some cases) by their morphological template.

(24) a. Dani xašav al   ze **xašiva** aruka.   - Type A
Danny thought about this thinking long
'Danny thought about this for a long time.'

   b. Dani xašav **maxševa** nora'it še-xaverto azva oto.   - Type B
Danny thought thought terrible that-girlfriend-his left him
'Danny had a terrible thought that his girlfriend had left him.'

Likewise, in Edo the two types of COs can be distinguished by different nominalization morphemes on the head-noun: Type A COs are formed by *u...mwèn* circumfix, while Type B COs are formed only by a vowel prefix.

(25) a. Òzó tié èbé ùtiémwèn.
Ozo read book NOM:reading:NOM
'Ozo read a book reading.'

   b. Òzó tue uyi otue.
ozo greet Uyi NOM:gretting
'Ozo greeted Uyi every greeting.'

In Biblical Hebrew, the two types of COs are distinguished by their position in the sentence: Type A COs appear in the preverbal position, whereas Type B COs follow the verb.

(26) a. va-jomer ha-naxaš el-ha-iša   lo-mot   tmutun.
and-said the-serpent to-the-woman not-death you:will:die
'But the serpent said to the woman , "You will not die..."'
[Genesis, 3:4]

   b. va-izbax   ja'akov zevax   ba-har.
and-sacrificed Jacob   sacrifice at-the-mountain
'And Jacob offered a sacrifice in the height.'
[Genesis, 31:54]

In Vietnamese, in contrast with Type B COs, Type A COs cannot occur in middle constructions (27) and cannot appear as complements in the light verb construction (28).

(27) a.* Mot su kinhtrong dacbiet kinhtrong de.
    a   CL respect special respect   easily
    'A special respect respects easily.'

    b. Mot gap gap de.
    a pick pick easily
    'A pick picks easily.'

(28) a. * Ti **lam** mot su thathu dedai.   b. Ti lam mot bo.
      Ti do an easy forgiveness   Ti do a chop
      'Ti does an easy forgiveness.'   'Ti did a chop.'

The last property distinguishing between the two types of COs to be mentioned here is that Type A COs must be modified (see examples from Vietnamese; also applicable in Russian and in Hebrew[5]).

(29) a. * Toi nho Hien mot noinho.   b.   Ti da   mot da.
      I   miss Hien a   miss   Ti kick a   kick
      'I miss Hien a miss.'   'Ti kicks a kick.'

To sum up, in this section I provided evidence for the distinction between two types of COs in Hebrew, Russian, Vietnamese and Edo. The same data also point out to the adverbial status of Type A COs: they are non-referential, non-extractable, can occur with a wide range of predicates and can be coordinated with manner adverbials. On the basis of the above observations, I propose to treat Type A COs as a special class of manner adverbial NPs (i.e., "cognate adverbials"). In the next section I argue for a structural analysis of these cognate adverbials. On the other hand, Type B COs are non-distinct in their properties from "normal" direct objects. Nothing special is to be said about them here. For more discussion, see Massam (1990) and Macfarland (1995).

3. Analysis

As shown in the previous section, cognate adverbials are in a predicative position. To capture this structurally, I propose that they are base-generated as DPs adjoined to a VP inside a small clause-like PredP (as in Bowers, 1993). A somewhat simplified structure is given in (30).

---

[5] This is not strictly true of Edo, where non-modified COs can be used contrastively.

(30)

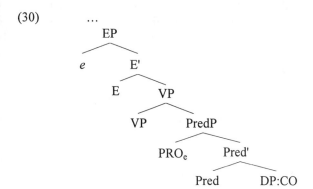

The cognate adverbial is a complement of a null Pred which assigns it case. The PredP is adjoined to the VP. The Spec, PredP is occupied by a PRO coindexed with the event argument generated in Spec, EP[6]. The PRO has to be controlled since it occurs in an adjunct clause (see Haegeman, 1994). Therefore, it has to be c-commanded by the controller. This in its turn requires that PredP should be adjoined no higher than VP (for the implications of this claim see below).

3.1. Alternative possibilities
In this section I investigate two alternative structural possibilities and reject them. The first alternative is to generate cognate adverbials inside VP. This analysis is analogous to Stroik's (1990) and Alexiadou's (1998) treatment of manner adverbial NPs in English and Modern Greek, respectively. However, this possibility should be excluded for several reasons. First of all, cognate adverbials do not "compete" for any object position, that is, even double object verbs can appear with COs of this type. Moreover, cognate adverbials can co-occur with resultatives (even though such sentences are marginal for information packaging reasons).

(31) a. * Ha-roceax   hika et   kurbano   [šaloš makot] [le-mavet].
The-murderer beat ACC victim-his three blows to-death.
'The murderer beat his victim (with) three blows to death.'

   b. #Ha-roceax   hika et   kurbano   [le-mavet] [šaloš makot].
The-murderer beat ACC victim-his to-death   three blows.
'The murderer beat his victim to death (with) three blows.'

---

[6] Note that this use of EP is different from that proposed in Travis (1994). I assume that the event argument is like other arguments and therefore should be generated in a Spec position. By generating the event argument in a particular syntactic position, I restrict the range of positions in which the event argument can be predicated of (contra Wyner, 1998).

In (31a) the cognate adverbial precedes the resultative, thus making the sentence ungrammatical. This shows that, unlike the resultative, the cognate adverbial is outside VP. If the order of the two phrases is switched, as in (31b), the resulting sentence is better. However, it sounds somewhat strange because the result precedes the manner of the action. The same judgment is reported for sentences with manner adverbs instead of cognate adverbials.

Furthermore, contra the claims of Stroik (1990) and Alexiadou (1998), it is impossible to bind an anaphor or to license an NPI from the direct object into the cognate adverbial. This is illustrated with Russian examples in (32) and (33)[7], respectively.

(32)   Andrej $_i$ poceloval Mašu $_k$ svoim $_{i/*k}$ nepovtorimym poceluem.
         Andrew kissed   Mary   self's   unique   kiss
         'Andrew kissed Mary with his own kiss.'

(33) *   On ljubil nemnogix zhenschin kakoj-libo ljubovju.
         He loved few   women   any   love
         'He loved few women with any love.'

Another reason to exclude the possibility of generating cognate adverbials inside VP is their behavior in VP-ellipsis resolution. More specifically, cognate adverbials are not necessarily reconstructed in the target conjunct.

(34) Dani kar'a et ha-sefer kri'a mehira ve-xafifa ve-ruti gam,
     Danny read ACC the-book reading quick and-superficial and-Ruthie too
           aval leat   u-vejesodijut.
           but slowly and-thoroughly
'Danny read the book a quick and superficial reading and Ruthie did too, but slowly and thoroughly.'

The sentence in (34) is fully acceptable and has no contradiction that would be expected if the cognate adverbial were to be copied into the target conjunct. Once again, the judgments for sentences with manner adverbs instead of cognate adverbials are exactly the same.

Another alternative possibility is to adjoin the PredP to EP instead of VP. This possibility is excluded because PRO in Spec, PredP must be controlled and therefore c-commanded by *e* (as discussed above). If PredP were adjoined to EP, PRO would still be in the m-command domain but not in the c-command domain of *e*. However, being in the m-command domain is not enough for control.

---

[7] On overt NPI licensing in Russian see Pereltsvaig (in press).

3.2. Implications

Assuming that the event argument is projected in Spec, EP (as in (30)), it should constitute a barrier for DP-movement through Spec positions. But obviously it does not. A possible solution (for which I am grateful to Mark Baker) is the following. Since both the event argument and the PRO coindexed with it refer to events (and not to individual entities), they are not DPs in the usual sense, but rather ZPs (as in Stowell, 1996)[8]. Therefore, they do not count for Relativized Minimality.

Another implication of this analysis of cognate adverbials has to do with their interpretation. As argued in Ernst (1997), the VP-adjoined position is restricted to manner adverbials. This explains why the range of modifiers of the cognate adverbial is limited to manner adjectives but not to speaker-oriented ones (in the sense of Jackendoff, 1972)[9]. Likewise, Cinque's (1996) "higher adverbs" (evaluative, evidential and epistemic) cannot be used to modify the head of the cognate adverbials.

(35) a. * Dani roce liftor et ha-beaja pitaron efšari.
   Danny wants to-solve ACC the-problem solution possible
   b. Dani roce limco pitaron efšari la-beaja.
   Danny wants to-find solution possible to-the-problem
   both: 'Danny wants to find a possible solution to the problem.'

Moreover, present theory explains why COs (unlike corresponding adverbs) can have only a manner interpretation. Thus, (36a) is ambiguous between the manner and the "higher" interpretations of the adverb. On the other hand, the cognate adverbial in (36b) can have only a manner interpretation.

(36) a. Dani maher kar'a et ha-mixtav.
   Danny quick(ly) read ACC the-letter
   ambiguous: (i) 'Danny read the letter fast/in a quick manner.'
               (ii) 'Danny read the letter right away.'

   b. Dani kar'a et ha-mixtav kri'a mehira.
   Danny read ACC the-letter reading quick
   'Danny read the letter fast.' [not: '... read the letter right away.']

In addition, this analysis of cognate adverbials allows a unified analysis of Instrumental case in Russian along the lines of Bailyn & Rubin (1991). Essentially, they propose that Instrumental case is assigned by an empty

---

[8] Stowell uses the term ZP for phrases referring to times. I assume that events and times are of the same type ontologically.

[9] This fact was noticed in Massam (1990). In the present theory it follows naturally from the analysis.

Pred head to its complement. This is exactly the configuration in which cognate adverbials occur according to (30).

This analysis also highlights the parallelism between cognate adverbials and secondary predicates (of arguments), which is illustrated in structure (37a) for sentences with secondary predicates (37b) and (37c) and with cognate adverbials (37d).

(37) a.

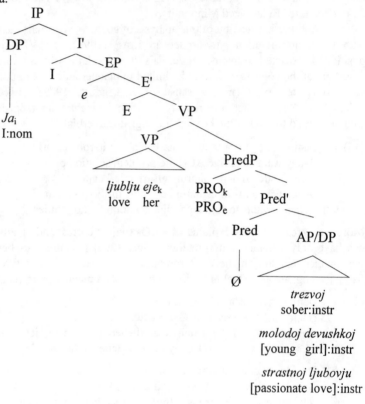

b. Ja ljubil eje trezvoj.
   I loved her sober:instr
   'I loved her sober.'
c. Ja ljubil eje molodoj devushkoj.
   I loved her [young girl]:instr
   'I loved her as a young girl.'

d. Ja ljubil eje strastnoj ljubovju.
    I loved her [passionate love]:instr
    'I loved her passionately.'

Last but not least, this analysis accounts naturally for the cognate nature of
the cognate adverbials. Since cognate adverbials are predicated of the event
projected by the main predicate of the sentence, they have to be compatible
with this event. Therefore, sentences like (38a) are excluded on the same
grounds as those in (38b) and (38c).

(38) a. * Hu kar'a et   ha-sefer ktiva   mehira.
        He read ACC the-book writing quick
        'He read the book a quick writing.'

    b. * I loved her diagonalized.

    c. * This boy is a girl.

However, cognate adverbials do not have to be strictly cognate (i.e.,
morphologically related). They can be based on a different root as long as
they are semantically related to the main predicate. More specifically, the
noun head of a cognate adverbial NP can be more specific than the verb. An
example is the Malagasy sentence in (22) repeated here as (39).

(39)   mihomehy ampikakakahana koto
        laugh:prs loc:chuckle   Kutu
        'Kutu laughs a chuckle.'

In this example, *ampikakakahana* is an onomatopoeic word that is more
specific than the verb *mihomehy*. In this case the requirement that the
cognate adverbial be modified is obeyed via "incorporating" modification
by using a semantically more restricted term.

4. Summary

In this paper, I argued for the distinction between two types of CO
constructions: argument cognate objects and cognate adverbials. I provided
data in favor of this distinction from four unrelated languages: Hebrew,
Russian, Vietnamese and Edo. I further argued for the adverbial status of the
latter construction. What is more, I provided a structural analysis that
accounts neatly for the observed facts. Last but not least this paper provides
evidence for VP-adjunction rather than VP-internal generation of manner
adverbials.

References

Alexiadou, Artemis (1998) *On Complement Adverbs*, paper presented at the 20th Annual Meeting of the DGfS, Adverbial Workshop, Halle.

Bailyn John, and Edward Rubin (1991) The Unification of Instrumental Case Assignment in Russian, in Almeida Toribio and Wayne Harbert (eds.) *Cornell Working Papers in Linguistics*, 9, Department of Modern Languages and Linguistics, Cornell University , Ithaca, NY, 99-126.

Bowers, John (1993) The Syntax of Predication, *Linguistic Inquiry*, 24, 591-656.

Cinque, Guglielmo (1996) *Adverbs and the Universal Hierarchy of Functional Projections*, Unpublished ms., University of Venice, Venice (to appear from Oxford University Press).

Doron, Edit (1986) The pronominal 'copula' as agreement clitic, in Hagit Borer (ed.) *The Syntax of Pronominal Clitics: Syntax and Semantics 19.* Orlando: Academic Press, 313-32.

Ernst, Thomas (1997) *The Scopal Basis of Adverb Licensing*, unpublished ms., Rutgers University, New Brunswick, New Jersey.

Haegeman, Liliane (1994) *Introduction to Government and Binding Theory*, 2nd ed., Blackwell, Cambridge, Massachusetts.

Hale, Kenneth & Samuel Jay Keyser (1993) On Argument Structure and the Lexical Expression of Syntactic Relations, in Hale, Kenneth & Samuel Jay Keyser (eds.) *The View from Building 20*, 53-109.

Jackendoff, Ray (1972) *Semantic Interpretation in Generative Grammar*, Cambridge, Mass., MIT Press.

Jones, M. A. (1988) Cognate Objects and the Case Filter, *Journal of Linguistics*, 24, 89-111.

Lefebvre, Claire (1994) On Spelling Out E, *Travaux de recherche sur le créole haïtien*, Département de Linguisitique, Université du Québec à Montréal.

Macfarland, Talke (1995) *Cognate Objects and the Argument/Adjunct Distinction in English*, Ph.D. dissertation, Northwestern University, Evanston, Illinois.

Massam, Diane (1990) Cognate Objects as Thematic Objects, *Canadian Journal of Linguistics*, 35, 161-190.

Mittwoch, Anita (1997) Cognate Objects as Reflections of Davidsonian Event Arguments, ms., to appear in Rothstein, Susan (ed.) *Events in Grammar*, Dordrecht, Kluwer.

Moltmann, Fredericke (1989) Nominal and clausal event predicates, *Papers from the 25th Annual Regional Meeting of the Chicago Linguistic Society*, 300-314.

Pereltsvaig, Asya (1998) Genitive of Negation in Russian, *Proceedings of the 13th IATL Annual Conference*, Jerusalem, Israel, 167-190.

Pham, Hoa (1996) *Cognate Objects in Vietnamese Transitive Verbs*, Ms., University of Toronto.

Stowell, Tim (1996) *The Phrase Structure of Tense*, ms., UCLA.

Stroik, Thomas (1990) Adverbs as V-sisters, *Linguistic Inquiry*, 21, 654-661.

Travis, Lisa deMena (1994) Event Phrase and a Theory of Functional Categories, in Paivi Koskinen (ed.) *Proceedings of the 1994 Annual Conference of the Canadian Linguistic Association*, University of Toronto, Toronto.

Williams, Ed (1994) *Thematic Structure in Syntax*, Cambridge, Mass., MIT Press.

Wyner, Adam Zachary (1998) *On Adverbial Modification and Ellipsis*, paper presented at the 20th Annual Meeting of the DGfS, Adverbial Workshop, Halle.

Zubizarreta, M. L. (1987) *Levels of Representation in the Lexicon and the Syntax*, Dordrecht, Forris.

ECM Constructions and Binding: Unexpected New Evidence[1]

ANNA PETTIWARD

University of London

1. Introduction

"ECM subjects" (e.g. *Bob* in *I believe Bob to be a genius*) differ from subjects of tensed clausal complements (henceforth, "TC subjects") in that according to standard tests, the former c-command certain elements belonging to the matrix clause. This difference has often been taken as evidence that ECM subjects undergo some form of movement into the higher clause (Postal (1974), Lasnik & Saito (1991)) (see Section 2).

In this paper I dispute such movement explanations of the contrast between ECM and TC subjects, beginning with the observation that *non-subjects* of infinitives also show signs of c-commanding matrix clause elements, in tests where locality is not a factor (Principle C, NPI licensing), thereby resembling ECM subjects, rather than TC subjects as expected (see Section 3). Unlike ECM subjects, there is no reason to think that non-subjects of infinitives raise into the matrix clause. Therefore, unless the subject and non-subject binding/licensing facts are analysed as separate phenomena, a DP-movement account of ECM subject behaviour seems out of the question. The potential alternative solution in terms of a Larsonian or cascade structure (Pesetsky (1995)) also seems inappropriate for the ECM binding facts (see Lasnik (1996)).

---

[1] For some helpful discussions relating to this paper, I would like to thank, with the usual disclaimers, Hiroto Hoshi, Ruth Kempson, Stavroula Tsiplakou, Andrew Simpson, Howard Gregory, Richard Breheny, Taeko Maeda, Justin Watkins, Jeanne Cornillon, and Julia Martinez Garcia.

Since appearing to c-command matrix elements is a property of DPs within *to*-clause complements of ECM verbs but never of DPs within corresponding *that*-clause complements, it seems that a "boundary" explanation is needed. In Section 4, I explore two alternative possibilities along these lines. The first, syntactic, approach sees the unexpected binding/licensing from lower to higher clause in terms of the construction being/becoming monoclausal (cf. restructuring in some Germanic and Romance languages). The other approach to the problematic binding facts which I consider just dispenses with the assumption that binding depends directly on c-command. I attempt to explain the binding abilities of DPs within *to*-clause complements of ECM verbs by assuming, following Williams (1994), that binding depends on thematic rather than configurational relations, and in addition, that *to*-clause complements are not true arguments of the ECM verb, which renders them transparent for binding not only from outside in (like *that*-clause complements) but also from inside out (unlike *that*-clause complements).

2. ECM constructions and binding: existing beliefs

As background to the discussion, I will summarize the asymmetries between ECM subjects and TC subjects mentioned above and outline approaches to this which seek to implicate raising of the ECM subject into the main clause. (Examples in this section are from Lasnik & Saito (1991) (henceforth L&S) unless indicated otherwise).

Firstly, consider (1): the Principle C effect in (1a) suggests that the ECM subject *him* must at some level c-command the main VP adverbial, in contrast with (1b), where coreference between the TC subject *he* and *Bob* in the adverbial is perfectly possible:

(1) a. * Joan believes him$_i$ to be a genius even more fervently than Bqb does.
     b.   Joan believes he$_i$ is a genius even more fervently than Bob$_i$ does.

L&S (p.327) observe that even after ruling out potential interference from reconstruction of the elided VP in (1a) (yielding ... *Bob$_i$ believes him$_i$ to be a genius*, which contravenes Principle B), by replacing the phrase *Bob* with *Bob's mother* as in (1'a), the example is still noticeably worse than the equivalent tensed complement example (1'b), confirming the presence of a genuine Principle C effect.

(1') a. *? Joan believes [him$_i$ to be a genius] even more fervently than Bob$_i$'s mother does.
      b.   Joan believes [that he$_i$ is a genius] even more fervently than Bob$_i$'s mother does.

Facts about the licensing of Negative Polarity Items (NPIs) also suggest that ECM subjects c-command matrix VP-adjuncts - witness the more or less perfect (2a); here again there is a contrast with TC subjects, which completely fail to license an NPI in the same position:

(2) a.   The DA proved [no-one to be guilty] during any of the trials.
     b. * The DA proved [that no-one was guilty] during any of the trials.

ECM and TC subjects also differ in their ability to license anaphors: thus, an ECM subject - (3a) - but not a TC subject - (3b) - may be the antecedent of a reciprocal contained within a matrix VP-adjunct:

(3) a. (?) The DA proved [the suspects to be guilty] during each other's trials.
     b. * The DA proved [that the suspects were guilty] during each other's trials.

In addition, following Burzio (1986) in assuming that binominal *each* is licensed more or less under the same conditions as anaphors (Principle A), (4a) once again shows ECM subjects behaving as if they were in the matrix clause, thereby contrasting with TC subjects:

(4) a. (?) Jones proved [the prisoners to be guilty] with one accusation each
     b. * Jones proved [that prisoners were guilty] with one accusation each

Safir & Stowell (1988), to whom L&S attribute (4a), actually dispute Burzio's contention that binominal *each* is subject to Principle A, one of their reasons being that there is no contrast between the *each*-DP as ECM subject and as TC subject, in contrast with anaphors ((5) = Safir & Stowell's (33), (6), their (32), p.439; judgements their own):[2]

---

[2] Safir & Stowell's other main argument against taking binominal *each* to be subject to Principle A of the binding theory is that c-command by the antecedent (their "R-NP") is not always necessary: they give the following examples in which binominal *each* fails to behave like "true reflexives and reciprocals":

(i)   Tom is depending on the boys for two ideas each.
(ii) Mat lived with Sue and Mo in one apartment each.

In fact, I find it a strain to get any interpretation for (ii) (*Mat lived with the women in one apartment each* is slightly better, though). But in any case, Safir & Stowell's objection is rendered questionable by the fact that "true reflexives and reciprocals" themselves appear not to require c-command by their antecedent in (among others) the environments in which *each* appears in (i) and (ii), i.e where the antecedent is contained in a PP. See for instance Reinhart (1983), and below (Section 4).

(5) a. * The boys expected one picture each to be on sale.
     b. * The boys expected that one picture each would be on sale.

(6) a.   The boys considered themselves/each other to be smart.
     b. * The boys considered that themselves/each other were smart.

However, I find that there is a contrast between (5a,b), with (5a) fairly good, a judgement also expressed in Postal (1974) and in L&S, the latter of whom (citing the former) give the following similar example (relevant reading = 'each student proved three formulas to be theorems' rather than the "floating quantifier" reading 'the students proved each of the three formulas to be theorems'):

(7) a. (?) The students proved three formulas each to be theorems.
     b. * The students proved that three formulas each were theorems.

Whatever the precise conditions involved in licensing binominal *each*, example (4), like (1)-(3), does show a decided syntactic difference between ECM subjects and TC subjects. ECM subjects actually resemble regular direct objects, as the examples in (8) (again from L&S) show:[3]

(8) a. *? Joan believes him$_i$ even more fervently than Bob$_i$'s mother does.
     b.   The DA accused none of the defendants during any of the trials.
     c.   The DA accused the defendants during each other's trials.
     d.   Jones prosecuted the defendants with one accusation each.

In order to explain the surprising properties of ECM subjects, it has been proposed, initially by Postal (1974), that they raise to the main clause. L&S themselves develop a modern version of this idea, reinterpreting the facts as evidence that ECM subjects, like direct objects, raise to the Specifier of a functional projection above the matrix VP (in their framework, AGR$_o$P) for Case-checking, as illustrated in (9). This explains how the ECM subject reaches a position where it c-commands the matrix VP - and why TC subjects never do, since their Case needs are met within their own clause.

---

[3] The ECM subject examples (and also the comparable direct object examples) mostly have a slightly marginal character: the NPI, reciprocal and binominal *each* cases are not quite perfect (Postal finds the *each* example in (3a) "somewhat strained" (1974, p.219); likewise, the Principle C effect in (1a) is perhaps not as bad as it might be (compare it with e.g. *she admires the people who work with Lola* or *Rosa tickled him with Ben's feather* (from Reinhart (1983)) both of which are hopeless under the relevant interpretation). That noted, the important point is of course the contrast between ECM and TC subjects, which is fairly clear.

(9)

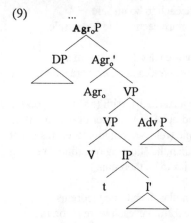

      Finally, note that the behaviour of ECM subjects as compared to TC subjects has been used by Lasnik (1996) as evidence that the former move *overtly* to their Case position, ultimately as support for the wider hypothesis that checking of Accusative Case is overt in English (as also proposed by e.g. Johnson (1991), Koizumi (1995), on other grounds). This argument that the alleged movement is overt relies on a further assumption, namely that only movement of a full category (i.e. overt movement), as opposed to just its formal features (in the sense of Chomsky (1995)), affects binding possibilities. This assumption appears to be supported by the contrast in (10) (from Lasnik (1996, p.5): the raised subject can antecede an anaphor in the higher clause, as shown by (10a), whereas the associate of expletive *there* cannot - (10b) - although covertly it will assume the same position.[4]

(10)   a.   Some linguists seem to each other to have been given good job offers.

        b. * There seem to each other to have been some linguists given good job offers.

---

    [4]   On the other hand, Chomsky (1995) concludes that covert movement *does* extend binding possibilities, citing the example in (i):

(i)   There arrived three men without identifying themselves.

Notice also that NPI licensing is possible by an associate of *there*, if (ii) is anything to go by:

(ii)   a.   No storms arose off any coast.
        b.   There arose no storms off any coast.

Incidentally, I find Lasnik's example (10b) ungrammatical independently of the binding problem: *there seem to us to have been some linguists given good job offers* is no better. However, it is possible to construct similar examples which make the point (see Pettiward (1997)).

3. A problem for movement accounts

I now turn to some further data involving ECM constructions which in my view undermines the hypothesis that raising of ECM subjects - overt, covert, "to object", to Spec,AGR$_o$P, or wherever - is responsible for their surprising relationships with DPs associated with the matrix clause. The asymmetry just reviewed between ECM and TC subjects takes on a different appearance in the light of the behaviour of non-subjects of infinitives (hereafter abbreviated to " 'ECM' objects", for want of a better name) which for some reason act more akin to ECM subjects than TC subjects. To illustrate this, consider the following:

(11) *? Joan expects [the DA to acquit him$_i$] even more confidently than Bob$_i$ does.

I find coreference between *him* and *Bob* difficult in this example, suggesting a Principle C violation. (11) is hardly better than (12), in which the pronoun is an ECM subject, and (11) and (12) collectively contrast with the examples in (13) where we have subjects and objects contained in finite complements.

(12) *? Joan expects [him$_i$ to be acquitted] even more confidently than Bob$_i$'s mother does.

(13) a. Joan expects [that he$_i$ will be aquitted] even more confidently than Bob$_i$ does.
      b. Joan expects [that the DA will acquit him$_i$] even more confidently than Bob$_i$ does.

Since ECM constuctions with a subject and object in the embedded clause can in general sound slightly unnatural for some speakers ((?)*I believe John to like Mary*, (?) *the DA proved Bob to have murdered them*), which may contribute irrelevantly to the unacceptability to (11), it is worth trying to remove this factor by considering passive examples, where this particular unnaturalness disappears[5] (*John is believed to like Mary, Bob was proved to have murdered them*). This amendment is made in (14a), but the example is still worse than the corresponding tensed complement example:[6]

---

[5] With some verbs, as is well-known, the construction is possible only in the passive * *everyone said Bob to be the murderer* versus *Bob was said by everyone to be the murderer*.

[6] Another potential complication to be aware of is that where there is an 'ECM' object, there will be an embedded 'real' verb - unlike the case of ECM subjects, where we can examine examples with *be* (as in (1) above). This increases the risk of adverbials being construable within the embedded clause, which would give rise to irrelevant effects.

(14)   a. *? Someone was proved [e to have murdered him$_i$] during Bob$_i$'s
            postmortem.
        b.   It was proved [that someone had murdered him$_i$] during Bob$_i$'s
            postmortem.

The degraded nature of (11) and (14a) is surprising; from a configurational
perspective they should be as acceptable as their tensed clause complement
counterparts, or, e.g., as an example like (15):

(15)   Those pictures of him$_i$ ruined Bob$_i$'s career.

    Unusual results are also found with NPI licensing: a negative 'ECM'
object seems able to license an NPI in the main clause adjunct, as in (16). Again,
the status of this example resembles that of an example with an ECM subject, as
in (17), though the expectation is that (16) should be as bad as the examples in
(18):

(16)   The DA proved [the guilt to lie with none of the defendants] during any
        of the trials.

(17)   The DA proved [none of the defendants to be guilty] during any of the
        trials.

(18)   a. * The DA proved [that none of the defendants were guilty during
            any of the trials].
        b. * The DA proved [that the guilt lay with none of the defendants
            during any of the trials].

We can also look at a passive example, in case (16) is less good than it might be
for reasons independent of the NPI's circumstances (see above). (19a) featuring
the 'ECM' object is quite clearly better than (19b) which features a tensed clause
object presumably situated at the same hierarchical level:

(19)   a. ? The defendants were proved [e to have committed no crime] by
            any lawyer.
        b. * It was proved [that the defendants had committed no crime] by
            any lawyer.

Although there are known to exist cases where NPIs seem to be licensed in the
absence of c-command (for example, *Nobody's articles ever get published on
time* (Kayne (1994:24)), it is surprising that (16) and (19a) are any better than an
example like (20), where the negative element would seem to be in a similarly
low position relative to *anyone*:

(20) *? Pictures of no-one ruined anyone's career.

Given the above-mentioned hypotheses (see §2) that ECM subjects appear to c-command matrix elements because they move into the matrix clause, the facts we have just seen are difficult to understand. The non-subjects of infinitivals get Case unexceptionally within their own clause, in common with TC subjects, and yet these objects act more like *ECM* subjects.

The behaviour of 'ECM' objects calls into question the movement type of account of the ECM subject facts - if this account were maintained, one would then need to come up with a separate explanation for the behaviour of the objects. That would not be desirable, given the similarity of the phenomena. The patterning of the facts suggests that what must be relevant is the nature of the boundary separating the DPs in question, and not simply their relative positions (see §4 below).

The argument that the binding/licensing asymmetries between ECM and TC subjects is not about ECM subjects raising into the higher clause obviously affects any account of that type, including Lasnik's (1996) overt movement version mentioned earlier.

Before concluding this section, let us consider reciprocals and binominal *each* again. In contrast with ECM subjects (see (3a) above), an 'ECM' object cannot serve as the antecedent of a reciprocal inside a matrix adjuncts: in the following examples, *the defendants* is the only possible antecedent for *each other*:

(21)   The DA proved [the defendants$_i$ to have assaulted the policemen$_j$] during each other$_{i/*j}$'s trials.

(22)   The defendants$_i$ were proved [e to have assaulted the policemen$_j$] during each other$_{i/*j}$'s trials.

It might be wondered whether this clear difference between ECM subjects and 'ECM' objects weakens the argument against raising explanations of ECM subject behaviour, which after all was based on the fact that the two behave in a similar way (with respect to Principle C effects, NPI licensing). In fact, the failure of 'ECM' objects to bind anaphors in the matrix clause is arguably not relevant to the issue. Obviously, unlike in the case of Principle C and NPI licensing, locality must also be taken into consideration where anaphors are concerned. It seems reasonable to speculate that the 'ECM' objects in (21) and (22) are blocked as antecedents of *each other* by the presence of the ECM subject/its trace - in other words, (21) and (22) are "backwards" instances of the more familiar Specified Subject Condition (Chomsky (1973)) type of effect illustrated in (23), where the ECM subject *the policemen* blocks binding of the reciprocal by the matrix subject *the defendants*. While in (21)/(22), the potential but blocked antecedent is in the embedded clause and the reciprocal in the matrix, in (23), the potential but blocked antecedent is in the matrix, with the reciprocal in the embedded clause; but in both cases, the ECM subject gets in the way.

(23)   The defendants$_i$ believed the policemen$_j$ to have assaulted each other$_{*i/j}$.

Turning to binominal *each*, relevant examples with 'ECM' objects are difficult to construct. However, if it should turn out that 'ECM' objects cannot antecede binominal *each* in a matrix adjunct, in contrast to ECM subjects (see (4a) above), it can again be argued that this does not undermine the main argument of this section, since it seems that the relation between binominal *each* and its antecedent is also subject to a locality constraint (as expected, if it obeys the same conditions as anaphors, as I assumed earlier (Burzio (1986))). Thus (24) can only have the interpretation 'the students proved each of the professors to know three formulas' (not 'each of the students proved the professors to know three formulas'.[7]

(24)   The students proved the professors to know three formulas each.

To sum up so far: in §3 we have seen that 'ECM' objects appear to c-command matrix VP-adjuncts: abstracting away from independent locality issues, their properties resemble those of ECM subjects, as shown by Principle C and NPI-licensing data. Given this, I argued that the movement approach proposed in relation to the ECM subject facts (Postal (1974), Lasnik & Saito (1991)) is inadequate, since it is incapable of extending to the similar non-subject facts.

4. An alternative account - some options

It is not simply that a raising account is inadequate for the unexpected binding/licensing facts: as long as the standard, biclausal, analysis of ECM constructions is maintained, then there is arguably no way of dealing with the problem in configurational terms at all.

Consider the alternative approach generally to moving unexpectedly c-commanding phrases to a higher position, i.e. positing a "novel" constituent structure such that the apparently c-commanded phrase is simply generated in an appropriately low position (Larson (1988), Pesetsky (1995)). A version of this method is used by Pesetsky (1995) to deal with some unexpected binding/licensing facts in monoclausal environments where, in some ways parallel to the contrast we have seen between DPs in ECM *to*-clauses and DPs in *that*-clauses, DPs inside PPs seem to c-command out (see Reinhart (1983)), in contrast

---

[7]   Although for some reason, getting the latter interpretation of (24) does not seem to me to be as difficult as construing (23) with *the defendants* as antecedent. And for some speakers, this interpretation of (24) is more or less possible.

to DPs inside other DPs, which do not (see (15), (20) above). The PP phenomenon is illustrated in (25), Pesetsky's cascade structure solution in (26):

(25)   a. *   I spoke to him$_i$ in Ben$_i$'s office.
      b.   Sue gave books to these people on each other's birthdays.
      c.   John spoke to Mary about no linguist in any conference room.

(26)

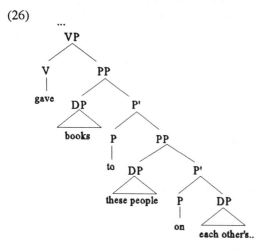

But unfortunately, as Lasnik (1996:7-8) points out in the process of promoting a raising approach to the properties of ECM subjects, a solution along these lines does not seem feasible for ECM constructions. This is what makes the 'ECM' object binding and NPI licensing data crucial: unlike the better-known ECM subject data, it is equally resistant to a raising approach.[8]

In this absence of any conventional means of getting the relevant phrases into the proper configurational relation to one another, the following options remain for explaining the unexpected binding facts: (i) say that ECM constructions have a different, flatter, structure to than is typically assumed; or (ii) take the binding facts "at face value" and assume that binding, NPI licensing etc. do not depend directly on c-command, a view that has sometimes been advocated for other reasons (see below).

The more conservative approach of these, i.e. that which is compatible with assuming as usual that the Binding Principles, NPI licensing and so forth are dependent on c-command, would be to analyse ECM constructions, though

---

[8]   A further and independent point against a raising approach - or at least, against an overt raising approach - is that it does not easily extend to the "object of preposition" cases; although it has been proposed that these DPs raise covertly to the Spec of an AGRP for some sort of checking purposes (Runner (1995)).

outwardly biclausal, as monoclausal at some syntactic level; that is, they involve, or by some process (cf. Rizzi (1982)) come to involve, a kind of verbal complex. Under such an analysis, it is possible that ECM subjects and 'ECM' objects would both move to Specifiers of functional projections above this verbal complex, placing them in a similar position to "matrix objects" in terms of c-command.

Although this is not exactly a standard view of ECM constructions as far as English is concerned, it is worth noting that such "restructuring" processes have been hypothesized in relation to various other languages where syntactic relations - scrambling, clitic movement - can unexpectedly hold cross-clausally in some environments.[9] In German, for instance, "long distance" scrambling from lower to higher clause, which is generally impossible, is allowed in constructions with certain matrix verbs, including ECM verbs. Consider the following example featuring the verb *sehen* 'see' which can appear in ECM-type constructions: (27a) is the version without scrambling. (27b) shows that long-distance scrambling is possible, but crucially, the scrambled item *sie* 'her' must be interpreted as the ECM subject, with *den Hans* the embedded object - i.e. (27b) is not a scrambled equivalent of (27a).[10]

(27) a. ... weil der Peter   den Hans   sie   schlagen sehen hat.
          ... since the Peter-NOM the Hans-ACC her-ACC hit   see has
          '...since Peter saw Hans hit her'

     b. ... weil sie der Peter den Hans schlagen sehen hat.

A non-subject of an infinitival complement in an ECM construction may undergo long-distance scrambling, if there is no overt ECM subject, as in (28) (from Wurmbrand (1997)). As in the example with *sehen* above, if there no overt ECM subject is present, then movement of the non-subject is blocked:

(28) a. ... weil der Peter   ihr   helfen lassen hat.
          ... since the Peter-NOM her-DAT help   let   has
          '...since Peter let somebody help her'

     b. ... weil ihr$_i$ der Peter t$_i$ helfen lassen hat.

(29) a. ... weil der Peter   den Hans   ihr   helfen lassen hat.
          ... since the Peter-NOM the Hans-ACC her-DAT help   let   has
          '...since Peter let Hans help her'

---

[9] See Grewendorf & Sabel (1994) for discussion of some theoretical problems associated with traditional restructuring analyses of this type of phenomenon.

[10] Thanks to Stefan Ploch for providing examples (27) and (29).

b. *   ... weil ihr$_i$ der Peter den Hans t $_i$ helfen lassen hat.

It is interesting that these movement facts bear a passing resemblance to the binding facts in ECM constructions: in both instances, embedded subjects can form an unexpected relation into the matrix clause; non-subjects also can, if no locality issue arises.

Finally let us consider the second of the approaches alluded to above: as opposed to manipulating the syntax, this would take the even less conventional path of assuming that binding does not directly involve configurational relations. Williams (1994) develops a framework in which "...the binding theory is less 'structural' and more based on 'argument of' relations, which have an imperfect relation to S-structure..." (p. 231). He claims separately (and nonstandardly, by Principles & Parameters standards) that there is a thematic difference between "equivalent" constructions with *to*-clause complements and *that*-clause complements. I will try to combine these two aspects of Williams's theory to give an account of the unexpected binding facts. Before coming to this, I will outline some basic notions of Williams's binding theory.

Williams takes binding to be a relation among theta-roles themselves, not among the phrases to which they are assigned, an assumption for which there is some independent evidence.[11] Along these lines, the usual binding principles A,B,C are reformulated in terms of *th(eta)-binding*, like binding except that c-command is replaced the relation of *th(eta)-command* which holds among theta-roles. Williams defines th-command as follows (1994, p.213), where two theta roles are *coarguments* if they are different arguments of the same predicate.

(30)   *th-command*
        For two theta roles X and Y, X *th-commands* Y if X is a coargument of
        Y; or, if X th-commands B, B is assigned to Z, and Z th-commands Y.

Hence, for example, Principle C will require that an R-expression (more accurately, the theta-role assigned to it) is not th-bound, that is, th-commanded by a theta role coindexed with it.

The important point is the second part of the definition, which allows an argument to bind elements inside one of its coarguments, but crucially not vice versa. This depends on taking theta role assignment to consist of assignment of the role to the external role of the "recipient", which connects the assigned theta role to *all* of the theta roles within the "recipient", in virtue of their own coargumenthood with the external role. The reverse does not hold, on the assumption that the assignment relation is asymmetric. In this way, a contrast like

---

[11]   Evidence for this comes from facts involving nominals, in which demonstrably unassigned θ-roles play a role in binding possibilities (see Williams (1994, p. 208)).

(31) is captured:[12]

(31) a.   Bob$_i$ saw [Joan's pictures of him$_i$].
      b. * He$_i$ saw [Joan's pictures of Bob$_i$].

Let us return to the problem: why do DPs within ECM *to*-clause complements manage to bind into the matrix clause, while DPs within a *that*-clause cannot? Some examples are repeated here involving Principle C contrasts:

(32) a. *? Joan believes [him$_i$ to be a genius] even more fervently than Bob$_i$'s mother does.
      b.   Joan believes [that he$_i$ is a genius] even more fervently than Bob$_i$'s mother does.

(33) a. *? Joan expects [the DA to acquit him$_i$] even more confidently than Bob$_i$ does.
      b.   Joan expects [that the DA will acquit him$_i$] even more fervently than Bob$_i$ does.

I will adopt the further proposal of Williams's that *to*-clauses in ECM constructions differ from *that*-clauses in their relation to the matrix verb: only *that*-clauses are *arguments,* in sense of being assigned a theta role. A *to*-clause complement is not licensed in an argument-of relation with V, but in virtue of a different relation, *function composition* (the verb and *to*-clause are said to be in a functor-complement relation). This relation "neither provides, nor uses up, theta roles" and as a result "is 'transparent' to theta relations" (1994, p.45).[13] Williams himself makes this assumption to allow for the possibility of passive in ECM constructions (*Bob was believed to be a genius*): a theta role of the embedded verb can "percolate" up to the higher V(P), if the latter loses its own role, and be assigned to the matrix subject.[14]

Under the function composition view, it seems reasonable to assume that effectively a single argument structure is involved in the ECM construction, meaning that arguments of the embedded verb also count as arguments of the higher verb. This would go some way to explaining why DPs in the *to*-clause behave like matrix objects (see (8) above). A question which remains to be

---

[12] This diverges from the standard binding theory in the case of arguments in subject position - see Williams (*op. cit.*, p.215).

[13] See Jacobson (1990) for a related proposal about what she calls "raising to object" constructions, motivated by different considerations, and within an entirely different framework.

[14] Williams assumes no NP-movement, so this method of passing up a role is necessary to deal with cases in which assigner and assignee are not in a local relation.

clarified is the relation between arguments and adjuncts with respect to binding.

Moving on to *that*-clauses, since these have the status of theta arguments, their behaviour with respect to binding of DPs within them may be assimilated to the case of nominal arguments discussed earlier. Binding of theta roles inside the *that*-clause by a coargument of the *that*-clause should be possible (*he_i believes that *Bob_i* is a genius) in virtue of theta role assignment (see (30) above),[15] but in the reverse direction, the *that*-clause will be opaque.

5. Summary

In this paper, I discussed the fact that non-subject DPs in the *to*-clause complement of ECM verbs act as if c-commanding matrix elements, as revealed by the existence of Principle C effects and the licensing of Negative Polarity Items. These properties of the non-subjects cannot be accommodated by the standard approach to the better-known but very similar behaviour of ECM subjects, which attributes this to the phrases raising into the matrix clause (for Case checking, in the recent analysis of Lasnik & Saito (1991)). I hypothesized two alternative approaches which would cover the properties of both subjects and non-subjects in ECM construction *to*-clauses. Obviously, further details and issues remain to be worked out with respect to each of these approaches. One possible drawback of the thematic approach is that it does not clearly extend to the NPI licensing facts, which if anything are more clearcut than the Principle C facts.

References

Burzio, Luigi. 1986. *Italian Syntax: a Government and Binding approach.* Dordrecht: Reidel.

Chomsky, Noam. 1973. Conditions on transformations, in S. Anderson and P. Kiparsky, eds., *A Festschrift for Morris Halle*, 232-286. New York: Holt, Rinehart and Winston.

Chomsky, Noam. 1986. *Knowledge of language: its nature, origin and use.* New York: Praeger.

Chomsky, Noam. 1995. *The Minimalist Program.* Cambridge, Mass.: MIT Press.

Chomsky, Noam and Howard Lasnik. 1993. Principles and Parameters theory, in J. Jacobs *et al*, eds. *Syntax: An international handbook of contemporary research*, 438-517. Berlin: de Gruyter.

---

[15] Although, unlike in the case of true nominal arguments, the "nominalizing" external role of the *that*-clause cannot be part of the embedded verb's argument structure (see Williams (*op. cit.*, p.35), and so strictly speaking should not be coargumental with the latter.

Emonds, Joseph. 1997 How clitics reveal the flat structure of complex verbs in Romance. Talk given at the Linguistics Department Seminar, SOAS.

Grewendorf, Günther and Joachim Sabel. 1994. Long Scrambling and Incorportion, in *Linguistic Inquiry* 25, 263-308.

Jacobson, Pauline. 1990. Raising as function composition. *Linguistics and Philosophy* 13:423-475.

Lasnik, Howard. 1993. Lectures on Minimalist Syntax. *University of Connecticut Working Papers in Linguistics: Occasional Papers Issue 1.*

Lasnik, Howard. 1996. Levels of representation and elements of anaphora. Ms, University of Connecticut.

Larson, Richard. 1988. On the double object construction, in *Linguistic Inquiry* 19:335-91.

Lasnik, Howard and Mamoru Saito. 1991. On the subject of infinitives. In L. Dobrin *et al*, eds., *Papers from the 27th Regional Meeting, Chicago Linguistic Society*, 324-343.

Pettiward, Anna. 1997. When does the English Object Shift, in S. Ploch and D. Swinburne, eds. *SOAS Working Papers in Linguistics* 7, 123-141.

Pesetsky, David. 1995. *Zero Syntax: Experiencers and Cascades*. Cambridge, Mass.: MIT Press.

Postal, Paul. 1974. *On Raising: one rule of English grammar and its theoretical implications*. Cambridge, Mass.: MIT Press.

Reinhart, Tanya. 1983. *Anaphora and Semantic Interpretation*. London: Croom Helm.

Rizzi, L. 1982. *Issues in Italian Syntax*. Dordrecht: Foris.

Runner, Jeffrey. 1995. Noun Phrase Licensing and Interpretation. PhD thesis, U.Mass.

Stowell, Tim and Ken Safir. 1988. Binominal *each*, in Proceedings of *NELS* 18, 426-450.

Williams, Edwin. 1994. *Thematic Structure in Syntax*. Cambridge, Mass.: MIT Press.

Wurmbrand, Susi. 1997. Deconstructing restructuring. Paper presented at the 3rd *Langues et Grammaire* conference, Université de Paris VIII.

In Defense of the T-Model

NORVIN RICHARDS

University of Massachusetts, Amherst

1. Introduction

There seem to be three main strategies for forming multiple-wh questions. In some languages, all wh-phrases undergo some type of wh-movement:

(1) *Bulgarian*

Kogo kakvo e   pital Ivan?

whom what AUX asked Ivan

'Who did Ivan ask what?'

We also find languages in which all wh-phrases remain in situ:

I am very grateful to Ani Petkova, Roumyana Slabakova, Kamen Stefanov, and especially Roumyana Izvorski for their help with Bulgarian facts; to Takako Aikawa, Shigeru Miyagawa, and Satoshi Oku for their help with Japanese; to Željko Bošković and Milan Mihaljević for their help with Serbo-Croatian; and to Lisa Cheng, Hooi Ling Soh, and Wei-Tien Dylan Tsai for their help with Chinese. I am also indebted to Željko Bošković, Noam Chomsky, Danny Fox, Paul Hagstrom, Kyle Johnson, Kiyomi Kusumoto, Idan Landau, Winnie Lechner, Martha McGinnis, Shigeru Miyagawa, Jon Nissenbaum, Junko Shimoyama, and especially David Pesetsky, as well as to the audiences at my Fall '97 Syntax Seminar at the University of Massachusetts, Amherst and at WCCFL 17, for helpful comments and encouragement. Responsibility for any remaining errors is mine alone.

(2)   *Japanese*

Taroo-ga   dare -ni   nani -o ageta no?

Taroo NOM who DAT what ACC gave Q

'Who did Taroo give what?'

Finally, there are languages in which these two strategies are mixed, with some wh-phrases moving and others staying in situ:

(3)   *English*

Who did John give t what?

A number of interesting questions now arise. For instance, what is the status of wh-phrases which have been left in situ? Should a movement relation be posited between such wh-phrases and their scopal positions? And if so, why does this movement relation have no visible effects?

There is one set of proposed answers to these questions, involving a model diagrammed in (4), which I will refer to here as the T-model (see Chomsky 1995 and much other work):

(4)

According to this model, syntactic structures are built up by the computational system, attaching a set of items from the lexicon to each other, eventually forming an LF. At some point in the course of the construction of the structure (referred to in recent work as SPELL-OUT), a representation is sent to the phonological component and pronounced, at PF. Movement may take place either before or after SPELL-OUT, but any movement which takes place after SPELL-OUT on the branch of the derivation which leads to LF will have no effect on the phonology, since they will not affect the representation which is sent to PF. Such movements will therefore be "covert".

This model has at least three properties which distinguish it from competing models which have been proposed, and which I will try to defend here. First, it is a derivational model; operations are described as occurring at times, and can precede or follow other operations in a derivation. Secondly, it is a model in which there is such a thing as a movement relation which cannot be seen; wh-in-situ in (2) and (3), for instance, is taken to undergo movement to a scopal position after SPELL-OUT. Thirdly, it is a model in which the difference between overt and covert movement is a syntactic one having to do with the timing of the operations; overt movements are ones which precede SPELL-OUT, while covert movements are ones which follow SPELL-OUT. All overt movements, then, precede all covert movements in the derivation.

All three of these claims about the computational system have been denied in recent work. Brody (1995) has claimed, for instance, that a representational approach to syntax is preferable to a derivational one. A number of recent works, including Cole and Hermon (1994) and Reinhart (1995), while still assuming the existence of a derivation, have denied that there is such a thing as covert movement; wh-in-situ, on this approach, is related to its scope position by a mechanism which is completely unlike movement. Finally, there is a class of approaches (including Bobaljik (1995), Groat and O'Neil (1996), and Pesetsky (1998)) which assume a derivation and a distinction between overt and covert movement, but deny that the difference between overt and covert movement is significant to the syntax. These approaches make crucial use of the Copy Theory of movement (cf. Chomsky 1993), and claim that overt movement involves pronunciation of the copy in a chain which is in the "landing site" of movement, while covert movement is pronunciation of the tail of the chain. On theories of this type, the distinction between overt and covert movement is purely a matter of phonology.

The T-model is unique among the models just discussed in that it can be seen as dividing the languages mentioned in (1-3) above into two groups on the basis of syntactic criteria. Languages of the Bulgarian type and languages of the Japanese type have something in common, to the exclusion of languages like English; they are the languages which do all wh-movement on a single cycle, either before or after SPELL-OUT. English, on the other hand, is unique in that it performs some wh-movement before SPELL-OUT and then some more wh-movement later in the derivation, after SPELL-OUT. None of the other models above have this property. In a purely representational model, there can be no division of languages into groups by their derivational properties. In a model in which there is no such thing as covert movement, Bulgarian and Japanese ought to have nothing at all in common, syntactically speaking; on such theories, these languages use completely different mechanisms for assigning scope to their wh-phrases. On the models in which overt and covert movement differ only phonologically, there should be no syntactic differences between the language types just described.

If we could discover properties of multiple-wh movement which were crucially sensitive to characteristics of the derivation, then, we might be in a position to choose among the models just outlined. If we find clearly syntactic phenomena having to do with wh-movement which discriminate between Bulgarian and Japanese on the one hand and English on the other, we will have an argument for the T-model. I will argue that such phenomena do in fact exist.

2. Preliminaries: Additional-wh Effects and the Derivation

In an approach which posits covert movement, the following well-known data are in need of explanation:

(5) *English*

    a. Which senator$_i$ t$_i$ denied [the rumor that he wanted to ban

           Under the Yoke] ?

    b.* Which book$_j$ did the senator deny [the rumor that he wanted to

           ban t$_j$]?

    c. Which senator$_i$ t$_i$ denied [the rumor that he wanted to ban

           which book$_j$]?

(5b) is ruled out by Subjacency, or its successor; wh-extraction out of a complex NP is banned. In (5c), covert wh-movement of *which book* will proceed out of the same island, just as overt wh-movement does in (5b), yet the resulting sentence is well-formed. A theory which posits covert movement, then, must explain why such movement is not subject to the same locality requirements as overt movement. One standard approach to this problem, following Huang (1982), has been to simply state that Subjacency constrains only overt movement, not covert movement. We might refer to this as a "levels approach"; on this approach, the relevant difference between (5b) and (5c) has to do with the level on which wh-movement takes place.

In Richards (1997, to appear a) I argued against the levels approach, claiming that in fact the relevant property of (5c) which distinguishes between it and (5b) is the presence of a second, Subjacency-obeying wh-movement (namely, that of *which senator*). I suggested that we might think of these data in terms of a "Subjacency tax"; Subjacency must be obeyed by one wh-phrase in a specifier of each interrogative C, but once one wh-phrase has "paid the Subjacency tax", Subjacency can be freely violated. In Richards (1997, to appear b) I developed a general theory of interactions between syntactic dependencies, claiming that phenomena of this type, in which a dependency which would be ill-formed in isolation is rendered well-formed by the presence of a well-formed dependency, are in fact pervasive in the grammar. I tried to formalize this property of the grammar as the *Principle of Minimal Compliance* (PMC); see Richards (1997, to appear b) for further discussion.

One argument in favor of a Subjacency tax approach, and against a levels approach, can be based on the fact that additional-wh effects like those in (5) can be found in languages in which the distribution of overt and covert movement is not the same as it is in English. Watanabe (1992) notes very similar facts from Japanese:

(6)   *Japanese* (Watanabe 1992)

a.   Taroo-wa [Hanako -ga kuruma -o   katta ka dooka]

Taroo TOP Hanako NOM   car   ACC bought whether

dare -ni   tazuneta no?

who DAT   asked Q

'Who did Taroo ask t [whether Hanako bought a car]?'

b.* Taroo-wa [Hanako -ga nani   -o   katta ka dooka]

Taroo TOP Hanako NOM what ACC bought whether

tazuneta no?

asked   Q

'What did Taroo ask [whether Hanako bought t]?'

c.   Taroo-wa [Hanako -ga   nani -o   katta ka dooka]

Taroo TOP Hanako NOM what ACC bought whether

dare -ni   tazuneta no?

who DAT asked   Q

'Who did Taroo ask t [whether Hanako bought what]?'

The data in (6) are structurally parallel to those in (5). All of these
examples involve an island. In the (a) examples, extraction takes place from
a position which is not inside the island, and the sentences are therefore
well-formed. In the (b) examples, extraction is from inside the island, and is
therefore ruled out. The (c) examples involve multiple-wh extraction, from
positions both inside and outside the island, and the result is well-formed.
On a Subjacency tax approach, this is an expected result; a well-formed
move can redeem a move which would be ill-formed in isolation, regardless
of whether the moves are overt or covert. On an approach which makes
crucial reference to the distinction between overt and covert movement, on
the other hand, the Japanese data are surprising; since all Japanese wh-
movement is covert, there is no reason for Japanese to behave like English
in this regard.

Similar data are to be found in Bulgarian, a language in which all wh-
movement is overt:

(7)   *Bulgarian* (Roumyana Izvorski, Ani Petkova, Roumyana
        Slabakova, p.c.)

  a.   Koj   senator$_i$ t$_i$ otreče

        which senator   denied

                [mălvata   če   iska da zabrani *Pod   Igotom*]?

                the-rumor that he-wanted to ban   under the yoke

        'Which senator t denied

                [the rumor that he wanted to ban *Under the Yoke*]?'

  b.*   Koja   kniga$_j$ otreče senatorăt

        which book   denied the-senator

                [mălvata če   iska   da zabrani t$_j$]?

                the-rumor that he-wanted to ban

        'Which book did the senator deny

                [the rumor that he wanted to ban t]?'

  c.   Koj   senator$_i$ koja kniga$_j$ t$_i$ otreče

        which senator which book   denied

                [mălvata če   iska   da zabrani t$_j$]?

                the-rumor that he-wanted to ban

        'Which senator denied

                [the rumor that he wanted to ban which book]?

The data in (7) are translations of the English data in (5), and the judgments
are the same, even though all the movements are overt. Again, the facts
seem to favor an approach to these phenomena which makes no reference to
the distinction between overt and covert movement. It seems to be the case
quite generally that a well-formed move can improve the status of a move
which would be ill-formed in isolation, regardless of whether the moves in
question are overt or covert.

     Investigating this kind of interaction between wh-dependencies further,
we discover that this effect makes crucial reference to properties of the
derivation. For a well-formed move to "pay the Subjacency Tax", thus
licensing a Subjacency-violating move, the well-formed move must precede
the ill-formed move in the derivation. This is shown by the data in (8):

(8)   a.   Which senator t said that [the rumor that he wanted to

            ban which book] had been spread by Communists?

       b.* Which book did the senator say that [the rumor that he wanted to

            ban t] had been spread by whom?

(8a) is another Subjacency Tax example; movement of *which senator* has
"paid the Subjacency Tax", licensing subsequent extraction of *which book*
out of an island. (8b) is an attempt to do the same thing in reverse. *Which
book* moves overtly out of an island, and well-formed movement of *whom*
will subsequently take place in the covert component. The ill-formedness of
(8b) shows that this has no effect; Subjacency Tax effects obtain only when
a well-formed move precedes the ill-formed move it is to redeem.
Subjacency Taxes apparently cannot be paid retroactively.

   Consider the Bulgarian Subjacency Tax example above in (7c), repeated
here as (9):

(9)   *Bulgarian* (Roumyana Izvorski, Ani Petkova, Roumyana
              Slabakova, p.c.)

       Koj   senator$_i$ koja kniga$_j$ t$_i$ otreče

       which senator which book   denied

            [mălvata   če   iska   da zabrani t$_j$]?

       the-rumor that he-wanted to ban

       'Which senator denied [the rumor that he wanted to ban which book]?

In this example, the well-formed move is that of *koj senator* 'which senator',
and the presence of this well-formed move licenses extraction of *koju kniga*
'which book' out of an island. We have just seen that this kind of
interaction between well-formed and ill-formed dependencies is only possible
if the well-formed dependency precedes the ill-formed dependency in the
derivation. We are led to the conclusion, then, that movement of *koj
senator* precedes movement of *koja kniga* in the derivation; more generally,
that derivations involving multiple wh-movement proceed as follows:

(10) a.. CP

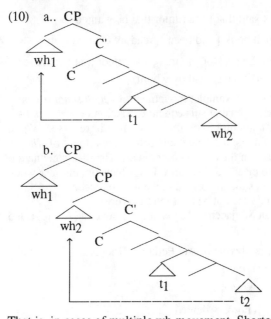

That is, in cases of multiple wh-movement, Shortest Attract forces movement of the highest wh-phrase first (as in (10a) above). When the second wh-phrase is attracted, it "tucks in" to a specifier below the existing specifier (as in (10b)). The relative c-command relations (and, in principle, the relative order) of the moved elements are thus preserved. See Richards (1997, to appear b) for some further discussion of this phenomenon. In what follows I will assume the derivation in (10) for multiple wh-movement. Of course, the parts of this derivation may occur at different times. In Bulgarian, both (10a) and (10b) occur in the overt syntax, while in English, only (10a) is overt, and in Japanese both movements are covert.

3. Arguing for the T-Model: The Path Containment Condition

English wh-movement, as has frequently been noted, is subject to Pesetsky's (1982) Path Containment Condition; informally, wh-movement paths which intersect must nest, rather than cross:

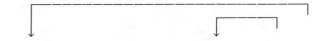

(11) a. Which violins are you wondering which sonatas to play t on t?

b.* Which sonatas are you wondering which violins to play t on t?

In languages like Bulgarian and Serbo-Croatian, in which all wh-movement is overt, and also in languages like Japanese and Chinese, in which all wh-movement is covert, the preference is the opposite; wh-movement paths which intersect must cross, rather than nest[1]:

(12) *Bulgarian* (Roumyana Izvorski, Roumyana Slabakova, Ani Petkova, Kamen Stefanov, p.c.)

    a. Koj se   opitvat da razberat kogo t   e   ubil   t ?
       who SELF   try to find-out who   AUX killed
    'Who$_i$ are they trying to find out whom$_j$ t$_i$ killed t$_j$?'

    b.*Kogo se   opitvat da razberat koj t   e   ubil   t?
       who SELF   try to find-out who   AUX killed
    'Whom$_j$ are they trying to find out who$_i$ t$_i$ killed t$_j$?'

(13) *Serbo-Croatian* (Željko Bošković, Milan Mihaljević, p.c.)

    a. Ko   si me pitao šta t može da uradi t?
       who AUX me asked what can   do
    'Who$_i$ did you ask me what$_j$ t$_i$ can do t$_j$?'

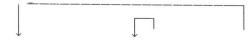

    b.* Sta   si me pitao ko t može da uradi   t ?
       what AUX me asked who can   do
    'What$_j$ did you ask me who$_i$ t$_i$ can do t$_j$?'

---

1 A caveat is in order here. There are speakers of these languages for whom crossing and nested paths are equally grammatical, or ungrammatical (and there seem to be cross-linguistic differences in the distribution of such reactions; see Richards 1997 for some discussion). The preference described above holds for all speakers that I have talked to who express a preference. The judgments indicated here are intended to be contrastive.

(14)   *Japanese* (Takako Aikawa, Shigeru Miyagawa, Satoshi Oku, p.c.; cf.
       also Nishigauchi (1990, 33), Saito (1994, 198))

Keesatu-wa [dare -ga   dare   -o korosita ka] sirabeteiru   no?

police   TOP who NOM who ACC   killed   Q   investigate Q

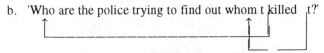

a.* 'Whom are the police trying to find out who t killed t?'

b.   'Who are the police trying to find out whom t killed   t?'

(15)   *Chinese* (Lisa Cheng, Hooi Ling Soh, Wei-tien Dylan Tsai, p.c.)

Jingcha xiang-zhidao [shei sha   -le   shei]?

police   want   know   who kill PERF who

a.* 'Whom are the police trying to find out who t killed t?'

b.   'Who are the police trying to find out whom t killed   t?'

Here we appear to have a phenomenon which sorts languages as the T-model
predicts they should be sorted; languages like English, which do some wh-
movement overtly and some covertly, exhibit Path Containment Condition
effects, while languages which do all wh-movement on a single cycle
exhibit anti-PCC effects. Let us consider how the distribution of PCC
effects may be explained using the T-model.

3.1   English: PCC

Kitahara (1997) notes that the effects of the PCC in English may be derived
from fairly general principles of the Minimalist Program. In the first step
of the derivation, after the tree is built from the bottom up until the lower
of the two interrogative complementizers is reached, the strong wh-feature
on C forces wh-movement. Shortest Attract requires that it be the higher of
the two wh-phrases which moves:

(16) CP

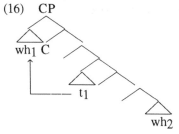

Construction of the tree then continues until the higher C is reached. The higher C must attract a wh-phrase. Shortest Attract would prefer that *wh₁* be attracted again, as this is still the higher of the two wh-phrases. This is not what happens, however; *wh₂* is attracted:

(17) CP

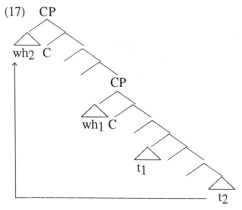

Apparently there is some principle which overrides Shortest Attract in this case, forcing attraction of the lower wh-phrase. The principle in (18) would have this effect:

(18) **No Orphaned C**

An interrogative C may not be deprived of its only specifier at any point in the derivation.

(18) will prevent attraction of *wh₁* at the stage of the derivation in (17).

We have seen how the English facts can be made to follow from fairly straightforward assumptions. In the next section I will show that these assumptions account for the distribution of anti-PCC effects as well.

3.2 Bulgarian, Japanese: Anti-PCC

Let us now consider the relevant derivation in languages like Bulgarian and Japanese, which perform all wh-movement on a single cycle. First, as in English, the tree is built up until the lower C is reached; in the next step, both wh-phrases are attracted to specifiers of C. As we saw in section 2, the paths of wh-movement to multiple specifiers must always cross:

(19)

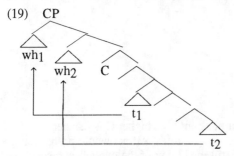

Construction of the tree continues until the higher interrogative C is introduced, and the higher C attracts a wh-phrase. As in English, Shortest Attract prefers that *wh₁*, the higher of the two wh-phrases, undergo movement at this point. In the derivation under consideration here, the lower CP has multiple specifiers by the time the higher C is introduced into the structure. As a result, Shortest Attract can be satisfied perfectly; there is no danger of "orphaning" the lower interrogative C by removing its only specifier. Shortest Attract therefore forces attraction of *wh₁*:

(20)

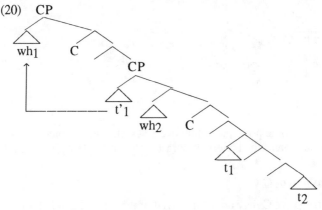

Thus, we derive the desired result; in a language in which all wh-movement is on a single level, intersecting wh-paths will preferentially cross, preserving the base c-command relations between the moving wh-phrases[2].

---

[2] In fact, this result could have been derived without crucial reference to the notion of building the tree from the bottom up. Perfect obedience to Shortest Attract will always involve derivations in which the c-command relation between the wh-phrases is maximally preserved; we have seen that there is one such derivation available in this class of languages (which is unavailable in English), so these languages will always prefer to preserve relative c-command relations between wh-phrases. On the assumption that in cases of multiple covert movement (e.g., in Japanese), the tree has been entirely built up by the

3.3 Postlude: the Role of Shortest Attract

The account just sketched of the distribution of PCC and anti-PCC effects claims that in a language like English, a ban on removing the only wh-phrase in the specifier of an interrogative C forces a violation of Shortest Attract, causing inversion of the c-command relations between wh-phrases; in other words, intersecting wh-movement paths must nest. In languages which perform all movement on a single level, on the other hand, Shortest Attract may be obeyed perfectly. Each attracting C can always attract the highest available mover, and as a result the wh-phrase which is highest at the beginning of the derivation is still the highest at the end. Anti-PCC effects, in other words, are a result of perfect obedience to Shortest Attract.

In fact, there is some additional evidence that Shortest Attract should play this role. Under certain circumstances, Shortest Attract may be violated freely, and under exactly these circumstances the anti-PCC effect in languages like Bulgarian and Chinese disappears.

Bošković (1995) discovers that the rigid ordering which typically holds between multiple wh-phrases in Bulgarian breaks down between the second and third of three fronted wh-phrases:

(21)   *Bulgarian* (Bošković (1995, 13-14))

    a.   Kogo$_j$ kakvo$_k$ e   pital Ivan t$_j$ t$_k$?

    whom what AUX asked Ivan

    'Whom did Ivan ask what?'

    b.* Kakvo$_k$ kogo$_j$ e pital Ivan t$_j$ t$_k$?

(22)   a.   Koj$_i$ kogo$_j$ kakvo$_k$ e   pital t$_i$ t$_j$ t$_k$?

    who whom what   AUX asked

    'Who asked whom what?'

    b.   Koj$_i$ kakvo$_k$ kogo$_j$ e pital t$_i$ t$_j$ t$_k$?

In Richards (1997) I attempt to relate this fact to the Subjacency Tax facts discussed in section 2 above; just as a Subjacency-obeying wh-movement may license subsequent Subjacency-violating wh-movement, a wh-movement which obeys Shortest Attract can allow subsequent violations of Shortest Attract. In (22), then, once the interrogative C has attracted *koj* 'who' first, it is free to attract the remaining wh-words in either order, either obeying Shortest Attract, as in (22a), or violating it, as in (22b), by attracting the lowest wh-phrase second.

Recall that anti-PCC effects, on the account given above, are taken to be a consequence of Shortest Attract, which can be obeyed perfectly in languages which perform all wh-movement on a single level. We have now

---

time wh-movement begins to occur, it is important that tree-construction play no important role in making this derivation the preferred one.

seen that the presence of a Shortest Attract-obeying wh-movement can "turn off" Shortest Attract, permitting Shortest Attract-violating movements to specifiers of the C which has hosted a well-formed wh-movement. We expect to find, then, that anti-PCC effects can be made to vanish by the presence of a well-formed wh-movement to the higher C. This expectation is borne out in Bulgarian and Chinese; nested paths, which are typically ruled out, are permitted just when a third wh-phrase has moved to the higher of the two Cs, licensing subsequent violation of Shortest Attract:

(23)   *Bulgarian* (Roumyana Izvorski, p.c.)

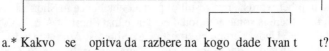

a.* Kakvo se   opitva da razbere na kogo dade Ivan t   t?
      what SELF   try to find-out to whom gave Ivan

   'What is he trying to find out to whom Ivan gave?'

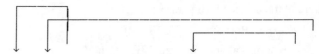

b. Koj kakvo t se opitva da razbere na kogo   dade Ivan t   t?
    who what   SELF try to find-out to whom gave Ivan

   'Who is trying to find out to whom Ivan gave what?'

(24)   *Chinese* (Lisa Cheng, Hooi Ling Soh, Wei-tien Dylan Tsai, p.c.)

a. Jingcha xiang-zhidao shei sha -le   shei?
    police want know who kill PERF who

   *'Who do the police want to know who t killed   t?'

b. Shei xiang-zhidao shei sha   -le   shei?
    who want know   who kill PERF who

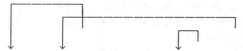

   'Who   who t wants to know who t killed t?'

4. Conclusion

In investigating interactions between wh-dependencies, we discover syntactic phenomena which group languages like Bulgarian (in which all wh-movement is overt) and languages like Japanese (in which all wh-movement is covert) together, to the exclusion of languages like English (in which some wh-movement is overt and the rest covert). In this paper I have discussed one such phenomenon, having to do with the cross-linguistic distribution of PCC and anti-PCC effects; I discuss this issue further in Richards (1997). The T-model is the one model which naturally groups languages syntactically in this way; in the other models discussed above, the effects considered here look suspiciously coincidental.

References

Bobaljik, Jonathan. 1995. *Morphysyntax: The Syntax of Verbal Inflection.* Doctoral dissertation, MIT.

Bošković, Željko. 1995. On Certain Violations of the Superiority Condition, AgrO, and Economy of Derivation. ms., University of Connecticut.

Brody, Michael. 1995. *Lexico-logical Form: a Radically Minimalist Theory.* Cambridge, Mass.: MIT Press.

Chomsky, Noam. 1995. *The Minimalist Program.* Cambridge, Mass.: MIT Press.

Cole, Peter, and Gabriella Hermon. 1994. Is There LF Wh-Movement? *Linguistic Inquiry* 25.239-262.

Groat, Erich, and John O'Neil. 1996. Spell-out at the LF Interface, in W. Abraham, et al., eds., *Minimal Ideas.* Amsterdam: John Benjamins.

Kitahara, Hisatsugu. 1997. *Elementary Operations and Optimal Derivations.* Cambridge, Mass.: MIT Press.

Nishigauchi, Taisuke. 1990. *Quantification and the Theory of Grammar.* Dordrecht: Kluwer.

Pesetsky, David. 1982. Paths and Categories. Doctoral dissertation, MIT.

Pesetsky, David. 1998. Some Optimality Principles of Sentence Pronunciation, in P. Barbosa, et al, eds., *Is The Best Good Enough?* Cambridge, Mass.: MIT Working Papers in Linguistics and MIT Press.

Reinhart, Tanya. 1995. Interface Strategies. Utrecht: OTS Working Papers.

Richards, Norvin. 1997. *What Moves Where When in Which Language?* Doctoral dissertation, MIT.

Richards, Norvin. To appear a. The Principle of Minimal Compliance. *Linguistic Inquiry* 25.4.

Richards, Norvin. To appear b. Shortest Moves to (Anti-)Superiority. *Proceedings of WCCFL 16.*

Saito, Mamoru. 1994. Additional-wh Effects and the Adjunction Site Theory. *Journal of East Asian Linguistics* 3.195-240.

Watanabe, Akira. 1992. Subjacency and S-structure Movement of Wh-in-situ. *Journal of East Asian Linguistics* 1.255-291.

Scope Reconstruction without Reconstruction*

ULI SAUERLAND

Massachusetts Institute of Technology

1. Introduction

This paper argues for a new analysis of so called ·'reconstruction' phenomena in A-chains. I propose that A-movement can take place in the PF-branch of the derivation and therefore be not noticed at the LF-interface. The argument for this proposal is based on the unavailability of reconstruction when the A-moved element doesn't c-command its trace in the overt form as first observed by Barss (1986). As I show, only the PF-movement analysis straightforwardly predicts this restriction on reconstruction.

Let me begin with a terminological convention. Since the term *reconstruction* presupposes a particular analysis of these phenomena, I use the term *narrow interpretation* instead of the term *reconstruction* in this paper. Hence, I speak of a narrow interpretation whenever a moved phrase seems to take scope lower or is bound lower than its overt position.[1]

In the remainder of the introduction, I summarize the evidence that

---

* Versions of this paper were presented in the MIT LingLunch series (September 1997), the LF reading group at MIT (October 1997), at the NELS 28 poster session at the University of Toronto (October 1997), and at WCCFL 17 at the University of British Columbia (February 1998). I would like to thank all the participants of these events for their comments. In addition, personal discussions of this material with Jonathan Bobaljik, Noam Chomsky, Danny Fox, Paul Hagstrom, Irene Heim, Kyle Johnson, Julie Legate, Jon Nissenbaum, David Pesetsky, Dominique Sportiche, Susi Wurmbrand, and Kazuko Yatsushiro helped me bring it into its current form. All remaining errors are of course my own. For lack of time, this version of the paper is identical to the one in the Proceedings of NELS 28.

[1] I'm largely concerned with A-chains, where the same position of the chains matters for scope and binding (cf. Fox (1997)). In section 4, I address A-bar chains.

narrow interpretations do occur in A-chains. May (1977) first noticed narrow interpretations in A-chains looking at quantifier scope. He observed that in raising constructions the raised subject is scopally ambiguous with respect to a scope bearing element that intervenes between the trace of the raised subject and its overt position. This is illustrated by the examples (1a) and (2a), where the two different readings are paraphrased in b. and c. In (1a), the wide scope reading (paraphrase (1b)) is salient because our world knowledge about skiing competitions at the olympic games tells us that the possibility of there being two gold medal winners in one competition is vanishingly small. In (2a), on the other hand, the narrow scope reading paraphrased in (2c) is the only one compatible with our world knowledge that, in a lottery, it's never the case that a particular individual has more than a very small chance of winning.

(1)   a.   [Two Germans]$_x$ are likely to t_x win the Gold Medal in this skiing race.

        b.   Two Germans have a good chance of winning. (two $\gg$ likely)

        c.   #There is a good chance that two Germans will win. (likely $\gg$ two)

(2)   a.   [Two people from New York]$_x$ are likely to t_x win the lottery next weekend.

        b.   #Two New Yorkers have a good chance of winning. (two $\gg$ likely)

        c.   There is a good chance that two New Yorkers will win. (likely $\gg$ two)

May's (1977) scope argument for the narrow interpretation of A-chains has never been given an alternative analysis.[2] Nevertheless, the existence of the narrow interpretation has sometimes been disputed in the literature (e.g. Chomsky (1993), Chomsky (1995)). For this reason and also because these tests will be useful later on, let me summarize two tests for the presence of a narrow interpretation in A-chains which rely on grammaticality judgements.

The first of these tests uses negative polarity licensing in addition to Scope as a test for the narrow interpretation (Linebarger (1980), (1987)). As is well known, a negative polarity item (henceforth NPI) must be c-commanded by negation or a downward entailing operator. What Linebarger shows is that the narrow interpretation of an A-chain can feed NPI-licensing. This is illustrated in (3). Neither in (3a) nor in (3b) does the negation c-command the NPI *anything* in the overt form. Nevertheless, the NPI in (3a) can be licensed and the NPI-licensing seems to force a scopal construal where negation takes

---

[2] It is quite clear that the suggestion that the scope bearing predicate *likely* can raise above the subject in (2) cannot be maintained, because the narrow interpretation is blocked if the subject binds a variable, which is higher than scope bearing predicate:

(i)   [Two men]$_x$ seem to themselves t_x to be likely to t_x win. (two $\gg$ likely, *likely $\gg$ two)

scope over the subject. Given that there is an A-trace of the subject below negation, it seems reasonable to assume that the narrow interpretation of the subject A-chain feeds NPI-licensing in (3a).

(3)   a.   [A doctor who knows anything about acupuncture]$_x$ isn't t_x available.

       b.   *[A doctor who knows anything about acupuncture]$_x$ i · t_x available.

In raising constructions as well, the narrow scope interpretation can feed NPI-licensing. This is illustrated in (4a), which contrast with example (4b), where there's no negation c-commanding the A-trace, as well as with (4c), where negation is present, but the A-trace is not c-commanded by it.

(4)   a.   [A doctor with any reputation]$_x$ is likely not to be t_x available.

       b.   *[A doctor with any reputation]$_x$ is likely to be t_x available.

       c.   *[A doctor with any reputation]$_x$ is t_x anxious for John not to be available.

A second test for the availability of a narrow scope interpretation using grammaticality was discovered by Burzio (1986).[3] It uses binomial *each* as test. The contrast between (5a) and (5b) shows that normally binomial *each* must be c-commanded by a distributive noun phrase in the overt form.

(5)   a.   The athletes demanded one translator each.

       b.   *One translator each welcomed the athletes.

As Burzio notes, there's one exception to this generalization which is illustrated in (6): Binomial *each* attached to the direct object can be licensed by a distributive *to*-phrase and, as Safir and Stowell (1987) point out certain other prepositional phrases.[4]

(6)   The Olympic Committee assigned one translator each to the athletes.

For our purposes, Burzio's most important observation is that the narrow interpretation in an A-chain can feed *each*-licensing in the pre-PP position before a prepositional phrase. This is shown in (7) for A-movement in passives, and in (8) for two-step A-movement, one step being movement to the subject position of a passive and the second step being movement to the subject position of a raising construction.

(7)   a.   [One translator each]$_x$ was assigned t_x to the athletes.

---

[3] Richard Kayne (p.c.) first drew my attention to Burzio's work.

[4] As David Pesetsky (p.c.) pointed out to me, licensing of direct object binomial *each* by the following PP might itself involve a narrow interpretation of an A-chain, assuming the direct object moved from a position below the goal-PP to its surface position. See Pesetsky (1994:221) for corroborating data.

b. *[One translator each] gave a speech to the athletes.

(8) a. [One translator each]$_x$ is likely to t_x be assigned t_x to the athletes.

b. *[One translator each]$_x$ is likely to t_x give a speech to the athletes.

The existence of a narrow interpretation in A-chains being established, consider the proposals that have been made to derive the narrow scope interpretation. The three proposals I know of are LF-lowering (May (1977), (1985), Chomsky (1995)), the Copy Theory of movement (Burzio (1986), Chomsky (1993), Hornstein (1995)) and Semantic Reconstruction (Cresti (1995), Rullmann (1995), Chierchia (1995)). I don't have room to summarize these proposals here in detail—in a nutshell, LF-lowering assumes that covert movement doesn't have to be to a c-commanding position in the tree and thereby can undo the effect of overt raising. The Copy Theory of movement assumes instead that a full copy of the moved phrase is left in the trace position and the interpretive component of grammar can look at this lower copy rather than the higher one. Semantic Reconstruction, finally, assumes that the semantics of an A-chain dependency can optionally be of a higher semantic type, which leads to a narrow interpretation. All three proposals have in common that they assume that overt A-movement is followed by an invisible undoing operation as the traditional term 'scope reconstruction' for the narrow interpretation suggests. I, as already mentioned, believe that the term 'reconstruction' is misleading and propose that no undoing of movement is necessary. Rather, I propose that A-movement in the cases of a narrow interpretation, is not seen by the interpretive component of grammar because it takes place in the PF-branch of grammar.

The remainder of the paper has the following structure: In the following section, I lay out the PF-movement proposal for the explanation of scope reconstruction phenomena. I then show that this proposal makes an interesting prediction, which I'll call the Scope Freezing Generalization. I go on to show, that this generalization is true building on work of Barss (1986). In section 4, I then address the question in what way A-bar movement differs from A-movement. In my conclusions, I show that none of the other approaches to narrow interpretations in A-chains can predict the Scope Freezing Generalization without additional stipulations.

2. PF-movement Account of Scope Reconstruction Phenomena

The question that needs to be answered by any account of narrow interpretation phenomena in A-chains is the following: What is the derivation of the PF-LF-pair in (9)?[5]

(9) PF: Two people are likely to   win the lottery.

LF: are likely to two people win the lottery.

---

[5] The PF-representations here and in the following are given in the form before real phonology has applied.

My answer to this question relies on the T-model of grammar (also sometimes called the Y-model or inverted Y-model) of Chomsky and Lasnik (1977), which I assume here in the form given in Chomsky (1995). The T-model embodies three partially interrelated assumptions: One, it assumes that complex representations are built up and modified by simple operations, generalized transformations, which are inherently ordered. Two, it assumes that operations can apply either having an effect on both LF and PF, or their effect can be limited to only LF, or only to PF. Three, there is a link between the ordering of operations and where they have an effect: namely the operations that are visible only to one of LF or PF follow operations that are visible to both. All three assumptions together have the consequence that LF-PF pairs are derived by a partially ordered set of transformations that has the graphical shape shown in (10).[6]

(10)   T-model (Chomsky and Lasnik 1977)

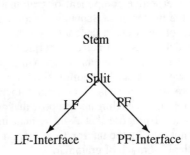

For the moment assumption two of the T-model, that an operation can have an effect at only one of the interfaces if it applies in one of the branches, is what we need. This allows us to analyze LF-PF mismatches as operations that apply in one of the branches. It seems natural to propose that (9) is derived by PF-movement of *two people* from the embedded subject position. This is the derivation I propose generally derives narrow interpretations in A-chains. In other words, I propose that A-movement in general can optionally take place in the PF-branch of the derivation, instead of taking place in the stem. For an illustration, consider (11).

(11)   [Two people]$_x$ are likely to t_x win the lottery.

The proposal is that (11) has two possible derivations. In one derivation raising of *two people* takes place in the stem and therefore the result of raising

---

[6]The T-model incorporates an additional assumption, namely that operations which take more than one simple representation as input (in Chomsky (1995) the only operation of this type is Merge) must have an effect at both LF and PF, if the inputs each contain both semantic and phonetic information. This assumption ensures that there is exactly one Split point in the derivation of one LF-PF pair and that the branch segments of any derivation are totally ordered. This assumption, however, is not important for anything I'll say in the following.

is visible to both LF and PF. This derivation therefore gives rise to wide scope of *two people* over *likely*. Crucially, I assume that there's no way raising in the stem can be covertly undone. So, this derivation yields only the wide scope interpretation. The second derivation is one where raising of *two people* is takes place at PF, and its application is visible only to PF, but not to LF. This derivation leads to a narrow scope interpretation of *two people* below *likely*, because raising is not seen by the LF-interface.[7]

One immediate ramification the PF-movement proposal makes concerns the level at which it is verified that obligatory movements have indeed taken place. The PF-movement approach is incompatible with the view taken by e.g. Chomsky (1995) that this verification takes place at LF. Rather, PF must be the level where the verification takes place. At least, the morphological requirement that triggers raising in (11)—the EPP-feature if current work on the topic is to be believed—must be checked at PF. This consequence however, as far as I can see, doesn't cause any new problems; on the contrary, it now follows that the EPP must universally be satisfied overtly (cf. Chomsky (1995)).

3. Prediction: Frozen Scope

In this section, I show that the PF-movement approach predicts a generalization Barss (1986) first hinted at regarding the availability of narrow interpretations, and then argue that the generalization is indeed true. This generalization is the following Scope Freezing Generalization (SFG).

(12)   *SFG:* A moved quantifier QP cannot be interpreted in an A-trace position, if the trace isn't c-commanded by the overt position of QP.

The SFG blocks a narrow interpretation in cases where the trace left by A-movement is inside a constituent that subsequently undergoes movement itself. One such case is example (13) from Barss (1986), who based solely on (13) suggests an analysis that would account for the SFG. In the next subsection, I present additional evidence for the SFG, and section 5 addresses Barss's account of the SFG.

(13)   [How likely to t_{QP} address every rally]$_{wh}$ is [some politician]$_{QP}$ t_{wh}?
        (some≫likely, *likely≫some)

The SFG is a consequence of the PF-movement analysis of narrow scope phenomena in conjunction with the three assumptions in (14). Each of these additional assumptions is independently motivated. I show that assumption (14a), that *wh*-movement and other types of A-bar movement take place in the stem, follows from the nature of A-bar movement in section 4. The c-command condition on movement in (14b) could follow from a better

---

[7] It is technically conceivable that in a derivation where raising is delayed until PF, quantifier raising applies in the LF-branch to bring about the wide scope interpretation. I don't have any evidence bearing on this possibility.

understanding of movement as discussed by Chomsky (1995). I also discuss this assumption in section 5 in the context of a quantifier lowering analysis. Of the T-architecture, I will make use of the order it imposes on the operations in a derivation; specifically, that movement in the PF-branch takes place after movement in the stem.

(14)   a.   A-bar movement must take place in the stem.

       b.   c-command: Movement must target a position that c-commands the moving item. (Chomsky 1995)

       c.   T-architecture: PF-movement must take place later than stem movement. (Chomsky and Lasnik 1977)

Consider now the derivations of a structure like (13) that would lead to narrow and wide scope respectively. First, look at a potential derivation for narrow scope in (15). For narrow scope, raising must be delayed until PF. But, *wh*-movement must take place in the stem by assumption (14a). Assuming the T-model, the derivation in (15) is forced. It violates either the EPP or the c-command condition on movement.

(15)   Failing Derivation for Narrow Scope

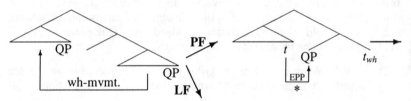

For wide scope, on the other hand, EPP-raising takes place in the stem, and can therefore precede *wh*-movement, as shown in (16). As the derivation in (16) shows, the EPP can be satisfied without incurring a violation of the c-command condition.

(16)   Derivation for Wide Scope

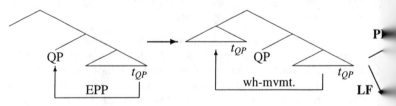

We see that the SFG is a consequence of the PF-movement approach to narrow scope phenomena. In the next subsection, I try to show that the SFG is also true.

3.1. More Evidence for Scope Freezing

Barss (1986) presents only the one example I repeated in (12) above in support of the SFG. In this section, I show that the SFG is a true generalization. The kind of constructions that are relevant to testing the SFG are ones where subsequent A-bar movement destroys the c-command relationship between an A-moved phrase and its trace, as it happened in (12). Example (17a) shows that such a stranded A-moved phrase is capable of taking scope below a c-commanding quantifier. (17b) shows that the stranded phrase can also take scope below a c-commanding *likely*. Therefore, the lack of narrow scope of the stranded phrase in (12) and the examples in the following must be due to the lack of c-command.

(17)   a.   [Every journalist]$_\forall$ asked [how likely to t_3 address every rally]$_{wh}$ [some politician]$_\exists$ is t_{wh}. ($\forall \gg \exists$, $\exists \gg \forall$)

   b.   John is **likely**$_1$ to find out [how likely$_2$ to t_3 address every rally]$_{wh}$ [some politician]$_\exists$ is t_{wh}. (likely$_1$ $\gg$ $\exists$, $\exists \gg$ likely$_1$)

The judgement in Barss's (1986) example can be sharpened by using *each*-licensing (see section **??**) as a test. As we see in (18), Barss's judgement now shows up as a grammaticality contrast: (18a) shows again that the narrow interpretation can feed *each* licensing. In (18b), where the SFG correctly blocks the narrow interpretation, *each* cannot be licensed. (18c), on the other hand, without *each* is grammatical, but it only has the reading with scope of *one* over *likely*.

(18)   a.   [One translator each]$_{QP}$ is likely to be assigned t_{QP} to the athletes.

   b.   *[How likely to be assigned t_{QP} to the athletes]$_{wh}$ is [one translator each]$_{QP}$ t_{wh}?

   c.   [How likely to be assigned t_{QP} to the athletes]$_{wh}$ is [one translator]$_{QP}$ t_{wh}?

In (12) and (18) it was *wh*-movement that destroyed the c-command relationship between the A-moved QP and its trace. The contrasts in (19) and (20) show that other types of A-bar movement, namely topicalization in (19) and *though*-raising in (20), have the same effect.[8]

(19)   a.   *... and [likely to be assigned t_{QP} to the athletes]$_{top}$ [one translator each]$_{QP}$ is t_{top}.

   b.   ... and [likely to be assigned t_{QP} to the athletes]$_{top}$ [one translator]$_{QP}$ is t_{top}.

---

[8]Examples of VP-fronting like (19) are best if they are preceded by the same sentence with a non-fronted VP as in (i). The dots preceding all examples of VP-topicalization serve as a reminder to look at them in such a context.

(i)   Martin said that one translator (each) is likely to be assigned to the athletes and, likely to be assigned to the athletes, one translator (*each) is.

(20)   a.   *[Likely to be assigned t_{QP} to the athletes]$_{tr}$ though [one translator each]$_{QP}$ is t_{tr}, there were still complaints.

     b.   [Likely to be assigned t_{QP} to the athletes]$_{tr}$ though [one translator each]$_{QP}$ is t_{tr}, there were still complaints.

While in questions NPIs are independently licensed, with topicalization and though raising we can also use NPI-licensing as a test for the availability of a narrow interpretation. As the data in (21) and (22) show, the result from NPI-licensing confirms the *each*-licensing data.

(21)   a.   *... and [certain to be not t_{QP} available]$_{top}$, [a doctor with any reputation]$_{QP}$ was t_{top}.

     b.   ... and [certain to be not t_{QP} available]$_{top}$, [a doctor from cardiology] was t_{top}.

(22)   a.   *[Certain to be not t_{QP} available]$_{tr}$ though [a doctor with any reputation]$_{QP}$ is t_{tr}, patients were waiting.

     b.   [Certain to be not t_{QP} available]$_{tr}$ though [a doctor from cardiology] is t_{tr}, patients were waiting.

A-movement of subjects has been argued to take place not only in raising constructions, but also with all other subjects from the VP-internal underlying subject position to the EPP-position. Hornstein (1995) and Johnson and Tomioka (1997) argue that inverse scope of the object over the subject in English transitive clauses requires a narrow interpretation of the subject chain from the VP-internal subject position to its overt position. Therefore, the SFG predicts that A-bar movement of the VP will block inverse scope in transitive clauses. In fact, this prediction seems to be a well-known fact (Fox, p.c. referring to Truckenbrodt, p.c.), though I don't know who first made this observation nor whether this has ever been made in print. The contrasts in (23) and (24) show the prediction. While (23a) and (24a) allow inverse scope, this interpretation is not available in (23b) and (24b).

(23)   a.   ... and [a policeman]$_{QP}$ t_{QP} stood in front of every bank. ($\forall \gg \exists$, $\exists \gg \forall$)

     b.   ... and [t_{QP} stand in front of every bank]$_{top}$ [a policeman]$_{QP}$ did t_{top}. ($\forall \gg \exists$, *$\exists \gg \forall$)

(24)   a.   Though [enough of us]$_{QP}$ were t_{QP} defending every gate, the enemy broke through. (enough$\gg \forall$, $\forall \gg$enough)

     b.   [t_{QP} Defending every gate]$_{tr}$, though [enough of us]$_{QP}$ were t_{top}, the enemy broke through. (enough$\gg \forall$, *$\forall \gg$enough)

Potentially, another case of scope freezing is shown in (25). If an object is stranded by VP-topicalization, as in (25b) and (25c), it can only take scope over the VP it originated in. If we assume that examples like (25b) and (25c) involve rightward A-movement, these fact fall under the SFG. However, the assumption that heavy NP-shift is A-movement is otherwise not standard and I'm not sure whether it can be argued for.

(25) a. ... and David gave every handout [to one of the students]$_{QP}$. ($\forall \gg \exists$, $\exists \gg \forall$)

b. ... and [give every handout t_{QP}]$_{top}$ David did t_{top} [to one of the students]$_{QP}$ ($\forall \gg \exists$, *$\exists \gg \forall$)

c. ... and [giving every handout t_{QP}]$_{top}$ David is t_{top} [to one of the students]$_{QP}$. ($\forall \gg \exists$, *$\exists \gg \forall$)

4. Reconstruction of A-bar Movement

A-bar movement shows a more intricate reconstruction pattern than A-movement. In this section, I summarize arguments from the literature that the Copy Theory of movement is the right approach to reconstruction phenomena in A-bar movement chains, and then show that this assumption derives necessary assumptions about A-bar movement for the account of the SFG above.

As Fox (1997) shows, in A-chains the position in the chain where scope is taken exactly matches the position in the chain that matters for binding theory. A-bar chains differ in this respect, as is well known and discussed by Fox and others in detail. Consider (26). In (26a), the overtly *wh*-moved phrase enters condition C as if it was in the trace position. In (26b), Condition C also applies when every friend of Mary's takes scope above the subject. This leads Fox (1997) to propose that A-bar movement leaves a copy, which is relevant for binding theory, even when a higher position in the chain determines scope. In Sauerland (forthcoming), I provide evidence that the copy in all positions of an A-bar chain not only matters for binding theory, but also is interpreted.

(26) a. *[Which friend of Susi$_i$'s]$_{wh}$ did she$_i$ meet t_{wh}?

b. *[A different boy] introduced her$_i$ to [every friend of Mary$_i$'s].

Therefore, I assume that traces of A-bar movement are always complex, containing a copy of most of the lexical material of the head of the chain. This, however, still leaves it open whether narrow scope in A-bar chains is derived by means of this copy or in some other way like PF-movement. At this moment, I have no conclusive evidence to offer on the question whether A-bar movement obeys the SFG or not.[9] For the moment, I follow Chomsky (1995) in assuming that the copy theory of movement accounts for all reconstruction effects in A-bar chains.

---

[9] Relevant examples would be those where an A-bar trace is left unbound by subsequent movement. Unfortunately, in English all examples of this type are ungrammatical for independent reasons (cf. Müller (1996)). In scrambling languages, like German, such constructions are possible if the A-bar movement involved is scrambling. But, the issue is more complicated since, at this point of the investigation, chains created by A and A-bar scrambling don't seem to me to differ in the relevant respect.

Now, consider again the explanation of the SFG given, especially for the failure of derivation (14) above. Two assumptions that need to be made about A-bar movement for the account to go through are the following:

(27)　(i)　A-bar movement has to take place before the split into PF and LF. (=(13-a))

　　　(ii)　The QP inside the bottom copy left by A-bar movement cannot move at PF.

Assumption (i) can now be derived from a proposal of Fox (1995). He argues that quantifier lowering must be motivated by a new scope possibility for the moving phrase itself. His condition translates on the PF-movement view into the condition that movement must take place in the stem (cf. Pesetsky's (1989) Earliness), unless delaying it brings about a new scope possibility. This predicts that A-movement will only be delayed until PF, if a reading that isn't equivalent to one available after stem-movement is achieved. For A-bar movement, however, this predicts that PF-movement is never possible, because, on the copy theory, stem movement doesn't restrict the scopal construals available.[10]

Assumption (ii) might be part of a more general requirement that two positions in an A-bar chain must contain identical material (except for adjuncts to the head of the chain). Alternatively, it might that the phonological deletion of the bottom copy in a non-trivial chain must precede movement at PF. Either account allows movement of the entire A-bar trace at PF, which is needed in (28). For the narrow scope reading of *many* with respect to *seem*, the A-movement of *how many men* or its silent copy across *seem* must be delayed until PF.

(28)　[How many men]$_{wh}$ t_{wh} seemed to Kazuko to be t_{wh} downstairs playing their guitar? (many≫seem, seem≫many)

5. Conclusion

In section 3 we have seen building on an observation of Barss (1986) that there is a significant generalization, the SFG, which restricts the narrow interpretation in A-chains to environments where the A-moved quantifier c-commands its trace. This generalization was shown to be correct across a number of different constructions. Furthermore we saw that the SFG follows more or less directly from the assumption that cases of a narrow interpretation in an A-chain, so called scope reconstruction phenomena in A-chains, should be analyzed as being derived by PF-movement.

Before I begin to consider serious alternatives, let me mention that both the copy theory as well a semantic approaches to scope reconstruction

---

[10]Because of the restriction to bringing about a new scope possibility for the moving phrase itself, it is not sufficient motivation for delaying A-bar movement in the SFG cases that the delay makes narrow scope possible for the A-moving phrase.

phenomena in A-chains seem to offer no perspective in accounting for SFG in an insightful way. On either account the operation bringing about the narrow interpretation is different from movement, and therefore a sensitivity of this operation to c-command would have to be stipulated. The strength of the PF-movement account, in this respect, is that the c-command sensitivity of movement is an independently argued for property of movement which carries over to PF-movement. Now, let me briefly consider two alternative explanations that might be given for the SFG. Note here, that the evidence for the SFG came entirely from examples with the structure in (29).

(29)

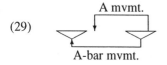

The first potential alternative was brought to my attention by David Pesetsky and Želko Bošković, and is based on two assumptions of Lasnik and Saito (1992): One, the generalized proper binding condition (GPBC), that traces must not be unbound at any point of the derivation, and two, the assumption that a control analysis is optionally possible in all raising constructions. These two assumptions force a control analysis for all examples that have the structure in (29) as Lasnik and Saito (1992:140-42) point out: Since control structures generally don't allow scope reconstruction, Lasnik and Saito's (1992) analysis of structures of type (29) predicts the SFG.

However, the assumptions underlying this account are at best controversial. As Takano (1993), Kitahara (1994), and Müller (1996) show, the GPBC is not correct in the form suggested by Lasnik and Saito (1992) and an empirically more accurate condition accounting for all data attributed to the GPBC follows from the general economy condition Shortest Attract. But, this condition allows a raising analysis for structure such as (29). Moreover, the assumption that a control analysis is possible for raising structures misses some distinctions between the two: As Wurmbrand (1998) points out, real control can be 'imperfect' as in (30a): The PRO can refer to a plural entity that the subject is a member of. Raising on the other hand doesn't allow 'imperfect' readings, as (30b) shows.

(30)   a.   The mayor decided to PRO$_{they}$ gather in the lobby.

       b.   *The mayor was likely to PRO$_{they}$ gather in the lobby.

The second potential alternative is the analysis Barss (1986) gives for the example (12). He relies on a Q-lowering analysis of scope reconstruction phenomena in A-chains and proposes that the c-command condition on movement cannot only be satisfied by the landing site c-commanding the origin site, but is also satisfied if the origin site c-commands the landing site. This modified, symmetric, c-command condition allows lowering, but only to a position that is c-commanded by the origin site. Barss (1986) claims that his account blocks lowering in a structure like (29) because the landing site inside the fronted constituent here isn't c-commanded by the origin site.

However, it is first of all not clear that Barss's (1986) accounts actually predict the SFG. Consider a derivation, where the position inside the fronted constituent is reached by two steps of movement: The first step raises the raised subject to a position above the fronted constituent, and the second step lowers the subject into the fronted constituent. This derivation doesn't violate Barss's weakened c-command condition. Secondly, Barss's (1986) account inherits the problems that Q-lowering has. In particular, the absence of overt lowering will need to be explained, which is not trivial in many cases: Consider e.g. Japanese scrambling: Saito (1992) shows that in Japanese a *wh*-phrase can be scrambled to a position outside of its scope domain as in (31a). He therefore argues that Japanese scrambling can be freely undone. Nevertheless, it is still impossible to scramble a phrase to a lower position in Japanese as the ungrammaticality of (31b) attests.

(31) a. dono hon-o$_i$ Masao-ga Hanako-ga t_i tosyokan-kara
          which book   Masao$_{NOM}$ Hanako$_{NOM}$ library-from
          karidasita   ka siritagatteiru
          checked-out Q want-to-know

          'Masao wants to know which book Hanako checked out from the library.'

      b. *Hanako-ga t_i Masao-ga Taro-ni$_i$ waratta-to   omowa-seta
          Hanako$_{NOM}$ Masao$_{NOM}$ Taro$_{DAT}$ laughed-that believe-made

Finally, it seems to me quite likely that a strict c-command condition on movement could easily be derived as a consequence of more general principles of syntactic derivations—an issue that has received a lot of attention in recent work (cf. Chomsky (1995)). The symmetric c-command condition of Barss (1986), on the other hand, seems to be a mere stipulation at this point, and it would be more natural to assume no such restriction on lowering. Therefore, I conclude that c-command is a general property of all movement. But then, the PF-movement account of scope reconstruction in A-chains is the only account of the SFG left.

References

Barss, Andrew. 1986. *Chains and Anaphoric Dependence. On Reconstruction and its Implications*. Cambridge: Massachusetts Institute of Technology dissertation.

Burzio, Luigi. 1986. *Italian Syntax: A Government-Binding Approach*. Dordrecht: Kluwer.

Chierchia, Gennaro. 1995. *Dynamics of Meaning*. University of Chicago Press.

Chomsky, Noam. 1993. A minimalist program for linguistic theory. In *The View from Building 20: Essays in Linguistics in Honor of Sylvain Bromberger*, ed. by Ken Hale and Jay Keyser, 1–52. MIT Press.

——. 1995. *The Minimalist Program*. Cambridge: MIT Press.

——, and Howard Lasnik. 1977. Filters and control. *Linguistic Inquiry* 8.425–504.

Cresti, Diana. 1995. Extraction and reconstruction. *Natural Language Semantics* 3.79–122.

Fox, Danny. 1995. Economy and scope. *Natural Language Semantics* 3.283–341.

——. 1997. Reconstruction, variable binding and the interpretation of chains. MIT Ms.

Hornstein, Norbert. 1995. *The Grammar of Logical From: From GB to Minimalism*. Cambridge: Blackwell.

Johnson, Kyle, and Satoshi Tomioka. 1997. Lowering and little clauses. University of Massachusetts, Ms.

Kitahara, Hisatsugu. 1994. Restricting *ambiguous* rule-application. In *Formal Approaches to Japanese Linguistics I*, ed. by Masatoshi Koizumi and Hiroyuki Ura, 179–209. Cambridge. MITWPL.

Lasnik, Howard, and Mamoru Saito. 1992. *Move α: Conditions on Its Application and Output*, volume 22 of *Current Studies in Linguistics*. Cambridge: MIT Press.

Linebarger, Marcia. 1980. *The Grammar of Negative Polarity*. Cambridge: Massachusetts Institute of Technology dissertation. Distributed by MITWPL.

——. 1987. Negative polarity and grammatical representation. *Linguistics and Philosophy* 10.325–387.

May, Robert. 1977. *The Grammar of Quantification*. Cambridge: Massachusetts Institute of Technology dissertation.

——. 1985. *Logical Form: Its Structure and Derivation*. Cambridge: MIT Press.

Müller, Gereon. 1996. *Incomplete Category Fronting*. Habilitationsschrift. Universität Tübingen.

Pesetsky, David. 1989. Language particular processes and the earliness principle. MIT ms.

——. 1994. *Zero Syntax: Experiencers and Cascades*. Cambridge: MIT Press.

Rullmann, Hotze. 1995. *Maximality in the Semantics of Wh-Constructions*. Amherst: University of Massachusetts dissertation.

Safir, Ken, and Tim Stowell. 1987. Binominal each. In *Proceedings of NELS 18*, 426–450. Amherst: GLSA.

Saito, Mamoru. 1992. Long distance scrambling in Japanese. *Journal of East Asian Linguistics* 1.69–118.

Sauerland, Uli. forthcoming. *The Making and Meaning of Chains*. Cambridge: Massachusetts Institute of Technology dissertation.

Takano, Yuji. 1993. Minimalism and proper binding. UC Irvine Ms.

Wurmbrand, Susi. 1998. Downsizing infinitives. In *The Interpretive Tract. MITWPL 25*, ed. by Uli Sauerland and Orin Percus. MITWPL. (to appear).

Rejection and Innovation in the Acquisition of an Artificial Language

KELLY STACK

University of California, Los Angeles

1. Introduction

If human beings are genetically endowed with the capacity to learn language, what happens when a child is brought up using an artificial language which differs in fundamental ways from natural human languages? This paper presents some of the results of a long-term case study of a child attempting to acquire an artificial language as her native language. There are stark differences between her acquisition patterns and those of children acquiring natural languages; she lags far behind in her acquisition of pronouns and grammatical morphology, while at the same time she invents grammatical systems (unattested in natural child language development) and "repairs" dysfunctional aspects of the artificial language.

The language in question is SEE, or Signing Exact English (Gustason, et al. (1980)). SEE was invented by a group of educators in order to make English accessible to deaf children. In essence, SEE contains a sign for each of over 4,000 English words and a sign for each bound morpheme in English. The vocabulary of ASL is used as the lexical foundation for SEE.

In (1) a single sentence is shown as in SEE, then in ASL, then as it would be spoken in English. In the SEE utterance, subscripted letters indicate the way SEE uses hand configurations to "initialize" signs. In the ASL utterance, simultaneous non-manual negation is shown with a superscripted bar which indicates its perseveration throughout the utterance. The dual form of WE uses phonological location (the physical position of the sign; see Stack (1988) for a complete description and for arguments that signed languages have phonologies) for agreement, and this is indicated with the subscripted (AGR).

(1) SEE vs. ASL vs. Spoken English

SEE: WE$_{(W)}$ ARE$_{(R)}$ N'T$_{(N)}$ GO$_{(G)}$ ING$_{(I)}$ TO DANCE.

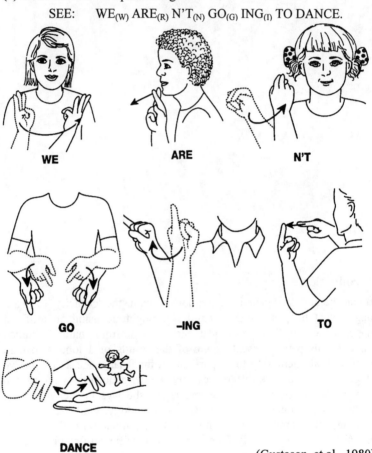

(Gustason, et al., 1980)

(1) (cont.)

<u>non manual head shake</u>

ASL: WE(AGR) DANCE.

(Humphries, et al, 1981)

English: We aren't gonna dance. (wɪ ˈɑrnt gənə ˈdæns)

The subject of this study is Jamie (not her real name), a deaf child who was exposed exclusively to SEE from both her hearing parents starting at the age of 11 months. The study period was from age 4;3 to 5;5. During that period she had at most very minimal exposure to the natural signed language ASL and no exposure to any natural spoken languages, due to her deafness. She conversed with her parents and teachers in SEE, and with other children in her SEE kindergarten class. As we shall see, Jamie's acquisition of SEE is only partial, with gaps that seem similar to those of children exposed to language after the critical period for language acquisition. But there is a dramatic difference between Jamie and post-critical period language learners: Jamie's linguistic innovations show that her internal Universal Grammar is alive and well and hard at work reinventing SEE in order to make it conform to UG.

Based on the fact that Jamie's developing grammar diverges from SEE in just those areas in which SEE is most unlike natural human languages, I argue that children bring substantial innate resources to the task of first language acquisition in the form of unconscious expectations about linguistic principles. I will focus first on the ways in which Jamie has rejected certain aspects of SEE, and second on the innovations she has made to SEE.

2. Rejecting SEE

2.1 Pronominal System
The SEE pronominal system is shown in (2).

(2) SEE Pronouns

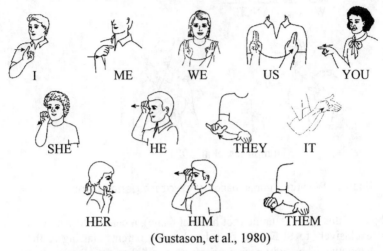

I   ME   WE   US   YOU

SHE   HE   THEY   IT

HER   HIM   THEM

(Gustason, et al., 1980)

Although children acquiring spoken English tend to master third person pronouns by around the age of 2, Jamie did not master SEE third person pronouns throughout the period of study. This is confirmed by the results of administration of the Curtiss-Yamada Comprehensive Language Evaluation (CYCLE) as shown in (3), which contains Jamie's results in the CYCLE-R (Receptive Measures) subtests on comprehension of pronouns. The CYCLE was developed to provide information about the development of specific grammatical structures and features, such as active voice word order, adjective scope, relative clause structures, and so forth.   In the pronoun subtests, the subject is asked to identify pictures corresponding to stimuli, such as "Point to them."

(3) Curtiss-Yamada CYCLE-R Results

Jamie's age	Name of Subtest	Jamie's results	Normal passing age
4;3	Object Pronouns: me/you	3/5 - not passed	3;0
4;3	Third Person Object Pronouns	2/5 - not passed	4;0
5;3	Third Person Object Pronouns	2/5 - not passed	4;0

In spontaneous conversation, in 572 contexts obligatory for a third person pronoun, Jamie supplied a SEE third person pronoun only 11 times (2%).

Jamie did, however, have greater mastery of first and second person pronouns in conversational contexts. Throughout the year of study, she used first person pronouns in 69% of obligatory contexts and second person pronouns in 93% of obligatory contexts. The results with respect to pronouns are summarized in (4).

(4) Third Person Pronouns in Spontaneous Conversation, 4;3 – 5;5.

SEE 1st Person Pronouns supplied in obligatory contexts	69%
SEE 2nd Person Pronouns supplied in obligatory contexts	93%
SEE 3rd Person Pronouns supplied in obligatory contexts	2%

Why did Jamie do so much better with first and second person SEE pronouns than with SEE third person pronouns? I argue that the answer lies not in grammatical person but in the morphophonemic structure of the pronouns. Jamie is able to acquire pronouns that make the same use of phonological location that ASL pronouns do. But in the place of the SEE third person pronouns which do not make use of space, Jamie has innovated a third person pronoun (similar to ASL's third person pronoun): a POINT.

Of those 572 contexts that were obligatory for a third person pronoun, Jamie used the POINT pronoun 225 times, or 40% of the time. A revised version of the Third Person Object Pronouns test was administered at 5;5 using POINT instead of using SEE third person pronouns. This time, just two months after she had failed the SEE version of the test for the second time, Jamie passed with 100% correct responses. These results are shown in (5).

(5) The Innovated POINT Pronoun

POINT 3rd Person Pronouns obligatory contexts (4;3 – 5;5)	40%
Results of revised Third Person Object Pronouns test (5;5)	5/5 - passed

Ignoring case and gender inflection found in SEE, Jamie's developing pronominal system instead uses location to mark person, making systematic use of a morphosyntactic feature of natural signed languages which is almost ignored by her target language, SEE.

3. Innovations – "Repairs" of SEE

3.1 Morpho-Syntactic innovation

Jamie's ability to innovate in order to fix Signing Exact English is also nicely demonstrated by her creation of an inflectional paradigm not existing in SEE or English, but apparently present in all natural signed languages

Padden (1983) divides ASL verbs into a four-part typology of Inflecting, Spatial, Classifier and Plain verbs. Inflecting verbs agree with their arguments in terms of person and number. Spatial verbs are marked for location, but not for person or number. Classifier verbs are those referred to by Supalla (1982) as "verbs of motion and location." Plain verbs do not inflect for person, number or location, but can inflect for aspect.

These classifications are useful in analyzing Jamie's JSL verb system. There are 9 verbs in her corpus that inflect for person and/or number agreement. There are 16 verbs that can be marked for location. There appear to be three classifier verbs and 9 innovated verb forms which are morphologically complex but not necessarily productively formed. Of the majority of verbs that cannot be classified in one of the first three categories, 11 are modified in non-locative adverbial ways.

In this paper, I will focus only on Inflecting verbs. Recall that inflecting verbs agree with their arguments in person and number. Lillo-Martin (1991:53) argues convincingly that in ASL "sentences with an inflectional argument and no overt pronoun are comparable to sentences with plain verbs and an overt pronoun." In other words, the theta requirements of Inflectional verbs can be satisfied by overt lexical arguments or by overt inflectional arguments (agreement morphology). The theta requirements of non-inflecting verbs can be satisfied only by overt lexical arguments.

This is summarized in (6), where the Inflecting verb TEACH may occur with or without lexical arguments (6a-b), but the Plain verb LIKE may occur only when accompanied by lexical arguments (6c-d).

(6) Overt Lexical and Inflectional Arguments with Inflecting vs. Plain Verbs

a.	$_1$INDEX	$_1$TEACH$_2$	$_2$INDEX
	1st person	1p-teach-2p	2nd person
	"I taught you."		
b.	$_1$TEACH$_2$		
	1p-teach-2p		
	"I taught you."		
c.	$_1$INDEX LIKE	$_2$INDEX	
	1st person	like 2nd person	
	"I liked you."		
d.	LIKE		
	like		
	*"I liked you."		

Jamie has not acquired the inflectional system of SEE. (In fact, Jamie acquired none of the bound morphology of SEE.) Instead we see a budding inflectional system that is similar to that of natural signed languages.

Jamie produces 10 verbs that appear to inflect for person and/or number agreement. These verbs, like ASL Inflecting verbs, can be modified in terms of their beginning or ending phonological location. For example, when shown a picture of shoes, I asked her teasingly if she would eat them. She responded, "NO! HATE$_i$ – STINK!" (No! I hate them – they stink!). The sign HATE was directed at the picture, and there was no overt lexical argument.

It is important to note that these are not static production variants; none of Jamie's Inflecting verbs is inflected 100% of the time, and they are not always inflected in the same ways. This is evidence that the system is still developing, and Jamie has not simply invented a different way of producing these signs, since the production varies in a principled way.

Although it might be tempting to view Jamie's verb inflections as ad-hoc mimetic extensions rather than truly grammatical innovations, her systematic treatment of these verbs with regard to argument structure strongly suggests the opposite.

Jamie provided required lexical arguments for Non-Inflecting verbs 83% of the time over the year-long course of study as shown in (7). This high percentage indicates a relatively solid grasp of theta requirements. We would expect to see a similar high rate for Inflecting verbs. However, Jamie provides required lexical arguments in only 52% of utterances containing inflecting verbs. Why would she suddenly lose track of theta requirements for just those verbs?

(7) Percentage of Lexical Arguments in Obligatory Positions

	Non-Inflecting Verbs	Inflecting Verbs
Lexical Arguments in Obligatory Position	83%	52%

The mystery is solved when we count agreement morphology as an additional way to satisfy theta requirements for Inflecting verbs. In this case, we find a combined total of lexical and non-lexical arguments appearing 92% of the time in obligatory positions, summarized in (8).

(8)   Percentage of Lexical and Non-Lexical Arguments in Obligatory Positions

	Non-Inflecting Verbs	Inflecting Verbs
Lexical Arguments in Obligatory Position	83%	52%
Non-Lexical Arguments in Obligatory Position	n/a	40%
TOTALS	83%	92%

3.1 Phonological innovation

We have seen Jamie's selective rejection of "broken" parts of SEE and her use of innovations to create a "repaired" grammar of her own demonstrated syntactically and morphologically. Now let us examine her phonological innovations.

Jamie produced seven SEE forms that violate ASL phonotactics. She did not produce any of these as they should be produced in SEE, even though she did not systematically alter the phonological structure of any of the hundreds of other SEE forms she used.

Four of the forms violate the Maximality Condition (Stack (1988)), which states that in ASL, syllables may not contain both a hand configuration change and a palm orientation change.

These signs were ALREADY, ANY, BEHIND, and PLANT. Each violates Maximality by containing both a hand configuration change and a palm orientation change (9). Jamie altered the production of these signs in ways that brought them into compliance with the Maximality Condition, as shown in (9).

9) SEE signs violating Maximality

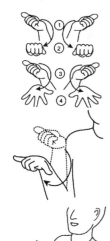

a. ALREADY
Violation: In second syllable there is both a hand configuration change and a palm orientation change.
Repair: Kept same hand configuration (5-Hand) throughout sign.

b. ANY
Violation: Both a hand configuration change and a palm orientation change.
Repair: Kept same hand configuration (Y-hand) throughout sign.

c. BEHIND
Violation: Both a hand configuration change and a palm orientation change.
Repair: Kept same hand configuration (A-Hand) throughout sign.

d. PLANT
Violation: Both a hand configuration change and a palm orientation change.
Repair: Kept same hand configuration (P-Hand) throughout sign.

Three signs (10) violated the Dominance Condition (Battison (1974)), which restricts the passive hand in a two-handed sign to one of only seven hand configurations. These signs and her repairs are shown in (10).

(10) SEE signs violating Dominance

a. RIBBON
Violation: Passive hand configuration of R is illegal.
Repair: Changed Passive hand to H-hand, horizontal, palm facing down. Changed Active hand to R-hand, horizontal, fingertips touching tips of fingers of Passive hand

b. HANG
Violation: Passive hand configuration of H is illegal.
Repair: Changed Passive hand to 1-hand.

c. BERRY
Violation: Passive hand configuration of I is illegal.
Repair: Changed Passive hand to 1-hand.

Let me make clear that I am not suggesting that Jamie was born with the phonotactics of ASL hardwired in her brain. In fact, the changes Jamie made to RIBBON are evidence that she is following general principles of signed languages, but not necessarily those of ASL. In RIBBON, the change in the Passive hand configuration from R to H itself does not solve the Dominance violation, since H is also an illegal hand configuration for the Passive hand in ASL. Jamie appears to be using the H hand as a size and shape specifier (a type of classifier), indicating a narrow flat object. It is possible that this production of RIBBON is a transitional form, with a form in which both hands use the H handshape (or even both hands use the R handshape) appearing in the future.

I offer two possible explanations for Jamie's phonological innovations. First, we must remember that the vocabulary of SEE is based on the lexicon of ASL and the majority of SEE signs do not violate the phonotactics of ASL. It is possible that Jamie has been able to induce ASL phonotactic principles from her observations of the conforming SEE signs. Second (and more likely), it is possible that the phonotactic principles discussed here are manifestations of signed language universals, and this is the reason why Jamie's output conforms to them.

4. Prosody and Morphophonology in SEE

There is a striking pattern evident in Jamie's rejections and innovations. In natural languages, various grammatical modules assist each other in drawing focus to critical structures and systems. In English, for example, the phonological properties of grammatical morphemes are different from those of content words, lending what appears to be a necessary redundancy to the signal. Prosodic phrasing and syntactic structure cooperate in the construction of grammatical utterances. This is as true of natural signed languages as it is of spoken languages.

In signed languages as in spoken languages, bound grammatical morphemes are generally unstressed, undergo phonological reduction and are underlyingly underspecified and sub-minimal. Phonological location, for example, is exploited in the morphology of every known signed language. Location is a morpheme that is unproduceable alone; it must be minimally bound to handshape and palm orientation in order to surface. As we have already seen, Jamie repeatedly turns to phonological location in her innovations.

What is it about SEE that induces Jamie's rejections and innovations? At the levels of syntax, semantics and morphology, SEE is an almost exact replica of English – the word order and rules for forming different structures, the set of words and their meanings, and the set of morphemes, their meanings and functions – are the same. But when it comes to the input-output channel of phonetics and phonology, SEE diverges drastically from natural language, both signed and spoken, and this divergence results in damage that permeates all its linguistic modules, as evidenced by Jamie's wide-ranging rejections and innovations.

The bound and grammatical morphology of SEE consists of mainly unreduced forms; an example can be seen in (1). There are no reduced forms in the SEE utterance; in fact, there are no forms in it that are reducible. The auxiliary verb, the clitic, and the inflectional morphemes are all underlyingly fully specified for handshape, location, palm orientation and movement. WE ARE 'NT GO ING TO DANCE. At most, a small degree of location assimilation is possible between GO and ING. Contrast this to the ASL translation, in which agreement is expressed by the subsegmental feature of location, and negation by a non-manual gesture delivered simultaneously with the utterance. And again, contrast the SEE to English, in which vowels are reduced and syllables are elided.

Jamie rejects the SEE pronominal system in part because it is phonologically incompatible with a larger system of agreement. She fails to acquire SEE morphemes such as –ING and –ED because they are prosodically ill-formed, and in their absence innovates other, more phonetically and phonologically natural, morphosyntactic systems. In this way the major failure of SEE can be seen to lie in its input-output channel, which of course is the most problematic area for mapping of a spoken language to a signed mode.

5. Summary

To summarize, we have seen here that, at the level of morphosyntax, Jamie rejected the parts of the SEE pronominal system that were inconsistent with natural signed language morphosyntax, and innovated more natural replacements for them. Ignoring case and gender inflection found in SEE, Jamie's developing pronominal system instead uses location to mark person, making systematic use of a morphosyntactic feature of natural signed languages which is almost ignored by her target language, SEE.

Turning to morphology, Jamie innovated a verb agreement system that is consistent with the use of phonological location for her innovated pronouns. We have evidence from her use of overt and covert arguments, where she differentiates between inflecting and non-inflecting verbs by supplying covert arguments for the former and overt for the latter, that this is indeed a grammatical system.

Finally, at the phonological level, Jamie repaired forms that violate certain phonotactics of ASL, and also possibly more general principles of signed languages.

Children normally acquiring natural languages do not reject grammatical systems in the target language, innovating their own systems. But Jamie has done just this with SEE. Jamie herself is normal, her acquisitional circumstances are nearly normal (early exposure to language from both parents). The problem lies with SEE. Jamie had to figure out which parts of SEE make sense and which parts don't, and that's just what she did, bringing substantial innate resources to the task of first language acquisition in the form of unconscious expectations about linguistic principles.

References

Battison, Robbin. 1974. Phonological deletion in American Sign Language. *Sign Language Studies*, 5.1-19.

Curtiss, Susan and Jeni Yamada. 1987. *Curtiss-Yamada Comprehensive Language Evaluation (CYCLE)*.

Gustason, Gerilee, Donna Pfetzing and Esther Zawolkow. 1980. *Signing Exact English*. Los Alamitos, CA: Modern Signs Press.

Humphries, Tom, Carol Padden and Terrence J. O'Rourke. 1981. *A Basic Course in American Sign Language*. Silver Spring, MD: T. J. Publishers, Inc.

Lillo-Martin, Diane. 1991. *Universal Grammar and American Sign Language: Setting the Null Argument Parameters*, The Netherlands: Kluwer.

Padden, Carol. 1983. *Interaction of Morphology and Syntax in American Sign Language.* Doctoral Dissertation, U.C. San Diego.
Stack, Kelly. 1988. *Tiers and Syllable Structure in American Sign Language: Evidence from Phonotactics.* M.A. Thesis, UCLA.
Supalla, Ted. 1982. Structure and Acquisition of Verbs of Motion and Location in ASL. Ph.D. Dissertation, UC San Diego

Contiguity, Metathesis, and Infixation

JOSEPH P. STEMBERGER & BARBARA HANDFORD BERNHARDT

University of Minnesota & University of British Columbia

1. Introduction

When morphemes are combined, languages may fail to respect the strict linear order of the two morphemes in several ways. In this paper, we discuss two types of reordering during morpheme combination, i.e., infixation and metathesis. An affix may appear within another morpheme through infixation. Alternatively, the expected order of two segments may be reversed through metathesis. It has been argued that both infixation and metathesis are driven by constraints on phonological form. This paper has several goals: (1) to identify one type of metathesis as a special type of infixation (just as some infixes are special types of prefixes or suffixes), (2) to argue that some infixes derive not from phonological constraints but from morphological constraints that require them to be infixes, (3) to address predicted but unlikely types of infixation/metathesis, and (4) to address issues of acquisition and learning that bear on these phenomena. We argue for an enriched set of ways to refer to edges in constraints.

2. Infixation as Phonologically-Driven

Prince and Smolensky (1993) and McCarthy & Prince (1993) have argued that there are two types of infixation, both being phonologically driven and both being special types of prefixes or suffixes. Type 1 infixes are prefixed or suffixed to a phonological category, so that they appear in the middle of the base. Type 2 infixes are prefixed or suffixed to a base morpheme, but their linear position is adjusted to within the base, in order to avoid the violation of high-ranked phonological constraints.

A typical example of a Type 1 infix is Ulwa -ka-:[1]

(1) (siwá)-**ka**-nak   'root'   (bás)-**ka**

The infix is suffixed to the foot that is the head of the prosodic word, via the morphological alignment constraint **Aligned([ka],L,Head-Foot,R)**. In order for the affix to appear in the middle of the base morpheme, the constraint **Contiguity(Base)** (which requires that all segments in the base morpheme that are contiguous in the input must also be contiguous in the output) must be low-ranked. This allows the first /a/ and the /n/ of /siwanak/ to be separated by the infix.

A typical Type 2 infix is Tagalog -**um**-:

(2) **um**-aral   'teach'   gr-**um**-adwet   'graduate'
     *****um**-gradwet

Prince and Smolensky (1993) analyze /um/ as a prefix that is forced rightward into the stem in order to avoid a coda. It floats leftward only far enough so that all segments of the affix and base can be expressed, without an additional coda being created by the affix. This derives from the ranking:

Not(Coda)   »   Aligned([um],L,Stem,L)
                 Contiguity(Base)

When the base word starts with a vowel, the prefix-final /m/ is in an onset, and thus the affix surfaces as a prefix. It is infixed only when the base starts with a vowel.

---

[1]Constraint names are from Bernhardt and Stemberger (1998).

3. Infixation for the Sake of Infixation

We believe that infixes do not have to be driven by phonology. Infixation is a basic kind of affixation, in which an affix occurs near an edge, but not at that edge. Type 3 infixes have only this motivation. In Type 4 affixes, the affix is an infix for morphological reasons, but its exact placement away from the edge is driven by the phonology.

An example of a Type 3 infix is the Cambodian nominalizer -əmn-, which follows the consonant at the beginning of the base word. (This is a common affix, but it is not the most productive nominalizer.)

a. *Vowel-initial roots* – ?none?
b. *Root begins with single consonant*
Affix follows the consonant; all segments of the infix survive.

(3)	čɔŋ	č-əmn-ɔŋ	'desire'
	sowk	s-əmn-owk	'bribe'
	tiəp	t-əmn-iəp	'low'
	kɔəp	k-əmn-ɔəp	'bury'
	?awi	?-amn-awi	'give'

c. *Root begins with two consonants*
Affix follows the first consonant; final /n/ deletes.

(4)	tŋʊn	t-əm-ŋʊn	'heavy'
	črow	č-əm-row	'deep'
	skɔːm	s-əm-kɔːm	'skinny'
	čluh	č-əm-luh	'quarrel'
	thɔm	t-əm-hɔm	'big'
	tɓañ	ɗ-am-ɓañ	'weave'
	traw	ɗ-am-raw	'right'
	khaŋ	k-am-haŋ	'angry'
	čŋay	č-am-ŋay	'remote'

If the base word begins with a single consonant, then the -əmn- follows the first consonant. All consonants of the affix can be syllabified, and so none are deleted. If the base word begins with two consonants, the -əmn- follows the first consonant. The /n/ at the end of the affix cannot be syllabified, and so is deleted. This can potentially be derived from the following ranking:

Aligned(Base,L,PrWd,L)   »   **Aligned([əmn],L,PrWd,L)**
Contiguity([əmn])   **Contiguity(Base)**

The higher-ranked alignment constraint guarantees that the first consonant of the base is ordered first. The affix -əmn- is a prefix, but its alignment constraint is ranked too low for it to actually appear before the base. Having *one* consonant of the base at the beginning of the word satisfies **Aligned(Base)**. **Aligned(əmn)** forces the affix to appear as close to the left edge as it can, immediately after the first consonant of the base. This placement is allowed, due to the low ranking of **Contiguity(Base)**. The high ranking of **Contiguity([əmn])** keeps the segments of the affix together.

Phonologically, it would be more sensible for -əmn- to follow the second consonant of the base morpheme, because all of the consonants in the affix could be syllabified:

(5)   *čŋ-αmn-αy   *čl-əmn-uh

However, such placement would increase the degree of mis-alignment from the left edge. This illustrates that the exact placement of this affix is *not* determined by the phonology; thus, -əmn- cannot be a Type 2 infix. We reject the idea that -əmn- is suffixed to the first consonant, since "the first consonant" is not a prosodic category. This is a Type 3 infix, in which the affix is forced internal to the base morpheme for morphological reasons only, via the constraints that are responsible for the placement/alignment of affixes.

However, in Type 4 infixes, the phonology does affect exact placement of the infix. An example of a Type 4 infix is the Choctaw instantaneous -h- (Niklas (1972)). Starting from the right edge of the stem (the base morpheme plus derivational affixes), the -h- is placed in the penultimate syllable, before any consonants at the end of that syllable. In the following examples, the base is underlined.

a. *Looks like suffix*:

(6) pisa-či   pisa-h-či   'show'

b. *Looks like infix in base*:

(7) pisa   pi-h-sa   'see'   lakna   la-ha-kna 'yellow'
    čito   či-h-to   'big'   iško   i-hi-ško 'drink
    ona   o-h-na   'arrive'   takči   ta-ha-kči 'tie'
    apa   a-h-pa   'eat'
c. *Looks like prefix*:

(8) sa-bi sa-h-bi   'he kills me'
    či-bi   či-h-bi   'he kills you'

d. *Looks like infix in prefix*:

(9) iš-bi   i-**hi**-š-<u>bi</u>   'you (sg.) kill him'
ī:-pa   i-**h**-ī:-<u>pa</u>   'eat (intrans)'

This infix is also a good illustration of the fact that the placement of an infix may be determined relative to an edge (here, the right edge): an infix is *not* necessarily placed specifically *within* another morpheme (as the name "infix" implies). If there are no derivational suffixes and the base morpheme has at least two syllables as in (b), the -**h**- is internal to the base morpheme. If there is a derivational suffix as in (a), the -**h**- appears between the base and the derivational suffix (looking like a suffix). If the base is particularly short as in (c) or (d), the -**h**- may appear directly before the base (looking like a prefix) or within another prefix.

These examples also show allomorphy. If there are already two consonants at the relevant portion of the word, then the -**h**- cannot be added without creating an impossible sequence of three consonants. In order to allow all consonants to be syllabified, a copy of the preceding vowel is also "infixed" after the /h/.

The placement of the -**h**- cannot be achieved through the ranking of different alignment constraints, because that would always place it in the same place relative to a particular morpheme, such as the base:

Aligned-R([či]) » **Aligned-R(Base)** » **Aligned-R([h])**   *pi-h-sa-či

Nor is {CCV} any form of prosodic unit, to which the /h/ could be prefixed; thus, -**h**- is not a Type 1 affix (affixed to a phonological category).

In order to derive the placement of -**h**-, we suggest that it is *mis*-aligned with the right edge of the stem:

Aligned([h],Right,Stem,NotRight)

The location constraint **NotRight** means that the affix appears as close to the right edge as possible, but not exactly at the right edge. This type of constraint is equivalent to constraints that have been used elsewhere. For example, the constraint **Nonfinal**, when used to account for stress patterns, guarantees that the rightmost syllable will be extrametrical (the rightmost foot ends one syllable from the right edge). In syntax, **Nonfinal** require that a syntactic element such as a clitic will be the second word in the sentence. We extend this notion to infixation. Below, we address a slightly different way to encode this notion formally, without making use of generalized alignment (which, as we show below, is problematic).

We have not yet explained the exact placement of the -h-. Why does the /h/ float in front of a consonant as in [pi-h-sa], and not a mere one segment into the word, as in *[pis-h-a]? The exact placement of the affix is determined by phonological constraints:

NotCo-occurring(Rime,C-Place)

This constraint states that rimes optimally do not contain C-Place. It holds on both vowels and coda consonants. (For discussion, see Bernhardt & Stemberger (1998).) The actual output [pi-h-sa] does not violate this constraint, because the coda consonant /h/ has no place features. In the alternative *[pis-h-a], the coda [s] has C-Place and consequently violates the **NotCo-occurring** constraint. If the **NotCo-occurring** constraint is ranked higher than the relevant alignment constraint, the /h/ floats further to the left, so that this constraint is not violated.

The /h/ floats leftward even farther when there are two consonants in the relevant portion of the word. Why is the optimal output [i-**hi**-ško], and not *[iš-**ih**-ko]? Another phonological constraint is relevant here:

Uninterrupted(V-Place)

This constraint requires that V-Place gestures should be continuous and uninterrupted. There can be no segment in the word that interrupts V-Place by not being *linked* to V-Place (= no embedded domains; no line crossing). In the above words in Choctaw, syllable structure constraints result in the insertion of a vowel between the first & second of three consonants, with the vowel assimilating to the place of the preceding vowel. The first consonant is in the middle of a doubly-linked V-Place node. Since /š/ has C-Place, V-Place would be interrupted by another place gesture (albeit C-Place). Since /h/ has no place information, V-Place is not interrupted.

The spreading of V-Place across glottals but not across true consonants is an often-reported phenomenon (Steriade (1987); Stemberger (1993)). Because

V-Place must spread across an intervening consonant here, the infix **-h-** is positioned so that **Uninterrupted(V-Place)** is not violated. In order to achieve this, the **-h-** is pushed three segments from the right edge of the stem.

Infixation can occur for the sake of infixation. It is a basic type of affixation which does not have to occur for phonological reasons. Type 3 and Type 4 infixes are infixes because they are mis-aligned with the edge of the base (**NotLeft** as in Cambodian, or **NotRight** as in Choctaw). Some of these infixes (Type 3) are not dominated by phonological constraints, and thus appear one segment from the edge, even though a phonological price may have to be paid (as in Cambodian, in the form of a deleted consonant). Other infixes (Type 4) are dominated by phonological constraints, and thus appear more than one segment from the edge (as in Choctaw).

4. Metathesis as Infixation

Infixes have the following characteristics: (a) the infix is a single segment, or (b) all of the segments of the infix remain contiguous. For infixes with two or more segments, **Contiguity(Affix)** must be high-ranked.

This ensures that all of the segments of the affix that are contiguous in the input will also be contiguous in the output (even though the contiguity of the base morpheme is violated, by definition).

If **Contiguity(Affix)** is ranked low, it is possible for just a part of the affix to be "infixed." This will appear to be "metathesis" at a morpheme boundary (see also Hume (1997)). This is not, however, "true" metathesis, in which the order of two segments is reversed. The segment at the edge of the base and the segment at the edge of the affix are not ordered with respect to each other in the input, since the two morphemes are not themselves ordered with respect to each other. The two segments have not been *reversed*, they are simply ordered in a (perhaps) surprising fashion when the two morphemes become ordered in the output. This can be viewed as a special type of infixation. We propose the name **interdigitation** to denote that the two morphemes are placed together in an interlocking fashion

An example of interdigitation can be found in the Basaa indirect causative suffix **-àhà** (Schmidt (1994)):

a. *After a vowel-final stem* (deletion of affix-initial vowel)

(10)	cí-**hà**	'destroy'
	lò-**hà**	'arrive'
	hé-**hà**	'put'

b. *After a base ending in two consonants*

(11)   kóbl-àhà   'peel'
        éŋl-àhà   'tell'
        sùgɓ-àhà   'rinse mouth'

c. *After a base ending in a single consonant*
   (deletion of middle V in CVCVCV)
   (metathesis of base-final C and /h/)

(12)   lé-h-l-à   'cross'
        tì-h-ŋ-à   'tie'
        ɓú-h-n-à   'promise'
        ɓó-h-l-à   'burst'

We address issues of allomorphy, and of placement of the /h/.

First, what motivates the interdigitation? Why is the optimal output [lé-h-l-à] (with interdigitation), and not *[lél-hà] (with a true suffix)? Interdigitation derives from the following ranking:

NotCo-occurring(Rime,C-Place) » **Contiguity(Base)**
Aligned([àhà],R,Stem,R)   **Contiguity([àhà])**

As in Choctaw, there is a preference for coda consonants not to have C-Place. As a result, it is preferable for the /h/ of the affix to be the coda (since it lacks place features) than for the base-final consonant to be the coda. Further, the entire affix cannot be infixed, because the high ranking of **Aligned** keeps the right edge of -**àhà** at the right edge. The low ranking of **Contiguity** allows the /h/ and the /a/ of the affix to be separated, as well as the consonants and vowels of the base morpheme. Interdigitation results, and not true suffixation or infixation.

Second, why are there any codas at all? Why not add the -**àhà** suffix without deleting the first vowel, as in *[lél-àhà]? The deletion of the suffix-initial vowel derives from the following ranking:

Not(V-Root) » **Survived(V-Root)**

This ranking looks like it could, in principle, lead to the deletion of every vowel: it is better to have no vowels than to faithfully produce any vowel in the input. There are two reasons why some vowels are present in the output. First, no consonants can be deleted, due to the following ranking:

Survived(C-Root) » Not(C-Root)

Given that there are no syllabic consonants in the language, syllables must be headed by vowels, and consonants require syllables to be present in order to be pronounced. Consequently, vowels must surface, to the extent that they are needed for the survival of consonants. This cannot be the whole story, however, because in Basaa initial and final vowels are not required for the survival of consonants. It appears that medial vowels are more likely to be deleted than vowels at the edge of a prosodic word. In our view, medial syllables are weak prosodic domains, in which faithfulness is ranked low (Cole & Kisseberth (1994); Bernhardt & Stemberger (1998); Beckman (1997)). **Survived(V-Root)** is ranked below **Not(V-Root)** only in weak prosodic domains. In the stronger domains of initial and final syllables, **Survived(V-Root)** is ranked higher, and so initial and final vowels are not deleted. Note that the deletion of the suffix-initial vowel in /cí-àhà/ [cí-hà] is deleted because it is not necessary to support any consonants, rather than because it is following another vowel.

In Basaa, suffixation plus vowel deletion leads to a non-optimal coda consonant. Because **Contiguity(Affix)** is ranked low, the /h/ of the "suffix" is separated from the following vowel of the suffix and infixed into the base morpheme. Interdigitation has occurred for phonological reasons.

We argued above that infixation can occur for morphological reasons, through **NotRight** or **NotLeft** placement relative to an edge. Such placement cannot force interdigitation, because the segments of the affix that are not infixed are still at the relevant edge. We know of no purely morphological constraints that could lead to interdigitation. It is a type of infixation that is purely driven by phonological constraints.

Interdigitation can result from any phonological constraints. In Basaa, the relevant constraints affected the optimal features within rimes. In other instances, the relevant features restrict sequences of consonants. Hume (1997) discusses several such instances. In Kui, a stem-final velar "metathesizes" with a suffix-initial /p/, as in /bluk-pa/ [blu-**p**-k-**a**] 'to break down.' This results from the constraint **NoSequence(Dorsal...Labial)**, which prohibits a velar from appearing before a labial (but allows a labial to appear before a velar); this is a common constraint across languages, and is often observed in language acquisition in English-learning children (Bernhardt & Stemberger (1998)).

5. A Typology of Infixation

The constraints discussed so far lead us to a typology of infixation. They define a class of phenomena that are predicted to exist, and also allow us to predict that other things will not occur. We summarize these predictions here. We point out that certain types of predicted phenomena do not in fact seem to occur. We argue that some of these should be considered possible, but that characteristics of learning make them unlikely. Others may require a refinement of the theory of alignment.

The following seems fairly secure. There may be *morphological conditioning* (with low-ranked **Contiguity(Base)**) leading (a) to infixation that is prefixation or suffixation to a prosodic category, or (b) to infixation that derives from a stipulation that an affix is not at the edge of a morphological or phonological category, but (c) *not* to interdigitation. There may be purely *phonological conditioning* (with low-ranked **Contiguity(Base)**) leading (a) to the infixation of a whole affix (with high-ranked **Contiguity(Affix)**), or (b) to the infixation of just part of an affix (with low-ranked **Contiguity(Affix)**), which we call interdigitation. There may be *both morphological and phonological conditioning*: morphological conditioning can require that an affix *not* be at the edge of a morphological or phonological category, but phonological conditioning will determine the exact location of the affix.

Other patterns could be predicted, but they do not seem to occur. First, combining both morphological and phonological conditioning, an affix could be infixed via suffixation or prefixation to a prosodic category, with the exact location determined by phonological constraints. For example, in Ulwa', -**ak**- could be suffixed to the head foot, but if all syllables must have onsets, the infix floats rightwards:

(13) Ulwa':   *(siwá)-**ak**-nak   'root'   (siwú)n-**ak**-ak

Similarly, with infixation to a prosodic category, there might be interdigitation via phonological constraints. In Ulwa", -**ha**- might be suffixed to the head foot, with interdigitation resulting from /h/ being a more optimal coda than most consonants:

(14) Ulwa":   *(siwák)-**ha**-nak   'root'   (siwá-**h**-k)-a-nak

The constraints discussed here also predict the occurrence of *circumfixes*, in which some material is prefixed but some material is suffixed. The following ranking (highest to lowest) derives a circumfix with no phonological conditioning (with one half of the circumfix showing odd orderings):

Aligned(Affix,L,Stem,L)

| Aligned(Base,L,Stem,L) |
| Contiguity(Base) |

| Contiguity(Affix) |

This ranking assures that the affix comes first and the base morpheme second, and that the contiguity of the base will be respected. Consequently, the first segment of the affix is a prefix, and the remaining segments constitute the first suffix following the stem; e.g. plural **nos-**, realized as /n-BASE-**os**-DerivationalAffixes/. Instead of the ranking of two alignment constraints driving the circumfixation, phonological conditioning (such as requiring syllables to have an onset) could drive the results. For example, the suffix -**nos** (as in /safat-**nos**/) could be a circumfix with a vowel-initial root: /**n**-afat-**os**/. Lastly, a prefix could always surface as a suffix, given this ranking:

> Aligned(Base,L,Stem,L)   »   Aligned(ka,L,Stem,L)
> Contiguity(Base)

(15)   ***ka**-siwa   siwa-**ka**

The approach taken here (and undoubtedly any approach within Optimality Theory) predicts types of affixation that, as far as we know, never occur. Is this a problem for the theory? We believe that it is not, because gaps in typologies can derive from characteristics of learning. Stemberger (1996) argued that many of the restrictions on morphological reduplication cannot be predicted by any theory likely to have enough power to account for occurring patterns. Some of the restrictions should be attributed to learning. For examples, radical changes in segmental content are often restricted to edge syllables, and it may be that the lower salience of nonedge syllables makes it more difficult for learners to notice differences from the base morpheme.

Learning may also account for some of the missing patterns here. By morphological stipulation, when affixing to a phonological category internal to the word, interdigitation does not occur, nor is the affix's exact placement affected by phonological constraints. Perhaps the low perceptual salience of the internal portion of the word makes it difficult for a learner to spot patterns there, making it less likely that such patterns would be learned. Even if they were to arise historically, this might make them unstable and unlikely to survive for long.

The unusual nature of circumfixes may derive from a different aspect of learning. Learners may treat the two parts of the circumfix as two separate affixes, if they are always split. The two affixes are redundant with each other in terms of meaning, which is an unusual circumstance. Because of this redundancy, one of such affixes tends to be lost historically, if this situation ever arises. Similarly, a child faced with a prefix will assume rankings that treat the affix inherently as a suffix, and not as a prefix that is always forced to the right of the base. There are ambiguities in the data, but learning always leads to one analysis, so the odd morphological patterns listed here, although allowed by the theory, never become a part of the grammar of any language.

6. Child Language Development: Consequences for Alignment

Bernhardt and Stemberger (1998) note that no English-learning children to date have been observed to produce suffixes as infixes (or prefixes) in phonological development, even if the affixes cannot be expressed for phonological reasons (because, for example, codas cannot be pronounced). But one could easily imagine patterns such as the following. (a) Syllables must have onsets, and thus the suffix floats to the left:

(16) *lions*   /layən-z/   *[lay-z-ən]
     apples   /æpəl-z/   *[z-apu]

(b) Suffixes become infixes or prefixes for morphological reasons. For example, plural -z might be suffixed to the head foot:

(17) *octopuses*   /ˈɑktə‚pʊs-əz/   [ˈʊktə-z-‚pʊs]

(c) There might be interdigitation at a boundary in order to avoid nonoptimal consonant sequences:

(18) *sadness*   /sæd-nəs/   [sæ-n-d-əs]

How can we account for the fact that no such patterns have ever been observed?

It does not work to stipulate that **Contiguity(Base)** is always ranked high, thereby ruling out infixation and interdigitation. **Contiguity(Base)** is often violated for phonological reasons, but not in interactions with *morphology*. For almost all English-learning children, a contiguity violation arises when word-initial clusters are simplified via the deletion of the more sonorous consonant in obstruent-sonorant clusters:

(19) *fly*   /flay/   [fay]

A too-high ranking for contiguity would prevent this. Some other explanation must be found.

It does not work to stipulate that **Aligned(Affix)** is always ranked higher than phonological constraints. Other morphological constraints must be ranked lower phonological constraints, and there is no reason why alignment should be special. For example, **Expressed(Affix)** may be ranked lower than phonological constraints, so that the affix is "deleted":

> NotComplex(Coda) » Expressed(pl,-z)
> Not(V-Root)

> (20) *rocks* /rɑk-s/   [wat]   (cf. *box* /bɑks/ [bas])

Since the same cluster is treated differently within a morpheme, this appears to be "deleting" the affix as one way to avoid a cluster. Similarly, a base-final segment can be taken as the realization of an affix:

> (21) *horses* /hɔrs-z/   [hors]

Through the low-ranking of **Distinct**, the base-final /s/ also corresponds to the plural **-z** suffix, in order to avoid violations on clusters of epenthesis of schwa (as in adult /hɔrsəz/). Lastly, **SinglyExpressed(Affix)** (assuring that one instance of an affix in the input corresponds to just one token on the affix in the output) may be violated, if the double expression of the affix allows the avoidance of nonoptimal clusters within a coda (such as stop-stop clusters):

> NotTwice_Coda(-sonorant)   »   SinglyExpressed(past,-d)
> Expressed(past,-d)

> (22) **breaked* /breykt/   [veyktəd]

Many morphological constraints are ranked lower than phonological constraints in phonological development. There is no obvious reason why **Aligned(Affix)** should be special.

Further, metathesis *does* occur in child phonology, but for phonological reasons. Metathesis may be motivated by **NotComplex(Onset)**:

> (23) *snow* /snow/   [nows]

If fricatives are allowed in codas, but not in onsets, metathesis may occur:

Co-occurring(Rime→+continuant)

NotCo-occurring(σ-Margin,+continuant)

Survived(+continuant)

(24) *fine*   /fayn/   [aynf]

Metathesis can occur to create more optimal consonant sequences:

NoSequence(+continuant...-continuant):   *sky* /skay/ [ksay]

Why can metathesis not occur for morphological reasons?

The absence of these patterns in language acquisition can be derived with constraints in which the specific or general location of the affix *is built into* the affixal constraints themselves. Generalized affix alignment constraints, separate from constraints on the realization of the affixes, *are not able* to explain the absence of the acquisition patterns. We propose three types of locations: (a) exact edge locations **Right** or **Left,** for true prefixes, (b) near-edge locations **NotRight** or **NotLeft,** for true infixes that are always infixes, and (c) vague locations **Right-ish** or **Left-ish**, i.e., near the edge (*possibly* at the edge, possibly not), for affixes that are infixes purely for phonological reasons. (This last constraint reflects observed variation in the location of the affix.)

In phonological development studies, we have not yet found any evidence of suffixes being converted into prefixes or infixes. This suggests that children consider exact location to be essential to the expression of an affix: **Expressed([um],Left)**. An affix will be deleted if it cannot be expressed in an exact location.

A true infix does not have a specific edge location, and therefore would have to be expressed as:

Expressed([um],Left-ish) OR   **Expressed([um],NotLeft)**

There must be an explicit *morphological* recognition that the placement of the affix is either vague, or expressly not at the edge. These marked locations are more complex conceptually. Learners do not appear to posit them unless they are motivated by evidence. This proposal opens the possibility that infixes may be difficult to learn, and that children may convert them into prefixes or suffixes. Nothing is known about the acquisition of infixation and interdigitation. Consequently, this possibility cannot be evaluated at the present time.

7. Conclusion

In this paper, using data from unrelated languages, we identified a typology of infixes, some of which showed morphological or phonological conditioning only, and some of which showed both types of conditioning. The typology suggests the interaction of a number of 'location' constraints with contiguity rankings. The location constraints vary in terms of location specificity. Acquisition data and learning issues support the need for a range of location constraints, and additionally suggest that location may need to be part of the affixal constraints themselves. Acquisition data in languages with infixation will further elucidate this issue.

8. References

Beckman, J. N. 1997. *Positional faithfulness*. Doctoral dissertation, University of .Massachusetts, Amherst. (ROA-234)

Bernhardt, B.H. and Stemberger, J.P. 1998. *Handbook of phonological development: From the perspective of constraint-based nonlinear phonology*. San Diego, CA: Academic Press.

Cole, J. S. and Kisseberth, C. W. 1994. An Optimal Domains theory of harmony. *Cognitive Science Technical Report* UIUC-BI-CS-94-02 (Language Series), University of Illinois. (ROA-22)

Hume, E. 1997. Towards an explanation of consonant/consonant metathesis. Unpublished paper: Ohio State University.

McCarthy, J.J. and Prince, A. 1993. Generalized Alignment, in G. Booij and J. van Marle, eds., *Yearbook of Morphology*, 1993, 79-153. Dordrecht: Kluwer.

Niklas, T.D. 1972. *The elements of Choctaw*. Doctoral dissertation, University of Michigan.

Prince, A. and Smolensky, P. 1993. Optimality theory. (Rutgers Univ. Cog. Sciences Center Tech. Report-2). Piscataway, New Jersey.

Schmidt, D. 1994. Phantom consonants in Basaa. *Phonology*, 11:149-178.

Stemberger, J. P. 1993. Glottal transparency. *Phonology*, 10:107-138.

Stemberger, J. P. 1996. The scope of the theory: Where does beyond lie? In L. McNair, K. Singer, L. M. Dobrin, and M. M. Aucoin, eds., *Papers from the Parasession on Theory and Data in Linguistics, CLS 23*, 139-164. Chicago: Chicago Linguistic Society.

Steriade, D. 1987. Redundant values. *Papers from the Twenty-Third Regional Meeting, Chicago Linguistic Society, 2*, 339-362. Chicago: Chicago Linguistic Society.

Robust Interpretive Parsing in Metrical Stress[1]

BRUCE TESAR

Rutgers University

1. Introduction

Most computational work to date within Optimality Theory (Prince and Smolensky 1993) has focused on generation, the mapping from an underlying form to its full structural description (Eisner 1997, Ellison 1995, Frank and Satta in press, Tesar 1995). While such a computation, labeled *production-directed parsing* by Tesar and Smolensky (1998), is a natural one, it is not the only function of interest related to an OT grammar. Language comprehension involves the interpretation of *overt forms*, forms consisting of the auditory information directly available to a listener. The function is not the inverse of generation, but the mapping from an overt form to its full structural description. The process of computing this latter function is *interpretive parsing*. Tesar and Smolensky (1996, 1998) have proposed that a particular

---

[1]The author would like to thank Paul Smolensky and Alan Prince for useful discussions. Beneficial interactions also took place with the participants of the Stanford workshop on Optimality Theory (December 1996), where some of this material was presented. The references with a listed ROA number can be obtained electronically, from the Rutgers Optimality Archive, at http://ruccs.rutgers.edu/roa.html.

form of interpretation, robust interpretive parsing (discussed below), has an important role to play not only in language comprehension but in language acquisition (see also Smolensky (1996)). Hammond (1997) has proposed a procedure specific to syllable parsing which is interpretive in nature, although it does not strictly enforce conformity of the interpretation to the overt form. Hammond's procedure is not "robust" in the sense discussed in this paper.

This paper presents an efficient algorithm for the interpretive parsing of forms for optimality theoretic systems for metrical stress. This algorithm has been used in learning simulations that have been presented elsewhere (Tesar 1997, Tesar in press). The system used for illustration in this paper has 8 freely rankable constraints, and can account for core metrical phenomena. The underlying forms are strings of syllables, and the full structural descriptions include foot structure and the assignment of stress levels to the syllables. The overt forms include the syllables and their stress levels, but not the foot structure. Overt forms are inherently ambiguous; the same pattern of stress levels is consistent with multiple foot structures. For example, a tri-syllabic overt form with main stress on the middle syllable, [˘ ˊ ˘], is consistent with a total of three distinct interpretations: a left-aligned iambic foot, [(˘ ˊ) ˘], a right-aligned trochaic foot, [˘ (ˊ ˘)], and a monosyllabic foot containing only the stressed syllable, [˘ (ˊ) ˘]. Interpretive parsing must recover the correct foot structure from the overt form, using the constraint ranking of the grammar. The algorithm presented here is based upon the dynamic programming approach of Tesar (1995), but includes extensions to deal with the non-localities of metrical structure.

Interpretive parsing poses an interesting issue that does not arise in generation: the issue of dealing with ungrammatical overt forms. By the principle of richness of the base (Prince and Smolensky 1993), an optimality theoretic grammar assigns a description to every possible input. But there can be overt forms which do not correspond to any optimal structural description of a grammar. Most traditional parsing techniques (such as those used in syntactic parsing) are designed to identify and reject ungrammatical overt forms. However, in language acquisition, the learner cannot simply reject and ignore forms which are inconsistent with their current grammar. To the contrary, such data are precisely what a learner needs to attend to; they indicate that the learner needs to modify their grammar, in such a way as to render the forms grammatical.

The point demonstrated here is that overt forms that are ungrammatical (by a learner's current grammar) are nevertheless interpretable. The interpretive parsing algorithm presented in this paper assigns the best possible interpretation to an overt form, whether it is grammatical or not. Thus, the procedure is called *robust* interpretive parsing. The ability to interpret ungrammatical overt forms depends crucially on the framework of OT; the algorithm selects, from among the possible interpretations of the overt form, that interpretation which best satisfies the ranked constraints.

Robust interpretive parsing has great significance for language learning. A child in the process of learning their native language does not yet have the correct grammar, and thus cannot rely on their grammar to judge the grammaticality of the overt forms they hear. Robust interpretive parsing allows a child to use what they have already learned to estimate a best interpretation of overt forms, which they can then use to perform further learning. Significant learning results, reported elsewhere (see Tesar (1997), Tesar (in press)), have already been obtained using this approach to learning. Those learning results are critically dependent upon the robust interpretive parsing procedure presented in this paper.

2. Computing Optimal Descriptions in Optimality Theory

Tesar (1995) developed algorithms that computing optimal descriptions for several classes of optimality theoretic grammars. Those algorithms compute production-directed parsing. A primary focus of that work was on algorithms that could deal efficiently with *faithfulness* in OT systems, that is, grammars that permit insertion and deletion of segments.

The types of OT systems discussed here don't involve faithfulness. The underlying form is an ordered list of syllables, and the grammar assigns stress levels to the syllables; no insertion or deletion of syllables is considered. However, the same basic dynamic programming approach works for these systems. This section describes an algorithm for production-directed parsing of metrical stress: given a string of syllables and a ranking of the constraints, this algorithm computes the optimal metrical structure for that string of syllables. The robust interpretive parsing algorithm, presented in section 3, will be based closely on the production-directed parsing algorithm presented here, differing only in the inclusion of one additional restriction.

2.1 The Metrical Stress System
The optimality theoretic analysis of stress described here is simplified for purposes of presentation; the eight constraints presented here are a subset of the constraints used in a larger optimality theoretic system of metrical stress grammars, used in the learning simulations investigated by Tesar (1997, in press). That larger optimality theoretic system uses ideas from several sources (McCarthy and Prince 1993, Prince and Smolensky 1993, Prince 1990, Hayes 1995, Hayes 1980), and includes analyses of quantity sensitivity and non-finality/extrametricality effects. The parsing approach presented in this paper is equally effective on the larger metrical system.

The metrical stress system for this paper has as possible inputs words consisting of strings of syllables, each labeled for weight (light or heavy). A candidate structural description for an input is a grouping of (some of) the syllables of the input into feet, under the following conditions: (i) a foot contains either one or two syllables; (ii) each foot assigns stress to exactly one of its syllables; (iii) each candidate has exactly one head foot assigning main stress, with any other feet assigning secondary stress. Condition (iii) implies that every language in the system has at least some foot structure. The system has 8 constraints, listed in (1).

(1) PARSE   a syllable must be footed
     MR   the head-foot must be rightmost in the word
     ML   the head-foot must be leftmost in the word
     AFR   a foot must be aligned with the right word edge
     AFL   a foot must be aligned with the left word edge
     IAMB   a head syllable must be rightmost its foot
     TROCH   a head syllable must be leftmost in its foot
     FOOTBIN   a foot must have two moras or two syllables

2.2 Categories for Candidates

The key idea is to build up candidate structural descriptions in stages, one syllable at a time. This section will illustrate the basic ideas, abstracting away from distinctions of main vs. secondary stress (that distinction will be added in the section 2.4). The algorithm is designed around a data structure, called the dynamic programming table. This table is used to store partial structural descriptions as they are constructed.

The ranking used for this first illustration is given in (2).

(2) FOOTBIN » PARSE » AFR » TROCH » {AFL, IAMB}

Table 1 shows the basic dynamic programming table for the input / ◡ – ◡ ◡ /, using the constraint ranking in (2). Each syllable of the input is the head of a column in the table. Observe that the column headed by the first syllable contains several partial structural descriptions, each containing the first syllable. The next column, headed by the second syllable (which happens to be heavy in this example), contains partial structural descriptions containing the first two syllables. Each partial description in the second column is obtained by taking one of the partial descriptions in the first column, and adding the second syllable to it in one way or another. The final column, headed by the final syllable, has structural descriptions containing all four syllables. The optimal description is selected from among the candidates in this final column; it is the description in row **F2**, [(◡̀ –) (◡̀ ◡)].

Table 1: Production-Directed Parsing for / ˘ ‒ ˘ ˘ / (without main stress).

	˘	‒	˘	˘
NoF	[˘]	[˘ ‒]	[(˘‒) ˘]	[˘ (˘˘) ˘]
F1NoS	[(˘)]	[˘ (‒)]	[(˘‒)(˘)]	[˘ (˘˘)(˘)]
F1S	[(˘)]	[˘ (˘)]	[(˘‒)(˘)]	[˘ (˘˘)(˘)]
F2		[(˘‒)]	[˘ (˘˘)]	[(˘‒)(˘˘)]

The labels at the far left of the rows indicate the categories for the partial structural descriptions in the rows. The label **NoF** (no-foot) means that the syllable just added to a partial description (the rightmost syllable) is unfooted. In the column for the first syllable, the partial description in row **NoF** contains the single syllable unfooted. In the subsequent cells in the row labeled **NoF**, the rightmost syllable of each partial description is unfooted. Partial descriptions are grouped into categories based upon the condition of the right-most syllable in the partial description. The four categories shown in the table are the four different ways of parsing a syllable into metrical structure.

The category **F1NoS** (foot-one-no-stress) means that the new syllable (the rightmost syllable) is the first syllable of a foot, and that the new syllable is unstressed. Because each foot must contain precisely one stressed syllable (the head syllable of the foot), a partial description in this row will only be a part of valid structural descriptions in which the next syllable is stressed and added to the same foot. Such a foot would be a bi-syllabic, iambic foot. The category **F1S** (foot-one-stress) means that the new syllable is the first syllable of a foot, and that the new syllable is stressed. Such a partial description can be legally extended in several ways: the next syllable could be added as unstressed to the same foot, creating a bi-syllabic, trochaic foot; or, the next syllable could be added outside the foot (either unfooted or beginning a new foot), leaving the current foot as monosyllabic.

The category **F1NoS** may appear useless in the context of this example, given that the ranking in (2) is in force. With that ranking, feet will always be either trochaic or, if the syllable is heavy, mono-syllabic. Because any continuation of a partial description in **F1NoS** will be a bi-syllabic, iambic foot, the partial description will never be a component of an optimal description in this language. The importance of category **F1NoS** might be more apparent when using a ranking in which some optimal descriptions contain bi-syllabic, iambic feet. This brings up a central property of this approach: the architecture of the computational system, including the identity of the row categories, is invariant across all languages (all possible constraint rankings) of the associated OT system. If the constraint ranking is changed, the computational system can function in exactly the same manner without modifying the form of the table; it merely consults the new constraint ranking when comparing partial descriptions.

The category **F2** (foot-two) means that the new syllable is the second syllable of a foot. Because feet are maximally bi-syllabic, this category need not be partitioned based on whether the new syllable is stressed or not; either the new syllable or the one before it must be stressed. A foot with two unstressed syllables is universally ill-formed, and is considered here to be banned by GEN from possible candidate descriptions. Thus, the algorithm will not generate or consider such structures.

Notice that in the column for the first syllable, there is no entry in the row for category **F2**. This is because at this point only one syllable has been processed, and the **F2** is only for partial descriptions ending on a foot with two syllables. Because insertion/deletion of syllables is not permitted in this system, there is no way to construct a partial description satisfying the requirements of that cell.

2.3 Filling the Table: A Single-Pass Method
The descriptions in the cells of the column for the first syllable are the different ways of parsing the first syllable. Cells in subsequent columns are filled by considering ways of adding the new syllable to the partial descriptions of the previous column. The key to the operation of the algorithm is that constraint violations can be assessed to partial descriptions, so that they may be compared with respect to the constraint hierarchy.

(3)   The candidate partial descriptions of the first two syllables competing to fill cell **NoF**.

		FOOTBIN	PARSE	AFR	TROCH
a.	[˘ -]		* *		
b.	[(˘)-]	*!	*	*	

Consider the cell in the column for the second syllable and the row **NoF**. Only partial descriptions with the second syllable unfooted can compete to fill this cell. There are two such candidates, shown along with some of their constraint violations in the tableau in (3). Candidate (3a) extends the partial description from the same row in the first column, [˘]. Candidate (3b) extends the partial description from row **F1S** in the first column, [(˘)]. Candidate (3b) has a violation of FOOTBIN (the top-ranked constraint), while its competitor does not, so it loses, and candidate (3a) is placed in the cell. By excluding the losing partial description at this point, the algorithm has successfully dismissed all structural descriptions of the entire word which have the first syllable footed by itself and the second syllable unfooted, without having to explicitly generate, evaluate, and compare all such candidates.

Consider two different partial structural descriptions of the first two syllables, candidates (4a) and (4b). After seeing only two syllables, it is premature to determine which of these two is more harmonic. The reason is that the (non-)existence of additional syllables in the word is crucial. If the word has no more syllables, then the foot in (4a) satisfies AFR, while (4b) violates PARSE. If there are more syllables to the word, then the foot in (4a) will ultimately incur a violation of AFR for each additional syllable. If there is exactly one more syllable, it would be added onto (4a) unfooted to become (4c) (to satisfy FOOTBIN), incurring violations of both PARSE and AFR, while the foot in (4b) could be extended as (4d), incurring a violation of PARSE but not of AFR. So, after only two syllables have been processed, both (4a) and (4b) need to be retained, pending further information.

(4)   Candidates for the first two syllables, and possible extensions with the third syllable.

		FOOTBIN	PARSE	AFR	TROCH
a.	$[(\,\breve{\;}-\,)]$				
b.	$[\,\breve{\;}\,(\,\acute{\;}\,)]$		*		
c.	$[(\,\acute{\;}-\,)\,\breve{\;}\,]$		*	*	
d.	$[\,\breve{\;}\,(\,\acute{\;}\,\breve{\;}\,)]$		*		

It is this issue that is successfully addressed by the row categorization of the dynamic programming table. Because **F1S** and **F2** are separate categories, the partial descriptions (4a) and (4b) don't compete with each other in the second column. Each is attempting to fill a *different* cell.

The appropriate time to directly compare two partial descriptions is when they qualify for the same cell. The categories defining the rows are designed so that the constraint violations incurred by the parsing of the remaining syllables will be dependent only on the category (the way in which the last syllable is parsed), and not on structural details that would distinguish different partial descriptions seeking to fill the same cell.

The rest of this section departs from the example of table 1. Consider candidates (5a), (5b), and (5c), competing to fill a cell in row **NoF**. The less harmonic members of the set may be discarded, because the constraint violations resulting from the addition of subsequent structure will be the same for all of these candidates. In (5d), (5e), and (5f), an additional foot is added onto (5a), (5b), and (5c), respectively. For the constraints shown, the violations to the right of the dotted line are the additional violations incurred when the new foot is added. The new violations are identical for each of (5d), (5e), and (5f). For any ranking, if (5a) is more harmonic than (5b) and (5c), then it is guaranteed that (5d) will be more harmonic than (5e) and (5f). Thus, all that needs to be retained is the most harmonic of (5a), (5b), and (5c). The unfooted third syllable which qualifies the partial descriptions for the category NoS acts as a shield: the additional constraint violations incurred by subsequent parsing decisions will not depend on the candidates' structure to the left of the unfooted third syllable.

(5)   Candidates for the same cell (a, b and c) will incur identical additional violations when more structure is added (d, e and f). The additional violations are shown after the dotted lines.

		PARSE		AFR		AFL	
a.	[(˘ -) ˘]	*		*			
b.	[˘ (˘) ˘]	* *		*		*	
c.	[(˘) - ˘]	* *		* *			
d.	[(˘ -) ˘ (˘ ˘)]	*		*	* *		* * *
e.	[˘ (˘) ˘ (˘ ˘)]	* *		*	* *	*	* * *
f.	[(˘) - ˘ (˘ ˘)]	* *		* *	* *		* * *

The additional violations of AFR shown for candidates (5d), (5e), and (5f) are all for the lack of alignment of the foot containing the first two syllables of each partial description. When candidates (5a), (5b), and (5c) are compared (when filling the NoF cell in the column for the third syllable), these violations have not yet been assessed, because the additional syllables added to the word have not yet been seen. But this is not a problem. Candidate (5f), which has more violations (four) of AFR than (5d) or (5e), would be derived from candidate (5c), which has more violations (two) of AFR than (5a) or (5b). Thus, when AFR is highly ranked, eliminating (5c) in favor of (5a) when filling the NoF cell in the column of the third syllable is correct and desirable; for any candidate of the whole word containing (5c), there will be a more harmonic candidate containing (5a).

2.4 Filling the Table: A Two-Pass Method

There is an alternative method of assessing alignment constraint violations to partial descriptions. This method makes two passes through the input. The first simply counts the number of syllables in the input. The second fills in the dynamic programming table as described above, except for the assessment of violations of constraints aligning to the right edge of the word. Given a count of the number of syllables, the number of align-right violations (constraints AFR and MR) incurred by a completed foot is simply the total number of syllables in the word minus the number of syllables already processed, so all the alignment violations for a foot can be assigned at once. Proper care must be exercised: when assessing partial descriptions ending with a mono-syllabic foot, the number of alignment violations incurred by the foot cannot yet be determined, because the foot might be extended in the next column to a bi-syllabic foot (reducing the number of align-right violations by one). Align-right violations can only be assessed to completed feet.

The extra pass means that this method is not strictly incremental, but it does simplify the alignment violation counting during the filling of the cells. The computational complexity of this method is the same as that of the one-pass method.

2.5 Keeping Track of Main Stress

GEN requires that every prosodic word have exactly one main stress. The actions of the processor must reflect and enforce this condition. Thus, care must be taken not to add a syllable with main stress onto a partial description already containing a syllable with main stress.

This is handled by the algorithm by splitting each of the previous row categories into two variants: one for partial descriptions in which no main stress has yet been assigned, and one for descriptions in which main stress has been assigned. The algorithm can only consider assigning main stress to a new syllable if it is adding the syllable to a partial description from a cell in a no-main-stress category to create a candidate for a cell in a main-stress category. As a result, there are a total of eight categories, as shown in table 2. The first four categories, with the prefix **NoM-**, are for partial descriptions lacking a main stress, while the second four categories, with the prefix **M-**, are for partial descriptions already containing a main stress.

The constraints specific to the head foot bearing main stress, ML and MR, can now be added to the working constraint hierarchy. The complete hierarchy is given in (6). One constraint on the location of main stress, ML, is near the top of the hierarchy.

(6)   FOOTBIN » ML » PARSE » AFR » TROCH » {AFL, MR, IAMB}

Table 2: Production-Directed Parsing for the Input / ˘ - ˘ ˘ / using all
categories, and including main stress.

	˘	-	˘	˘
NoMNoF	[˘]	[˘ -]	[(˘ -) ˘]	[˘ (˘˘) ˘]
NoMF1NS	[(˘)]	[˘ (-)]	[(˘ -) (˘)]	[˘ (˘˘) (˘)]
NoMF1S	[(˘)]	[˘ (˘)]	[(˘ -) (˘)]	[˘ (˘˘) (˘)]
NoMF2		[(˘ -)]	[˘ (˘˘)]	[(˘ -) (˘˘)]
MNoF		[(˘) -]	[(˘ -) ˘]	[(˘ -) ˘ ˘]
MF1NoS		[(˘) (-)]	[(˘ -) (˘)]	[(˘ -) ˘ (˘)]
MF1S	[(˘)]	[˘ (˘)]	[(˘ -) (˘)]	[(˘ -) ˘ (˘)]
MF2		[(˘ -)]	[˘ (˘˘)]	[(˘ -) (˘˘)]

Once all of the cells in the table have been filled, the algorithm selects the optimal description from among those in the last column. Not all entries in the final column are considered, however; several are not valid full structural descriptions. None of the candidates in the first four rows qualify as full structural descriptions, because they do not contain a main stress, and any well-formed full description must include a main stress. Among the four categories including main stress, the **MF1NoS** category is also ruled out, because the final foot does not have a head (a stressed syllable).

The optimal candidate, then, will be one of the entries in the final column for row categories **MNoF**, **MF1S**, and **MF2**. A tableau showing these three candidates and their violations of the top few constraints is shown in (7). The optimal candidate, (7c), assigning initial main stress and penultimate secondary stress, is thus correctly selected by the algorithm.

(7)   The final three full candidate descriptions and their high-ranked constraint violations; candidate c is the optimal one.

		FootBin	ML	Parse	AFR	Troch
a.	[(ˊ -) ˘ ˘]			*! *	* *	
b.	[(ˊ -) ˘ (ˋ)]	*!		*	* *	
c.	[(ˊ -) (ˋ ˘)]				* *	

3. Robust Interpretive Parsing

The interpretive parsing algorithm is similar in many respects to the production-directed parsing algorithm: the table for storing partial descriptions is structured exactly the same, the same categories are used, and the procedure for filling the cells of the table is similar. The difference comes with the addition of one extra restriction: when a new syllable is added to a partial description, the stress level of the new syllable must match the stress level it bears in the overt form. In other words, the candidate set being optimized over in interpretive parsing is really a subset of the candidate set used in production-directed parsing: interpretive parsing selects from among those candidates (defined by GEN) which match the overt form in the assignment of stress levels to the syllables.

Table 3 shows the full parsing table for interpretive parsing. The syllables at the top of each column now constitute the overt form, and each reflects the stress level assigned to it in the overt form: the third syllable bears main stress, and the other three syllables are unstressed.

Observe that many of the cells in the table are empty. This is because many of the cells could only contain partial descriptions that would fail to match the overt form. The cell for category NoMF1S for the first syllable cannot be filled, because such a description would necessarily assign a secondary stress to the first syllable, contra the overt form. The same kind of reasoning explains why a majority of the cells in the table are empty.

Once the table has been completed, the algorithm must select the optimal interpretation of the overt form, from the candidates in the final column. The candidate in the row for category MF1NoS is excluded, as it is in production-directed parsing, because the final foot has no head. This leaves two candidates, shown with their high-ranked constraint violations in (8). The more harmonic of the two, (8a), is selected as the optimal interpretation.

Table 3: Interpretive Parsing for the Input [˘ - ˘̌ ˘] using all categories.

	˘	-	˘̌	˘
NoMNoF	[˘]	[˘ -]		
NoMF1NoS	[(˘)]	[˘ (-)]		
NoMF1S				
NoMF2				
MNoF				[˘ (- ˘̌) ˘]
MF1NoS				[˘ (- ˘̌) (˘)]
MF1S			[˘ - (˘̌)]	
MF2			[˘ (- ˘̌)]	[˘ - (˘̌ ˘)]

(8)   The two full descriptions for interpretive parsing, and their high-ranked constraint violations; candidate a is the optimal one.

	FootBin	ML	Parse	AFR	Troch
a. [˘ (- ˘̌) ˘]		*	* *	*	*
b. [˘ - (˘̌ ˘)]		* *!	* *		

Interpretive parsing uses the same data structure (the dynamic programming table) and basic construction operations as production-directed parsing. All that is added is an additional restriction that the stress levels match the overt form. As a consequence, interpretive parsing proceeds even more quickly, and more candidates are eliminated early due to failure to match the stress levels of the overt form (yielding many empty cells in the parsing table). Generation and comprehension can both be accomplished with the same core optimization machinery.

4. The Role of Interpretive Parsing in Language Learning

Robust interpretive parsing plays a central role in an approach to language learning proposed by Tesar and Smolensky (1996), an approach that has more recently been implemented and investigated by Tesar (in press). Due to space limitations, only a brief outline of the approach will be given here; details and further discussion can be found in the works just cited.

The learning algorithm takes as input an overt form. Robust interpretive parsing is then applied to the overt form, using the learner's current constraint hierarchy. The learner then extracts the underlying form from the interpretation (recall that, for metrical stress, the underlying form is the syllables without any stress levels), and applies production-directed parsing to the underlying form, using the same constraint hierarchy. The learner compares the results of the two parsing procedures, in essence checking to see if they would pronounce the form in the same way as they just heard. If the descriptions are identical, no modification of the constraint hierarchy results; as far as the learner can tell, their grammar is fine. However, if the two do not match, then the learner will assume that the interpretation of the overt form assigned by robust interpretive parsing is the grammatical structural description, and will attempt to modify the constraint ranking in order to make the interpretation optimal.

The procedure used to modify the constraint ranking is called *constraint demotion*. Given the learner's current constraint ranking, and two descriptions, one that is intended to be optimal, called the *winner*, and a competing structural description that is currently more harmonic than the winner, called the *loser*, constraint demotion modifies the ranking so that, with respect to the new ranking, the winner is more harmonic than the loser (if this in fact possible). It does this by identifying the highest-ranked constraint violated more by the loser, and demoting all constraints violated more by the winner to just below it.

Recall the constraint hierarchy used in the illustrations of the previous sections, given again in (9).

(9)   FOOTBIN » ML » PARSE » AFR » TROCH » {AFL, MR, IAMB}

Given the overt form [ᴗ - ᴗ́ ᴗ], the learner applies robust interpretive parsing to that overt form, and production-directed parsing to the underlying form, the results being exactly as shown in the examples of the previous sections. The respective descriptions are shown in (10), with the result of production-directed parsing labeled the winner (10b), and the result of interpretive parsing labeled the loser (10a).

(10) The loser and winner before constraint demotion.

Overt: [˘ - ˊ˘]	ML	PARSE	AFR	TROCH
a. Loser [(ˊ-) (ˊ˘)]			* *	
b. Winner [˘ (- ˊ) ˘]	*	* *	*	*

Constraint demotion is applied to the pair, identifying the constraint AFR as the highest-ranked constraint violated more by the loser, and demoting constraints ML and PARSE down below AFR into the stratum already occupied by TROCH (the constraint FOOTBIN, not shown in the tableau , is not violated by either candidate, and remains at the top of the hierarchy). The full resulting hierarchy is shown in (11).

(11) FOOTBIN » AFR » {TROCH, ML, PARSE} » {AFL, MR, IAMB}

Now that the constraint hierarchy has been changed, both production-directed parsing and interpretive parsing can be re-applied, using the new hierarchy. The results are shown in (12), with the loser row (12a) showing the outcome of production-directed parsing, and the winner row (12b) showing the outcome of interpretive parsing.

(12) The new loser and winner, after constraint demotion.

Overt: [˘ - ˊ˘]	AFR	PARSE	ML	TROCH
a. Loser [˘ - (ˊ˘)]		* *	* *	
b. Winner [˘ - (ˊ˘)]		* *	* *	

The loser and the winner are now identical; so far as the learner can tell from this data, the new constraint hierarchy is correct. The overt form was clearly ungrammatical with respect to the previous ranking. However, because of the robustness of the interpretive parsing algorithm, the learner was able to assign a best possible interpretation to the overt form, rather than simply declaring the overt form ungrammatical and returning nothing. Notice that the result of robust interpretive parsing with the previous hierarchy, (10b), was incorrect (it has one foot stranded in the center, not aligned with either word edge), as a result of the incorrect constraint hierarchy. The best interpretation still contained enough information indicate to the learner how to modify the ranking. The application of constraint demotion to the best interpretation (as the winner) allowed the learner to end up at a constraint hierarchy for which the overt form is indeed grammatical.

References

Eisner, Jason. 1997. Efficient Generation in Primitive Optimality Theory, in *Proceedings of the 35th Annual Meeting of the Association for Computational Linguistics* (ROA-206).

Ellison, T. Mark. 1995. Phonological Derivation in Optimality Theory, in *Proceedings of the Fifteenth International Conference on Computational Linguistics*. 1007-1013 (ROA-75).

Frank, Robert and Giorgio Satta. Optimality Theory and the Generative Complexity of Constraint Violability. In press, *Computational Linguistics* (ROA-228).

Hammond, Michael. 1995. Syllable Parsing in English and French. Ms., University of Arizona (ROA-58).

Hammond, Michael. 1997. Parsing in OT. Ms., University of Arizona (ROA-222).

Hayes, Bruce. 1995. *Metrical Stress Theory: Principles and Case Studies*. Chicago: University of Chicago Press.

McCarthy, John and Alan Prince. 1993. Generalized Alignment, in G. Booij and J. van Marle, eds., *Yearbook of Morphology*, 79-154. Dordrecht: Kluwer (ROA-7).

Prince, Alan. 1990. Quantitative Consequences of Rhythmic Organization, in K. Deaton, M. Noske and M. Ziolkowski, eds., *CLS26-II: Papers from the Parasession on the Syllable in Phonetics and Phonology*, 355-398.

Prince, Alan and Paul Smolensky. 1993. Optimality Theory: Constraint interaction in generative grammar. Technical report, TR-2, Rutgers University Center for Cognitive Science, and CU-CS-696-93, Department of Computer Science, University of Colorado at Boulder. To appear in the Linguistic Inquiry Monograph Series, MIT Press.

Smolensky, Paul. 1996. On the Comprehension/Production Dilemma in Child Language. *Linguistic Inquiry* 27. 720-731 (ROA-118)

Tesar, Bruce. 1995. Computing Optimal Forms in Optimality Theory: Basic Syllabification. Ms., University of Colorado at Boulder (ROA-52).

Tesar, Bruce. 1995. *Computational Optimality Theory*. Doctoral dissertation, University of Colorado, Boulder (ROA-90).

Tesar, Bruce. 1997. An Iterative Strategy for Learning Metrical Stress in Optimality Theory, in E. Hughes, M. Hughes and A. Greenhill, eds., *The Proceedings of the 21st Annual Boston University Conference on Language Development*, 615-626. Somerville, Mass.: Cascadilla Press (ROA-177).

Tesar, Bruce. An Iterative Strategy for Language Learning. In press, *Lingua*, special issue on conflicting constraints.

Tesar, Bruce and Paul Smolensky. 1996. Learnability in Optimality Theory (long version). Technical Report JHU-CogSci-96-4, Department of Cognitive Science, the Johns Hopkins University (ROA-156).

Tesar, Bruce and Paul Smolensky. 1998. Learnability in Optimality Theory. *Linguistic Inquiry* 29:2. 229-268.

The Syntactic Locality of Temporal Interpretation[*]

ELLEN THOMPSON

University of Puerto Rico

1. Introduction

Recent work on the syntax of tense shows that there is a principled relationship between the meaning and the phrase structure representation of temporal information (Hornstein (1977), (1990), Zagona (1988), Giorgi and Pianesi (1991), Stowell (1993)). I contribute to this discussion here by arguing that syntactic locality at LF constrains the interpretation of temporal relations; temporal dependency between times requires the times to be in the same checking domain at LF.

Based on this claim, I present an analysis of the syntax and semantics of gerundive relative clauses in subject position. I argue that gerundive relatives are temporally dependent on the main clause tense and are thus required to be within the checking domain of a matrix time at LF. A gerundive relative within a subject which is located in VP at LF receives a reading where the gerund is temporally dependent on the time associated with the head of VP, while a gerundive relative associated with a subject interpreted in TP is temporally dependent on the time of the head of TP.

* I would like to thank Juan Uriagereka, Norbert Hornstein, and Jairo Nunes for very helpful suggestions on this work. An earlier version of this paper appeared in the Fortieth Anniversary of Generativism On-line Conference, December, 1997, and was presented at the LSA Meeting, 1998. I am grateful to those audiences for comments and questions. I would also like to thank the organizers of WCCFL XVII for all of their help.

This paper is organized as follows: in section 2, I outline the Reichenbachian (1947) aproach to tense adopted here, and I sketch a proposal for the syntactic representation of tense. Section 3 shows that the temporal interpretation of gerundive relatives is dependent on the tense of the main clause; a gerundive relative may be interpreted either with respect to the Event time or the Speech time of the main clause.

Section 4 presents a syntactic analysis of these temporally dependent readings. Evidence for this proposal is discussed from constructions involving coordination, existential *there*, scope of quantificational adverbials, and presuppositionality effects, in section 5. Section 6 discusses the behavior of gerundive relatives with respect to binding-theoretic reconstruction effects, and section 7 turns to an analysis of extraposition with gerundive relatives.

2. Framework

2.1 Semantics of Tense
Within the framework of Reichenbach (1947), tenses are composed of three times: the Event time, the Reference time, and the Speech time. This system is illustrated in (1), where the Event time is the time of Mary's leaving, the Reference time is the time by which Mary's leaving takes place (2:00 in this sentence), and the Speech time is the time at which the sentence is uttered.

(1)   At 2:00, Mary had left.

I assume Hornstein's (1990) Reichenbachian approach to tense, according to which the structures of the basic tenses of English are as in (2), where the linear order of the Speech, Reference and Event times reflects their temporal order. If two times are separated by a line, the leftmost time is interpreted as temporally preceding the other time. If two times are separated by a comma, they are interpreted as cotemporal.[1]

(2)   S , R , E   present   E _ S , R   present perfect
        E , R _ S   past   E _ R _ S   past perfect
        S _ R , E   future   S _ E _ R   future perfect

2.2 Syntax of Tense
In the spirit of much recent work on the syntax of tense, I assume that times are the syntactic, as well as the semantic, primitives of tense

---

[1] The term "time" is used here as a cover term for temporal points and intervals.

(Hornstein (1977), (1990); Zagona (1988); Giorgi and Pianesi (1991); Stowell (1993)).

I adopt Hornstein's (1990) proposal that the Event time is associated with VP, whereas the Speech and Reference times are associated with Inflectional projections. I propose that the Event time is a semantic feature of the head of VP, the Reference time a semantic feature of the head of Asp(ect)P, and the Speech time a semantic feature of the head of T(ense)P, located above AspP.

Evidence for the structural hierarchy of Event and Reference times comes from the distribution of temporal point adverbials. In clause-final position, these adverbials may modify the Event time or the Reference time; (3) may mean that the leaving event takes place at 3 p.m. (Event time reading), or that the leaving event takes place sometime before 3 p.m. (Reference time reading).

(3)   Mary had left the store at 3 p.m.

However, when a temporal point adverbial is unambiguously associated with VP, it modifies only the Event time; in the VP fronting construction in (4), the leaving event takes place at 3 p.m., not sometime before 3 p.m.

(4)   Mary claimed that she had left the store at 3 p.m., and left the store at 3 p.m. she had.

In contrast, when the adverbial occurs above VP, as in (5), with a clause-initial temporal point adverbial, this adverbial modifies the Reference time only; the reading is that the leaving takes place sometime before 3 p.m., and not at 3 p.m.

(5)   At 3 p.m., Mary had left the store.

The discussion of the syntax and semantics of gerundive relatives presented here will provide evidence that the Speech time is located in TP and the Event time in VP.

3. Interpretation of Gerundive Relatives

Enç (1987:645) notes that the temporal interpretation of finite relative clauses is independent of the tense of the matrix clause (see also Ladusaw (1977), Dowty (1982), Abusch (1988) for discussion of the temporal interpretation of relative clauses). This is shown by (6), where the matrix event of complaining and the gerund event of waiting are both interpreted as occurring in the past relative to the Speech time, but are temporally independent of one another; the complaining or the waiting may take place first, or they may take place at the same time.

(6)   A passenger who was waiting for flight #307 complained to the flight attendant.

Hudson (1973) points out that in contrast to finite relative clauses, gerundive relatives are interpreted as temporally dependent on the main clause (see also Comrie (1985)). The gerund event of waiting in (7) may take place at the time of the matrix event of complaining (Hudson's "derivative" reading), with the meaning 'A passenger complained to the flight attendant while he was waiting for flight #307'. The event of waiting may also take place at the Speech time (Hudson's "deictic" reading), with the meaning 'A passenger who is now waiting for flight #307 complained to the flight attendant'. However, a temporally independent reading, for example with the waiting taking place sometime in the past before the complaining, is not possible.

(7)   A passenger waiting for flight #307 complained to the flight attendant.

3.1   Temporal Dependency of Gerundive Relatives

In order to account for the temporal dependency of gerundive relatives, in this section I analyze their tense structure. Following Hornstein (1990:115-117), I assume that gerunds have a reduced tense structure with no Speech time, consisting of only Reference and Event times, as in (8).

(8)   R , E

Evidence that gerundive relatives lack a Speech time is that they do not permit tense markers, as shown in (9). Since the tense morpheme orders the Reference time with respect to the Speech time (see Hornstein (1990)), given that there is no Speech time, there can be no tense marker.

(9)   *The passengers were waiting for flight #307 left the room.

A tense structure may be interpreted by being temporally linked to the time of the event of utterance, the Speech time, or by being linked to another time which is in turn linked to the Speech time. Because the tense structure of a gerund cannot be anchored to a Speech time within its own clause, it must be interpreted by being linked to the matrix tense.

I claim that the two readings of (7) (which is repeated in (10)) are due to interpretation with respect to different times of the matrix tense. The reading of (10) where the waiting is interpreted as occurring at the time of complaining (Event time reading) results from the tense structure of the gerund linking to the Event time of the main clause, as shown in the structure in (11b).

(10)   A passenger waiting for flight #307 complained to the flight attendant.

(11)   a.   Event time reading - event of gerund (waiting) is interpreted as occurring at time of matrix Event (complaining)

        b.   E , R _ S
              |
              R , E

In contrast, the reading where the waiting occurs at the time of Speech (Speech time reading) results from the tense structure of the gerund linking to the Speech time of the main clause, as in (12b).

(12)   a.   Speech time reading - event of gerund (waiting) is interpreted as occurring at time of Speech

        b.   E , R _ S
                    |
                    R , E

4. Syntax of Subject Gerundive Relatives

4.1 A Restriction on Time Linking

In this section, I turn to a discussion of the syntactic representation of the Event and Speech time readings.

I propose that the Event time reading requires the gerundive tense to be in a syntactically local relation with the Event time of the main clause, and the Speech time reading requires the gerundive tense to be local with the Speech time of the main clause. This locality requirement is formulated in (13a), the Condition on Time Linking, which states that in order for times to link in tense structure, they must be located in the same checking domain at LF. The definition of checking domain assumed here is illustrated in (13b), where the checking domain of V contains DP_1 and H (Chomsky (1995: 325)).

(13)   a.   Condition on Time Linking - In order for time α to link to time β, α and β must be within the same checking domain at LF.

b.

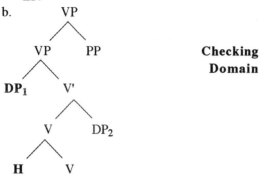

Checking
Domain

Event and Speech time readings of gerundive relatives thus correlate with the position of the subject at LF. Adopting the VP Internal Subject Hypothesis, the subject is generated within VP (I assume that this position is Spec, VP), and moves from this position to Spec, TP (see Zagona (1982), Kitagawa (1986), Speas (1986), Koopman and Sportiche (1991)). Subjects interpreted within VP at LF therefore result in gerundive relatives being temporally dependent on the Event time, since VP is the position of the Event time. On the other hand, subjects interpreted inside TP at LF result in gerundive relatives being temporally dependent on the Speech time, since TP is the position of the Speech time.[2]

(14)   Temporal interpretation   LF interpretation site of subject
       Event time reading   Spec, VP
       Speech time reading   Spec, TP

5. Structural Evidence

In this section, I present evidence for the proposed analysis of the syntax of

---

2 Note that a "Reference time reading", with the event of the gerund interpreted with respect to the Reference time of the main clause, does not seem to be available. In (i), the Reference time (the time by which the getting water event takes place) is made salient; it is 2:00. (i) may be interpreted with the leading event taking place at the time of getting some water (Event time reading), or as taking place at the time of utterance (Speech time reading); however, (i) cannot be interpreted with the leading event taking place at 2:00 (Reference time reading).

(i)   The runner leading the race had gotten some water by 2:00.

This is as expected, given that the subject may be interpreted either in Spec, VP (Event time reading) or in Spec, TP (Speech time reading).

gerundive relatives from constructions involving coordination, existential *there*, the scope of quantificational adverbials, and presuppositionality effects.[3]

5.1 Coordination

Full relatives which are coordinated in subject position may receive independent temporal interpretations. This is illustrated in (15), where the first relative *who entered the department in 1993* is interpreted as past with respect to the Speech time (the entering takes place before the Speech time), and the second relative *who finish their work on time* is interpreted as past with respect to the time of the event of going to the conference (the finishing takes place before the time of going to the conference, but may be after the Speech time).

(15)   Three students [who entered the department in 1993] and [who finish their work on time] will go to the conference next month

In contrast to full relatives, when gerundive relatives are coordinated in subject position, they must be evaluated with respect to the same time. In (16), the events of waiting and suffering may be both interpreted as occurring at the Event time, with the reading 'Three passengers called the manager at the time that they were waiting for the next ship and suffering from seasickness'. The waiting and suffering may also be interpreted with respect to the Speech time, with the meaning 'Three passengers who are now waiting for the next ship and who are now suffering from seasickness called the manager'. However, although it is pragmatically plausible, it is not possible to interpret the waiting as occurring at the utterance time and the suffering as occurring at the time of calling the manager, with the meaning 'Three passengers who are now waiting for the next ship called the manager at the time that they were suffering from seasickness'.

(16)   Three passengers waiting for the next ship and suffering from seasickness called the manager.

---

[3] In this paper, I focus on the syntax of gerundive relatives in subject position and I do not consider objects. As is well-known, objects participate in determining the interpretation of the temporal contour of the event in a way in which subjects do not (for example, see Verkuyl (1972)). Recent research suggests that the contribution of the object to the aspectual structure of the sentence is reflected in its syntactic position. Given the added variable of the influence of the syntax of objects in determining the temporal contour of the sentence, I put them aside here, leaving exploration of this area for future research.

Since distinct temporal interpretations for coordinated relatives are possible with full relatives, it does not seem to be purely due to a semantic problem that coordinated gerundive relatives cannot be interpreted with respect to different times. This effect is predicted on the current analysis of gerundive relatives; since the subject including the conjoined relatives must be interpreted either in Spec, TP, or in Spec, VP, both gerunds must be interpreted either with respect to the Speech time or with respect to the Event time.

5.2   Existential Constructions

Support for the claim that subject gerundive relatives are interpreted within VP when they relate to the Event time and within TP when they relate to the Speech time comes from existential constructions. Note that (17a) is ambiguous; it can have an Event time reading, where the waiting is interpreted with respect to the time of storming into the room, or it can have a Speech time reading, where the waiting is interpreted with respect to the utterance time. However, the existential construction version of (17a) in (17b) does not permit the Speech time reading; the waiting here is necessarily interpreted with respect to the event of storming into the room.

(17)   a.   Three passengers waiting for the flight stormed into the room.
        b.   There stormed into the room three passengers waiting for the flight.

I assume, following den Dikken (1995) and Groat (1995), that existential constructions involve interpretation of the associate of the expletive within VP. Evidence for the VP-internal position of the associate discussed by den Dikken (1995) comes from contrasts in reciprocal licensing. In (18a), the subject *some applicants* can bind *each other* in the PP *to each other*, but binding is not permitted in the existential construction version of (18a) in (18b). Assuming that the reciprocal *each other* must be c-commanded at LF by its antecedent, this contrast shows that whereas the subject of (18a) c-commands the reciprocal, the associate in (18b) does not c-command the reciprocal at LF. This is explained if the associate is interpreted within VP.

(18)   a.   Some applicants$_i$ seem to each other$_i$ to be eligible for the job.
        b.   *There seem to each other$_i$ to be some applicants$_i$ eligible for the job.

Given that the associate of the expletive is interpreted within VP at

LF, the present analysis correctly predicts that only the Event time reading is permitted in the existential construction, since when the subject is located within VP, it is in the checking domain of the Event time.

5.3 Scope of Quantificational Adverbs

Certain quantificational adverbs show a scope ambiguity with respect to the subject. This is illustrated in (19), which may be interpreted with the adverb taking scope over the subject, with the meaning 'It is usually the case that there are some three passengers or other such that they get stranded here', or may be interpreted with the subject taking wide scope, meaning 'There are three particular passengers such that they usually get stranded here'.

(19)   Three passengers usually get stranded here.

This scope ambiguity correlates with the Event or Speech time reading of gerundive relatives. When the gerund receives an Event time reading, the subject is interpreted as within the scope of the adverb. On this reading of (20), the meaning is 'There are usually some three passengers or other such that they get stranded here when they are waiting for flight #307'. It is not possible for the subject to take wide scope, meaning 'There are three particular passengers such that they usually get stranded here when they are waiting for flight #307'. However, when the gerund receives a Speech time reading, the subject is interpreted as outside the scope of the adverb; here, the meaning of (20) is 'There are three particular passengers who are waiting for flight #307 such that they usually get stranded here'. The reading with wide scope for the adverb is not possible: 'There are usually some three passengers or other who are now waiting for flight #307 such that they get stranded here'.

(20)   Three passengers waiting for flight #307 usually get stranded here.

Given that the quantificational adverb is located between the TP subject position and VP, since on the present analysis the Event time reading is linked to VP-internal interpretation of the subject, we correctly predict that on this interpretation the subject is within the scope of a quantificational adverb. Conversely, given that the Speech time reading is linked to TP interpretation of the subject, on this interpretation, the subject is outside the scope of the quantificational adverb.[4]

---

[4] I assume here that the quantificational adverb does not raise at LF, an assumption which is in the spirit of current Minimalist non-QR analyses of scope effects (see Kitahara (1992), Hornstein (1994), (1995), Beghelli and Stowell forthcoming for discussion).

5.4 Presuppositionality Effects

The interpretation of the subject as cardinal or presuppositional influences the temporal interpretation of the gerundive relative. Cardinal subjects result in the Event time reading only; in (21), the event of waiting is interpreted as occurring relative to the time of complaining, not relative to the time of Speech. For example, (21) with *few* may mean 'Few passengers who were waiting for flight #307 complained to the flight attendant at the time that they were waiting', but may not mean 'Few passengers who are now waiting for flight #307 complained to the flight attendant'. This is predicted by the current analysis, if we assume, following Diesing (1992), that cardinal DPs are interpreted within VP at LF, and are therefore within the checking domain of the Event time.

(21)   Passengers/Few passengers waiting for flight #307 complained to the flight attendant

In contrast to cardinal subjects, presuppositional subjects permit both Event and Speech time readings, as shown by the examples in (22a) and (22b); (22a) with *every* may mean 'Every passenger who was waiting for flight #307 complained to the flight attendant at the time that they were waiting', or it may mean 'Every passenger who is now waiting for flight #307 complained to the flight attendant'.

(22)   a. Every/Each/All/Most passenger(s) waiting for flight #307 complained to the flight attendant
         b. Most/Some/All of the passengers waiting for flight #307 complained to the flight attendant

Given that analyses of presuppositionality claim that cardinal DPs are within VP at LF, and presuppositional DPs outside VP at LF (Diesing (1992)), the fact that presuppositional subjects are temporally ambiguous seems to be a puzzle. However, deHoop's (1993) analysis of presuppositionality may explain this issue. deHoop shows that in languages such as Dutch with overt scrambling of presuppositional DPs, scrambling is optional; although only presuppositional DPs may scramble, they also may remain inside VP. Carrying over this view of scrambling to English, which shows presuppositionality effects at LF, the interpretation of presuppositional DPs in VP-external position can be seen as optional, accounting for the data discussed in this section. [5]

---

[5] The present analysis of the temporal interpretation of gerundive relatives in subject position may be extended to subject nominals in general, which also show presuppositionality effects.

6. Reconstruction Effects and Gerundive Relatives

It has been noted in the literature that relative clauses contrast with complement clauses in that they do not show binding-theoretic reconstruction effects with WH-movement (see van Riemsdijk and Williams (1975), Freidin (1986), Lebeaux (1988) for discussion). In (23a), with the complement clause *that John was asleep*, the WH-phrase *which claim that John was asleep* behaves as if it is located in its pre-movement position; *he* cannot be coreferent with *John*. However, in (23b), with the relative clause *that John made*, *which claim that John made* behaves as if it is outside the c-command domain of the subject; *he* can corefer with *John*.

(23)   a.   *Which claim that John$_i$ was asleep did he$_i$ say was false?
        b.   Which claim that John$_i$ made did he$_i$ say was false?

Gerundive relatives, unlike full relatives, do not seem to circumvent reconstruction effects. This is illustrated in the contrast between (24a), with a full relative, and (24b), with a gerundive relative; in (24a), *Chomsky* and *he* can corefer, but in (24b), coreference is not permitted. The gerundive relative, unlike the full relative, behaves as if it reconstructs.

(24)   a.   Which student who was reading Chomsky's$_i$ book did he$_i$ say
              was smart?
        b.   *Which student reading Chomsky's$_i$ book did he$_i$ say was
              smart?

The analysis of gerundive relatives presented here, in combination with Lebeaux's (1988) proposal for the anti-reconstruction effect of relative

---

Musan (1995) discusses examples such as (ia) and (ib), where the subject of (ia) is interpreted either as people who were professors in the forties, or as people who are now professors, whereas (ib) allows only the reading where the people were professors in the forties (data from Musan (1995:75-76)).

(i)   a.   In the forties, all professors were young.
        b.   In the forties, professors were young.

Musan considers but rejects an analysis of this contrast according to which presuppositional subjects, such as in (ia), are interpreted in IP (TP), and are therefore outside the scope of the tense operator, whereas cardinal subjects are interpreted within VP, and are thus within the scope of the tense operator. However, even if we assume that there is a tense operator, it is not clear how being outside the scope of this operator would result in the reading where the description is evaluated relative to the time of utterance. This proposal can be reformulated within the framework adopted here; in (ia), the subject may be interpreted within TP, where it is evaluated with respect to the Speech time, whereas in (ib), the subject may be interpreted in VP, and is therefore evaluated with respect to the Event time. I leave development of this analysis for future work.

clauses, makes possible an explanation of this contrast between full and gerundive relatives. Lebeaux (1988) argues that the relative clause of (23b), unlike the complement clause of (23a), is not present before WH-movement takes place, but is adjoined to the WH-phrase by generalized transformation after the WH-phrase moves to Spec, CP. Since the relative clause is never in object position, it cannot reconstruct to object position.

I claim that although full relatives can be adjoined by generalized transformation after WH-movement has taken place, this option is not available for gerundive relatives because they are temporally dependent on the main clause. If a gerundive relative were to adjoin to the WH-phrase after the WH-phrase moves to Spec, CP, the relative would not be within the checking domain of a time of the main clause, since the times are located in TP and VP. Hence the gerund would not receive a temporal interpretation. Therefore, gerundive relatives must be present before movement takes place in order to be interpreted relative to a matrix time, and thus they show reconstruction effects.

7. Extraposition

Williams (1975) notes that gerundive relatives, unlike full relatives, do not undergo extraposition, as shown in the contrast between (25a) and (25b). ((25b) is unacceptable on the relative clause reading of *wearing a fedora*.)

(25)   a.   A man said hello to me who was wearing a fedora.
        b.   *A man said hello to me wearing a fedora.

This contrast is predicted by the present analysis of gerundive relatives. We have seen that gerundive relatives are interpreted with respect to the Speech or Event time of the matrix clause by being located within the checking domain of TP or VP at LF. An extraposed relative, since it is adjoined, is not within the checking domain of any time. Hence an extraposed gerundive relative cannot be temporally interpreted.[6]

Note that if it were possible for an extraposed gerundive relative to reconstruct, it should be able to be interpreted with respect to the time that the subject is within the checking domain of. However, it seems that extraposition does not permit reconstruction, as shown in the binding data in (26), from Guéron (1980:650). Coreference is possible between *Mary* and *her* in (26a), but not in (26b), with extraposition of *of Mary*, showing that

---

[6] Note that this analysis supports Chomsky's (1995:325) definition of checking domain, which excludes adjuncts, as opposed to Chomsky's (1995:178) earlier formulation, which includes adjuncts.

reconstruction in order to avoid a Binding Condition C violation is not possible with extraposition.

(26)   a.   A picture of Mary$_i$ was sent to her$_i$
         b.   *A picture was sent to her$_i$ of Mary$_i$

The same effect is seen with extraposed relative clauses as with PPs, as seen in the contrast between (27a) and (27b).[7]

(27)   a.   A picture that Rembrandt$_i$ painted was sent to him$_i$
         b.   *A picture was sent to him$_i$ that Rembrandt$_i$ painted

8. Conclusion

In this paper, I have shown that the LF syntax of subjects provides evidence that the Event time of tense structure is associated with VP, while the Speech time is associated with TP. Gerundive relatives in subject position are temporally dependent on the matrix Event or Speech time. Assuming the proposal that temporal dependence requires times to be in the same checking domain, a subject located within VP at LF results in an Event time reading for a gerundive relative, while a subject located within TP at LF results in a Speech time reading for a gerundive relative.

Constructions involving coordination, existential *there*, scope of quantificational adverbials, and presuppositionality effects have provided

---

[7] Reduced *-ed* relatives are also impossible in extraposed position, as seen in (i) ((ib) is unacceptable on the intended interpretation, where *arrested in London* modifies *three men*).

(i)   a.   Three men arrested in London shot a police officer.
        b.   *Three men shot a police officer arrested in London.

I follow Hudson's (1973) analysis of these constructions whereby they involve a covert perfect tense, and therefore the tense structure of the relative clause is E _ R. The two meanings of (ia) are thus derived in the same way that the readings for gerundive relatives are; the reading where the relative event of arresting takes place before the matrix event of shooting is represented by the tense structure in (iia), where the Reference time of the relative links to the Event time of the main clause. The reading of (ia) where the event of arresting takes place after the time of shooting is represented by the tense structure in (iib), where the Reference time of the relative tense links to the Speech time of the main clause. The analysis of gerundive relatives in extraposed position thus carries over to *-ed* relatives.

(ii)   a.   E, R _ S
                                    |
                            E _ R

        b.   E, R _ S
                                    |
                              E _ R

evidence for this proposal. The analysis also explains why, unlike full relatives, gerundive relatives do not circumvent reconstruction effects with WH-movement, and do not undergo extraposition.

The broader goal of this paper has been to show that it is possible to advance our understanding of the connection between the semantic and syntactic representation of time in natural language by making use of core notions of the Minimalist Program; the semantic relation of temporal dependency between times requires those times to be within the same checking domain at LF.

References

Abusch, Dorit. 1988. Sequence of Tense, Intensionality and Scope, in Proceedings of the West Coast Conference on Formal Linguistics 7, 1-14. Stanford Linguistics Association, Stanford University, Stanford, CA.

Beghelli, Filipo and Tim Stowell. To appear. *The Direction of Quantifier Movement.*

Chomsky, Noam. 1995. *The Minimalist Program.* Cambridge, Mass.: MIT Press.

Comrie, Bernard. 1985. *Tense.* Cambridge: Cambridge University Press.

Diesing, Molly. 1992. *Indefinites.* Cambridge, Mass.: MIT Press.

Dikken den, Marcel. 1995. Binding, Expletives, and Levels. *Linguistic Inquiry* 26:347-353.

Dowty, David. 1982. Tenses, Time Adverbs, and Compositional Semantic Theory. *Linguistics and Philosophy* 5:23-55.

Enç, Murvet. 1987. Anchoring Conditions for Tense. *Linguistic Inquiry* 18:633-657.

Freidin, Robert. 1986. Fundamental Issues in the Theory of Binding, in B. Lust, ed., *Studies in the Acquisition of Anaphora, volume 1,* 151-188. Boston: D. Reidel.

Giorgi, Alessandra and Fabio Pianesi. 1991. Toward a Syntax of Temporal Representations. *Probus* 3:1-27.

Groat, Erich. 1995. English Expletives: A Minimalist Account. *Linguistic Inquiry* 26:354-365.

Guéron, Jacqueline. 1980. On the Syntax and Semantics of PP Extraposition. *Linguistic Inquiry* 11:637-676.

Hoop de, Helen. 1992. Case Configuration and Noun Phrase Interpretation. Doctoral dissertation, Rijksuniversiteit Groningen.

Hornstein, Norbert. 1977. Towards a Theory of Tense. *Linguistic Inquiry* 8:521-557.

Hornstein, Norbert. 1990. *As Time Goes By.* Cambridge, Mass.: MIT Press.

Hornstein, Norbert. 1994. An Argument for Minimalism. *Linguistic Inquiry* 25:455-480.

Hornstein, Norbert. 1995. *Logical Form: From GB to Minimalism.* Oxford:

Blackwell.

Hudson, R.A. 1973. Tense and Time Reference in Reduced Relative Clauses. *Linguistic Inquiry* 4:251-256.

Kitagawa, Yoshihisa. 1986. Subjects in English and Japanese. Doctoral dissertation, University of Massachusetts at Amherst.

Kitahara, Hisatsugu. 1992. Checking Theory and Scope Interpretation without Quantifier Raising, in H. Thráinsson and S. Kuno, eds., *Harvard Working Papers in Linguistics* 3, 51-71. Cambridge, Mass.: Harvard U.

Koopman, Hilda and Dominique Sportiche. 1991. The Position of Subjects. *Lingua* 85:211-259.

Ladusaw, William. 1977. Some Problems with Tense in PTQ, in *Texas Linguistic Forum* 6, University of Texas, Austin.

Lebeaux, David. 1988. Language Acquisition and the Form of the Grammar. Doctoral dissertation, University of Massachusetts at Amherst.

Musan, Renate. 1995. On the Temporal Interpretation of Noun Phrases, Doctoral dissertation, MIT.

Reichenbach, Hans. 1947. *Elements of Symbolic Logic*. New York: The Macmillan Company.

van Riemsdijk, Hans and Edwin Williams. 1981. NP-Structure. *The Linguistic Review* 1:171-217.

Speas, Margaret. 1986. Adjunction and Projections in Syntax. Doctoral dissertation, MIT.

Stowell, Tim. 1993. The Syntax of Tense. Ms., UCLA.

Verkuyl, Hank. 1972. *On the Compositional Nature of the Aspects*. Dordrecht: Reidel.

Williams, Edwin. 1975. Small Clauses in English, in *Syntax and Semantics*, volume 4, ed. J. Kimball, 249-273. New York: Academic Press.

Zagona, Karen. 1982. Government and Proper Government of Verbal Projections. Doctoral dissertation, University of Washington at Seattle.

Zagona, Karen. 1988. *Verb Phrase Syntax*. Dordrecht: Kluwer.

A-Templatic Reduplication in Halq'eméylem

SUZANNE URBANCZYK

University of British Columbia

1. Introduction[1]

Recent approaches to reduplication have eschewed prosodic templaticism (defining invariant shape by positing prosodic templates) in favour of a-templaticism, where there are no templates *per se* (see McCarthy and Prince *to appear*, Urbanczyk 1996, Spaelti 1997, Gafos 1998 for example). This paper adds to this growing body of research by illustrating a new type of a-templatic reduplicative phenomenon in Halq'eméylem (Central Coast Salish). The 'continuative' morpheme is expressed in a variety of ways, as can be seen by the data in (1).

(1)   Halq'eméylem 'continuative' (Galloway 1993)

a.   wíqəs   wíwəqəs   'yawn/ yawning'
b.   máq'ət   hámq'ət   'swallow s.t./ swallowing s.t.'
c.   łəxʷáłtsɛ   łáxʷəłtsɛ   'spit/ spitting'
d.   ʔíməx   ʔí:məx   'walk/ walking'

Galloway (1993) observes that the 'continuative' can be formed by reduplication (1a), hə- prefixation (1b), stress shift (1c) or vowel

---

[1] I would like to thank everyone at the Stó:lo Shxwelí for generously sharing their knowledge and insights about Halq'eméylem with me. I would also like to thank Laura Benua, Strang Burton, Laura Downing, Ewa Czaykowska-Higgins, Kimary Shahin, John McCarthy, Doug Pulleyblank, Lisa Selkirk, Pat Shaw, Bernard Tranel and Moira Yip as well as audiences at the University of Calgary, UC Irvine and WCCFL 17 for helpful feedback as this research has evolved over the past year. All errors are mine.

lengthening (1d).[2] This paper proposes that the morpheme is essentially reduplicative in nature (RED^{cont}), and that the non-copied forms of the morpheme emerge in order to avoid a marked reduplicant. This pattern of reduplicative allomorphy is termed 'avoidance of the marked' to highlight the parallels with 'emergence of the unmarked' (McCarthy and Prince 1994) where marked structure is eliminated in the reduplicant. However, rather than having unmarked structure emerge in the reduplicant, in the 'continuative', reduplication is avoided altogether. The driving force behind the non-reduplicative allomorphy is to produce a phonologically distinct 'continuative' stem. No other input specifications are necessary.

The paper begins by outlining the theoretical assumptions (§2). An abreviated analysis of each of the Halq'eméylem patterns of 'continuative' allomorphy is presented next (§3). This is followed by a summary and discussion of the conditions necessary for a language to exhibit 'avoidance of the marked' (§4).[3]

2. Optimality Theory and Correspondence

The analysis is set within Optimality Theory, where constraints on phonological well-formedness are ranked and violable (henceforth OT: Prince and Smolensky 1993). In OT, alternations occur when some high ranking constraint on well-formedness compels violation of some lower ranked constraint on identity. Correspondence Theory defines the identity relations that exist between related strings (McCarthy and Prince 1995, *to appear*).

(2) Correspondence

Given two strings, S_1 and S_2, **correspondence** is a function $\Re$ from the elements of S_1 to the elements of S_2. Elements $\alpha \in S_1$ and $\beta \in S_2$ are referred to as **correspondents** of one another when $\alpha\Re\beta$.

Correspondence relations have been shown to hold between input and output (IO), base and reduplicant (BR), and output words (OO). All three will be referred to in the analysis and will be illustrated as needed below.

---

[2] All data cited here are of the Upriver (or Stó:lō) dialect of Halq'eméylem. The sources are Galloway's (1993) *Grammar of Upriver Halkomelem* and the classified wordlist contained in *Tó:lméls ye Siyelyólexwa*. All data are phonemicized consistently with the grammar and presented using the IPA.

[3] The analysis presented here is a radical departure from Urbanczyk (1998a), where the 'continuative' is argued to be non-reduplicative. It is hoped that the analysis developed here proves that a reduplicative analysis is possible. Given space limitations, rather than delve into a formal comparison of both analyses, the reader is referred to Urbanczyk (1998b).

3. Halq'emeylem 'continuative' Allomorphy

Halq'eméylem, like other Salish languages, has a rich system of reduplicative and non-concatenative morphology. This section presents an abbreviated analysis of the four basic patterns of 'continuative' formation. For the most part, the choice of allomorphs is predictable, based on the phonological shape of the base. The central goal here is to show the rankings necessary to derive 'avoidance of the marked'.

3.1 Reduplicative Allomorph
If the 'non-continuative' begins with a single consonant and a stressed full vowel, the 'continuative' is formed by CV- reduplication (3).

(3)	CV- prefix		
a.	t'í:ləm	t'ít'ələm	'sing/ singing'
b.	xákw'əm	xáxəkw'əm	'bathe/ bathing'
c.	p'ɛ́tθ'	p'ɛ́p'ətθ'	'sew/ sewing'
d.	p'ɛ́tθ'ət	p'ɛ́p'ətθ'ət	'sew it/ sewing it'
e.	yíq	yíyəq	'fall (snow)/ snowing'
f.	yáqw'əm	yáyəqw'əm	'perspire/ perspiring'
g.	wíqəs	wíwəqəs	'yawn/ yawning'

Being a reduplicative morpheme, 'continuative' (RED^cont) is segmentally empty in the input, acquiring its phonological exponence via a BR-relation present only in the output. The stem to which RED^cont is attached achieves its exponence via an IO-relation, as below. The reduplicant is underlined.

(4)   Basic Model of Reduplication (McCarthy & Prince *to appear*)
        Input: /RED^cont - wiqəs/
                                    ⇕   *Stem I-O Faithfulness*
        Output: wí ⇐⇒ wəqəs
                Reduplicant   Base   *B-R Identity*

Faithfulness constraints are formulated in a general way, to evaluate the identity between S_1 and S_2. In the model above, S_1 is the input or the base, while S_2 is the output or the reduplicant. Each relation has a distinct set of constraints evaluating identity. Total identity satisfies all faithfulness constraints. Partial reduplication and deletion violate Max, which requires every element of S_1 (base or input) to be in S_2 (reduplicant or output).

The CV- shape can be derived without reference to templates, by assuming that it is an emergent property of the reduplicant. 'Emergence of the unmarked' or TETU effects are achieved by having phono-constraints intervening between high-ranking IO-Faith and low-ranking BR-Ident (5).

(5)   Emergence of the Unmarked (McCarthy and Prince *to appear*)
       IO-Faith >> Phono-constraint >> BR-Ident

Mono-syllabism can be derived by any constraint which penalizes syllables or segments. Following Urbanczyk (1998c), the relevant constraint is proposed to be *Struc-Syll, which penalizes all syllables in the output (a specific version of the more general *Struc - Zoll p.c. cited in Prince and Smolensky 1993: §3.1). A violation is incurred by each syllable in the output. The output allows more syllables because IO-Max is high-ranking. The reduplicant minimizes the number of syllables because BR-Max is low-ranking. CV- shape is achieved by minimizing NoCoda violations. The fact that the reduplicant has any exponence at all follows because the 'continuative' must be phonologically distinct from the 'non-continuative' (this point is discussed further below). The following tableau verifies that these TETU rankings will select a CV- shaped reduplicant as optimal.[4]

(6)   IO-Max >> *Struc-Syll, NoCoda >> BR-Max

REDᶜᵒⁿᵗ wiqəs	IO-Max	*Struc-Syll	NoCoda	BR-Max
a ☞ wí-wəqəs		σσσ	*	qəs
b wíqə-wəqəs		σσσσ!	*	s
c wiq-wəqəs		σσσ	**!	əs
d wíq-wəq	*!*	σσ	**	
e wí-wəqə	*!	σσσ		qə

The optimal candidate (6a) fares the best on the phono-constraints (cf. 6b

---

4 The base virtually always has a reduced vowel in Halq'eméylem, reduplication leading one to question how the vowel in the reduplicant can be reliably obtained. There are several devices available to ensure that the base vowel is accurately reflected in the reduplicant including an Input-Reduplicant-relation (McCarthy and Prince *to appear*), having the base be the related 'non-continuative' stem (in the spirit of Downing *to appear*, Steriade 1997), proposing a sympathetic candidate (McCarthy 1997), or by having the feature parsed in the reduplicant satisfy IO-Faithfulness (Struijke 1998; Pulleyblank 1998). I leave this interesting question for further research, noting that the basic analysis is not affected.

and 6c) and IO-Max (cf. 6d and 6e). CV- shape is derived as an emergent property of the reduplicant without reference to templatic constraints. These effects are obtained because BR-Max is ranked lowest. The low-ranking of BR-Max will turn out to be crucial in explaining the other forms of 'continuative'.

3.2 /hə- hɛ-/ Allomorph

If the 'non-continuative' begins with a sonorant-stressed schwa sequence, the 'continuative' is formed by /hə-/ prefixation, as exemplified by the data below.[5] Note also the loss of the base schwa.

(7)   hə- prefix

	'non-contin'	'continuative'	
a.	məq'ət	həmq'ət	'swallow s.t./ swallowing s.t.'
b.	ləp'əx	hɛlp'əx	'eat s.t/ eating s.t.'
c.	ləqəm	hɛlqəm	'dive/ diving'
d.	yə́θət	hɛ́yθət	'talk about st/ talking about st'
e.	yə́θəst	hɛ́yθəst	'tell it/ telling it'
f.	yə́q'əs	hɛ́yq'əs	'file/ filing'

A reduplicative allomorph is marked in these stems for two reasons. First, it is marked to have stressed schwa in the reduplicant. Second, it is marked to have a sonorant onset.[6] The analysis of these sonorant-schwa stems is contrasted with the sonorant-full vowel stems.

Bianco (1996) shows that stress and vowel quality interact in interesting ways in Cowichan (Island Hul'qumi'num'), where stress prefers to fall on /a/, and resists falling on schwa. In order to explain interactions of this sort, Kenstowicz (1996) proposes the following set of harmonically ranked constraints where vocalic sonority and stress are linked. Because /a/ is the most sonorous vowel, it makes the best peak. This translates to *P/a being ranked the lowest. Schwa is the least sonorous vowel and is the worst peak, hence highest ranked *P/ə (8a). The reverse ranking is made for unstressed vowels in margin (M) position (8b).

---

5 There are actually two vowels: [ə ɛ]. Thanks to Catalina Renteria and Helen Joe for pointing out a strong tendency for the front vowel to occur before coronals.

6 Evidence that this the correct avenue of explanation comes from the following form, which is the only case in the corpus which begins with an obstruent-stressed schwa sequence. Here reduplication occurs, and stress stays on the base vowel.

i.   χə́ylt   χəχə́ylt   'write it/writing it'

(8)   Sonority-Driven Stress   (Kenstowicz 1996)
a.   *P/ə   >>   *P/i, u   >>   *P/e, o >>   *P/a
b.   *M/a   >>   *M/e, o   >>   *M/i, u   >>   *M/ə

Tableau (9) shows that for full-vowelled stems, regardless of the ranking of the *P and *M constraints, reduplication is prefered to hə́...prefixation. Candidates with non-initial stress are ruled out because, with relatively few exceptions, 'continuatives' have initial stress.

(9)   RV... Stems

REDᶜᵒⁿᵗ wiqəs	*P/ə	*M/i,u
a ☞ wíwəqəs		
b hə́wiqəs	*!	*!

A third candidate, not indicated, is *[híwəqəs], which also obeys these constraints. It is ruled out by either IO-Linearity ([i] and [w] are reversed) or BR-Anchor (the initial segment of the base is not initial in the reduplicant). If we look at schwa-vowelled stems, it is clear that they fare they same on the *P and *M constraints as can be seen by the following tableau. Some other constraint must be active to rule out candidate (10b).

(10)   Rə- Stems

REDᶜᵒⁿᵗ mq'ət	*P/ə	*M/i,u
a. hə́mq'ət	*	
b. mə́mq'ət	*	

As mentioned above, it is proposed that a constraint against sonorant onsets is active in choosing between candidates.

(11)   *SonOnset: Supralaryngeally articulated sonorants are marked
                         in the Onset.   (cf. Itô & Mester *to appear*)

There are two types of evidence that this constraint is active in Coast Salish. First, syllable contact effects can be explained by appeal to this constraint. Urbanczyk (1996) notes that syncope is blocked in Lushootseed diminutive stems if the result would be a hetero-syllabic cluster of rising sonority. Second, some glides in Mainland Comox (Northern Coast Salish) alternate with obstruents. The conditioning factor is syllabic position: obstruents are found in the onset and glides in the coda (Blake 1992).[7]

(12)   Mainland Comox (Blake 1992)
         obstruent   glide
a.   d͟ʒúθʋt   dʒú-jθotəs   'to push/ pushing it'
b.   qégəθ   qéw͟   'deer/ Deer (mythical name)'

*SonOnset must be ranked higher than BR-Max, in order to compel maximal violation with schwa-vowelled stems, but lower than *P and *M because it is violated with sonorant-V stems. When there is no reduplicative exponent at all BR-Max is maximally violated (as in Gafos 1998). The following tableau verifies the ranking, and that both patterns can be successfully derived.

(13)   *P/ə, *M/i,u >>*SonOnset >> BR-Max

RED^{cont} wiqəs	*P/ə	*M/i,u	*SonOn	BR-Max
☞ wíwəqəs			**	qəs
hə́wiqəs	*!	*!	*	həwiqəs
RED^{cont} məq'ət				
☞ hə́mq'ət	*			həmq'ət
mə́məq'ət	*		*!*	q'ət
mə́mq'ət	*		*!	q'ət

The analysis proposes that schwa and /h/ are epenthetic and are inserted in order to make the 'continuative' distinct from its non-continuative counterpart.[8] The existence of epenthetic schwa in Salish is non-controversial (Kinkade 1992). Vowel insertion violates Dep-V and /h/-insertion violates Dep-C (Dep says every element in S_2 has a correspondent

---

[7] Not all glides alternate, leaving some analysts to posit that the voiced obstruent is basic. However, many of the non-alternating palatal glides are derived historically from /l/.

[8] This differs from Hukari's (1977) analysis of Cowichan Hul'qumi'num' where the /h/ is derived by a type of debuccalization rule affecting reduplicative sonorants. If this turns out to be correct for Halq'eméylem, then this allomorph is reduplicative as well. In any case, the debuccalization would presumably be triggered by *SonOnset .

in S_1). /h/-insertion satisfies high-ranking ONSET, which is unviolated in Salish in general. The question arises as to why the more faithful [mə́q'ət] is not optimal. Briefly, it is not phonologically distinct from the non-continuative form. Thus, a constraint requiring stems to be phonologically distinct - DistinctStem - must be active in Halq'eméylem.[9] Distinctness or Identity of stems is checked via an OO relation between 'continuative' and 'non-continuative', as illustrated below (obeyed in 14a, violated in 14b).[10]

(14)   OO-Identity Checking for DistinctStem

O: 'non-continuative'   a.   mə́q'ət   b.   mə́q'ət

O: 'continuative'   hə́mq'ət   mə́q'ət

Tableau (15) verifies the ranking of Onset & DistinctStem above IO-Dep-C.

(15)   ONSET , DistinctStem >> IO-Dep-C

RED^{cont} məq'ət	ONSET	DistinctStem	IO-Dep-C
☞ hə́mq'ət			*
mə́q'ət		*!	
ə́mq'ət	*!		

Evidence that /h/ is in fact epenthetic comes from an /h/ ~ ø alternation that occurs between 'continuative' and 'resultative' stems. The data in (16ab) and (17a) show that resultatives are formed by adding the /s-/ 'stative' prefix to intransitive 'continuative' forms in both Upriver and Island dialects. If a root begins with a sonorant-schwa sequence, only /s-/ occurs, the /h/ is lost, as can be seen in (16c) and (17bc).

(16)   Upriver Halq'eméylem 'resultatives' (Galloway 1993)
a.   p'íw   sp'íp'əw   'freeze/ frozen'
b.   t'έːl   st'έt'əl   'go out of sight/ shade'
c.   lə́c'ət   səlíc'   'fill it/ filled'

---

[9] Note that the relevant constraint must be something like DistinctStem (cf. Rose 1997) and not MorpReal (cf. Gafos 1998, Walker 1998) because the 'continuative' has only a single input and when there is no reduplication, there is no exponence, in violation of MorphReal.

[10] See Alderete (in prep) for a formal and fully developed Anti-Faithfulness approach to obtaining phonologically distinct stems, relying on OO-Correspondence.

(17)   Cowichan Hul'qumi'num' 'resultatives' (Hukari 1978)

a.   yákʷ'ət   syáy'əkʷ'   'break it/ broken'

b.   nə́qəm   sə́n'qəm'   'dive/ dived & still under'

c.   snə́xʷəɬ   sənxʷíɬ   'canoe/ arrived by canoe'

If /h/ is epenthetic, then there is a ready explanation for the /h/ ~ ø alternation: /h/ is inserted only when necessary. When the 'stative' prefix supplies an onset, there's no need to insert /h/.[11]

    To summarize, 'avoidance of the marked' occurs with sonorant-schwa stems because high-ranking Phono-constraints (*P, *M and *SonOnset) compel violation of IO-Faith and total violation of BR-Max.

3.3 Vowel Lengthening Allomorph

If the 'non-continuative' stem begins with a glottal, then 'continuative' words are formed by vowel lengthening.

(18)   V lengthening

a.   ʔíməx   ʔíːməx   'walk/ walking'

b.   ʔítət   ʔíːtət   'sleep/ sleeping'

c.   ʔíwəst   ʔíːwəst   'teach/ teaching'

d.   ʔəmə́t   ʔá́ːmət   'to sit up, down/ sitting'

e.   héwə   héːwə   'hunt/ hunting'

f.   hékʷ'ələs   héːkʷ'ələs   'remember st/ remembering st'

g.   hάqʷət   hάːqʷət   'smell s.t./ smelling s.t.'

    The analytic task is to determine why reduplication is marked with glottal-initial stems. The general tack is to examine Halq'eméylem glottal phonology/phonotactics more closely. In the following discussion ʔ refers to glottal stop and /h/, C is any supralaryngeally articulated consonant, V is any non-schwa vowel. Interestingly, glottal-schwa sequences are extremely rare in Halq'eméylem. An examination of the over 2,000 words contained in *Tó:lméls ye Siyelyólexwa* reveals thousands of Cə and CəC syllables. Only twenty ʔə syllables were found, all of which are prosodic-word initial. There were only six ʔəC syllables, half of which are derived from CəC

---

11 Also, while rare, some [s-h] initial words have been observed, suggesting that the alternation is not phonotactically motivated.

reduplication.[12] On the other hand, there are over a hundred ʔV syllables, initially and internally. Thus it appears that the only time schwa is found after a glottal is when the root is glottal-initial. The relative rarity of ʔə syllables, and their restriction to initial position can be explained if we assume that they are glottal-initial stems. There are no ʔC initial stems in the corpus, so schwa must be epenthetic in this context. The lack of ʔə stems internally is explained if there is a constraint against ʔə. Internal epenthesis would produce əʔ instead (which is also marked). The fact that about half of the ʔəC syllables are inherently reduplicated also receives explanation if the glottal is present underlyingly, and schwa is epenthetic.

Furthermore, if one examines diminutive stems, it turns out that of the 21 diminutive stems with full vowels, six don't reduce the base vowel to schwa. (Diminutives are also accompanied by initial stress.) Lack of vowel reduction is unexpected, because reduplication virtually always occurs with vowel reduction. For diminutives (CV-), its the stem vowel that's reduced, for plurals (CVC-), its the reduplicant vowel that reduces. Of these exceptional diminutives, two are the only glottal-initial diminutive stems found (19ab). This is significant because it means that there are no CV-reduplicants which allow vowel reduction when the first consonant is a glottal. Of the remaining exceptions, one has an irregular vowel (19c) and the rest maintain pitch accent (19d) or stress (19ef) on the base vowel.

(19)   Non-Reduced Diminutives

a.	ʔáχəθ	ʔiʔaχíθ	'lie down/ baby lying down'
b.	héwt	hihéw t	'rat/ little rat'
c.	yiláw	yáyilaw	'after/ a little after'
d.	χèːm	χíχèːm	'cry/ to sob'
e.	ɬíːm	ɬiɬíːm	'pick berries/ picking a little'
f.	sqéːq	kikék	'younger sibling/ little sister'

Thus it seems that glottal-schwa syllables are marked in general, making reduction of the base vowel to schwa marked when C_1 is a glottal. Candidates with glottal codas are not an option either because historically, glottal codas have been lost in Upriver Halqʼeméylem compared to Downriver (Musqueam) and Island (Cowichan) Halqʼeméylem where they are

---

12 A notable exception is /h/-epenthesis which occurs with continuatives. There was a correlation between vowel quality and glottal type, where high vowels are only followed by a glottal stop and low vowels prefer to be preceded by the glottal fricative. This may explain why the epenthetic glottal is the fricative and not the stop with schwa.

retained (Elmendorf and Suttles 1960).[13]   The survey of the wordlist is consistent with the comparative data. There were no glottal codas.

These observations can be translated into the following constraints and interactions. First, the phono-constraints. If glottals and schwa are placeless, then these types of syllables are marked because they do not have a head (or articulatory target). The lack of a featural head also entails a lack of prominence. The example in (18d) above is particularly interesting, because the initial [ʔə] resists being stressed altogether - stress falls on the second syllable instead. The usual situation is for stress to fall on the first schwa in schwa-only stems. Further research on Halq'eméylem glottals is needed to verify these proposals regarding glottal-schwa interactions, but we will use them in the analysis for now. The anti-lengthening IO-Identity constraints Ident-μ, Dep-μ, and *VV, defined informally below.

(20)   *ʔə]   Placeless syllables are not permitted.

       *ʔ]$_\sigma$ Glottals are not allowed syllable-finally.

       Ident-μ Moraic specification of vowels is identical.

       Dep-μ Every μ in S_2 is in S_1.

       *VV   Long vowels are not permitted.

The following tableau illustrates that the glottal phono-constraints must dominate anti-lengthening IO-Faith and BR-Max. The optimal candidate (21a) violates a number of constraints. However, other candidates are worse.

(21)   Glottal-initial stems

RED^{cont} ʔiməx	*ʔə]	*ʔ]$_\sigma$	Ident-μ	Dep-μ	*VV	BR-Max
a. ☞ ʔíːməx			*	*	*	ʔiməx
b. ʔíʔməx		*!				məx
c. ʔíʔəməx	*!					məx

Once again we see that high-ranking phono-constraints compel violation of IO-Faith and total BR-Max violation.

3.4 Stress Shift Allomorph

The final set of stems show that if the 'non-continuative' stem has non-initial stress, the 'continuative' is formed by shifting stress word-intially.

---

[13] Of related interest, the markedness and rarity of əʔ] sequences is wide-spread in Interior Salish, as been noted by Bessel and Czaykowska-Higgins (1991) and Shaw (1998).

(22)   Non-Initial Stress [14]

a.	łəxʷółtsɛ	łóxʷəłtsɛ	'spit/ spitting'
b.	tsʼətłʼóm	tsʼótłʼəm	'jump/ jumping'
c.	tˢsɛ́θà:m	tˢósətəm	'you were told/ being told'
d.	tθʼəχʷásəm	tθʼóχʷəsəm	'wash face/ washing one's face'
e.	səqʼɛ́t	sóqʼət	'split s.t./ splitting s.t.'
f.	pətɛ́:mət	pótmət	'ask s.o./ asking s.o.'
g.	kʷʼəxɛ́:t	kʷʼɛ́xtəs	'count s.t./ he's counting'

An analysis of the stress patterns of these forms would take us too far afield, so lets jump straight to the chase - to understand why reduplication does not occur.

Recall that, with a few exceptions, 'continuative' stems have initial stress. So, one aspect of any analysis is to have an account of the stress pattern. This could be accomplished by having a separate stress requirement. Interestingly, the effect of initial stress can be achieved without requiring an input specification. Using the constraints already motivated - and the idea that 'continuative' stems are formed in the most harmonic way - the best way to make the 'continuative' distinct from the 'non-continuative' is to shift stress to the initial position. Actually, stressed schwas and morphological stress aside, this happens to be the default position for stress in Coast Salish in general (Urbanczyk 1996 - Lushootseed; Bianco 1996 - Cowichan; Bar-El & Watt 1998; Dyck 1998 - Squamish; Blake 1992 - Mainland Comox). Unable to avoid a stressed schwa, the 'continuative' stems avoid having the marked stress pattern.

More technically, the 'avoidance of the marked' occurs with these stems because IO-Dep dominates BR-Max. The following tableau shows that this must be the case. If we compare the stress-shift candidate (23a) with reduplicated (23b) or epenthesized (23c) candidates, stress-shift is optimal because it is most faithful to the input. Candidates (23bc) both violate IO-Dep-C. Reduplication always violates IO-Dep. For the most part, we don't count violations of IO-Dep in tableaux because we assume that for reduplication to occur BR-Max must dominate IO-Dep. Here we see that the reverse ranking is possible. Candidate (23d) is out because it is not phonologically distinct from the 'non-continuative'.

---

[14] The following exception was found, which takes a reduplicative prefix. Note that the stressed syllable is followed by a glide, suggesting that it might not be formed by stress-shift because reduction of the stressed vowel would lead to glide vocalization.

| i. | χʷəlá:ystəm | χʷəχʷəlá:ystəm | 'to stagger/ staggering' |

(23)   *P/ə, *M/i,u, Distinct >> IO-Dep-C >> BR-Max

	*P/ə	*M/i,u	Distinct	IO-Dep-C	BR-Max
a ☞ ɬə́xʷəɬcɛ	*				ɬəxʷəɬcɛ
b. ɬə́ɬxʷəɬcɛ	*			*!	xʷəɬcɛ
c. hə́ɬxʷəɬcɛ	*			*!	hə́ɬəxʷəɬcɛ
d. ɬəxʷə́ɬcɛ	*		*!		ɬəxʷəɬcɛ

4. Summary

To summarize, the 'continuative' morpheme has been analyzed as an a-templatic reduplicative morpheme, whose shape is determined by the shape of the base to which it is attached. Phonotactic considerations (formalized as phono-constraints) play a role in determining whether or not the morpheme is realized as a reduplicant, or as a minimal change in the base, such as epenthesis, vowel-lengthening, or stress-shift. In the first two, the avoidance of the marked occurs under compulsion of a high-ranked phono-constraint. With sonorant-schwa stems, reduplication and epenthesis both result in a stressed schwa. Epenthesis avoids a sonorant onset. This differs from stress-shifted stems where having a stressed schwa is also unavoidable with reduplication and epenthesis. Stress shift is preferred because it is the most IO-Faithful option. Vowel-lengthening successfully avoids a glottal-schwa sequence which would occur with a reduplicative allomorph.

The analysis has led to the following constraint interactions. The central ranking that emerges to produce 'avoidance of the marked' is that some Phono-Constraint compels violation of IO-Faith and maximal violation of BR-Max.

(24)   Ranking Summary
a.   CV- shape
         IO-Max >> *Struc-Syll, NoCoda >> BR-Max
b.   Reduplication with full vowels, not with schwa
         *P/ə, *M/i,u >>*SonOnset >> IO-Dep-C >> BR-Max
c.   Epenthesis with sonorant-stressed schwa roots
         DistincStem, Onset >> IO-Dep-C >> BR-Max
d.   Vowel-lengthening with glottal-intial stems
         DistinctStem, *ʔ]σ, *ʔə] >> IO-Ident-μ, IO-Dep-μ, *VV, BR-Max

e.   Stress shift with non-initial-stressed stems
      DistinctStem, *P/ə, *M/i,u >> IO-Dep-C >> BR-Max

The ranking in (24a) is a TETU ranking as generated by the schema in (5). In terms of defining a ranking schema for 'avoidance of the marked', a pattern is found, where Phono-Constraints dominate IO-Faith, with BR-Max as the very lowest constraint. This is consistent with either one of the following rankings (where 25a is a case of 25b).

(25)   Avoidance of the Marked
a.   Phono-Constraint >> IO-Faith >> BR-Max
b.   Phono-Constraint >> IO-Faith, BR-Max

Finally, let us compare these rankings to the typology developed in McCarthy and Prince (*to appear*). The ranking in (25a) is similar to the ranking which derives 'normal application' in reduplication, where phonological alternations are not restricted to any one domain, nor is identity forced in any one domain. Thus, a varied pattern of stem allomorphy is the result of a set of phonological conditions compelling a variety of changes to input-output pairings. The type of alternation that a stem undergoes is directly related to its phonological shape and the phonological patterns of the language. Avoidance of the marked is simply another way that phonological constraints affect the shape of morphemes, and in this case, the shape of a stem, in true a-templatic fashion.

Bibliography

Alderete, John. in prep. *Morphologically Governed Accent in Optimality Theory.* Doctoral dissertation, University of Massachusetts, Amherst.

Bar-El, Leora and Linda Watt. 1998. What determines stress in Sk̲wx̲ú7mesh? *Proceedings of the 33rd ICSNL*: 407-427.

Bessel, Nicola and Ewa Czaykowska-Higgins. 1991. Interior Salish evidence for placeless laryngeals, *Proceedings of NELS 22*: 35-50.

Bianco, Violet. 1996. *The Role of Sonority in the Prosody of Cowichan*. MA Thesis, University of Victoria.

Blake, Susan. J. 1992. *Two Aspects of Sliammon (ɬáʔamɪnqən) Phonology: Glide/obstruent Alternation and Vowel Length*. MA Thesis, UBC.

Coqualeetza Elders Group, Stalo Heritage Project Elders Group, the Halkomelem Workshop of the Nooksack Tribe, and Brent Galloway. 1980. *Tó:lméls ye Siyelyólexwa: Wisdom of the Elders*. Coqualeetza Centre: Sardis, BC.

Downing, Laura. *to appear*. Morphological correspondence constraints on KiKerewe reduplication. *Proceedings of WCCFL 16*.

Dyck, R. 1998. Stress assignment & syllable structure in Squamish. m.s. UVic.

Elmendorf, William & Wayne Suttles. 1960. Pattern and change in Halkomelem Salish dialects. *Anthropological Linguistics*: Vol. II, no. 7. 1-32.

Gafos, Diamandis. 1998. Eliminating long-distance consonantal spreading. *Natural Language and Linguistic Inquiry*: 16: 223-278.

Galloway, Brent. 1993. *A Grammar of Upriver Halkomelem*. University Publications in Linguistics 96: University of California Press.

Hukari, Tom. 1978. Halkomelem non-segmental morphology. *Proceedings of the 13th ICSNL*: 157-209.

Itô, Junko and Armin Mester. *to appear*. Realignment, in Kager, van der Hulst, and Zonneveld, eds., *The Prosody - Morphology Interface*. Cambridge: CUP.

Kenstowicz, Michael. 1996. Quality-sensitive stress. *Rivista di Linguistica*.

Kinkade, M. Dale. 1992. The chemirical status of schwas. m.s. UBC.

McCarthy, John. 1997. Sympathy and phonological opacity. m.s. University of Massachusetts, Amherst.

McCarthy, John and Alan Prince. 1994. Emergence of the unmarked: Optimality in Prosodic Morphology, in Gonzàlez ed. *Proceedings of NELS 24*: 333-79.

McCarthy, John and Alan Prince. 1995. Faithfulness and reduplicative identity. in Beckman, Walsh Dickey, & Urbanczyk eds. *Papers in Optimality Theory: UMOP 18*. GLSA: 249-384.

McCarthy, John and Alan Prince. *to appear*. Faithfulness and identity in Prosodic Morphology, in Kager, van der Hulst, and Zonneveld (eds) *The Prosody - Morphology Interface*. Cambridge: CUP.

Prince, Alan and Paul Smolensky. 1993. *Optimality Theory: Constraint Interaction in Generative Grammar*. Technical Report #2 of the Rutgers Center for Cognitive Science, Rutgers University.

Pulleyblank, Douglas. 1998. Markedness-based feature-based Faithfulness. Talk presented at SWOT 4: University of Arizona.

Rose, Sharon. 1997. Multiple correspondence in reduplication. *Proceedings of Berkeley Linguistics Society* 23.

Shaw, Patricia A. 1998. Escher effects in morphology. Talk presented at CLA.

Spaelti, Phillip. 1997. *Dimensions of Variation in Multi-Pattern Reduplication*. Doctoral dissertation, UC Santa Cruz.

Steriade, Donca. 1997. Lexical conservatism and its analysis. m.s. UCLA.

Struijke, Caro. 1998. Reduplicant and output TETU in Kwakwala: A new model of Correspondence. *University of Maryland Working Papers* 7: 150-178.

Urbanczyk, Suzanne. 1996. *Patterns of Reduplication in Lushootseed*. Doctoral dissertation, UMass, Amherst.

Urbanczyk, Suzanne. 1998a. Segment doubling and Integrity violation, m.s. University of British Columbia.

Urbanczyk, Suzanne. 1998b. Avoidance of the marked, m.s. UVic.

Urbanczyk, Suzanne. 1998c. Reduplicative shape and segmentism: A unified approach, m.s. University of British Columbia.

Walker, Rachel. 1998. Minimizing RED: Nasal copy in Mbe. m.s. University of California at Santa Cruz.

Island Insensitivity of Focus and Wh-Phrase

HAE-KYUNG WEE

Indiana University

1. Introduction

Among the currently available focus theories, a long standing controversial
issue is whether focus phrases undergo wh-movement or not: In generative
syntax tradition, it has been believed that focus phrases require a variable
binding structure for interpretation, that is, they undergo wh-movement.
Chomsky (1976) argued for this scoping approach because focus structures
trigger Weak Crossover effects, similar to other quantifiers and wh-phrases.

Under this scoping approach of focus, one can expect that they show
the movement constraints. However, focus does not show island sensitivity
which other quantifiers show as illustrated in (1a - 1c).

(1) a. The professor rejected the proposal that [John]_F submitted.
    b. The professor rejected the proposal that no/every student submitted.
    c. * Who did the professor reject the proposal that [ ]*i* submitted?

Focus can have scope outside the complex noun phrase as in (1a) whereas
other quantifiers cannot as in (1b) and (1c). This island insensitivity of focus
has been the grounds to refute the scoping approach to the LF of focus, and

accordingly the movement of focus. As an alternative, Rooth's (1985) recursive definition of alternatives provides an account of focus interpretation in situ. Rooth's non-quantificational approach to focusing, which generates a set of alternative propositions, does not run into this problem. Alternatives of the following type are generated to the proposition expressed in the sentence (1a): *The professor rejected the proposal that MARY submitted; The professor rejected the proposal that BILL submitted;* and the focus is the constituent that has different values in the alternatives.

One problem of Rooth's alternative semantics approach is that, as pointed out by Kiss (1995), it does not represent the exhaustiveness involved in focusing. Rooth's representation will not imply that of the set of alternatives only the alternative *the professor rejected the proposal that JOHN submitted* is true. The second problem of Rooth's method is that the quantification is performed over the set of propositions. But, the quantificational domain of the focus *John* in the sentence like (1a), for instance, should be the set of the individuals including *John*, rather than the set of the alternative sentences as enumerated above. In addition, as acknowledged by Rooth (1995) himself, there exist other cases of island escaping operators, for example, indefinites and certain wh-questions including wh-in-situ. Given this semantic similarity among the group of island-escaping operators, Rooth suggests that it might be possible to replace the focus-specific definition with a theory in which focus is one of a family of island-insensitive operators. I believe this paper can be a step towards establishing such a more general theory that can treat focus as one of its part.

In this paper, I support the scoping approach. I provide a solution for the problem of island insensitivity of focus phrases by adopting and expanding the analysis independently developed for the study of some wh-in-situ phrases and weak island insensitive wh-questions, especially the notion of Pesetsky's (Pesetsky 1987) 'D-linking' (Discourse-linking) or 'referentiality' (Cinque 1991), based on the parallelism between wh-questions and the corresponding focus structures. More specifically, the goal of this paper is as follows: First, I will show that the characterizing property of the kind of *wh*-phrases that can occur inside of a scope island is that they presuppose the existence of a variable that can replace the wh-phrase; that is, they are definite. Then, I will show that the focal phrases are also definite based on my observation that they also have existential presupposition. Second, following Pesetsky who argues for *unselective binding* for some wh-in-situ phrases by treating them as *variables* rather than operators, I propose that focus phrases as well as definite wh-phrases also should be treated as variables to be unselectively bound by an operator, whereby they can be scoped without movement. Third, I will provide a mechanism that could incorporate the parallelism between the definite wh-phrases and focal phrases, which will be free from Rooth's problems mentioned above.

2. Island Insensitivity of Wh-phrases and Narrow Foci

First, let us observe the sentences that include a focus constituent embedded in the scope island, that is, those constructions that would violate the island constraints under the assumption of focus movement. All focus phrases in (2) and (3) are embedded in an island:

(2)   a. Mary wonders whether to invite [John]$_F$.
        b. I didn't invite [John]$_F$.
        c. I regret that she talked to [John]$_F$.

(3)   They caught the thief who stole [the Volvo]$_F$.

Each of these sentences in (2) can be an answer to a corresponding wh-question as shown in (4). Such wh-questions as those in (4) have prompted a lot of researches due to its peculiar behavior that selectively allows the movement of wh-phrases out of the island as shown in (4a-c). Since these islands, *i.e., wh*-clause, negation, and the complement of certain factive verbs, allow only certain kinds of wh-phrases, but not all, to move out of the island, they are called weak islands as opposed to strong islands such as the complex noun phrase in (4) which completely blocks the movement of the wh-phrases in English as illustrated by the ill-formed wh-question in (5).

(4)   a. A: Which man$_i$ does Mary wonder whether to invite t$_i$?
           B: Mary wonders whether to invite [John]$_F$.
           cf) ?Who$_i$ do you wonder whether to invite t$_i$?

        b. A: Which man$_i$ didn't you invite t$_i$?
           B: I didn't invite [John]$_F$.
           cf) ? Who$_i$ didn't you invite t$_i$?

        c. A: Which man$_i$ do you regret that she talked to t$_i$?
           B: I regret that she talked to [John]$_F$.
           cf) ? Who$_i$ do you regret that she talked to?

(5)   A: * Which$_i$ car did they catch the thief who stole e$_i$?
        B: They caught the thief who stole [the Volvo]$_F$.

(6)   A: Mu-sun cha-rul   humchin   pemin-ul   capassni?
           Which car ACC stole   REC thief -ACC   caught
        "For which car, the thief of that car was caught?"

The type of the sentences as in (5A), however, is allowed in other languages like Korean and Japanese as in (6).

The key observation here is that both focus and certain kind of interrogative wh-phrases show island insensitivity with respect to scoping structure. This seems to suggest that the nature of the commonality between this type of wh-phrases and foci might be related to island insensitivity. The characterizing property of the wh-interrogatives in (4-5) can shed some light to the island insensitivity of a focus, too. So, I will take advantage of some proposals that have been put forward for this type of wh-phrases.

There have been various studies on the nature of wh-phrases extractable from a weak island. Szabolsci and Zwarts (1993) and Cresti (1995) argue that they should be *individual type* variables, Kiss (1993) defines their nature as *specificity*, and Cinque (1991) defines them as *referents*, etc. Another early proposal for the wh-questions that have a conceptually close relationship with the weak island extractee is found in Pesetsky (1987).

2.1 D-linking and Unselective Binding

Pesetsky(1987) argues that the wh-in-situ phrases that violate the Superiority Condition, which is a movement constraint, do not move at LF. Since wh-phrases must have the scope at LF, whether they undergo LF movement or not, Pesetsky claims that such wh-phrases violating movement constraints remain in situ and they can have scope by some other mechanism. According to him, among wh-in-situ phrases, *which* phrase and *normal* occurrence of *who* or *what* are discoursally different in that *which*-phrases are discourse-linked (D-linked), whereas *who* and *what* are normally not D-linked. When a speaker asks a question like *which book did you read?*, the range of felicitous answers is limited by a set of books both speaker and hearer have in mind. No such requirements are imposed on normal use of wh-phrases like *who, what,* or *how many*. He claims that the wh-phrases which are D-linked such as *which-phrases* (including other wh-phrases which are forced to be D-linked by context) can be left in situ. He suggests that D-linked wh-phrases are exempted from moving either in syntax or in LF because they are not operators but variables unselectively bound by an interrogative operator in COMP. By being bound by an interrogative operator in COMP, the D-linked in-situ wh-phrases can get a relevant scope without movement and accordingly without any movement violation. He assimilates the mechanism of obtaining the scope of this type of wh-phrases to that of *Existential Closure* of indefinites in the sense of Heim (1982) in that indefinites that remain free are unselectively bound by an existential quantifier which is inserted at the text level.

Pesetsky provides the representation that incorporates his idea of treating D-linked wh-phrases as variables bound by the interrogative operator Q as in (7) for a sentence with multiple interrogations such as *who read what?*, for instance.

(7) $[[_{COMP} Q_{i,j}$ *which man$_i$*$]$ e_i read *which book$_j$*$]$

He extends this idea for the kind of Japanese wh-questions that corresponds to the Korean counterpart in (6) which occurs in strong island environments such as Complex NP. The wh-phrase in (6) is D-linked and hence it does not have to move from the complex NP to COMP.[1]

Given that *which*-phrases are typical examples which are extractable from weak island as in (4a-c), this notion of D-linking can be applicable to weak island extractee if his analysis for in-situ which-phrases in multiple interrogations is correct.

However, there is a problem in the notion of D-linking as the criterion for the island extractee. Cresti (1995) and Szabolsci and Zwarts (1993) claim that D-linking cannot be the proper condition to characterize the island extractee given the availability of wh-phrases that are not D-linked but can extract from a weak island as shown by the question like (8). (8) can be felicitously uttered in a context where someone sees another person "madly searching through the dictionary":

(8)   What the hell do you still not know how to spell?[2]

(8) shows that even *wh-the-hell* phrases, which guarantee non D-linking, can be extracted from wh-island. Szabolsci and Zwarts (1993) and Cresti (1995) argue that the condition for the island insensitivity is that the wh-variable must be an **individual type** (*e* type) and that, when set in a context where an individual answer is easily available, non D-linked wh-phrases can be extracted from a weak island. According to them, D-linking is relevant only so far it facilitates individuation.

From an empirical point of view, the claim of Cresti (1995)and Szabolsci and Zwarts (1993) for an individual type variable as the requirement for the wh-phrase extractee from the weak island context seems to be a correct generalization, but it does not provide any explanatory reason for why a constraint like that should hold, as Cresti herself noted. This requirement on the extractee operates on the sentential level, and I believe an explanatory account must be available from the discoursal point of view.

In the sense that he tries to give a discoursally oriented account, Pesetsky's notion of D-linking has some truth, even though D-linking is not the exact property for the requirement for the island insensitivity. Pesetsky's mechanism of obtaining scope by unselective binding and its similarity to Heimian existential closure of an indefinite can shed some light on the account

---

1. Watanabe (1991) and Aoun & Li (1993) provide a similar proposal for Japanese *wh*-phrases and Chinese *wh*-phrases respectively.

2. One might claim that the source of existential presupposition involved with the example (8) is the adverb *still* rather than the construction. Whether *still* is the trigger for the presupposition or not, the point here is that the condition that allows the extraction of *what* phrase, that is, the existential presupposition, is satisfied. Hence, what the source of the presupposition is does not seem to matter here.

for the island insensitive commonality shared by wh-phrases in (4-6), indefinites, and foci, which can be a crucial contribution for developing the more general theory that has been suggested by Rooth, as mentioned in the introduction. What I want to do now is to propose such an account by adapting Pesetsky's. In the next section, however, I will first argue that the genuine requirement for a *wh*-phrase to be extractable from an island is that it has a presupposition of existence rather than Pesetsky's D-linking.

2.2 Existential Presupposition

I propose that the criterion that characterizes the extractee from weak islands is whether an **existential presupposition** is available in the context.

Consider the sentences in (4-6) and (8). None of these sentences can be properly uttered without the presupposition that there exists a referent that can fit the wh-phrase. For example, (4A) presupposes the information in (9a), and the sentence (8) which includes a *what*-phrase, but not a *which*-phrase, does also presuppose an existential information like (10):

(9)   a. $\exists x$ [man(x) $\wedge$ Mary wonders whether to invite x].
        b. $\exists x$ [man(x) $\wedge$ I didn't invite x].
        c. $\exists x$ [man(x) $\wedge$ I regret that she talked to x].
(10) $\exists x$ [word(x) $\wedge$ I still don't know how to spell x].

In the context which lacks this presuppositional information, the sentences in (4-6) and (8) cannot be properly uttered. This existential presupposition is different from Pesetsky's D-linking in the following sense: *D-linking* requires that a concrete set of discourse referents must be available, from which an answer for the interrogative wh-phrase can be chosen. But, the true requirement for the extractee is the **existence** of a variable that meets the description of the question, without necessarily any prior information about its identity, as those in (9-10). The identity of the variable can be completely unknown previously. This presuppositional information can become available by actual introduction in the prior discourse, by *accommodation* as a normal presupposition, or by non-linguistic inference. A sentence like (8) belongs to the case of presupposition accommodation by non linguistic inference. Without the assumption that there is a word that the hearer does not know how to spell in a certain context, a sentence like (8) cannot be felicitously uttered. This presupposition can be accommodated based on the non-linguistic cue that the hearer is madly searching the dictionary. According to Pesetsky, *what-the-hell* context guarantees non D-linking of a wh-phrase. If D-linking in Pesetsky' sense is the real factor that can explain this type of wh-phrase, a sentence like (8) should not be possible. As mentioned above, Pesetsky's D-linking requires a set of individuals that are candidates as an answer for the wh-phrase, that is, a familiar discourse domain that the wh-phrase can quantify over. As the *what-the-hell* phrase in (8) suggests, however, the familiarity of the domain is not a genuine requirement. The existence of an individual that fits the presuppositional frame as represented in the interpretation in (9) and (10) without any further information about the identity of that individual would suffice as the requirement. The familiarity of the domain for a *which*-phrase is not a discoursally required condition, but is the lexical information of a *which*-phrase, since *which*-phrase is inherently partitive, and it requires a restricted familiar set of the possible answers. Because of this presupposition that is lexically associated with *which*-phrases, *which*-phrases are typically good candidates to be extracted from a weak island. The condition for the extractability of a wh-phrase from a weak island, however, is just the existential presupposition, but not the familiarity of the quantificational domain of the wh-phrase.

Now, I will provide a mechanism that overcomes the island violation problem. The mechanism that I propose is the possibility of scoping of wh-phrases and focal phrases without movement based on the similarity of these phrases to indefinites or pronouns. I will show that the wh-phrases in (4-6) and (8) and the narrow foci such as the corresponding answers to these wh-questions have commonalities in that 1) they must be treated as variables rather than operators and 2) both have the property of definites like pronouns, which will account for the semantic similarity of indefinites, the group of wh-phrases at hand, and narrow foci.

3. Function of Wh-phrase and Focus and Double Indexing

3.1 Definite vs. Indefinite Wh-phrase

Let us consider what the existence presupposition really means. Existence presupposition means the discourse referent of the wh-phrase is not new, in other words, it should be a **definite**.[3] This idea is essentially the same as

---

3. The condition that Cresti (1995) and Szabolsci and Zwarts (1993) proposed as a sentential level condition can be restated in terms of discoursal properties. The condition for the individual type variable has essentially the same nature as the existential presupposition. There are some supporting arguments available. It is well known that definite NPs may not occur in these contexts, as illustrated in (ia-c):

(i)   a. There is a man at the door.
                    b. *There is John at the door.
                    c. *There is he/him at the door.

Heim (1987) points out that individual variables, because of their name-like properties, should be classified as definite and hence be subject to the Definiteness Restriction in the same way as overt names like John in (ib). She proposes the filter in (ii) as a special case of the Definite Restriction:

(ii)   *There be x, when x is an individual variable.

In Cresti (1995) this observation is used as an account for the absence of wide scope readings for NPs in the postcopular position of sentences like (iii).

Pesetsky's original idea. He suggests treating his D-linked *wh*-phrases like a pronoun since it must be an old referent if it is D-linked. This idea seems to be on the right track, but as its original form, his idea does not work through. Let us suppose that a sentence like (3a), which is repeated in (11), is represented as in (12) following Pesetsky's suggestion:

(11)   Which man$_i$ does Mary wonder whether to invite t$_i$?

(12)   [[$_{COMP}$ Q_i which man$_i$] does Mary wonder weather to invite e$_i$]

If *which man* is a pronoun, according to the *familiarity condition* of Heim, the index that can represent a discourse referent must be an already introduced one, so it must be bound by the antecedent variable introduced as the presupposition.

However, treating the definiteness property of a wh-phrase in the same way as that of a normal NP seems to be problematic. The problem can be stated from two perspectives:

The first one is the structural aspect. Let us suppose the index of a wh-phrase is *i*, which is treated as a variable. The variable *i* will be bound by the antecedent which is an existentially quantified variable such like those in (9-10). The problem is that once it is bound by the antecedent, it will no longer be able to be bound by the interrogative operator Q in COMP. The variable *i* would be doubly bound by the existential quantifier and the Q operator resulting in an undesirable situation.

The second aspect is more cognitively or functionally oriented. The function of a normal definite description is to pick a proper antecedent among the previously introduced discourse referents and nothing more. But, the function of a definite wh-phrase is not just to pick an antecedent. The main function of an interrogative wh-phrase is to ask the identity of a variable, regardless whether it is a definite or indefinite. Hence, a definite wh-interrogation must perform both tasks. To accommodate this functional property of an interrogative wh-phrase and overcome the structural problem mentioned above, I propose that a wh-phrase introduces two variables and expects them to be equated to each other. In other words, the wh-phrase must

---

(iii)   a. Ralph believes that someone is spying on him
                            Believes > someone; someone >believes
                         b. Ralph believes that there is someone spying on him.
                            Believes > someone; *someone > believes

Since an individual variable should not be in the existential construction, *there is___*, and should be considered as definite as pointed out by Heim, an individual variable must be associated with a certain kind of presupposition. I claim that the nature of this presupposition is existential. The requirement of existential presupposition for an individual variable prevents it from occurring in existential construction and forces it to be a kind of definite. Therefore, the condition of individual variable and the condition of existential presupposition are the same phenomenon descried from two different perspectives, sentential and discoursal. So, every occurrence of a wh-question in an island environment requires existential presupposition and hence must be an individual variable.

carry not one but two indices. A wh-phrase must introduce another discourse referent in addition to the discourse referent already introduced as a presupposition. With one index, the double duty of a wh-phrase cannot be completed. The second index variable will be identified later when an answer is successfully provided. Suppose the other variable is j. Then, the LF representation for (11) will be like (13).

(13)   [[$_\text{COMP}$ $Q_{i,j}$ which man $_{i,j}$]does Mary wonder weather to invite e $_{i,j}$]

The first index i must be old, if the wh-phrase is definite, and it must be new, if the wh-phrase is indefinite. The definiteness property of a wh-phrase is represented by the first index. As implied in the previous discussion, wh-phrases which do not carry existential presupposition are indefinite, whereas wh-phrases which carry existential presupposition like the examples discussed so far are definite.

In the next section, I will provide the analysis that can treat focus in a parallel fashion with interrogative wh-phrases using the double indexing mechanism. The motivation for double indexing can be justified from the perspective of focusing, which will clarify the conceptual relationship between a wh-question and its corresponding focus structure.

3.2 Definiteness of Focus
In many of the current theories of focus, it is believed that the semantics of focus must include the presupposition that there is a set of alternatives contrasting with the actual sentence. For example, in Rooth (1992), (1995), the focus interpreter ~ introduces a set consisting of the sentence itself and other alternatives. However, I claim that introducing alternatives and contrast might be a pragmatic **effect** of a sentence with a narrow focus, but not the **function** of focusing. The semantic function of narrow focus is just identifying the variable presuppositionally introduced. I claim that the function of narrow foci is **identification**. My analysis shows that the semantics proper for focus does not involve anything other than identification of a presupposed variable. This variable can be identified by being equated with an individual either from a closed set whose members are transparently known to the hearer or any individual who has never been introduced previously. Consider a sentence like *John introduced [Bill]$_F$ to Sue*. Given that the constituent *Bill* is the only focus, this sentence can be uttered in a situation when the identity of the *somebody* is completely unknown as well as when the set of the potential individuals is already introduced. Hence, the only requirement for the sentence at hand to be felicitously uttered is that it is presupposed that *John introduced somebody to Sue*. Whether the domain of possible individuals is closed or not does not matter for the semantics proper of focus. The function of narrow focus is mere identification of the variable which is introduced as presuppositional information. The same discoursal requirement, which is the existence of the

individual as a presupposition, holds for both the weak island extractee and narrow focus, and hence both the questions and their corresponding answer in (4-6).

The question now is how we can represent the focus constituent distinguishably from a normal linguistic expression, while keeping the parallelism with wh-questions. How can we distinguish the focal **Bill**, for instance, and the normal *Bill?* Rooth, for this question, proposes an additional semantic value for a focus constituent called *focus semantic value*. He employs the two-dimensional alternative semantics for focus, which defines a semantic interpretation of the focus feature. The focus semantic value of **Bill**, for instance, can be a set of individuals that are contextually relevant. Roberts (1996) also employs the notion of focal alternatives which match with alternatives as the denotation of a question under the assumption that every focus sentence presupposes a question under discussion to which the focus sentence could be a relevant answer. In *structured meaning* approach, von Stechow (1991) and Krifka (1991) posit an ordered pair for a structured meaning which reflects the focal structure, dividing the utterance's meaning into focus and ground to capture the semantic characteristics of focus constituents distinguished from normal phrases.

Along the same lines as my analysis for interrogative wh-phrases, I will make use of an indexing mechanism in order to distinguish a focus constituent from ordinary linguistic expression and accommodate the function of *identification* of a narrow focus. My proposal is that a focal constituent also carries two indices. The fundamental assumption for this is that every focus constituent is very closely related with the corresponding wh-question. My position, however, is not the same as Roberts'. The existence of a question is not a requirement for the well-formedness of a focus constituent in my framework, whereas in Roberts the existence of question is the essential part that licenses a focus structure. So, in Roberts' framework, when the question is not overtly asked in a dialogue, the system must accommodate a relevant question to make the focus sentence felicitous. In other words, every focus construction **presupposes** its licensing wh-question in Robert's analysis. But, in my framework, the existence of a wh-phrase is incorporated into the focus constituent under the assumption that a focus has the property of a wh-phrase inherently. And I believe that the nature of this inherent property can be captured by my double indexing mechanism.

I claimed that the function of an interrogative wh-phrase is to introduce two variables and expects one to be identified by the other by equating them. Likewise, the function of a focus is to introduce two variables and *asserting them to be identified*. As in a wh-phrase, the first index is for the definiteness feature and the second is for the identifier. As I previously claimed, the job of a narrow focus is identification of a variable presumed to exist already. In that sense, a narrow focus is always definite. So, the first index must be bound by an antecedent. When the corresponding wh-phrase is physically present, the first index of a focus is bound by that of a wh-phrase, and otherwise, it is bound directly by the existentially presupposed variable. Therefore, a **definite** wh-phrase is redundant from the perspective of focus, whereas an **indefinite** wh-phrase is essential, since it must introduce the antecedent for the first variable of the focus. In this way, the double indexing mechanism for a wh-phrase and a focus can accommodate the relationship and parallelism between them. What distinguishes a focus constituent and wh-interrogatives on the one hand and the other linguistic phrases on the other is that the former is relating two variables whereas the latter assumes only one variable for its referent. Relating two variables by *expecting* them to be equated to each other is the function of an interrogative wh-phrase and relating two variables by *asserting* them to be equated to each other is the functions of a narrow focus. This property of a focus can be understood as the property of its answerhood to a potential question. So, even when the question is not explicitly asked, the double indexing representation of focus can represent this property of answerhood. Double indexing enables us to keep the trace of asking with a wh-phrase and answering with a focus constituent even when this route is not overtly taken.

So far, I have tried to provide the conceptual justification for double indexing mechanism. In the next section, I will show that the structural problem stated above can be properly solved.

4. Representation for Focus and Definite Wh-phrase

4.1 LF Representation
In order to let a definite wh-phrase and a narrow focus to have scope, I adopt Pesetsky's suggestion of treating D-linked *wh-in-situ* as variables to be unselectively bound by a Q operator in COMP. To overcome the technical problem of potential double binding of the wh-variable by both the antecedent and the Q operator, I stipulate that the operators Q and F look at only the second index of a constituent, resulting in (unselectively) binding every occurrence of a definite wh-phrase or a narrow focus in a sentence. LF representations for a definite wh-phrase question in (4a) and a narrow focus as in (4b) would be as follows.

(14)   a. $[[_{\text{COMP}} Q_j]$ does Mary wonder whether to invite *which man* $_{i,j}]$
        b. $[[_{\text{COMP}} F_j][$Mary wonder whether to invite JOHN$_{i,j}]$

As (14) suggests, this operator binding mechanism enables the definite wh-phrases and focus-constituents to be scoped without movement at LF. After the second index of a definite wh-phrase and a narrow focus is bound by the relevant operators, the remaining free variables are supposed to be bound by the proper antecedents. The process of anaphora resolution of the second variable will be exactly the same as that a normal pronoun. The following discourse representation of the form of Heim (1982) will properly capture the discoursal context of the question-answer pair of (4a).

(15)   Mary wonders whether to invite a man$_x$.
        [[$_{COMP}$ Q_j] Mary wonders weather to invite *which man* $_{i,j}$]
        [[$_{COMP}$ F_j] I wonder weather to invite JOHN$_{i,j}$]

(16)   [$_T$ [$\exists_x$[Mary wonders whether to invite a man$_x$.]
            [[$_{COMP}$ Q_j] Mary wonder weather to invite *which man* $_{x,j}$]
            [[$_{COMP}$ F_j] I wonder weather to invite JOHN$_{x,j}$]]]

The discourse representation of (15) obtained by the operator binding of Q and F will be further processed into (16) by *existential closure* at the text level and unselective binding of the free variables and the normal anaphora resolution procedure of definite descriptions for the first index.[4]

The semantics for a definite wh-phrase and a narrow focus are informally representend as in (17) and (18). I will just mark the representation of a *question* as ?, leaving the issue of the exact semantics of a *question* open:

(17)   Semantics of the interrogative operator Q for a question S$wh_{x,y}$ which contains a definite *wh*-phrase $wh_{x,y}$:
        (i)   Presupposition: $\exists x Sx$ where x is a variable replacing the definite *wh*-phrase
        (ii)   Proferred Content: $?\lambda y(x = y)$[5]

The focus operator F binds every occurrence of a free focus constituent in the sentence with the meaning of exhaustive identification. The semantics of the focus operator F for the case of free focus can be paralleled with that for a definite wh-phrase as follows:

(18)   Semantics of the focus operator F for the sentence S$t_{x,y}$ which contains a focused NP $t_{x,y}$:
        (i)   Presupposition: $\exists x Sx$ where x is a variable replacing the free focus t
        (ii)   Assertion: $\lambda y(x = y)t$; $x=t$ (by lambda conversion)

4.2 DRT Analysis
The discourse representation provided in 4.1 can be implemented again in Kamp & Reyle (1993) style DRT framework. I will call any context information state S. Information states are representations containing a set of

---

4. Indefinite *wh*-phrases move at LF as an operator, so both indices for an indefinite *wh*-phrase would be coindexed between the moved operator and the trace.
5. The term *proferred* is adopted from Roberts (1996), which covers both asserted and asked information.

discourse referents and a list of conditions about these referents. Following Vallduvi & Vilkuna (1997), I allow conditions to be underspecified, departing from standard DRT, so that an information state S_1 may contain a lambda-abstracted formula. A *wh*-question is represented by this lambda-abstracted condition. The discourse in (4) can be represented again as in (19) in this DRT framework[6]:

(19) S_1:

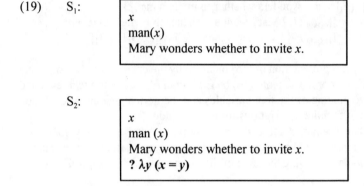

Information state S_1 represents the context which satisfies the existential presupposition which makes the question (4a) felicitous. The question (4a) corresponds to the stage S_2 with the presupposition and the assertion signified by the bold, which is asking the identity of the referent x. As shown in S_2, the referent x is already introduced in S_1 so that it represents the wh-phrase in (4a) as a definite. The variable y is converted to the focus phrase in the answer. The stage S_3 represents the process of the conversion of y to *John*, whereby the referent x is identified as *John*. Since the variable y is clause-bound as represented in (15) and (16), it is not updated as a discourse marker in the

---

6. The exact DRT construction algorithms for narrow foci are developed in Wee (in preparation).

DRS.[7]

5. Conclusion

In this paper, I proposed a mechanism that could account for the island insensitivity associated with definite wh-phrases and narrow foci, which enables them to have scope without movement. This mechanism could uniformly account for the family of island insensitive phrases, *i.e., definite wh-phrases, narrow foci, definite and indefinite NPs,* by capturing the semantic similarity shared by this group of linguistic categories while maintaining the difference between wh-phrases and narrow foci on the one hand and other categories. The semantic similarity can be analyzed as due to the fact that they are variables rather than operators which must be unselectively bound by a relevant operator. What distinguishes wh-phrases and narrow foci from other categories can be viewed as the fact that wh-phrases and narrow foci must carry double indices.

The theoretical contribution of this paper can be summarized as follows: 1) Considering that there have been many arguments on the issue of the relation between Wh-questions and focus structures (Roachmont 1986), it is important in that it reveals the nature of the strong connection between wh-questions and focus structures. 2) It provides a relevant syntactic, semantic and discoursal property which can properly characterize focus phenomenon and the different kinds of wh-questions, the lack of which was the source of the failure of a proper explanation for focus in general. 3) It can be a step towards a general theory that could provide a unified account for the family of island insensitive constructions, *i.e.* wh-in-situ, weak island extractee, wh-phrases in strong islands in Korean, Japanese, and Chinese, narrow focus, and indefinites.

References

Aoun, Joseph and Yen-hui Audrey Li. (1993). Wh-elements in Situ: Syntax or LF? *Linguistic Inquiry* 24: 199-238.

Chomsky, Noam. (1976). Conditions on Rules of Grammar, *Linguistic Analysis* 2: 303-351.

Cinque, Gugliemo. (1991). *Types of A'- Dependancie.* Cambridge, Mass.:MIT Press.

---

7. The identificational process of an existentially presupposed variable performed by the question-answer pair, *i.e.,* wh-phrase and focal phrase pair, resembles the process of anaphora resolution. The difference lies in that the identificational process by focusing is an explicitly asserted information, whereas the normal anaphora resolution process is performed implicitly, that is presuppositional information. Therefore, once a DRS undergoes a normal anaphora resolution process such as a Van der Sandt type, the process cannot be traced in the resulting DRS, whereas the identificational procedure performed by a question-answer is overtly kept in the resulting DRS as illustrated in S_3 in (19).

Cresti, Diana. (1995). Extraction and Reconstruction. *Natural Language Semantics* 3: 79-122.

Heim, Irene. (1982). *The Semantics of Definite and Indefinite Noun Phrases.*Doctoral dissertation, University of Massachusetts, Amherst.

_____. (1987). Where Does the Definiteness Restriction Apply? Evidence from the Definiteness of Variables, In E. Reuland and A. ter Meulen., eds., *The Representation of (In)definites*, Cambridge, Mass.: MIT Press: 21-42.

Kamp, Hans and Uwe Reyle. (1993). *From discourse to logic.* Dordrecht: Kluwer.

Kiss, Katalin É. (1995). *Discourse Configuratinal Languages.* Oxford.: Oxford University Press.

Krifka, Manfred. (1991). A Compositional Semantics for Multiple Focus Constructions. *SALT* 1:127-158.

Pesetsky, David. (1987). Wh-in-situ: Movement and Unselective Binding, In E. Reuland and A. ter Meulen., eds., *The Representation of (In)definites*, Cambridge Mass: MIT Press: 98-129.

Roberts, Craige. (1996). Information Structure in Discourse: Towards an Integrated Formal Theory of Pragmatics. Ms., The Ohio State University.

Rochemont, Michael S. (1986). *Focus in Generative Grammar.* Amsterdam: John Benjamin.

Rooth, Mats. (1985). *Association with Focus.* Doctoral dissertation, University of Massachusetts, Amherst.

_____. (1992). A Theory of Focus Interpretation. *Natural Language Semantics* 1: 75-116.

_____. (1995).*Focus*, in L. Shalom, ed., *The Handbook of Contemporary Semantic Theory.* Cambridge, Mass.: Blackwell: 271-291.

Szabolcsi, Anna and Franz Zwarts. (1993). Weak Islands and an Algebraic Semantics for Scope Taking. *Natural Language Semantics* 1: 235- 284.

Vallduví Enrich and Maria Vilkuna. (1997). On Rheme and Kontrast. Ms., Unisersitati Pompeu Fabra, Barcelona.

von Stechow, Arnim. (1991). Current Issues in the Theory of Focus, in A.Stechow and D. Wunderlich eds., *Semantik/Semantics: An International Handbook of Contemporary Research.* Berlin: de Gruyter: 804-825.

Watanabe, Akira. (1991). Wh-in-situ, Subjacency, and Chain Information. Ms., MIT. Cambridge, Mass.

Wee, Hae-Kyung. (In preparation). *Definitness of Narrow Focus.* Doctoral dissertation. Indiana Universtity, Bloomington.

Transparent Free Relatives

CHRIS WILDER

Zentrum für Allgemeine Sprachwissenschaft, Berlin

1. What it's about

The literature recognizes two types of Free Relative with *what*. Ordinary FRs as in (1) function like definite or universal argument DPs (Jacobson 1995). In specificational pseudocleft sentences (2), the wh-clause has been argued to form the predicate of the matrix clause, taking the adjective as its subject (Williams 1983, Iatridou & Varlokosta 1996).

(1)   John likes [what(ever) I cook]

(2)   angry is [what John is]

The examples in (3) belong to a third type which does not reduce to either of the first two, although it shares properties with both. This type has gone largely unnoticed—the only discussion I have seen is in McCawley (1988). I call them *Transparent Free Relatives* (TFRs), for reasons that will become clear. TFRs occur as arguments (3a), predicates (3b) or attributes (3c):

(3)   a.   [what seems to be a tourist] is lying on the lawn.
        b.   John is [what you might call a fool / stupid]
        c.   a [what you might call tricky] example

This construction shows syntactic behaviour which leads to a kind of paradox; with respect to various syntactic tests, the free relative behaves as if it were invisible. The goals of this paper are to sort out the relevant properties of TFRs, by contrasting them with ordinary FRs, and to suggest how to resolve the paradox they present. Section 6 adds some remarks on the relation of TFRs to specificational pseudoclefts.

2. Transparent Free Relatives *vs.* Ordinary Free Relatives

Ordinary FRs have the internal syntax of complement wh-clauses. The same wh-phrases (ignoring the *-ever* morpheme) are used in both: *what(ever)* (N); *which(ever)* (N); *who(ever)*. However, free relatives have the distribution of DPs, being licensed in DP-only positions, such as the goal argument position of ditransitive verbs (4)-(5). I shall assume a structure like (6), where a zero determiner takes a wh-CP complement:

(4)   he gave whoever she named a kiss

(5)   *   he V [whether I failed] NP   (*there is no such verb*)

(6) $[_{DP} \varnothing_D [_{CP} \text{what}_j \varnothing_C [_{IP} \text{you ordered } t_j]]]$

FRs also get interpreted like DPs, rather than interrogatives. In particular, they get a definite or universal reading, rather than an indefinite reading (7) (Jacobson 1995). As expected, they are also barred from the indefinites-only position in *there*-sentences (8).

(7)   [what you ordered] is on the desk
           ≠ something which you ordered ...
           = the thing(s) which you ordered ...

(8)   *   There is [what you ordered] on the desk.

The properties of bare *what* are important in what follows. Jacobson (1995) notices that Free relatives with bare *what* are semantically vague with respect to the cardinality of the sets they can denote. Thus, while example (9a) denotes a properly plural set, and (9b) denotes a singleton set, (9c) can be used to denote either a singleton or a plural set.

(9)   a.   whatever dishes John ordered   *proper plural*
       b   whatever dish John ordered   *atom*
       c.   what(ever) John ordered   *either*

However, bare *what* is grammatically singular, regardless of interpretation: cf. (10), where *what* itself triggers singular agreement inside the FR; and the FR itself triggers singular agreement in the higher clause:

(10)   [what(ever) is (*are) on the table], belongs (*belong) to me.

Also, FRs with bare *what* cannot be used to refer to humans. The deviance of (11a,b) is due to the fact that *invite* selects a [+human] object. Neither bare *what* nor an FR headed by *what* can fulfill that requirement.

(11)   a. # I liked what he invited   (*ok:* what students)
        b. # I invited what he recommended

Note that neither [singular] nor [−human] is a rigid property of *what*, which as a determiner combines freely with [+human] NPs and with plural NPs.

Transparent FRs have the form of wh-CPs headed by bare *what* with the specific format (12). They always contain an internal small clause whose subject is *what*, and whose predicate XP can either be a DP or an AP. The wh-pronoun can be moved from a nominative or an accusative position, depending on the governing verb, cf. typical frames given in (13).

(12) $[_{CP}$ what$_j$ ... V $[_{SC}$ t$_j$ XP$_{PRED}$] ...]

(13)   a.   *trace of what (DP*)=Acc*
             ... V $[_{SC}$ DP* to be XP]   (V = consider, take *etc*)
             ... V $[_{SC}$ DP* as XP]   (V = describe, regard *etc.*)
             ... V $[_{SC}$ DP* XP]   (V = call *etc.*)

        b.   *trace of what (DP*) =Nom*
             $[_{IP}$ DP* .. V $[_{SC}$ t$_{DP}$ to be XP]]   (V = seem, be considered *etc.*)
             $[_{IP}$ DP* .. V $[_{SC}$ t$_{DP}$ as XP]]   (V = be described *etc.*)
             $[_{IP}$ DP* .. V $[_{SC}$ t$_{DP}$ XP]]   (V = be, be called *etc*)

All Transparent Free Relatives have this structure, but not all free relatives that have this structure are necessarily transparent, as we will see.

As noted, TFRs can function as arguments, predicates or attributes. When they appear in argument position, they appear to be ordinary referential DPs, like ordinary free relatives. But they differ with regard to the properties just reviewed, and more besides. (14) lists six important differences:

(14) a. *Ordinary FRs*
        i) definite/universal reading only
        ii) barred from 'indefinites-only' position
        iii) singular agreement only with bare *what*
        iv) [−human] only with bare *what*
        v) wh-phrase can also be *whatever* (N), *who(ever)* etc.
        vi) strong island for extraction

    b. *Transparent FRs*
        i) weak indefinite reading also possible
        ii) can appear in 'indefinites-only' position
        iii) plural agreement possible with bare *what*
        iv) [+human] possible with bare *what*
        v) wh-phrase can only be bare *what*
        vi) no island effect w.r.t. extraction from XP_{PRED}

In contrast to ordinary free relatives, TFRs can have indefinite or weak existential interpretation, cf. (15a) (McCawley 1988:733); and can also stand in the indefinites-only position (15b):

(15) a. [what could best be described as pebbles] were strewn across the lawn.
    b. there were [what could be best described as pebbles] strewn across the lawn.

This case is a first illustration of the paradoxical properties of TFRs. The XP in the small clause clearly acts as a predicate within the FR. However, the FR is 'transparent' in the sense that XP simultaneously determines properties of the whole free relative. Thus, in (15), the FR seems to inherit indefiniteness from the XP predicate, which is an indefinite DP (*pebbles*).

This transparency is both syntactic and semantic. The predicate XP seems to form the semantic head of the TFR consituent; while the remainder of the FR functions as a modifier, cf. the paraphrase in (16):

(16) a. there is [what appears to be an error] in this program.
    b. there is [an apparent error] in this program.

Syntactically, also, the predicate XP shows all signs of being the head of the construction. Most strikingly, it is *the category of XP* that determines the distributional possibilities for a TFR. If the predicate XP is adjectival, the TFR must be in an AP-position (17); and if the predicate is a DP, the TFR must be in a DP-position (18) (note that while copular sentences accept DPs or APs in predicate position, subject positions accept DPs but not APs and prenominal attributes inside DP can be AP but not DP):

(17) a.   John is [what you might call <u>stupid</u>]   *predicate*
      b. *   [what you might call <u>stupid</u>] just walked in   *subject*
      c.   a [what I'd describe as <u>stupid</u>] decision   *attribute*

(18) a.   John is [what you might call <u>a fool</u>]   *predicate*
      b.   [what you might call <u>a fool</u>] just walked in   *subject*
      c. *   a [what I'd describe as <u>a failure</u>] decision   *attribute*

Where the predicate XP is a DP, it also determines other properties of the FR, such as definiteness and number. If the predicate is definite (19b), the whole TFR takes on a definite reading, and can no longer appear in the *there*-sentence:

(19) a.   there is [what appears to be [a virus]] in this program
      b. *   there is [what appears to be [the virus]] in this program

If the predicate is plural, the TFR triggers plural agreement (20) (cf. also (15)); and if the predicate is [+human] (21), the FR takes a human referent:

(20)   [what seem/*seems to be [tourists]] are/*is lying on the lawn.

(21)   she invited [what I took to be [a policeman]]

Recall that ordinary FRs headed by bare *what* do not trigger plural agreement even if denoting a semantically plural entity; nor do they permit human referents. However, in wh-questions (22), we see plural agreement with *what*, though only in (22a), i.e. in precisely the TFR configuration (12). This can be related to facts (23) showing that a plural DP predicate as in (22a) is incompatible with a singular subject. So arguably, the plural in (20) does not show that the predicate DP directly determines the number features of the FR; as the transmission may be mediated by wh-movement of *what*:

(22) a.   what seem to be *t* the worst problems?   (*seems)
      b. *   what seem to be *t* on the table?   (*ok:* seems)

(23) a. *   this seems to be [*t* the worst problems]   (*ok:* these seem...)
      b.   I consider [these (*this) terrible scissors]

A similar line might be attempted with [+human]—it could be that *what* may inherit [+human] from its DP predicate and transmit it via wh-movement to the whole FR. However, in wh-questions, even those with the TFR-configuration (12), *what* seems far less compatible with human reference:

(24) a. ? what did you take to be a policeman?
      b. * what do you consider to be your best friend?

TFRs are not only transparent with respect to category and other features, they are also transparent with respect to extraction. Ordinary FRs form strong islands, like complex NPs (expected if FRs are in fact DPs):

(25) a. * the student that Mary invited [who(ever) likes t]
      b. * something that Mary invited [whoever is angry about t]

Now consider (26). As far as extraction out of the predicate XP is concerned, TFRs are not islands at all. The contrast between (26) and (25) is huge. In terms of grammaticality, the extractions in (26) exactly match those in (27), where there is no FR at all containing XP:

(26) a. ? the professor who I met [what you might call [a student of t]]
      b.   something that John is [what you might call [angry about t]]

(27) a. ? the professor who I met [a student of t]
      b.   something that John is [angry about t]

To summarize: with respect to a range of syntactic tests, a Transparent Free Relative seems to have no interaction with the matrix clause containing it. Rather, it is the XP constituent—apparently a predicate contained *inside* the TFR—that interacts directly with the matrix clause.

3. XP$_{PRED}$ is the head of the TFR constituent

McCawley (1988:732-733) cites a proposal from Kajita (1977) to account for the special properties of what I am calling TFRs. This invokes a process of 'Reanalysis' which transforms the structure (28a), with the predicate XP contained within the FR, into (28b). XP becomes the head of the structure, the FR becomes a kind of modifier or adjunct:

(28) a. [$_{FR}$ .... XP$_{PRED}$] → b. [$_{XP}$ [$_{FR}$ ....] XP$_{PRED}$]

(29) a. John bought [$_{FR}$ what he took to be [$_{DP}$ a guitar]]
      b. John bought [$_{DP}$ [$_{FR}$ what he took to be] a guitar]

This is intuitively correct. (29) is ambiguous. In one reading, associated with the ordinary Free Relative structure (29a), the object of *bought* is a definite: 'the thing that he thought was a guitar'. In the second reading, the object of *bought* is indefinite: 'a guitar (or so he thought)'. In this reading the Free Relative is transparent; it merely modifies the indefinite *a guitar* (as McCawley notes, this modification has a metalinguistic flavour—the FR 'hedges' the description in the NP).

Assuming that TFR's have a structure like (28b) offers an immediate solution to most of our problems. The reason why XP (and not the free relative) determines grammatical properties of the TFR constituent, is that XP is the head of that constituent. This goes for number agreement, human reference, definiteness, and for the syntactic category of the constituent. As for why the free relative does not interfere with extraction out of XP, the reason is simple—the free relative does not contain XP.

How does the structure (28b) arise? There can be no transformational rule of Reanalysis deriving (28b) from (28a)—such a rule would alter theta-relations, turning an argument (the Free relative) into a modifier, and turning a predicate (XP) into an argument. Hence, we must assume that (28a) and (28b) are two independently generable structures.

Looking more closely at the transparent structure (28b), it becomes apparent that the free relative is incomplete. The trace of *what* is an argument variable; it needs a theta-role. Yet there is no predicate in the relevant position to assign that theta-role. The missing predicate is of course XP. Thus, XP in the 'reanalyzed' structure is in fact a 'shared constituent'—it needs to be in two places simultaneously. Transparency dictates that XP is outside the FR; but XP must also be inside the FR where it acts as a predicate, theta-marking the trace of *what*.

So we have reached three conclusions about TFRs: (i) XP heads the TFR constituent, as in (28b); (ii) the structure (28b) is not transformationally related to ordinary FRs; and (iii) XP is in some sense a 'shared constituent'. We now face two further questions about (28b):

(30) a. What is the relation of the FR to the host sentence?
      b. What is the nature of constituent-sharing?

For (30a), I see two possible answers. Either the FR is an adjunct—i.e. is adjoined to XP in syntax; or the FR is some kind of parenthetical expression. There are grounds for assuming that the FR is a parenthetical, which I take to mean that it is syntactically disconnected from the host sentence, and that it gets inserted into the host sentence only in the PF-component (this is only tentative—other approaches to parentheticals are conceivable). In section 5, it is argued that TFRs have more in common with parenthetical expressions than with classical adjunct modifiers.

With respect to constituent sharing (30b), there are also two possible answers. In one view, sketched in (31), XP is literally simultaneously the daughter of two VP nodes, the VP in the FR and the VP of the matrix clause. This approach requires a theory of phrase structure which gives up the unique mother condition, to permit multiple dominance (cf. Moltmann 1992 for such an approach to constituent sharing in coordination):

(31)

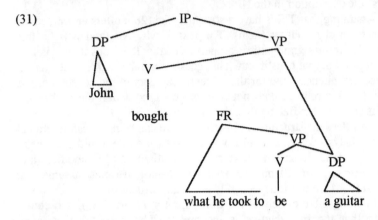

The alternative, preserving standard assumptions about phrase structure, is to assume an ellipsis approach: there are two copies of XP, one in the FR and one in the matrix, one which surfaces as an empty category, giving one of the two options in (32):

(32) a. John bought [$_{FR}$ what he took to be [$_{DP}$ a guitar]] [$_{DP*}$ ∅]]

      b. John bought [$_{FR}$ what he took to be [$_{DP}$ ∅]] [$_{DP*}$ a guitar]

Here, I will adopt the ellipsis approach. In particular, I will argue for (32b)—the deleted copy of XP is the copy inside the TFR. There is no known ellipsis rule that could give us (32a); but there is an ellipsis rule that could generate (32b). This is Backward Deletion, also involved in so-called Right Node Raising constructions (see Wilder 1997).

Combining these two answers, my proposal is summarized in (33). In syntax, only XP is present in the matrix clause, where it interacts directly with the matrix with respect to argument/predicate status, category, definiteness, agreement, and extraction. Deletion takes place in the PF-component, following parenthetical placement (only then is the input configuration for Backward Deletion created).

(33) a. *Syntax: independent phrase markers*
          [he bought [$_{DP}$ a guitar]]   [what he took to be [$_{DP}$ a guitar]]

b.   *Phonology: parenthetical placement and deletion*
      John bought < what he took to be ~~a guitar~~ > a guitar

Two additional stipulations are needed to ensure correct placement and to guarantee that deletion takes place. If either of the conditions (34) is not met, the construction simply fails. (34a) excludes cases like (35a)—the FR cannot be placed farther left from the matrix XP, though there is no reason why Backward Deletion should not apply in such cases. (34b) is needed to exclude (35b)—if there is no deletion in the FR, we get gibberish:

(34)   a.   the TFR must be left-adjacent to XP in the host sentence
       b.   XP in the TFR must be deleted

(35)   a. * <what he took to be ~~a guitar~~> John bought a guitar
       b. * John bought <what he took to be a guitar> a banjo

4. Evidence for Backward Deletion

This section gives two arguments to support the Backward Deletion approach. One concerns identity, the second concerns word order.

4.1 Identity
We have already seen that deleted and overt XPs can fulfill different syntactic functions. The deleted XP is always a predicate in a small clause, while the overt XP can be an argument, a predicate or an attributive adjective. If there really is phonological deletion in TFRs, we might expect that the deleted constituent and its overt antecedent would need to be identical phonologically, but not necessarily morphosyntactically. Evidence for this is provided by the contrast between (36a) and (36b). In the frame *call YP XP*, cf. (37), the predicate XP can be nominal or adjectival but not verbal. This takes case of (36b). In (36a), though, the verbal form *snoring* is able to license deletion of the homophonous nominal gerund in the FR, as in (38):

(36)   a. ? John is what I'd call snoring
       b. * John what I'd call snores

(37)   I'd call that [$_{AP}$ boring] / [$_{NP}$ snoring] / * [$_{VP}$ snores]

(38)   John is < what I'd call [$_{NP}$ ~~snoring~~] > [$_{VP}$ snoring]

4.2 Word order: placement of the overt copy of XP

The second argument for Backward Deletion concerns word order. The shared constituent of TFRs underlies the restriction (39): it must be positioned in the surface string so as to stand at the right edge of the Free relative. In other words, the shared constituent cannot appear properly contained within the FR. If we assume Backward Deletion, this is exactly what we expect—the spelled-out copy must be outside and to the right of the FR. Add to this the assumption about placement (34a), and (39) follows.

(39)   The 'shared XP' must appear at the right edge of the FR

The data in (40)-(42) illustrate this condition. Recall that TFRs in DP position can be ambiguous between an indefinite transparent free relative and a definite ordinary free relative (40a). If (39) is not met, as in (40b), the transparent indefinite reading disappears. The same goes for TFRs in predicate position (41). (41a) is ambiguous between a 'hedged AP' reading and a 'definite DP' reading; (41b) loses the 'AP' reading. In prenominal modifier position (42), only the transparent structure is available, and the structure fails if the AP is not at the right edge of the free relative.

(40)   a.   John bought [what I described as a guitar   *ambiguous*
       b.   John bought [what I described as a guitar to him]   *TFR*

(41)   a.   This was [what I described as stupid   *ambiguous*
       b.   This was [what I described as stupid to John]   *TFR*

(42)   a.   a [what I described to John as stupid decision   *TFR only*
       b. * a [what I described as stupid to John] decision

4.3 The 'right edge' condition on the deletion target

There is a further fact that supports the generalization of constituent-sharing in TFRs to right node raising in coordination. Example (43a) is excluded because the *to*-PP cannot intervene between *as* and its adjective, cf. (43b). However, this account depends on an additional assumption, viz. that the AP-gap in the FR must be at the right edge of the FR. (43a) could have had another derivation (43c), based on the word order in (41b), with the deleted adjective preceding the PP:

(43)   a. * a <what I described as to John ~~stupid~~> stupid decision
       b. * I described this as to John stupid
       c. (*) this is a <what I described as ~~stupid~~ to John> stupid decision

We can rule out (43c) by appealing to the condition (44), which holds of Backward Deletion generally (cf. Oehrle 1991, Wilder 1997). The deletion site must be right-peripheral in the TFR (the domain referred to in (47); in coordinations, this corresponds to the conjunct):

(44)   A Backward Deletion target is at the right edge of its domain.

With respect to 'Right Node Raising', (44) accounts for contrasts like (45):

(45)   a.   Sue gave _ to Bill ~~that old diary of mine~~ and
            Mary will read <u>that old diary of mine</u>
       b. * Sue gave _ roses ~~the boy next door~~ and
            Mary visited <u>the boy next door</u>
       c.   Sue gave _ to Bill [that old diary of mine]   *ok HNPS*
       d. * Sue gave _ roses [the boy next door]   ** HNPS*

In (45a), the deleted NP can be at the right edge of its conjunct, if it undergoes Heavy NP-shift. In (45b), the deleted NP is the goal object of a double construction. Such NPs cannot undergo Heavy NP-shift—cf. (45d), hence there is no way for the deleted NP in (45b) to be at the right edge of its conjunct.

4.4 OV-languages

These facts about TFRs seem to hold cross-linguistically as well. We predict that a language can only have a TFR modifying a prenominal adjective if the word order rules of that language allow an adjectival predicate to stand at the right edge of the free relative, that is, in postverbal position.

German is an OV language that does not allow predicative APs to follow the verb in free relatives (46); and German does not have TFRs (47). In Dutch, another OV language, predicative APs can follow the verb in free relatives (48)—and Dutch does have TFRs (49) (Dutch data from Marcel den Dikken, p.c.):

(46)   a.   Dies ist [was ich <u>als dumm</u> bezeichnen würde]
            this is what I as stupid describe would
       b. * Dies ist [was ich bezeichnen würde <u>als dumm</u>]

(47)   a. * eine [was ich als dumm bezeichnen würde] Entscheidung
            a what I as stupid describe would decision
       b. * eine [was ich bezeichnen würde als] dumm-e Entscheidung
            a what I describe would as stupid-AGR decision

(48)   Dit is [wat ik beschouw als <u>tamelijk stomm</u>]
            this is what I regard as fairly stupid

(49)   een <wat ik beschouw als > tamelijk stomm-e beslissing
            a what I regard as fairly stupid-AGR decision

5. TFRs as parentheticals

Turning now to the claim that TFRs are parentheticals and not standard adjuncts, it is a quite general fact about English that finite clauses are not tolerated inside premodifiers of adjectives, cf. (50a). If TFRs were adjuncts, then in prenominal position they would have to be analysed as pre-modifiers of the prenominal adjective, a blatant counterexample to the generalization. On the other hand, sentence parentheticals can pre-modify adjectives (50b):

(50) a. * an [$_{AP}$ [as clearly as mine is] stupid] decision
      b.   This is a, [she thinks], stupid decision

Sentence parentheticals and TFRs also share properties of intonation and information structure. In (50b), the host sentence is foregrounded, and the parenthetical backgrounded. In a TFR, the shared constituent in the matrix is foregrounded, and the free relative (minus the shared XP) is backgrounded.

Ordinary sentence parentheticals do not have the 'constituent sharing' property of TFRs, but there is another type of parenthetical which does. This is the *Sluice Parenthetical*, discussed by Lakoff (1974) (cf. also McCawley 1988:739). (51) involves a sentence parenthetical containing a sluiced interrogative complement (*Sluicing*=IP-ellipsis), which serves to meta-linguistically 'modify' the matrix object, much like TFRs do.

(51)   John invited <you'll never guess what kind of> people
            to his party

Sluice parentheticals involve constituent sharing at the right edge of the parenthesis—the noun of the wh-phrase is simultaneously the (bare indefinite mass or plural DP) object of the matrix clause. This is shown by the fact that neither clause of (51) is complete without the noun *people*:

(52) a.   John invited people to his party
      b. * John invited to his party
      c.   You'll never guess what kind of people [$_{IP}$ $\varnothing$]
      d. * You'll never guess what kind of

The analysis developed for TFRs can be applied directly to Sluice Parentheticals—parenthetical placement followed by Backward Deletion:

(53)   John invited <you'll never guess what kind of ~~people~~> people
         to his party

In German, word order rules are such that the wh-phrase in a sluice ends up
at the right edge of its clause. This means that we expect Sluice
Parentheticals (unlike TFRs) to be possible in German, as indeed they are:

(54)   Hans hat <du kannst dir nicht vorstellen, was für ~~Leute~~>
         H. has you can REFL not imagine what-sort-of
         Leute eingeladen
         people invited

Notice also that we have to make the same two stipulations (55) for Sluice
Parentheticals as we did for TFRs, to guarantee that the parenthetical is
placed correctly and that deletion takes place, excluding examples like (56):

(55) a.   the Sluice-SP must be left-adjacent to XP in the host sentence
      b.   XP in the Sluice-SP must be deleted

(56) a. * <you'll never guess what kind of ~~people~~> John invited
            [people] to his party
      b. * John invited <you'll never guess what kind of people>
            [idiots] to his party

These similarities between Sluice Parentheticals and TFRs underscore the
claim made here that TFRs are a species of parenthetical expression.

6. TFRs and Pseudoclefts

One difference between ordinary FRs and TFRs still to be addressed (cf.
(14) above) concerns the "*what*-only" restriction—TFRs can only be formed
with bare *what*, cf. (57)-(58). Interestingly, this is also a property of
specificational pseudoclefts (SPCs) (cf. Iatridou and Varlokosta 1996).

(57) a.   John is what/*whatever I'd call angry   *TFR*
      b.   I'd call what/*whatever John is angry   *SPC*

(58) a.   John is what/*who (I thought) was a policeman   *TFR*
      b.   what/*who John is is a policeman   *SPC*

The *what*-only restriction has two subcases. First, *whatever* is not possible.
Secondly, it concerns the choice between *what* and *who* in FRs with

[+human]; *who* is not possible in (58).[1] To conclude, I comment briefly on the relation between the two constructions.

The SPCs in (57)-(58) are like the sentences containing TFRs, only turned inside out, as it were. The predication relation *inside* the TFR, between the trace of *what* and *angry* in (59a), is the same as the *external* predication in the SPC (59b), between the Free Relative and *angry*:

(59) a. John is < what I'd call [$_{SC}$ *t* ~~angry~~] > angry   *TFR*

       b. I'd call [$_{SC}$ what John is angry]   *SPC*

This suggests that the *what*-only restriction may reflect a common property holding of the internal predication (the small clause) inside TFRs and of the external predication between the FR and its associate in SPCs.

Suppose that the predications marked in (59) are underlyingly predications involving bare *that* as its subject, as in (60).

(60) a. I'd call [that angry]   *TFR*

       b. I'd call that (John is that) angry   *SPC*

The *what*-only restriction follows on the reasonable assumption that bare *what* is the only wh-pronoun that can realize *that*.

If this is on the right track, then TFRs and pseudoclefts should have other properties in common with predications having bare *that* as their subject (cf. Higgins 1979:ch.5 for relevant discussion copula sentences with *that* as subject). There is another restriction that holds of all three cases, illustrated in (61) to (63)—none of them works with *remain* or *become*:

(61)   * what John is remains / has become angry   *SPC*

(62)   * John is < what remains / has become ~~angry~~ > angry   *TFR*

(63)   (Did you hear him shouting?)   *that-predication*
       a. that was (what you'd call) angry
       b. * that remains / has become (what you'd call) angry.

---

[1] The facts are complicated by (i)-(ii); however, it might be that (i) with *who* is not a genuine TFR (but an ordinary FR), and that (ii) with *who* is not a genuine SPC:
(i)   I saw who (?what) I thought was John
(ii)   who (?what) I thought I saw was (actually) John

The correlation with predications having bare *that* as their subject may prove important in understanding why TFRs can only be formed from free relatives having the format (12). Also suggestive is the fact that the contrast in (64) between ordinary FRs headed by *what* and TFRs with respect to [+human] also correlates with the compatibility of *that* in (65a) but not (65b) with [+human] denotation.

(64) a.   \<What I'd call a~~policeman~~\> a policeman just walked in.

      b.   I invited [who / #what you met last night]

(65) a.   That's a policeman / I'd call that a policeman
      b.   I met him / #that last night.

Of course, the ideas sketched in this section need careful working out, but that's a topic for another paper.

References

Higgins, Roger. 1979. *The Pseudo-Cleft Construction of English*. New York: Garland.

Iatridou, Sabine & Spyridoula Varlokosta. 1996. A crosslinguistic perspective on pseudoclefts. *NELS* 26:117-131

Kajita, Masaru. 1977. Towards a dynamic model of syntax. *Studies in English Linguistics* 5:44-66.

Jacobson, Pauline. 1995. On the quantificational force of English free relatives, in E. Bach, E. Jelinek, A. Kratzer & B. Partee, eds., *Quantification in Natural Languages* [Vol. 2]. Dordrecht: Kluwer.

Lakoff, George. 1974. Syntactic Amalgams. *Chicago Linguistic Society* 10:321-344.

Moltmann, Friederike. 1992. *Coordination and Comparatives*. Doctoral dissertation, MIT.

Oehrle, Richard. 1991. Categorial frameworks, coordination and extraction. *WCCFL* 9:411-425.

McCawley, James. 1988. *The Major Syntactic Phenomena of English*. Chicago: Chicago University Press.

Wilder, Chris. 1997. Some properties of ellipsis in coordination. In: A. Alexiadou & T. Hall, eds., *Studies in Universal Grammar and Typological Variation*. Amsterdam: Benjamins.

Williams, Edwin. 1983. Semantic vs. syntactic categories. *Linguistics & Philosophy* 6:423-446.

Free Relatives as Indefinites

MARTINA WILTSCHKO

University of British Columbia/University of Vienna

0. Introduction

It is a well-known fact that free relatives (henceforth FRs) can be interpreted in two different ways. For example, the FR in (1) is standardly paraphrased as in (2):

(1) *What (ever) annoys Mary* also annoys Chris.

Cooper 1983, p.79, (1c)

(2) a   Everything which annoys Mary also annoys Chris.
   b.   The thing that annoys Mary also annoys Chris.

The reading in (2a) corresponds to the so-called universal interpretation and the reading in (2b) has traditionally been called the 'definite reading' of FRs. Previous analyses of FR reflect these two readings in one way or other.

   In this paper[1], I will argue that the readings associated with FRs have been misidentified, and so the analyses that capture the readings in (2) are not empirically adequate. The main proposal of this paper is summarized in the next section.

---

[1] I would like to thank the audience of WCCFL XVII in Vancouver for fruitful comments, many of which I am unable to incorporate in this short paper. Special thanks are due to Strang Burton and Hamida Demirdache. All remaining errors are of course my own. The research on this paper was funded by the Austrian Academy of Science (APART 435)

1. The Proposal.

In the main part of this paper I will argue for the following claims:

(3) a. FRs are interpreted as indefinites.
     b. The Indefiniteness of the FR has to do with the indefiniteness of the wh-words used in FRs.

For this reason, we do not need a special analysis for the semantics of FRs: since their heads are indefinite, FRs are indefinites as well: whatever analysis is chosen for indefinites will carry over to FRs.

How does this view derive the two readings of FRs? Since FRs are indefinites, they are best paraphrased with an indefinite head as in (4):

(4) *Something which annoys Mary* also annoys Chris.

Observe that this one paraphrase is sufficient. It is itself ambiguous between a generic and a non-generic (in this case specific) reading. This paper argues that this is exactly how FRs are interpreted.

First, FRs can receive a generic interpretation (and this is the interpretation that has previously been identified as the universal reading). Secondly, FRs can receive a specific indefinite interpretation (which has previously been identified as the definite interpretation).

In order to compare the present approach to previous analyses of FRs, let me briefly introduce some of them.

2. Previous Proposals.

On the one hand there is the view that FRs are either Definites or Universals, as for example advocated by Cooper 1983 who "*interpret[s] a headless relative such as 'what Mary says' as if it contains a hidden universal quantifier....*" (p. 96)

More recently there are several approaches that treat FRs as uniformly definite. For Jacobson (1995) the FR in (1) denotes the unique maximal individual satisfying the description. Noun phrases indicate morphologically whether quantification is over atoms or pluralities. The lack of number morphology in FRs makes them ambiguous: maximality can operate over the domain of atoms or pluralities. So a definite reading arises if there is only one atomic individual with that property. If there are more such individuals, a (quasi)-universal reading arises.

For Dayal (1996) FRS are generalized quantifiers, with uniqueness/maximality built into their interpretation. The two readings arise in essentially the same way as in Jacobson's approach. Crucially for both authors FRs are <u>uniformly</u> treated as definites.

In what follows I will argue that FRs are interpreted as indefinites. Obviously this claim makes different predictions than either of the previous analyses. In (5) I have summarized several properties of FRs that I will discuss.

(5) A comparison of predictions:

Property	FR=Indefinite	FR=Definite
1. FRs are associated with a uniqueness presupposition?	NO	YES
2. FRs can have a (3rd) non-specific reading?	YES	NO
3. Tense/Aspect restricts the universal (=generic) reading?	YES	NO
4. FRs can behave like (semantically) plural definites?	NO	YES

Crucially, I will show that the claim that FRs are indefinites makes the correct predictions for all of these properties.

3. Evidence from non-uniqueness.

Obviously, Jacobson's and Dayal's analysis predicts that FRs are associated with a uniqueness presupposition, whereas if FRs are indefinites, no such presupposition is predicted. There is a number of arguments that FRs are not associated with a uniqueness presupposition.

3.1. Coordination.
Let me start with the sentence in (6) involving coordinated sentences:

(6) Peter explained the thing people needed to know and Mary explained the thing people needed to know.

Since the definite determiner presupposes uniqueness this sentence says, that Peter and Mary both explained the same thing. Indefinites do not presuppose uniqueness. A sentence like (6) with an indefinite head can mean that Peter and Mary can have explained different things:

(7) Peter explained a thing/something people needed to know and Mary explained a thing/something people needed to know.

Crucially, FRs pattern with indefinites: they do not presuppose uniqueness. The sentence in (8) can mean that Peter and Mary have explained different things:

(8) Peter explained what(ever) people needed to know and Mary explained what(ever) people needed to know.

3.2. Adverbs of frequency.
A second argument has to do with adverbs of frequency. Consider the sentence in (9) involving a definite object:

(9) #Mary repeatedly killed the ant.

This sentence is infelicitous because on the one hand the definite DP *the ant* presupposes uniqueness (there is only one ant), but on the other hand one cannot repeatedly kill one and the same ant.
Again, indefinites behave differently as shown by the felicity of (10):

(10) Mary repeatedly killed an ant.

The indefinite *an ant* does not presuppose uniqueness. The sentence means that Mary killed several different ants, one after the other. Again, FRs behave just like indefinites:

(11) Mary repeatedly killed what(ever) was in her way.

(11) can mean that Mary killed more than one thing that was in here way. Adding an adverb of frequency does not render the sentence infelicitous.

3.3. Adverbs of Quantification: quantificational variability effects
We find a similar effect with adverbs of quantification and subject FRs (so far we have only seen object FRs). FRs exhibit quantificational variability effects (QVE).[2] Consider (12):

(12) What Peter says is always intelligent.

(12) says that all the things Peter says are intelligent. This variable reading is predicted under the assumption that FRs are interpreted as indefinites, since

---

[2] Dayal (1996) observes the same effect in Hindi correlatives (and attributes the same observation for English FRs to Kratzer 1988)). Since she assumes that FRs are definites, QVE constitute a problem for her analysis, which she solves by letting the adverbial quantifier quantify over situations.

indefinites pattern in exactly the same way, which is a well-known fact exemplified in (13):

(13) A talk by Peter is always intelligent.
=All talks by Peter are intelligent.

The variable reading however is not expected under the view that FRs pick out a unique individual. The sentence in (14) with a definite DP is ill formed.

(14) ?*The talk by Peter is always intelligent.
≠ All talks by Peter are intelligent.

3.4. Scopal interactions with other quantifiers.

Another piece of evidence against the uniqueness of FRs concerns scopal interactions with other quantifiers. It is a well-known fact that the an indefinite in an example like (15) allows for a distributive construal, where the number of studied subjects can vary with the number of students.

(15) Every student studies a subject that is useful for society.

Again, because definites induce a uniqueness presupposition, the distributive construal is not available in (16).

(16) Every student studies the subject that is useful for society.

In (16) every student has to study the same subject. Again, FRs behave like indefinites:

(17) Every student studies what(ever) (subject) is useful for society.

In (17) the distributive construal is possible. The sentence can mean that every student can study a different subject.

4. Evidence from the non-specific reading.

Assuming that FRs are indefinites, predicts that the non-generic reading is itself ambiguous between a specific and a non-specific reading. This third reading is not expected under the treatment of FRs as definites.

4.1. FRs under the scope of an intensional operator.

Consider the examples in (18). *'Write'* is a verb of creation. The existence of its object cannot be presupposed. An indefinite, does not induce a presupposition of existence, and therefore the non-specific (narrow scope) reading is possible:

(18) John wants to write a book that sells well.

Definites crucially differ. They induce an existence presupposition, which is incompatible with the narrow scope reading in (19)

(19) *John wants to write the book that sells well.

Again, FRs behave like indefinites, they do not induce a presupposition of existence, as the well-formedness of (20) shows:

(20) John wants to write whatever sells well.

4.2. FRs under the scope of negation.
The same point can be made on basis of FRs under the scope of negation. It is a well-known fact that indefinites induce a specific/non-specific ambiguity in the scope of negation:

(21) John didn't marry a Canadian girl (because there is no Canadian girl).

Adding the clause in parenthesis does not induce a contradiction because indefinites allow for a non-specific reading, which is compatible with the non-existence of the discourse referent. Definites on the other hand presuppose existence, thus the oddity of the bracketed clause in (22):

(22) John didn't marry the Canadian girl (#because there is no Canadian girl).

Again, FRs behave like indefinites, they allow for a narrow-scope non-specific reading:

(23) John didn't marry who he loves (because there is nobody he loves).

In this section, we have seen that FRs allow for a non-specific reading, which is only expected under the assumption that FRs are interpreted as indefinites.

5. Evidence from the interaction with tense and aspect.

There is a peculiar restriction on the availability of the 'quasi-universal reading' (which is the generic reading) of FRs, which is unexpected under the view that FRs are definites.

Indefinites are not inherently generic. They can receive a generic interpretation in a generic (or characterizing) sentence (cf. Krifka et al. (1995)) as shown in (24a). The same is true for FRs: (24b) allows the generic (or quasi-universal) interpretation:

(24) a. A dog barks.
         = Every dog barks.
     b. What(ever) John does bothers me.
         = Everything John does bothers me.

If the generic reading of a sentence is excluded, then the generic interpretation of the indefinite is excluded as well. For example, the progressive excludes a generic interpretation, and the indefinite in (25) cannot be interpreted generically:

(25) A dog is barking.
     ≠ Every dog is barking.

Again, FRs behave exactly like indefinites. The generic reading is not available in (26):

(26) What(ever) John does is bothering me.
     ≠ Everything John does is bothering me.

Similarly, the generic reading of indefinites and FRs is excluded with perfect aspect as shown in (27):

(27) a. A dog has barked.
         ≠ Every dog has barked.
     b. What(ever) John did has bothered me.
         ≠ Everything John did has bothered me.

Also, the generic reading of indefinites and FRs is excluded with episodic tense, no matter whether episodic tense occurs in the matrix clause as in (28):

(28) a. Something John did, bothered me yesterday at 4 o'clock.
         ≠ Everything John did bothered me yesterday at 4 o'clock.
     b. What(ever) John did, bothered me yesterday at 4o'clock.
         ≠ Everything, John did bothered me yesterday at 4 o'clock.

or whether episodic tense occurs in the relative clause itself:

(29) a. Something John did yesterday at 4 o'clock bothered me.
≠ Everything, John did yesterday at 4 o'clock bothered me.
b. What(ever) John did yesterday at 4o'clock bothered me.
≠ Everything, John did yesterday at 4 o'clock bothered me.

The restriction on the availability of the generic (i.e. the quasi-universal) reading is exactly the same for FRs and indefinites, which supports the claim that FRs are indefinites. No such restriction on the universal reading is expected under the assumption that FRs are definites (or under the assumption that they are universally quantified NPs for that matter).

6. Evidence from the lack of plural-like behaviour

So far, I have argued that FRs behave like indefinites, implicitly assuming that they behave like singular indefinites. Jacobson (1995) argues that FRs denote the unique maximal **plural** entity (to allow for the quasi-universal reading). This means that there is another property that distinguishes the present approach from Jacobson's. We predict that FRs behave like singulars whereas Jacobson predicts that they behave like (semantically) plural definites. There are a number of phenomena that show that FRs don't behave like pluralities.

6.1. Collective vs. distributive interpretation.
Consider the sentences in (30). Without *together* these sentences allow for a collective or a distributive interpretation with plural subjects. Adding *together* forces the collective interpretation:

(30) a. The boys are lifting a piano (together).
b. Peter and Mary are building a table (together).
c. These authors have written a book (together).

(Generic) indefinites only allow for the distributive interpretation, indicated by the ungrammaticality of *together:*

(31) a. A strong man lifts a piano (*together).
b. A worker in this factory builds a table (*together).
c. An expert writes a book (*together).

Again, FRs behave like indefinites rather than plurals. They do not allow for the collective interpretation, as shown by the ungrammaticality of *together* in (32):

(32) a. Who(ever) is strong lifts a piano (*together).
b. Who(ever) works in this factory builds a table (*together).

    c.   Who(ever) knows about this topic writes a book (*together).

Note also, that the impossibility for the collective reading is independent of the syntactic singularity of indefinites and FRs. Collective nouns do allow for the collective reading even though they are syntactically singular as shown in (33):

(33) a.   The family lifts a piano (together).
     b.   The group builds a table (together).
     c.   The class writes a book (together).

6.2. The collective property interpretation of generics.

There is another interesting point at stake here. One could maintain the view that FRs are definites and still account for the possibility for the generic reading because definites can be interpreted generically as well. However, this possibility can be rejected on basis of the following argument.

    Krifka et al (1995) identify a variety of generic readings, and it is crucial that indefinites can assume only a subset of them, which is the same subset as for FRs. In the present context the reading, which has been labeled the 'collective property interpretation' is relevant (given that we just discussed collectivity). Both bare plurals and definites can receive this interpretation as shown in (34):

(34) a.   Linguists have more than 8000 books in print.
     b.   The German customer bought 11.000 BMWs last year.

Krifka et al 1995, p.78 124b

Here the property of *having more than 8000 books in print* applies collectively to all existing objects of the kind *linguist*. The property can be projected from the objects to the kind and so the interpretation arises that the kind *linguists* together has 8.000 books in print, and not each one individually.

    Crucially, indefinites cannot be used to induce the collective property interpretation:

(35) a.   A linguist has more than 8000 books in print.
     b.   A German customer bought 11.000 BMWs last year.

(35) has only the implausible reading that each linguist has 8.000 books in print. FRs behave just like indefinites: they do not allow for the collective property interpretation. (36) has only the implausible reading:

(36) a.   Who(ever) is a linguist has more than 8.000 books in print.
     b.   Who(ever) is a German citizen bought 11.000 BMWs last year.

6.3. 'Plurality seeking elements'.

Another argument against the assumption that FRs denote a plurality has to do with, what Schwarzschild (1996) calls, plurality seeking elements. One such element is shown in (37). *Unanimously* is only licensed in the context of a plural subject:

(37) a.   The students unanimously voted for the proposal.
   b.   *The student unanimously voted for the proposal.

Crucially, FRs do not license *unanimously* as shown in (38):

(38) *Whoever was asked unanimously voted for the proposal.

Note again, that this is independent of the syntactic singularity of FRs. Collective nouns can license *unanimously*:

(39) The group unanimously voted for the proposal.

7. The indefiniteness of the wh-word

In the rest of this paper I will show that it is not at all surprising that FRs are interpreted as indefinites given that the wh-words used in FRs are indefinite. This simply means that FRs are indefinites because their heads are indefinite.

Let us briefly go over some of the evidence for the indefiniteness of the wh-words used in FRs.

7.1. The wh-words used in FRs are indefinite
One piece of evidence is very simple. Across languages the wh-words that are used in FRs are consistently the ones that can be classified as indefinite wh-words.[3]

We know at least since Katz & Postal (1964) that wh-phrases differ in their status w.r.t. definiteness. Wh-words like *who* and *what* are indefinite whereas *which N* is argued to be definite. Now, in FRs we always find *who* and *what* but not *which*.[4] This correlation is summarized in the table below:

---

[3] There are exceptions to this generalization. For languages (like Greek) that make use of a definite wh-word in FRs the present proposal predicts that they behave differently. Note, that given the denial of 'constructions' as primitives in the theory, we do actually expect different types of FRs.

[4] Smits (1989) notes one exception to this generalization. In English *which* can be used in FRs. For now, I set this aside, noting that a) this is cross-linguistically a marked option and b) even in English there are several restrictions on the use of *which* in FRs:

i)   I buy you whichever hat you like.
ii)   *I buy you which hat you like.   *I buy you which(ever) you like.

Note that i) is marked in one further respect. Cross-linguistically, attributively used wh-words are generally very rare in FRs.

(40) English wh-words:

WH-word	Definite	Indefinite	used in FRs
what/who	-	+	+
which	+	-	-

This does not seem to be an accidental property of English. According to Smits (1989) other Germanic languages and Romance languages behave just like English in this respect: They all use indefinite wh-words in FRs *"Typically, what we find in FRs are the ordinary interrogative pronouns, in as much these can occur without an antecedent themselves."* Smits (1989), p.143. (Smits uses "being able to occur *without an antecedent*" as a test-criterion for the indefiniteness of FRs.)

7.2. There insertion[5]

The indefiniteness of the wh-phrase is further supported by the fact that (at D-structure) they can occupy a position reserved for indefinites, namely the postverbal position in there-insertion contexts. It has been shown in Heim (1987) that wh-words differ as to whether they can be base-generated in the post-verbal position of there insertion contexts. As shown below only the indefinite wh-word *what* is well formed. The definite *which* is ill formed.

(41) a.   ??Which one of the two men was there in the room/*drunk?
     b.   What was there in Austin?   Heim 1987: 27, (15); (18)

Crucially, the wh-word of a FR can be base-generated in this context as shown in (42):

(42) Peter likes what$_i$ there was t$_i$ in Austin.

This shows that the wh-word is still indefinite when it is used in a FR.

7.3. Aggressive non-D-linking

There is another argument for the indefiniteness of the wh-word in a FR. It has been observed in Pesetsky (1987) that D-linked (or definite) wh-phrases cannot be aggressively non-D-linked as shown in (43)

(43) a.   What the hell book did you read that in?
     b.   *Which the hell book did you read that in?   Pesetsky 1987: 111 (40)

---

[5] It has to be noted here that FRs are not licensed in there-insertion context, contrary to what we would expect under the present analysis. To account for this fact, I assume that FRs are of category CP, and that the postverbal position of there-insertion contexts is reserved for NPs., but this goes beyond the scope of this paper.

Crucially, wh-words in FRs can be aggressively non-D-linked as shown in (44)

(44) Whatever the hell you are doing doesn't bother me.

This further supports the claim that the wh-words in FRs are indefinite.

7.4. Coordination of FRs and the Novelty Condition.
Finally consider the following fact,

> *Free relatives can be coordinated, but the conjoins have different referents, especially when both introduced by* what(ever). *If both must refer to the same referent, then the combination* what ... and/but which.... *is obligatory."*   Smits (1989) p. 296f.

In (45) the two coordinated FRs have to denote two different things, whereas in (46) they denote the same thing:

(45) What he did and what he said were two different things.
(46) He only wished to assert what I cannot believe to be true but which would vanquish all our hopes if it were really true.

                                                        Smits p.297, (3)-(4).

This surprising pattern follows straightforwardly from the assumption that the wh-word in FRs is indefinite. Being indefinite however, means being subject to the Novelty Condition (in the sense of Heim (1982)). Therefore they have to introduce a new discourse referent, which results in the fact that the FRs in (45) have to denote two different things.

8. Conclusion.

Let me briefly summarise the main claim of this paper. I showed that FRs are interpreted as indefinites. We have seen a variety of contexts in which they clearly behave like indefinites rather than singular or plural definites. I have also pointed out that the indefiniteness of FRs correlates with the indefiniteness of the wh-words used. For this reason, we do not need a special analysis for the semantics of FRs: the head of a FR is indefinite and therefore FRs are indefinites.

9. References.

Berman, Steve. 1989. An Analysis of Quantificational Variability in Indirect Questions. *MIT Working Papers in Linguistics* 11.
Bresnan, Joan, Jane Grimshaw. 1978. The syntax of Free Relatives in English. *Linguistic Inquiry* 9, 331-391.

Cooper, Robin. 1983. *Quantification and Syntactic Theory.* Dordrecht: Reidel.

Dayal, Veneeta. 1996. *Locality in WH-Quantification.* Dordrecht: Kluwer.

Dayal, Veneeta. 1997. Free Relatives and *Ever: Identity* and *Free Choice* Readings. *Proceedings of SALT VII.*

Heim, Irene. 1982. *The Semantics of Definite and Indefinite Noun Phrases.* Doctoral dissertation, University of Massachusetts, Amherst

Heim, Irene. 1987. Where does the Definiteness Restriction Apply?, in E.J. Reuland, A.G.B. ter Meulen, eds., *The Representation of (In)definiteness.* Cambridge, Mass.: MIT Press. 21-42.

Iatridou, Sabine, Spiritoula Varlakosta. 1996. A Crosslinguistic Perspective on Pseudoclefts. *Proceedings of NELS 26.*

Jacobson, Pauline. 1995. On the Quantificational Force of English Free Relatives, in E. Bach, E. Jelinek, A. Kratzer, B.H. Partee, eds., *Quantification in Natural Languages.* Dordrecht: Kluwer. 451-486.

Katz, Jerry, Paul Postal. 1964. *An Integrated Theory of Linguistic Description.* Cambridge, Mass.: MIT Press.

Kratzer, Angelika. 1988. Comments on P.Jacobson's 'The Syntax and Semantics of Free Relatives in English. Paper presented at the Annual Meeting of the Linguistic Society of America, New Orleans.

Kratzer, Angelika. 1989. An Investigation into the Lumps of Thought. *Linguistics and Philosophy* 12, 607-653.

Krifka, Manfred, Francis Jeffry Pelletier, Greg Carlson, Alice ter Meulen, Godehard Link, Gennaro Chierchia. 1995. Genericity: An Introduction, in G. Carlson, F.J. Pelletier, eds., *The Generic Book.* Chicago & London: The University of Chicago Press. 1– 124.

Link, Godehard. 1983. The Logical Analysis of Plurals and Mass Terms: A Lattice-Theoretic Approach, in R.Bäuerle, C. Schwarze, A.v.Stechow eds., *Meaning, Use and Interpretation of Language.* Berlin: de Gruyter.

Pesetsky, David. 1987. Wh-in-situ: Movement and Unselective Binding, in E.Reuland, A.G.B.ter Meulen, eds., *The Representation of (In)definites.* Cambridge, Mass.: MIT Press. 98-129.

Schwarzschild, Roger. 1996. *Pluralities.* Dordrecht: Kluwer.

Smits, R.J.C. 1989. *Eurogrammar. The Relative and Cleft Constructions of the Germanic and Romance Languages.* Dordrecht: Foris

Tredinnick, V; 1994: 'On the Interpretation and Distribution of –ever in English Free Relatives.' *Proceedings of Console 2.*

Index

713